PRESERVING THE TRUTH

Preserving the Truth:

The Church without a Name and Its Founder, William Irvine

By Cherie Kropp-Ehrig

CherieKroppEhrig.com

Associated with *Telling The Truth* Website
TellingTheTruth.info

Clarion Call Publishing

Preserving the Truth: The Church without a Name and Its Founder, William Irvine

Published by Clarion Call Publishing
6333 Mockingbird Lane #147, PMB 2074
Dallas, Texas 75214
E-mail: Truth@TellingTheTruth.info
CherieKroppEhrig.com

The author has made every reasonable effort to ensure the accuracy and validity of the content of this book. All information is provided on an "as is" basis with no guarantee as to completeness. Because knowledge of the past is subject to change, the author assumes no responsibility or liability for errors and omissions. Historical information discovered after publication may possibly affect the material presented herein.

Publisher's Cataloging-in-Publication Data

Names: Kropp-Ehrig, Cherie, author.
Title: Preserving the truth : the church without a name and its founder, William Irvine / Cherie Kropp-Ehrig.
Description: Dallas, TX : Clarion Call Publishing, 2022. | Includes bibliographic references and index. | Contains maps and photographic illustrations. | Summary: History of the Two by Two Church/Sect, a restoration movement modeled after the New Testament primitive church, and its founder.
Identifiers: ISBN 9798985625011 (hardback) ISBN 9798985625004 (pbk.) | ISBN 9798985625028 (ebook) |
Subjects: LCSH: Two-by-Two's (Christian sect) – History. | Cooney, Edward, 1867-1960 – Biography. | Irvine, William, 1863-1947 – Biography. | Primitivism – Religious aspects – Christianity. | Ireland – Church history. | BISAC: BIOGRAPHY & AUTOBIOGRAPHY / Religious. | RELIGION / Christianity / History. | RELIGION / Christianity / Protestant.
Classification: LCC BX9798.T854 K76 2022 | DDC 289.9 K--dc23

Credits: Cover design by Elizabeth Coleman. Author's photograph by Katherine Hershey. Maps and artwork created by Galen Berry. Photograph restoration by Thomas Teegarden and Galen Berry. All rights reserved.

ISBN 979-8-9856250-0-4; ISBN 979-8-9856250-1-1
ISBN 979-8-9856250-2-8 (electronic version may exclude images)

Contents

Appendices

~~~~~

Maps

Maps by Galen Berry

Abbreviations

Countries

N. Ireland	Northern Ireland
UK	United Kingdom of Great Britain and Northern Ireland (includes England, Scotland, Northern Ireland and Wales)
US	United States of America

Websites

EXP	Expressions by Ex-2x2s, Ex2x2.info
RIS	Research and Information Services, workersect.org
TTT	Telling The Truth, TellingTheTruth.info

General

2x2	Two by Two
aka	also known as
Co.	County
C.O.	Conscientious Objector
Ed.	Edition
Ex-2x2	Former member of 2x2 Sect
FM	Faith Mission
n.d.	no date provided
n.p.	no place specified; no publisher given
Non-2x2	Outsider; not a 2x2 member
PC	Personal Computer

Bible Versions

KJV	Authorized King James Version
NASB	New American Standard Version
NIV	New International Version

All Scripture quotations are from the *Authorized King James Version*, unless otherwise noted.

Hebrew and Greek translated words are shown without diacritics.

*Condemnation before investigation
is the highest form of ignorance.*
(Albert Einstein)

*There are just two types of people ...
Those people to whom their beliefs are more precious
than the truth ...
Those people to whom the truth is more precious than
their beliefs.*
(A.E Wiggam)

*For we can do nothing against the truth,
but for the truth.*
(2 Corinthians 13:8)

Preface

All books have a story behind them, and this book is no exception. My story began in 1989 when I received an envelope in the mail from Threshing Floor Ministries of Spokane, Washington, US, containing about 50 old articles from an Irish newspaper, the *Impartial Reporter and Farmer's Journal,* relating to a new religious sect that was making "big news" in Ireland.

As I pored over the articles from the early 1900s, I read about William Irvine, the founder of a peculiar new religious sect in Ireland, and a large Christian convention he arranged in Enniskillen in 1904. This new sect had no name, and its itinerant preachers went about the countryside preaching in pairs. To my amazement, I saw the familiar names of some preachers, such as George Walker and Jack Carroll—both these men and Carroll's sisters, Fannie and May, had visited in my family's homes!

The more I read, the more certain I became that the articles were about the nameless church my family and I had been attending for three generations. My grandparents entered this church in the early 1930s when my parents were children. Devout followers, my parents hosted the annual statewide convention in Jackson, Mississippi, where I grew up.

As I studied these old newspaper articles, I wondered why my family and church friends had never heard an inkling about this preacher, William Irvine. Nor had we been aware that our church started in Ireland around the turn of the twentieth century. Having been immersed in this church from birth, these discoveries turned my world upside down.

Most children born and bred into this church were told that there was no earthly founder; that Jesus Himself had started it, and that our ministers had continued in a direct line from the first century apostles to the current ministers (a concept known as *apostolic succession*). That is, our church began when Jesus sent out His disciple from the Sea of Galilee to preach in Matthew 10. We believed this without question—it never occurred to us that it might not be true. Countless followers believed and still believe this particular nameless church is the *only* church that was not founded by man.

After mulling over this surprising new information, I began a quest to prove or disprove if William Irvine had really started our church. I discovered his senior ministers had quietly expelled him in 1914 and deliberately erased his name and role from their church history. The church continued much the same as usual.

I was initially aided in my research by a book published in 1982 that revealed many hidden details surrounding the life and ministry of William Irvine. The title was *The Secret Sect* written by Doug and Helen Parker from Australia. Over time, I independently verified the facts contained in the Parkers' book. During my investigation, I made two research trips to the UK and Ireland where I found additional evidence.

Over the past 25 years, I have been dedicated to researching, collecting, preserving, publishing and revealing the hidden history of this nameless sect. It has been a daunting challenge to compile an accurate account of a sect that purposely does not take a name, does not record its own history and even goes to great lengths to prevent it from being documented by others. The content of some of this book is being published for the first time.

Truth is a precious commodity, and I place a high value on it. Devoted to the pursuit of truth and its preservation, I am strongly opposed to deception and unwilling to remain silent. For this reason, I created a website in 1997, where I have shared my research documents publicly. I believe everyone who has ever been associated with this church has a right to know the truth about its history and deserves access to the facts. Arrangements have been set in place for this book and my associated website, *Telling The Truth (TellingTheTruth.info)* to continue indefinitely, long after I leave this world.

Ultimately, I hope this book will give the reader insight into who, what, when, where, why and how the 2x2 Sect started and developed. It is a well-established principle that understanding the linkage between the past and present is essential for a good understanding of the present.

Researching the history of the 2x2 Sect has been a very fulfilling and enjoyable quest. To the best of my knowledge, I have preserved and reported the facts currently known to me. I am deeply indebted and grateful to countless sources all over the world who have assisted me in compiling this book.

Written for the love and preservation of Truth,

Cherie (Berry) Kropp-Ehrig

My Mission is:

- To safeguard and preserve early historical documents regarding the development of the 2x2 Sect; this goal inspired the book's title, *Preserving the Truth*.
- To present a reliable, well-documented historical record supported by accurate and verifiable sources dating from the beginning of the 2x2 Sect.
- To make easily accessible the historical facts about the 2x2 Sect, its origins, ministers, organization, growth, progression and importantly, its founder, William Irvine.
- To cause William Irvine's name and role to become common knowledge among 2x2 members, former members and others.
- To offer the opportunity to assess the past, review lessons learned, benefit from mistakes and avoid future pitfalls by sharing history, its positives and negatives, similar to the Bible that recorded good, bad, meritorious and unsavory events.

Am I therefore become your enemy, because I tell you the truth?
(Galatians 4:16)

Acknowledging the Contributors

Whatever successes, victories or achievements we attain in life, we are never the sole accomplisher. I am very grateful to former and current Two by Two Church members, non-members and helpers worldwide who supplied information, support and encouragement for over 25 years. Without their generous ongoing assistance, suggestions and material, along with providential intervention, this book would not be a fraction of what it is today.

I am especially thankful for the invaluable comments of my dear husband, Chester Ehrig, who has championed this project from its beginning and spent untold hours assisting in this lengthy endeavor; for my mother, Dorothy "Dot" Berry, and my brother, Galen Berry, who were remarkable sources of material, maps, artwork, photography; and for my father, Raymond Berry (1920–2014), who was proud of my research. There is a special place in my heart for my two children, Kelly and Julie Krista, who grew up while their mother was writing this book. To their oft repeated impatient question, "Mom, are you *ever* going to finish your book?" I can now answer with a resounding, "Yes! It is finished!"

For those who volunteered to edit and proofread, their constructive comments have been immensely helpful. In alphabetical order they are, Galen Berry, Russell Cooney, Kevin N. Daniel, Alistair Henderson, Jerry Hopkins, Julene Jones, Thomas Teegarden, Andre van der Merwe, Alan Vandermyden and four 2x2s who wish to remain anonymous. I was fortunate to find a professional editor, Elizabeth M. Garrett of Polish Point Editing, whose expert assistance was invaluable.

Those who helped financially, performed research, provided letters, notes, lists, photographs, etc., and paid shipping/postage to send me items include (in alphabetical order):

United States: Paul Abenroth, Jeff and Lorraine Armstrong, Beverly Bafus, Dorothy "Dot" Berry, Galen Berry, Maria Bodey, Mark Burrell, Bob, Joan and Kevin Daniel, Katherine "Kay" Curtis Arvig-Downs, Jeanie Dudley, Sharon (Heisler) Edmundson, Lee Fryer, James Ferguson, Derrick Hahn, Carol (Staack) Hammond, Roy Hedahl, Randy Hohenfeldt, Ilylo, Tim Jones, J. Frank Kelly, Donn Klor, Martha Knight, Larry and Bonnie Lindemann, Stephen Magowan, Darrell Mansur, Michelle (Storck) Matthews, Marie (Gooding) Micheletti, Julie Olson, Kathleen Overby, Mary Ann Schoeff, Charles Storck, Tom Teegarden, Judy Temple, Jim Vail, John, Thelma and Alan Vandermyden, Louise Warnes, the family of Cordia and Henry White and Marguerite Fern (White) Petersen of Scappoose, Oregon, Edward K. Williams, Bob Williston and Linda Wotipka.

Australia: Ross Bowden, Nola Davies, Joan (Fleming) Frost, David Mansur, Stan and Rose Perry, Geoff and Esther Schmidt, Mervyn Schmidt and Alan Stone.

New Zealand: Ian Carlson, Russell Cooney, Lynn Cooper, Elizabeth Freebairn and the 2x2 history website owner.

Canada: Fred and Verna Alder, Don Galloway, Sandi Gunther, Halena Halpin (granddaughter of Edward Cooney's sister Mary Elizabeth), Walter Holt, Iver, Bonnie and Tammy Kleven, Alvin and Diane Kroeker, Ellen McLane, John Mitchell, Bruce Murdoch, Valerie (Stokes) Pike and Marge Reynolds.

Ireland, Northern Ireland, England and Scotland: Alison (Pearson) Chambers, Mervyn Dane (*Impartial Reporter* newspaper, Enniskillen), Louise (Napier) Dawson, Myrtle Doherty, James Hutchison, Robert Kee, David Killicoat, *Kilsyth Chronicle*, Shonagh Love, David and Daniel Magowan, Jim and Philomena Mallon, Ron Morris, Maeve Plower (Weirs of Baggot Street, Dublin, Ireland), Public Records of N. Ireland (PRONI), Patricia (Melia) Reynolds, Mary (Wood) Rogers, Kate Sutcliff, John and Joyce Swanton.

Vietnam: Nguyễn Huu Bau and his daughter Nguyễn Minh Thanh with her husband Nguyễn Xuân Hoàn; Nguyễn Thanh Hoa, an unrelated Brother Worker.

Book Authors/Compilers: Daurelle Chapman, *Reflections*; Elizabeth Coleman, *Cult to Christ*; Lynn Cooper, *The Church with No Name*; Kevin Daniel, *Reinventing the Truth*; Joan F. Daniel, *Reflected Truth*; James Hutchison, *History of Kilsyth* and *Canal Boats & Miners Rows: Kilsyth 1750—1970*; Kathleen Lewis, *The Church without a Name*; Mr. and Mrs. John Long, *Journal of John Long*; Gene and Grace Luxon, *Has the Truth Set You Free*; Seamas Mac Annaidh, Editor *Fermanagh Miscellany 2*; Doug and Helen Parker, *The Secret Sect*; William Paul, *They Go About 2x2*; Dr. Patricia Roberts, *The Life and Ministry of Edward Cooney*; and Henry Robinson with Ballinamallard Historical Society, *Ballinamallard, A Place of Importance.*

William Irvine's Letters: Nancy Cusick, Llewellyn "Lew" Fountain, Bruce Hartman, Barbara "Briza" James, Leila Muller, Marie (Judd) Parsons, Princeton University, Nancy Sue Rodríguez and Margaret Turner.

Ancestry of William Irvine: Dr. Betty J. Iggo, A.S.G.R.A. (Scotland Genealogist); David Clelland and Daniel Bruce (descendants of Helen Irvine Clelland); David Forrester Mitchell, David Killicoat, Liz Kwasnik and her mother Elizabeth Kwasnik (regarding John Irvine); Lizbeth Freebairn and John Freebairn (descendants of Agnes Irvine Freebairn); and Linda Stopforth (regarding James Irvine).

Faith Mission Assistance: Bobby Dukelow, John G. Eberstein, Rev. Colin N. Peckham, Keith H. Percival, Sandy Roger, John Townend; Valerie Robertson and Catherine Briggs, librarians.

To all of you, especially to the One above, who guided, supported and enabled me to compile this book, I am deeply grateful! "In all thy ways acknowledge him, and he shall direct thy paths" (Prov. 3:6). My sincere apologies to any whose names I have inadvertently left out. For those who provided invaluable assistance but prefer to remain anonymous, your contribution and anonymity are priceless.

Introduction

Sources. Numerous sources were used to compile this book. Over 120 years later, there are, of course, no surviving witnesses to verbally testify about the sect's beginning, but there are volumes of written documents that provide firsthand details by witnesses, reporters and recorders who were present at the sect's formation and early development. Primary materials include diaries, journals, speeches, interviews, memoirs, manuscripts, photographs, autobiographies, letters, published materials (books, magazines and newspapers), official records, court cases, ship passenger lists, genealogies, etc. Many of these are posted on the associated website, *TellingTheTruth.info.*

Newspapers. In this book, quotations from the newspaper, *The Impartial Reporter and Farmers Journal*, outnumber any other source; they produced more articles than any other newspaper. This was largely due to their location in **Enniskillen, Co. Fermanagh, N. Ireland**, the hometown of prominent early preacher, Edward Cooney, and the site of their first large-scale Convention in 1904 and thereafter. Their reporters attended and wrote numerous firsthand, detailed articles about the new sect's emergence, early missions, conventions, baptisms, preachers and members, which provided glimpses into its early development. On January 15, 1903, *The Impartial Reporter* printed their earliest article found to date about the new sect.

Impartial Reporter Newspaper, 8 and 10 East Bridge Street, Enniskillen, N. Ireland (2004)

The very earliest mentions of the sect in the press found to date were on April 12, 19, 26, 1900, when the *Kings County Chronicle* printed some letters to their editor relating to the "malicious destruction" of a wooden hall used by some evangelists in Co. Tipperary, Ireland. Most newspapers cited in this book are available at the British Library in London and also on the associated website, *Telling The Truth* at *TellingTheTruth.info*.

Letters. In bygone centuries, word of mouth and correspondence were the major methods of communication. Fortunately, many letters by primary witnesses have survived. The founder, William Irvine, penned thousands of letters to his followers from 1911 to 1947. *See* website *TellingTheTruth.info* in Founder, Irvine's Letter Collection.

Faith Mission Records. The monthly periodical, *Bright Words*, published by the Faith Mission (FM) headquartered in Edinburgh, Scotland, provided detailed records of their Pilgrim workers and mission locations. William Irvine preached with them for about five years. *See* Chapter 4 and Appendix G.

Historical Accounts. In the past 20 years, several excellent primary sources have come to light providing additional details about this nameless movement. One is a document written in 1935 titled "Account of the Early Days" by Goodhand Pattison of Cloughjordan, Co. Tipperary, Ireland. An early convert and father of two Brother Workers, Pattison is recognized by many members as a reliable firsthand historian of their sect. *Read* on website *TellingTheTruth.info* in Publications.

One of the most informative newly discovered primary sources regarding the movement's early years is the comprehensive *Journal of John Long*, written by John Long, an early preacher who assisted William Irvine at his first independent revival mission in 1897. A former Methodist, Long was a one of Irvine's preachers until 1907. *Read* on website *TellingTheTruth.info* in Publications.

Photography as a Witness. Photography may be viewed as an accurate and objective medium for documenting and preserving historic moments. A film record of the view from the camera's lens, photos bear witness to history. Pictorial history provides glimpses into past lives, long ago events and forgotten places. A powerful aid in chronicling events and telling stories, photos often influence our knowledge and understanding of historical narratives.

Books Published. Four books have been published about Edward Cooney by his official biographer, Dr. Patricia Roberts. *See* Appendix D. *The Secret Sect* by Doug and Helen Parker. *See* Chapter 33.

Internet. With the arrival of the Internet, genealogy resources are readily accessible, providing verification of family, ship passengers, census, immigration and emigration records. Ancestry.com has been a valuable resource.

This book is centric to the United States as I am an American and speak American English. Some quotations are reproduced in their original British English. The examples and perspective in this book do not represent a worldwide view. I regret so little information and few photographs have been included about some countries, due to lack of information.

Divided into Sections A-D, this book presents the 2x2 Sect's history in chronological order in Section A, although some topics or events may also appear in other chapters due to their relevance to multiple subjects. Doctrine and traditions are reviewed in Section B. International expansion is covered in Section C, with a summary of various divisions, purges and revolts worldwide. Section D ends with the Finale. To limit the number of pages in this book, many in-depth details have not been included; however, they are available on the associated website, *TellingTheTruth.info.*

A few unverified comments from unknown sources are prefaced with the words *allegedly, purportedly* or *reportedly,* indicating they are unconfirmed reports. Where there is conflicting, debatable information, all known versions are provided to enable readers to form their own opinions. I strived to portray an unbiased presentation; however, in the literary world, it is recognized that a degree of bias, even unconsciously so, appears in most writings.

Although some errors no doubt exist in this book, much effort has been expended to provide a truthful, accurate account. I apologize for any unwitting errors or unintentional omissions. Should you find any errors, ask yourself if they are significant. Do they jeopardize the accuracy or affect the integrity of the historical facts in this book?

This book and website are not investigations into, nor intentional expositions of, the doctrine and beliefs of the 2x2 Sect, although some are mentioned. When it comes to matters of faith, doctrine and history, I strongly encourage individual examination.

As its title, *Preserving the Truth,* indicates, the purpose of this book is to safeguard and preserve the early historical details of the 2x2 Sect. The past is what it is—it is set in stone. There are many benefits in knowing the past. Although this sect in no small way owes its existence to William Irvine, today few of its followers have ever heard of, or recognize, his name.

Section A –   Development through the Years

All truth passes through three stages.
First, it is ridiculed.
Second, it is violently opposed.
Third, it is accepted as being self-evident.
(Misattributed to Arthur Schopenhauer, 1788–1860)

Facts do not cease to exist because they are ignored.
(Aldous Huxley)

This above all: to thine own self be true
And it must follow, as the night the day
Thou canst not then be false to any man ...
(William Shakespeare, *Hamlet*)

William Irvine (1863–1947)

1

From the Ashes of Despair

New Year's Day, 1893. Looking forward to a diverting, pleasurable time celebrating the New Year, the young, handsome, broad-shouldered Scotsman, William Irvine, invited several of his friends to a Pantomime event. He expected to be entertained and amused; instead, he left the theater feeling disappointed and empty. In fact, he was so depressed and disillusioned with his circumstances that he seriously considered taking his life that very night (to Kerrs, Dec. 4, 1921, *TTT*).

With few career options available in his small hometown of Kilsyth, Scotland, Irvine had followed in the footsteps of many of his male relatives, including his father, grandfather, uncles, brothers and cousins by becoming a collier (coal miner). Mining was a dangerous industry; miners faced possible injury or death daily.

At age ten in 1873, he went underground to work in the coal mines. Through grueling, hazardous, dirty work, he gradually rose to the position of General Manager of Baird's Collieries at Bothwell, Lanarkshire, overseeing two pits and supervising many men. At age 30, making a good salary of about £300 a year, he had the best of prospects ahead.

Professional success aside, Irvine was far from content with his personal life. He disclosed, "1893, on January first, I thought on finishing my course, so much disgusted was I with what the world looked upon as a successful life. It seemed so hollow and disappointing, both in pleasure, place and power" (to Dunbars, Oct. 13, 1920, *TTT*). With his 30th birthday approaching on January 7, the future was weighing heavily on his mind. He longed for a career outside of colliery work.

Unknown to him, a solution loomed on the horizon that would exceed his wildest dreams. Within a week, he would make an unexpected choice that would transform his life. In Irvine's words, the resolution to his dilemma was "quite unexpected and in a way that was quite foreign to any of my plans or calculations." This decision radically altered the future course of his life and the lives of many others worldwide during the following decades.

It all started on a whim. The day after his 30th birthday, Irvine was invited by a friend to attend a revival mission conducted by well-known Evangelist Rev. John McNeill in the nearby town of Motherwell. During the service, Irvine was so deeply moved that he surprised himself by publicly deciding "to serve the Lord, no matter what it meant or cost" (to Wood, Jan. 9, 1946, *TTT*). This surprising small event would have a big impact on the future—*the butterfly effect*.

On the anniversary date of his spiritual decision, he would often reminisce, "My grandfather was born in 1803, my father in 1833, I in 1863, and born again in 1893 on 8th January" (to Newby, April 11, 1946, *TTT*). Irvine entered a lifelong pursuit of God. Before this time, he had taken little interest in the Scripture, explaining, "I followed the blind leaders of the blind 'til I was 30."

Soon, his choice led him to abandon his career, give up his home, move in with his parents (where his illegitimate son may have resided) and attend the Glasgow Bible Training Institute for the next two years.

No one could have guessed how far-reaching the effects would be when Irvine zealously embarked on his spiritual odyssey. From contemplating on taking his life, he would go on to establish a revolutionary religious movement that rapidly spread worldwide.

Main Street at Westport Street Intersection, Kilsyth, Scotland (1915)

❖❖❖

2

1863–1893 – The Man Behind the Movement, Wm. Irvine

To understand the man, William Irvine, it is important to become familiar with his family, culture, values and background. His parents married on December 9, 1858, and over the next two decades they had eleven children. Their third-born child was William Irvine, born on January 7, 1863, in Newtown, Kilsyth, Lanarkshire, Scotland. No middle name was provided on his birth registry. Nevertheless, the initials W.E.I. were engraved in gold on his Bible cover; a few publications identified him as William *Weir* Irvine.

Main Street, Kilsyth, Scotland (circa 2004)

Irvine's mother, Elizabeth (Grassam), was born in Larbert, Scotland, on November 10, 1833, and died November 25, 1897, aged 64. His father, John, was born in Falkirk, Scotland, on July 8, 1833, and died August 12, 1913, aged 80. In birth order, their 11 children were John, Margaret, William, James, Agnes, Henry No. 1, Henry No. 2, Elizabeth, Jane "Jeanie," Helen "Nellie" and Janet "Jennie." The two Henry sons passed away in 1868 and 1870, aged 15 months and 2 years. *See* Appendix B, Irvine Family Tree.

Before his marriage, John Irvine "served with the 79th Cameron Highlanders during the Crimean War (1853–1856) where he saw action in the Battles of Alma, Inkerman and Balaclava and witnessed the famous Charge of the Light Brigade" (Hutchison 2018, 79). He was employed by William Baird & Co. Ltd. in their collieries. For 30 years, he and his two sons, John and James, managed their Dumbreck pit near Kilsyth.

According to local historian James Hutchison, "In 1860, the famous business family, the Bairds of Gartsherrie, began operations in Kilsyth when they leased the Curriemire pit and then began mining for ironstone above Neilston ... In addition, Bairds developed Queezieburn into a coal mining village by opening the Dumbreck pit ... They also built several 'miner's rows' to house their workers in Queenzieburn and in Kilsyth ... by the end of the nineteenth century, Kilsyth was almost entirely a coal mining town with seven local collieries employing between 4,000–5,000 men" (1986, 124–128).

Religious Landscape. Raised by Presbyterian parents, Irvine attended the Burns Free Church of Scotland in Kilsyth. Built in 1816, it was demolished in 2002.

From 1899, Rev. William Jeffrey was the pastor (Hutchison 1986, 72). The Burns Free Church and Old Parish Church united in 1975, becoming the Kilsyth Burns and Old Parish Church, currently located at Eleven Church Street (Anton 1893).

Kilsyth Burns and Old Parish Church

John Irvine, was "one of Dr. [William] Jeffrey's most stalwart supporters and a manager of the Free Church ... As a young boy he ... was greatly influenced by the great revival meetings of that period," pointed out James Hutchison (2018, 79). William Irvine remarked, "I was brought up in that way and was a member of the Kirk till I was 30—but never heard or could hear the voice of the Living God" (to Fred Hill, Feb. 14, 1930, in author's possession). The *Kirk* is a Scottish word for church and particularly refers to the Church of Scotland, that country's national church.

The marriages of Irvine's sisters are further confirmation he was raised Presbyterian. Jane, Helen and Janet were married by Rev. Jeffrey of the Free Church of Scotland; Agnes was married by Rev. Peter Anton of the Church of Scotland. Marriages usually took place in the bride's home.

Family Residences. The 1861 Scotland Census records show Irvine's parents living in Kilsyth, Lanarkshire, where John, Margaret and William were born. Rarely staying in one place for long, the family lived in Strone, Kirkintilloch and Dunbartonshire, during 1864–1868 when James, Agnes and Henry No. 1 were born.

The 1871 Scotland Census indicated the Irvine family had moved to 113 Henderson Street, Kinning Park, Govan, Glasgow, Lanarkshire, when Henry No. 2 and Elizabeth came along. The Irvines were back living in Kilsyth during 1874–1876, when Jane and Helen made their entrance.

The 1881 Census for No. 16 Auchinstarry Row in Cumbernauld, Dunbartonshire, for the Irvine household included John (47), Elizabeth (47), William (18) and James (16), both working as ironstone miners, Agnes (14), Elizabeth (9), Jane (7), Helen (5) and Janet (1). Margaret (20) was working as a live-in servant for the Sommerville family in Kilsyth.

William Baird & Co. typically provided housing for their employees and deducted the rent from their wages. Between 1860 and 1875 they constructed many colliery villages set in open country areas of Lanarkshire and Dunbartonshire, Scotland. Records indicate the Irvine family occupied some of their miners' row houses. Irvine recalled that he refused to wear a cap because he had plenty of rough, curly hair and had "always lived in the country."

Row houses were built of brick or stone in long rows of 10–12 houses all joined together, situated row behind row. A miner's house typically consisted of two rooms connected by a door, with no indoor drainage, toilets or running water. The front room had an entry door, one window and a wood floor. The kitchen contained a fireplace, small stove on a brick or concrete floor. Each room measured about 10–12 by 15 feet.

A renovated miners' row cottage in Kilsyth (circa 1995).
The Irvine family resided in similar homes.

Both rooms had set-in beds containing wooden bed slats. With curtains surrounding them, the recessed beds gave a modicum of privacy. Mattresses were made from feathers, cornhusks, straw, hay, grass, etc. stuffed into a cloth bag. Every dwelling had to store fuel; many did so under the kitchen bed. Outside toilets were shared with several families. Often residents collected their water from wells. Domestic washing was done in a tub in the kitchen or outside. Refuse was deposited in an outside stone-built ashpit serving 10–12 families. *See* photos and details on the Scottish Mining Website, *Housing of Scottish Miners* Report at *scottishmining.co.uk/379.html*.

Births and deaths occurred within the confines of miners' row homes. Mining was dangerous work and tragedies were not uncommon; a death or serious injury could cost the miner's family their home. It is possible the home provided to John Irvine, as General Manager, came with more amenities. Some row houses have been renovated and continue to be occupied.

Ten years later, the 1891 Census showed the Irvine household at Nos. 7 and 8 Auchinstarry Row in Cumbernauld had shrunk to John, Elizabeth, Jane, Helen, Janet and grandson, Archibald Irvine, age four. In this census, William Irvine (28) was a lodger of Robert Condel in Bothwell, Lanarkshire, working as a colliery manager.

Sometime after 1891, the Irvine family moved to Queenzieburn, Kilsyth, where Jane, Helen and Janet were married and their mother, Elizabeth, died in 1897.

1868–1871: Education. In 1868, when Irvine was five years old, he may have started school in Kirkintilloch, Dunbartonshire. It was not until 1880 that an Education Act made it compulsory for children ages five to ten to attend school; this was extended to age twelve in 1899. In 1868 when Irvine was five years old, he may have started school in Kirkintilloch, Dunbartonshire.

After they moved to Glasgow, Irvine attended school there, dropping out in the fourth grade when he started his first job. From age 20 to 30, he made up for his lack of education by attending night school after a long, hard day at work, 12 miles from home. Travel at that time was by foot, bicycle or horse.

1871–1893: Employment Record. As a grocery message boy, eight-year-old Irvine earned £3 a week at his first job. At his second job at the Gray Dunn Biscuit Factory, he worked 72 hours a week for £4 a week. His third job was with Nelson's Foundry for £5 a week, making cores and little kettles. When he was ten years old, he started working underground in the coal mines for his father's employer, William Baird & Co.

The 1833 Factory Act regarding child labor was broadened from textiles to all industries in 1867. The basic act during Irvine's childhood specified: No child workers under nine years (raised to 12 years in 1901); two hours schooling each day; women and children under 18 could not work more than ten hours a day.

A strong, husky boy by age 16, Irvine was earning more than his father. By the time he was 20, he earned £200 a year. He and his older sister, Margaret, moved away from home; she was his housekeeper for three years until her death in 1886. From 20 to 30 years of age, Irvine held various mining jobs, working his way to the top through very hard work.

At the colliery in Calderbank, he worked for nearly a year; Haugh No. 1 at Kilsyth for four years; Meiklehill Nos. 4 and 5 in Kirkintilloch for a year; and he ended his career in 1893 at Bairds in Bothwell Park, Lanarkshire, where at age 30, he held the position of general manager, earning £300 per year.

Courtship. Only once in Irvine's correspondence did he mention a sweetheart. "Bella Jarvis, who became Mrs. Shaw. She was a very nice, sweet girl. When I gave her up, I went to Calderbank" (to Lauchlin, Jan. 1, 1944, *TTT*). He never married, confiding, "what a tragedy it would have been for me to have married and dragged the woman I loved through all the conflict of these 34 years" (to Lauchlin, Feb. 23, 1927, *TTT*).

1884, January 23: Freemasonry. Irvine was 21, when he became a lifetime member of the Masonic Lodge. Years later, he disclosed in letters his status as a Freemason, "I also am a Free and accepted Master Mason. My Mother Lodge being 547 Stewart Scotch" (to Sheeley, Jan. 30, 1929, *TTT*). "I am a Mason for over 50 years, though I don't take any stock in it" (to Berglinds, Sept. 10, 1937, *TTT*). He claimed the last time he set foot in a Mason's Lodge was in 1894, when he was 31.

Irvine's membership in the Grand Lodge of Antient Free and Accepted Masons of Scotland was verified in a letter to Cherie Kropp by James L. Noble, Grand Secretary, dated November 19, 2010. "I ... can confirm that the records held within my office do show that Brother William Irvine was Initiated within Lodge Steuart [*sic: Stewart*] No. 547, Kilsyth, Stirlingshire, on 23 January 1884; Passed to the Fellowcraft Degree on 7 January 1885; and Raised to the Master Mason Degree on 17 January 1885. His occupation is shown as a miner, age 25 years. Unfortunately, this Lodge was declared dormant in 1898."

Arguably, Noble's records for a William Irvine who was 25 years old in 1884–1885 may not be the same William Irvine born in 1863 (who would have been about 21 in 1884) who stated in 1937 that he had been a Mason for over 50 years. It is possible there was an error in transcription in the date in Irvine or Noble's letters, or perhaps Noble's record was for another Mason by the same name.

Very little is known about Irvine's connection to Freemasonry. The adage "Masonry is generational" was certainly true in the Irvine family. His grandfather, John A. Irvine, was the Grandmaster of the Kilsyth Lodge 1866–1867. Freemasonry was well represented by other Irvine family members, including his father, Uncle Walter, several cousins, his brother-in-law, John Freebairn, and likely more.

1886–1887: Deaths of Two Sisters. Margaret, Irvine's older unmarried sister, who roomed with him, died on July 18, 1886, aged 25, from phthisis (tuberculosis). He reminisced, "I lost my sister when she was 25 and I, 23. She was like a second mother to me, and we were more to each other than any of the others younger could be" (to Pincetl, Feb. 21, 1946, *TTT*). Less than a year later, his unmarried sister, Elizabeth, died on June 15, 1887, aged 15, of periostitis.

1886, April 23: Birth of William Grassam. According to Lizbeth Freebairn,* an Irvine family descendant, it was common knowledge in their family that Irvine fathered an illegitimate son when he was in his early twenties.

The 1891 Scotland Census showed grandson, Archibald Irvine, age four, living with John and Elizabeth Irvine. Any of their three sons could be the father of this grandson. James never had any children; John had no sons named Archibald; and William was known to have an illegitimate son. Could it be the four-year-old grandson Archibald was the son of William Irvine?

Ms. Freebairn located a birth register entry for William Grassam, born on April 23, 1886, to Margaret Helen Grassam, a domestic servant. In place of the father's name was the notation *illegitimate*. Wm. Irvine was 23 in 1886. The mother was born on April 16, 1859, in Larbert, Stirlingshire, Scotland, to Archibald (1831–1874) and Marion (Howden) Grassam (1832–1891). Since Margaret's father and Wm. Irvine's mother were siblings, Margaret and William were first cousins.

In 1888, when William Grassam was nearly two years old, his mother, Margaret Grassam, age 28, married John Hastings, age 36, in Falkirk, Scotland. He was a widower with three sons. Together they had two more children. Four years after they married, John Hastings died in 1892, aged 41. Margaret died on October 5, 1915, aged 56. The first Scotland Census taken after William Grassam's birth was in 1891 when he was four years old. It did not show him living in the Hastings household.

Archibald Grassam Irvine and William Grassam share the same birthdate (April 23, 1886) and birthplace (Glasgow, Scotland). These vital statistics are consistently shown on the records of Archibald Irvine's death, tombstone, marriage, university, church, World War I military service and in the *Register of New Zealand Presbyterian Church Ministers*.

A birth record has not been found for Archibald Grassam. Possibly John and Elizabeth Irvine adopted their son's illegitimate offspring prior to the 1891 Census and changed his name to Archibald Grassam Irvine (name of Elizabeth's father and grandfather). At that time, adoptions were arranged on a private basis by individuals and charitable agencies. Since the Scotland National Archives hold no adoption records prior to 1930, an adoption cannot be confirmed.

Archibald used his grandparents' names for his parents on various legal documents, except for one. An Attestation for General Service in New Zealand Expeditionary Force in World War I showed Margaret *Irvine* as his mother and John Irvine as his father. (His mother was Margaret *Grassam* and his grandmother was *Elizabeth* Irvine.)

In summary, there are two records of male children born into the same family with identical birthdates and birthplaces, with the names William Grassam and Archibald Grassam Irvine. Although there is no proof, Lizbeth Freebairn* and I agree there is sufficient evidence to reasonably conclude that William Grassam's name was changed to Archibald Grassam Irvine, and that they are one and the same person.

From this point forward in this book, Archibald "Archie" Grassam Irvine is treated as Wm. Irvine's son.

The 1901 Scotland Census did not include John Irvine's household, as and he and Archie were out of the country. His wife, Elizabeth, had passed away in 1897, when Archie was 11 years old.

On July 19, 1900, Archie (14), his widowed grandfather, John Irvine (66), along with John's son, James (40), his wife Catherine (35) and a cousin, William McCallum, departed from Scotland for New Zealand aboard the SS *Whakatane*. For 30 years, from age ten, James had been working at the Dumbreck pit managed by his father. They went to visit John Irvine's brother, James, and his wife, Jane, who immigrated to Dunedin, New Zealand, in 1863, where they started the House of George, a thriving canning factory. In 1902, John Irvine was the only one of the five travelers to return to Scotland. His son, James, and wife, Catherine, were buried in 1928 and 1940, respectively, in Dunedin, Otago, New Zealand.

Archie became a permanent New Zealand resident and graduated with a Master of Arts (M.A.) degree in 1916 from the University of New Zealand at Otago. Since the Irvine family members were strong Presbyterians, it is not surprising that Archie became an ordained Presbyterian minister at Waiareka in 1916. During World War I, he was a chaplain with the New Zealand Expeditionary Force. He became a minister of the Presbyterian Church at Ashburton in 1924 and in Hawera in 1933.

Archibald Grassam Irvine, age 30, married Mary Jamieson Murray, age 27, on October 24, 1916; they had no children. His marriage certificate shows John and Elizabeth Irvine as his parents. Soon after he retired in 1950, Archie passed away on June 14, 1952, aged 66; Mary died December 19, 1982, aged 93; both were buried in Bromley Cemetery, Christchurch, New Zealand. His father, William Irvine, died in 1947, aged 84; his son Archibald was not mentioned in his will. *See also* Chapter 30 and Appendix B.

*Lizbeth Freebairn, an avid genealogy researcher of the Irvine family lineage, is the granddaughter of Wm. Irvine's sister, Agnes, who married John Freebairn. She has resided both in Kilsyth, Scotland, and New Zealand. Her voluntary contributions of time, information and photographs are very much appreciated.

3

1893–1895 – The Turning Point

The January 7, 1893, *Motherwell Times* contained an announcement that revival services would be held on January 8–13, 1893, in Motherwell, Lanarkshire, Scotland, conducted by Evangelist Rev. John McNeill. According to his official biography, *Rev. John McNeill, His Life and Work* (Gammie 1933), he was affiliated with Dwight L. Moody's evangelistic campaign from 1892 to 1907. *See* Appendix F.

On January 8, 1893, the day after he turned 30, William Irvine made his choice to serve the Lord in Rev. McNeill's first service held in the Motherwell Town Hall. On the anniversary date of his conversion, he would often recall in his letters the unexpected decision he made that day in 1893 that altered the course of his life. "Seventy-two years ago, I was born into a Presbyterian family; forty-two years ago, I was born into the family of which Jesus is the head, as Adam is of the human family. A Presbyterian preacher was the means" (to Billett, Jan. 8, 1934, *TTT*).

Motherwell Town Hall, site of Rev. McNeil's mission where Irvine was born again

Presbyterian minister John McNeil, through whom Irvine was converted on January 8, 1893

Documents written by his close friends, Edward Cooney, John Long, Joe Kerr and Goodhand Pattison, as well as newspaper accounts, provide further confirmation that Irvine was converted through Rev. John McNeill.

1893: Employment Resignation. Five days after his decision to serve the Lord, Irvine openly confessed his choice to the men over whom he was taskmaster. He began his 30th year deciding whom he would and would not serve. He jettisoned habits, friends and activities (to Kerrs, Dec. 4, 1921, *TTT*). Irvine "very soon found out that neither church nor world fitted the New Testament service of the Master I had chosen ... I was not satisfied with my knowledge of the Book and wanted to get rid of much of my old infidelity and other things which I had learned. I had been in the yoke since I was eight years of age and could afford to take a little look around; and in spite of all my friends and enemies, I did what the Lord was prompting me to do" (to Dunbars, Oct. 13, 1920, *TTT*).

Eight months later in September, he turned in his resignation to Baird & Co.; he walked away a free man on November 1, 1893, on what many thought was a "wild goose chase." Considered foolish for throwing away his successful career, some scoffed, "You're not preacher material!"

Regardless of opposition from family, friends and enemies, he steadfastly continued with his plans. He later stated, "I got saved and left the company 45 years ago to follow and serve Jesus in the Gospel, which created much talk and stirred people up to oppose doing such a foolish thing ... but in spite of opposition in home, friends and enemies, I went" (to W. Edwards, Feb. 18, 1938, in author's possession).

1893: Bible Training Institute. After Irvine left his job, he moved in with his parents (where his son, Archie, may have resided). He stipulated in a legal document that he "studied in the Bible Training Institute, Glasgow, for two years" (Irvine 1913, Statement, Appendix B). He acknowledged, "I benefited in the Bible Institute by getting to know the Book according to the teachings of the best and most holy and evangelical missionary people in the world" (to Dunbars, Oct. 13, 1920, *TTT*).

The Bible Training Institute opened in 1892, with John Anderson as principal. In 1991, the name was changed to Glasgow Bible College, which merged in 1998 with the Northumbria Bible College to become the International Christian College. Its doors permanently closed on June 30, 2018.

Influence of Irvine's Sister. Irvine claimed his spiritual turn-around in 1893 was influenced by the death of his sister, Margaret. He reminisced, "My favorite and elder sister died 51 years ago; but it broke my infidelity and rebellion against God" (to Grims, May 20, 1937, *TTT*). "I owe more to the loss of my sister when she was 25 and I, 23, than to all other circumstances and events" (to Duncan, May 12, 1934, *TTT*).

1895: William Irvine's Call to Service. Following the example of Madam Jeanne Marie Bouvier De La Motte Guyon, the author of a book he had been reading, Irvine opened his Bible and randomly placed his finger on a verse. From that time forward, he took that verse to be his personal *Call to Service* from God. The verse was Isaiah 41:15:

"Behold, I will make thee a new, sharp threshing instrument having teeth: thou shalt thresh the mountains, and beat them small, and make the hills as chaff."

Irvine believed God had called him to protest the evils of Christendom. "The Lord gave me Isaiah 41:10–20 ... and it has always been before me ... It was in June 1895, that I bowed my head and asked the Lord to give me encouragement, as He had given Madam Su Yen [*sic:* Madame Guyon], whose book I was reading. She opened the Book and put her finger on this spot, and when I opened my Book, it was at the same place" (to Edwards, March 3, 1924. *TTT*).

Irvine took his Call to Service very seriously and believed God intended for this verse to be his life's mission. It was no secret he viewed himself as the thresher with sharp teeth, beating down mountains of clericalism. Later, he proclaimed "What John the Baptist was to Jesus as forerunner, John the apostle from Heaven will be to Jesus' second coming. Isaiah 40 is his work and Isaiah 41 is my work, as Jacob, with a few who share my anointing" (to Billetts, Jan. 8, 1934, *TTT*). According to historian Goodhand Pattison:

> Mr. Irvine regarded Isa. 41:15–16 as his 'Call to Service' and certainly seemed to fit in with the description given there. The threshing instrument was to be new and sharp, having teeth, and most people who knew him in those and subsequent days can well remember how well he could thresh and how sharp could be his bite ... being a 'new' instrument, very 'uncommon' in his methods and his 'like or equal' unknown or unheard of ... there was not another in all the world who could or would have dealt such deadly blows to the 'mountains' of clergy, and of clericalism and so-called organizations, or to the 'hills' of traditional social customs and usages. (1935, Threshing, *TTT*)

Faith Mission Headquarters, Gilmerton, Edinburgh, Scotland (2004)

Mount Clare, Rothesay, Isle of Bute, Scotland 1897–1910
Site of Faith Mission Headquarters, Training Home and Annual Convention

☘☘☘

4

1895–1901 – The Faith Mission

1895, June 14: Irvine Joined the Faith Mission. After completing two years at the Bible Institute, Irvine carefully considered his options. On June 14, 1895, he "finally chose to join the Faith Mission, which showed the most spiritual (*sic:* spirit) and fire" (to Dunbars, October 13, 1920, *TTT*).

The Faith Mission (FM) is a Protestant evangelical movement founded in Scotland by John George Govan (J. G. Govan). According to their monthly periodical, "Faith Mission was founded in 1886, for the promotion of spiritual life and godliness through the evangelising of the country districts of Scotland, and farther afield if God leads, on unsectarian lines. Evangelists, called *Pilgrims,* generally work in pairs. They visit a place for several weeks, more or less, according as circumstances and the leadings of the Spirit of God seem to indicate advisable, visiting among the people and holding meetings for the unsaved and for Christians, in which they welcome the cooperation of all who love the Lord Jesus in sincerity" (*Bright Words,* Sept. 1900, 200).

Faith Mission Pilgrims were instructed to lead sinners to accept Christ as their Lord and to set up Prayer Unions. Those interested in becoming Pilgrims were referred to the founder, John Govan. After an approved volunteer went through a training session, the new Pilgrim was paired with an experienced Pilgrim in the mission field. Pilgrims did the work of an evangelist (not pastors). "And he gave some, apostles; and some, prophets; and some, *evangelists*; and some, pastors and teachers" (Eph. 4:11).

The FM is still in operation. Its headquarters and Bible College are in Edinburgh, Scotland. Their Pilgrims evangelize in Scotland, England and Ireland. Affiliated branches are established in Australia, Canada, South Africa, France, etc. Their website explains, "As an interdenominational agency, it works closely with all Christian churches that share a similar concern for passionate evangelism and evangelical truth, especially in areas where there is little or no biblical witness."

Irvine's affiliation with FM was described by Goodhand Pattison. "I must ... introduce the 'Faith Mission' ... [which was] quite new to me until William Irvine's arrival in these parts, and while he made no secret of the fact, either publicly or privately, that in preaching the Gospel he was connected with and owed allegiance to that association, and would continue to do so ... until he found better; yet he never for a moment sought to preach up the Faith Mission so as to obscure his hearers' vision, or hide for a moment his Lord from their eyes. First and last, it was 'Jesus Only.' "

Irvine's name was first mentioned in August 1895 in the FM's monthly publication, *Bright Words*: "In the south a mission is being worked by two brothers who have recently joined us, William Irvine, from Queenzieburn, and Angus M'Lean, from Tiree" (1895, *TTT*). At that time, there were 45 FM Pilgrims; 6 years later when Irvine left, there were 60.

J. G. Govan's father, William Govan Jr. (1819–1883), worked in the family business, William Govan & Son, a textile manufacturer in Glasgow, Scotland, which can be traced back at least to the late eighteenth century. His mother, Margaret Arthur Govan (1822–1891), was the daughter of a Congregational Church minister.

J. G. Govan's early life was influenced by Christian parents, grandparents and godly examples in their family and home, e.g. D. L. Moody and Rev. William Booth, founder of Salvation Army, with their holiness messages. When he was 12 years old (1873), he accepted Christ through an address given by his father. In 1879, his parents re-joined the Congregational Church founded in 1812. J. G. joined in 1881. In 1882, he was profoundly moved while attending about 40 of Moody's meetings in Glasgow. While five of the six Govan brothers "could preach the gospel and preach it well; but probably James would be accepted as the preacher of the family" (William Govan Family Account by James Eustace Govan, June 1980, in author's possession).

John George Govan (1861-1927)
Founded Faith Mission in 1886

With no ecclesiastical credentials, J. G. Govan (age 25) started the Faith Mission on October 14, 1886. He declared,

I believe God gave us the name [Faith Mission]. Faith was to be the principle of the mission: faith in God, and in Him alone; absolute dependence upon Him for everything necessary, for guidance, for health and strength besides food and clothing; faith for the future, as well as faith for the present. Faith lives on distinct promises such as: 'They who preach the gospel shall live by the gospel' and 'They that seek the Lord shall not want any good thing.' And the word 'I will never leave thee nor forsake thee' covers all contingencies ... We want those who will forswear all the comforts of home, all the ambitions of life and the pleasures of the world to go out as 'Pilgrims and strangers on the Earth,' and live entirely for God. (*First!*, Sept-Oct 2011)

Originally, FM concentrated mainly on enlisting unmarried youth. Many sacrificed home, family, financial security and marriage to be entirely free to reach the lost and unsaved. They did not accept candidates who used tobacco or liquor. Only superintendents were allowed to marry. Generally, Pilgrims were given one month to rest annually during the summer.

Agnes Jack and Annie Martin, the first female Pilgrims, were accepted in March 1887. In September 1894, J. G. Govan married Annie Martin wearing her Pilgrim uniform; they had four children. John George Govan was one of thirteen children born to William and Margaret (Arthur) Govan. Born in Glasgow, Scotland, on January 19, 1861, J. G. Govan died October 3, 1927, in Perth, Scotland, aged 66. Annie, born in 1870, and died July 26, 1932. The family tombstone is in Dean Cemetery, Edinburgh, Scotland.

Determined not to start a sect, FM refrained from administering baptism or communion. They began forming interdenominational midweek Prayer Union meetings in June 1887, a place where Christians could fellowship, pray and encourage one another. **The Prayer Unions did not take the place of a church—the members retained their church memberships and attended the churches of their choice.**

From *Faith Mission Aims and Principles*: "We do not wish in any way to interfere with denominational preferences and distinctions, but leave those who get help through our missions, to attach themselves to whatever church, chapel, or meeting house they choose." They were unsectarian. According to Govan, "The mission does not seek to advance its own interests, to draw away members from existing organizations, or run down other sects. Its aim is to build up the Kingdom, and for this purpose to have fellowship with all God's people" (1978, 40). *See* Appendix G.

IMPORTANT! The reader needs to understand that the Faith Mission is NOT a sect, church, denomination or religion. They do not have organized churches, do not baptize or serve communion in their Prayer Union services. As their name states, they are a *faith* **mission.**

Faith Mission Dress Codes. Early in the twentieth century, FM Pilgrims followed a strict dress code. Their bonneted female Pilgrims were well-known by their long, dark skirts worn over black stockings and court shoes into the 1950s and '60s. The male Pilgrims wore coats with lapels and a FM motif on their pockets.

Faith Mission Workers Lists. Annually, a Staff of Workers List was updated in FM's monthly magazine *Bright Words.* It showed each Pilgrim's name and the date they entered FM. Under the founder's name (J. G. Govan 1886) at the top, the Pilgrims were listed by seniority.

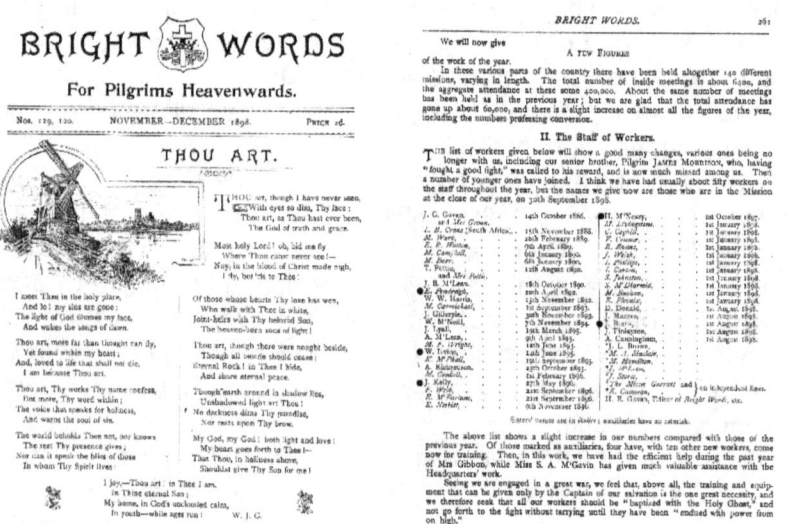

"Bright Words," Faith Mission's monthly magazine
Cover and Staff of Workers list (Dec. 1898)
Later, names marked •joined Irvine's movement

Faith Mission Finances. Open about their finances, financial reports were printed in their monthly publication, *Bright Words.* Each September they published a Statement of Accounts summarizing their annual income and expenses. The Fourteenth Annual Report in *Bright Words* began with the following statement by their founder: "The Mission is maintained on the faith principle, by freewill offerings during missions and unsolicited contributions to headquarters" (Sept. 1900, 200). Quarterly, they published a list of donations for each fund, e.g. General, Special, Foreign, Resting.

Each Pilgrim received an allowance. For the year ending September 1900, *Bright Words* reported, "The amount for maintenance of our workers is £10 less [than in 1899], and when the total amount ... is divided by the number of Pilgrims in the mission ... it gives the average cost of about £28 each for maintenance, which is exceedingly moderate" (Nov.–Dec. 1900, *TTT;* £28 divided by 12 months is £2.33 per month in 1900). *See* this report and the Annual Staff of Workers List on the website *TellingTheTruth*.info in History, Newspaper Articles-Old, *Bright Words*.

They were truly, in the literal sense of the term, a *faith mission*. They did accept donations for heating, lighting, halls, lodgings, etc. Quarterly, FM Pilgrims sent a report to headquarters that included income, expenses and attendance figures. Any surplus money was forwarded to headquarters who met any deficits (personal communication, Dukelow to R. Kee, April 16, 2002). Historian G. Pattison elaborated:

> While conducting missions they did not take up collections, but at or near the close of a mission, if not before, they intimated or allowed it to be understood that they would accept a thank-offering from those who felt like giving one, for blessing received. These offerings were sent to Headquarters ... In their preaching they did not usually attack clergy or churches, but when the mission was over and any professed to have got saved, or otherwise helped by their ministrations, they sought to establish 'Prayer Unions,' with cards of membership pledging the members to attendance of united prayer meetings at various centres, etc. (1935, Faith Mission, *TTT*)

Supporting Archibald Irvine. When Irvine entered FM in 1895, his son, Archibald, was nine years old. The question sometimes arises: How was Archie Irvine supported between 1895 and 1900 while William Irvine was a FM Pilgrim? Did Irvine use funds intended for the FM to support his son?

It is possible, but no evidence has been found that he did so. Since the records are silent, all we know for certain is that we do not know. However, the allowance for FM Pilgrims was barely enough to survive on, a mere £2.33 per month in 1900. Perhaps, Irvine had saved money from his working days that he gave his parents to provide for his son.

See also Chapter 2 and Appendix B.

the different townships were resorted to. Never, we think, has Christian work been more successful in the district, and, considering the number that have openly professed Christ, the results are really pleasing and happy. Even on the coarsest nights there was always a good attendance, while in good weather the house was often crowded. It was pleasing to see so many coming over bad roads, amid pelting rains and in the darkness of winter nights. Many who were rather remiss in their attendance at church heretofore, could very often be seen taking their seat among the audience. On December 31st a watch-night meeting was held, which was largely attended, and in meditation and prayer the New Year was ushered in. It was the first meeting of its kind ever held in this particular district, and it was a very solemn occasion. On the night of 12th January, again, a most successful tea-meeting was held. This was New Year in the old style, and the attendance of young people on that occasion was most remarkable. The Rev. Mr Brown, Baptist minister, and the Rev. D. M'Lean, Bunessan, took part in the proceedings. The Rev. Mr Dewar, of Iona, and the Rev. Mr Stewart, of Ross of Mull Free Church, though not present at this meeting, encouraged the pilgrims during their stay in the district.

A Prayer Union has been formed, and the young converts meet every Tuesday for prayer, Bible reading, and singing.

J. M.

ACHOSNICH.—After our special Old New-Year gatherings we are once more " on a mission "—this time to ARDNAMURCHAN, where there are a good number who truly love the Lord. It was about this time last year that the first mission was opened, and, after almost a year's experience of living for Jesus, the converts' only desire is to know more of their blessed Lord and Master, and they are not afraid to tell it out. Night after night, as one looked across the crofts in the direction where the meeting was to be held, it was really inspiring to see here and there a little company of old and young climbing

the hill, lamp in hand, and singing as they came, if not audibly, truly in the heart. Several have professed since our coming this time, and others been helped. Two sister-pilgrims paid them a brief visit this winter, which was a real help to them all, especially to those that were not so strong in the faith.

Now we must pass on elsewhere, for we are *pilgrims.* Let each of us remember these friends continually in our prayers. The people are above measure kind ; if any-one doubts Highland hospitality, let him come to Ardnamurchan.

M'L. and P.

Ireland.

Place.	Pilgrims.	Opened.	Closed.
KILLYMAN,	Barr, M. R. Wright.	Nov. 29.	Feb. 1.
BALLINDERRY,	Morrison, Taberner.	Dec. 27.	
BALLYNURE,	M.F.Wright, Goodall.	Jan. 3.	
TULLYARRAN,	Lyall, Kelly.	Jan. 10.	
KILLYBEGS,	M. and H. Garratt.		
ENNIS,	Irvine and Deathe.		

Beside the missions that are reported, let me add a few notes about the others.

BALLYNURE is very encouraging, and souls are deciding for Jesus nightly. Praise the Lord.

TULLYARRAN (Co. Tyrone) has had a good opening, and the attendance and interest are very satisfactory. Up to the present, after-meetings have not been held, but we hope that by the time this reaches *B. W.* readers there will be a harvest of souls.

KILLYBEGS (Co. Donegal) has good meetings, many of the converts of the Aughay-eougue mission coming nightly.

For long we have been praying and hoping to go to the more neglected parts of this island. At length we have made a start, and Pilgrims Irvine and Deathe have gone to the south-west. At present their work is mostly pioneering. Let us pray much that the Lord may open a door before them, and that fruit may be won for Jesus from the dark places of this land.

Pilgrim M'Lean has, besides visiting various P.Us., had a week of Christians' meetings at PORT STEWART. Though the attendance was small, we trust that there shall be fruit that will remain. He and Mr Estall probably begin a Gospel mission soon.

Faith Mission Publication "Bright Words" (February 15, 1897)

5

1896–1897 – Pilgrim's Progress in Ireland

1891: FAITH MISSION EXPANDS INTO IRELAND. In their beginning, Faith Mission limited their work to Scotland. After J. G. Govan made his first visit to Belfast, Ireland on May 27, 1891, they began working missions in Co. Antrim, Ireland. *"By 1894 the work was firmly established and on 12th of July 1895, conferences were held in a tent at Ballymena* [N. Ireland] *which was packed with more than 1,500 people present"* (Peckham 1986, 38).

1896, May: William Irvine Sent to Ireland. After joining FM in 1895, Irvine preached in Scotland until he was sent to Ireland in May 1896. *Bright Words* reported, "Ireland: For long we have been praying and hoping to go to the more neglected parts of this island. At length we have made a start, and Pilgrims Irvine and Deathe have gone to the Southwest. At present their work is mostly pioneering" (Feb. 15, 1897, 39, *TTT*).

Irvine wrote, *"In November 1896, I was sent to the West of Ireland to the hottest Roman Catholic spot in the world ... After 6 or 7 months there, I got to where the Carrolls were in Nenagh; and there began the work that has spread so far ... that stirred the whole of that country for years to come, as I did in Southwest Ireland and finally all over Ireland"* (to Dunbars Oct. 13, 1920, *TTT*).

From January 1 to November, 1897, Irvine preached in the southern Irish counties of Clare, Trim, Kerry, Tipperary and Meath (*Bright Words*, June 15, 1897, 146, *TTT*), except for the time he spent with his seriously ill mother in the Spring (to Kerrs Dec. 4, 1921, *TTT*).

1897, March: Kilrush, Co. Clare. According to FM records, Irvine was holding a mission in Kilrush, Co. Clare from March 30 to May 15, 1897. They reported, "Kilrush is a very Roman Catholic town. Pilgrim Irvine, joined recently by Pilgrim Taberner, is working away quietly. They have had one or two interesting lantern meetings. Those in such stiff fields specially need our prayers" (*Bright Words*, May 15, 1897, 113, *TTT*). A magic lantern was essentially a slide projector. A very modern concept in 1897, it was an ingenious way to arouse curiosity and interest in an evangelistic mission. John Long, a Methodist colporteur, was present and explained:

> He had announced for a magic lantern address, in order to influence the Roman Catholic people to come into the little Methodist Chapel to hear singing, and the Gospel Message. The lantern refused to work that night … so he turned it into a sermon. Some Romans were in the meeting and the evangelist [William Irvine] spoke with great vehemence, love, power; placing Catholic and Protestants on the same natural condition, namely all are sinners, all need salvation or regeneration … After the meeting I was introduced to him; then he took me down a street, where he put tracts under doors in the homes and dropped them on the footpath … Next day being the Sabbath, he took me where we had private prayer together. (March 1897, *TTT*)

Dora and Harry Holland. After a long dry spell of preaching with no response, finally, a young woman named Dora Holland attended Irvine's mission in Kilrush and converted. It is generally accepted that Dora was Irvine's first Irish convert. Harry Holland, Dora's brother, stated in a letter (1966), "My sister, Dora, was 90 on January first. She was the first person to profess in Ireland … That was … before I left Ireland … in 1899."

Dora Holland (1876–1968) and her brother Harry Holland (1877–1967)
Dora, Irvine's first convert, entered the work in 1902, and Harry in 1908

J. G. Govan remarked, "Our brothers in the Southwest, after closing the mission at Kilrush, spent a week or two itinerating—visiting farms, selling literature, distributing tracts, singing, praying and talking with the people, and continually holding a meeting … Pilgrim Irvine has had to go home for a little on account of the serious illness of his mother" (*Bright Words*, June 15, 1897, 146, *TTT*).

The 1901 Irish Census confirmed that Dorathy Holland (24), a Methodist governess, resided in the household of Mary E. M. Peacocke in Kilrush, Co. Clare. Dora explained, "It was while I was there that two preachers came along and held meetings in the town. I attended the services. They were held by a Mr. William Irvine from Scotland, and his companion. It was at that time that I made the choice I would yield my life fully to God's control. I decided then that I would give my life to Gospel Work sometime but continued teaching for a few years" (to Dear Brother, Aug. 11, 1913, *TTT*).

Besides 1897, two other years (1895 and 1896) have been given for Dora's conversion. During a trip to Ireland in 1985, Dora's nephew, Sydney Holt, Overseer of Washington, US, composed several letters to his American "Fellow Laborers and Friends." He visited "Mother's three sisters in their nineties ... [who] filled me in on more family history dating back to Aunt Dora Holland hearing the gospel in **1896** in Kilrush in the western part of Ireland" (May 1, 1985, *TTT*). Dora's eulogy contained the statement, "She heard the gospel and professed in **1896**."

A transcript of a talk by Dora's niece, Hazel Hughes, provided **1895** as the year Dora professed through Irvine, which also inconsistently stated Irvine did not arrive in Ireland until 1896. Additional discrepancies in this account are reviewed on the website *TellingTheTruth.info*, in Workers Early, Gill-Hughes (Hughes 1971, *TTT*).

Dorathy "Dora" Holland was born on January 1, 1876, in Galway, Ireland, and died on August 1, 1968. She became a preacher in 1902. Along with 16 other missionaries, she arrived in Montreal, Quebec, Canada, aboard the SS *Virginian* on August 4, 1905. Her brother, Henry "Harry," was born February 6, 1877, in Galway, Ireland, and died April 30, 1967; he preached in North and South Dakota. Buried beside each other, the two siblings share a tombstone in Graceland Cemetery, Madison, South Dakota, US. Four more of their sisters were also preachers: Maud, Kathleen, Mable and Muriel Holland.

John Long

John Long's son (also John) with his wife Mollie

6

1897 – Genesis of the Irish Revival – John Long

1897, February: Profile of John Long. The first time John Long heard of William Irvine was when the Methodist minister Rev. Charles Cronhelm asked him to meet two Faith Mission (FM) evangelists in Kilrush, Co. Clare, Ireland. Long complied and spent an interesting weekend with Irvine (Long Feb. 1897, *TTT*).

One of eight children, John Long was born on September 15, 1872, at Burntwood, Cloughjordan, Co. Tipperary, Ireland, to Gilbert and Ann (Turner) Long; he died July 4, 1962, aged 90. He began attending Sunday school in the Episcopal Church when he was 12 and was confirmed at age 16. He also signed the Temperance Pledge against alcoholic liquor and was a total abstainer all his life.

In 1890, Long left the Episcopal Church and joined the Methodists because "Episcopalianism lacked the preaching of conversion, the witness of the Spirit, the present possession of eternal life, confessing Christ with the mouth, family prayer and liberty for laymen to preach in the churches. Methodists preached those essential and vital truths" (Sept. 1893, *TTT*). According to John Wesley, the founder of Methodism, "a Methodist is one that lives according to the method laid down in the Bible."

In November 1890, when he was 18, Long left home and became a domestic servant for Rev. Leopold O'Sullivan, the Methodist rector for Cloughjordan. On Saturday evenings, as a member of the Methodist Preacher's Plan, Long, a layman, preached in meetings in nearby towns and villages.

Feeling that God was calling him to go *fully* into the Lord's Work, at age 23 on February 19, 1895, Long became a colporteur in the Methodist society, the only branch of mission work open to him. As a colporteur, he lived on "a salary of £1 a week; it took ten shillings a week for lodging besides travelling expenses and clothing, and a tenth to the Lord and postage, etc., so as that a colporteur had barely maintenance" (Sept. 1895, *TTT*).

Long explained that there were no Bibles in most Roman Catholic homes, bookstores or libraries. Christian Protestants "tried through the agency of the colportage work to place the Scriptures in the hands of all who desired to have them. The colportage work was really a mission work. It consisted in selling the Scriptures and other Christian books to all denominations; also personal conversations with the people about their soul's salvation, together with giving away tracts, and reading and praying in the homes and occasionally holding Gospel Meetings" (1895, *TTT*). "While in the colportage work ... in round numbers, I must have sold and circulated upwards of 100,000 literature, from the Bible to the tract" (Nov. 1898, *TTT*).

1897, June: John Long and William Irvine happened to be on the same ship en route to Kilkee. Irvine was returning from Scotland where he had been visiting his ailing mother. Soon after, Long went to Tarbert, Co. Kerry, where he lodged for two weeks in the same house as Irvine and Pilgrim Fred Tapp.

In July 1897, Long found Irvine, "very happy, but at times repining over the spiritual laxity of the churches, and was spending much time in prayer for a revival ... He [Irvine] was out of an opening, and one day when he was praying, it was revealed to me by the Holy Spirit, to write to Goodhand Pattison, the Cloughjordan Methodist Steward, about an opening for a mission" (July 1897, *TTT*).

The Red-Hot Evangelist. G. Pattison recalled, "I got a letter from John Long ... He said, 'There's a man here, an evangelist who would cause a stir in Cloughjordan if you ask him along' ... we had not much to lose, and at least the possibility of gain, by the incoming of a red-hot evangelist, even if a bit off orthodox lines" (1935, John Long, *TTT*).

1897: First Nenagh Mission. Long's letter resulted in Irvine holding a very successful four-week revival mission in the Nenagh Methodist Church in Co. Tipperary, from August 15 to September 16, 1897. "At his [Irvine's] first meeting only 5 persons attended; but at the closing meeting, there were 100 present ... altogether upwards of 30 persons of position and note got converted; most of them afterwards gave up all that they had to follow Jesus," reported Long (Aug. 1897, *TTT*). (The Nenagh Methodist Church was demolished in 2004.)

G. Pattison recalled, "Nenagh ... yielded quite a crop of decisions for God," including Jack and May Carroll and many others (1935, Burning and Shining Light, *TTT*). Irvine recounted, "After six or seven months there [West of Ireland], I got to where the Carrolls were in Nenagh; and there began the Work that has spread so far ... that stirred the whole of that country for years to come, as I did in Southwest Ireland and finally all over Ireland" (to Dunbars, Oct. 13, 1920, *TTT*).

A friend invited Jack Carroll to Irvine's Gospel Mission in Nenagh. He went, saying to himself: " 'This is just going to be like every other meeting. I will go and listen and that will be the end of it.' ... when the meeting was over, I was the first out and down the street, but I was a different man. As I sat in that meeting that night, I was careless, hopeless, Godless and Christless; didn't care if there was a God in Heaven or a Devil in Hell. But I felt I had run into something I had never heard of before ... I stumbled on the 'hid treasure' ... I listened, and in three weeks I paid the price and made that 'hid treasure' my very own" (Matt. 13 Sermon, *TTT*).

Long asserted that Irvine and Fred Tapp went to Nenagh, "where the revival began"; however, FM records do not show a Co-worker with Irvine at the Nenagh missions, nor at the following Rathmolyon missions held in 1897 (*Bright Words,* Sept. 1897, *TTT*).

Faith Mission's monthly publication carried this report: "Nenagh: Eight months ago [i.e. September 1897] ... it would have been almost impossible to unearth more than a dozen live Christians in this town; but now, praise the Lord, we have 41 Prayer Union members, all trusting in Jesus, together with a number of other Christians who received blessing and help during the missions held by Pilgrim Irvine and Pilgrims Pendreigh and M'Lean" (*Bright Words,* April 1898, *TTT*).

About the Nenagh September 1897 mission, Long proclaimed, "**That revival was the origin of the Go-Preacher Fellowship** (Roberts 1990, 12–13, *TTT*). In Long's words, he and Irvine were "the two instruments used of God at the origin of that movement" (June 1907, *TTT*). Irvine considered this revival mission the starting place where the Work began and spread out from; where he "got the Seal of God."

From the start, Long was present at many momentous occasions. As Alfred Trotter phrased it in an unpublished letter to his sister Edith, "He [John Long] ... fired the first shot in a campaign which was destined to re-echo around the world" (Jan. 8, 1968, in author's possession). The *first shot* was Long making arrangements for Irvine to hold a mission in the Nenagh Methodist Church.

After the book *Heresies Exposed* came to Long's attention in 1932, he contacted the compiler, W. C. Irvine. The subsequent editions contained the footnote, "Mr. John Long has written us that he was the man who obtained for William Irvine the first opening for a mission in Nenagh, August 1897 ... That William Irvine is the name of the original leader of the Go-Preachers ... He declares that the movement dates from 1897" (W. C. Irvine 1935, 73; W. C. Irvine was unrelated to Wm. Irvine or Irvine Weir).

**The origin of the Go-Preacher Fellowship
was the 1897 Nenagh Revival Mission.
(according to John Long)**

As a Methodist colporteur, Long often assisted other ministers in their missions, and he frequently helped Irvine. He stated, "It was a great privilege for me to get the benefit of those meetings and to be a fellow-helper in pointing anxious souls to Christ" (March 1898, *TTT*). It appeared that Irvine was the main, perhaps the only, speaker during most of his early Irish missions. Although Long was physically present in both the Nenagh and the following Rathmolyon missions, he never implied in his *Journal* that he preached alongside Irvine. He did mention that he was asked to speak in both of Irvine's missions at Borrisokane and Cloughjordan (Jan. 1898, *TTT*).

As G. Pattison pointed out, "Meanwhile, John [Long] held on in increasingly close association with William Irvine, as of course in his particular calling, one locality was nearly the same as another, and in many ways, they were useful to each other, undoubtedly thought a lot about each other. I believe that in the Templederry mission ... and probably some others ... John was Irvine's sole companion" (1935, Oak and Ivy, *TTT*).

"Both John Long and Mr. Gilbert," disclosed G. Pattison, "incurred some of Mr. Whittaker's [Methodist minister] displeasure because of allowing themselves to attend so frequently and persistently upon the ministrations of *the man* [Irvine] who at this time had become the great centre of attraction, the former [Long] keeping in touch with him nearly all the time, while still doing a little at his book scattering, etc." (1935, All-Day Meetings, *TTT*). Overall, Long affirmed that he was with Irvine for 83 missions.

Perhaps following the Methodist model of John Wesley's Journal spanning 50 years, Long wrote a detailed journal spanning the years 1872–1956. His *Journal* is a valuable primary source of recorded history about the new religious sect founded by Irvine. He made three copies; one was lost and the family has the other two. Unfortunately, the family has very few photographs of John Long, author of the Journals.

While it was known that John Long's journal existed, the whereabouts of the Journal and the Long family remained a mystery for many years. Finally, in 2002, two original copies of the Journal surfaced.

John Matthews, the Faith Mission administrator, was teaching a customary series of classes about cults and exclusive movements such as the Jehovah Witnesses and the Mormons, including a movement started by a former Faith Missioner, William Irvine, assisted by John

Long. During his class, Ruth Long, a student, exclaimed, "John Long was my Grandfather!"

Subsequently, in August 1999, while visiting the Faith Mission, Ex-2x2 Paul Abenroth, an American, was told this story by Matthews. Abenroth relayed this information to Irishman Robert Kee, who located John Long (son of the author of the *Journal*; Ruth was his daughter) and arranged to photocopy Long's handwritten *Journal* in February 2002. I cannot thank Robert Kee enough for his diligent, persistent efforts in acquiring and providing me with this and other valuable historical Irish documents; without them, this book would not contain many interesting factual details.

Cherie Kropp-Ehrig and Robert Kee
at Faith Mission Bookshop, Belfast, N. Ireland (2004)

We appreciated and enjoyed the hospitality of Robert Kee and his family in 2004. Kee kindly toured my husband and me around Northern Ireland and escorted us to visit John and Mollie Long (son of author John Long). I was allowed to handle, read and photograph the Journals. Mr. Long was happy to provide me with written permission to publish it. *See* website *TellingTheTruth.info* in Publications, *John Long's Journal.*

John Long's son (also John) with Cherie Kropp-Ehrig,
reviewing his father's Journal notebooks (2004)

1897: Rathmolyon Revival Mission. The Faith Mission Location of Pilgrims report showed Irvine holding a mission October 10–31, 1897, in Rathmolyon, located about 94 miles (150 km) east of Nenagh (*Bright Words,* Dec. 1897, 277, *TTT*) and 29 miles (47 km) northwest of Dublin.

According to Long, Bill Carroll (brother of Jack and May) "got the use of the Church of Ireland schoolhouse in Rathmolyon for a mission for William Irvine, where 40 persons got converted; most of them afterwards gave up their situations to go fully on the Lord's Work" (Sept. 1897, *TTT*). Records do not show Long being present at this mission, although he may have been. It appears the Carrolls were friendly with or related to the William Weir family of Dublin and invited Irvine Weir to come hear Wm. Irvine preach. This resulted in many of the Weir family and their descendants being followers today.

Cherie Kropp-Ehrig toured the Rathmolyon schoolhouse in August 2004 and walked about in the room used for Irvine's Gospel Mission.

In 1897, Irvine held his first Mission in this Rathmolyon schoolhouse

G. Pattison recalled that "from Nenagh's first visit, William [Irvine] went to Rathmolyon through the Carrolls' introduction, where ... he had another very successful mission, getting hold of nearly all the best type of character in the place, including the Gills, Carrolls, Hastings, Winters and others, and from there back to Nenagh a second time, after which he booked for here" [Cloughjordan, G. Pattison's hometown] (1935, Burning and Shining Light, *TTT*).

Jack Carroll's sister, Fannie, from Rathmolyon, recollected that "The meetings only lasted for three weeks, but fourteen Workers [missionaries] went out of that mission ... Willie Gill ... was the first from the Mission we had professed in to go into the Lord's harvest field" (F. Carroll 1964, *TTT*). Willie Gill entered the Work in 1900, and Fannie followed in 1904.

Terminology. From their start, Irvine's ministers referred to themselves as *Workers* or *Servants*, *Go-Preachers* and *Tramp Preachers* and *Tramps*. The laity were called *Friends* or *Saints.* Becoming a full-time itinerant Worker (aka preacher, evangelist, missionary, minister) was referred to as *going into* or *entering the Work.*

~~~~~

Carroll Family of Rathmolyon, Ireland. Six Carroll children were born to William and Cecelia (Christie) Carroll, who married in 1875 in Dublin, Ireland. Their father was only 47 years old when he died on January 23, 1897, leaving behind a widow and six unmarried children: William "Bill" (21), John "Jack" (19), May (18), Agnes (15), Frances "Fannie" (13) and Primrose (7).

Seven months after their father died, Jack and May were working for their Uncle Pat in Nenagh when Irvine opened his revival mission there. Some of the Carrolls attended those meetings. Jack, May and Fannie all made their choices in 1897. These three plus Bill and his wife, Margaret "Maggie," entered the Work in this order: 1903, May (age 24), with Bill (age 26) and wife Maggie (age 25); 1904 Fannie (age 21) and Jack (age 26); 1910–1911, Primrose (age 20–21). All but Primrose "died in the harness" (remained in the ministry till death).

Jack Carroll became Overseer of Western North America, and Bill Carroll became Overseer of Victoria, Australia. Bill and Maggie were one of the few married Worker couples. Agnes married Harry Weir of Dublin. Not long after their mother, Cecelia Carroll, died in March 1909, May returned to Ireland. In 1910, she escorted her youngest sister, Primrose, age 20, to North America.

Siblings Bill, Jack, Fannie and May Carroll

Primrose, Fannie and May are all shown on the 1912–1913 Workers List in Washington, US. The 1920 US Census showed Primrose married to John Richard Perrott and residing in Alameda, California, US. Perrott was a Brother Worker who came to the US from Ireland in 1916. Of the six Carroll siblings, Primrose (and her husband), was the only one who did not remain a follower of the 2x2 Sect. It remains a mystery why they disassociated themselves.

William Irvine   *L–R Carroll Siblings: Jack, Primrose, Fannie,*
Bill and Jack Carroll   *May, Bill and Agnes*

1897: Second Nenagh Mission. Irvine returned to Nenagh to conduct a week-long second mission on November 1–6 in the Presbyterian Church. Afterwards, he held several missions, all within a 20-mile radius of Nenagh: Roscrea, Cloughjordan, Borrisokane, Templederry and Finnoe.

Other missions held in, or nearby Tipperary Co. were Lorrha, Portumna, Moneygall and Behamore. G. Pattison clarified, "Neither do I remember how or by whom the Lorrha or Portumna missions were held, at which probably John and Tom Clarke, Richard Dagg, Tot Dane, the Hodgins family and others were brought in. I think there must have been meetings at Bailey's home below Portumna where Tom Turner heard the message and accepted it" (1935, Big Ingathering, *TTT*).

1897: Roscrea Mission. Long recalled, "On hearing of the revivals in Nenagh and Rathmolyon, Pastor Crookshanks invited William Irvine to have a mission there [Roscrea], when many young people decided for Christ, and the endeavour meetings got great blessing" (Oct. 1897, *TTT*).

The FM Location of Pilgrims report in *Bright Words* confirmed that Irvine held a mission in Roscrea, Co. Tipperary on November 7–21, 1897.

It also showed John Kelly (joined FM on May 27, 1896) was preaching in Scotland. Later, Kelly joined Irvine's movement (Dec. 1897, *TTT*).

1897: Death of William Irvine's Mother. Irvine arrived in Scotland in time to see his mother before her death. Elizabeth Irvine died on November 25, 1897, aged 64. He was the informant on her death certificate. He recalled, "My mother broke her heart in trying to hinder me from doing what I did ... But both Mother and Father on their deathbed said I was right, and the best son they had" (to M. Canada, Aug. 23, 1933, *TTT*).

1897, December: Cloughjordan Mission. A ten-day mission was held in Cloughjordan, the hometown of both Long and Goodhand Pattison, in which several persons were converted. Long recalled:

> Pastor Whittaker started a mission in Cloughjordan to prepare the way for the coming of William Irvine to that needy town; I left Roscrea and went to help there ... During his [Irvine's] stay in Cloughjordan, I invited him out to our home in Burntwood, for a cup of tea, and the humble and loving way by which he dealt with my brothers and sisters sowed the seed and prepared the way for their conversion which happened within one year afterwards.

> The mission [Cloughjordan] ended up with an all-day conference when the Christians from Roscrea and Nenagh came to our help. Open-air preaching, for years was an unknown thing in the town of Cloughjordan ... In the evening William Irvine suggested an open-air march through the street which took the inhabitants by surprise. Outside the Methodist Church, we formed a circle and sang the best of all hymns. (Nov.-Dec. 1897, *TTT*)

The Borrisokane Methodist Church
First meeting place of William Irvine and Edward Cooney

William Irvine

7

1898 – Matthew 10 Bible Study

1898, February: Edward Cooney. During his business trips, Edward Cooney, an ardent Christian lay preacher and commercial traveler from Enniskillen N. Ireland, met and was impressed with some of William Irvine's young converts. He arranged to meet Irvine at the Methodist Church in Borrisokane where he was holding a mission. Lasting reverberations and historic impact worldwide would result from this eventful meeting.

1898: Borrisokane and Finnoe Missions. Faith Mission (FM) records indicate Irvine and Fred Hughes preached in Borrisokane, Co. Tipperary, Ireland, from January 16 to February 6, 1898. Afterwards, they held a mission in Finnoe in a barn offered by a farmer (*Bright Words* March 1898, *TTT*). John Long reported, "The special revival efforts continued with lasting results; in that barn, whole families got converted, including my aunts" (March 1898, *TTT*). From the "Corcoran Family Story of Faith":

> There was a mission held at Borrisokane in 1898, and it was here that the mother of Finnoe House, Jane Ann Corcoran, made a profession in this faith; some who did so with her were several of her family, the Dennison family, (whose sons, Frank and Harry, and their sister, Mae, entered the ministry); possibly John Corcoran's brother George's family; another Robinson couple, the Longs, Brays and Falkiners ... Another mission was held a little later, near Finnoe House in the home of the Burgess family. John and Jane's children Lydia, Jim and probably Bill Corcoran embraced the faith at this time. Eight years later in 1906, John Corcoran, the father of Finnoe House, made a profession but died only two years later. Four of John and Jane's ten children went into this ministry: Sally, Jack, Bill and Jim. (Corcoran, *TTT*)

1898, March: Faith Mission reported in *Bright Words*:

> Pilgrims Pendreigh and M'Lean have just closed a 16 days' mission ... with a tea-meeting, which proved a complete success, and a time of refreshing in every sense of the word. Pilgrims Irvine and Hughes came

over from Borrisokane for the occasion. All present were delighted to see our two brothers again ... The meeting was then left open for testimonies, each one telling what the Lord had done for them, and several praising God for the Faith Mission, and for Pilgrim Irvine in particular, and also for sending the sisters to Nenagh.

The Lord's work is progressing in this neighbourhood in face of a lot of opposition. Missions have already been held in Roscrea, Cloughjordan, Finnoe and Borrisokane, and at present, Pilgrims Pendreigh and M'Lean are working in Shinrone; Pilgrim Irvine in Templederry; Pilgrim Hughes and Mr. Henry Gilbert in Portumna, all within a radius of 20 miles from Nenagh. (April 1898, *TTT*)

1898, April, May and June Missions. Moving further afield, according to FM records, Irvine held missions in Templederry, Cahir, Limerick City and Kilkee. Possibly, he was assisted by John Long.

Matthew 10 Bible Study

1898, June 19–30: Kilkee Mission. By this time, Irvine had been with FM for about three years, and Long had been a Methodist Colporteur for three years. Irvine held a mission in Kilkee June 19–30, 1898 (*Bright Words,* August 1898, *TTT*). Per Long, "While in Kilkee we had a Bible reading on Matthew 10." Their attention was particularly drawn to Matthew 10:5–10:

> *These twelve Jesus sent forth, and commanded them, saying, 'Go not into the way of the Gentiles, and into any city of the Samaritans enter ye not: But go rather to the lost sheep of the house of Israel. And as ye go, preach, saying, The kingdom of heaven is at hand. Heal the sick, cleanse the lepers, raise the dead, cast out devils: **freely ye have received, freely give. Provide neither gold, nor silver, nor brass in your purses, nor scrip for your journey, neither two coats, neither shoes, nor yet staves: for the workman is worthy of his meat.**'* (Matthew 10:5-10)

According to *The Secret Sect,* Irvine asked Long, "When did God change this? Does He mean it to be the same today?" Long replied, "I suppose it has never changed." However, no documentation has surfaced confirming this exchange. A 2004 review of two of Long's original *Journals,* with *particular* attention given to the Matthew 10 study, did not contain the above comments, and *The Secret Sect* did not include a reference to its source (Parker 1982, 2).

The earliest extant documentation of the concept of a faith missionary, relative to the 2x2 Sect, is found in Long's Journal.

How differently things would have turned out had Long replied, "Jesus changed it in Luke 22:35–36: 'When I sent you without purse, and scrip, and shoes, lacked ye any thing? And they said, Nothing. Then said he unto them, But now, he that hath a purse, let him take it, and likewise his scrip: and he that hath no sword, let him sell his garment, and buy one.' "

It would seem Irvine and his early band of preachers did not realize that Jesus' instructions to the twelve and seventy in Matthew 10 and Luke 10 were intended for two specific short missions (about six weeks) to the Jews only, after which the disciples returned to and remained with Jesus. After Jesus' death, the method changed regarding how Jesus' message was to be spread. Jesus explained, "As my Father hath sent me, even so send I you. And when he had said this, he breathed on them, and saith unto them, Receive ye the Holy Ghost" (John 20:21–22). From that time forward, the Holy Spirit would supply guidance and directions that superseded Jesus' earlier Matthew 10 instructions.

1898, July: Edward Cooney. Long commented, "It was a very remarkable coincident that Edward Cooney turned up next day, [after the Matthew 10 Bible study] for he ... went fully on the Lord's Work and became a great advocate of preachers going without a stated salary" (July 1898, *TTT*).

The Protestant Missionary Movement's goal was to carry out Jesus' Great Commission: "Go ye into **all the world** and preach the gospel to every creature" (Mark 16:15; Matt. 28:19–20). When the movement began around 1800, reportedly, there were only a few hundred Protestant missionaries in the world; one hundred years later in 1900, there were about 15,000. Allegedly, it began in May 1793, when English Baptist missionary William Carey went to proselytize India. It was supported by a number of missionary societies, denominations and organizations.

A well-known faith mission society was founded in Britain by J. Hudson Taylor in 1865, the non-sectarian **China Inland Mission** (CIM). The "new mission [CIM] ... had a number of distinctive features, including this: **its missionaries would have no guaranteed salaries, nor could they appeal for funds**; they would simply trust God to supply their needs" (*Christianity Today* Issue 52, 1996).

Thus, at the time Irvine was forming his new sect, the concept of missionaries preaching without guaranteed financial support was not a novel idea. Possibly Irvine had interviewed the China Inland Mission when he was deciding what group to affiliate himself with, eventually choosing the Faith Mission. Similar to the CIM's faith missionaries dressing as the Chinese did, even to the men wearing pigtails, Irvine's early Workers also adopted the attire of the common man and became known as *tramp preachers* or *the Tramps*, as they, along with many other Protestant missionaries, passionately spread the New Testament Gospel (*good news*) to foreign countries "without purse" (Luke 22:35).

~~~~~

1898, July: About his visit to Co. Tipperary in July, J. G. Govan, FM founder, reported: "I attended five meetings at Nenagh ... It was a joy ... to see so much satisfactory fruit remaining from the missions held by Pilgrim Irvine and the sisters during the past 12 months. I had also a number of candidates for the mission to interview" (*Bright Words,* Aug. 1898, *TTT*).

1898, July: Galway Mission. Irvine went to Galway, where he met Wilson and Annie McClung from Belfast. Mrs. McClung stated in a letter to My Dear Brother: "My conversion, as well as my husband's, took place in Galway in year 1898 through the preaching of Mr. William Irvine in that town, and on my husband's resignation from the Prison Service, we went out to preach November 1903 ... in Ireland for a year, then in England ... until our leaving for Australia in October 1908" (Aug. 31, 1913, *TTT*).

A newspaper provided a complimentary description: "The chief missioner is a bearded Irishman named M'Clung, who is assisted by his wife ... He is a handsome man, with magnetic eyes, a rich voice and very nice white shapely hands" (*Impartial Reporter,* June 21, 1906, 3, *TTT*).

1898: William Irvine Became FM Superintendent. In July 1898, J. G. Govan visited Co. Tipperary. Apparently, he was sufficiently pleased with Irvine's performance that he promoted him to Superintendent of South Ireland. Irvine's name first appeared as Superintendent in *Bright Words* Location of Pilgrims report in August 15, 1898; the last time was December 1900 (*Bright Words,* Aug. 15, 1898, *TTT*).

1898, November 5–26: Birr Mission. Long reported, "We went to Birr, [formerly Parsontown] where we again met with William Irvine who was having a mission in Soldiers' Home ... That was the only mission in which Irvine said, so far as he could judge, there was no conversions" (Oct. 1898, *TTT*).

1898, November: Roscrea Mission. Long noted, "William Irvine, Thomas Turner [working with Todd's Mission] and I went to Roscrea to have a mission in the Methodist Church ... Ben Boles, a shopkeeper from Roscrea, and John Sullivan, a School Master from Moneygall, gave up their occupation to go fully on the Lord's work" (Dec. 1898, *TTT*).

❧❧❧

8

1899 – Bicycle Mission Trip to Scotland

After three years and nine months, John Long resigned from colportage work in November 1898. He continued to be a member of the Methodist Church and the local Faith Mission Prayer Union. Irvine encouraged Long to join the Faith Mission staff. Although he had been accepted, Long considered the matter for a year before deciding not to join them (Jan. 1900, *TTT*).

1899, January 1: John Long, First Independent Evangelist. Bicycling from town to town, Long became a traveling evangelist. From his *Journal*: "On the first of January 1899, I started on the new Lines of Faith in God; that morning £1 came to me by post" (Jan. 1899, *TTT*). Long was the first to independently start preaching fully on *Faith Lines*—before Irvine, Eddie Cooney, George Walker or any other Worker.

Long defined *Faith Lines* as, "a preacher going forth without any fixed or stated salary, neither any public collections at meetings, but just trusting in God to put it into the hearts of God's people to give to the support of them who ministered in spiritual things. If more came in than necessary, learning to abound; if less, learning to suffer lack" (Jan. 1899, *TTT*).

Depending solely on the Lord's guidance through prayer for his mission work, Long had no supervisor or co-worker, and was not a part of any church or missionary group. Up until the 1903 Rathmolyon Convention, he was in close contact with Irvine, but was not working directly under him.

Long explained, "Desiring to consecrate my life forever to God, as an act of ordinance and sanctification with the burial and resurrection of our Lord Jesus Christ, I got baptized by immersion" (May 1900, *TTT*) in a stream by Rev. George C. Grubb, who at that time was an evangelist for the Church of Ireland. At this time, Irvine's movement had not yet been organized, did not baptize converts, nor did FM.

1899, February–May: Scotland. Irvine and John Burns preached with FM in Scotland at Ballinluig, Dalguise and Stanley. Since Irvine failed to send monthly reports to FM headquarters from June to December 1899, his name was not shown on their *monthly* Location of Pilgrims report, except for one mission he held alone in January 1900, at Finnoe, Ireland. However, his name remained on their List of Superintendents for the years 1899 and 1900.

1899, April: Wooden Halls. William Irvine appeared to be orchestrating the movements of his growing band of independent Workers and the wooden hall building process. *Bright Words* reported, "Pilgrim Irvine is in the South of Ireland ... he has been building two movable wooden halls" (March 1900, *TTT*).

In the British Isles, in one year at least a dozen portable wooden halls were built and used by Workers for Meetings and living quarters. The wooden halls, also called *baches* or *batches*, generated the nickname "Wooden Hall Preachers." Goodhand Pattison recounted:

> It would probably be in the second year after the Cloughjordan mission when the Methodist ministers and leaders having taken great offense at the turn things had taken were now refusing admission to chapels, schoolrooms or other buildings over which they had control, and while as yet there were pretty large numbers interested ... So the idea of movable wooden halls took hold of a few.
>
> The first hall was built in our yard mostly by amateur labor, including, I think, John Cavanagh, W. Williams, John Sullivan, Henry Culbert and others, and cost in all, outside the labour, about £30. Its first move for service was Finnoe ... a second was built in Mr. Cooke's premises in Moneygall, engineered and superintended by John Sullivan ... being even then more than half a carpenter, although teaching his school most successfully. (1935, Wooden Halls, *TTT*)

According to Long, "The downside was the difficulty in relocating the wooden halls. The labour attached to it was heavy for evangelists. It took one day for two men to take it down; one day to remove it; and it took two days to put it up; and one day to clean it; then there was occasional repairs, painting, etc. to be done" (April 1903, *TTT*).

Ballinamallard residents were "awakened on Sunday afternoon by a party of religious enthusiasts variously called *Cooneyites, Tramps,* or *Pilgrims*, who entered the village on brakes and cars singing hymns. The occasion was the opening of a wooden hall erected on what is known as *The Commons*. It is a comfortable building, possessing four windows, lighted by two lamps and heated with a suitable stove. Seating accommodation is commensurate with the intended requirements, and the hall is nicely boarded inside, but the entire structure is unadorned with paint" (*Impartial Reporter*, Feb. 16, 1905, *TTT*).

A special correspondent for the *Morning Leader* writing from Ipswich commented on the wooden hall used by the McClungs for Gospel

Meetings: "Chapels and schoolrooms having been denied them … Belfast sent them a collapsible, portable chapel big enough to hold 60 souls. That chapel now stands on a waste corner of ground near the Derby Road Station. It is a black shed with a tin roof, and its doors are ornamented with big posters announcing that: 'Jesus will be preached in This Hall Nightly. Come, Hear and Think!!' The chief missioner is a bearded Irishman named McClung, who is assisted by his wife [Annie] and one or two newly made Tramps" (June 11, 1906, *TTT*).

Not all the Workers appreciated the wooden halls—Edward Cooney objected, believing they indicated a lack of faith in God. Eventually, the wooden halls gave way to tents that were easier to erect. As recently as the '50s–'60s some of the Workers in Southern US, New Zealand, and perhaps elsewhere, occasionally used tents for Gospel Missions and living quarters. A portable hall was still used in New Zealand in the 1960s, and tents were still used in Europe in the 1970s.

Walter Frank and Frank Phillips outside their portable hall, assembled from standard panels bolted together, as used in New Zealand in early 1960s

1899: Elizabeth Pendreigh. In 1899, after seven years' service with FM that began on April 20, 1892, Elizabeth Pendreigh resigned and married Thomas A. Betty on September 9, 1899. Her name and work were often mentioned in *Bright Words*, as preaching in South Ireland where Irvine was her superintendent.

The 1901 Irish Census shows Pendreigh from Scotland, married to Thomas A. Betty, a Co. Fermanagh farmer, with a son named *Moore* (no age); two more sons would follow. Tom Betty was a long-time friend of Edward Cooney. On the 1905 Workers List, Tom is shown as entering the Work in 1905. Elizabeth later joined him; they were a married

Worker couple on Irvine's Worker staff. They are included in the 1921 Dimsdale Hall, Staffordshire, England Workers Convention photograph.

1899: West County Cork Pioneers. Converts Thomas Turner and Alex Givan were preaching with Todd's Mission, and together they pioneered the West Cork area in Ireland, producing some highly successful missions, as well as more converts who wanted to be missionaries like them. G. Pattison confirmed that these two men "went to my old home at Inchinadreen, Dunmanway, [Co. Cork, Ireland] ... where in a sense they may be called the pioneer apostles to West Cork, opening up and having meetings all around Dunmanway, Lisbealad, Drinagh, Kilmeen, etc." (1935, Pioneers, *TTT*). *See* Todd's Mission in Chapter 10.

1899: May Carroll. May Carroll professed in Irvine's first Nenagh revival mission in 1897. FM secretary, Tillie Thompson, stated, that "Mae [May] Carroll joined the Faith Mission on October 11, 1899, and it is intimated in our magazine that she left in November 1903, and 'joined Mr. Irvine's band of Workers.' We can find no record that any other members of the Carroll family were in the Faith Mission" (to Cherie Kropp, Oct. 30, 1991, in author's possession) *See also Bright Words*, Nov/Dec 1900, *TTT*.

Separation from Faith Mission

From 1897 on, it appeared that Irvine worked toward becoming independent of Faith Mission. His progress during the next four years may be traced in the FM magazine, *Bright Words*. There are conflicting statements regarding how and when Irvine fully separated from FM. Some reports indicate he resigned and others that he was expelled. Irvine supplied several dates for when he was "put out" of FM: in September 1897, 1898 and 1899. However, FM did not drop his name from their roster until January 1901.

1897–1898: Irvine stated in a letter, "I was put out of Faith Mission September **1897** ... because I was not of them and [not] willing for all their discipline, which I felt was not of God or according to the Book" (to Kerrs, Dec. 4, 1921, *TTT*). Similarly, he also declared, "In September **1898**, I was put out of the Faith Mission for not being willing to conform to all their piccadilly discipline, etc." Adding even more confusion to the year Irvine was put out, in this same letter he stated, "Was put out of the Faith Mission and had Convention in Ireland in **1899**" (to Dunbars, Oct. 13, 1920, *TTT*). *See* Appendix B. Due to the similarity of the first two statements and considering the events that transpired in 1898, the 1897 year is likely an error in memory or transcription. (He acknowledged uncertainty regarding another date in the 1921 letter.)

1899, September: Annual Faith Mission Convention. Long's *Journal* reports that Irvine, Long, and Sister Falkiner attended the annual week-long convention beginning the third weekend in September 1899 at the Faith Mission headquarters in Rothesay, Scotland. It is feasible that Irvine was "put out" during this convention in 1899. Soon after, on December 26, he held an all-day Special Meeting/Convention in the Nenagh Methodist Church. *See* details below.

Regardless of the reason and date, beginning on June 14, 1895, Irvine had been a Pilgrim with FM for about five years when they parted ways. He stated, "I joined the Faith Mission, which was controlled by J. G. Govan, and I preached in various parts of the Kingdom *for something like five years*" *(Lloyd's Weekly*, Feb. 3, 1907, *TTT*). Five years was also confirmed in Irvine's 1913 Statement in *Burfitt v. Hayward*. Neither Long nor G. Pattison supply a date for his separation.

1899 Bicycle Mission Trip to Scotland

Long explained, "After the Convention, [Faith Mission 1899 Rothesay Conv.] William Irvine invited me over to his sister's home in Queenzieburn, Kilsyth. At the same time, he went to meet some young men that came over from Ireland, with the intention of going fully on the Lord's Work" (Oct. 1899, *TTT*). This expedition came to be commonly known as the "1899 Bicycle Mission Trip to Scotland."

Taking a step toward independence from the Faith Mission, on October 1899, Irvine led a group of eight or nine young men on an experimental bicycle preaching tour of Scotland, putting into practice the Matthew 10 instructions insofar as they could. Although they were not evangelizing under the auspices of FM, the young men did accept the hospitality of FM converts.

It was a Great Experiment (William Irvine, 1938)

In shepherding this group, Irvine well knew he was going against FM policies. Govan's position was, "No workers can be said truly to belong to the Faith Mission, unless they acknowledge our direction and adhere to the aims and principles set forth in our official pamphlet" (*Bright Words,* Dec. 1903, 275, *TTT*). Their pamphlets, *"Aims and Principles"* and *"Pilgrim Life,"* were to be read at least once a quarter.

Jubilantly, the young men returned. Having gained some converts, they considered their experimental tour a success. They had proved for themselves that *Faith Lines* worked! Possibly speaking of this trip, John Hardie reminisced to Irvine many years later, "Those cottage meetings we had in Kilsyth **that gave the Work of God a start in our day** often come up before me" (Nov. 2, 1937, *TTT*).

Irvine Weir, one of the young men who entered the Work in 1900 recalled, "Then in October 1899, *William Irvine, still in the Faith Mission, but not satisfied*, got seven men and with himself we toured Scotland using the Faith Mission converts to entertain us." Referring to the photograph taken of the young men on their bicycles, Weir announced that this **"in my mind was the start of the work of William Irvine outside the Faith Mission"** (Parker 1982, 37, Fn. 23).

Weir shared that "Irvine's ideas of preaching and Tramp preaching were founded entirely on his idea of the tenth Matthew … William believed that what was good for the apostles was also good for the preachers of that day. He forgot that this message was given to the apostles to give to the Jewish nation only" (Parker 1982, 2, 9, Fn. 5).

> **The October 1899 Bicycle Mission Trip to Scotland was considered the starting point when William Irvine began working independently of the Faith Mission, by early Workers Irvine Weir and John Hardie.**

Jack Douglas | William Gill 1899 | George Walker 1900 | John Hardie 1900 | William Irvine Pre-1899 | Bill Carroll 1903 | Irving Weir 1900 | Warren Hastings

October 1899 Bicycle Mission Trip to Scotland

The widely distributed picture of eight young Brother Workers with their bicycles was taken on this 1899 trial expedition. Some photos have this notation: "Picture taken in Ireland before these men professed." Under the men's names are the years they entered the work. Hastings and Douglas were only in the Work a short time. Some sources include

Sam Boyd on this trip. Four of these men spent the remainder of their lives in the work.

1899, December 26: St. Stephen's Day Meeting. After their successful trial mission in Scotland (October–November), Irvine held an all-day Meeting on December 26, St. Stephen's Day (honoring the life of Stephen, the first recorded Christian martyr stoned to death, Acts 6–7). This meeting may be the "Convention" Irvine was referring to in his comment: "Was put out of the Faith Mission and had Convention in Ireland in **1899**" (to Dunbars, Oct. 13, 1920, *TTT*). G. Pattison's description of the Meeting/Convention:

> I remember very distinctly seeing and hearing Tom [Turner] ... at an all-day Meeting in Nenagh Methodist Chapel on a St. Stephen's Day ... we had in our gathering ... the great Rev. George Grubb ... also ... two or three other clergymen ... and a whole crowd from Cloughjordan, Borrisokane and Finnoe, etc., as well as those belonging to Nenagh; and I believe the two Faith Mission workers were also present and spoke, viz. Miss Pendreigh ... and a Miss McLean ... of course, John Long ... and also our evangelist Mr. Gilbert ... some from Rathmolyon for the first time. (1935, All-Day Meetings, *TTT*)

It appears Pattison was mistaken about Long and Miss Pendreigh attending. Long does not mention this large meeting in his *Journal*. In December 1899, he and Sam Boyd were across the Irish Sea in Scotland holding short Missions, where they "spent the watchnight (New Year's Eve) in Queenzieburn School Room" (Dec. 1899, *TTT*). Also, Miss Pendreigh married on September 9, 1899, and was no longer with FM.

While Pattison does not portray it in this manner, and Long does not record it, some refer to this meeting as "the moment of consolidation of the various contributing elements" (Jaenen, 2003, 524).

1900: Rev. George Carleton Grubb became a Keswick Missioner in 1889 when he was 33. It was rumored in 1895 that he sometimes privately taught an unorthodox doctrine (Conditional Immortality) that some identified as heresy. To muzzle him and others, Keswick drafted a general statement: "Guidance of Speakers at all Conventions Connected with Keswick." It required all Keswick Missioners to pledge not to teach during the Convention or Mission any doctrines or opinions except those upon which there was a general agreement among the convention promoters. Grubb declined to sign, dropped out of the Keswick team and became an independent evangelist in 1896. (Born in 1856, married in 1906, died in 1940, aged 84).

Full of humor and spiritual fire, Rev. Grubb was also a popular guest speaker at widely scattered conventions and missions, including some of Irvine's during his movement's infancy. A native of Co. Tipperary, he possibly remained in Nenagh after the St. Stephen's Day Meeting to hold this mission Pattison described:

> No. 2 [wooden] hall was sent to Nenagh for Mr. Grubb to hold a Mission in. It was set up in a field at the left side of the courthouse facing it. A good bit of hostility was manifested by some of the rougher element ... In conducting that mission, he had laid aside his clerical garb, dressed in dark grey tweed, and was thought completely won to The Testimony, but whether it was the bit of reproach frightened him, or that he failed to agree with all that Mr. Irvine stood for, I don't know, but I believe that was his first and last mission in the fellowship. (G. Pattison 1935, Wooden Halls, *TTT*)

Even so, a short time later in May 1900, Rev. Grubb helped John Long in a mission in the Rathmolyon school house and was a speaker at Irvine's July 1900 Rathmolyon Convention.

To date, the earliest newspaper reporting on Irvine's new sect was the *King's County Chronicle* (now Co. Offlay) for April 12, 1900. Regarding the wooden mission hall placed on Mr. C. Butler-Stoney's land in Bourney, Co. Tipperary, they reported, "For some reasons the preachers, who principally came from Roscrea, met with great opposition and almost personal violence by crowds assembled nightly with the avowed object of disturbing the worshippers; bands playing up and down the road, followed by groans, boos and epithets of a most grossly vulgar type ... several police had to be present nightly to afford protection ... However, a more effectual means of putting an end to the meetings was adopted last week when the hall was practically demolished, and the organ carried out and smashed into pieces. This has led to a claim being lodged for £50 as compensation for the malicious damage."

Faith Mission Updates

J. G. Govan stated in 1900, "Pilgrim Irvine is in the south of Ireland. We have not had regular reports from him lately, but he has been building two movable wooden halls and has also had meetings at Cloughjordan, Roscrea, Moneygall, Kildare and other places, attended with a good deal of blessing. The wooden halls are cheaply put up, and he writes of them as a great success, proposing that we should have some for Scottish counties. This we will consider. The friends at Rathmolyon, Co. Meath, are also building one to be used in that county" (*Bright Words*, March 1900, *TTT*).

Later that year, *Bright Words* carried this comment: "We should mention that work in south of Ireland has not been reported, and thus is not included in our statistics, much of the time Pilgrim in charge [William Irvine] having been taken up with building movable wooden halls, nearly all of which are worked on independent lines by workers unconnected with, and not under the direction of the Faith Mission" (Nov-Dec. 1900, *TTT*).

The last time William Irvine's name appears on FM's Annual Staff of Workers List was December 1900, when he was shown as the Superintendent in South Ireland (*Bright Words,* Nov-Dec 1900, *TTT*). Finally, beginning January 1901 his name was dropped from their publications.

Keith H. Percival, the General Director of Faith Mission who retired in 2004, provided a copy of the FM's Official List of Workers for the years 1895 through 1902. This list shows Irvine left in January 1901, with the notation, "founded Cooneyites in S. Ireland." It also showed John Kelly's departure in September 1901, with the notation, "joined Cooneyites" (Eberstein, Official List, in author's possession). This list was not an ongoing record or register posted as each person joined and/or left the Faith Mission; it was reconstructed long afterwards by Mr. Eberstein researching earlier FM records. Therefore, the list is not a primary source of evidence.

Cherie Kropp-Ehrig with Keith H. Percival (July 2004)

The Secret Sect book contains this statement: "In 1901, Irvine resigned officially from the Faith Mission. George Walker and Matthew Wilson witnessed his formal resignation" (Parker 1982, 6; Irvine Weir was the source). No further documentation has been found regarding a resignation. John G. Eberstein, Principal of Faith Mission, clarified, "Faith Mission has no copy of Irvine's resignation," and his personal opinion was that his name was simply dropped from their rolls (to Jim Vail, Dec. 24, 1988, in author's possession).

In 1901, FM reported: "During the year, several have dropped out of our list of workers. Pilgrim Irvine has been working on independent lines chiefly in Ireland. Then quite recently Pilgrim Kelly has resigned and also aligned himself with these independent workers" (*Bright Words,* Sept. 1901, *TTT*).

John Kelly appears to be the first Faith Missioner who left and aligned himself with Irvine. Over a span of two to six years, there were six Faith Missioners who eventually joined Irvine's staff—some left FM before Irvine did and some after. Those who left *after* Irvine did were John Kelly (1901), Joe Burns (1902), May Carroll (1903) and Sandy Hinds (by 1904). The two who left *before* Irvine separated were Harry McNeary (1900) and Elizabeth Pendreigh (1899).

That being the case, the oft repeated rumor is false that several Faith Missioners accompanied Irvine when he left and that together they formed a spin-off, offshoot, breakaway, or splinter movement. In fact, no records have surfaced showing any Faith Missioners left with Irvine.

Explanations for Why William Irvine Left the Faith Mission

William Irvine: "It was whilst I was working in the south of Ireland that I came to the conclusion that my position was still inconsistent with the example set by Christ, and I left the [Faith] Mission to preach *alone*" (*Lloyd's Weekly*, Feb. 3, 1907, *TTT*).

John G. Eberstein, former President of Faith Mission: "I know that the founder of the Faith Mission, J. G. Govan, had a little private means and did not himself look to Faith Mission funds for support, which was one of Irvine's objections to him" (to Jim Vail, March 22, 1989, in author's possession).

Goodhand Pattison:

> What exactly were the things with which William found fault and probably testified against, I do not consider myself an authority, but believe it was something he had seen more particularly at convention in Rothesay, such as giving place to outsiders, who while very able and attractive speakers were not the principle (*sic*) doers, and making of such very prominent to the exclusion of others who had faced the music and bore the brunt of the battle. This would naturally meet with disapproval. More especially would this be the case when the persons concerned were the clergymen class which even then had been receiving unfavourable attention at his hands ... and protesting, he would naturally grow lax in his dealing with and fidelity to Mr. Govan's authority and arrangements, becoming irregular in his reports, thereby making it difficult for Mr. Govan to carry on; and so little by little relations were becoming more strained until they reached breaking point. (1935, Difficulties, *TTT*)

The Impartial Reporter:

> William Irvine gave up his connection with that sect [Faith Mission] for two reasons … First, because the leader was alleged to have been a 'hypocrite,' in that while teaching Pilgrims to live by faith, he himself had over hundreds of pounds. Second, because Mr. Irvine's converts always lapsed and were lost among the clergy by going back to their own congregation or what is known as the churches. (Aug. 25, 1910, *TTT*)

John Long:

> William Irvine left the Faith Mission. All who knew the man was acquainted with the fact that he did not covet or desire to start a new sect or mission; and his leaving the Faith Mission was not without feeling the risk and responsibility of doing so; but circumstances and events rendered it necessary. Some Workers who gave up their situations to go fully in the Lord's Work were not accepted by the Faith Mission; others did not feel led to join it; and others believed in being more like the pattern as seen in Jesus and reforming according to the ideal church in the Acts of the Apostles; among the latter was Edward Cooney, who had newly started out, became a strenuous advocate. Most of these Workers were either young converts or disciples of William Irvine; and it became impossible for him to be true to the rules of the Faith Mission and to them; so, he resigned the one and entered enthusiastically into the other. (Dec. 1900, *TTT*)

There appears to be sufficient reason to conclude that Irvine mentally disconnected from FM at least by September–October 1899, and transitioned to preaching independently on *Faith Lines*, although he did not notify FM of same. Until January 1900, Faith Mission continued to list him as one of their Superintendents.

Faith Mission Warnings

Because Irvine copied many FM practices, the public sometimes confused Irvine's Workers with their Pilgrims. Concerned J. G. Govan issued several statements in *Bright Words* during 1900–1903 to set the record straight. He tactfully reported:

> **1900.** Several brothers who have received blessing in connection with Faith Mission work have been holding missions in various places where we understand they are on faith lines and in sympathy with our work … It should be understood that they are not directly connected with the Mission or under its control. (March 1900, *TTT*)

1901. When in Ireland I came into closer contact with a movement that has been going on for the past year or two. A number of young people are going out on quite independent lines, holding missions in various parts both of Ireland and Scotland. While there may be much that is good in the devotion and earnestness of those who thus leave all, believing that the Lord has called them thus to follow Him, a number of features of this movement do not commend themselves to us.

There is no one to judge of the fitness of these workers except themselves; being independent, they are not able to profit from the experience of others older in the work, as they would if there was some organisation; and then some of them have not been long enough converted themselves before going out and, wanting in Christian experience, are very apt to be unbalanced and one-sided. While we can quite believe that a few of those who have gone out have been truly called of God, we fear that a number of others have been more called of man or moved by their own impulses and are really not fitted for the work. As some have been mistaken for Pilgrims, we think it necessary to say that the Faith Mission is not responsible for this movement. (Aug. 1901, 75–76, *TTT*)

1903. We regret that it seems needful ... to state plainly that we have no responsibility for the work carried on in Ireland and elsewhere by Mr. Irvine and his fellow workers ... the agents of this anonymous work have in some places been mistaken for our Faith Mission Pilgrims, and misleading references have in consequence appeared in the public press. While we honour the zeal and devotion of these workers ... their lines of work differ essentially from those of the Faith Mission, as an unsectarian agency, and are such as we could not endorse or approve. (May 1903, *TTT*)

1903. It seems necessary to again point out that missions are being held ... by persons who represent themselves to be 'Faith Mission' workers, but who are not in any way under our control or direction. This movement ... was started by Mr. William Irvine ... there are various points, both in method and teaching, that we do not approve of and in which they widely differ from us. Then we hear ... some of these irresponsible workers have misrepresented and spoken against the Faith Mission, while taking personal advantage of it by ... seeking the support of our Prayer Unions. (Dec. 1903, *TTT*)

9

1899–1901 – Conventions

Keswick Conventions. The *Impartial Reporter* mentioned that Edward Cooney attended the Keswick Conventions held in July 1907, 1908 and 1909. Fred Wood and others claimed the early 2x2 Conventions were patterned after Keswick Convention (1985, *TTT*).

The first Keswick Convention was assembled on July 28, 1875, by Canon Dundas Harford-Battersby of St. John's Church, Church of England. There were 300–600 attendees. In 1888, Keswick began sending out missionaries. By 1895, convention attendance had risen to 3,000.

The Keswick Conventions continue to this day. Currently, various ministers of Protestant denominations assemble annually in July in Keswick, England, for a two-week convention. Auxiliary Keswick Conventions with a strong family likeness are held in many other countries, although they may not use the word *Keswick* in their publicity, e.g. in the UK, Australia, Asia, Europe, Caribbean and North America. Together they form a Keswick movement that reaches hundreds of thousands of people across many nations and cultures.

The Keswick Conventions include sermons of speakers from many denominations, prayer and Bible studies. It is not a school of theology, a seminary, sect, or church. Keswick is regarded as a *mission* to Christians. Classified as a *Holiness Movement*, the Keswick Convention popularized Bible conferences (conventions). Its "persistent theme was the concern for practical holiness; a holiness that was biblically based, Christ-centered and was empowered by the Spirit" (Price 2000, 54). Its purpose is the promotion of scriptural and practical holiness. Their goal is to foster genuine unity among Christians of various denominations. From their start, their motto has been "All One in Christ Jesus." *See* Appendix E.

Faith Mission Conventions. As described by Long, "An annual convention was held for the deepening of spiritual life, when the whole staff of Pilgrims, and Prayer Union representatives, etc. gathered together and spent a week in prayer, praise and preaching, together with setting and arranging for future service, companions and districts.

At these gatherings, G. C. Grubb, F. B. Moore, J. G. Govan and others gave stirring and searching addresses" (Sept. 1899, *TTT*).

Their annual week-long conventions were held at the Faith Mission headquarters in Rothesay, Scotland, beginning the third weekend of every September. Since all FM Pilgrims were expected to attend, Irvine should have been present in 1895, 1896, 1897, 1898 and 1899. Long's *Journal* reports that Irvine, Long, and Sister Falkiner attended in 1899, but does not mention the conventions for 1898 or 1900.

In the spring of 1994, an American Ex-2x2 man attended the 77th Annual FM convention in Bangor, Ireland, and provided a written review. It began with an evening meeting on Friday and continued through Tuesday evening. Three meetings were held each day, lasting from 90 minutes to two hours each. Estimated attendance was 300–500.

The meetings were opened with hymns, followed by prayers, testimonies of Pilgrims and sermons from invited speakers. Their terminology was very similar to that of the 2x2s. They used the hymnbook *Selected Hymns from Songs of Victory,* containing 185 hymns, many of which are also in the current 2x2 hymnal, *Hymns Old and New*. At the end of their Sunday meeting, the invitation was extended to any willing to give up their earthly possessions and pursuits, give the rest of their lives to Christ and become Pilgrim Workers. Those who were moved to do so walked to the front while a hymn was sung.

There are many similarities in the conventions held by the Workers, FM and Keswick. Both Keswick and FM held their annual conventions on Saturday through Tuesday; likewise, Irvine's large-scale Conventions also convened on those days and still do in the UK and Ireland.

Rathmolyon Convention, 1900. By this time, it seems the movement had begun to assume a distinct identity under Irvine's leadership. He assembled the first general Convention in connection with the Work in the South of Ireland in July 1900. About 40 Christian Workers met together, including George C. Grubb, Robert Miller, Robert Todd, William Irvine, Edward Cooney and others (July 1900, *TTT*).

At times, Irvine invited evangelists such as George C. Grubb, John Chalmers and John Ramsay to be guest speakers at some of his Special Meetings. Rev. Grubb was a Church of Ireland (Anglican) evangelist and a popular speaker at various Christian conferences and missions.

Gill Family of Rathmolyon, Ireland

William Gill, one of the young men who accompanied Irvine on the Bicycle Mission Trip to Scotland, was destined to fill a prominent role in the 2x2 Sect. He was the second child and oldest son of Garrett and Ann

(Pigott) Gill. William "Willie" John Gill was born on June 12, 1863. All nine Gill children were baptized in the Church of Ireland in Rathmolyon, per church baptismal records. The Gill parents, all their children and their spouses were converted by Irvine or his Workers, except for Garrett Gill (son), who remained in the Church of Ireland. Willie, Emma and Jennie Gill all joined Irvine's movement around 1900.

Willie Gill, William Irvine and George Walker

When Garrett married Ann Pigott on March 11, 1861, Ann's brother, William John Pigott, transferred several pieces of property to them. Around 1872, Garrett Gill built a family home on acreage he called *Ashmount* in Kill, Rathmolyon, Enfield, Co. Meath, Ireland. Paul, Jennie and possibly Emma Gill were born at Ashmount. For most of his teenage and young adult years, Willie Gill lived at Ashmount, helping his father farm the land.

In 1895, Garrett Gill purchased a farm and home from John Fox in Dalystown, Co. Meath, located about six miles from Rathmolyon. All the Gill family moved to Dalystown, except Philip Henry "Harry" and his wife, Lilian, who remained at Ashmount.

In 1897, Garrett Gill transferred ownership of two properties located in Rathmolyon to his oldest son, William Gill. One was a rather remote small farm of 40 acres with no dwelling. The other property was

Ashmount and surrounding acreage. Arguably, the last site was likely where the early Conventions at Rathmolyon took place. It was private and also convenient to the cooking, washing and latrine facilities of Ashmount.

Ashmount, Rathmolyon, Co. Meath, Ireland
The home Willie Gill gave up to enter the Work

Jack Jackson stated at Willie Gill's funeral at West Hanney, England, on June 5, 1951, that by his calculations, it was 53 years and 8 months since Willie and some others at Rathmolyon made their choice. This calculates to October 1897, the date of the Rathmolyon mission. Jack Forbes recollected: "When we think of what our Brother referred to those days in Rathmolyon ... you have heard him speak of those days when he attended that Convention and got so very little out of it, but in his bedroom when he thought of Elisha [1 Kings 19:19–20] taking those oxen and sacrificing them, and he asked himself the question would he be willing to do that" (1951, *TTT*).

While visiting in Rathmolyon in 2004, my husband and I were invited to Ashmount by the current owners, John and Joyce Swanton. We were shown Willie Gill's small, narrow, upstairs bedroom where reportedly, he spent all one night in turmoil, struggling to make the decision to give up his inheritance and go into the Work on *Faith Lines*. The Swantons have kindly accommodated groups desiring to tour Ashmount.

As a wealthy landowner, Willie Gill's decision to give up his farm, possessions and inheritance to enter the Work made quite an impression on the community. He became the Overseer of the 2x2 Sect in England at least by 1914 until his death in 1951, aged 88.

According to the Irish National Land Registry, William Gill transferred the title to his real estate to his brother, Harry Gill. Confirming this transaction, their niece, Hazel Hughes reported, "Uncle Willie made up his mind to go in the Work, and he sold his farm Ashmount to his brother Harry. Harry paid a certain amount of money into the Work till the farm was paid for" (1971, *TTT*).

Harry Gill died February 12, 1961; his son, Herbert Norman Gill, inherited Ashmount; he had no children and died on March 14, 1985. Upon his death, Herbert provided his wife with a life estate at Ashmount and willed the Ashmount home and land to his nephew, John Swanton.

*Fred and Mary Ann (Gill) Hughes'
wedding picture (Feb. 25, 1891)*

Jennie and Emma Gill, 1899

Before Irvine came to Rathmolyon, Fred Hughes immigrated to America in 1887. Willie Gill's sister, Mary Ann, arrived in the US in October 1890. They were married in North Dakota on February 25, 1891, and made their home in Cando, North Dakota. Their five surviving children were: Lincoln, Hazel, Garrett, Joe and Eunice.

Garrett Hughes told of the first time his parents heard from their family in Ireland about Irvine's missions. "Ninety years ago [1897], a letter came from Ireland. We heard about those with no home, no name, etc. Forty people made their choice. Sixteen went out in the Work—that was the beginning" (Erling Omdal Funeral Service, Eagle Bend, Minnesota, Oct. 6, 1987).

Emma Gill was the first Worker to share the Gospel with her sister Mary Ann and family. She arrived at their home in North Dakota in December 1904. Subsequently, Fred and Mary Ann Hughes professed in a mission held by some Brother Workers. Two of their children, Garrett and Hazel, went into the Work in America, where Garrett became a Regional Overseer. He died July 19, 1991, and Hazel was killed on September 19, 1975, by a passing motorist as she was crossing the road at the Utica, South Dakota Convention.

Four of the six children from another family in Rathmolyon, Thomas Maddock and Deborah Hughes, became early Workers. William and Charles entered the Work in 1906. Willie pioneered Victoria, Australia, was Overseer of South Australia and New Zealand. Charlie was the US Overseer of Virginia and New York. Annie spent her life in the work in the UK. Thomas preached for seven years after 1905, left and married. Some 2x2 Hughes currently reside in Rathmolyon.

Charlie and Willie Hughes

Willie Hughes, Adam Hutchison and Willie Gill

1902: Rathmolyon Devastated by White Mice. When Irvine came to Rathmolyon in 1897 to recruit new members, there was great concern among the Roman Catholic population. They feared Irvine might attract many Catholics to his group. The local parish priest dismissed the entire situation in words similar to the following: "My dear people, don't be the least concerned about this new sect which has formed in our parish. It will all fizzle out, and in a short while they will be as scarce as white mice." His words turned out to be partially true. There is no evidence that a single Catholic in Rathmolyon converted to Irvine's sect; as for it fizzling out, he could not have been more wrong.

From that day forward, the 2x2 Sect members have been known as *White Mice* in the Rathmolyon Parish although many Rathmolyon residents are unaware of the origin of the term, *White Mice* (*Dair Rioga*, 2005, 326).

Church of Ireland Fallout. The Catholics were not the only concerned church. The exodus of so many members was viewed as a major disaster in the Church of Ireland community in decrease of membership and loss in finances. The Church lost the income from farming tithes. At the time of the White Mice exodus, the rector was Rev. Fred W. Weatherell of the St. Michael and All Angels Church, established in 1797. On our visit to Rathmolyon, I was allowed to use the very old key to unlock and enter the Church of Ireland and walk around.

St. Michael and All Angels Church, established 1797
(Church of Ireland in Rathmolyon, Ireland)

In just three weeks' time, (October 10–31, 1897), Irvine successfully recruited "nearly all the best type of character in the place, including the Gills, Carrolls, Hastings, Winters and others" (G. Pattison, 1935, *Burning and Shining Light, TTT*). Irvine sapped the lifeblood and effectively split the church in two. Most or all of the Gill and Carroll families became *White Mice,* along with three of the Hastings children.

The young people mentioned, Gills, Carrolls, Hastings and Winters, had been baptized in the Church of Ireland and were actively involved in it. They held positions of esteem, such as vestrymen, secretary, treasurer and church warden (church documents in author's possession). The *vestry* was an assembly of parishioners who met to discuss parochial business that took place in the vestry room in the church (where the minister's vestments were kept). The vestry raised funds for local services, such as poor relief and church socials.

Living just a short distance from each other, they attended church socials together and were members of upstanding Church of Ireland families. Their active participation in church affairs at such early ages boded well for the future of the Church of Ireland in Rathmolyon. All that changed when 40 of them forsook the church of their birth.

The legacy of this event lives on. The Church of Ireland community in Rathmolyon began loathing the White Mice soon after Irvine's arrival.

This feeling is exacerbated by a number of factors. Ownership of property is one source of irritation. Previously, many of the farms now owned by *White Mice* were exclusively owned by Church of Ireland people at the time of Irvine's coming.

Upon their owners' conversion to Irvine's group, these farms became *White Mice* property and have remained so. In the greater Rathmolyon region, a large acreage of land is owned by *White Mice*, e.g. the families of Hughes, Chambers, Buttimer, Hendy, Clarke and Jackson. Since the *White Mice* usually intermarry, this prevents the properties from going on the market for sale. It also prevents prospective Church of Ireland purchasers from buying and returning the property to what they believe is its traditional place in history.

Adding insult to injury, when a member of the *White Mice* community dies, they are buried "in their ancestral burial ground," which is the Church of Ireland cemetery surrounding the church. The Church reluctantly allows the burial to take place but refuses to register the death and burial in their parish records. Often the *White Mice* erect headstones without permission and beyond the recommended size in height. In everyday life the Church of Ireland people can avoid or refuse to meet or do business with the *White Mice*, but they are forced to view their headstones whenever they visit their relatives' graves or attend their church services. These are a constant reminder of a bitter past and serve to prolong it. (Information provided by Co. Meath residents.) In 2004, my husband and I walked through the graveyard surrounding the Church of Ireland where many 2x2s have been and continue to be buried.

Methodist Church Loss. The Methodist Churches in Ireland also experienced disruption accompanied by significant loss of members. "The Springfield [Co. Fermanagh] Methodist Church Membership and Class Roll Schedules for 1900–1911 show that many of the leaders and some local preachers left Methodism to join the [2x2] movement, with up to 100 references to people becoming Pilgrims at this time ... the damage the Cooneyites [2x2s] did to Springfield was very substantial and to evangelicalism in the area in general" (Roddie 2013, 150). Tom and Ellen Elliott left the Springfield Methodist Church to become a married Worker couple in Irvine's movement.

10

1897–1903 – Robert R. Todd's Mission

The Faith Mission reported in 1900, "Since we started in Ireland some seven or eight years ago, several agencies have followed suit on somewhat similar lines. A Mr. Duff has a mission in the north with a number of workers, and in the south, there is the mission conducted by **Mr. and Mrs. Todd,** formerly workers with us" (*Bright Words,* March 1900, 56–57, *TTT*). *See* website *TellingTheTruth.info* in History Articles, Walter Duff.

Profile of Robert Todd. On July 12, 1888, Robert R. Todd, a single man, became a Faith Mission Pilgrim *(Bright Words,* June 1950, 117, *TTT*). Born in Newmilns, Ayrshire, Scotland, on February 24, 1866, Todd died March 27, 1950, aged 84. The woman who would become his wife, Jane "Jeanie" Moodie Mitchell, became a FM Pilgrim in June 1888. Born in Kincardine, Perthshire, Scotland, on May 12, 1868, she died in June 1932, aged 64. They were married in Edinburgh, Scotland, on August 28, 1895, and were buried in Leominster, Herefordshire, England (*Bright Words,* 1932, *TTT*).

According to their daughter, Margaret B. (Todd) Davis, "He … was enrolled as a Queen's Scholar at Glasgow Training College, entering the teaching profession. In 1888, however, he joined Faith Mission and was one of the first band of Pilgrims, whose pioneer work must be an inspiration to those who carry on the work today" (*Bright Words,* June 1950, 117, *TTT*).

1897, November: Todd was District Superintendent of the Irish Work, with headquarters at Antrim, Ireland. For two years after they married, Mr. and Mrs. Todd preached together with the FM. Then, in the fall of 1897, Govan announced, "After nine years' service in the Mission, during which time they have been much used of God in many different parts … [they] have retired from among us. They intend going out on independent work in Ireland, unconnected with any mission" (*Bright Words,* Nov. 1897, 266, *TTT*). The arrival of their first child, Matthew Thomas in 1897, the first of six children, may have contributed to their resignation.

William Irvine's time in FM overlapped the last two years of Todds' service. After their departure from FM, the two men remained on good terms and kept in contact. Todd was a speaker at Irvine's Conventions held in Rathmolyon in July 1900, and in Dublin in 1901 also attended by Long (Long, July 1900; June 1901, *TTT*).

Irvine had quite a number of young people willing and anxious to go preach. Fortunately, Robert Todd "took on the direction and oversight of such, and in a short time had a pretty nice number in the field, including Tom Turner, John Hardie, Emma Gill, Annie Holland, Sarah Sullivan and probably Alex Givan, etc." (G. Pattison 1935, Workers, *TTT*). It was commonly called *Todd's Mission.*

Todd's Mission was also known as the Evangelistic and Missionary Alliance. In the August 17, 1901, *Freeman's Journal* newspaper, Andrew Robb stated he was an evangelist and a member of the Evangelistic and Missionary Alliance (Todd's Mission). Robb, William Jackson and George Buttimer, all missionaries in Todd's Mission, were subjected to malicious property damage. According to the June 29, 1901, *Kildare Observer:*

> A wooden gospel hall was erected at Camolin, Co. Wexford, by Mr. A. H. Robb, of the Evangelistic and Missionary Alliance ... a crowd of about 400 persons gathered and attacked the hall with stones. Two police constables ... were utterly powerless. One man in the crowd gave the order, 'Line up,' and a rush was made, the hall was knocked down and the woodwork smashed up. Four cycles, cooking utensils that belonged to the evangelists were also smashed, the men themselves having to take refuge in the police barracks. One of them was knocked down by the mob when on his way.

1903: Todd's Mission Disbands. After about six years (1897–1903), Robert Todd, by that time father to three sons, accepted employment elsewhere. Eight or nine of Todd's Workers joined Irvine's movement: Emma Gill, John Hardie, Thomas Turner, Andrew Robb, George Buttimer, Alex Givan, John Stanley, William Jackson and possibly his brother, Jack Jackson. Todd's Mission became a thing of the past.

Jack and William Jackson

John Hardie

11

1898 – Unsectarian Early Days

Irvine had quite a number of young people willing and eager to leave all and work toward restoring the methods of primitive Christianity as practiced in the New Testament. The Workers were increasing in numbers and were scattered about. Some "young converts [of Irvine] began to hold missions ... Some joined the Faith Mission, others joined Todd's Mission in the southeast of Ireland, and others went out preaching not connected with any mission" (Long June 1898). At this time, the Workers were not sectarian or exclusive.

William Irvine, Edward Cooney, Willie Gill and Andrew Robb were some of the oldest Workers in the early days. Born in 1863, Irvine, Gill and Robb were all about 34, Cooney was about 30 and John Long was about 25.

Most of the volunteer Workers were quite young, around 20–22 years old. Therefore, there were very few older, experienced Workers. George Walker remarked, "In the early days, most of the young Workers ... found they looked older with hair on their faces." In many photographs, Walker (22 when he entered the Work) sported a beard. Irvine permitted female preachers, and three Irish women entered the Work in 1900.

Willie Clelland (aka Cleland) entered the Work in 1900 and observed, "When the Work first started, we were a band of young men and women, as we were nearly all of that age. I was all of 21. Irvine was around 35. Being young, we were easily influenced by the older members of the band, such as Cooney and Irvine, and of course, got to thinking as they did, and that without much scriptural backing" (Parker 1982, 10, Fn. 20).

Many of the young Workers were born around 1880 when education was compulsory for children five–ten years old; thus, most were probably not educated beyond the fifth grade when they were ten years old. Many, like Irvine, began working full time at age ten.

A reporter noted, "One purpose of the convention was to educate the 'young workers,' many of whom may be diamonds, but they are diamonds in the rough state. They are full of zeal, they lead good lives, they exhort others to be reconciled to God ... and [are] for the most part, uneducated and of the servant or small farmer or artisan class" (*Impartial Reporter,* Oct. 13, 1904, *TTT*).

Tramping for the Lord. The early Workers were called *Tramp Preachers* for good reason; most only had one set of clothing. "The brethren could be easily recognised by their unshaven beards, rubber collars and coarse clothing" (*Irish Weekly,* Aug. 24, 1907, *TTT*). At that time, men's shirts did not have attached collars or cuffs; instead, detachable collars made of fabric or rubber were purchased separately. Upper class men wore fabric collars, while the working man and Workers wore reusable rubber collars that did not require high maintenance laundering. Their brown undershirts caused them to appear dirty. *See* Chapter 34.

Grit, grace, gumption and go were all needed by the early Workers. Sometimes they worked odd jobs when they needed money. They accepted financial help, no matter the source, regardless of their religious background. Workers sometimes placed a bag or box to receive donations in the back of their mission facility.

Having a hard time finding lodging, a Co-worker remarked to Alfred Magowan that it would have been nice if God had made Workers like turtles—where their homes were on their backs. Once when their audience went home and left them to fend for themselves under the stars with empty bellies, John Burns remarked, "I think they take us for angels. They give us credit for having wings, but no stomachs" (Parker 1982, 33).

First Full-Time Worker Recruits (1899)

John Long, Thomas Turner, Alex Givan, George Walker

On the various 1905 Workers Lists (the oldest list found to date), John Kelly's name is shown immediately under Irvine's name, before the other Workers' names, with three different starting years. The correct year is 1901–1902. Following Kelly are the four Workers who entered the Work in 1899: Alex Givan, John Long, Thomas M. Turner and George Walker. Previously, Long and Walker preached independently while

Turner and Givan preached with Todd's Mission. Their earlier time spent in evangelistic service appears to have been grandfathered into Irvine's ministry.

Profile of John Kelly. Born to James and Matilda (Dinsmore) Kelly on April 6, 1872, in Connor, Co. Antrim, Ireland, John had at least five siblings. A list titled "Early Conventions" shows a Convention held in Taylorstown, Co. Wexford, Ireland, on Kelly's' property (possibly related).

When he was around 24, Kelly became an evangelist with FM on May 27, 1896. Later, sometime before September 1901, he resigned to "become a Cooneyite." The 1901 Scotland Census shows Kelly and Harry Sherratt as "Tramp Preachers," lodging in Duns, Berwickshire, with Janet Buckham.

The 1911 Irish Census showed Kelly, 39, evangelist, as a visitor of Esther Ekin, 73, widow, born 1838. Kelly left the Work in 1928, married, and had at least one child, a daughter, but little else is known about him. A letter indicated that he passed away sometime after December 1960. Fred Wood relayed, "We received a letter from John Kelly's daughter saying that her father was very ill. She told us he was nearly 90" (Roberts 1997, 12, *TTT*).

Profile of John Long. *See* details in Chapters 6 and 19. Long's *Journal* does not state when he relinquished his independent evangelist status and submitted to Irvine's authority/leadership; presumably it was at the 1903 consolidation Convention at Rathmolyon. However, the starting date for Long on the 1905 Workers List was grandfathered back to 1899, when he left the Methodist colportage work and began preaching independently on *Faith Lines*.

Profile of Thomas "Tom" McCausland Turner. Born September 1, 1877, in Swatragh, Maghera, Londonderry, Ireland, Turner died on April 19, 1959, in Brisbane, Queensland, Australia, aged 82, and was buried in Mt. Gravatt Cemetery.

Turner professed in 1898. G. Pattison disclosed, "Tom had only been a very short time saved when he decided to give up teaching ... "Even in that little Templederry mission ... there was one who took his stand, who through thick and thin has kept faithful, and ... surely the winning of a soul like Tom M. Turner was ... well repaid whatever effort was put into it" (1935, Oak and Ivy, *TTT*). For a time he preached in Todd's Mission before joining Irvine's ministers; he went to Australia in 1905. *See* Chapter 41.

Profile of Alexander "Alex" Givan (often misspelled as Given or Givern) was born in Slane, Co. Meath, Ireland, on March 12, 1874, and died in Glasgow, Scotland, on May 28, 1948, aged 74. He was employed by Fawcetts in Roscrea. The first time he preached was in the Cloughjordan-Behamore mission with Tom Turner and Dick Norman. He joined Todd's Mission, then segued to Irvine's movement. He sailed on September 22, 1911, to New York aboard the SS *Cameronia*, age 37. He preached in Ireland, Pennsylvania, Kentucky, New York, Ohio and West Virginia, US.

Profile of George Walker. The ninth of eleven children, Walker was born on February 12, 1877, in Cavantillycormick, Coa, Maghercross, Co. Fermanagh, N. Ireland, to John and Jane (Fawcett/Faussett) Walker. His mother died on June 21, 1888, when he was 11 years old. Walker had been preaching in America since 1903 when his father died on May 6, 1910, leaving one shilling to George in his will.

Walker recollected, "I spent the teen years of my life working in a store. The man I worked for was very religious, but his whole idea of a successful life was making money" (Walker, 1970). Walker was a draper's apprentice employed by Edward Cooney's father, W. R. Cooney, a successful Enniskillen clothier merchant (*Impartial Reporter*, July 28, 1910, *TTT*).

14 High Street, Enniskillen, Ireland
Site of W. R. Cooney's business, now Graham's Store

Local lore indicates Walker also worked at the Dublin store McBirneys & Co. Although another tenant now occupies this building, the inscription *McBirneys* remains engraved in stone. The pediment above the main door of McBirneys carries the name *Hibernian House*, which was also the name of W. R. Cooney's Enniskillen store. There are several conceivable business relationships where Walker could have worked at both locations.

Walker was contemplating becoming a Methodist preacher when he first met Irvine in March 1898, in Rathmolyon. He recounted at Brother Worker Charles Hughes' funeral: "Seventy-four years ago last March

[1898], I went down near Charlie's home and going to that place changed my whole course of life, and it is the cause of me being here today. Charlie was only 14 then; I was 21" (1972, *TTT*).

Shortly after his encounter with Irvine, on April 11, 1898, while walking across the Broadstone Railway Train Station in Dublin, Walker surrendered his life to God and said, "If this is what it takes, I'm willing for it" (Walker 1988, *TTT*).

After 1914, Walker rarely ever admitted he professed through William Irvine; yet other Workers, including Edward Cooney, stated that he did, and documents confirm it. Irvine's name is noticeably absent from all of Walker's accounts retelling how he became a Worker.

Walker was 21 years old when he entered the Work in 1899, month unknown. His first Co-worker was Matthew Wilson, age 22–23, who had been "preaching the gospel before he ever met any of the Faith Mission. Then he met William Ervine [Irvine] and joined hands with him, and George Walker and Matt preached together the first mission George ever preached" (Ralph Derkland to Our Many Friends, 1955, *TTT*). Two brothers of Walker's mother, John and James Fawcett, entered the Work in 1904.

Details are scarce regarding Walker's ministry in the British Isles from 1899–1903. He was one of the young men who went on the 1899 Bicycle Mission Trip to Scotland. Reportedly, he was one of several Workers who preached in the London Gospel Mission when Lizzie/Lily Coles embraced the faith. Soon after he arrived in America in 1903, he preached in Philadelphia, where Mrs. Abernethy (mother of Overseer Andrew Abernethy) was among his first converts. Walker frequently used her home for his mailing address.

During his lifetime, Walker preached in Ireland, England, Scotland, US and Canada and was a speaker at Conventions all over the world. Overseer of the Eastern US until he died on November 6, 1981, aged 104, he was buried in North Wales Cemetery, Montgomery Co. Pennsylvania, US. Andrew Abernethy succeeded him as Overseer.

Walker told a reporter that "he thinks some Christians have believed as his people do since the days of Christ. **About 22 years ago** ... church members in England and North Ireland became interested in the doctrines, and out of this has come the spread of the faith into this country, Canada, Australia and New Zealand ... South America. **William Irvine, a Scotchman, one of the original leaders**, is not now affiliated with this group because of a difference over the prophecies of the Revelations" [1921 minus 22 years = 1899 start date] (*Indianapolis News*, Sept. 26, 1921, p. 11, *TTT*).

Profile of Alfred "Alfie" Magowan (often misspelled as McGowan or McGowen). Age 19, Magowan professed in a Gospel Mission held in 1902 by Joe Kerr and Edward Cooney in the Balteagh School, Co. Armagh, Northern Ireland. He immigrated to America in 1903, destination Detroit, Michigan, occupation bookkeeper. Around 1907, he entered the Work. John Burns is shown as his Co-worker on the 1907 Pittsburgh US Convention List.

When Magowan (age 24), and John Burns (age 19) held their first Gospel Mission in Kentucky in October 1907, they only had $5.00 between them. (Magowan July 1, 1957, TTT).

Magowan spent twelve years in the Work in Alabama, Indiana, Ohio and Indiana before he married Sister Worker Sarah K. Dawson, also from Ireland, in 1917. They continued preaching as a married Worker couple until Alfred was excommunicated at the 1919 Illinois Convention. *See* Chapter 28.

Sarah, aged 55, died at Rossahilly (John West's home) on May 30, 1934, and was buried at Sydare Cemetery in Irvinestown, Co. Fermanagh, Ireland. In 1939, Alfred married Isobel Waugh; they had four sons and made their home near Portadown, Co. Armagh, N. Ireland. Born October 24, 1883, in Drumgor, Co. Armagh, Ireland, Alfred died November 13, 1960, aged 73; Isobel died November 11, 2005.

Magowan was a prolific letter writer; many quotes from his eloquent writings are included in this book. He published a hymnbook, some essays, and an insightful, fictional play inspired by 2x2 events that he was privy to, titled *Outline of the History of a Peculiar People from 1900–1931. See* website *TellngTheTruth.info* in Publications.

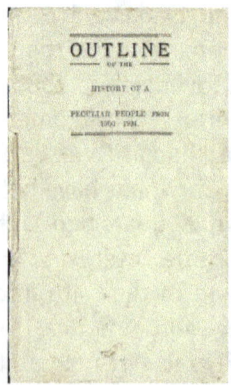

"Outline of the History of a Peculiar People from 1900–1931" by Alfred Magowan

Alfred Magowan

(1883–1960)

Unsectarian – Non-exclusive

1898: The Early Days. According to Long, the Workers, who then called themselves *Go-Preachers* and *Tramp Preachers*, were unsectarian evangelists in 1898. That is, they were not a sect or church, and they were not associated as preachers or evangelists with any other particular church, denomination or religion. They were not yet *exclusive*. Religious exclusivism, or exclusivity, is the doctrine or belief that God has *only* one true church.

Alfred Magowan recalled in a letter to Brother Worker Wilson McClung on January 21, 1931, that in their beginning, forming a sect did not enter the young Workers' minds:

> There were no regulations and no asserting of authority. The Lord had mercifully set us free in spirit to worship and serve him under the guidance of the Holy Spirit through a good conscience; and there was neither machinery nor any of those things that religious people think necessary, and which are necessary in sects under human control. There was nothing in the vision we had of 'the way in Jesus' that would have led us towards another kind of sectarianism, nor did we ever anticipate a time when we would become a strong people in an evil world.
>
> We had only one commission and that was to make disciples as we had been made; and we had only one authority, viz., if the Lord was with us, we would so live and speak that He would use us in getting people saved. And as they listened to us, they would recognize the voice of Him because of the anointing. That was the simple outline in the days of our beginning.

According to John Long:

> As long as the Work kept from exclusiveness and remained unsectarian in manifestation, it was wonderfully used of God in the salvation of sinners and the making of disciples ... the Workers occasionally went to the various churches and at times preached in them, whenever the way opened up, that helped to disarm prejudice, and get at the unconverted to win them for Christ, leaving them to the option of their own will as to where they worship and get the most spiritual food. (June 1898, *TTT*)
>
> While God was reviving His work in Scotland and raised up that godly man and his brethren, J. G. Govan, etc.; and God raised up William Irvine and Edward Cooney for Ireland; and there was a great redemption of fallen humanity. In Wales also, God was at work and raised up Evan Roberts. Though the revival manifestations under the labours of each of these evangelists varied as much as the seasons, it only fulfilled the

> Scripture: 'Now there are diversities of gifts, but the same Spirit. And there are differences of administrations, but the same Lord. And there are diversities of operations, but the same God which worketh, all in all 1 Cor. 12:4–6. (Jan. 1905, *TTT*)

IMPORTANT NOTE! Before delving deeper into the history, **it is essential to understand that those who were converted by Irvine's Workers in the very early days did not form a church. They continued to attend the church of their choice.** This was the policy of the Faith Mission with which Irvine was still associated. Fellowship Meetings in homes had not yet been set up.

Gospel Meetings and Missions

The early Workers used many methods to reach out to others, such as open-air and street preaching on the town diamonds and squares, marches through the streets singing hymns, home visitations, Matthew 10 tours, doorstep evangelizing and magic lantern meetings.

In addition to nightly Gospel Meetings, Long also "occasionally took mothers' meetings, Bible classes, children's meetings, while also some house-to-house visitation, personal talks and tract distribution. [Preached] in the churches of all Protestant denominations, in mission halls, tents, barns, cottages, schoolrooms, public halls, etc." (Jan. 1907, *TTT*).

John Long's Description of Meetings:

> Concerning conducting Meetings and Missions, something could be learned from Irvine's methods; he had no fixed forms or stereotyped methods of prayer, praise and preaching; yet he did it with order and reverence. He seldom prepared his sermons beforehand ... He occasionally threw his Meetings open for prayer but encouraged shortness and definiteness. He had plenty of singing and was careful in selecting hymns suitable for the occasion ... He always valued God's gifts in others and utilised any person who could sing solos effectually to the glory of God.

> He seldom had after-meetings but tested his Meetings immediately after his sermon, without dismissing his audience and nearly always was successful. He often had Testimony Meetings; and encouraged shortness and up-to-date testimonies; and always tried to get young converts to speak, sing and pray. Sometimes he closed the Meetings by singing the doxology; and at times made them grasp each other's hands and sing 'Keep me true Lord to Thee.' (April 1898, *TTT*)

Goodhand Pattison's Description of Meetings:

> Reports reached us at Cloughjordan about this strange man [William
> Irvine] and his strange methods, etc. Nearly everything was highly
> unconventional—forms, rules and usages were either discarded or flung
> ruthlessly aside, instead of the beaten path. One never knew ... what
> was going to come next with him, sometimes hardly any sermon—at
> other times nearly all sermon; sometimes give out a hymn and ... [other
> times] never sing a hymn at all ... sometimes nearly all racy anecdotes
> with plenty smiles and laughter; at other times soul-stirring exhortation,
> backed by sad and tragic experiences, etc. All this added freshness and
> life to the words of one whose intense earnestness and wholehearted
> zeal and devotion none of us had seen before. (1935, Burning and
> Shining Light, *TTT*)

Their Nomenclature

Most specialized subjects or groups develop a special language.
Newcomers soon begin using the group lingo or jargon which may
introduce novel meanings that differ, often widely, from their common
definitions.

In their formative period, sects frequently employ the doctrines,
traditions, terminology and organization already in use by
contemporary Christian churches. For example, the Quakers use the
honorific English words "thee," "thou" and "wouldst," which were
commonly used when they were founded in mid-seventeenth century
England.

The terminology Irvine employed for his movement was not unique.
As a Faith Mission Pilgrim, Irvine would have used their commonly used
terminology. Faith Mission books and publications contain the typical
language and nomenclature prevailing among English Protestantism in
the nineteenth and twentieth centuries, including such terms as:
*profess, decided, made their choice, took their stand, testimony, take
part, fields, friends, saints and servants, elders, laborers, workers,
companions, two by two, the Work, entered* and *offered for the Work,
great harvest field, missions, conventions, meetings, lead* and *test the
meeting, special meetings, gospel meetings/missions* and *testimony
meetings.*

These terms are commonly used in the 2x2 Sect today. When a group
has distinctive practices and language that can be traced to the
nomenclature commonly used in a particular time period, it is highly
probable the group initially came into existence around that time.

❧❧❧

George Walker and William Irvine

12

What Was William Irvine Like?

1900: G. Pattison speculated, "*I believe* the Workers jointly and individually felt Mr. Todd was not the man to superintend and direct such an important movement and *probably* pressed Mr. Irvine into accepting the responsibility of superintending what one would think rightly belonged to him." The fact that up to that point he [Irvine] had not sought out place and any authority which one would think rightly belonged to him spoke volumes for the character and worth of both men, and perhaps we may leave it at that, only to say that 'Todd's Mission,' as it was then called, shortly became a thing of the past. And the Workers now in fellowship with William Irvine went on and increased in numbers, and perhaps I may add increased in their attachment to and respect for their chief's leadership, possibly more so than was good for him or them" (1935, Leaders, *TTT*).

PLEASE NOTE: The above was not a definitive statement by Goodhand Pattison. He was speculating as to how Irvine *may* have arrived at his decision to leave FM when he did. He used the speculative terms, *I believe*, and mentioned that the Workers "*probably* pressed Mr. Irvine into acceptance of responsibility to superintending "what one would think rightly belonged to him." G. Pattison's speculations should not be considered historical facts.

Descriptions of William Irvine

What was unusual about Irvine? How did his preaching generate such large turnouts and large numbers of converts? He was ebullient and charismatic. His enthusiasm provoked men to think along fresh lines with a vigor that persisted after he was long gone. Firsthand witnesses, John Long, Goodhand Pattison and Alfred Magowan provided insightful memories.

John Long's Description:

> In either secular or religious matters, he was a born leader of men; he was a holy man and practical. In personal dealing, he was pre-eminently the best conversationalist I ever met and skillful in soul winning. He had

a marvellous insight into the deep things of God's Word, and like his Master, was an apt teacher of all who received the truth with pleasure. He always set forth the cross and was a swift witness against all pride, vainglory and hypocrisy; he was severe on Christians, but merciful to sinners. In prayer, praise and preaching he excelled in joy, liberty and power. He was very much opposed and misunderstood by religious people; nevertheless, the common people liked him and heard him gladly. (March 1897, *TTT*)

Goodhand Pattison's Description:

But here comes a man, a complete stranger, without pedigree, prestige, or credentials worth the meaning, only on fire with loyalty and love for God and souls, unfettered and unhindered by traditions and opinions of men, and with an untiring energy and consuming zeal. He dared to be, do, or suffer in obeying God (as he then understood it) whatever it meant or cost 'in labours more abundant,' 'through evil report and good report,' he just went on in face of much within and without to thwart and hinder; becoming in a comparatively short time the wonder and admiration of many and the object of envy and opposition of many others. (1935, Practice, *TTT*)

Particularly noticeable were his [Irvine's] constant and oft repeated references to his own experiences, or as we might call it, 'the work of his testimony' ... so realistic did he make this truth of 'Christ in You' and 'Christ in Me' that it seemed like a new revelation, although we had been familiar enough with the words 'Christ in you the hope of glory' and also 'For me to live is Christ' and others like them.

Another expression he was fond of using in the first days was Jesus was a common man. And although at first to our Pharisaic ears, it sounded very irreverent ... yet none of us could contradict or deny the simple fact; and admitting and thinking it over and ... changing completely my conception of who and what Jesus was and is, from the fictitious 'Gentleman Jesus' to the Jesus of the New Testament, whom the 'common people heard him gladly' and who had always been, both at home and abroad, from cradle to grave, the poorest and lowliest. (1935, Christ in You, *TTT*)

Alfred Magowan's Description:

I will cherish grateful recollections of his striking lightning, his crashing thunder and the gentle winds, and refreshing showers which followed. His storms of wrath against humbug and hypocrisy were dreadful to see and to hear; and his sympathetic understanding of weak and troubled souls made him the most loved man I have ever met. He was the only preacher I ever heard who made clear distinctions between weakness and wickedness; weakness was of the flesh and the will; wickedness was of the heart and showed itself mainly in religious and respectable iniquity—in the ordinary ways of strong men taking advantage of the weak; rich men exploiting the poor; religious rulers tyrannizing over the fearful … in the name of Christ and His church …

And had he been a revolutionary, inciting men to the violent overthrow of iniquitous and tyrannical government, he would have made such men as Lenin and Trotsky seem tame and commonplace by comparison. And where the common run of preachers murdered the Scriptures by elocutionary reading of them, or by dull and flat interpretations and applications of them, he brought them to life by the abundance of his own life from his childhood among hard working people. And he was well acquainted with hard work himself–in the 'bowels of the earth.' He had also a grand sense of humour and of the fitness of things … He was the most sensitive-spirited preacher I ever met … And of course, he never used notes: that would have been like going to a dinner and taking his own food with him … He could not endure religious ostentation of any kind … And distinctive religious garb filled him with a deep disgust. (1948, 4–5)

The *Impartial Reporter's* Description:

[William Irvine] thrives on the excitement and his burning zeal impresses itself on any who listen … he is rather of the fiery Peter nature, and however amiable in private life, as a speaker, he is a rather repugnant type of Christian, with a hard and harsh voice; rugged, denunciatory, argumentative, Pharisaic, self-sacrificing, full of earnestness, consumed by the idea that he is God-sent, and that he has a great mission to fulfil. Mr. Irwin [Irvine] is absolutely adamantine in his manner. No sweetness or graciousness. Nothing winning or attractive. (Jan. 29, 1903, *TTT*)

The sacred name is bandied about in the public street as if it were Jack or Tom, and while without intentional irreverence, yet with hurtful familiarity. (Jan. 15, 1903, *TTT*)

Leader and Supervisor

From the Nenagh Revival mission in August 1897 to mid-1898, Irvine was instrumental in the conversion of over than 100 individuals; many would become Workers in his movement. Although he was still associated with FM, many of Irvine's converts were looking to him for guidance and direction as they were busily persuading others to join them. They considered him their leader.

From Long's comments and Irvine's actions, it is obvious Irvine was in charge of and oversaw the operation. Behind the scenes, he was busily orchestrating the movement of the wooden halls, organizing all-day Special Meetings and Conventions, and marshaling and training his and Todd's new Workers. Long explained, "The strain of continuous ministry [for Faith Mission]; also, the care and charge of young converts affected much the physical health of the Evangelist [Irvine]" (March 1898).

Although Long preached independently, Irvine frequently sent him new, young Workers for brief training sessions. Long reported, "About that time, Joseph Kerr left me, and Richard Meikle joined me. For knowledge of the Scriptures, Kerr was the finest companion I ever had; and he was only 21" (Oct. 1902, *TTT*).

In his *Journal,* Long faithfully recorded Co-workers who joined him, dates they arrived, left and locations of missions they worked together. These included Thomas Turner, Irvine Weir, Samuel Boyd, Willie Clelland, Matthew Wilson, Thomas Hastings, Joseph Gillis, John Hardie, Harry Weir, Richard Meikle, Sam Jones and Joe Kerr. All these men would become Workers in Irvine's movement when it coalesced; none had been FM Pilgrims. Some of Long's Worker trainees were associated with Todd's Mission.

At times, Irvine attempted to supervise Long, even though he was an independent preacher; they did not always see eye to eye. Long complained, "While I was originally helped by William Irvine, yet he often interfered with my providential leadings" (Oct. 1900, *TTT*). On occasion, Long refused to follow Irvine's instructions. "At that time some misunderstanding arose between me and William Irvine; he was leaving Ireland and crossing to Scotland, and he wrote me to go over and take the oversight of the Work in the south of Ireland. I felt that it was God who opened up the way when I came first to Scotland, and that I would not leave until He showed me His will in the matter" (March 1900, *TTT*).

Another area of contention between Irvine and Long was that Long, "Owing to lack of courage in conducting after-meetings, I had not the visible results of other evangelists in many of my missions; and because of that, I suffered a good deal of reproach from William Irvine ... I did not get the credit for the amount of day work regarding house-to-house visitation and literature that was attached to my missions; also the continuous preaching, night after night, without any gap or rest or holiday; and that for years without much break" (Feb. 1900, *TTT*).

1900, July: Rathmolyon Convention. According to Long, Irvine held the first general Convention in connection with the Work in the South of Ireland at Rathmolyon, Co. Meath, Ireland. "About 40 Christian Workers met together to consider the word of the Lord. At that conference, I met G. C. Grubb, Robert Miller, Robert Todd, William Irvine, Edward Cooney and others. It was a spiritual time, and we will not forget that hymn of William Gill's sung 16 times, 'Rich are the moments of blessing' " (July 1900, *TTT*).

1900: Twelve new Workers came on board in the UK and Ireland: nine Brothers (Willie Gill, Albert Quinn, Irvine Weir, John Sullivan, Ben Boles, John Hardie, Matthew Wilson, William Clelland, A. Alexander and possibly Samuel Boyd); and three Irish Sisters (Sarah Rogers, Emma and Jennie Gill), making a cumulative total of 18 or 19 new Workers. *See* Appendix A.

Following the Convention, John Long "spent a week helping Sister Gill at a mission in a Wooden Tent, newly built. While in that district [Ballymena, Ireland], Irvine had a meeting so powerful that the people refused to go home, and it lasted all night" (Aug. 1900, *TTT*).

1901: Second Rathmolyon Convention. An Irish "Early Conventions" list indicates another Rathmolyon Convention was held in 1901. Long did not mention it, however, G. Pattison commented that two Conventions were held at Rathmolyon prior to the 1903 Portadown Convention (1935, Conventions, Fn. 49, *TTT*).

1901 Irish Census. Three unmarried male visitors were shown at the residence of James Wilson Robinson at Three Castle Street, Nenagh, Co. Tipperary, Ireland. They were **William Irvine** (age 37, unmarried; birthplace Stirlingshire, Scotland; religion Presbyterian); **Irvine Weir** (age 22, unmarried; birthplace Dublin, Ireland; religion Presbyterian); and **Alexander W. Bradley** (age 20, unmarried; birthplace Co. Down, Ireland; religion Methodist). Obviously, as of 1901, they had not yet separated from their church affiliations.

1901: Ten more Workers entered the Work that year in the UK and Ireland, nine Brothers and one Sister Worker (Martha "Mattie" McGivern), making a cumulative total of 28 Workers (four Sisters and 24 Brothers, including Irvine). *See* Appendix A.

Accounts Predating William Irvine

County Cork. Some residents from Co. Cork, Ireland, claim their families were meeting in homes for fellowship before the Workers' arrival, including some of the Bateman, Burchill and Buttimer families. After meeting Irvine and/or some of his Workers, they merged with them. (No supporting documentation found.)

Irvine's Sister. An unsupported story circulated that Irvine's sister worked for a family in Ireland who were following the practice of their ancestors in their homeland country on the European continent. This family held meetings on Sunday morning in their home. Reportedly, William Irvine's sister introduced their faith to her brother. Some versions of this account suggest these people had fled from their homeland to escape persecution; the stories vary as to location, e.g. Switzerland, the Alps, France, Armenia and Germany.

This story is usually credited to early Worker, Robert "Rob" Darling, who entered the Work in 1905, seven years after the movement began. He was not present at its genesis. Reportedly, he told this account to some Brother Workers in the 1960s. One of them, George Gittins, frequently repeated the story to groups, interlaced with his personal thoughts and speculation. Typed notes of Gittins' talks have circulated that do not include any dates, names or places. Both accounts by Darling and Gittins are based on hearsay with no verifiable primary supporting documents.

Several things mitigate this theory. No records have been found of Irvine repeating this story about his sister, nor is it found in any of the countless letters he sent his followers. There is no evidence of anyone who professed prior to Irvine starting his movement. Also, there is no documentation relative to a group of ministers in Ireland matching the characteristics of Irvine's ministry or in places from where people may have fled to Ireland. Further, no Worker going to preach in another country has found any people worshiping in the same manner.

As stated in Chapter 3, Irvine credited his favorite sister Margaret's death with his spiritual awakening, although it should also be noted that there is no substantiation that Margaret ever visited or worked in Ireland; she died in Scotland.

Gill Family. Sister Worker, Hazel Hughes, daughter of Fred and Mary Ann (Gill) Hughes, remarked in her account, "Our parents' people heard the gospel in **1888**" (1971, *TTT*). This is inconsistent with several other records indicating that the Gill family first heard Irvine in **1897** in Rathmolyon, Ireland. The 1888 date is only found in this single secondary document (based on hearsay). Hazel Hughes was not yet born in 1888—she was born in 1894; she is not a firsthand witness of the event she described. Possibly, the 1888 date is an error in communication or transcription.

13

Tenets of Irvine's New Belief System

Matthew 10: *Faith Lines* Concept. Since one reason given for Irvine's separation from FM was because he objected to the founder living on private means, rather than faith, it is not surprising he made the *Faith Line* concept in Matthew 10 the central bedrock in his new movement and the foundation for the Workers' ministry. It is one of the key fundamental principles that sets the 2x2 ministry apart from most other Christian ministries.

Faith Lines consists of preaching solely on faith with no prearranged support and relying totally on God for natural provisions. The source for this model is Matthew 10:8–10, "Freely ye have received, freely give. Provide neither gold, nor silver, nor brass in your purses." George Walker, Overseer of Eastern US, explained the *Faith Lines* method to the US Selective Service:

> In due time a number of these people went forth to devote their lives to the preaching of the gospel according to the teaching and example of Christ as given in the New Testament, i.e. 'two by two,' and without salary or making appeals for financial assistance, putting implicit trust in God and His promise that as they 'sought first the Kingdom of God,' their natural needs of food and raiment would be added to them. (1942, *TTT*, RIS) [Matt 6:33]

Two by Two Itinerant Preachers. Following Jesus' method of pairing his disciples two and two (Luke 10:1, Mark 6:7), Irvine grouped his Workers in same-sex pairs, as did Faith Mission. Irvine's staff was required to abandon their homes, donate their money and possessions, resign from their employment and become itinerant, living off the generosity of others. Possessing no permanent operation base, they were truly Go-Preachers, preachers-on-the-move, holding short missions here and there, rarely staying in one place long. According to the *Impartial Reporter*:

> One feature in connection with these people is one of the saddest. Their idea is that a 'saint' cannot remain in the world but must go out to

preach the (i.e. their) gospel and hunt for 'saints.' To this end they give up their situations. Mr. Irwin [Irvine] himself gave up a comfortable business. He had £300 a year when 20 (*sic:* should be 30) years of age. (Jan. 22, 1903, *TTT*)

The Pilgrims imagine that each of them has the gifts of preaching and teaching. They do not concede that you serve God where you are placed; you must leave your place and family and go out with them ... They think God will give them the power to speak and teach, but for so far, the Almighty has not done much in this direction ... The 'Tramps' ... must forsake 'the world,' and go about from place to place, preaching, because the Lord did. They put themselves in His place, and consider that the state of things existing now justify them copying the Master's methods 1900 years ago. (Jan. 29, 1903, *TTT*)

The misconception has been circulated that in the early days, *every* convert left all and went out preaching in Irvine's ministry. In other words, there were no laymen (aka Friends, Saints) who remained with their families in their homes. History shows this was not the case.

Some who converted but did not become Workers were John and Sara West (owners of Crocknacrieve Convention grounds); Goodhand and Eleanor Kate Pattison; William West and some of his family; and Workers' family members, such as the Gills, Carrolls and Hastings of Rathmolyon. There were also those who were too elderly to be Workers (parents and grandparents), or too young like Fannie Carroll, who was 14 when she professed, and some with large, young families.

Irvine's Doctrine and Principles According to John Long:

Concerning the principals of the doctrine of Christ, he [William Irvine] was sound. He believed in the fall of man, in the Atonement, in the Trinity, in the Divinity of our Lord, in the immortality of the soul, in the Resurrection of the body, the Inspiration of the Bible, in Heaven for the saved and in Hell for the lost. He believed in a personal Devil, the enemy of God and man. He believed and taught Repentance and that every person can be saved and know it, and that the conditions of salvation were 'If thou shalt confess with thy mouth the Lord Jesus, and shalt believe in thine heart that God hath raised Him from the dead, thou shalt be saved,' Romans 10:9 ...

He taught that every saved soul is indwelt by the Spirit of Christ ... and that the life of Jesus is the pattern for everyone to imitate and follow; and that the life of forsaking all for Christ's sake was the best to live. The fruits of that teaching resulted in farmers, shopkeepers, domestic servants, schoolteachers, police, soldiers and persons of every occupation forsaking all that they had to follow Jesus and to preach the Gospel of the Kingdom of God. (March 1898, *TTT*)

Refusal to Take a Name. From their beginning, Irvine declined to brand his new belief system with an official name, based on Acts 4:12, "Neither is there salvation in any other: **for there is none other name under Heaven given among men, whereby we must be saved.**"

For a brief time, the Workers referred to themselves as *Go-Preachers*, from the injunction in Matthew 10:7, "As ye go, preach." The title of their first hymnal was the *Go-Preacher's Hymn Book* (1909, *TTT*), but this appellation was soon discarded. Early Worker Wilson McClung asked, "And who are we? We have no name ... but the ribald multitude give us many. Some call us *Cooneyites*, some call us *Tramps, Faith Missioners, No-Secters, Women-Thieves,* and so on ... Our Mission was started by William Irvine, a Scotchman, seven or eight years ago. Others followed him" (*Morning Leader,* June 11, 1906, *TTT*).

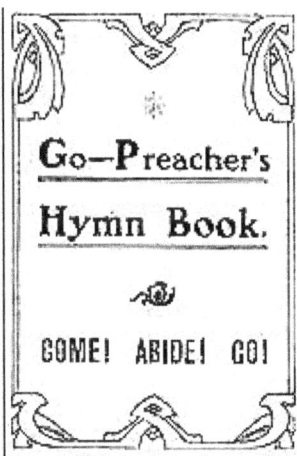

Go-Preacher's Hymn Book, published 1909

In the absence of an official name, for identification purposes, the press and public have provided a variety of nicknames for the nameless sect, including Irvinites, Cooneyites, Reidites, The Jesus Way, Tramp Preachers, Wooden Hall Preachers, Dippers, Black Stockings/Socks, White Mice, Two by Twos (2x2s), etc.

Two by Twos. In publications, "Two by Twos" is their most frequently used moniker, including *Wikipedia* and the US Library of Congress. Like the term *Christian* in the New Testament, *Two by Two* (abbreviated 2x2) is not used by members. Coined by outsiders, this descriptive nickname was derived from their core belief that ministers should travel in same-sex pairs (two by two), as Jesus instructed the twelve and seventy disciples.

For the sake of convenience, this book uses the term *Two by Twos* (abbreviated 2x2), as well as *sect, church, movement, ministry* and *belief system*. These are not derogatory terms used in a perjorative sense. The definition of the word *sect* is a nonconformist church; a religious faction united by common interests or beliefs; a religious group that has separated from an established church. These descriptions accurately portray the nameless 2x2 Sect.

Cooneyites. By 1904, three years after Edward Cooney joined, the group had become well known as the *Cooneyites*. A reporter quoted Cooney declaring, " 'I am a Tramp Preacher.' Therefore, if the writer describe the latest phase of religious enthusiasm by the name given by one of themselves, it cannot be misunderstood ... and the two leaders are Mr. Wm. Irvine and Mr. Edward Cooney" (*Impartial Reporter,* October 13, 1904, *TTT*).

Cooney commonly referred to the group as *God's Saints and Servants.* He declared, "Please note that I am not a Cooneyite, but a Christian. Those in fellowship with me as fellow Workers and Saints are not Cooneyites, but Christians" (*Fermanagh Times,* April 18, 1907, *TTT*). An Enniskillen resident, George Coalter, commented in his Memoirs, "The membership of the churches was greatly reduced and so *Cooneyism* found its way into a leading dictionary as a new word or sect."

Letters dating from 1910 onward by early Scottish Workers Willie and Elisabeth Jamieson referred to the group as the nonspecific: *Way of God, Way of Jesus, Jesus Way, God's Way* and *God's Truth and Way.* Similarly, current followers, among themselves, commonly refer to their church as *The Truth* (most common term in the US), *The Way, The Fellowship, The Fold, God's Kingdom/Family/People,* etc.

During the first 15 years, some members referred to their church as *The Testimony of Jesus,* a name Willie Gill reportedly registered with the UK Government during WWI. The name *Christian Assembly* was used in during WWII in Australia and New Zealand, while the US and Canada used the name *Christian Conventions Representing Assemblies of Christians Assuming This Name Only.*

Women Preachers Accepted. It was considered a scriptural mandate until the late 1800s for women to "keep silence in the churches" (1 Cor. 14:34). Phoebe Palmer played a major role in changing this. In 1859, she published a book titled *The Promise of the Father* defending women's rights to preach. Her argument was primarily based upon the prophecy in Joel 2:28–29, quoted by the Apostle Peter in his Pentecost sermon

(Acts 2:18), in which he proclaimed that in the New Covenant both men and women would prophesy (preach). This became the principal scriptural justification for women preachers throughout the nineteenth and early twentieth centuries.

The Salvation Army, founded in 1854 by William and Catherine Booth, made notable inroads for women to become ministers or evangelists. Mrs. Booth was a powerful and popular preacher. From its beginning around 1840, the Holiness Movement permitted women to speak/preach. Women were vital to the China Inland Mission. From its inception in 1878, single female missionaries were permitted to work in teams in the interior of China.

The Faith Mission, a holiness ministry, accepted its first two female Pilgrims in 1887. Accustomed to working with female preachers in FM, Irvine also accepted them. At the turn of the twentieth century, the 2x2 Sister Workers were among the few female evangelists and missionaries in the world. The new sect was on the progressive end of a trend—a rarity.

No Collections or Institutional Support. From their start, the Workers have received monetary support through members' *spontaneous, unsolicited, freewill* donations, along with provisions for their other needs (food, clothing, transportation, medical treatment, electronics, etc.). Legacies and estates upon the death of a 2x2 are sometimes left to the Work.

To this day, the *Faith Lines* concept is an integral, inseparable, uncompromisable 2x2 core doctrine. Following Matthew 10:8–10, "Freely ye have received, freely give. Provide neither gold, nor silver, nor brass in your purses," the Workers did not appeal for money or take up collections. As Jack Carroll put it, "If we knew of any of us ever lifting a collection or asking for money, we would immediately see to it that he would be excluded from our Fellowship as a preacher of the Gospel" (1934, *TTT*).

Nevertheless, concerning their early practices, Long explained, "By experience we learned that it was not inconsistent with *Faith Lines* to have a box at the door of our tent for freewill offerings; so as that the poor widow could give her mite, as well as the rich their abundance" (2 Kings 12:9) (Jan. 1901, *TTT*).

The Impartial Reporter observed, "The Tramps say they have no collections. In strict parlance, this may be correct, but it is not the whole truth. They may not 'collect,' but they receive donations. At the houses in which they hold meetings, a bag is placed for the receipt of the gifts" (Aug. 27, 1908, *TTT*).

"There is a lot of 'rot' spoken about 'no collections' at Tramp meetings ... The Tramps do receive donations from their own people, (not from the general public) and generous gifts, too. The bag which they place in the houses of their people 'collects' the donations, and the 'brethren' give freely" (Sept. 30, 1909, Art. 5, *TTT*). Receptacles for donations were discontinued sometime after 1909.

Claim of No Published Literature. From their beginning, other than a hymnal, the 2x2 Sect has not published any literature for or about their sect for outside distribution. The first *Go-Preacher's Hymn Book* was printed in 1909. It was replaced in 1913 by *Hymns Old and New;* successive editions have been printed, and the 1987 edition is used currently. Their only written material (strictly for internal use) includes copies of letters, poetry, lists, Convention summaries, funeral accounts, Meeting and sermon notes (aka gems).

Claim of No Ministerial Training. Workers pride themselves in not attending seminaries, religious schools, or receiving any formal theological training. Unlike the new Faith Mission volunteers, whose trainees complete a training program, the 2x2 Sect maintains no schools. For their apprenticeship training, new Workers are assigned to older experienced Workers. There are no written principles, doctrinal statements or rule books to guide them.

Claim of No Organization. There is no worldwide head, president, chairman, secretary or treasurer. As explained by Overseer Jack Carroll, "We have no organization or regular system—we are a strange and peculiar people" (n.d. Minister Statement).

No central worldwide fund is known. However, it has come to light in recent years that some substantial trust funds, investments and properties are controlled by Regional Overseers, and some individual Workers have personal bank accounts and credit cards.

The sect has a developed a highly organized hierarchy that governs the sect. A group of Senior Overseers have oversight of Regional Overseers on state, provincial and national levels. Under them, by rank, are the older male Workers, the younger male Workers, the older female Workers, the younger female Workers and lastly, the lay members. Distinctions exist among the laity as well.

Non-sectarian (Unsectarian). In their early years, their mission was unsectarian; that is, it was not affiliated with a particular religious sect, church or denomination. The Workers were chiefly non-sectarian evangelists holding recruiting missions. Their chief aim was to bring souls to Christ. New converts continued to attend the Protestant church of their choice.

On the 1901 Irish Census, many 2x2 converts and Workers gave their religion as Presbyterian, Methodist, Church of Ireland, etc. They did not separate from other denominations until sometime in/after 1902 when they began establishing Sunday Fellowship Meetings in members' homes, serving communion and holding baptisms.

Until 1905, evangelists, missionaries and preachers of other Christian denominations were looked upon as fellow laborers in Christ. Several times in his *Journal*, Long listed names of preachers outside their sect who were speakers at their Special Meetings. Also, some of Irvine's Workers attended the Keswick Convention in England, where the speakers were preachers and evangelists from various denominations worldwide.

~~~~~

Holiness Movement. William Irvine adopted elements from a variety of pre-existing movements and sources in formulating his independent belief system. A significant amount of Faith Mission (FM) terminology and practices were carried forward, while others were altered and jettisoned.

Many FM practices for daily living were applications of the Holiness Movement doctrine. Some believe Irvine was influenced by the Holiness Movement that began in the mid-1800s and that he borrowed or adapted some of its beliefs and principles.

While there are many similarities in the terminology and perspectives of Irvine's belief system and the Holiness Movement, there are also significant differences. The Holiness Movement was not a church or sect; its doctrine transcends denominational lines. The Keswick Convention, Faith Mission, Salvation Army, Church of the Nazarene and Methodists all taught traditional Holiness concepts—not to be confused with the Pentecostal and Charismatic Holiness Movements.

The core tenet of the Holiness Movement was the doctrine of sanctification, defined as being "set apart" for the Lord's use and the possibility of achieving personal perfection and spiritual maturity. This was also a core tenet of Irvine's belief system and of FM. Both movements promoted a life of obedience, self-denial, abstaining from the appearance of evil, separating from and not conforming to the world, "walking in the light," etc.

It appears that sanctification was a 2x2 core tenet also. Western US Overseer Jack Carroll declared in a Convention, "If you don't believe in sanctification, you are not in the Kingdom, are not yet a child in the Kingdom, and if you don't believe in being wholly sanctified, it is doubtful whether you have entered at all" (Carroll n.d., n.p., Matthew 13, *TTT*).

Irvine's belief system also shared several characteristics found in other nineteenth century movements during that era's resurgence in religious interest and vigor, sometimes known as the *Second Great Awakening* and the *Missionary Movement*. These were typically characterized by large revivals, emergence of new denominations and active mission work.

The Tent
Seventh and E Streets

Dear Friend:

We give you a hearty invitation to the undenominational Evangelistic Talks on the LIFE AND MINISTRY OF JESUS and HIS Apostles in THE TENT, SEVENTH AND E STREETS, continuing Sundays at 2:30 and 7:30 P.M. Evenings (except Saturdays) at 7:45.

We will endeavor to make these services instructive and helpful to all. We are gladly giving our lives in telling the "Old, Old Story" of HIM who "lived to show us how to live" and died as our Redeemer that HE might live again, in the power of HIS resurrection life, in all who will make room for HIM

The services will be sane, practical, and not unduly prolonged. THE TENT IS COMFORTABLY HEATED.

We will value your kindly interest in coming to the services and bringing others.

Your "Servants for Jesus' sake"

JOHN CARROLL
HENRY HANSON
RASMUS PRIP

The Portable on the Scappoose School Grounds

Dear Friend:

We give you a very cordial invitation to the

EVANGELISTIC MEETINGS
that will be conducted
In the Portable on the Scappoose School Grounds.
Meetings every evening at 7:30 P. M.
except Mondays and Saturdays
Beginning on Sunday, Nov. 22nd

Your friendly co-operation in attending and making the services known will be much appreciated.

We are gladly giving our lives in preaching the Gospel of our Lord Jesus Christ in simplicity and sincerity. There will be nothing extreme or sensational in any of the services. Our purpose is to give simple, sane, practical talks on the fundamentals of the "faith of Jesus" and to make clear HIS plan of Salvation and Service for all.

Come and bring others.

Your "servants for Jesus' Sake"

A. STEVENS

H. R. MATHEWS

Invitations to Tent and Portable Hall Gospel Meetings

14

The Great Experiment – Alfred Magowan

Death of Queen Victoria. The 2x2 Sect was founded during the Victorian Era (1837–1901). Born on May 24, 1819, Victoria was Queen of the United Kingdom of Great Britain and Ireland from June 20, 1837, until her death on January 22, 1901, aged 63; her reign was called the *Victorian Era*. She was succeeded by her son, King Edward VII, who reigned from January 22, 1901, to May 6, 1910; his reign was called the *Edwardian Era*.

William Irvine's initial success may have been somewhat due to his being in a fortunate time and place. He raised his voice to protest against the religious beliefs and practice, social conditions and values of the late Victorian Britain. His style of preaching appealed to those who had few of the educational and social opportunities afforded the upper classes.

Reminiscing in 1953, Alfred Magowan eloquently explained the nature of Irvine's revolutionary experiment that prompted young men and women to offer their lives for the harvest field (ministry) and become Workers in Irvine's new sect.

> It was a revolution against the respectable and comfortable members of the community who, while claiming to be Christians, were in high positions, looking down on the improvidence of the poor. Many of us were moved to go forth ... We forsook all we had. We emptied ourselves of all worldly ambition ... We were so zealous that no arguments against us could have made the slightest effect. Minds were unalterable and irrevocably made up. The need seemed so great. It was a chance to live heroically in an age afflicted with dullness ... We were fanatical ...

> We believed that we were the last hope of the world and that ours was an honest hearted revolt. We set out to form a brotherhood where all would be equal. We wanted to break from all tradition and become a people neither Catholic nor Protestant with no regulations, no authority, no machinery or human control, to be free to serve God and make people free like ourselves. We put all worldly ambition behind us, none of this world's satisfactions or regards held any attraction, we had

no theology to propound, no congregations to please, we saw ourselves as workers, but not bosses. (Parker 1982, 26, Fn. 10)

It was a Great Experiment (William Irvine, 1938)

In retrospect, Irvine made the shocking comment to Magowan in 1938 that, **"It was a great experiment,"** to which Magowan replied, "It was a great experience" (1956, 5, *TTT*). Magowan eloquently expressed the Workers' perspective of "the experiment":

> An experiment in brotherhood, where all were on one level; where possessions had no power over the hearts of men; where there was no desire for honours or titles or distinctions; where men could walk together and call each other by their first names; where there was faith enough to believe preachers would not starve if they went out into the world without visible means of support.

> An experiment in passing through this world without conforming to it; and where spiritually minded men could maintain their pilgrimage, when establishment was calling to them and pulling at them from every side. An experiment in serving, without expectation of reward in this life; where something of the sufferings of Christ was to be expected; and where the soul could be disciplined by all that it would be required to pass through—unto the final purifying of the heart. **A very great experiment indeed**, and in which thousands of young men and women took part—to be made in an image and likeness not to be attained in any other way or by any ordinary means. (1958, 8–9, *TTT*)

A contrasting perspective from the world:

> 'Giving up all' to 'win souls for Christ', as they put it ... They say the Lord calls them when they yield to their own wishes. They say they 'forsake all' and go out for Him, after the manner of Peter, when they have little to forsake ... Some young man has been selling tea or hardware or setting potatoes and some young lady who has been selling yards of ribbon, think it would be well to go out to 'work for the Lord,' and in a spirit of self-sacrifice 'go out for Him.' And because they like the idea, they imagine the Lord has called them to His work ... Then they imagine the Lord Himself inspires them to speak, tells them to speak, tells them what to say, etc. when whatever we know of inspiration tells the direct contrary. (*Impartial Reporter*, Jan. 29, 1903, *TTT*)

Condemning the Clergy and Churches

From the perspective of Irvine and his Workers, everyone fell into one of three categories: sinners, saints or servants. Irvine believed the institutional church was apostate. Taking Isaiah 41:15 as his "Call to Service," he viewed himself as God's personally appointed "thresher," whose task was to expose the unscriptural aspects of clericalism. A reporter's summary: "They think the churches have lapsed or back-slidden, and that they are called by God to rouse people to a sense of their danger from hell-fire" (*Impartial Reporter,* Jan. 15, 1903, *TTT*).

Not one to be reticent, Irvine's lambasts of clergy seemed bizarrely improper to some of his audiences who reacted with outrage, vengefulness and even rioting. He challenged religious authorities, insulted and mocked various preachers and claimed they are or would be in Hell, including such highly revered men as John Wesley, Charles Spurgeon and the popes.

Irvine's unkind accusations were frequently reported in newspapers and caused him to be denied access to church buildings and facilities for missions. According to Long, "A good deal of opposition arose at that time because William Irvine spoke with great authority against the unfaithfulness of the clergy; many threw on the brake, but he refused to be corrected by them, believing that God had raised him up to 'thresh the mountains' " (March 1898, *TTT*).

In condemning the clergy, Irvine and his Workers believed they had a precedent with Jesus who said to the scribes and Pharisees, "Ye serpents, ye generation of vipers, how can ye escape" (Matt. 23:33), and with John the Baptist who said, "O generation of vipers, who has warned you to flee" (Matt. 3:7). Their severity and disrespect for clergy and church members were addressed in a blistering critique by the *Impartial Reporter:*

> Various speakers at the meetings say the townspeople are going to Hell. They are all very cocksure about it. No pope ever claimed the power of loosing and binding in Hell and Heaven stronger than these Pilgrims or Tramps claim to know those who will go to the hot place ... Every other sentence almost of Mr. Irwin's [Irvine's] oration one night had Hell mentioned in it ... and they assume with the most sublime audacity to take upon themselves to say who is and who is not going to Hell ...
>
> The Pilgrims know they are not liked, and for that reason they say they are 'persecuted.' One of their dogmas—for they have no doctrines—is that if you are 'really saved' you must be persecuted; and argue if you are not persecuted, you cannot be saved ... No one persecutes them, as they are generally credited with being soft-headed—perhaps an unkind

thing—but nevertheless, this is the attitude of the public, and this is the kindest way of viewing their extravagances. (Jan. 22, 1903, 8, *TTT*)

Pastors and Evangelists

To the question, "What is your occupation?" Workers sometimes reply they are *evangelists,* e.g. early ship passenger lists. Long opined, "For a pastor to say of an evangelist, *"I have no need of thee"* is a mistake; and for an evangelist to say of a pastor *"there is no need for thee"* is a mistake; the work and office of both are scriptural and should not be done without" (Jan. 1900, *TTT*).

Five distinct roles of ministry (aka five-fold ministry) are provided by the Apostle Paul: "And he gave some, apostles; and some, prophets; and some, **evangelists;** and some, **pastors** and teachers; For the perfecting of the saints, for the work of the ministry, for the edifying of the body of Christ" (Eph. 4:11–12). Each term describes a unique facet of ministry.

The word *pastor* (Latin, meaning *shepherd*) refers to a leader of a Christian congregation. A **pastor** guides, directs, leads, protects feeds and dispenses advice and counsel to his congregation *who come to him.* Pastors generally remain stationary.

The word *evangelist* (from the Greek word *evangelistis,* meaning a messenger of good news) is someone *who goes to others* and publicly delivers the good news (gospel) of Jesus Christ. Evangelists are not pastors of a church. Preaching the Gospel is the central work of evangelists; most do not go from church to church preaching to the converted, nor do they oversee and guide a church. The Apostle Paul uses the term *evangelist* three times. He instructed Timothy to "preach the word," and "do the work of an evangelist," (2 Tim. 4:2). *See* Jesus' instructions for evangelizing in Matthew 28:19–20.

While evangelists share the same goal, their approaches vary. Some hold evangelistic indoor or outdoor rallies, revivals, campaigns or crusades; others have been successful with open-air street preaching and at factories and dockyards at midday meal break, prisons, etc. Some evangelists remain in their home country while others, also called *missionaries,* cross geographical boundaries into other countries.

Not all evangelists represent a particular Christian sect or denomination; some are non-sectarian. John McNeill (1854–1933, through whom Irvine was converted) was a well-known ordained Presbyterian preacher, dubbed the *Scotch Spurgeon,* who was both an evangelist and pastor (not at the same time); *see* Appendix F. Some prominent American international evangelists have been Dwight L. Moody (1937–1999, non-sectarian); Billy Sunday (1862–1935, non-sectarian); and Billy Graham (1918–2018, Southern Baptist minister).

Means of support varies for evangelists. Some Christian groups or churches pledge to support a particular evangelistic Christian mission and/or an evangelist. The Keswick Convention has been hosting missionaries and their families for well over 100 years. Some agencies fund a particular evangelist for a specified length of time. Some evangelists are supported by donations given at their meetings. Pilgrim evangelists worked under the auspices of FM, a non-sectarian mission.

Faith Lines in reference to an unsalaried ministry did not originate with Irvine's ministers; many across the centuries have and continue to practice *faith lines*. Charles Parham, James McKeown and others, in what became the Pentecostal movement, had experimented with faith lines years before Irvine and Long. China Inland Mission missioners (and groups that modeled themselves after them) also went about on *faith lines* with no salary or support. Roman Catholic mendicant preaching orders avoided owning property, did not work at a trade, and embraced a poor, often itinerant lifestyle, depending for their survival on the goodwill of the people to whom they preached.

Years later in retrospect, Long gave the following advice regarding Matthew 10:

> However, as a guide to preachers, Matthew 10 should only be taken in conjunction with the other Scriptures and Acts of the Apostles after Pentecost. This is a very important point lest young preachers should attempt that which our Lord never meant and run into catastrophe; as in Matthew 10, that tour was only for a few days to meet a need and prepare the way for His visit to them, vs. 10–25. In Matthew 10 they were not to go to the Gentiles, nor to the Samaritans; after Pentecost they were to be 'Witnesses unto me both in Jerusalem, and in Judea and in Samaria, and unto the uttermost parts of the Earth,' Acts 1:8. In Matthew 10 they were to take neither gold, silver, or brass, in their purses nor any luggage; after Pentecost they used money and carried necessary luggage (Acts 4:34–35; 21:15; 28:30–31; 1 Cor. 9:14). (July 1898, *TTT*)

The Impartial Reporter expounded, "The conditions of those commands ... given during the earlier part of His ministry, were cancelled in the 22nd chapter of Luke, after the Lord's Supper, when new conditions had arisen ... The 10th of Matthew, on which the Tramps affect to base their whole code of ethics, has now no binding force whatever, as it was repealed by the same authority which had created it, in addition to the fact, that it was addressed to the 'twelve' alone.

Thus, the code and ideas which the Tramps built on a wrong foundation crumble to the dust" (*Impartial Reporter,* Oct. 7, 14, 1909).

1902 Events

As time marched on and as the need arose, Irvine, Cooney and their Co-workers developed their teachings (aka doctrine), rules and traditions. Cooney appropriately called it "groping their way." On a learning curve, their methods and beliefs evolved. Irvine did not start out with a complete master plan for assembling a ministry and church. It developed over the years. The new sect was a work-in-progress.

The Workers received strong criticism because they did not administer the ordinance of communion (aka Lord's Supper, Eucharist, Emblems, Breaking of Bread). The *Impartial Reporter* editor objected on the following grounds: "But there is harm ... of their ignoring the solemn rite of the Lord's Supper commanded by the Lord Himself. What excuse can possibly be offered for ignoring the most solemn and sacred of all Christian institutions ... to disregard the command—'As oft as ye do this, do it in remembrance of me' " (Oct. 27, 1904, *TTT*).

1902, January: In late 1901, Irvine had a mission in Edinburgh, Scotland where 70 persons were converted. Long reported that Irvine "newly returned from his recent mission with a number of the young converts with him; and he spoke with great power and authority; he emphasized aggressive labor in the Lord's vineyard; and showed the possibility of doing a work for the Lord, even by giving away tracts."

Twenty-three more Workers entered the Work in 1902 in the UK and Ireland, 10 Sisters and 13 Brothers, including Sam Jones, the renowned hymn writer, for a cumulative total of 51 Workers. *See* Appendix A.

Derrygonnelly Convention, Co. Fermanagh, Ireland. This Convention was held in a wooden hall with the Workers staying with David Donaldson, according to a list of Irish "Early Conventions."

Enniscorthy Convention, Co. Wexford, Ireland. According to G. Pattison, two Conventions had been held in Rathmolyon and one in Enniscorthy (1935, Conventions, Fn. 49, *TTT*).

Portadown Convention, Co. Armagh, Ireland. Referring to this event, Alfred Magowan mentioned to Wilson McClung, "My own experience goes back to 1902, and my most real recollection of fellowship was that gathering in Portadown 28 or 29 years ago" (June 21, 1931, *TTT*). G. Pattison noted, "It would *probably* be within four or five years from the start when a Convention was arranged for Portadown in a hall ... I made it my business to be at that Convention" (1935, Conventions, *TTT*).

Long reported, "Joseph Kerr and I went to a conference held in Portadown; about 60 Workers met together to consider missions, doctrines, companions, etc., also to exhort one another in the Lord our God" (July 1902, *TTT*). The British term *conference* was called *convention* by Americans.

Baptisms. After G. Pattison arrived at the 1902 Portadown Convention, he observed, "Messrs. Irvine and Cooney together spoke to me on the subject of baptism, as at that Convention for the first time to my knowledge, they started to baptize ... the subject of baptism before this time formed no part of William Irvine's teachings ... as also in the matter of forming churches" (1935, Conventions, Baptisms, *TTT*).

"The Ulster Herald" Waiting for the 'Dippers' (October 22, 1904)

Home Church Meetings. About this time, declared Long, "Edward Cooney began to baptize his converts and form assemblies according to the model in the Acts, namely meeting together on the first day of the week for fellowship, breaking of bread and prayers. The opposition against the Work from the clergy and churches rendered it necessary to reform, also the responsibility of shepherding young converts. William Irvine shrank from this great and responsible undertaking; but afterwards went into it. This produced fresh opposition especially when important persons left their churches to go in with an improved testimony," explained Long (July 1902, *TTT*).

Up until this time, new converts continued to attend churches of their choice. In 1902, when Sunday Fellowship Meetings with communion were installed in members' private homes, 2x2 members withdrew from their church affiliations, leaving behind hard feelings, resentment and disruption. While Workers held Gospel Missions in almost any available facility, including church buildings, they began gathering for Fellowship Meetings *only* in private homes of members—never in a public building.

Edward Cooney (1867–1960) entered the Work in 1901

15

1901 – Edward Cooney – The Master Marketer

Two of the most prominent early leaders and marketers of the 2x2 Sect were William Irvine and Edward "Eddie" Cooney from Enniskillen, Northern Ireland. Cooney, a Christian lay preacher, first met Irvine in January 1898, and joined his movement three and one-half years later in June 1901.

Cooney explained, "I travelled for my father's business and preached ... as occasion offered ... Whilst doing so, I met William Irvine through whom George Walker, Jack Carroll, William Carroll, Willie Gill and a number of the present leaders professed ... William Irvine and I were drawn together as Brothers in Christ, each of us claiming liberty to follow Jesus as we received progressive light from God by the Spirit ... He was at that time Pilgrim Irvine, a preacher in the Faith Mission ... At that time, we believed that all who were born anew, including ourselves, in the denominations were children of God" (to Alice Flett, 1930, Appendix D).

As Irvine's right-hand man and as an outstanding, well-respected early leader in the 2x2 Sect, Cooney was frequently discussed and quoted in newspapers. "At last Sunday evening's service there were five men and two women on the platform, and of the former were two of the chief pioneers of the movement—Mr. William Irwin [Irvine] and Mr. Edward Cooney" (*Impartial Reporter,* July 18, 1907, 8, *TTT*). "Mr. William Irvin [Irvine], the founder of the sect, is in attendance, and Mr. Edmund [Edward] Cooney, his chief lieutenant, is returning from Canada to take part in the deliberations" (*Irish Independent,* July 5, 1910, 5, *TTT*).

By 1904, the press had dubbed Cooney the "Hot Gospeller of his time." The new sect was commonly referred to as *Cooneyites or Cooneyism,* an eponym derived from Edward's surname. The moniker *Cooneyites* continues to be used today in various publications.

THE IMPARTIAL REPORTER AND FARMERS' JOURNAL

'PILGRIM' CONVENTION

AT CROCKNACRIEVE.

---

600 IN CONFERENCE.

HOW THEY ARE CATERED FOR.

A NEW IDEA OF HELL.

MR. WM. IRWIN AND THE CLERGY.

The annual convention of those who are popularly known as Pilgrims or Cooneyites, and who style themselves 'Tramp preachers,' is at present being held at Crocknacrieve, the residence of Mr. John West, within a mile of Ballinamallard. The convention which met last week will continue for a month. At present there are about 600 in conference, and more are expected to arrive during the coming week.

To cater for and find sleeping accommodation for such a large concourse of people is no small undertaking. For a month previous to the meeting of the convention arrangements were being made for their habitation. Crocknacrieve is a large house, with many spacious rooms, and its roof at present cover 200 women and children. Most of the rooms are at present bedrooms having over an average four double beds each. The beds are mostly made on the floor and in some instances three occupy the same bed, some rooms are occupied solely by mothers and their children. The large stable loft, which has been the scene of many meetings in the past, is now converted into one large dormitory for women, in which there are about 50 beds and with a few exceptions all are double beds.

The men, excepting those far advanced in years, sleep out in large marquee tents of which there are seven. 70 are accommodated at Mullaghmeen and 50 at Ballinamallard.

The cuisine arrangements are complete in every detail. Two large boilers are constantly in use for cooking. The old wine cellar is turned into a bakehouse and on last Saturday as many as 160 loaves were baked by two members of the convention who were old soldiers and had served their country at home and abroad. The meat for use is brought from Belfast and it is not a question of ordering a sirloin or round, but whole carcases. Those of the 'tramps' who understand butter-making are busy in the dairy where a separator is kept in use.

Practically every trade is represented at the Convention. There are mechanics, tailors, dressmakers, joiners, carpenters, cobblers, tinsmiths, and even a watchmaker is there with his tools and bench and is kept busy doing repairs.

Most of the 'tramps' have bicycles, and to enter one of the spacious lofts where the machines are kept one would imagine they were looking into a store of some large Coventry cycle warehouse. It would be impossible to describe fully all that has been done for the comfort of the visitors, but even to a writing room and a post box for letters, an hospital for the sick, are they provided with.

Each day of the week (including Sunday) three services are held in the large tent on the west side of the house. The first is in the morning from 11 a.m. till 1 p.m., then another is held in the afternoon from 3 p.m. till 5 p.m., and the evening service lasts from 7 p.m. till 9.30 p.m. On last Sunday at the afternoon and evening services fully 1,000 people were present. The men and women according to the old Jewish custom sit apart from one another and do not mingle. Their dress is plain. The women mostly wear black skirts, cotton blouses and sailor hats. The male attire does not in any way vary except that in some cases no collars or ties are worn. To look upon the vast gathering one would wonder where they all came from. There are English, Scotch and Irish. Some come from the Far East and some from the wild West. There are even half-caste Indians from North America there. They all formerly belonged to all sects and creeds—not only Protestants, but some had been members of the Greek and Roman Churches. Two of their number were Ministers, and Suffolkshire is represented by no fewer than 30 souls.

At last Sunday evening's service there were five men and two women on the platform, and of the former were two of the chief pioneers of the movement—Mr. Wm. Irwin and Mr. Edward Cooney. The meeting opened with the singing of hymns and prayer. The most interesting address was that of Mr. Wm. Irwin, who dealt solely with the clergy and the terrors of hell. The others did not practically touch either of those subjects. Mr. Irwin is a forcible speaker, and has a very convincing manner. He spoke of the clergy of all denominations in scathing terms and stated that in all ages the clergy were the marks of the devil. Jesus, he said, would never have a clergyman, and his own personal belief was that every clergyman would go to hell unless he turned and worked in what he called 'the Jesus way.' He also added—'No one in heaven believes in the clergy, and no one in hell either.' His idea of hell is rather novel. He described it thus :—'Hell is a place where every man will be made to serve God in the Jesus way.' Mr. Cooney gave a short address. In the course of his remarks he made the momentous announcement—' We believe this is the last message to the people of Fermanagh.' He also referred to their sect as '.God's saints and servants.' At the close of his remarks he called on those who were saved since the beginning of the convention to stand up and remain standing, the idea being to confess God openly as their Saviour. Seven did so. Mr. Cooney also requested those who had not been publicly baptised, and wished to be, to stand up. Nineteen signified their wish. A baptismal service was then announced for next Sunday.

It has often been said that a Monday evening meeting is tame compared with that of any other evening. At the meeting last Monday evening the addresses were simple homilies which might be heard any time in a Salvation Army Hall. They lacked in vigour the vim and force of ordinary revival addresses. It is pleasing to note that there is practically nothing said that would offend anyone, the services being nicely conducted and remarkable for the freedom from abusive language which used to characterize them. There are occasional visitors. A Mr. Kelly delivered a lengthy address and spoke earnestly. The only marring feature in it

was a personal reference to four persons who attended on Sunday night. When they came in to the meeting, he said they prayed and afterwards giggled and talked. They were devil possessed, added the speaker, and must have been Methodists. The same gentleman made reference to unsaved people praying to God. His theory was that it was far better for them not to pray to God at all, until they live in the 'Jesus way.'

"Impartial Reporter" July 18, 1907, page 8

*William Irvine and
Edward Cooney*

Cooney Family

The third of eight children, Edward (middle name unknown) was born on February 11, 1867, in Enniskillen, N. Ireland, to William Rutherford and Emily (Carson) Cooney. His five brothers were William McEffer,

Henry "Harry," Frederick George, Alfred Carson and James Ernest; his two sisters were Edith Emily and Mary Elizabeth. (*See* Appendix D, Cooney Family Tree). They resided at Lakeview House in Enniskillen. According to a local historian:

> On August 31, 1863, Dr. Magee conducted the marriage ceremony of William Rutherford Cooney to Emily Carson. W. R. Cooney (1836–1924) had come to Enniskillen from Cootehill, Co. Cavan and ... he served his time with a local businessman, married his daughter and eventually succeeded him. W. R. Cooney's wife Emily was the only child of ... William Carson (1816–1900) ... in July 1850, he moved [his business] across High Street to No. Four, the Hibernian House ... a great clothes emporium and it remained a highly successful business under W. R. Cooney. The site is now Graham's Menswear, but the original ... building was destroyed by a bomb which devastated the town centre in the 1970s. (Mac Annaidh 2008, 45–6; the building was rebuilt in 2014).

W. R. Cooney was a prominent citizen and a successful, if not wealthy, owner of an extensive clothier business headquartered on High Street in Enniskillen. His business card read, "W. R. Cooney, Woollen & Linen Draper, Silk Mercer Haberdasher &c., Military & Merchant Tailor and General Outfitter." (A *draper* was a retailer of cloth used mainly for clothing.)

The Cooneys were members of the Church of Ireland (Episcopal), where Edward and his siblings were baptized when infants. They attended Sunday school at the Enniskillen Parish Church, now St. Macartin's Cathedral. However, after joining Irvine's ministry, Cooney renounced his previous church affiliation, declaring that "since he had been sprinkled in the Episcopal Church, he had been a child of the Devil. Sprinkling was no good, 'You must be born again' " (*Impartial Reporter*, June 9, 1904, *TTT*).

Cooney and all his brothers received their primary education at the Enniskillen Model School under Catholic Headmaster Charles Morris. They received their higher education under Rev. William Steele at Portora Royal School in Enniskillen, known as the *Eton of Ireland*. Notable Irish poet, Oscar Wilde, and Samuel Beckett, Irish novelist and winner of the 1969 Nobel Prize in Literature, also attended Portora.

Since the Portora records are sketchy from their opening to 1936, they were not able to verify the attendance of Edward Cooney but confirmed that his brothers H. Cooney and F. Cooney were students. Cooney's grandfather, William Carson, was an active member of the Portora Board of Education and was well positioned to ensure acceptance for his grandsons (Mac Annaidh *Fermanagh Miscellany 2,*

46). After he finished school at age 14, Edward was sent to Armagh as an apprentice to learn the family business.

The oldest Cooney son, William, was about 19 when he contracted tuberculosis. Impressed with his brother's Christian life, Edward became a Christian at age 17, through prayer without the assistance of a clergyman or church, and long before he met William Irvine. He often proclaimed, "I was born anew in the city of Armagh, Ireland, sometime during 1884."

For his health, William went to stay with an uncle in Australia. After Edward was also diagnosed with tuberculosis, he followed his brother there in 1887. William died a week after he returned to Ireland on May 29, 1887, aged 22 (Roberts 1990, 6, *TTT*). Recovered, Edward returned home in 1890 and worked as a commercial traveler in his father's business. His younger brother, James Ernest Cooney, went to Colorado for his health and died in December 1898 on his way home aboard the SS *City of Rome*, aged 25.

Edward's brother, Frederick, immigrated to New Zealand in 1924 with his wife and four children. His unmarried brother, Alfred, a successful solicitor with one of the largest law firms in Co. Fermanagh, committed suicide or was murdered on August 29, 1909, aged 38. No suicide note was discovered. From the September 4, 1909, *Anglo-Celt*:

> On Sunday afternoon, Mr. Alfred Carson Cooney, a well-known Enniskillen solicitor, was found dead in his room at Lakeview, the residence of his parents, under tragic circumstances. A member of the family on entering his room found the unfortunate gentlemen lying in a large pool of blood with a deep gash in his throat and a razor beside the body ... blood flowed freely from a wound in the throat ... He was then dead ... No reason can be assigned for the tragic occurrence. The deceased gentleman ... appeared in the best of health and spirits and no cause whatever can be assigned for the dreadful occurrence.

Mr. and Mrs. W. R. Cooney moved from Lakeview House (since demolished) to 15 Willoughby Place, Enniskillen, where the Carsons (Mrs. Cooney's parents) lived their last years. Emily Cooney died on December 18, 1917, aged 75. W. R. Cooney died September 12, 1924, aged 86.

~~~~~

Spiritual Meetings. Edward Cooney, John West, Tom Betty, Andy and Sam Boyd and some other like-minded Christians occasionally met together. Cooney commented, "a number of us who had been through the same experience, met in a room from time to time, to encourage one another to follow Jesus, still attending the same denominations we belonged to ... In Enniskillen, my native town, we met in a Presbyterian man's home Sunday afternoons and preached in the slums in a schoolhouse granted the use of by the Methodists" (to Alice Flett, 1930, Appendix D).

Sara West, wife of John West, declared, "I grew up in the same town as Edward Cooney and knew that he, with Tom Betty and my husband John West, held evangelical meetings together in connection with the different churches" (S. West 1954, *TTT*). John West was a leader and local lay preacher at the Ballinamallard Methodist Church.

1901: Edward Cooney Capitulated. Regarding the extraordinary night Irvine convinced Cooney to leave all and join his ministry, G. Pattison recounted:

> Then one night while on his travels he [Cooney] and William [Irvine] arranged to meet at our house and ... the two men discussed so fully the subject of preachers and preaching of Matthew 10. William pointing out the need, etc. in the face of the greatness of the harvest and fewness of laborers; Eddie seeking to escape the issue in one way or another, even to the extent of offering all he could make out of his job as traveller, to be used by William as he thought fit, for evangelistic purposes. William would meet such an offer with, 'It isn't your money the Lord wants, but yourself.' So about 2:00 a.m. he had won, and Eddie had decided to give up his job and go forth ... after this discussion on Matthew 10, they came to the decision to live and go as Jesus taught in that chapter. (1935, Wrestlers, *TTT*)

Dr. Patricia Roberts, Biographer of Edward Cooney. According to Dr. Roberts, "Edward, however, having found the pearl of great price, gladly gave up both his inheritance and fine business prospects. His own personal wealth, which was considerable, **he gave to the poor.** And so, in 1901, at the age of 34, in fellowship with Irvine and his associates, Edward too forsook all and went forth to preach depending on God to move the hearts of others to minister to his needs" (Roberts 1990, 9, *TTT*).

1901, June: Cooney's Entrance. In 1901, at age 34, Cooney gave up his business interests, disposed of his funds and possessions and became a Worker on Irvine's fast-growing staff. Reports vary as to the beneficiary of Cooney's money; the poor, the cause (the developing movement) and Irvine have all been named as recipients. John Long recalled, "Edward Cooney ... gave up a very good situation, and **distributed £1,300 to the poor**, and went fully on the Lord's work, and became a great advocate of preachers going without a stated salary" (July 1898, *TTT*; £1,300 was a small fortune at that time).

The *Impartial Reporter* quoted Cooney saying, "Three years ago the Lord said to me, 'Go, Edward Cooney, without scrip, and go into all nations, baptising them in the name of the Father, Son and Holy Ghost, and teach them to observe all things whatsoever I have commanded you.' Then He gave me His promise, 'Lo, I am with you until the end of the world,' and He has kept it" (June 9, 1904, *TTT*; "three years ago" was 1901).

Cooney's first test of faith after entering the Work came as he was traveling to the wedding of Bill Carroll and Margaret Hastings on June 6, 1901. He had a train ticket as far as Dublin, but no money to purchase a fare from there to Borrisokane.

Fortunately, a commercial traveler offered him a ride from Dublin to the home of a friend's mother. She gave him a hearty welcome and invited him to spend the night. The next morning on the breakfast table he found an envelope addressed to him with a note. Having heard of Cooney's life plans, the writer was moved to get up in the night and deliver money for his fare to the wedding. When Cooney went to purchase his ticket, the stationmaster refused his money and handed him a ticket with the words, "In the name of the Lord" (Roberts 1990, 20, *TTT*).

He worked his first mission in 1901 in Edenderry, Co. Offaly, Ireland. Co-workers Irvine Weir and William Gill visited him there (Parker 1982, 86). Cooney's bold, sincere, earnest style of preaching attracted large crowds and won many converts. He was a tremendous asset to the nascent movement, and the early days of his ministry were extraordinarily successful. Following are some descriptions of Cooney from his hometown newspaper, the *Impartial Reporter*:

> However, the chief motive power was latent until Edward Cooney heard William Irvine and offered him money and even a salary yearly, which was refused by Irvine. At all events £1,300 from Mr. Cooney alone was **applied to the cause,** and has been preached as having been **'given to the poor,'** on the authority of 'Sell all that ye have, etc.' Yet as a matter of fact, this **sum was mostly paid to transport preachers to places abroad** and not to the poor, as is sometimes understood. (Aug. 25, 1910, 8, *TTT*)

> Cooney can talk; by dint of practice he can pitch his voice without shouting; he can reason; he can enforce his argument with chapter and verse; and therefore, he is listened to and his reasoning has power and force. (Oct. 20, 1904, *TTT*)

He was described in the *Irish Presbyterian* periodical in an article titled "A New Sect": 'As to the evangelist himself, [Edward Cooney] ... he is an exceedingly earnest and devoted man who has relinquished fine business prospects to occupy his whole time and energies with Christian work. He is an attractable and forcible speaker, well educated, and gentlemanly in his manners, overflowing with zeal and enthusiasm ... Being naturally a man of strong will and considerable mental gifts, he exercises a great influence over those whose minds are weaker than his own, and over those who have not hitherto had any very definite or settled religious convictions' " (Scrutator 1905, *TTT*).

The press soon recognized Cooney as the second-in-command and a leader in the sect: "The speakers at this service were the two leaders of the movement, Mr. William Irwin [Irvine] and Edward Cooney. Both speakers denounced the various churches and the clergy in no unmeasured words" (*Impartial Reporter*, July 23, 1908, 8, *TTT*).

Some reporters were unsure of Cooney's title and position and often mistakenly labeled him. He was called its *co-leader, co-founder, chief lieutenant, a chief pioneer* and occasionally (and erroneously) the founder, especially around his hometown of Enniskillen. For example, the *Impartial Reporter* speculated "so far as the outside world can judge, Mr. Edward Cooney (after whom they are generally called *Cooneyites*) seems to be the accepted high priest or leader" (Sept. 29, 1904, *TTT*).

Cooney was definitely NOT the founder, as he joined Irvine's band of Workers in 1901, four years after Irvine's new sect began. Cooney stated, "the man who finally moved me to go to preach was William Irvine" (Roberts 1990, 18, *TTT*).

Family Estrangement. When Cooney entered the Work in June 1901, it "left a gulf fixed between my father and mother, sisters and brother, whom I love dearly" (*Impartial Reporter,* August 12, 1909, 8, *TTT*). His sister, Mary Elizabeth (Cooney) Boyton Smith, was married to an Episcopalian rector. After she became a widow in June 1923, she began following Cooney's beliefs. For a time, his brother, Fred, living in New Zealand, also embraced the faith.

Upon his death in 1924, Cooney's father left a remarkable, *provisional* bequest in his will. A Dublin newspaper article stated: "$500 a Year to Stop Preaching. A novel bequest and ban on preaching appears in the will of Mr. William Rutherford Cooney ... He directs that in the event his son Edward stating in writing that he has ceased to preach and has returned to allegiance to the Church of Ireland, thereby abandoning his means of living, £100 per annum shall be paid to him so long as he adheres faithfully to his decision" (Dec. 12, 1925, *TTT*). His son was not enticed.

Cooney is shown on the 1905 Workers List as entering the Work in 1901 and is identified as No. 69 on the 1921 photograph of Workers taken at Dimsdale Hall, Staffordshire, England Convention.

Some view Cooney as one of the prime founders of the 2x2 Church **practices**, and view Irvine as the prime founder of the 2x2 **Ministry**, which eventually consolidated to become the 2x2 Sect/Church.

Although the 2x2 Sect gained considerable impetus from Cooney's evangelism, and regardless of the significant role he played in the sect's early days, he would be excommunicated in 1928. Attempts would be made to erase his name and role from the history of the 2x2 Sect; the same would happen to Irvine in 1914.

~~~~~

1909: *Go-Preacher's Hymn Book.* The first 2x2 hymnal, titled the *Go-Preacher's Hymn Book,* was printed in 1909, containing 130 hymns (words only). It contained no date, publisher or authors' names. However, Edward Cooney's initials ("E.C.") were shown as the author for 12 hymns: Nos. 14, 16, 57, 91, 92, 95, 98, 99, 100, 110, 115 and 130. *See also* Chapter 27 and Appendix D. Four of Cooney's hymns mention Matthew 10, illustrating the importance the new sect gave to literally following Jesus' instructions in that passage:

No. 91: "Whilst thousands say Lord, Lord, through men who preach, but won't live *Matthew Ten.*"

No. 95: "For well we ken, through *Matthew Ten,* the way that pleases God."

No. 99: "Tramp about and preach. Saints will give you bread. This you'll find full described in *Matthew Ten.*"

No. 100: "Poor men who left their homes and then launched out to live like Jesus as told in *Matthew Ten.*"

16

1903 – Inaugural Rathmolyon Convention

Conditions in Ireland. At the turn of the twentieth century, opportunities were severely limited for the younger generation in the small towns and rural villages of Ireland. Full of frustrated young men looking for something more out of life than becoming a farm laborer, miner or shop clerk, and young ladies looking for other jobs than becoming a domestic, caregiver, governess or salesperson, these conditions provided a particularly ripe environment for the new sect to take root in its first decade.

Irvine's propitious timing and location may have played a large part in its initial success and rapid expansion. The new sect was one of many that blossomed and flourished during this period. Author Doug Parker provided a glimpse into the state of affairs:

> The nineteenth century in Britain was a period of great change in economic and social life when, through the effects of the Industrial Revolution, in which she pioneered the way, changes in the balance between agriculture and industry necessitated the urbanization of large areas, and involved population upheavals ...

> Although the churches were finding a great indifference to organized religion among the working people, there were, concurrent with the rising status of the working man, greater opportunities for lay evangelism, and there was a growth of movements that depended upon the efforts of lay people: Plymouth Brethren, Mormons, Christadelphians, the Salvation Army, Jehovah's Witnesses, the Student Volunteer Movement, the Irish Workers Christian Union and the Faith Mission all arose during the nineteenth century. Revivalism on an intensive scale, from the Primitive Methodists to the great campaigns of Finney, Moody, Pearsall Smith and Torrey had made the earnest lay leader an increasingly common phenomenon.

> Irvine's teaching excited the imagination of young Christians in the country districts of Ireland and also appealed to men and women living in a drab existence of routine in the towns and suburbs. Young converts

eagerly abandoned their strictly limited environments to capture the opportunity that Irvine offered to become preachers, and they were excited by the promise of God's care for them if they were to give up everything. (1982, 4–5)

Searching for the reason some were leaving the established churches and associating themselves with the Go-Preachers, *Watchman* sent a perceptive letter to the editor of the *Impartial Reporter*:

As a watchman on the walls of Zion, but without the camp, I have been observing for a long time … I have been forced to ask myself, is there not a cause? Is there not a cause for it in the settled routine forms of worship (Episcopal, Presbyterian and Methodist) that obtain amongst us. We cannot do now with the services that satisfied our parents and grandparents. The sad white-washed walls, the cold services, and the long sermons, and the old psalm singing and hymn singing that satisfied the religious needs of a century or half century ago, do not satisfy the present age … the feeling all round is that our ministers are wanting in earnestness, that our religion is growing to be somewhat like the religion the Divine Master denounced—a religion without heart, a religion as dry as dust, full of infantile forms that satisfied no longing of the soul. Our people … are growing tired of this heartless religion, and so it is coming to pass that our settled congregations are growing small, while those at Crocknacrieve [Convention] are growing large … (*See* Chapter 18.)

As time and years go on, our ministers have less of a 'draw' … The result of all is, when the services are ended, our people leave such places of worship dull and heavy, far less scriptural in heart, less cheerful in soul than when they entered. It is no marvel that many of our young and middle-aged people are glad to find some other meeting place to satisfy their religious needs and longings. (Aug. 13, 1908, 8, *TTT*)

Filled with spiritual zeal and repelled by what they perceived as the apostate church, Irvine's listeners were drawn by the magnetic power of his words. At times, he was known to preach for three to five hours at a time to a mesmerized, riveted audience.

1903, April: Irvine became so discouraged with the disorganized state of the Workers he was superintending that he considered giving up his place to become an independent evangelist. John Long suggested another plan:

He was in a strait between two as to whether he should go from the Work as leader and labour for God independently in a new district, as he shrank back from forming a new mission or sect; and the Work and Workers at that time were very scattered and disorganized. He was very downcast and disheartened and humbled before God ... I encouraged him not to forsake the Work ... but to call a conference and get the Workers united together and form the young converts into assemblies where they could get spiritual food, but to be open and unsectarian in attitude towards all other sects, missions and persons. (April 1903, *TTT*)

Alfred Magowan recollected:

My memory takes me back to the time when we appeared to be at a crossroads or at a junction of roads, when William Irvine and E. Cooney, under a variety of influences pulled in different directions and finally came to agreement about the lines our witness should take. William spoke of it as 'giving The Testimony of Jesus'; and Edward put emphasis on getting people baptized and following Paul's example in 'forming churches.' William appeared to think that we were called and sent to be a savour or influence of Christ in a Christendom that had gone badly wrong under the evil influences of clericalism and mammonism. Edward was strong on separation and his view prevailed apparently, unto this day. (1956)

1903, July: Rathmolyon Convention. After vacillating between separation and collaboration, acting on Long's suggestion, Irvine held what some view as the sect's inaugural Convention at Rathmolyon, Co. Meath. Here it was where the new sect's fundamental belief system was set in motion; where Irvine initially articulated his ideals, principles and methods; and where orientation for the young Workers took place.

Vow of Celibacy. Beattie recollected, "Seventy of Irvine's converts met at William Gill's farm at Rathmolyon late in 1903 for a Convention that lasted three weeks. They passed the severe test of entry to the new fellowship by giving over all to the common purse and by casting off allegiance to their former ways of life ... he laid down the values and standards that were to be kept ... and a strict form of asceticism was made the rule of life ... at the close of the Convention the men and women took a vow of poverty, chastity and obedience ... Irvine would not recognize anyone unless they gave up *all*" (Parker 1982, 12, 20, Fn. 3).

During an interview, Willie Clelland related to Parker, "Regarding the Meeting in Rathmolyon when the Vow of Celibacy was taken by the Brother Workers, I was there at the Meeting and promised like the others to observe it. This happened in 1903. It then became the recognized thing for all Workers, and anyone failing to observe it was just not right and looked upon gravely with suspicion" (1982, 20, Fn. 3).

This vow resembled the three-fold vow taken by the Franciscan Friars of Poverty, Chastity and Obedience. It entailed surrendering the opportunity to marry or have children. Entering the Work was a lifetime commitment. Once a Worker had "put their hand to the plow" (Luke 9:62), there was no going back—their goal was to "die in the harness." In time, this type vow by new Workers was discontinued.

Irvine, their unquestioned leader, united them into a single group who submitted to his authority and standards. These included some who had already been preaching independently on *Faith Lines*, such as John Long, George Walker, George Beattie, Willie Clelland, some from Todd's Mission, and May Carroll from Faith Mission.

Irvine drew boundaries, initiated rules and procedures. He told them how to behave and what to believe and teach as they went about proclaiming their Gospel message and way. Before the Workers left that Convention, there was no doubt in their minds as to Irvine's expectations, although not formally committed to paper. The FM had a printed booklet of their guidelines for Pilgrims. Since FM's rules and discipline had been a source of irritation to Irvine and were part of the reason he left, it is not surprising that he did put together a rule book.

**Some view the 1903 Rathmolyon Convention
when the Workers formally united under William Irvine's leadership
as the sect's beginning.**

What Event Was the Starting Point? There are several possible answers to this question. Most groups start with an idea they experiment with and develop. Over time, the idea evolves, endures, diminishes or disappears. The 2x2 Sect started by experimenting with *Faith Lines*. *See* Chapter 13.

The Sect did not start all at one time or take form overnight. It took place in stages over about six years. First, the ministers volunteered. Second, Irvine consolidated the ministers into a single body. A few years later, the sect/church emerged, i.e. meetings in homes, communion and baptism.

The year 1897 is used for the 2x2 Sect's initial start date in many historical documents. Irvine's first highly successful mission was held at Nenagh, Ireland, (August 15–September 16, 1897) where about 30 professed. His second very successful mission was held at Rathmolyon, Ireland, (October 10–31, 1897) where over 40 professed. Many or most from these missions entered the Work.

If William Irvine had not preached those two revival missions in the manner that he did, those converts would never have offered for the

Work. Instead, they would have become Faith Mission Prayer Union members and attended the church of their choice. Irvine came first, and the Workers came after him. William Irvine was "the first," the founder and the original leader, according to Irvine himself; early Workers, John Long, Ed Cooney, Wilson McClung, Jack Jackson; and the historical accounts of Goodhand Pattison, Alfred Trotter, and John Long.

The year 1899 is preferred by some as the 2x2 Sect's start date. They speculate that the first group of Workers coalesced into a loose-knit body at the St. Stephen's Meeting in Belfast, Ireland, on December 26, 1899, shortly after the 1899 Bicycle Trip to Scotland.

Another possible start date is the 1903 at Rathmolyon Convention, when Irvine united and consolidated the Workers into one body and set out its basic tenets and practices, i.e. he formed the ministry. In 1902–1903, the first Sunday Fellowship Meetings were started in homes with communion and baptisms were introduced, i.e. the sect/church was formed. Summarized, the four possible starting dates are:

1. Irvine's revival mission at Nenagh, Ireland, when over 30 people professed (August 1897).

2. After the Bicycle Trip to Scotland at the all-day Meeting at Nenagh? (December 26, 1899)

3. Irvine's consolidation Convention at Rathmolyon. (1903).

4. Around the turn of the twentieth century (from 1897 to 1903).

The author believes there is sufficient evidence to show that the 2x2 Sect started in 1897 with Irvine's first mission at Nenagh, which was the viewpoint of first-hand witness John Long. Therefore, this book uses 1897 as the starting date, and also at times, the all-inclusive blanket date range: *the turn of the twentieth century.*

~~~~~

1903: Fellowship Meetings. Instituting Fellowship Meetings in homes and conducting baptisms began earlier in 1902 and continued after the July 1903 inaugural Rathmolyon Convention. *See* Chapter 14. "The Workers began to baptize," reported Long, "and separate their converts; form them into assemblies to meet together on the first day of the week for fellowship, breaking of bread and prayers, Acts 2:42. Also, they appointed Bishops or Elders over them. William Irvine emphasized separation but not exclusiveness" (July 1903, *TTT*).

Sunday Fellowship Meetings were installed in members' private homes. Modeled after the home church meetings in the New Testament, a universal protocol for participatory worship was agreed upon; that is, each member participated with singing, prayer, a short spiritual commentary and communion, overseen by a group leader (aka an *Elder*) designated by the Workers. If Workers happened to be present, they led the Meeting and participated along with the others.

Long recollected, "At William Irvine's request, I went to Co. Tipperary and baptized many disciples and helped to form their assemblies. One in Cloughjordan in the home of Goodhand Pattison; also, in the home of Falkiners, Hillsborough, Borrisokane and in the home of Hodgins, Lorrha" (Aug. 1903, *TTT*).

First Sunday Fellowship Meeting. Historical accounts do not agree as to the location of the very first 2x2 Sunday Fellowship Meeting. Two sites have been reported. One location, mentioned only in one source, is the gate lodge, a very small building at the entrance to the Crocknacrieve estate in Ballinamallard, Co. Fermanagh, Ireland (Roberts 1990, 29, *TTT*; Ballinamallard, 2004, 65).

Weirs of Baggot Street, 21 Upper Baggot Street, Dublin, Ireland
Site of first Sunday Morning Meeting
Early 1900s and 2014
weirsofbaggotst.ie

The other location is the home of William C. and Susan (Tinkler) Weir situated over their store, Weirs of Baggot Street, at 21 Upper Baggot Street, Dublin, Ireland. The three floors above the store were living quarters for the Weirs and their ten children.

William and Susan Weir (1875), Owners of Weirs of Baggot Street

Presumably, their son, Irvine Weir, was the first one to profess in the Weir family. The Carrolls had invited Irvine Weir to travel from Dublin to the Rathmolyon mission to meet the "rough Scotsman," Irvine. Subsequently, Weir went on the 1899 Bicycle Mission Trip to Scotland, was one of the first 12 Workers to enter the Work (in 1900), was one of the first three Workers to go to America (1903) and pioneered the Work in California before he was expelled around 1950. *See* Chapter 32.

After William Weir Sr. died in 1931, his son, Charles M. Weir, inherited the business. The Fellowship Meetings continued over Weir's Store where their daughter, Rebecca Edith "Edie" (a former Worker), resided until she passed away in 1959. After a brief stint in the Work, their son, Harry Cecil Weir, married Agnes Carroll in 1908 and immigrated to the US; two of their daughters, Primrose and Gladys, became Workers. Of the ten Weir children, four did not become 2x2s.

The Weir's Store building is in good condition and is currently a retail variety store now known as Weirs Home Gift & DIY. My husband and I visited this store in August 2004 and again in 2014. The owners graciously gave us a tour of the upper rooms; we stood in the very room where the first Meeting took place. *See* brochure of business and building in website *TellingTheTruth.info* in Workers & Conventions by Country, British Isles, Ireland, Dublin.

Before moving on, a dating error needs further explanation. *The Secret Sect* erroneously stated the first home church Meetings were set up in, "*1908* when Irvine sanctioned house church meetings, and the body of believers was divided officially into Saints and Workers" (Parker 1982, 24–25). When Parkers' book was published, the *Journal of John Long* and Goodhand Pattison's "Account of the Early Days" were not available to him. Both these primary sources provide 1902 as the year Sunday Fellowship Meetings were first established in members' homes.

Midweek Evening Meetings. At the turn of the twentieth century, Protestant church members customarily met for social activities on Wednesday night, e.g. barn dances, bridge, etc. Reportedly, Workers decided to add a competing Meeting on the same night to keep the Friends occupied and prevent them from backsliding to their former church activities.

"The church in the home and the preacher without a home."

A New Sect

Several sources have attested that there was no pre-existing movement in Great Britain or Ireland similar to Irvine's burgeoning new sect, and that William Irvine was the sole founder. "William Irvine, one of the founders of the Go-Preachers' Society, said it was Protestant evangelical ... In cross-examination, witness [William Irvine] said he had never known of a *new sect* being founded without opposition" (*Impartial Reporter,* July 17, 1913, *TTT*).

George Walker, Eastern US Overseer, clarified to the US Government that the 2x2 Sect was not a continuation of an existing religious group. He explained how some men studied the *Bible* and decided to "return" to the methods of Christ and his first disciples (Statement, 1942, *TTT*, RIS).

Rev. Colin N. Peckham, Principal of Faith Mission declared, "William Irvine definitely did not leave the Faith Mission to take over or become a part of an existing ministry. There certainly was no movement of that kind existing over here before Irvine's breakaway movement. As

William Irvine spent some time in the Faith Mission before leaving it, there is no possibility that he founded the Cooneyite Sect before 1886 ... [when] John George Govan began the Faith Mission" (May 29, 1991, Appendix G).

J. G. Govan affirmed, "This movement was started by Mr. William Irvine" (*Bright Words*, Dec. 1903, *TTT*).

Irvine's very successful revival missions in Irish counties drew attention. Reporters began referring to the nameless religious movement as a *New Sect* as early as 1903–1904 and identified Irvine as its founder and leader. Worldwide, hundreds of newspaper articles about the sect were printed during the first 20 years of the movement.

The Impartial Reporter

Telephone: (0365) 24422 Proprietors: William Trimble Ltd. Member of Northern Ireland Network and Audit Bureau of Circulations.	and Farmers Journal 8 & 10 East Bridge Street, Enniskillen. Northern Ireland. BT74 7BT	London Office: Newspaper Representations Ltd. 52/53 Fetter Lane, London EC4A 1ER. Tel.: 01-583 6077 and 111 Piccadilly, Manchester M1 2DQ. Tel.: 061-228 7643

Stationery heading for Impartial Reporter

On January 15, 1903, the *Impartial Reporter* newspaper in Enniskillen, Ireland, printed the oldest article found to date about the new sect. The third oldest newspaper in Ireland, it was owned and operated by the Trimble family from 1825 to 2006. When the new sect began making headlines, the proprietor was William Copeland Trimble (aka W.C.T.).

Everything about this unusual new sect came under scrutiny: its lack of a name, its charismatic founder, its inexperienced, uneducated preachers, its missions, conventions, practices, teachings and its members' distinctive mode of dress. First appearing in rural villages and towns, the new sect soon gained a large following with most converts becoming roving missionaries.

The *Impartial Reporter* newspaper not only established that Irvine was the founder of this new sect, but also investigated his background, including his previous religious associations: "William Irvine, the founder and supreme authority of what is known as *Cooneyism*, is a Scotchman. His native place is Kilsyth, a small town near Glasgow. Before he became a Tramp, he had attached himself to the sect known as the Faith Mission or Pilgrims and was the manager of a coal mine under Baird & Co., Glasgow ... William Irvine left this employment and joined the Faith Mission" (Aug. 25, 1910, 8, *TTT*).

From an article titled "A New Sect" in the March 1905 *Irish Presbyterian*:

> A few years ago, a religious movement was started in the North of Ireland by a few former members of the Scotch organization—the Faith Mission. These Pilgrims, or Tramp Preachers, as they are commonly called, being dissatisfied with the quieter methods of Christian work advocated by the parent Society, seceded from it and developed what may best be described as a New Sect, distinguished for its bitter hostility to all existing churches, and to a regular paid ministry of any kind ... It is believed that the originator of this somewhat erratic development was a Scotchman called Irwin, [Irvine] who at an early stage of this work enlisted the sympathy and help of an earnest young man, a native of Enniskillen, Mr. Edward Cooney, formerly an Episcopalian, who devoted himself to evangelistic work in various parts of Ireland, and a member of a most respectable family, several of whom have long been distinguished for their zeal in many branches of religious and philanthropic work. (*TTT*)

Although at first, Irvine may have reluctantly assumed the position of founder and leader, William Clelland recollected that in all the Conventions, Irvine was always the leader of the Meetings and chose all the speakers. "There was only *one* boss in the Tramp Preachers in those days, and they all knew who he was" (Parker 1982, 34–35, Fn. 6). Irvine was the leader and highest authority of the 2x2 Sect.

Irvine exercised the office of founder without applying that official title to himself. He was recognized as being more than "just a Worker" by his Co-workers and the Friends. Far more than just a figurehead, he ruled over the other Workers worldwide in every sense of the word *rule*.

It should be mentioned that most 2x2s do not recognize Irvine as the *founder* of their church. Instead, they regard the origins as a *group initiative* with Irvine being the nucleus around whom the movement went forward. They view him as the central figure involved with its formation whom God raised up for this unique role as leader (but not founder). According to those of this persuasion, the 2x2 Sect/Church was started by a "group of men" at the turn of the twentieth century.

~~~~~

1903: Todd's Mission Disbands. After about six years (1897–1903), Robert Todd, by that time father to three sons, accepted employment elsewhere. Todd's Mission became a thing of the past.

J. G. Govan announced, "Mr. Todd is now appointed to the home secretaryship of the South American Evangelical Mission with offices in Liverpool, and at the suggestion of himself and his Workers, we [Faith Mission] have agreed to take over the superintendence of their missions" (*Bright Words,* May 1903, 102, *TTT*). Six months later, J. G. Govan stated, "Of these, Sisters Stanley, Winter, and Halliday have come to us from Mr. Todd's Mission in Ireland, now dissolved ... Pilgrim Carroll joined Mr. Irvine's band of workers" (*Bright Words,* Nov. 1903, *TTT*). The Todds and J. G. Govan remained loyal lifelong friends.

Eight or nine Workers in Todd's Mission came over to Irvine's movement: Emma Gill, John Hardie, Thomas Turner, Andrew Robb, George Buttimer, Alex Givan, John Stanley, William Jackson and possibly his brother, Jack Jackson.

Married Worker Couples

Regardless of the Vow of Celibacy, four married couples were accepted for the Work and their names appear on the 1905 Workers List. They were:

- 1902 Mr. and Mrs. Thomas Elliott, no children.

- 1903 Mr. and Mrs. William (Bill) Carroll, one daughter, May, born in 1901.

- 1903 Mr. and Mrs. Wilson McClung, no children.

- 1905 Mr. and Mrs. Thomas Betty, three sons.

Two other married couples (Dicksons and Downies) entered the Work in 1905 but are not shown on the 1905 Workers List.

Finney and Ernest Punke   Frank and Hilda Quick   Joe and Minnie Kleven

Appendix A contains a list of all known married Workers. Over the years, at least 50 married couples were in the Work at various times, but they were the exception rather than the rule. For a time, there was no clear, consistent policy regarding married Workers being allowed to enter the Work. Most likely, Irvine reviewed them on a case-by-case basis. After Irvine left the Work in 1914, permission appeared to be left up to the Regional Overseers.

Q: Has your society ever discouraged marriage of their preachers?

Ans: Our views on marriage are no different from those of orthodox people, they have never differed from what is expressed in I Cor 7, where Paul shows that he sees advantage from the standpoint of the Gospel in his position of an unmarried man. But he clearly states in this chapter that those who marry commit no sin. In another place he (supposedly the writer to the Hebrews) states that marriage is honourable in all. Heb 13:4.

Willie Hughes answer to one of the questions submitted by Evangelical Lutheran Pastor C. A. Wiebush, April 23, 1931

Tracing the married Workers on Workers Lists shows they preached together most of the time, but not always, and often not at first. Some started out preaching as a married pair. Others married after they were in the Work, such as Robert and Maude Graham, Erne and Finney Punke, George and Ella Johnson, Bob and Martha Smith, Joe and Grace Brown, and Dave and Emily Christie.

Without obtaining prior permission, Dave Christie married Sister Worker Emily Wilson in 1923. Their Overseer and cousin, Jack Carroll, allowed them to remain in the Work, provided they went to Hawaii, where no Workers had ever preached. Carroll's blessing on the Christies' marriage appeared to have a rippling effect for the three following years. *See* Chapter 28.

Emily (nee Wilson) and Dave Christie with their two children (1930s)

On the 1922 North American Workers List, there were six married couples (Klevens, McIllwraths, Dunshees, Doaks, DeGroots and

Richters). Three years later, the 1925 List showed nine married couples (Walkers, Gards and Christies were added). One year later, the 1926 List included 12 married couples (Grahams, Byes and Browns were added); the 1928–1929 Workers List contained thirteen married couples (Winegards were added).

It appears that sometime during the 29 years between 1923 and 1952, the Senior Workers enacted a new worldwide policy of not permitting any additional married Worker couples to enter the Work; nor for Workers to marry each other and remain in the Work. Carroll may have been the first Overseer to enforce this new policy when he refused to allow Workers Chester Sweetland and Clara DenHerder to remain in the Work after they married on September 3, 1952, in Alpine, California.

Will Sweetland, father of Chester, protested, "You have also recently made a ruling relative to Workers who marry and desire to continue in the ministry. You state that to marry is proof of a diminished sacrifice and a limited service and is what you consider to be a change of status, not acceptable to 'Christian Conventions' administration. Such reasoning is obviously neither scriptural nor reasonable. God alone can measure degrees of sacrifice and will determine rewards accordingly. Compulsory celibacy is commonly recognized as the soil upon which immoral conduct and behavior thrives. To make such a ruling is clearly in conflict with God's laws and human right ... It is exactly the opposite to what the Scriptures teaches and what we heard and believed from your lips 30 years ago [when Christies married] (to Jack, Willie and Brethren, April 15, 1954, *TTT*).

It has been suggested that the new policy was spawned from the Workers' disapproval of the lifestyle of married Australian Overseer Bill Carroll who passed away in 1953, and the after-effects of the Guildford Report. *See* details in Chapter 48 and Appendix J.

A few exceptions were made. Martin and Betty Medica entered the work in 1962 and labored in the Caribbean. At least twice, two Workers married in order to preach in certain countries. Alexander "Sandy" and Eva (Idso) Scott married in 1954 to preach in Italy; Scott stepped down from being Overseer. Previously in 1917, John and Annie (McBride) Micheletos married so they could preach in Greece, John's homeland.

Regardless of the change in policy, the existing married Worker couples were allowed to remain in the Work. When their spouses died, some surviving spouses continued in the Work.

In the late 1960s and early '70s, according to author Willis Young, "there began to be what I can only call a 'clamp-down,' and one by one, the [married Worker] couples within my own personal purview

[Canada] were gradually encouraged to leave the Work, and, if they didn't do so quietly and willingly, they were subjected to many sorts of pressures, not the least of which were accusations of unfaithfulness, wrong-spiritedness, drunkenness, preaching false doctrine and—perish the thought—collusion with the 'weaker Saints' " (2000, 146, *TTT*).

1962: Demise of Married Workers. Martin and Betty Medica were the last married Worker couple in the world to *enter* the Work (1962), and Martin was the last of the married couples to die. They labored in the Caribbean. Betty passed away in 2012 and Martin in 2019, aged 95.

By 1970, nearly all the early married Workers had retired. Worldwide, the practice of allowing married Workers to preach has been entirely phased out. Workers can no longer choose to exercise their right as expressed by Apostle Paul in 1 Corinthians 9:5, "Have we not power to lead about a sister, **a wife,** as well as other apostles, and as the brethren of the Lord, and Cephas?" If the current Worker shortage continues, perhaps this policy will be revisited.

The 2x2 policy regarding marriage of Workers shares similarities with that of FM. When a FM Pilgrim became engaged or married, s/he could not remain in the ministry. However, their superintendents were allowed to marry and maintain semi-permanent residences for several years, while overseeing several itinerant FM Pilgrims. Likewise, the married 2x2 Sect Worker couples, Carrolls, McClungs, Grahams and Micheletos were all 2x2 Regional Overseers.

Children of Married Workers. Some married Workers had children while they were in the Work (Christies, Beatties, Grahams), indicating that celibacy among married Workers was not strictly followed. *See* list of Married Workers in Appendix A.

While Irvine was the international leader, he required married couples desiring to be Workers to leave their children behind. Reportedly, Bill and Maggie Carroll's daughter, May, was cared for by Bill's mother in Ireland, who died in March 1909. May immigrated with her parents to Australia in 1913. After the Beatties entered the Work in 1911, a relative raised their 18-month-old son. After Irvine's exit in 1914, according to a Beattie family account, their three subsequent children stayed with them during some or most of the time they were preaching, as was the case for the Christies in Hawaii.

1903: Thirty-four more Workers entered the Work in the UK and Ireland; 20 Brothers and 14 Sisters, bringing the cumulative total to 85. *See* Appendix A.

17

1903–1904 – Worldwide Outreach

The year 1903 was a pivotal year for William Irvine and for the extension of the 2x2 Sect. It began with the Kilsyth church wanting to be Irvine's headquarters. He refused and was expelled. According to Irvine, "In September 1903 I was put out of [the] church I had formed in my native town [Kilsyth] because I would not make it the head of the Work I was doing" (to Dunbars, Oct. 13, 1920, *TTT*). No further details are known.

1903: First Workers Venture to America. Soon after the July Rathmolyon Convention, Irvine and two young Brother Workers departed from Glasgow, Scotland, aboard the SS *Columbia*, on September 5, 1903, and arrived at the Ellis Island immigration station in New York on September 14. They were the first three Workers to set foot in the US: William Irvine (40), Scottish; George Walker (26), Irish and Irvine Weir (25) Irish. They sailed as steerage passengers, the least expensive ticket. (Ellis Island passenger records).

Irvine remarked, "George Walker and Irvine Weir ... quarreled the first night they went out without me, which was the second day there. Then [I] began pioneering and setting George and other to work (to Dunbars, Oct. 13, 1920, *TTT*).

~~~~~

At that time, Theodore "Teddy" Roosevelt was the US President (1901–1909). The 1900 US Census showed over 76 million people were living in the US before the Workers ever arrived, with 60% being rural. New York was the most populous state, and New York City was the nation's largest city (3.4 million people), followed by Chicago, Philadelphia and St Louis; San Francisco was the 10th largest city. The average annual income was $3,000, and the average work week was 66 hours. About 13% of women worked outside the home. Only four Western states allowed women to vote.

Life expectancy was 48 years for whites and 33 years for blacks. Households averaged 4.8 people. The percentage of illiterate (unable to read or write) was about 11 percent of those age 14 and over. Few citizens (14 percent) completed high school and less than 2 percent graduated from college. The average family had no indoor plumbing, telephone or automobile. There were no movies, radio, or television and only about 8,000 cars in the country.

For over 60 years, Ellis Island was a US immigration station in the New York Harbor. Twelve million immigrants approached America's *"front doors to freedom"* in the early twentieth century through Ellis Island, including many Workers. During its peak years, 1892–1924, thousands of immigrants arrived every day. Over 100 million Americans can trace their ancestry in the US to someone whose name passed from a steamship manifest sheet to an inspector's record book in the great Registry Room at Ellis Island.

Ellis Island is where the American Family Immigration History Center is located. The passenger records for persons passing through Ellis Island between 1892 and 1924 are posted on their website. They include name, gender, marital status, ethnicity, occupation, age, port of departure and arrival, ship name, person's name they were to visit, amount of money on them, etc.

My husband and I visited Ellis Island in 2013, including the main building which was restored to its former grandeur in 1990. It now houses the impressive Ellis Island Immigration Museum which is "dedicated to commemorating the immigrant's stories of trepidation and triumph, courage and rejection and the lasting image of the American dream."

A statement by George Walker to the US Selective Service contained the following paragraph about the beginning and development of the 2x2 Sect in America (without mentioning its founder, Wm. Irvine):

> During the closing years of the last century and the first years of this century, a number of people in the British Isles and in America were exercised in heart and mind, through their study of the Scriptures, in regard to the methods of preaching and worship in the several churches of which they were then members. They were deeply concerned about spiritual things and became fully convinced that there should be a return to the methods and purpose taught and carried out by Christ and His first disciples. This conviction led ... to religious meetings, and in due time a number of these people went forth to devote their lives to the preaching of the gospel ... in the year 1903, ministers of this Christian body began their labors in the United States and in the year 1904 in Canada. In these and subsequent years through the preaching of the gospel, assemblies were formed in homes. (1942 Statement, *TTT*)

At Walker's funeral, Andrew Abernethy spoke of Walker *"coming to Philadelphia 78 years ago this month* [November 1903] and having his first mission near Independence Hall and the Liberty Bell. Said the gospel he and his companion preached promised liberty and independence from the bondage of sin, false religion and wrong doctrine" (Walker 1981, *TTT*).

1903: Recruitment of Workers. In the early days, many Workers volunteered to labor in foreign countries. Fannie Carroll recounted, "At Christmas time, Jack and I went to the City of Belfast to Special Meetings. Those Meetings were tested to see how many would go in the Work, and several said they would. We were amongst them. Tom Lyness was another. Sam Jones, who wrote so many of our hymns, was another … Then in 1905, many Workers, over 60 of them, left for overseas" (F. Carroll 1964, *TTT*).

In 1904, it became customary after the Crocknacrieve Convention for volunteer Workers to venture to foreign lands to preach. They first pioneered the Work in the British Isles, then in the English-speaking countries of the US, Canada, Australia, New Zealand and South Africa. At the Convention, "The call for volunteers for Work in distant lands met with a response, a large number offering their services for America, South Africa and Australia" (*Impartial Reporter,* July 23, 1908, *TTT*).

1903: First US Sister Worker. While the first three Brother Workers were aboard the ship to New York, they met a young woman, Maggie Rowe, who professed and became the first American Sister Worker to go in the Work. She later left the Work and married (H. Hughes 1971, *TTT*).

In those days when Workers were planning to go to foreign lands, they often went to visit relatives. Also, it was not uncommon for Irish and British converts to provide them with contact information for family members who had previously immigrated abroad. Through these introductions, they gained many converts. Workers today also use similar introductions to invite outsiders to their recruiting Gospel Missions. This was the case with the McIntyres.

1903: First US Converts. Mr. and Mrs. George McIntyre (aka McIntire or MacIntyre) met the Workers' ship and were the Workers' first American converts. From talks given by George Walker:

> He [George Walker] and a couple others [William Irvine and Irvine Weir] arrived in New York Harbor September 14, 1903, … One of the Friends in Ireland had a relative that lived in New York, a young lady, Mrs. McIntire. She and her husband received a letter … asking that they would meet the boat … so she and her husband stood calling out the name 'George Walker' from behind a fence there at Ellis Island until

George heard them. They took them home for the night and later the McIntires professed—the first of those in America that George knew of. (Walker 1979, *TTT*)

So, her husband took off from work, and they rented an apartment for two weeks for these three strangers. They told them, 'We will take you to our home and you can have dinner, then we will take you to this apartment since we only have a four-room apartment and no room to keep you overnight.' The name of this couple was George and Edith McIntyre, and they were the first to profess in the Workers' Meetings. Not long afterward, his brother, Dan [McIntyre] and wife, professed out on Staten Island. (Walker 1988, *TTT*)

The Ellis Island ship passenger lists include a column for the name and address of the relative or friend the passenger planned to visit. Many of the early Workers coming to the US gave one of two names: George McIntyre (80 Coffee Street), or Dan/Don McIntyre (132 Van Dyke Street), both in Brooklyn, New York; also C. B. Wilson, 6401 Leeds Street, Philadelphia, Pennsylvania, and Mrs. Abernethy.

A column is also included for each passenger's occupation. The majority of Workers gave evangelist, preacher or missionary. Many gave their previous occupation, e.g. domestic, servant, laborer, carpenter, painter, grocer, clerk, laborer, teacher, baker, blacksmith, draper, gardener, draper, dressmaker, tailor, etc. The second most common occupation for men was farmer. An interesting notation was made on an early list of Bookings Abroad: *If questioned, go in as farmers etc.* Several early Workers bound for Canada, Australia and New Zealand used *farmer* as their occupation.

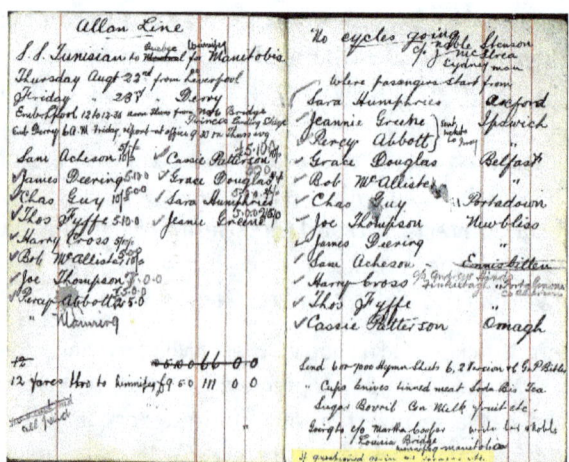

Extract from Ship Booking Notebook (Public Record Office of N. Ireland)

1904, May: Second Group of Workers Go to America. According to the Ellis Island passenger list for the SS *Furnessia*, six Workers, including the first two Sister Workers, departed from Londonderry Port, Ireland, on May 6, 1904, and arrived in New York on May 16. They were Mary "May" Carroll (24), Irish; Sarah Rogers (30), Irish; John "Jack" Carroll (25), Irish; Hugh Matthews (26), Irish; William Clelland (26), Scotch and Charles Glenn (27), Scotch.

SS Furnessia

1904, November: Third Group of Workers Go to America. According to the Ellis Island records for the SS *Oceanic*, eight Workers, including three more Sister Workers, departed from Liverpool, England, on November 30, 1904, and arrived in New York on December 8. They were John "Jack" Jackson (24), Irish; James Jardine (20), Scotch; Francis "Frank" Scott (20), Irish; William Weir (22), Scotch; David Lyness (26), Irish; Bella Cooke (23), Irish; Emma Gill (33), Irish; Lizzie M. Coles (26), Irish (should be English; aka Lily, Elizabeth, Mary).

Jack Jackson reminisced at the 1960 Freedom, New York Convention, "One morning towards the end of November 1904, my companion and I were in the East of England and were preaching there … and a knock came on the door and a telegram came for me, 'Be in Liverpool Tuesday and sail for New York Saturday.' That was short notice … we landed in New York on the 9th of December."

1904: There were 42 more Workers who entered the Work that year in the UK and Ireland; 25 Brothers including Jack Carroll and 17 Sisters, for a cumulative total of 127 Workers. *See* Appendix A.

1904–1908: In the following years, after Crocknacrieve Convention, according to Ellis Island ship passenger lists, several groups of Workers left the UK for the US. On August 14, 1905, 12 Workers including Willie Jamieson, arrived on the SS *Numidian*. Eleven Workers arrived on September 14, 1906, aboard the SS *Lusitania*. Ten Workers arrived on September 10, 1907, aboard the SS *Caledonia*. Nine Workers arrived on September 4, 1908, aboard the SS *Cedric*.

1904: Workers Head for England. From Ireland, several Workers arrived in England in 1904, including Willie Gill, Wilson Reid and Andy Robb. Gill held a mission in West Hanney. Starting in 1915, a Convention was held there through 2012. The first Sister Workers to go preach in England were Alice Pipe, May Carroll, Annie Smith and Lizzie Sargent. Both Irvine and John Long had worked missions there prior to 1900.

1904–1905: First Four Workers Venture to Canada. Four UK Brother Workers arrived in Quebec, Montreal, on August 13, 1904, destination Souris, Manitoba. *See* Canada, Chapter 40.

1904: First Two Workers Venture to Australia. John Hardie (often misspelled "Hardy") and Alex "Sandy" Alexander sailed on the SS *Medic* from the UK to Melbourne, Victoria, arriving on July 24, 1904. After two months, Sandy Alexander became discouraged and left the Work. *See* Australia, Chapter 41.

SS Medic

1904, September 25: First Worker Arrived in New Zealand. Not long after Sandy Alexander deserted him, John Hardie left Melbourne to visit his Irish friend, Tom Hastings in Wellington, New Zealand, arriving on September 25, 1904. *See* New Zealand, Chapter 42.

1904–1905: Irvine's Activities. After returning from his first trip abroad on September 5, 1904, Irvine remained for a year in the British Isles. According to John Long, "Everywhere he went he preached that the clergy were unsaved men going to Hell. He believed that it would be iniquity to believe a thing and not preach it; or to preach it in one place and not in another; that only made him the more faithful in his error. Long believed that "God used William Irvine to witness against clericalism; but in doing so he ran into the opposite, in going beyond truth when he preached that every clergyman is a false prophet and unsaved" (Long, July 1907, *TTT*).

During this time, Irvine was inundated with numerous converts volunteering to enter the Work and to venture to foreign fields. His time was likely occupied with instructing, directing, financing 50 to 60

Workers who left the "Old Country" (UK) to go preach abroad during 1904–1905.

According to Overseer Eldon Tenniswood, "The brethren in England, Ireland and Scotland knew they [the Workers] had to have their needs met and the fares to go to their respective fields. Some of those people had real nice homes; they sold their nice fancy furniture, some of their heirlooms which had been handed down and were valuable and gave this to the Kingdom for the Work of God to progress. With their whole heart, they made an investment—both the Workers and the Friends" (1977, *TTT*).

1905, August 25: First Eight Workers Venture to South Africa. The SS *Geelong* departed on August 25, 1905, from London (headed for Australia) and arrived in Cape Town on September 17, where Wilson Reid (24), Joe Kerr (24), Martha Skerritt (22) and Barbara Baxter (24) disembarked. Alex Pearce (29) and John Cavanagh (27) went ashore at Port Elizabeth; and Mary Moodie (38) and Lily Reid (26) went on to Durban. *See* South Africa, Chapter 46. Also aboard were Irvine (42) and eight more Workers who continued to Australia and New Zealand.

Not Without Opposition. The Workers' ministrations were sometimes met with excessive physical resistance. Their derogatory comments kept them in the center of controversy; some were enraged and retaliated with vandalism. In Ireland, Irvine Weir's wooden hall and organ were demolished in Co. Tipperary. In 1904, John Hardie's tent was set on fire in Co. Kilkenny. Thomas Elliott's wooden hall was overturned, and later in 1907, his wooden hall and furniture were burned in Co. Londonderry. Edward Cooney's wooden hall at Makeny, Co. Fermanagh, was burned in 1912. In Suffolk Co., England, McClung's wooden hall was smashed, doors wrenched off, windows broken, and organ destroyed in 1906.

Even further afield in North America, tents were burned, and shots were fired at a Convention in Baltimore, Maryland. Similar violence erupted at Meetings at St. Eleanor's, Prince Edward Island, with stones, revolvers and fierce fighting also figuring into the clash (*Lethbridge Daily Herald,* Aug. 29, 1910, 7). Newspapers reported that monetary compensation was sought and granted for most, but not all, of these losses.

See Section C and Appendix L for additional details about outreach to foreign countries in successive years.

1872

Chap. 1

I John Long, am a sinner saved by the Grace of God. I was born in Burntwood, Cloughjordan, County Tipperary on the 15th September, 1872. I confess that I am a stranger an pilgrim upon the earth; as all our Fathers were. Psa. 39-12.

My Grandmother, Jane Long, was a Godly woman and was sister to Thomas Carter, a famous Methodist, Local Preacher, in Cloughjordan circuit. Under his ministry my father Gilbert Long, was converted, and for some time attended class, though he backslid from it, but was restored before he died. I used to read the Bible for my Grandmother, in her old age; and I owe much to her prayers, which I believe were abundantly answered. My mother Ann Long, was of a religious family named Turners; she was a quiet person, and naturally tried to live good, and do good. Reader. "Honour thy father and mother which is the first commandment with promise" Eph. 6-2. Many die when young, and do not live out half their days because of ingratitude and unkindness shown to parents: they may not be all that they should be, nevertheless we should cover their faults; and bare with their infirmities. 1 Peter 4-8.

At the young age of seven I began to work on a small farm, also for many years during the summer months was occupied in wheeling, footing, and selling turf, one

John Long's Journal, Chapter 1, Page 1

18

1904–1906 – First Crocknacrieve Convention

1904, September–October: First Crocknacrieve Convention. About four miles northeast of Enniskillen, N. Ireland, near the little village of Ballinamallard, a Convention was installed on the West's property called *Crocknacrieve* ("the hill of the branched tree"). Sara West explained, "William Irvine and Edward Cooney asked my husband [John West] and I if we would be willing to have Convention in our home. We were willing and Conventions were held there until 1920 when we sold it" (1954, *TTT*).

Since Irvine was abroad from September 5, 1903, to September 5, 1904, he was not physically involved in preparation of the new Convention on the West's property. Possibly, Edward Cooney, Bill Carroll and Willie Gill were responsible. The Convention started prior to September 29; the exact day is unknown.

For about a month, around 300 attendees from the British Isles arrived and departed as their schedules permitted. Baptisms were held in the nearby Ballinamallard River. By this time, there were around 150 Workers worldwide: 50 in England, 30 in Scotland, 50 in Ireland and 20 in America (*Freeman's Journal,* Oct. 14, 1904, *TTT*).

Crocknacrieve House and 250 acres were purchased from Sir Edward Archdale for £2000 in 1901 by John James and Sara (Duff) West, the same year they married; all 12 West children were born there. John West also owned a sawmill in Ballinamallard. According to John Long:

> John West, Crocknacrieve, Ballinamallard, near Enniskillen, gave his premises for a Convention that year. William Irvine had newly returned from the United States; and was in good form. The weather was very fine during the whole month, which suited the camps set up for the Saints and Workers to sleep in …
>
> A great effort was made at every conference to put up both Workers and Friends free of charge; and all who had learned trades, such as bakers and butchers, their services were utilized on the occasion … there were no appeals for money; and no public collections; the strength and fruits of the teaching produced the necessary money

which was given freely to defray the expenses which amounted to nearly £1500; including the passages of those who went foreign ...

Flirting or courting was not allowed, and the flesh or selfish life strongly condemned. Marriage was not forbidden; yet the unmarried life was commended as the freest for Workers. The necessity of keeping prophet's chambers and entertaining strangers was strongly set forth.

At the close of the conference, every Worker threw his or her money into one common purse; then it was equally divided on departing to the varied districts and fields of labour. At that Convention, Irvine warned the Workers of speaking against men of God, such as J. G. Govan ...

Edward Cooney, who was in great form, tested the meetings every night when the unsaved came in, and a gospel effort was made to win them. Those efforts were very fruitful, for upwards of 100-some decided for Christ; and about the same number was baptized by immersion in a river nearby. (Sept. 1904, *TTT*)

Crocknacrieve House, Ballinamallard, N. Ireland
Site of first large scale Convention in 1904

Alfred Magowan informed George Beattie about the 1907 Crocknacrieve Convention: "The proportion of preachers to laymen was about ten to one ... whatever else may be said about it, our religion was a religion of preachers—a heroic religion making such an appeal to youth that hundreds of young men were prepared to do violence to desire and ambition that they might be counted among those who were sent on holy missions before them" (Sept. 28, 1954, in author's possession).

Baptisms. Newcomers were baptized by full immersion and earlier converts were rebaptized. Much of the baptizing was performed by Tom Elliott, fondly called *Tom the Baptist*, possibly due to his robust physique. These changes did not escape the attention of reporters: "Lately is the rebaptism by laymen of persons who have already received baptism in their infancy ... There is not a single instance in the Bible that such a ceremony [rebaptism] was ever performed by the Lord, or by his disciples, or by any of the apostles" (*Impartial Reporter*, Nov. 10, 1904, *TTT*).

The first baptism reported by the *Impartial Reporter* occurred on June 2, 1904, at Newtownards, Strangford Lough, N. Ireland. Several subsequent baptisms held in the Enniskillen area were reported in detail, accompanied by artists' illustrations.

> **"Ballinamallard has become the Jerusalem of Pilgrim Tramps, and the Ballycassidy River their Jordan"**
> **(*Impartial Reporter*, September 29, 1904).**

Newspaper illustration of baptism

From the book *Ballinamallard, a Place of Importance*, "Baptisms took place in the Ballinamallard River on a Sabbath evening in September 1904 and drew a large crowd of onlookers. These took place ... behind what was then the creamery, now the Masonic Hall. This place in future years would be known locally as *Cooney's Hole*" (Ballinamallard Historical Society 2004, 66). Since 1903, Masonic Hall No. 315 has been located on Baragh Road in Enniskillen. The *Impartial Reporter's* description:

> The party congregated near the bank of the river and sang a hymn, while those to be immersed undressed themselves in a barn at the mill. As the neophytes approached, the party divided itself into two lines ... and a Mr. Robert Elliott [*sic:* should be Thomas] ... a strong man of powerful build, clad in woollen shirt and trousers, entered the water up to his waist, while the neophytes came one by one through the living lane made for them. First came five young men, and Mr. Elliott, repeating the name of the person to be immersed, said, 'I baptize thee in the name of the Father, of the Son and Holy Ghost.' He then ducked the neophyte completely under the water, neatly and without splashing; his great strength enabled him to restore the ducked person to an erect position again easily. (Sept. 29, 1904, *TTT*)

Outdoor public baptisms in natural waters by immersion were uncommon at that time. Curious spectators came in droves to watch the unusual spectacle of the "dipping," which generated the new nickname for the sect, "Dippers." Often, there were hecklers and scoffers. Sometimes police intervention was needed.

THE COONEYITES.

LIVELY SCENES AT A BAPTISM.

The new religous sect named the Cooneyites, after their founder, have during the last two years created much interest in Ulster wherever they have held missions. They practise Christian baptism by immersion in the open air, and on Sunday last at a place known as the Bush, Dungannon, having banked up a farm stream to a depth of four feet, they baptised a number of converts. The ceremony was carried out in the presence of a big crowd, who regarded the proceedings as a cheap and novel entertainment, and repeatedly interrupted the hymn singing and the addresses.

Five men were duly immersed to the accompaniment of enthusiastic cheering and encouraging remarks from the men, while the women present evinced their interest by hurling cabbage stalks, turnips, and other missiles at the shivering subjects. A special tent for eight lady converts had been erected, and the immersions were carried out successfully, but when they returned to the tent a rush was made to overturn it. At this development some of the crowd took the side of the converts, and a well-directed blow laid the leader of the rush prostrate. A free fight followed, in which one assailant was immersed in a liquid manure heap, an incident which convulsed the crowd.

When the fight ceased the unsympathetic portion of the crowd caricatured the ceremony by subjecting a number of dogs to baptismal rites.

"Huddersfield Daily Examiner," England, May 7, 1907

The press observed, "Their views on baptism are perhaps better known than any of their other beliefs. All infant baptism is, in their opinion, useless ... and adult baptism—by immersion, of course—is insisted on, as well as complete separation from the churches, before full membership can be granted, and the fullness of gospel blessing, of which they apparently claim a monopoly, can be enjoyed" (*Impartial Reporter,* March 23, 1905, *TTT*).

Additional articles regarding baptism and rebaptism are printed in the *Impartial Reporter* issues June 2, Oct. 13, 20 and 27 and Nov. 10, 1904; and in the March 14, 1907, *Fermanagh Times,* posted on the website *TellingTheTruth.info* in History, Newspapers Old.

~~~~~

1904: James Irvine Weir. From New York, Weir arrived in California where he found lodging with a newly married couple, Clyde and Grace Brownlee. "Irvine Weir was the first Worker to come to California in 1904. He met Mr. and Mrs. Brownlee in December 1904, in Long Beach. Mr. Brownlee tried to help Weir with the Gospel Work for a while, but as the family increased, they advised him to establish a home and support his family" (Bone 1975, *TTT*). Their son was Brother Worker, Harry Brownlee, who entered the Work in 1934 and died in 2010.

1905: Walter Slater – First US Brother Entered the Work. Irvine Weir persuaded Walter Slater to accompany him on some missions in 1905, and thus, Slater became the first American-born Brother Worker on the West Coast—possibly, the first in all of America. "There was a tent put up in Paso Robles in the fall of 1905 ... and Irvine Weir, being impatient to get started ... invited Walter Slater to join him ... so when Walter was asked rather suddenly by Irvine Weir to join him in this tent ministry, he was too impressed with all this to refuse ... Walter always said he got saved after he went in the Work" (Milton n.d., Gospel to Weibes, *TTT*).

1905, July: Earliest Workers List. So far, the earliest list of Workers discovered bears the title "Names of Workers at July 1905." Many copies of this list exist with small differences, but the lists substantively agree. It contained the names of 201 Workers: 76 Sisters and 125 Brothers. *See* Appendix A. *See also* Comparison of 1905 Workers Lists at www.2x2church.info/early-workers.

This list, commonly referred to as the *1905 Workers List,* shows only Workers from the British Isles. It does not show those who started and dropped out before July 1905. Nor does it show those who entered the Work after July 1905, e.g. Elisabeth Jamieson, John Winter, Mr. and Mrs. Nat Dickson and Mr. and Mrs. Frank Downie, etc.

In comparing 11 different versions of the 1905 Workers List, the names of Irvine and John Kelly are consistently shown at the top as the first two Workers. Curiously, on nine lists, the year these two men entered the Work was left blank: one list shows 1897 and another 1899.

Coincidentally, the 1905 Workers List followed the same format that Faith Mission used for their 1905 Annual Staff of Workers List, published in their magazine, *Bright Words*. The first person shown was the founder (J. G. Govan – 1886), and under that, the Pilgrim workers were listed in order by the year they entered FM service. Likewise, on the 1905 Workers List, following the names of Irvine and Kelly were the first four Workers who entered the Work in 1899.

1905: Seventy-four more Workers entered the Work in the UK and Ireland this year, 31 Sisters and 43 Brothers, making a cumulative total of 201 Workers. *See* Appendix A.

Violet, Elisabeth and Willie Jamieson   *Elisabeth and Willie Jamieson*
(circa 1911)   *(West Coast US Workers)*

1905: Willie, Elisabeth and Violet Jamieson Enter the Work. William Rankin Jamieson, age 23 (from Scotland) attended his first Gospel Meeting on January 2, 1905; he professed in that Meeting. According to his sister, Elisabeth:

> After Willie heard and accepted the Gospel ... he asked the Worker [Ed Cooney] who held that Meeting, if there would ever be an opportunity for him to go into this ministry? This Worker asked him, 'How soon could you be ready?' 'In two weeks,' replied Willie. It was a little longer than this before he went, but during this time of waiting, he came to Edinburgh, where my older sister, Violet, and I were working. He told us about the Truth he had found every day for a whole week. One morning, by my bedside, I yielded my heart to God, and at the same time, offered

my life for God's great harvest field. My sister, Violet, went out then in the work in July or August 1905, and I followed on the 27th of October. I was 19 … It hurt Father and Mother to have Willie go, and then Violet, but it nearly broke their hearts when I left … They were Presbyterians; Father, an elder for as long as I could remember. (E. Jamieson 1969, *TTT*)

Overseer Sydney Holt recalled his tour of Scotland:

Just outside the town of Duns where we saw the home where Uncle Willie Jamieson was raised … Drove down the road Uncle Willie walked down after he said goodbye to his parents who weren't in agreement with his going forth to preach. Also saw the spot where he sat down and looked back wondering if he were making the right choice! Then the train depot (not in use now) in Duns where he caught the train … We then drove to Chirnside where Uncle Willie worked for a butcher in his shop. Saw the very hall in Reston where Uncle Willie first heard the Truth at a Special Meeting! In Chirnside we saw the farm where the first Convention was held (1911) in this part of Scotland. Across the road is a very old church (still in use) with a large cemetery … Five Workers were buried here (saw John Martin, Jean Gibson and Sarah Skerrit's graves). (to Fellow Laborers and Friends, May 1, 1985, *TTT*)

California Missions. Ellis Island records show that William Jamieson (male, Scotch, single, 25, residence Chirnside) disembarked from the SS *Numidian* in New York on August 14, 1905. He arrived in California on August 22, 1905, and joined Irvine Weir. Family accounts record that:

Willie Jamieson went straight to California from New York, September 1905. Irvine Weir was in California and Walter Slater was with him. The Waites professed in the third Meeting they were in at that time … Their home was the first in California that was opened and which continued so. Through the efforts of the Waites, the Workers went to Paso Robles and set up a tent in November where Willie Jamieson joined them. (McPhail, n.d., Early California, *TTT*)

They had a lot of opposition—the baser sort were put up to throwing things at them and making holes in the tent. There they found the Waite, Weibe, McPhail and Hill families, Esther Hanson, Hilma Johnson, Maude Hilton and some others. Most were baptized in Lake Isabel near Creston. (Wood 1977, *TTT*)

Reportedly, Thomas Purves, a young Scotsman, invited his good friend, Willie Jamieson, to Ed Cooney's Gospel Mission where Jamieson professed in his first Meeting. Purves, age 17, also entered the Work in 1905. Both volunteered to preach in the US and travelled to California separately, arriving in August and September. After preaching there from 1905 until 1911, Purves died alone of tuberculosis in Riverside, California, aged 24. The county buried him in Evergreen Memorial Cemetery. Some years later Friends learned of his grave and placed a tombstone on it. It is said that Friends took flowers from Jamieson's funeral (1974) and placed them on Purves' grave.

Thomas Purves (1887–1911)

During World War II, on January 6, 1942, Willie Jamieson, along with some other Brother Workers were imprisoned by the Japanese in the Philippines. They were liberated on February 23, 1945. Jamieson's account about their experiences is posted on the website, *Diary of a POW: Deliverance has Come!,* owned by John Beaber, son of Herman Beaber (my uncle). *See* Chapter 38.

Willie Jamieson passed away October 11, 1974, and was buried in the Pacific Crest Cemetery, Redondo Beach, California. Much loved, 2,500 attended his funeral.

1906, September: Elisabeth Jamieson entered the Work on October 27, 1905, and arrived in California in September 1906, where her brother had a Co-worker waiting for her, a convert of Irvine Weir. She explained, "I got a letter just then from Willie, offering me a place in the Work in California. He and Walter Slater were at Pismo Beach, 'a grand training ground for preachers,' he wrote … So, I came then to California, at the age of 20. I had been in the Work less than a year. Florence Langworthy, age 22, became my companion. We came to Paso Robles and worked in that area" (Jamieson 1969, *TTT*).

1905–1906, June or July: No Conventions were held at Crocknacrieve during 1905 and 1906. Instead, a smaller Irish Convention was held on Leadbetter Street in Belfast.

1905–1907, August: Not much is known about Irvine's activities while he was abroad for this two-year period. UK newspapers that formerly reported about him and the 2x2 Sect were silent those years. He was likely busy visiting and advising his many new young Workers who were gaining footholds while disseminating their Gospel Message in foreign countries.

Irvine's custom was to travel around the world every year to Conventions, leaving after the Irish Convention in August and arriving back prior to the Convention in June or July. Irvine disembarked in Adelaide, South Australia in 1905. Five months later, on March 19, 1906, he departed from Sydney aboard the RMS *Moana* bound for Vancouver, Canada. He returned home in 1907 in time to attend the summer Conventions.

1906: San Francisco Earthquake. Irvine arrived from Victoria, Canada, on the SS *City of Topeka* just a few days before a massive earthquake shook San Francisco for less than a minute at 5:10 a.m. on April 18, 1906. Its estimated magnitude was 7.8. Devastating fires lasted for several days. About 3,000 people died, over 80% of the city was destroyed and half the city's 400,000 residents became homeless. At that time, this was one of the worst and deadliest natural disasters in the US history.

Unharmed, Irvine left the burning city on his first trip down the California coast, headed for Paso Robles where the first Convention in California began on Sunday, April 22, 1906 (possibly the first Convention held in America). From there, he went south to Los Angeles for two weeks before returning to the UK. Aboard the SS *Empress of Britain,* he departed from Quebec, Canada, and arrived in Liverpool, England, on June 30, 1906, in time for the Irish Convention.

1906: William Irvine's Alleged Baptism. According to Charles "Charlie" Ross, Irvine was baptized in 1906 in Eastern Canada, possibly by Ross. Born in N. Ireland in 1881, Ross entered the Work in 1905 and immigrated to Canada in 1906. He preached in England; in North Dakota, US; in Manitoba, Canada, in 1906–1909 and in Saskatchewan in 1910. Workers Lists show Ross paired with Irvine in Manitoba in the Fall of 1909. While no other available source corroborates this baptism, it remains a possibility. Around 1918, Ross married Ethel Wagstaff and had two sons. He died in Nelson, B.C., Canada, in 1961, and she in 1953.

A purported, and probably unwanted, baptism was processed by the Church of Jesus Christ of Latter-day Saints (LDS/Mormon) of children of William Irvine's parents. LDS records show that all the children, except their two youngest daughters, were "Baptized, Endowed and Sealed" to their parents (1980–1986). John and Elizabeth Irvine were *sealed* to each other in the LDS Church on March 16, 1982. These ordinances were performed by proxy in the Church's temples by (unknown) living person/s, for the deceased.

1906–1907: First and Only 2x2 Church Building. Alfred Magowan told Jack Carroll about the construction of a church/meeting house in Gesto, Ontario, Canada, in the year 1906–1907. "I saw the church or meeting house put up by a grateful community after a spiritual 'moving of the waters' under the ministry of James Jardine and Willie Edwards … When William Irvine heard about it, he made that strange pronouncement*: 'All public worship is an abomination to God' "* (April 6, 1954, in author's possession). From that time on, no church buildings were constructed, although portable halls continued to be used for Gospel Meetings.

First and Only Sunday School. A Sunday school was arranged for 2x2 children but was very short lived. The *Impartial Reporter* commented, "The same absurd reasoning of the Tramps that nothing could be adopted unless it was mentioned in the Bible was urged against a Sunday school in Enniskillen for children. When it [the Sunday school] was started, the recognized leader of the schism, Mr. W. Irwin [Irvine], sent word that it *must* be stopped, that there was no scriptural authority for it" (Sept. 16, 1909, Art. 3, *TTT*).

1906: Hawkins Family Professes. James E. and Annie (Farring) Hawkins professed in 1906 through George Walker and David Christie in Brooklyn, Maryland, US. Christie arrived in the US on August 28, 1905, aboard the SS *Parisian*. Convention was held at Hawkins' place 1908–1953. Six of their seven children entered the Work; two remained in the Work until death; three married other Workers and one of these, Edgar and his wife, Olga, left the 2x2 Sect. *See* Chapters 31, 32.

1906, September 8: Ten Workers departed from Liverpool on the SS *Caledonia* and arrived in New York on September 16.

1907, September 7: Ten more Workers departed from Liverpool, England, on the SS *Lusitania* and arrived in Philadelphia on September 14.

19

1905–1907 – Birth of Exclusivity – God's Only/Right Way

Recall that during the first five to six years after the sect began in 1897, the Workers were primarily evangelists who held recruiting missions. Their goal was to help people get right with God. Like the Faith Mission, they were *unsectarian*—not a Christian sect, church or denomination.

According to John Long, in their early days, William Irvine and his Workers all believed that "salvation of the soul is by grace through faith to *everyone* that repents and believes in Christ Jesus; and the experience, testimony and fruits of many clergymen bear witness to the indwelling of the Spirit of Christ. Up until that time [1905] they all believed that" (July 1905, *TTT*).

Their early goals were described by Alfred Magowan, "We had only one commission and that was to make disciples as we had been made ... There was nothing in the vision we had of 'the way in Jesus' that would have led us towards another kind of sectarianism" (to McClung, June 21, 1931, *TTT*).

Eventually, the Workers' viewpoint narrowed radically. While training for the Methodist ministry, Joseph Kerr, a Scotsman, was converted by Edward Cooney. Born in 1881, Kerr entered the Work in 1902, age 21. In John Long's opinion, Joe Kerr was "one of the most gifted and talented of the Workers." Kerr was so disgusted with the clergy's preaching at a 1905 conference at the Bridge of Allan, Scotland, that he concluded there were no clergymen saved.

1905 July: Beginning of Exclusivity. Soon after, at the July 1905 Crocknacrieve Convention, Joe Kerr, "without any charitable consideration of the conscience or opinion of others" preached from the platform that no clergymen (preachers) were saved. Irvine defended Kerr's declaration; Cooney opposed it (*Journal,* July 1905, *TTT*). *See* website *TellingTheTruth.info* in Workers Early, Joe Kerr.

Against this backdrop, Irvine came down hard on Long at this Convention, insisting that Long's converts must cease attending their denominational churches. Believing Irvine had no right to take from him his liberty to be led by the Spirit of God, Long was bothered. "All through that year [1905] I felt in my heart that the Go-Preachers' Testimony was running fast into exclusiveness and extremes that I could never accept as right" (Dec. 1905, *TTT*).

Living Witness Doctrine (LWD). Now we turn our attention to a new religious theory called the *Living Witness Doctrine,* derived from the popular book published in London in 1884, *Natural Law in the Spiritual World.* The author, Henry Drummond (1851–1897), was a Scottish evangelist, writer, lecturer and professor at the Free Church College in Glasgow, and a minister of the Free Church. Irvine and Drummond were not associated.

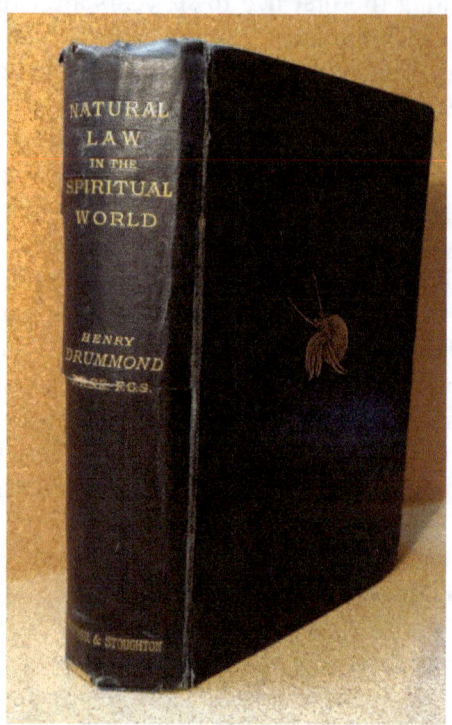

"Natural Law in the Spiritual World" by Henry Drummond (1884)

Joe Kerr was the harbinger who brought the LWD concept to Irvine's attention and proposed that this doctrine might apply to Irvine's belief system. Drummond proposed in his chapter titled "Biogenesis" that what occurs in natural life also occurs in spiritual life. He put forward two choices regarding the origin of spiritual life.

One choice was that spiritual life can be generated spontaneously without the help of man. The other was that spiritual life can only come from pre-existing spiritual life or from a living witness. In other words, there could be no spiritual life without a previous life, i.e. *life begets life.*

Every living thing has an ancestry, e.g. in nature, animals and plants reproduce in like kind. Applying this theory to spiritual life, spiritual sheep could only be reproduced from spiritual sheep. Thus, the *Living Witness Doctrine* theory was that spiritual life could only be transferred person-to-person—through a living witness. *"Without life, there can be no life."* (Drummond 1884, 59–94, *TTT*)

The Workers and Irvine accepted the LWD and rejected spontaneous conversion. Concluding that the Scripture by itself could not give spiritual life, they made Irvine the spiritual progenitor of the Christians of their generation, the Father of a latter-day spiritual family, outside whose genealogy there was little hope of salvation. From then on, salvation was only available via a living witness (Irvine or one of his "sons of the Gospel," i.e. Workers). In essence, the Workers became mediators between man and God.

The LWD was not a part of the sect's original belief system. Cooney explained, "William had been partially persuaded by Joe Kerr to accept the heresy that no one could be born again without meeting a 'Living Witness.' Others held that that witness must be a Worker who had heard William or a Worker who had heard one of them" (Cooney 1947, *TTT*; Appendix D).

1907: Compulsory Belief in Living Witness Doctrine. Irvine made his pivotal decision to add, adopt and apply the LWD to his burgeoning belief system circa 1905–1907. Thus, a decade after the 2x2 Sect started, the LWD was incorporated as an integral, inseparable tenet of the sect's fundamental teachings and beliefs. Members continue to hold this basic entrenched belief even though they may not recognize the term *Living Witness Doctrine*.

Irvine's Belief System Became "God's *Only* Right/True Way." Irvine and his Workers concluded that God intended for the *Faith Lines* method to be used to spread the Gospel universally for all time. They viewed themselves as God's only *true* ministers on Earth because they alone had "paid the price" and were willing to preach in the sacrificial manner that Jesus instructed His twelve disciples in Matthew 10. They considered their method to be unique.

Carrying this forward, it followed that only those who converted to Christ through God's only *true* ministers (Irvine and/or his Workers) had a hope of receiving eternal life. Thus, salvation was restricted to only those who entered through "the door" held open by Irvine, his Workers and their successors.

As such, the Workers were essential for salvation—they were God's only conduit to spiritual life. This reasoning provided Irvine's staff a monopoly on salvation. It tilted the odds decisively in their favor. As

God's "only true church" and "only true ministers," they dismissed all other churches as "false churches," and other preachers as "false prophets." They were guardians of "God's only/right true way."

They began preaching a *Way*, meaning a *way* of going to preach; a *way* of meeting together; a *way* of excluding outsiders. Rather than preaching a person (Jesus), they went about making proselytes to their way (method).

Jack Carroll succinctly framed their way, "There are two *fundamentals* of the faith of Jesus that are *vital* to a true understanding and interpretation as recorded in the New Testament. First, is the church in the home, and in the home only, and secondly, the preacher without a home. These two are *foundational*. We cannot, we dare not, depart from either of them" (J. Carroll 1951, *TTT*). Referring to Carroll's definition of the word *vital*, Magowan differed, "That is like saying that the two main parts of a motor car are the horn and the signalling arm."

The definition for the noun *fundamental* in *Webster's New International Dictionary of the English Language* (1911) is: "A principle, rule, law or article which serves as the groundwork of a system; an essential part; as the fundamentals of Christian faith."

Irvine made it mandatory upon his Workers and followers to believe that their church was *the only right/true church on Earth,* i.e. they were the only Christians. Worldwide, the Workers began teaching that eternal life could only be obtained through (1) hearing, believing and professing through Irvine or through one of his 2x2 Workers; and (2) disassociating from their current churches, following Irvine's 2x2 belief system and meeting in homes for worship.

Similarly, the Catholic Church has long considered it to be the "one true church" set up by Jesus Christ who appointed the twelve apostles to continue His Work. They regard the pope as the successor of the Apostle Simon Peter, and their church as the only "universal sacrament of salvation for the human race."

The Apostle Paul stipulated, "There is one God and one mediator between God and man, the man Christ Jesus" (1 Tim. 2:5). His simple criterion for salvation was, "if thou shalt confess with thy mouth and believe in thine heart that God hath raised him from the dead, thou shalt be saved … For the scripture saith '*Whosoever* believeth on him shall not be ashamed' " (Rom. 10:11).

When the Living Witness Doctrine was incorporated into the sect's belief system, most Workers were in their early twenties. None of them were born and raised in this church, for it did not exist when they grew up. These youths came from a variety of backgrounds, some having received orthodox religious instruction. They were full of zeal and zest, but lacking in life experience, training, logic and education.

The Living Witness Doctrine was based on a comparison or analogy. One item in a comparison may illustrate another, but an illustration is not proof. If the items are not in the same class, it is comparing apples to oranges.

Natural life and spiritual life are not in the same class; therefore, what is true in natural life does not always hold true in spiritual life. The Living Witness Doctrine compares two items that are not in the same class. Therefore, nothing can be reliably inferred from one life to the other.

The sect's narrowed perspective and changed doctrine was described in 1910 by a reporter attending the annual Crocknacrieve Convention:

> Change and development of doctrine prevails, and doubt in many cases, even in Mr. Edward Cooney's and Mr. William Irvine's cases, which have been confessed openly ... Many people professed to have been saved before meeting the Tramp Preacher ... Change of doctrine has made things different for many, especially for those who were not originally converts of Mr. William Irvine or Mr. Edward Cooney, because unless you hear or believe through a Tramp Preacher, they say there can be no possibility of spiritual, divine life, past, present or future.
>
> It is immaterial how definite your aspirations or what quickening towards God may have been wrought in your heart or soul previously. So that, in other words, derivative or successive Christianity is now re-established via William Irvine and Edward Cooney only. This is all the more remarkable and contradictory since William Irvine has a great difficulty to determine his own spiritual Father, and he professedly the great grandfather of all! Some say it was the Rev. John McNeill; some say William Irvine's sister was the means of spiritual life to him, and some are not very sure, but that since Thomas was a doubting apostle, they are contented to be a brother of his. (*Impartial Reporter*, Aug. 25, 1910, *TTT*)

Joe Kerr's Renunciation: In retrospect many years later, Joe Kerr recanted:

> The mistake I made in my ignorance was that I failed to take into account the sovereignty of God—God who could speak from Heaven and save one, as He saved Paul, Acts 9. He could save Timothy through reading of the Scriptures, 2 Timothy 3:15. I forgot that the greatest preacher that the Lord had was the firmament of Heaven, and that there was no place in the universe where the voice of that preacher cannot be heard, Psalms 19:1–4. That is the preacher to whom Paul was

referring in Romans 10:14–18, when he asked, 'How could they hear without a preacher?' For he immediately quotes from that Psalm; Romans 10:18.

I gave instances such as that found in Acts 8:35, how the Lord sent Philip to preach to the eunuch but while I emphasized the need of a preacher, it did not mean that the preacher had to be one of us. The idea that the preacher had to be William Irvine or one of his disciples was added to their doctrine after I had delivered my part ... When I saw the mistake I made, I tried to correct it, but it was too late! It was something new for people who had not been in the habit of thinking for themselves, and so off they set with it to the ends of the Earth! Then it grew until they had it that the preacher had to be one [of the] Testimony, and one who had either professed through William Irvine or one of his direct descent. I could not have preached that, for I believe I was saved before I met The Testimony, and I know that William Irvine had professed through the Rev. John McNeill. (to unknown addressee, Jan. 28, 1956, *TTT*)

Rebaptism of Christians. Transition to the newly adopted Living Witness Doctrine was problematic. It led to the ritual of rebaptism of believing, baptized Christians, a practice that continues today. Long recalled, "Edward Cooney emphasized rebaptism into their Fellowship; which was the beginning of refusing fellowship with Christians of all other denominations; and raising a sectarian barrier which made their Fellowship exclusive and sectarian; that I could not receive without a struggle. Believers have no authority for repeating baptism, unless they are first convinced that the former was not a scriptural one. *See* Acts 19:3–5. Baptism is ... into the name of the Father, and of the Son and of the Holy Ghost ... 'One Lord, one faith, one baptism,' Eph. 4:5" (July 1906, *TTT*).

Un-Christianizing the Christians. Irvine's sect members stopped worshiping and taking communion with Christians outside themselves. The newly adopted Living Witness Doctrine made it necessary for those who believed they were saved before they met Irvine or his Workers to reject and renounce their personal born again experiences. Some could not in good conscience deny or renounce their previous, wholehearted submission to the Lord. It also unsaved many of their Christian family members and friends and placed them on the road to Hell paved with good intentions.

Questions were raised: How did God work with people in countries where Workers had never been? What was the eternal disposition of those who died before Irvine started this church? What about those before Irvine came to America? Some went along with the doctrine, others left the group, and yet others were forced out for not embracing it.

John Long recollected, "The definite article *The* used in such a narrow way as *The* Truth, *The* Way, *The* Testimony, etc. unto the exclusion of all other sects and missions outside their own became at that time very common. **They 'un-Christianized' all Christians outside themselves;** and refused fellowship with them, and I could not go that length conscientiously; and indeed, the instructions of Christ, given in Matthew 10 to His apostles appear to be so contrary to that belief and spirit that it must have been blindness on the part of Irvine and Cooney not to have seen it" (June 1907, *TTT*).

William Irvine's "Revelation." It was well known, however, that Irvine received his spiritual birth in 1893 through Presbyterian minister Rev. John McNeill. He claimed, "Seventy-two years ago I was born into a Presbyterian family; forty-two years ago, I was born into the family of which Jesus is the head, as Adam is of the human family. A Presbyterian preacher was the means. He told me the right thing—to believe on the Lord Jesus Christ and thou shalt be saved. But I began to live by what God revealed through Jesus" (to Billett, Jan. 8, 1934, *TTT*).

Remember, according to the Living Witness Doctrine, Presbyterian ministers were considered *false* preachers. When applying the Living Witness Doctrine theory "life begets life" to Irvine, it breaks down. It does not follow through. Who was before Irvine? How could Irvine truly be saved since he professed through Presbyterian minister John McNeill who had not professed through a Worker?

Irvine and his Workers resolved these questions by reasoning that it was not necessary for Irvine to hear through a living witness—he was *exceptional*. They convinced themselves he had been called, raised up and used by God to restore the methods and ministry of the New Testament church. God had given Irvine "a special revelation."

Irvine's role in founding the 2x2 Sect was explained by Magowan as, "God began His human creation with Adam. There only needed to be one act of creation. Afterward every man came by natural descent. So, with His work of the Gospel. There was a break in the line of spiritual descent, so it was necessary for God to start a new line by special act again" (1931, 7, *TTT*). In turn, this made Irvine the Father or "Spiritual Adam" through whom all successive Workers received their spiritual life.

Cooney viewed Irvine's role in the following way: "Undoubtedly God called us and separated us to be His people in the beginning; and most prominent and most used in this calling out a people for God's name was William Irvine" (to My Dear Sister, 1930, Appendix D). *See* Chapter 27.

From the dialogue in a fictional play inspired by real events titled *Outline of the History of a Peculiar People from 1900–1931* by Alfred Magowan:

> **First Visitor:** They speak of him as a man raised up.
> **Second Visitor:** They trace their spiritual genealogy to him.
> **First Visitor:** I hear they are doing it now and many have already given up what they call their old profession and refer to him as the beginning of a new order, as Adam was the beginning of human descent. (1931)

IF it were true that going out to preach by the Matthew 10 *Faith Lines* method was "God's only right/true way" for all time, then this could only have been a *revelation* from God. The definition of the word *prophet* is one who receives a message or revelation from God. Therefore, by definition, Irvine was speaking from the place of a *prophet*—IF it were true.

There are two kinds of prophets, true and false. The Israelites asked in Deuteronomy 18:21–22, "How may we know the word which the Lord has NOT spoken? When a prophet speaketh in the name of the Lord, if the thing follow not, nor come to pass, that is the thing which the Lord hath not spoken, but the prophet hath spoken it presumptuously." In other words, a prophet was proved by the test of time—by whether or not his prophecies came to pass.

Later in life, Irvine made prophecies that did not come true. He predicted the Apostle John would return and that he and John would be the two witnesses (prophets) in Revelation 11:3–11. This unfulfilled prediction and others are contained in letters Irvine wrote over 26 years to his followers. Irvine died in 1947 from mouth cancer without his prophecies coming to pass. *See* list of Irvine's failed prophecies in Appendix C.

John Long's Excommunication

In 1907, there were over 500 workers laboring in the British Isles, US, Canada, Australia, New Zealand and South Africa (Long July 1907, *TTT*). Arriving at the 1907 Crocknacrieve Convention, John Long discovered that most of the Fellowship had turned against him, believing he had been disloyal to Irvine.

When it was made mandatory for the Workers to preach that all clergy and Christians outside of their sect were unsaved, Long did not acquiesce. He declared, "I have no doubt that God used William Irvine to witness against clericalism; but in doing so he ran into the opposite, in going beyond truth when he preached that every clergyman is a false prophet and unsaved. Because I tried to correct him and did not accept all he said as truth, I became unpopular among the Workers. He [Irvine] remained that year in the British Isles, and everywhere he went, he preached that the clergy were unsaved men going to Hell" (June 1907, *TTT*).

John Long

At the 1907 Crocknacrieve Convention, Irvine used his authority to excommunicate Long, his long-time fellow-helper who had been assisting him for ten years, from the very beginning, 1897 to 1907. Irvine made him a public example, leaving no doubt in the minds of his audience as to what would befall any other Worker who did not accept and teach that Irvine's new belief system was God's only right/true way and that all other churches and ministers were false.

While Long was speaking on the Convention platform, Irvine interrupted him. In the words of the *Impartial Reporter*:

> Like every other sect, the 'Tramps' have their backsliders and recalcitrant workers. One of their workers, John Long was accused of loafing for the past 12 months, instead of working zealously and bringing converts to the 'Jesus Way' of living. His ideas, evidently, were not far-fetched enough for his chiefs. At one of the services the suspected 'loafer' was called forth to give an address, and in the course of that address, John Long spoke of the ark of Noah. What was in it and not in it? There was no tobacco or pipes in it, he said. The speaker was interrupted by Mr. Irwin, [Irvine] who said to him 'Say there were no clergy in it.' 'No, there were no clergy in it,' quietly remarked the speaker. 'Say it strong' commanded Mr. Irwin [Irvine] in his gruff tone. But the speaker did not repeat it. It is understood that J. L. [John Long] was given notice to quit and left on Tuesday last. (July 25, 1907, *TTT*)

Long recounted that Irvine asked those to stand who believed there never was and never could be a born again clergyman. Everyone stood except Long, Goodhand Pattison and two Englishmen (possibly the Twiss brothers. *See* Chapter 38). Irvine then announced, " 'See the majority is against you, John.' Then he denounced me again with two untrue accusations. One that I never got on well with any Worker ... The other that I lived for years on his testimony ... during the ten years since the revival began, I ... received very little financial help from him [Irvine]" (July 1907, *TTT*). Irvine chided Long for not being willing to forsake his old ways.

With that pronouncement, the two preachers most used at the origin of the 2x2 Sect separated and never again worked together. Irvine gave Long 12 months' probation, instructing him not to visit any of the Friends' homes and to preach only in areas where no Workers had been, and after a year, if he still believed there were saved clergymen, they would look upon him as being unsaved, too.

Cut to the heart and in tears, Long left the sect. He revealed that it was "the saddest event and most painful, trying and unexpected that I met with during my life's experience; namely having to leave the Go-Preacher Fellowship; which God used me so much in, from its beginning, ten years ago ... Of the wrong done to me at that time, there has been no public confession or acknowledgment; it severed me from some of my near relatives; and robbed me of my privilege, namely the right of fellowship in the mission I helped to start" (June 1907, *TTT*; July 1907, *TTT*).

"The time came, I regret to say so, when the Go-Preachers' Mission became too exclusive and narrow ... it was a great pity for me to have to leave them; yet because of the exclusiveness and error they went into, it was a great liberation as well ... God saved me from exclusiveness ... and ever since, I claim the right of having fellowship with every member of the body of Christ; and preaching the Gospel to every creature, entering every open door" (Long, "Why I am an Unsectarian Evangelist," *TTT*).

For the rest of his life, Long continued with his independent, unsectarian, itinerant ministry "fully in the Lord's Work and a Go-Preacher, though not in fellowship with them" (Long July 1907, *TTT*).

In 1920, Long (age 48) married Margaret Keegan (age 28). Between 1923 and 1931, they had four children and made their home at Oldstone, Muckamore, Co. Antrim, Ireland. He died in 1962, aged 90, and was buried in Co. Antrim, Ireland. The Bible and prayer were his primary authority for spiritual teaching and standards—he knew what he believed and why. When he mentioned a teaching or belief in his *Journal* for the first time, he nearly always supplied supporting Scripture. His *Journal* entries during the 2x2 Sect's early days go into much detail about their beliefs, teachings, practices and changes that greatly troubled him.

Long recollected, "It is now 20 years since I withdrew from the Go-Preacher Fellowship, because I could not accept the development of their teaching along the lines of un-Christianizing all other churches, and persons; yet I do not hate them, nor despise them when I come in contact; but try to treat them as I do all other Christians with the Spirit of Jesus; and give them the credit for all excellencies found in their sect, but I don't get this in return" (July 1927, *TTT*).

Resistance to the New Doctrine. Long was not the only one who did not agree with the new Living Witness Doctrine concept. Long wrote, "William Irvine, John Hardy [Hardie] and some others [including Percy Abbott] at the beginning believed they were born again in Babylon." Although some found the new LWD doctrine hard to swallow, they later acquiesced and cooperated. Others "went back and walked no more with him."

In 1907 from the platform, Irvine forced Percy Abbot to make "his choice at a large convention of going home— not allowed to preach any more— or go out to America and prove himself ... so, rather than being sent home, he came to America" (W. Edwards to B. McCann, June 15, 1941, in author's possession).

At first, Ed Cooney opposed the Living Witness Doctrine, but he eventually went along with it—against his better judgment. In 1914, after Irvine fell from favor, Cooney and Tom and Ellen Elliott renounced the Living Witness Doctrine. Cooney bitterly regretted that he had ever gone along with it. *See* Chapter 27.

They 'un-Christianized' all Christians outside themselves...

(John Long, June 1907)

Cooney recounted, "Two heresies arose amongst us at this time, started largely by Joseph Kerr, who said no one could be saved who had not met William Irvine, or some of those in fellowship with him. Others held that only through Sister or Brother Workers could any be saved, and that these Workers must be William Irvine's associates. In 1914, I declared that I returned to the Gospel William Irvine and I with others preached for some years before these heresies were introduced" (to My Dear Sister, May 1930, Appendix D).

Alfred Magowan informed George Walker, "We had a visit from E. Cooney ... and he was telling us that Joe Kerr has repented of his 'Living Witness Doctrine' which made us the most exclusive body of people making the Christian profession. He has repented, but the teaching ... will still go marching on" (Feb. 21, 1954, *TTT*).

Current 2x2 Sect Beliefs

Regardless of John 3:16 ("that *whosoever* believeth in him should not perish, but have everlasting life"), most 2x2s still believe their belief system is God's only right/true way on Earth; that without the Workers, there would be no *true* church; that all other churches and ministers are *false,* and that everyone who is not following their method of worship and ministry will go to Hell. This includes all Christians in other churches with whom they will not share communion or recognize their baptisms.

The sentiment that no one can be saved unless they profess and are baptized through 2x2 Workers is not usually expressed in those words, but rather by invoking Romans 10:13–15: "For whosoever shall call upon the name of the Lord shall be saved. How then shall they call on him in whom they have not believed? and how shall they believe in him of whom they have not heard? and how shall they hear without a preacher? **And how shall they preach, except they be sent**? as it is written, How beautiful are the feet of them that preach the gospel of peace and bring glad tidings of good things!"

Verses 13–14 build the foundation of their argument. To be saved, you must call on the name of the Lord. But you cannot call on Him unless you believe in Him. And you will never believe in Him until you hear about Him *through a preacher*—and not just any preacher, but *one that was sent.* Here some Workers insert *sent as it is written* and then use Matthew 10 and Luke 10 to define this to mean going in pairs, homeless, poor, forsaking family, taking no salary or collections, etc. Further, if a preacher is *not sent as it is written* (as the twelve disciples did in Matthew 10 and Luke 10), then it follows that there can be no valid preaching, no valid hearing, no valid believing, no valid "calling on Him" and thus, no salvation.

Sydney Holt, Overseer of Washington, US, stipulated, "We do NOT accept those of different denominations as one in spirit or belief with our Fellowship" (to Paul Abenroth, Oct. 4, 2001, in author's possession).

After the Internet arrived, documentation became easily accessible showing the 2x2 Sect started around the turn of the twentieth century, rather than when Jesus sent out His twelve apostles on the shores of Galilee; and that it was not handed down in a succession from the apostles to the current Workers. It is not difficult to trace the Workers through verifiable documents from the present back to and stopping with Irvine at the turn of the twentieth century.

Although it is frequently mentioned or implied in their Meetings, and it continues to be taught to succeeding generations by professing parents, grandparents and Workers, it is rare for a 2x2 to admit to an outsider that they believe they are the only ones who have a chance of making it to Heaven. They will usually attempt to evade the question with a reply something like God is the Judge, or that God is fair and merciful, etc.

Sometimes a 2x2 may concede that it is possible that some members of other Christian denominations will be saved; the unspoken condition is IF they listen to a Worker in the future, become a 2x2 and leave their church. Exceptions are made for those in countries where Workers were not allowed to enter, and those who never had the opportunity to hear the Workers before their death.

Former Texas Overseer Hubert Childers, deceased, believed his mother was in Heaven, although the Workers did not arrive in their area until after her death. Reportedly, William Lewis, deceased Texas Overseer, remarked, "Don't be surprised if you see Abraham Lincoln in Heaven someday." Lincoln died in 1865, 38 years before the 2x2 Workers arrived in America. On occasion, some Workers have indicated that Massachusetts Governor (1880–1883) John Davis Long may have been saved, due to his poem *I Would, Dear Jesus.*

As noted above, the source of the Workers' methods and doctrine was not by a clear revelation, but rather, a gradual progressive evolution. In their beginning, they did not consider their *Faith Lines* Matthew 10 method to be *God's only right/true way.* History shows the sect has not been, as is sometimes claimed, "the same yesterday, today and forever." Examining their development in the decade between 1897 and 1907, it is obvious the outlook of the Workers changed considerably. Even so, adaptation and innovation are not characteristics of the 2x2 Church.

JULY 1907   CROCKNACRIEVE
BALLINAMALLARD, CO FERMANAGH.

A LARGE TENT WITH A PLATFORM & SEVERAL PREACHERS ON IT. ABOUT A THOUSAND PEOPLE FACING IT. J. L. PREACHING.

J. L.—There was no tobacco in the Ark.
(Voice of W. I. from behind)—John', tell them there were no Clergy in the Ark!
(The preacher is thrown off his line by this strange interruption, and sits down as soon as he can bring his speech to a hasty conclusion)
W. I.—John was always the Brake on our Progress. When we set out to follow Jesus, he was selling Books and settled as a Methodist. He was convinced that we were right and cast in his lot with us. But he was not convinced that the Clergy were wrong, and there has always been a holding back in him. For years he has been dragging his feet on the ground to hinder our going on, and we have decided to part company with him so that he can go his way and we ours, and let him prove whether God will be with him as He has been with us. All those stand up who believe that J......W...... is in Hell!!
(Nearly all stand up, those who remain seated provoke W. I. to wrath, and he makes uncomplimentary remarks about their quadruped connections!)
(One of John's English friends rises and begins to speak).
Englishman—It is not for us to discover the present whereabouts of the souls of men who are dead. They may not be where we think they are, and what we say about them can neither injure them nor help us. It is for us to look to ourselves that we may not come to where we say they are.

W. I. John can go and take his friends with him.
(They go out).

(E. C. gets up to answer some things John had said, or to make some points clear, and W. I. slips out of the Tent, by the platform. While E. C. is still speaking, W. I. slips in again with a piece of paper in his hand. His imperious manner makes itself felt immediately. He begins to tear the paper, and to speak as he tears it into very small pieces, which he drops one by one—dramatically).
W. I.—That is paper, and that is paper, and that is paper. And that also is paper. It is all paper!
(This is his way of correcting E. C's manner of speech, and all the people sit awed by his commanding presence, and cutting words. E.C. now seated, straightens himself, and looks straight ahead. W. I. goes on speaking, and soon the people are leaning forward to hear, as he opens up the Scriptures. Nobody can hold their attention like him; and he is so full of energy and wit that hours follow one another, and still he goes on—and still they listen eagerly.)

(Some hours later two visitors go for a walk, and talk together).

First Visitor—What do you think of it?
Second Visitor—You mean what do I think of HIM!
First Visitor—I suppose so. It seems to be him, and he seems to be it, and the people seem satisfied to have it so. There is something strange about it.
Second Visitor—Is it a weakness in them?
First Visitor—No, it seems to be a power in him. He has a strong personality, and they like it.
Second Visitor—Did you see how they looked after him when he walked across the court yard?
First Visitor—I would like to come back a few years from now, and see how this work grows.

8   9

Extract from Alfred Magowan's Play "Outline of a Peculiar People"

❧❧❧

20

1900–1906 – Apostolic Succession – Restorationism

Apostolic Succession. At some point, possibly after 1914, the Workers began claiming that the Two by Two Church started when Jesus sent His twelve apostles on a mission to the Jews in Matthew 10, and that it has continued down to them.

Starting from this end, that claim would mean that the current Workers have come from a direct, uninterrupted lineage of successive Workers going back through time, worker to worker, faith to faith, literally and physically, to the first century apostles. More simply stated, the current-day Workers come from a series of Workers in an unbroken chain, each having professed through another Worker, going back to the apostles.

This term for this concept or doctrine is *apostolic succession.* Within Christendom, it is the claim that the current ministry of the Christian Church hails from the apostles through a literal continuous line of successive ministers. It is widely known that the Catholic Church believes it is of apostolic succession; they claim an unbroken line of succession popes back to the Apostle Peter to Jesus Christ.

The concept of apostolic succession is not found in Scripture. No one has ever successfully traced the 2x2 Sect back to the New Testament primitive church—because it is demonstrably *not* of apostolic succession. Years later, when the truth became known about the 2x2 Sect's original founding and history, they would lose many members due to this misrepresentation.

Dr. Cornelius Jaenen, author and Professor Emeritus of History at the University of Ottawa, and a 2x2 member, disclosed that he found no evidence of apostolic succession: "In our efforts to trace the continuity of primitive Christian ideals over the centuries, no unbroken successions or continuous activities of a particular identifiable group have been documented" (2003, 535).

Early Worker William Clelland stated, "It might be a good question to ask those who say they are from the beginning: 'Who was ahead of William Irvine?' William Irvine was entirely responsible for the creation of this movement ... he had the idea that he could facilitate the spreading of the Gospel by having a few men and women join themselves to him. His ideas of preaching were entirely on his ideas of Matthew 10. And yet, they have the hide to tell one that it went back to time immemorial. It went back to exactly 1899 when the first Workers gathered around Bill Irvine" (Parker 1982, 96).

Some members denied their church was a "new sect" as the newspapers proclaimed. Disregarding the sect's literal, traceable lineage and referring to their *spiritual* beginning, a correspondent using the pseudonym "Within" wrote the editor, "We are not starting a new religion. We are 'earnestly contending for the faith once delivered to the saints' [Jude 1:3] and trying to separate it from the 'traditions of men,' [Mark 7:8–9] because there is not a doctrine in the word of God that has not been corrupted by the professing church" (*Impartial Reporter,* Oct. 7, 1909, 8 *TTT*).

Similarly, Edward Cooney stated, "We did not start this 'Jesus Way' ... It was started and planned by God before we were ever thought of, and if you go any other way, you will go to Hell ... If I started the Cooneyite Sect, I would go to Hell myself and all my followers. It's not Cooney's or another body's way, it is God's plan and way" (*Impartial Reporter,* Aug. 5, 1909, *TTT*; to an audience of more than 2,000 at Crocknacrieve Convention).

Just as Campbell's Soup only goes back to Joseph Campbell, and not to Jacob making a pot of soup for Esau or to the first creator of a pot of soup, the 2x2 Sect did not historically begin when Jesus sent out His disciples on the shores of Galilee, as can be seen from the previous 19 chapters. Even so, that claim continues to have a large following among its members. The records show, however, that the sect originated at Irvine's first Revival Mission at Nenagh, Ireland, in 1897 at the earliest.

However, Dr. C. Jaenen classified the 2x2 Sect as a "restoration movement," declaring "Several events coalesced to produce a *restorationist movement* in Southern Ireland" (2003, 520).

~~~~~

Restorationism. The term *restorationism,* also described as *Christian primitivism,* is the concept of restoring the beliefs, methods and practices of the early New Testament Church. The aim of restorationism is to separate from denominations and return to the original, essential and universal features of Christianity, using the early church as a normative model. In other words, to replicate the primitive church style of worship. The 2x2 Church/Sect fits the definition of a *restorationist movement.*

Countless newspapers printed details surrounding the commencement of the "new sect." The early Workers focused on restoring what they perceived as the methods used by the primitive New Testament ministry and church. Workers have portrayed Irvine variously as a man God raised up, the Lord's anointed, first leader, the restorer or finder of the literal New Testament church and the apostles' ministry. They did not yet claim their sect was of apostolic succession. That would change.

Variations on the restoration theme have also been disseminated. Today, the most common explanation of their beginning is that the 2x2 Sect was restored, regenerated, restarted, revived, resurrected, resurfaced, jump-started or raised up again; all of which involve bringing back after an interval or decline and require a start-up person/s. Restoration illustrations have been promoted suggesting that it came from an existing "remnant;" or sprang up from "the same seed" (that lay dormant for 1900 years); or grew out of "the stump" of the original New Testament ministry and church that had been cut off.

Through the years, various restorationist movements have implemented their restorative visions with assorted focuses, e.g. structure, key doctrines, traditions, methods, ministry, the role of the Holy Spirit, etc. Among the best known restorationist movements are the Hussites, Anabaptist, Puritans, Mormons, Seventh-day Adventists and Waldensians, as well as adherents to the Stone-Campbell Restoration Movement.

A few pre-Reformation groups, such as the Waldensians, Moravians (Germany), Eastern Orthodox, Mar Thoma Syriac Orthodox, Armenian Apostolic Church and in Africa, the Coptic (Egyptian) and Ethiopian Orthodox; etc. have survived as organized religious bodies into the modern era. Dr. C. Jaenen declared that although the Waldensian "movement claimed it was a continuation of pure and uncorrupted primitive Christianity, its origins are commonly traced to the decision by Pierre Waldes (Valdes), a rich merchant and usurer, in or soon after 1173" (2003, 442).

Some 2x2s, seeking to find a non-Catholic apostolic succession through church history, have looked for a descent through a succession of groups, rather than individuals. For example, some believe a line can be traced from Jesus' apostles to the Waldensians (aka Vaudois) to the Moravians to John Wesley (Methodism) to the Holiness Movement to the Faith Mission to the 2x2 Sect. However, there are gaps and contradictions in this historical lineage bridge. A noticeable inconsistency is evident when 2x2s link the Waldensians to their apostolic succession argument prior to 1897—while refusing to accept the Waldensians as their Brothers in Christ after 1897. The Waldensians still exist as a distinct church.

In addition, there are serious inconsistencies between the above "bridge" groups and the distinctive practices and beliefs of the 2x2 Sect, such as using the Bible only, baptizing adults only by immersion, women preachers and worshiping on Sunday rather than Saturday.

Irvine's experiment to restore the primitive New Testament church and to return to the faith and practices of the Apostolic Age was not a novel or uncommon approach. Other religious leaders also entertained the same ideals and goals.

The Restoration Movement. During the Second Great Awakening (1790–1840), the *Restoration Movement* took place. In the US, one of these was the *Stone-Campbell Movement.* Some Christian men attempted to return the church to its original state in the New Testament and to the simple teachings of the Bible only. They abandoned man-made creeds, traditions, confessions, teachings and took no name. Calling themselves *Christians only,* they did not believe they were the *only* Christians. Committed to the restoration principles and to the inspiration and authority of Scripture, they did not consider their return to primitive Christianity to be a new denomination or sect. Today, its three derivative groups assemble as the Church of Christ, Disciples of Christ and the Christian Church.

Also during the nineteenth century, several religious movements claim God broke through hundreds of years of silence to provide their particular self-proclaimed leader with a personal "revelation" to restore the true interpretation of God's truth, will and church on Earth. Some of these leaders were Joseph Smith, founder of the Church of Jesus Christ of Latter-day Saints (Mormons, 1830); Mary Baker Eddy, founder of Christian Science (1879); Charles T. Russell, founder of Jehovah's Witnesses (1870s).

During the same time period, some believe Irvine was given a "revelation" to restore God's only right/true way to Earth. This begs the question: What made Irvine's self-proclaimed revelation or experiment more accurate or superior to that of other founders' self-proclaimed revelations?

In the opinion of the Workers and Friends, their method was superior because Irvine's revelation followed Jesus' teachings and the New Testament church model more closely than any other Christian church. Therefore, their method restored the original New Testament church and ministry model to its fullest extent possible. From this conclusion, largely based on the *method* used by their ministers and the *location* of their worship meetings (in homes), they reasoned that Irvine's particular method IS "God's only right/true way" on Earth today and that Jesus intended it to be followed universally for all time.

How Well Did William Irvine's Method Work?

In the early days, some Workers suffered appalling hardships. Magowan observed, "Tramp Preachers did everything but sweat blood in the days of their going forth in strange lands and without visible means of support. They knew what it was to live on raw turnips in Scotland and on oranges in California. They also knew what it was to go for days without anything to eat ... We slept under the stars, in schools and churches, and halls and empty store buildings—with neither bed nor bed covering. We tramped through snow from morning to night in more than 40° of frost" (1956, 5, *TTT*).

Fannie Carroll who entered the Work in 1904, remembered, "We were tested sore. We had nothing to eat. We went out one afternoon to visit, though we weren't able for it. We were weak but it didn't bother us."

Willie Jamieson confessed, "We're living on bread and water" at Pismo Beach, California. His sister Elisabeth disclosed, "We paid 25¢ a night for a room and lived on bread and canned milk. I was young and always hungry! Once ... we found an apple a child had bitten into. We cut out the bitten part and divided it, and that was our supper" (1969).

Three times the *Go-Preacher's Hymn Book* mentions hungry Workers. Some Workers were wet, cold and slept outdoors in all kinds of weather. Others suffered malnutrition, experienced mental breakdowns, illness, early deaths and retained lasting handicaps from being unable to afford urgently needed medical or dental treatment. While sleeping overnight in hay in a barn in Washington, Harry Cross died from a spider bite in 1908.

In Australia, Sam Jones' Co-worker left him. "Being discouraged Sam letting him have what little money he could give, but getting worn out with the journey, took shelter in an empty house. Next day he found himself so weak he couldn't walk and was there for 18 days till some gipsies [*sic:* gypsies] found him half dead, but giving him some food, restored him to life again" (B. Pattison 1951, *TTT*).

Profile of Arthur McCoy. In 1914, McCoy entered the Work in his home state of South Australia. Between 1922 and 1927, he labored in New South Wales under Overseer John Hardie. Following are some of McCoy's comments concerning the suffering experienced by some of the Australian Workers:

> John's [Hardie] practice was, just after each Convention, to ask each Worker in turn, 'How much have you got?' and hold out his hand for it,

acting as controller. We saw and had part in his doing this after the 1923 Convention, handing each Worker back £2 and in some cases also a train or coach fare to go to his or her new field.

Because we were reduced to severe straits there, we repaired and erected an old windmill to help pay our way, mended cartwheels and dried our one set of wet clothes as best we might ... When our rent was six shillings a week, we worked as builders' labourers, but when they heard that McMurray, Helms and I worked to earn a little during missions, Edward Cooney and Adam Hutchison found fault. Edward Cooney said it was a 'travesty of Matthew 10', and ... I replied that, 'Paul worked in necessity and wrote of it' ...

Preachers were forbidden to carry a change of clothes, so Adam Hutchison got round the difficulty of having only one pair of trousers by his ingenious method of having a double seat; he sewed on an extra piece of cloth so that when it wore through from the continuous cycling he was able to take it off and sew on another patch. So strict was he that during a cycling trip of 160 miles in Northwestern Tasmania, we did not spend a penny for refreshments, then to be had for sixpence—we got water from creeks and roadside tanks. For three years in Tasmania, he and his companions lived in poorest rough huts and were often wet with no possibility of changing clothes.

At the end of 1922 ... I cycled 109 miles up to Glen Innes and took the opportunity of finding Jim Gordon, whom I met briefly. He noticed my boots, worn into holes and even wanted to buy me a new pair. I declined this kind offer, not seeing the fairness of it.

We went on to Bellingen, Repton and Uranga on the Bellinger River. We found an old empty cottage near the river; our water supply was from part of an iron tank which contained a foot of water, and there were mosquitoes in swarms, so we bought a quarter yard of mosquito netting to make two face covers; otherwise, rest was impossible. Fleas were on the floor by our two rugs like Caesar's legions, so Harry and I poured hot water on them but more came up out of the cracks. A dentist in Bellingen told me he would charge ten shillings to fix up a damaged tooth which cost was beyond us—so I filed it off with a small file and had to leave it; an abscess came later.

McCoy worked hard to make the Australian Friends and Workers aware of the pitiful, deplorable conditions under which the Workers labored. The Matthew 10 *Faith Lines* concept had not worked well for him and many other Workers. After enduring some extremely hard survival experiences, McCoy jettisoned his belief that Jesus intended for future ministers to follow the Matthew 10 *Faith Lines* concept forever.

He explained that the Matthew 10 directions were given against the background of Jewish social customs at the time of Christ, and that the law, customs and traditions of Israel provided for the needs of messengers and prophets who were to go empty-handed and were to be treated as honored guests. This same assurance was not given to Workers who followed Irvine's Matthew 10 experiment.

It was McCoy's opinion that the Overseers were not competent to interpret the Scripture. He expanded, "No properly organized and effective attempt was made to stop short, overhaul and examine fully the whole matter and the reason for the views held and laid down by the one who started this 'way' in 1900 and by the group of early leaders following him, including John Hardie, Jack and William Carroll, George Walker, Sam Lang, Willie Gill, Ed Cooney" (Parker 1982, 44–45).

Some Workers and Friends reason that if the 2x2 method was not according to God's will, then it would not *work* or would come to nothing; that God would hinder its progress, no one would convert, and the Workers' needs would not be met.

Man's acceptance or rejection is not and has never been a true gauge of what God approves. Whether something appears to *work* or feels right is not a measure of God's favor. Communism, slavery and Satanism all *work*. If the Workers' needs being met and their acquisition of converts were proof that God endorsed a particular ministry, then to be consistent, the same would also be true for other denominational Christian ministers whose needs were also met and acquired converts.

From the above examples, it appears that in their early days, faithfully following the *Faith Lines* method did not work out very well for some Workers.

Crocknacrieve Sisters/Brothers/Workers/Cooks (1913)

21

1907–1913 – Early Conventions

Second Crocknacrieve Convention. Three years after the first Crocknacrieve Convention was held in 1904, the second took place in 1907. An estimated 2,000 people attended from various English-speaking countries. This was the first large-scale Convention, and it lasted about four weeks. Beginning this year, this Convention was held annually from early July to early August.

Visiting reporters from the local newspaper, the *Impartial Reporter,* described various venues of the proceedings:

> The 'Tramp Preachers' to the number of 600 have continued in conference for the past week at Crocknacrieve ... there are about 300 workers ... The conference is lasting for a month and the workers remain all this time ... The saints and bishops come and go ... The women folk ... do not wander about with the brethren ... [a] Tramp Preachers remarked, 'This is not the time for courting. They can court elsewhere. They come here to work, not to court.' (July 25, 1907, 8, *TTT*)

> At last Sunday evening's service there were ... on the platform two of the chief pioneers of the movement, Mr. William Irwin [Irvine] and Mr. Edward Cooney ...

> Each day ... three services are held in the large tent ... The first is ... from 11 a.m. till 1 p.m., then another ... from 3 p.m. till 5 p.m., and the evening ... from 7 p.m. till 9:30 p.m. On last Sunday ... fully 1,000 people were present ... There are English, Scotch and Irish. Some come from the Far East and some from the Wild West.

> The meeting opened with the singing of hymns and prayer. The most interesting address was that of Mr. William Irwin [Irvine] ... a forcible speaker and has a very convincing manner. He spoke of the clergy of all denominations in scathing terms and stated that in all ages the clergy were the marks of the Devil ... his own personal belief was that every clergyman would go to Hell unless he turned and worked in what he called 'the Jesus Way.' (July 18, 1907, 8, *TTT*)

Sunday morning the 'Tramps' celebrated Holy Communion ... in the large tent where they dine and hold their meetings. Thanks having been offered up by Mr. Edward Cooney, bread was handed round by men workers ... A loaf is cut into six parts and one of these parts is given to each row. The first person ... breaks off a small piece and eats it, passing on the bread to the next ... [then] the wine is sent round ... in ordinary earthenware jugs poured into mugs which are then handed round.

To cater for and find sleeping accommodation for such a large concourse of people is no small undertaking ... The cuisine arrangements are complete in every detail. Two large boilers are constantly in use for cooking. The old wine cellar is turned into a bakehouse and on last Saturday as many as 160 loaves were baked ... The meat ... is brought from Belfast ... whole carcasses. Those of the 'Tramps' who understand butter-making are busy in the dairy ... Most of the 'Tramps' have bicycles, and to enter one of the spacious lofts where the machines are kept, one would imagine they were looking into a store of some large Coventry Cycle warehouse ...

Bathing is the order of the day, the men making full use of the Ballycassidy River, while the women use a pond specially dug out for them beside a stream" (Aug. 1, 1907, *TTT*). "The Baptismal font is the ladies' bathing place ... there were twenty-seven to be baptized; two of the workers performed the ceremony of immersing the converts in the water so that a considerable amount of time was saved. (July 25, 1907, 8, *TTT*)

After the Convention closed, William Irvine, age 44, departed on the SS *Ivernia* on August 6, 1907, from Liverpool, England, for Boston, Massachusetts, US, for his third trip around the world. From 1907 to 1913, between the annual Irish Conventions, he continually globe-trotted worldwide to Conventions.

1908: Conventions were held at Crocknacrieve, Rathmolyon and Willsburgh that year. Penny Barton's sermons were mentioned in the *Impartial Reporter* from July 1908 through 1909. *The Irish Independent* reported, "A Miss Barton, a member of an old Fermanagh Co. family, told one evening how she had given up her fine dresses and money and ease, and her horses, in order to go out and preach the gospel" (Aug. 24, 1907, *TTT*).

Penny Barton and Maggie Johnston were the first Workers to go preach in Italy and Switzerland. Barton appeared at the 1914 Crocknacrieve Convention, "Two preachers, one of whom is Miss Barton, Pettigo, have lately returned from North Italy and Switzerland"

(*Impartial Reporter,* July 9, 1914, *TTT*). Barton left the Work and married Simon Loane in 1918; they purchased Crocknacrieve in 1921.

1909: A New Phase – Separation of Sexes. Possibly 2,000 attended the 1909 Crocknacrieve Convention. The segregation of sexes commenced; men and women sat on opposite sides for meetings and meals. "In former years, the people sat anywhere in the spacious tent without distinction of sex, but on Sunday, the women sat on the right and the men on the left" (*Impartial Reporter,* Aug. 12, 1909, 3, *TTT*).

The following year the reporter remarked: "[At] Crocknacrieve ... A man stands at a cross way and directs the males one side and females the other, and thus do the folk proceed till the tent is reached ... Some 1,000 people are present, the sexes sitting at different sides" (*Impartial Reporter,* July 28, 1910, *TTT*).

Irvine stated, "Women and men observe strict separateness in meetings, at meals and quarters for sleeping; and any violation of these conditions would at once be disciplined by asking them to go home" (Statement for trial of *Burfitt V. Hayward,* July 1913). *See* Appendix B.

Until the 1980s, in Convention dining areas, the practice of separating the sexes was still used in South Africa, Australia, New Zealand and in the Eastern US under Overseer George Walker, but not in Western US.

After the Crocknacrieve Convention, on his annual trip around the world, Irvine, age 46, departed on September 12, 1909, from Queenstown, Ireland, for New York aboard the SS *Campania.*

1909: First English Convention. The first annual Convention in England assembled in Debenham, Suffolk Co. in 1909 and continued until 2007. For many years, Debenham was the longest running Convention in the world.

1910: According to reporters, the following year, "The Convention of Tramp Preachers at Crocknacrieve, near Enniskillen, has exceeded all expectations. Each day brings fresh arrivals to swell the large concourse, and on Sunday last the large tent ... was incapable of holding all who wished to enter it ... many had to remain outside ... on Sunday last no fewer than 1,150 dinners ... were served" (*Impartial Reporter,* July 21, 1910, 8, *TTT*).

As was his custom, after the Convention, Irvine, age 47, left for his sixth annual trip around the world on August 18, 1910. He boarded the SS *Royal George* from Bristol, England, bound for Quebec, Canada. He returned to London, England, on July 12, 1911, aboard the SS *Geelong* from Australia in time for the Crocknacrieve Convention.

1911: Last Large-Scale Crocknacrieve Convention. Described as the *Mecca of the Tramp Preachers,* thousands attended the last grand Convention. "From ten o'clock in the morning every road that one would look to were to be seen crowds of people flocking to Crocknacrieve, the scene of the Convention, by bicycles, motor cars and a large number by foot" (*Impartial Reporter*, July 27, 1911, 6, *TTT*). At the Sunday meeting, some 2,000 people were present. "Mr. Irwin [Irvine], the leader and founder of the movement was the principal speaker" (*Impartial Reporter,* July 6, 1911, 5, *TTT*).

Although Irvine was scheduled to leave on his seventh world tour on August 23, 1911, and on his eighth world tour in August 1912, no confirming ship records have surfaced. However, it is almost certain he left the UK as usual these two years. A US border crossing record from Canada shows he arrived at Eastport Boundary in Idaho in December 1912.

1911: Scotland Convention. Passenger records for the *SS Baltic* show that William Jamieson, age 30, returned to Scotland for a home visit on June 11, 1911. He attended the first Convention to be held at Chirnside, Berkwickshire (possibly the first held in all of Scotland) and remarked in a letter, "There were very large crowds all the time. William Irvine, as usual, did the most of the preaching and I never heard him better" (to Whites, Aug. 1, 1911, *TTT Photo Gallery*). Jamieson returned to America in November 1911.

1912: Irish Conventions. From 1912 forward, at least three smaller regional Conventions took place in Ireland. One was held in Belfast on Leadbetter Street in a shed. Another two-week Convention was held at Nutfield, Brookeborough, Co. Fermanagh.

1912 Nutfield Convention

Francis David McClung (brother of Brother Workers Wilson and Walter) and his wife, Ruby, retired from a military career in India, moved to Ireland and purchased Nutfield, a large farm. It was reported, "The sect commonly called 'Pilgrims' or 'Go-Preachers' opened their annual Convention at Nutfield House, a mile from Brookeborough on Sunday ... a beautiful country seat recently purchased by a County Antrim gentleman named Mr. M'Clung, a prominent member of the sect" (*Impartial Reporter*, July 25, 1912, 5, *TTT*).

A third Convention took place at Carrick, Rathdowney, Co. Laois, southwest of Dublin. John Pearson (1856–1938) professed in 1902 and purchased his old homeplace, Carrick House, around 1906. Currently, this home, with 24-inch thick stone walls, is well over 200 years old. In 2022, Carrick is the oldest Convention continuously held in Ireland and the second longest running Convention in the world. John's son, Irvine Pearson (1908–1997), Overseer of Ireland, was born and raised in this home.

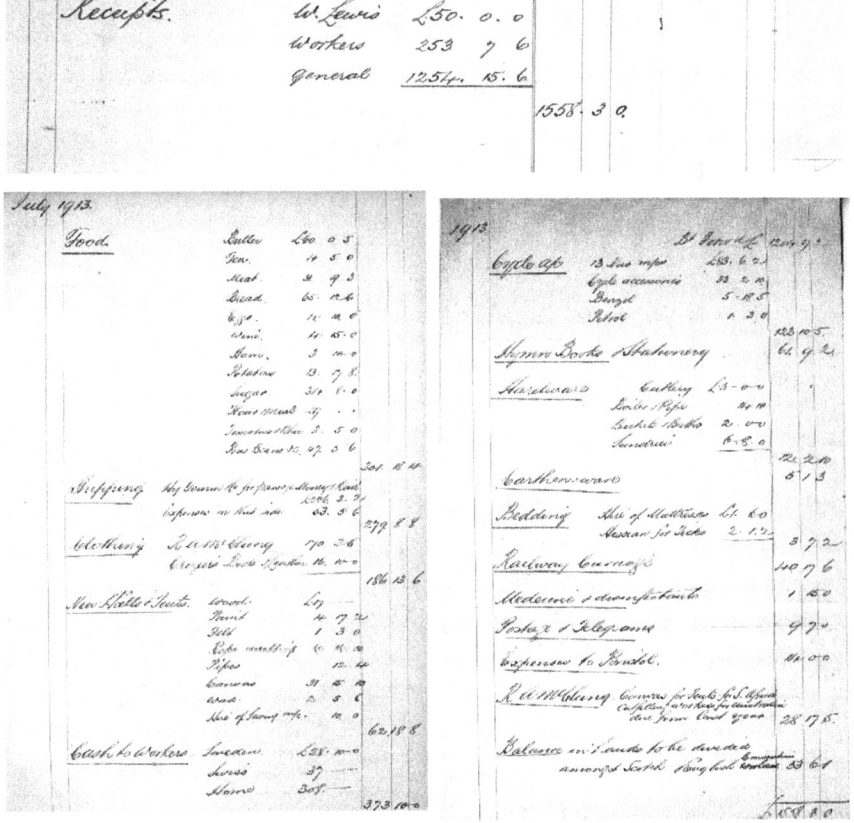

Records of Crocknacrieve 1913 Convention Receipts and Disbursements

1913: Small-Scale Crocknacrieve Conventions. From 1913 to 1916, around WWI, smaller scale Conventions were held at Crocknacrieve.

"Dinner was served at midday to about 750 people and the numbers which arrived later brought the gathering up to probably 1,000 … two large tents were erected, each to seat about 800. One is used as a meeting tent and the other as a dining tent ... The whole establishment was lighted by electricity, generated by suction gas, and water was pumped by an electric motor" (*Impartial Reporter,* July 3, 1913, 8). Possibly Goodhand Pattison, whose personal generator provided electricity in Cloughjordan, was responsible for electricity at this Convention (Williams 1999, 202).

Irvine, age 50, delivered the Convention's closing message. Little did he (or anyone else) realize this would be the last Crocknacrieve Convention he would ever attend. Afterwards, on August 23, 1913, he departed from Liverpool, England, for New York, US, aboard the SS *Lusitania* on his ninth and last world tour. After he returned in 1914, Irvine was excommunicated from the sect he had founded, guided, directed and controlled for 17 years. *See* Chapter 23.

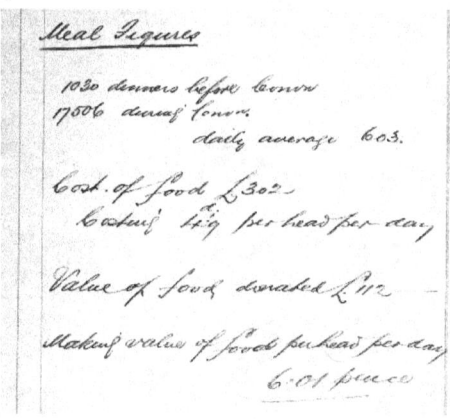

Crocknacrieve Meal Costs (1913)

1913: New Hymnal. "On Sunday last, a new hymnbook entitled *Hymns Old and New* made its appearance ... The *Go-Preacher Hymn Book* is no longer used" (*Impartial Reporter,* July 3, 1913, 8, *TTT*). *See* Chapter 38.

1914: A small-scale four-day Convention opened at Coolkill, Eglish, Dungannon, Co. Tyrone, Ireland, on James Richardson's place with about 400 attendees and lasted 4 days with a baptism (*Impartial Reporter,* July 9, 1914, 8, *TTT*).

1917–1922: Irish Conventions. Due to the War, likely compounded by the accompanying shortages and rationing, no Conventions were held in 1917 and 1918. Instead, many small Special Meetings took place. According to an "Irish List of Early Conventions," in 1919, Conventions were held in a tent on McKeekin's property at Knock, Belfast, and also at Scarva, Co. Monaghan on Bothwell's property during 1919–1921. In

1922, a large Convention was held in Eglish, Co. Tyrone; another at Derrybard, Co. Tyrone; and one at Downpatrick, Co. Down.

1920: Final Crocknacrieve Convention. The last Convention held at Crocknacrieve took place in 1920. The owners, John and Sara West, moved nearby to a larger place called *Rossahilly* in 1921. Succeeding Co. Fermanagh Conventions from 1923 to 1928 were held nearby at Mullaghmeen, Ballinamallard, the home owned by William and Harriett West, where John and William West were born and raised. When William died in 1935, his son Harry, age 17, inherited Mullaghmeen.

John and William West's sister, Emily, married William Hamilton Roberts. One of their eight children was Dr. Patricia Roberts (1919–2014), who published a biography of Edward Cooney and three more books about his followers known as *Cooneyites*. *See* Appendix D.

New Owners of Crocknacrieve. Simon Christopher and Penelope "Penny" (Barton) Loane purchased Crocknacrieve. Loane, a cattle dealer, was born October 22, 1883, and died March 1, 1940. On August 27, 1918, he married former Sister Worker Mildred Penelope "Penny" Matilda Barton, born April 25, 1885, in Irvinestown, Co. Fermanagh, Ireland, who died August 6, 1971.

Penny left the 2x2 Sect, and their four sons were not raised in the faith. Their son, Warren Loane, who inherited the property in 1940, died in 2007; presumably, his son is the current owner. In 2004, the Loanes graciously invited my husband and me for a visit on our trip to Ireland. We enjoyed the memories they shared and especially the interesting tour around their property.

Warren and Anne Loane, Crocknacrieve Owners, with Cherie Kropp-Ehrig
(2004)

Penny was the eighth child, and her sister Susannah "Susie" Cecil Grace was the ninth child, of Capt. Charles Robert and Henrietta Martha Mervyn (Richardson) Barton, members of the landed gentry class. The Bartons of The Waterfoot in Pettigo, Co. Fermanagh, have a long history in Ireland, England and France. It has been said that the Barton girls played with Queen Victoria's children. Susie Barton remained in the Work until she died on March 2, 1968. No one else in the Barton family adopted the 2x2 faith. *See* website *ThePeerage.com.*

First Conventions Outside of Ireland: 1906–1911
North America

1906: First Convention in North America. Leaving San Francisco after the earthquake on April 18, 1906, Irvine began his first trip down the California Coast to Paso Robles where the first US Convention was held on James and Ina Hill's ranch (to Dunbars, Oct. 13, 1920, *TTT*). The Convention was small.

1906: Philadelphia, Pennsylvania, US. The first Eastern US Convention assembled in August 1906 in Philadelphia. A second followed in 1907.

1907: Ina Hill reminisced, "must have been in April 1907, the time the river flooded, and Pa got in a boat and tried to get to the other side to get the preachers as they were at McPhail's and the crowd all at our place. William Irvine got in the boat, and it tipped over and he almost drowned ... the Workers were Willie Jamieson, Irvine Weir, William Irvine, and (Jack Carroll?). Later on, Florence Langworthy, Elisabeth Jamieson and Edie Wier [Weir] came" (Hanson 1987, 9).

In "Account of the Spread of the Gospel in the Early Days in California" James Bone gave the year of the flood as 1909, rather than 1907. "The Workers went to Paso Robles and were there for the Convention in 1909 on the Jim Hill place ... during that Convention a flash flood came down the river and separated the Workers from the rest of the people as they were staying at McPhail's ... across the river. Jim Hill and some others made a boat, and Jim Hill and ***another man*** got into it to bring the Workers across the river. The boat upset in the current and ***the other man*** got hold of a tree. They threw a rope to him and pulled him back" (1975, *TTT*). Note: The ***other man*** was Irvine.

The second California Convention was held six months later in December 1907 at San Luis Obispo; Jack Carroll attended (McPhail n.d., Early California, *TTT*).

1907: Pittsburgh, Pennsylvania, US. The list of attendees at this Convention shows a total of 80 Workers in attendance: 48 men (including Irvine), 30 women, plus one married Worker couple, Mr. and

Mrs. Matt Wilson. One list for Pittsburgh appears to be mislabeled "1907 Pittsburgh *and Chicago.*"

The first Midwest Convention was held in Chicago, Illinois, in October 1907. About 65 people attended, including 38 Workers (Walker 1979, *TTT*). From this Convention, "On October 21, 1907, eight of us took that first train journey together: you [George Beattie] and Tom Grooms to Alabama; Willie Clelland and Tom Clarke to Tennessee; and John Burns and I [Alfred Magowan] to Kentucky" (Magowan, Sept. 28, 1954, in author's possession). Also in 1907, first Conventions took place at Petersburg, Nebraska, and Janesville, Wisconsin.

1908: Additional US Conventions. Five more states held their first Conventions: Niagara, New York; Minneapolis, Minnesota; Zanesville, Ohio; Brooklyn, Maryland; and Sunshine, Michigan. Overseer Eldon Tenniswood recalled, "There was a Convention in Sunshine on Dad and Mother's farm. That year, 1908, the Workers dug a well on Grandpa Tenniswood's farm to provide plenty of water for the Convention" (1981).

The 1908 Brooklyn, Maryland Convention was held on the farm of James E. Hawkins, Sr. While the members slept nearby, two large tents of the **Irvinites** were set on fire after midnight, and a nearby house containing provisions was partially destroyed by a mob of men. "Hardly had the flames appeared when four of the **Irvinites** dashed up to the place and were met by the attacking party with pistols ... The principal cause of the trouble, it is thought, was the vigorous preaching of the **Irvinites,** in which they denounced the people of the town generally ... founder Irvine, it is alleged, used some offensive language toward the women of Brooklyn" (*Washington Post*, Sept. 17, 1908, *TTT*; *Washington Times,* Sept. 16, 1908, *TTT*). Notice: As early as 1908, the sect was called *Irvinites,* an eponym of their founder's name.

1911: Washington, US Convention. The first Convention on the Silvernail farmstead at Milltown, Washington, was small. "Meetings were held in the barn in the center isle between the cow and horse stalls ... Conventions have been held continuously at Milltown since 1911 until the present time ... Milltown Convention may have one of the longest tenures on one site under one family name" (Silvernail 1984, *TTT*).

1911: Kentucky, US Convention. The 1911 *Central Record* newspaper printed an article about the Lancaster, Kentucky Convention. A photograph of the 1912 Convention there shows Irvine, Cooney, George Walker, Alfred Magowan and others.

1913: Michigan, US Convention. The Carsonville, Michigan Convention, first held in 1913, holds third place for the oldest ongoing Convention worldwide.

No conventions are held in Nevada, Maryland or West Virginia. Friends living in the small New England states of Maine, Rhode Island, Connecticut, Delaware or Vermont usually attend the New Hampshire Convention. Many US states and countries have multiple Conventions.

1906: First Three Canadian Conventions. In a rented house and tent, the Toronto, Ontario Convention assembled in June 1906. The Workers List showed 63 Workers: 37 men (including Irvine), 24 women and one married Worker couple. In November 1906, Workers held a Convention in Minnedosa, Manitoba; another was held in 1908 in Halifax, Nova Scotia. "Mr. William Irvine, the leader of the organization, has set sail for [North] America and is to open a Convention in Halifax on Sunday 16th" (*Impartial Reporter,* Aug. 13, 1908, *TTT*).

Leaders Ventured Abroad

1909–1912: Edward Cooney's Trips Abroad. Cooney's four trips to North America were made in 1909, 1910, 1911 and 1912. Each year he returned to Ireland in time for the annual July Convention at Crocknacrieve. The passenger lists showed his occupation as evangelist.

1907–1913: William Irvine's Trips Abroad. Except for two years, Irvine went on a worldwide Convention speaking tour every year until 1913. "Mr. William Irvine, the leader of the movement, has set sail for America ... Altogether he has to attend nine Conventions before he returns to Crocknacrieve again next year" (*Impartial Reporter,* Aug. 13, 1908, *TTT*). *See* Ancestry.com for ship records.

Since he was abroad most of the year, Irvine did not have an assigned preaching field nor did a Co-worker accompany him. He was primarily a Convention speaker; yet most of the Friends abroad were not aware he was their founder and the supreme leader; it was not publicized. He was sometimes introduced as "an Elder Brother from the British Isles." No record for Irvine was found in the 1910 Ireland or Scotland Census records; perhaps, he was abroad at the time.

Deaths of First Workers

1907: On May 15, 1907, Brother Worker James "Jim" Hodgins, from Queens County, Ireland, aged 23, died of tuberculosis and was buried in the Greytown Public Cemetery, South Wairarapa, New Zealand. From the time the sect began, Jim was the first Worker to die; he was also the first to die of those shown on the 1905 Workers List.

The first Sister Worker to die was Rebecca Dane, cause of death unknown. She entered the Work in September 1904, went to America to preach in September 1906, died in Liverpool, England, on July 5, 1907, aged 28, and was buried in West Derby Cemetery, England.

1908: Death of First US Workers. Abbie Barton, from Massachusetts, professed through Jack Carroll and Hugh Matthews in 1904. She entered the Work in October 1907 and began preaching with Agnes Hutchison in West Virginia. Four months later, Barton was stricken with typhoid and died in February 1908, aged 27. Her tombstone states, "She hath done what she could 1880–1908." US Brother Worker Harry Cross died on July 2, 1908, from a spider bite obtained while sleeping in a haystack. He was buried in Dayton, Washington. Tom Purves, from Scotland, entered the work in 1905, died, aged 24, of tuberculosis in 1911 in Riverside, California.

Two New Publications about Cooneyites

1910: Pamphlet Published. *The Impartial Reporter* was owned and operated by the Trimble family from 1825 to 2006. When the 2x2 Sect began making headlines, the proprietor was William Copeland Trimble (aka W.C.T.). This newspaper carried a series of articles about the Workers, pursuing the question: Did they, in their doctrines and practices, follow what they called "the Jesus Way"? Following readers' suggestions that these articles be preserved, the author, W. C. Trimble, published a pamphlet titled *The Tramp or Go-Preachers* (1910, *TTT*).

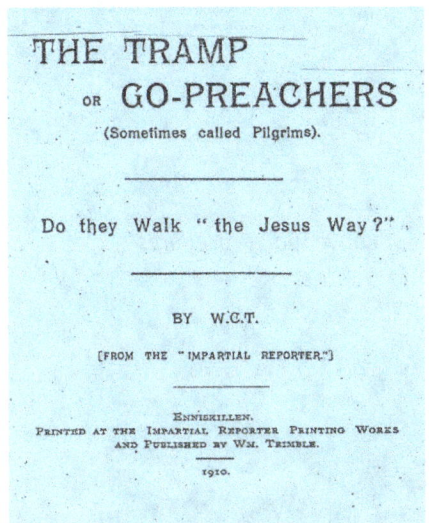
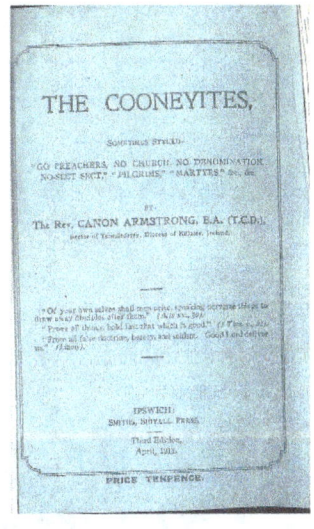

Perhaps W. C. Trimble's avid interest in Irvine's new sect was sparked when some of his family became involved. William Copeland (1851–1941) and Letitia Jane (Weir) Trimble (1854–1892) were married in Dublin on October 3, 1881, and had five children. Two of their relatives were connected to the new sect. Mrs. Trimble's brother was

William Weir in Dublin (a prominent 2x2 Sect family). Also, their son, Ernest Lionel Delmege Trimble, was married to his first cousin, Susan Weir, daughter of William Weir. Susan never embraced the faith of her parents.

1910: Second Publication. A pamphlet titled *The Cooneyites or Dippers* by Rev. S. C. Canon Armstrong was printed and advertised in the *Nenagh Guardian* newspaper as "a plain refutation of the principle errors of the Go-Preachers." The book preface stated: "Our people should be warned against the pernicious teaching of these so-called Pilgrims, who come amongst us ... seeking to draw away disciples after them. While the writer realizes his treatment of the subject to be very inadequate, he yet hopes it may serve this purpose. The Cooneyites openly avow that their object is to uproot and destroy the church ... and to set up their own system" (1910, *TTT*).

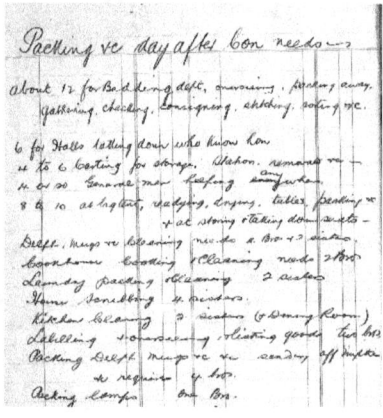

1913 Notebook "Records of Convention Procedures"

Truck load of ticks (straw-filled mattresses)
Every year the ticks were filled with fresh hay and placed in dormitories
Carsonville, Michigan, US Convention

22

1906–1914 – Recourse Through Court

White-Slave Trafficking. There was a worldwide increase in awareness regarding the phenomenon of trafficking in human beings in the early twentieth century. *White slavery* hysteria developed. Journalists fueled the craze with sensational stories of innocent girls kidnapped off the streets, smuggled out of the country and forced to work in brothels. White-slave trafficking found its way into novels and films, e.g. the 1911 movie, *A Victim of the Mormons*.

The white-slave trafficking situation became a public concern and drew intense interest and high emotions. It led to the International Agreement for the Suppression of White-Slave Traffic being adopted in May 1904, by 13 Western European States. Six years later in 1910, the US adopted the White-Slave Traffic Agreement, better known as the Mann Act.

Alice Pipe's Mission. The largest town and county seat in Suffolk Co., England, is Ipswich, where the regional newspaper, the *East Anglian Daily Times,* was based.

After arriving in Suffolk in March 1904, Sister Worker Alice Pipe contacted W. D. Wilson, Chairman of the School Board, requesting permission to use the Cretingham, East Suffolk schoolroom for a mission. Wilson allowed it—although he later bitterly regretted doing so. The Gospel Mission was successful. Afterwards, William Irvine arrived to baptize the new converts.

W. D. Wilson. Agriculture has been a major economic activity in Suffolk Co. since the eighteenth century. The owner of Rookery Farm in Cretingham, Framlingham, East Suffolk, was a prosperous farmer in good standing in the community named William Dennis Wilson. He was "the largest farmer in the whole of Suffolk and farms some thousands of acres ... he is known as a great dealer in pigs, always having near two thousand fattening for market ... and as touching any matter agricultural, Mr. Wilson is certainly the great authority in the countryside" (*People,* July 14, 1912, *TTT*).

Another newspaper observed, "Mr. Wilson's wife is alive, as are his seven children: Edward 27; Emily 26; William Frederick 25; Ellie

Elizabeth 24; Edith 23; John 22; and Minnie 14" (*Lloyd's Weekly,* Feb. 3, 1907, *TTT*).

W. D. Wilson attended Alice Pipe's first Gospel Meeting and afterwards remarked that he "found things queer." The second Meeting he pronounced *diabolical*. He claimed he heard "recruiting for Chinese white-slave traffic" in the third Meeting. Wilson directed the Secretary of the East Suffolk Co. Council Schools at Ipswich to issue warnings to all the school managers in his jurisdiction and not to allow any evangelists to use schoolrooms without satisfactory references.

1906: Workers Accused of White-Slave Trafficking. W. D. Wilson mounted a crusade wherein he harassed the Workers from 1906 through 1913. According to him, the Workers, "began their mysterious work in Cretingham about three years ago. First of all, came a pretty girl—Alice Pipe by name. She visited many houses in the district and telling how she came as the forerunner of a marvellous mission, made eyes at the young men and said sweet things to the young women with encouraging results. A hard-faced Scotsman followed in about nine months. He was William Irwin [Irvine], the founder of the Tramps and Chief Baptiser. Alice, with her sweet voice and wily ways, did the converting, and William ... completed the business" (*Morning Leader,* June 9, 1906, *TTT*).

Alice Pipe related, "I knew the Wilsons ... On my return from one of the Conventions, I brought back May Carroll. We two started Work at Monk Soham—not far from Cretingham. A short time afterwards, Miss Carroll left, and a girl named Annie Smith took her place. She too departed, and I was joined by Lizzie Sergent [Sargent]. Afterwards the work in Cretingham was taken up by Annie Smith" (*Lloyd's Weekly,* Feb. 3, 1907, *TTT*).

In a letter to "My dear Brother," Pipe explained, "[Wilson] came along to a village in which we were preaching, and after using very bad language, he took a stone and broke our windows. We had to pay £6 to get them repaired. He broke Sam Cole's windows and damaged the wooden hall belonging to W. McClung, but both was taken before the Magistrates and he had to make right" (Oct. 19, 1913, *TTT*).

A London newspaper ran an article that claimed, "Some 36 persons, mostly girls, have been sent away by these people, ostensibly for missionary purposes to foreign countries, and that requests for information as to their whereabouts, and the conditions under which they are living have been refused." The readers were warned of the danger of some becoming victims of circumstances and were advised not to encourage or assist the 'No Sect Missionaries' " (*Lloyd's Weekly,* Jan. 27, 1907, *TTT*).

Edith "Edie" Easy, the schoolteacher in the village of Brundish, Suffolk Co., was converted. Born in 1885, she professed and entered the work in 1905. After attending the 1905 Belfast Convention, she announced to her parents that she was going to America to preach. Her father contacted Edward Cooney and forbade him to send his daughter, a minor age 20, out of the UK. Undeterred, Easy preached in the UK until she turned 21. She then bid her parents farewell and sailed away to South Africa (*Lloyd's Weekly,* Jan. 27, 1907, *TTT*).

In the Suffolk area, an appeal was published in the June 12, 1906, *Morning Leader,* signed by 21 ministers. An extract in the publication *Ideas,* titled "Missing Converts" stated:

> They began preaching in the villages and very soon their enthusiasm and the novelty of their mission began to gather in converts. A large farmer's two daughters and one of his sons were converted by the Cooneyites and gave up their homes to join the sect. They simply disappeared, and the Cooneyite evangelists refused to give any information as to their whereabouts. At the same time, other young people began to disappear from Suffolk homes, and their parents were frantic with grief.
>
> The ... farmer ... wild with grief and anger ... commenced a bitter campaign against the Cooneyites ... He covered the dead walls round Debenham ... with posters setting forth his view of their conduct and morals. He followed them across the county to Sudbury in West Suffolk and roused a crowd of 3,000 people who drove the Go-Preachers out of the town. He gradually extended his campaign to other parts of England ... He wrote letters to newspapers and printed handbills and posters that he exhibited wherever he could find a sympathizer. (July 13, 1917, *TTT*)

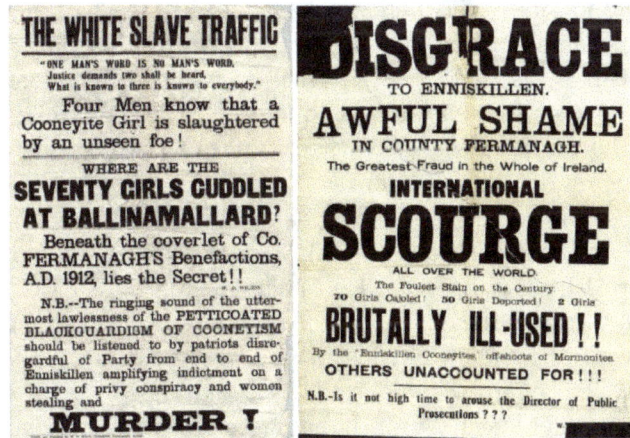

Examples of propaganda circulars W. D. Wilson distributed

Indignant at Wilson's allegations and the negative press the Workers were receiving, John Coles, father of Sister Worker Lizzie Coles, gave an interview to a London reporter in 1906. "Three years ago ... Mr. Irwin [Irvine], Mr. Cooney and five others held Meetings at my mission hall under the auspices of the London City Mission." His daughter, Lizzie, had professed in 1898 in this mission, and entered the Work in 1903. Mr. Coles provided evidence that his daughter was alive and well in America and vouched for the integrity of both Edward Cooney and William Irvine (*Morning Leader,* June 15, 1906, *TTT*).

Irvine informed a reporter, "No one is ever coerced into becoming a preacher. For that very reason I don't see how it would be possible to interfere with a man or a woman who feels the call so strongly as to leave home ... At the Convention held annually in Belfast, Brothers and Sisters volunteer for the Work in the Colonies, which is very much the same as the Work here [England]" (*Lloyd's Weekly,* Feb. 3, 1907, *TTT*).

In May or June 1906, Wilson McClung and his wife, a married pair of Workers, began holding missions in the Ipswich area in a movable wooden hall about 20 miles from Wilson's home (*Morning Leader,* June 11, 1906, *TTT*). They suspended their mission in July 1906 to attend the Belfast Convention.

W. D. Wilson's Children. Making matters worse for W. D. Wilson, three of his seven children entered the Work and those still living at home were "in full sympathy with the Go-Preachers." After the July 1906 Belfast Convention, Ellie (age 24–25) notified her parents, "Am not coming home. You know my intentions for being here, and I must seek to go on and be about my heavenly Father's business."

All the Wilson children had received an inheritance. "Under the will of their grandfather, who died about 14 years ago, each of Mr. Wilson's children became entitled to a sum of £500, on coming of age" (*Lloyd's Weekly,* Feb. 3, 1907, *TTT*). Both Willie and Ellie gave or loaned their £500 inheritance to their brother, John, to purchase a farm when they entered the Work. Conceivably, their father feared his children might be conned out of their inheritance.

Perhaps Wilson feared his eldest daughter, Ellie, would follow other Workers who had gone abroad—he was determined to find her and prevent this from happening. He finally located her at the home of Robert McClung in Belfast. Fully intending to take Ellie home with him, Wilson went to McClung's twice, where he used "some very abusive language." Police removed him from the premises.

Nor was a detective Wilson hired successful in persuading Ellie to return home. He was followed by two women, one employed by a newspaper, who went to visit Ellie and investigate her father's claim that his underage daughter had been stolen from his home and was being used as a servant. Subsequently, several newspapers carried a sensationalized, exaggerated report of these events, including some false information. Robert McClung's solicitor contacted the newspaper; they published a full apology and admitted the report was groundless (*Lloyd's Weekly,* Dec. 9, 1906, 15, *TTT*).

On November 26, 1906, on behalf of many aggrieved parents, Wilson signed a document titled "New Emigration Scheme," as Chairman of the School Board and Chairman of the Parish Meeting in Cretingham. It was distributed to 73 bishops of the Church of England, including the Primate of all the Church of Ireland clergymen in Belfast, and published in the December 6, 1906, *Stowmarket News,* and in the June 22, 1907, *Free Press* of Dublin, Wexford and Waterford.

According to W. D. Wilson, McClung had "bamboozled" several people. On December 3, 1906, Wilson took matters into his own hands and drove McClungs out of Stowmarket, Suffolk Co. by maliciously destroying McClung's mission hall, organ and contents.

> Before a crowded court at Ipswich on Thursday, William Dennis Wilson … was charged with willfully damaging the mission hall … The evidence showed that about three weeks ago he obtained two crowbars from a blacksmith, saying he wanted to smash the mission hall in question, and that he wanted the work of destruction to be effectively done. Doors were wrenched off, all the windows broken, and the organ knocked to pieces … The Bench fined Wilson £1 with £4 19s 6d damage and £2 3s costs in all, or one month's imprisonment. (Lloyd's Weekly, Dec. 23, 1906, *TTT*)

On December 7, 1906, Ellie Wilson wrote her parents, "I expect to be soon leaving here to start a mission with another Worker. Will let you know my address, so you needn't trouble yourself about me. When I see an opportunity, I hope to come home for a few days to see you all, although it will not be at Christmas." Her father was not pacified.

At this time, it was reported that the Go-Preachers "have spread to nearly every shire [county] in England, to Scotland, Australia, Canada and most of the English Colonies, whilst there are not less than 120 of the Go-Preachers at Work in the United States" (*Irish Independent,* Aug. 24, 1907, *TTT*).

~~~~~

1907, September 23: Enniskillen Town Hall Meeting. Since the Workers' largest Convention was held every July at Crocknacrieve, W. D. Wilson assumed it was their headquarters. He took his grievances and accusations across the sea to that community, where he held a lively meeting in the Enniskillen Town Hall.

Seated in the front row were several of the Friends and Workers, including John West, William West, William Carroll, Tom Betty, Edward Cooney and others. Wilson had no supporters on the platform. He read extracts from one of his pamphlets relating to his fears the Workers were recruiting young girls to leave their parents' homes and shipping them to China, South Africa and other foreign lands for white-slave trafficking purposes (*Impartial Reporter*, Oct. 3, 1907, *TTT*).

William West rose and declared that no person should take Wilson's comments seriously; that he had been going about making foul and filthy charges of women-stealing against a body of respectable people because his two daughters and a son had volunteered to be preachers in the sect in Ireland. He asked Wilson to provide the name of a single person he could prove was guilty of the charges.

John West rose and stated it was only reasonable when a man comes all the way from Suffolk, England, and mounts a platform to address an audience, that he should come with facts and not with insinuations; that it was only fair to provide the names of those Wilson claimed were lost in a harem in China.

Wilson refused to provide any names or addresses; instead, he asked where various girls were presently located. His questions were answered with, "In Philadelphia; in New Zealand; in South Africa," etc.

After receiving no name of the person/s who had supposedly stolen girls, the West brothers announced they were leaving. Wilson urged them not to be in a hurry—to stay and thresh out this matter, as he had come several hundred miles to do so. West reiterated that Wilson made charges he had utterly failed to prove. Wilson then instructed loudly, "Keep the door blocked—don't let them out. Lock the doors." Resolutely, they departed (*Impartial Reporter*, Oct. 3, 1907, 8, *TTT*).

1908: At the 1908 Crocknacrieve Convention, Irvine mentioned that every member of Wilson's family was saved, except for two (perhaps Wilson and his wife) and called on Wilson's two daughters and son to speak" (*Impartial Reporter*, July 30, 1908, 8, *TTT*).

Wilson began sending abusive telegrams to Cooney and the West brothers, continued to publish placards, pamphlets and tracts, and harassed members of the sect to the point it unfairly damaged their relationships with their employers and/or customers.

W. D. Wilson Taken to Court. It appeared that strong action was necessary to silence Wilson. Between 1910 and 1913, eight lawsuits were filed by various sect members in England and Ireland against

W. D. Wilson for distributing libelous propaganda. Two suits involved Cooney. No suits were filed by Irvine.

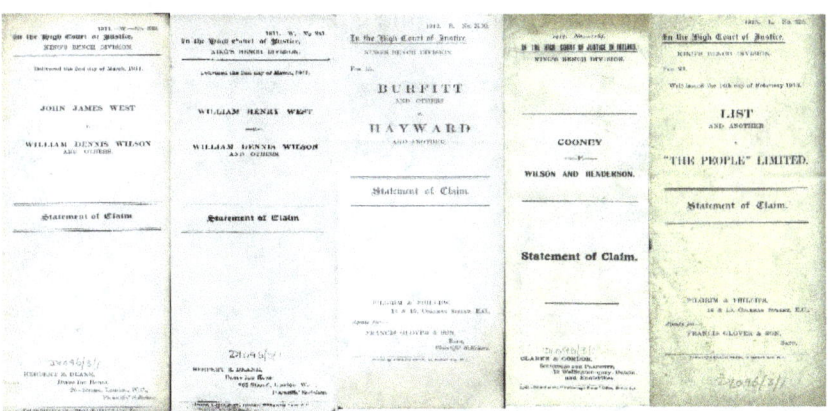

Suits filed by 2x2s for White-Slave Trafficking libel

The first suit was filed in 1910 by English merchant Charles Thomas Partridge. It was settled out of court with Wilson publishing a public apology in the newspaper and paying Partridge's legal costs.

Four suits were filed in 1911 by plaintiffs John and William West of Ireland. When Wilson's allegations put their livelihood at risk, it was reported that "the Messrs. West brought this action simply and solely for the purpose of vindicating their own character and that of the religious body to which they belong" (*Fermanagh Times,* Nov. 1911, *TTT*). The suits were settled out of court with Wilson paying damages, all costs, withdrawing all his assertions and publishing a full apology.

Another libel suit was filed in 1912 by Convention owner Joseph Burfitt of Bruton, Somerset Co., England, against Rev. D. L. Hayward, Vicar of Bruton. During the Convention, Hayward was responsible for distributing some of Wilson's libelous propaganda claiming Burfitt was engaged in white-slave trafficking under the cloak of religion. The jury awarded Burfitt damages.

In 1913, Cooney and Convention ground owner Ernest Walter List of Debenham, England, jointly filed a libel suit after *the People of London,* a weekly UK newspaper with a large circulation, printed an article on July 14, 1912, containing false allegations accusing Workers of white-slave trafficking (1912, *TTT*).

Cooney generated volumes of mostly handwritten documents for these cases. They included worldwide lists of Worker locations after the 1912–1913 Conventions, scores of testimonial letters from UK Sister Workers laboring abroad, Convention expenditure lists and copies of checks signed by Workers Bill Carroll and Willie Hughes. In 2014, my husband and I visited the Public Record Office of Northern Ireland (PRONI). We manually reviewed these original documents and Cooney and Irvine's written statements for the Court.

Cherie Kropp-Ehrig at entrance to PRONI, Belfast, N. Ireland (2004)

List and Cooney v *The People* Ltd was settled in court on December 11, 1913: "His Lordship ... said the defendants were satisfied that with regard to Mr. List and Mr. Cooney, there were no grounds for the charges that they led a movement which led, designed or otherwise, to the kind of immorality suggested, and that having been satisfied that Mr. List's and Mr. Cooney's characters were perfectly clear, they consented to judgment in the action in accordance with the terms stated" (*Impartial Reporter,* Dec. 18, 1913, *TTT*). Judgment was entered for the plaintiffs for £100 damages and £50 costs.

During court proceedings, Judge Justice Darling asked Cooney, while he was under oath: "Were you the founder of this sect?" Cooney replied: "No, William Irvine was the first, about 16 years ago. I cast in my lot with him as a fellow-preacher and preached a good deal in the North of Ireland. I recognise the name, but others have nicknamed us 'The Cooneyites.' I do not like it myself" (*Impartial Reporter,* Dec. 18, 1913, *TTT*).

NOTE: Two newspapers summarized the Wilson saga. The July 14, 1912, *People of London*, provided the basis of Cooney and List's lawsuit and gave a general outline of events leading up to it. The July 13, 1917, *Ideas* (a periodical) summarized the previous years. *See* more details and read Irvine and Cooney's statements for these cases on the website *TellingTheTruth.info* in History Articles, Court Cases.

1912–1913: W. D. Wilson's harassment was not restricted to the British Isles—it extended across the ocean to Canada to Newfoundland, New Brunswick and Nova Scotia, where newspaper articles hindered the progress of Workers and nearly prevented some converts from being baptized (Burgess, 1915, *TTT*). Also, various US newspapers (South Carolina, Tennessee) reprinted reports from UK newspapers.

W. D. Wilson's son, William Frederick Wilson, wrote to a Napan, New Brunswick, Canada, newspaper in 1912, "At present, they [his sisters] are all four living in this village [Cretingham, Suffolk Co., England]. One was out preaching in the same scriptural way as the two who are in your village but returned to try to stop her father from spreading such evil reports. Another was away for health reasons. Those two are now living with my brother, as does another who has not been away. The other is also at home" (March 5, 1912, *TTT;* some of Wilson's children did not continue in the Work).

1914: During WWI, W. D. Wilson fell on hard times and failed to pay his settlements. Cooney filed a judgment enforcement claim. In March 1915, a summons was issued, and a writ rendered against Wilson for non-payment for £191:1:9. Documents indicate that by April 10, 1915, he had paid all but £6:15:5.

1912: November Parliamentary Investigation. W. D. Wilson's white-slavery accusations and court cases attracted sufficient negative publicity that it generated an Oral Question in the UK House of Commons session in 1912. The Rt. Hon. A. Birrell, K.C., M.P. and the Chief Secretary and Keeper of the Privy Seal for Ireland replied: "The police inform me that there is no truth in the statement that Enniskillen is a centre of the White-Slave Traffic" (*Parliamentary Debates, 1912*, Great Britain. Parliament, House of Commons, 10th vol. Session 1912, 2063–4, *TTT*).

Founder of Two by Two Sect, William Irvine (no date)

23

1914–1919 – Irvine Forced to Abdicate

William Irvine's Discontentment. In 1914, William Irvine, the founder and leader of an international religious movement for 17 years, was at the zenith of his power and influence, but he was not satisfied. To the Ritzmans, owners of the Fillmore California Convention grounds, Irvine recalled, "The very success of The Testimony never gave me any satisfaction, while to others it seemed to give them the very desire of their heart, and many of the most enthusiastic were only a weariness to my heart ... I felt for long that The Testimony was not my home or rest" (Oct. 10, 1920, *TTT*).

The Workers' Discontentment. The senior Workers were no longer naïve idealistic youngsters but were now men in their 30s and some approaching 40. They were no longer prepared to give Irvine their unquestioning obedience. He reprimanded the Workers in public and rarely praised them.

Irvine had favorites. In one of the Meetings at Rathmolyon, he gave out a list of his preferred Workers. Willie Clelland recalled, "Here's how he put it: 'I would rather have Willie Gill, George Walker, Joe Kerr and Eddie Cooney than all the others of you put together' " (Parker 1982, 34–35, Fn. 6). Resentment built up over the years. Not recognizing the changing circumstances, he failed to change his leadership style. His ideas were becoming more bizarre and his high opinion of himself was embarrassing. A showdown was inevitable.

In a fictional play inspired by real events titled *Outline of the History of a Peculiar People from 1900–1931*, Alfred Magowan presented in uncomplicated but striking detail the perspective of two visitors at the Crocknacrieve Convention:

> **First Voice:** There are a thousand people in the tent and not one of them dare resist his will. The men on the platform nod to everything he says, whether they like it or not, and when he turns to them for approval, they draw their faces into the appearance of a smile, knowing that their lives as preachers depend on his favor.
>
> **Second Voice:** How did he get this power over them?

First Voice: He is a strong man by nature and used to be a mine boss, and never allowed his will to be resisted. He brought the same spirit into this work and uses the same methods in dealing with these people.
Second Voice: Do you think they will ever rebel and throw off his yoke?
First Voice: They are inwardly rebelling now, especially those who sit on the platform with him, but at the present time they can do nothing because he is master of the situation in every way ... The others are only poor echoes of his voice and in his presence are not able to throw off the incubus of fear that almost paralyzes them. (1931, 11–12, *TTT*)

Irvine's Strange Preaching. Some of Irvine's messages had been noticed for their bizarre, belligerent and even apocalyptic content. At the first South Australian Convention held at Woodside in 1910, "Wilson McClung hung his head when William spoke. This impression was further confirmed the following year at the 1911 Convention which William Irvine again attended" (Bethel Mission 1910, *TTT*). Reportedly, at the 1911 or 1912 Warrandyte Convention in Victoria, Australia, Irvine accused the entire congregation of having a bad spirit and sent them home early.

Alfred Magowan recalled, "What I especially remember about the Conventions that year [1913] was the oddness of his [Irvine's] preaching ... he spoke about stars as other worlds and held before us the strange possibility of going to them and doing for them the work of saviours as Jesus had done for this one!" (to Cooney, 1953, *TTT*).

From Jack Stancliff's account: "William Irvine made the statement to Uncle Willie [Jamieson] and Jack Carroll that he felt like he had gotten beyond the place of needing to pray; and it was then they realized that he had strayed from the lowly way" (Early History of the Gospel in Bakersfield, California 2009, *TTT*).

In 1913, Hardie was concerned about the effect Irvine's strange, new ideas might have at the Woodside, South Australia Convention. He decided to curtail his influence by not allowing him to appear or speak in the Meetings. Irvine stayed inside the farmhouse. Meanwhile, worldwide, the Senior Workers colluded together and provided Irvine with no further opportunities to air his strange ideas in their territories by refusing to allow him to speak at their Conventions.

According to Jack Carroll, Irvine "is also under the delusion that the 'day of grace ended in August 1914,' and that since that date 'the voice of God has not been heard in any Meeting on Earth.' This means that, according to him, none have been truly born again during the last four and a half years, and that the labor of all the Workers in every field has been utterly in vain. We believe on the contrary, that during the last four and one-half years, in spite of greater difficulties than ever before, men and women were as truly born of God as in all the years before" (to Brother or Sister, April 16, 1919, *TTT*).

Irvine's newfound "revelation" put the Workers' way of life at risk. If followed, they stood to lose power, position, influence and careers. This was not a gamble they were willing to take, especially after they had worked so hard to get where they were.

The Usurpation

1914: World War I. At the beginning of the twentieth century, the British Empire covered over 11 million square miles of territory, making it the largest empire ever known. The First World War officially began after the assassination of Archduke Franz Ferdinand, the Austro-Hungarian heir. The British Empire, which included all of Ireland at the time, joined WWI on August 4, 1914.

1913–1914: Irvine Forced to Step Down. July 1914 saw the beginning of the first World War. It also saw the end of William Irvine's leadership and rule. Irvine had been the leader of what he called *a great experiment* for 17 years: from age 34 to 51, from 1897 to 1914. As he did when he was a colliery supervisor, he also ruled over the Workers under him with an iron rod. In 1914, his Senior Workers galvanized a mutiny against him and refused to submit to his leadership any longer (J. Carroll to My Brother or Sister, April 16, 1919, *TTT*).

Reportedly, Bill Carroll delivered the ultimatum and supplied Irvine with his fare back to the UK. After he returned from his world tour in the summer of 1914, Willie Gill and Edward Cooney informed him of his status change before the Irish Conventions started.

Although forced out of leadership, Irvine was not expelled from the sect. The Senior Workers offered him the position of an ordinary Worker or that of a Friend; Irvine refused both and withdrew. From 1914 to 1918, the Workers warily continued to count Irvine as a Brother who was out of service. It would be 10 years later, in 1924, before the divorce was made official.

Irvine railed, "Those who thought I ceased to be their Father in the Gospel and became their Brother, as so many tried to make out ... surely are their own condemners ... Their attempts to prove that I should not have a right to overlooking of the whole Ark is clear evidence of where they were" (to Edwards, July 6, 1921, *TTT*).

Irvine's "sons of the Gospel" carried on without him. At the 1914 Coolkill, Eglish, Ireland Convention, "Mr. Edward Cooney and Mr. Robert Humphreys, two Fermanagh men, were the leaders at this Convention. Mr. Wm. Irvine is in County Meath. His health is stated not to be as good as usual" (*Impartial Reporter*, July 9, 1914).

Irvine inconsistently provided three different months in 1914 for when he was removed from leadership: April, August and September. He stated, "Six years ago in April, I was rejected, and despised and cast out to die, my birthright divided among my children and enemies" (to William Carroll, June 29, 1920, *TTT*). He reminded Cooney, "Tenth August 1914, the day of my rejection by Willie Gill and you, and you will long remember it to your sorrow" (Aug. 19, 1923, *TTT*). In other letters, he also gave the month of September for his ousting (to Dunbars, Oct. 13, 1920, *TTT*; to Percy Abbott, Oct. 3, 1930, *TTT*). (Recall that he supplied three different years for when he was put out of the Faith Mission in Chapter 8).

Why Irvine Was Removed as Leader. The four reasons most often provided for Irvine's rejection are: (1) he was guilty of womanizing or immorality; (2) he became *"lifted up with pride"* (1 Tim. 3:6); (3) he "got on the wrong track" and was preaching false doctrine; and (4) he became mentally unbalanced. Perhaps it was a combination of these reasons, or something entirely different; regardless, he was demoted.

Reason 1: His Womanizing or Immorality. A recurrent, whispered rationale implied that Irvine's sexual improprieties led to him being rejected by his peers. Irvine revealed, "It was out of Christchurch, New Zealand, came The Scandal ... he [Eddie Cooney] read a letter to me written by a dog outside The Testimony ... on this he slew his Brother" (to Loitz, Aug. 9, 1924, *TTT*). Irvine neither acknowledged nor denied such lapses in morality. In letters written soon after his dismissal, however, he frequently referred to some unspecified *scandal* and *sins of the flesh*. He countered, "I had many helpers of all kinds, was much loved and over loved by the sister" (to Friends, Dec. 24, 1921, *TTT*).

About the man they made their king, Irvine Weir compared Irvine's fall to King David, who gave into temptation and committed adultery with Bathsheba. Cooney compared Irvine to Samson who was a strong man until Delilah influenced him to put her wishes before God (Cooney 1947, Appendix D).

The Scandal possibly concerned Irvine's attendance at a New Zealand Convention in 1913. Whereas the 1912 Workers List included ten Sister Workers, the 1913 List had none. A story has circulated that the Brother Workers decided to continue the Work in New Zealand without any Sister Workers because they were concerned that women preachers were not scriptural. An alternative story is that the Sister Workers were sent away after the Convention until it was determined if any were pregnant by Irvine. That year the Brother Workers' missions produced no converts. No offspring was born. The Sister Workers were reinstated the following year, and six Sister Workers' names were on the 1914 Workers List.

In connection with Cooney's lawsuits against W. D. Wilson, William Hughes, Overseer of New Zealand, sent a letter to Willie Gill dated February 12, 1913, providing the location and occupation of all the New Zealand Sister Workers in 1913. The Sisters from the UK had been removed to Australia, and he explained the absences of the others.

It is doubtful the Scandal was the discovery of Irvine's illegitimate son, since Archibald was born in 1886 when Irvine was 23, long before his spiritual awakening in 1893. Archie was nine years old when his father entered the Faith Mission in 1895 and was likely residing with his grandparents. It would have been difficult over the long term for Irvine to hide the fact that he had an illegitimate son.

Reason 2: He Became *Lifted Up with Pride* (1 Tim. 3:6). Cooney thought the Living Witness Doctrine (LWD) was largely responsible for Irvine believing he was above and better than his Co-workers. Viewing Irvine's downfall as proof that the Living Witness Doctrine was false, Cooney declared, "In 1914, God showed me that the pre-eminence William [Irvine] got through this error [LWD] led ... to his ceasing to be the humble Brother among brethren that he was in the beginning" (to My Dear Sister, May 1930, Appendix D). This would not have been the view of most Senior Workers who continued to support the Living Witness Doctrine.

Alfred Magowan expressed grief over the harsh sentence Irvine received from the Workers:

> I have often wondered if those responsible for exalting our great man in preparation for his casting down, ever repented of giving him that lift which led to his degrading by them ... There are histories to all things; and as there were many things leading up to the final folly of King Saul, so was it also with our King William ... You saw it 40 years ago as violated morality. I have seen it in all the years since as God's answer to unchristian ambition. (to George Walker, Feb. 21, 1954, *TTT*)

> This is what I see: He [Irvine] became exalted and needed to be humbled. His 'sons in the Gospel' contributed to his spiritual delinquency by giving him a place that not even a pope might claim, making him the spiritual progenitor of all Christians in our time. They helped to seat him on that most unusual throne; and would have kept him on it all the days of his life if 'sin' had not intervened to cast him from it. (to Willie Hughes, 1957, *TTT*)

G. Pattison observed, "And the Workers now in fellowship with William Irvine ... increased in their attachment to and respect for their chief's leadership, possibly more so than was good for him or them ... when deference, loyalty, obedience, to leadership, etc. goes beyond a certain point, it is very apt to ... [be] bad for both sides making the leader a sort of demigod, filling him with notions of his own indispensability and importance and making of the led ones mere tools and chattels" (G. Pattison 1935, Leaders, *TTT*).

Reason 3: He Preached False Doctrine. According to this explanation, Irvine was demoted because he "got off on the wrong track," expounding a new doctrine, twisting the Scripture, making predictions and no longer being guided by the Holy Spirit. Jack Carroll explained, "For a number of years, it was becoming ... more painfully evident that the Lord was not with him; and in the last two years this has been made very manifest both in his manner of life, letters and foolish wresting of the Scriptures" (J. Carroll to Clyde, April 12, 1919, *TTT*).

"During the last few months, William Irvine has written many letters to Saints all over US and Canada," declared Jack Carroll, "urging them to sell their homes and farms and invest their money in railroads, fisheries, canneries, shipping, etc. He ... prophecies [*sic*] a worldwide drought and famine beginning August 1 of this year" (to Brother or Sister, April 16, 1919, *TTT*).

Irvine advised his correspondents to "encourage everybody to prepare by buying a little food for three months emergency when they can do it" (to Edwards and Kerrs, July 9, 1920, *TTT*). "Bury and hide. The less you have in men's eyes, the safer you will be" (to Fladungs, July 9, 1920, *TTT*).

George Walker was quoted in the September 26, 1921, *Indianapolis News*: "William Irvine, a Scotchman, one of the original leaders, is not now affiliated with this group because of a difference over the prophecies of the Revelations."

It was not until late 1918, over four years after he was demoted, that Irvine received his newfound understanding of the Book of Revelation. He recounted, "Toward Armistice Day [November 11, 1918] for about three weeks, night after night, His Spirit began to open up and put in order the truth we find in Revelation, and since that [time], has increased and become as simple as the gospel revealed in Alpha Jesus ... slowly, line upon line, the whole Message or program for the last days of the age has been unfolded" (to Andrew Walker, Feb. 21, 1929, *TTT*).

Reason 4: He Became Deranged, Unbalanced, Unfit to Lead. Some claimed Irvine had a mental breakdown, "went off the deep end," or as Jack Carroll concluded, was "delusional." No evidence has surfaced to confirm Irvine was ever under psychiatric care. Until the last few months before his death, he was able to live by himself and was well spoken of by those who knew him personally.

No documented proof has turned up to support any of the above reasons. However, in various letters, Irvine referred to a *sin* he had committed. For example, he proclaimed, "Every tongue, hand, or back that turned against me for *my sin* these past seven years must repent and find mercy—or perish to be tormented by the memory of their evil words" (to Willie Abercrombie, March 2, 1921, *TTT*; Worker on the 1905 Workers List). "Think of all I did for you and others in spite of *my sins*! ... Fancy the labor in building a house for God, and the pain of seeing it become a den of thieves!" (to John Hardie, Aug. 28, 1920, *TTT*; Worker on 1905 Workers List and Overseer of NSW Australia)

William Abercrombie (1877–1934) from Scotland
entered the Work in 1901, labored in US.

Under the circumstances, some Workers believed forcing Irvine out of leadership was the only course of action open to them. While the Workers were not proud of rejecting and ejecting their leader, some felt they were compelled to do so. A side benefit of Irvine's misbehavior provided a convenient opportunity for his "sons of the Gospel" to take the helm themselves.

Irvine's Reaction

Usurped, he became *persona non grata* and went from hero to zero. The *Thresher* was threshed out by his colleagues. When the very men he had appointed to fill powerful roles expropriated his kingdom, he did not surrender his position quietly. Severely wounded and hurt, Irvine suffered grief, pain and agony from the rejection and betrayal of his best friends. He viewed them as thieves who robbed him of his rightful place of pre-eminence in the sect. He reminded Cooney, "If you read the parables in Matthew 20–21, you will find I planted the vineyard, and it has fallen into the hands of wicked husbandmen" (March 2, 1923, *TTT*).

Stung with indignation, he protested, "While The Testimony claim I was only ONE of the twelve apostles … God surely has given them all their recompense in attempting to steal what God gave me. They put crowns on their own heads and shone by the reflections of what they got from me" (to Dunbars, Sept. 12, 1923, *TTT*).

To Brother Worker Fred Hanowell, he remarked, "Those who sat (*sic*) themselves up as leaders of The Testimony and use their horns of authority to hurt others and are claimed by men as leaders … [are] the greatest set of robbers in the world history—who thought they could rob me" (Aug. 17, 1921, *TTT*).

In his anger, Irvine railed to Bill Carroll, "Rejected of the seed in The Testimony … it was grasped greedily … The Jesus Way was stolen, confiscated, misappropriated … I was there to feel it … the victim of the heel bruisers; the theme of the scandal-mongers, and the dirty slut Sisters; the man without a parallel in history, whose back has been plowed upon [*see* Ps 129:3], who has been vanquished—no fear of him now!" (June 29, 1920, *TTT*).

Irvine disclosed to Ritzmans, "During these past years whether I have smoked or worked with my hands, gone to a picture show, or whatever I have been doing, it has only been to deaden the pain and relieve the suffering" (Oct. 10, 1920, *TTT*).

Magowan pondered, "The wonder is the man who, in his earlier years so bravely ran, was not driven raving mad when he surveyed his world of friendships falling round his head!" (1958, 27, *TTT*). "The men who crowned and throned him in their unchristian idolatry stripped and cast him down and drove him forth into the wilderness as one of the strangest scapegoats of the ages" (Parker 1982, 113).

1914–1918: First Schism and Exodus. For the first time in the Two by Two Sect history, a schism occurred. The group split into two factions when the First Exodus of Friends and Workers occurred. Irvine went his way with some of his loyal Friends and Workers, while the majority of the Friends and Workers continued as usual. Both the Workers and Irvine firmly believed they were the sole stewards of God's only right/true way.

24

The Workers Regroup – Erasing Irvine

Some, but not all, of the Workers remained certain their church was God's only right/true way and accepted the Senior Workers' decision to banish William Irvine as a righteous action. Now what? How should they continue without their leader? Who would take his place? His power had been removed, but his teachings remained. What beliefs and practices should they keep, change or jettison?

Originally, the question of how Irvine was saved, since he was converted through a Presbyterian preacher and not through a Living Witness, was resolved by making a special exception for him. They viewed him as a man God raised up for the particular mission of restoring, re-establishing or restarting the methods and ministry of the New Testament church. In turn, this made Irvine their *Father* or *Spiritual Adam*, through whom all successive Workers received their spiritual life. *Life begets life*. They had revered him as God's *Anointed One* and a prophet God raised up. This perspective was the underpinning for the claim that their belief system was God's only/right true church.

The Workers' Dilemma. Banishing Irvine was problematic. Assuming it was true that God had given Irvine a divine revelation to restore God's only right/true way, how could the Workers explain their audacity to arbitrarily separate Irvine from his God-directed mission?

Alfred Magowan summed up the Workers' predicament in a fictional drama inspired by real events, titled *Outline of the History of a Peculiar People from 1900–1931:*

> **Third Overseer:** He made us what we are. Except for him, I might still be what and where I was when he discovered me.
> **First Overseer:** It's going to upset our Family Tree!
> **Second Overseer:** You mean uproot it! Perhaps we made too much of him as our Father in the gospel. I begin to think I was right before I met him.
> **Third Overseer:** Fathers sometimes go wrong without ceasing to be fathers.
> **First Overseer:** Yes, but spiritual fathers are different. When they fall

away, they carry away the whole ground of relationship with them.
Second Overseer: Do you think then that we should give up the
Foundation of Teaching because he is not what he used to be?
First Overseer: We can still refer to the time we met him and the
necessity of genealogy, without committing ourselves any further.
Third Overseer But supposing somebody asks us who our spiritual
Father was and where he is now?
Second Overseer: In that case, it would be wise to change the subject!
(1931, 16–17, *TTT*)

Dispensing with William Irvine.

Irvine's downfall and forced departure was a colossal *fly in their
ointment.* What justification could they use to explain and counteract
their controversial actions? What damage control measures might
offset or minimize damages to their reputation and credibility? How
could they best navigate the future question, "Who was the founder of
this sect?"

The Senior Workers' solution was to cover up Irvine's involvement
and purge out his loyal Friends. They also concealed and redacted their
early history regarding how, when and by whom their sect began, by
obscuring or removing every known trace, mark, or visible sign of Irvine.
His name became anathema.

The difficulty of explaining their rejection of their founder was
overcome by ignoring Irvine and claiming their church was "from the
beginning" or had started on the shores of Galilee when Jesus sent out
His twelve disciples. Some pretended the sect had no known or
traceable founder/history. Others claimed a *group of men* founded it.
Still others minimized the question as unimportant and changed the
subject. Thus, the origin and development of the 2x2 Sect began to fall
into obscurity. Little did they realize the unintended consequences of
this action (future exoduses) they would encounter down the road—
consequences that continue to this day.

Willie Edwards (an Irvinite) recalled George Walker's plans for
phasing out the old: "Everything was going to be different. They would
not even sing the old songs. Nothing that would bring back old
memories, and he says, 'in two years, his [Irvine's] name will be
forgotten, and new people will never know that such a man lived' " (to
Fountains, Oct. 1, 1936, *TTT*). Irvine was vanquished.

The Purge. In history or religion, a purge is the removal of an
undesirable person or group by those in power. A purge of the Workers
and Friends followed Irvine's removal. Irvine's loyalists, who still held a
high regard for him and had not voluntarily deserted the sect, were

excommunicated or persecuted until they left. The repercussion for visiting purged members was excommunication. Irvine provided purging details:

> There were over one hundred Workers rejected and as many hundred Saints these past seven years ... and yet the treatment has been the same: unmerciful judging of their brethren, casting and shutting them out of fellowship. For anyone to have my name in honor, or in grateful memory, or to plead my cause means to be cast out ... and nothing pleases them better than when someone can speak more evil of the man to whom they owe all they have. (to W. Abercrombie, March 2, 1921, *TTT*; Brother Worker on the 1905 Workers List)

> The men who would fail in mercy and become the wicked accusers of the hundreds in The Testimony, whom they have treated violently and put out ... I count myself happy in finding a few hundred who have suffered for being true to my name and being rejected and cast out for having fellowship with me ... No man can mention my name lovingly in The Testimony and not suffer for it. (to Cooney, Feb. 23, 1921, *TTT*)

Erasing the Memory of William Irvine

Damnatio Memoriae. Irvine's name became anathema—a full-fledged *damnatio memoriae* transpired. Irvine took this as a compliment, "Since the parting of our ways—your desire to forget and dishonour my name and treat me as dead ... To burn my letters is the highest compliment they could pay me. Some have been foolhardy enough to openly blaspheme against the Holy Ghost and say that me and my words of warning are of the Devil" (to Wilson and John, April 1, 1923, *TTT*).

Damnatio Memoriae (Latin for *condemnation of memory*) was one of the most severe punishments the Roman Senate could impose upon traitors or others who brought dishonor on the Roman State. It forbade the mention of a particular person and required the destruction of all historical records indicating they ever existed. The intent was to erase someone from history; to cancel every trace of the person from the life of Rome, as if he never existed, in order to preserve the honor of the city. This included abolishing portraits and books, demolishing statues, doctoring paintings and images, smoothing out coins and removing all other traces of the disgraced person.

The Workers attempted something similar when they attempted to wipe out every vestige of Irvine's name, life and memory and placed his skeleton in the closet. However, as Irvine accurately predicted, "When the world and Testimony set out to bury me and forget my name, person, presence—they failed" (to Bill Carroll, June 29, 1920, *TTT*).

A *memory hole* is any mechanism for the alteration or disappearance of inconvenient or embarrassing documents, photographs, transcripts or other records to give the impression something never happened. The concept was first popularized in George Orwell's novel *1984*. In essence, the Workers dug a memory hole for Irvine, and later, another one for Cooney. Some photographs were cropped to remove Irvine. His name and presence in narratives and accounts were disguised or eliminated.

Jack Carroll   Moe Carroll   Willie 'Elizabeth   William
                                         Jameson   Irvine

Jack Carroll   May Carroll   Willie + Elizabeth Jamieson

West Coast Photo of Jack and May Carroll, Willie and Elisabeth Jamieson with William Irvine, and then with Irvine cut off, except for his hand (circa 1910)

For example, at the 1964 Santee, California Convention, Fannie Carroll reminisced about the time their family first heard a Worker. "Jack was having his vacation and *one of the Workers* came with him to our home, because he was taking him to Scotland for his vacation [the 1899 Bicycle Mission Trip]. When he came to our home, we saw he was different to any preacher we had ever met" (F. Carroll, 1964, *TTT*). Other sources reveal the unnamed Worker was Irvine. Another time, Carroll was observed ripping out the pages referring to the Cooneyites from the book *Heresies Exposed* (*See* Chapter 28) and burning them in the metal trash can in her bedroom. The book belonged to her host.

Brother Worker Eldon Tenniswood recounted, "The next year [1908] there was a Convention in Sunshine [Michigan] on Dad and Mother's farm ... I think the Workers were Jimmy Jardine, John Patterson, **a Scotchman who had been coal miners** [*sic*], Charlie Hughes" (1981, *TTT*). Note: the Scotchman was Irvine.

Walker was no exception. When telling about the first Workers coming to America, he mentioned that he "and *a couple others* arrived in New York Harbor September 14, 1903" (1979, *TTT*). The other two Workers were William Irvine and Irvine Weir. Walker did not admit that he professed through William Irvine; yet other documents verify he did so.

Walker made a statement to the US Selective Service dated March 24, 1942, in which he omitted Irvine's name as founder of the sect: "During the closing years of the last century and the first years of this century, *a number of people* in the British Isles and in America were exercised in heart and mind, through their study of the Scriptures, in regard to the methods of preaching and worship in the several churches of which they were then members."

The damnation of Irvine's memory continued until 1954, when a pamphlet titled *A Spiritual Fraud Exposed* filled in the memory hole. Written and published by Doug Parker, it was distributed worldwide to various sect members. The pamphlet exposed the sect's origins, early history, the roles of Irvine and Cooney, and much more. Nearly 30 years later, in 1982, Parker published a 125-page book about the history of the 2x2 Sect, titled *The Secret Sect,* which created an uproar and led to defections by numerous sect members. *See* Chapters 31 and 33.

The Workers were not entirely successful in erasing Irvine from their history. They did not anticipate Goodhand Pattison, or John Long writing detailed historical accounts or Alfred Magowan's letters that turned up many years later. They could not wipe out earlier newspaper records, published books and pamphlets. They were blindsided when Parker published his pamphlet and book.

The Internet was their undoing. Their whitewashing, deception, misrepresentation, suppression and concealment failed; worse, it backfired on them. In the words of William Shakespeare, "truth will out" (*Merchant of Venice*, 1596).

It does not pay to underestimate the power of history.

Cooney disapproved of the Workers' erasing Irvine's memory. He protested, "An attempt has been made to give an account of God's dealings with us, ignoring William Irvine. *This is not honest.*" *See* Appendix D.

Referring to the 2x2 Sect as *The Testimony*, Irvine emphatically declared to John Hardie: "No honest man who knows the facts can ever doubt that The Testimony was my work. **No William—No Testimony**" (Feb. 7, 1937, *TTT*). He insisted to Ed Cooney, "And if I was not the Father, certainly I was not the Brother of any. God never gathered brethren but by a Father **... No William, no Testimony**" (March 2, 1923, *TTT*).

Copy of Wm. Irvine's letter to   March 11, 1923, Bx 553 P.O.
Eddie Cooney.   Jerusalem, Palestine.

My Dear Edward (tho I like Eddie best):-

    I was pleased to see your letter and to hear of some *precede?* evidence of returning humanity in 3 of you; for that will proceed any hope of getting deliverance from the snare of the Devil into which you all have fallen, and which accounts for the deadness and corruption which characterize the whole Testimony these past 8 years, and if nobody else knows of it, I do—and always know more of those conditions than any one else, and rightly so. For the Testimony was the Seal of God and proof of my anointing; and if I was not the Father, certainly I was not the brother of any; God never gathered brethren but by a Father, and all your attempts to change these facts only reveals the secrets of your hearts and leaves you where you began; and as you begun without God and knowing it not; the full of zeal, knowledge and profession and fruit which you long ago recognized was only adding to the wickedness of the world.

    The Scriptures take no notice of anything which has not been produced by Prophets Sealed and sent of God. The Foundation of the Church in every age is the true Prophet and Apostles whom He has sent. False Prophets may be produced by the historical and traditional, or by the true Prophet and Servant of God. Cain and Abel were the seed of Adam – natural and Spiritual but at the end of days—or the lap as you call it—we see the greatest and the Least, the strong and the weak, the Kings and the slaves, the Rich man and Lazarus, the elder brother and the prodigal, the killer and the killed, the rejectors and the rejected, the judge and the judged, the one not fit to live on the earth going home to Heaven to wait the day of the manifestation of the sons of God, the other going forth on the Earth to multiply and build cities and all their abomination, which have characterised these past 6000 years, and finding himself at the end of a long life protected by God, with the cry of the Rich man in Hell, and the gulf fixed.

    I am the one God used altogether,—not most. No William, no Testimony. The Mountains echo and re-echo the human voice; and so the Testimony was the echo and re-echo of the Voice of God thru my lips, tho I knew it not then as I do today; for the Prophets and Apostles only got to know who they were, when they found themselves the victim of the Iniquity and Scandal of those who were called the church—or seal—of their anointing. Paul, Peter, James, Jude and John speak in the days of their rejection with a much more certain end. And I know from experience how these things can be and the need for it when the church is left desolate and Godless, to have the secrets of their hearts made manifest, so that the few may be gathered out and the many gathered in bundles to burn, as we see being made manifest in these days in fulfilling Matt. XIII: 34-43.

    The bride is the few who cleave to the anointed of God; for many are called, but few chosen, and the first in mens eyes are the least in God's, and vice versa. Let both grow together till the harvest, is true of every generation, as well as for the last and finish of the age we are in now. The harvest came in Paul's work in 60 A.D. when he was apprehended and put in jail. Tho the secrets of mens hearts were revealed, and Paul had to learn by experience as all God's chosen have, the meaning of it all, bit by bit. The Man who then or now could believe that God was in the churches or Apostles who forsook Paul, were neither human nor divine, but Devil

William Irvine's March 11, 1923 letter, as retyped by one of his followers

Who Was William Irvine?

A labyrinth of replies has been supplied to this question. Before his fall from grace, Irvine was portrayed variously as a man God raised up, the Lord's anointed, the chief leader or the restorer/finder of God's only/right way.

Today, it is a rare Worker who will voluntarily bring up the name of Irvine—to whom they owe their way of life and profession. Workers' replies differ widely regarding Irvine's role in 2x2 history and what became of him. The short answer given by some is that Irvine was "just a Worker who went wrong."

Workers are quick to disassociate Irvine from their church and have variously responded that he was expelled from the Work because: "he lost his anointing," "got off track," "preached false doctrine," "lost his mind," "was a womanizer," "became overly proud," etc. Some claim Irvine was one of a collective group or a number of men who started the sect circa the turn of the twentieth century. This begs the question: Why do the Workers pretend that Irvine played only a minor role in the formation of the 2x2 Sect?

Or questions are diverted with suggestions that history is not important; that the past is irrelevant and unimportant; that one should be primarily concerned with their current relationship with God; that genealogies are unprofitable (Titus 3:9). It may be implied their questions indicate they lack faith, have not received "the revelation," or do not have a "good understanding."

Many consider the failure of 2x2 leaders to acknowledge the founder and relatively recent origin of their sect to be at the very least dishonest, if not an act of ministerial malfeasance. Granted, some uninformed Workers have been unaware of Irvine's role and merely repeated what they were told. Many Workers made their decision to enter the Work with this critical information unfairly withheld.

> If you lack the humility to go back and tie up the loose ends in your past, then be prepared to forever be haunted by her ghosts, all of whom will come into your present and your future— staining everything and everyone with their leftover emotional and mental garbage. Humility is the master key that can get you out of all your cages; why do you choose your ego and stay in your prisons? (C. JoyBell C.)

❧❧❧

Founder of Two by Two Sect, William Irvine (no date)

25

1914–1919 – Irvine's Life After His Rejection

1914: Irvine Returned to the US. After his dismissal, he retreated to his family in Kilsyth, Scotland. On October 10, 1914, about a month after WWI began, Irvine, age 51, giving his occupation as miner, boarded the SS *Olympic* in Gourock/Glasgow for New York, US, to visit Mrs. Abernethy in Mt. Pleasant, Pennsylvania, US (possibly Andrew Abernethy's mother, Martha, George Walker's first convert in the US). He did not leave with empty pockets. Ship records reveal that he declared $7,000 USD in his possession, a value of about $190,000 today. During WWI, he remained in the US.

Information is scarce about William Irvine's activities during World War I after his fall from grace into ignominy. Tidbits gleaned from comments in his letters indicate he drove around America where he "sought in every way and place if I could find a man with God in him; and the end of the quest was to find out that what I sought—I was. The cheapest way of traveling in US is by auto … For £100, I got a good machine with tent, blankets and all I needed. This … enabled me to be free to go anywhere I wanted. I covered 1,200 miles first year … I sold the machine after three years' service. I look on it as one of the best and wisest choices I ever made" (to Mrs. Adams, Oct. 21, 1921, *TTT*).

Alfred Magowan mentioned that Irvine wrote him from Jerusalem that "after 1914, he went to New York … got an old car and drove on to California. And apparently, he took heart again when you [Jack Carroll] and others had that reunion with him in Santa Barbara. Then disheartenment overwhelmed him again, when … George [Walker] wrote … that he would have nothing more to do with him" (to J. Carroll, Dec. 1, 1954, *TTT*).

We next find Irvine in 1915–1916 "alone in San Diego in a shack. For five years I was in every kind of meeting in US … with an honest, hungry heart ready for any blessing they professed to have and only to find out that wickedness was in them all. They could all kill, but none of them could make alive, The Testimony included. And I found less wickedness in a picture show than any meeting I went to" (to Lees, April 28, 1921, *TTT*).

Irvine reminisced about traveling to the Dunbars in Placentia, California: "Here we are at the same date, or thereabout, I reached your door in 1916, twelve years ago, after being in the tunnel from Alpha to Omega; from the Jesus of the Gospel to the Jesus of Revelation 1" (to Dunbars, Nov. 27, 1928, *TTT*).

After his unsuccessful four-year quest searching for God in various venues, he again turned to Scripture, as he had done earlier when he opened his Bible and randomly placed his finger on a verse which he took to be his "Call to Service" (Isa. 41:15; *See* Chapter 3). This time he discovered a new calling for himself.

As God's "Prophet of the Last Days," he jettisoned the first belief system he founded (the 2x2 Sect). It was over, finished. There was no need for Workers anymore. God had begun His *New Thing* ("Behold, I will do a **new thing**," Isa. 43:19) in which Irvine figured prominently. As salvation had only been via Irvine in the 2x2 Sect, so now salvation was only via Irvine in his new belief system he dubbed the "Omega Message."

This new program came as a surprise to Irvine, "I did not know we were in the days of Judgment till four months ago [November 1918]. The Lord opened up Revelation to me. It's a program for the end of the age—covers 12 years from the beginning of the War. He spued the churches, all kinds, out of His mouth," Rev. 3:14–22 (to Edwards, March 31, 1919, *TTT*).

Irvine divided his teachings into two time periods—before and after World War I. Alpha was pre-War and Omega was post-War. In letters, he referred to the time period when he was leader of the 2x2 Work as the *Alpha Days* and that doctrine as the *Alpha Gospel*. He labeled the new vision he received in 1918 as his *Omega Message*, taken from verses in Revelation, "I am Alpha and Omega."

The first letter in the Greek alphabet is *Alpha* and the last letter, *Omega*. There are four verses in the Book of Revelation that refer to Alpha and Omega, meaning the *beginning and ending*, or the *first and last* (Rev. 1:8, 11; 21:6; 22:13). Hence the sobriquets *Alpha Gospel* for the starting group and *Omega Message* for the latter group.

According to Irvine, Jesus ceased to intercede in Heaven and took the throne as Judge on August 4, 1914 (Rev. 4). This event marked the end of the Age of Grace, also the end of the Alpha Gospel Days. Simultaneously, it was the beginning of God's Judgment Program which would end with the Day of Wrath.

The Prophet. Irvine believed God selected a new prophet for His Judgment Program. Deuteronomy 18:18–19: "I will raise them up a **prophet** from among their brethren, **like unto thee** [Moses], and will put my words in his mouth; and he shall speak unto them all that I shall command him. And it shall come to pass, that whosoever will not hearken unto my words which he shall speak in my name, I will require it of him." *See also* Acts 3:19–26. Therefore, Irvine reasoned that the prophet "like unto thee" (like Moses), would be a common man born to two human parents. Further, Irvine concluded that he was that prophesied prophet. *See* Appendix C, Irvine's explanation of the need for a prophet.

Irvine expounded, "There is to be only ONE Prophet in the Last Days ... I tell you frankly, I am *The Prophet* whom Moses speaks of in Deut. 18:18–19 and Acts 3:19–26 ... A Prophet must be a man of the people of the time of his day; raised up by the Lord alone, like unto Moses; and his words will mean life or death to the whole world according to the way people receive them" (to Laws, Dec. 21, 1927, *TTT*).

He avowed, "To hear and obey God's Message for today by his sent servant [Irvine] is the *only* faith that can save from Wrath. My prophesy (*sic*), like Noah's, Abram's and Moses', is the *only* foundation for faith that can save" (to Beard, Nov. 15, 1932, *TTT*).

The Two Witnesses. In late 1918, Irvine made the surprising discovery that God had chosen him to be one of the Two Witnesses in Revelation 11:3–11, the other witness being the Apostle John. "In [Revelation] chapter 10, you see John the Apostle come down from Heaven to be my companion, and you see the meeting of the two in Rev. 22" (to Craigs, Jan. 28, 1946, *TTT*). According to Jack Carroll, "He [Irvine] is under the awful delusion that he is one of the witnesses of Rev. 11 and prophecies (*sic*) a worldwide drought and famine beginning August 1 of this year [1919]."

Irvine was not the first; many others have self-proclaimed they would be one of the Two Witnesses. The Bible does not identify the Two Witnesses of Revelation 11. Bible scholars differ in their opinions. Some suggest they are Elijah and Enoch, as they were the only two recorded human beings who never died and were translated to Heaven. Others believe they will be Elijah and Moses.

Tribulation. According to Irvine, a drought would occur in the first half of the seven-year Tribulation period (Matt. 24). After three and one-half years, the Beast would be loosed. The Two Witnesses would be killed, and their dead bodies would lie in the streets of Jerusalem. After three and one-half days, the Two Witnesses would come to life again, and they, along with the faithful Omega Message followers, would all ascend to Heaven in a cloud with their enemies watching (Rev. 11:1–13).

The Reader. Irvine began in 1918 to view the entire Bible as prophecy for future events foretold in the Book of Revelation and considered it to be the only relevant book in the Bible. He believed God chose the Apostle John to *write* the Book of Revelation and chose Irvine to *read and interpret* the book.

He interpreted Revelation 1:3, "Blessed is **he that readeth** and they that hear the words of this prophecy and keep those things which are written therein," to mean the Book of Revelation was written specifically for the Reader (Irvine), and no one else could understand it. No longer could mankind be saved by independently reading the Scripture. He declared, "It's all dead; and life comes ONLY by receiving my *reading* of Revelation. It's a *New Thing*" (to Moores, Nov. 11, 1934, *TTT*). *See* Appendix C, Irvine's explanation of the Book of Revelation.

During the "New Thing," to be accepted by God one had to believe that Irvine was God's prophet, and that his interpretations were from God. How one treated Irvine would determine whether one would be blessed or cursed. "**The Reader ...** is **The Test** by which all who are His will be known" (to Hooes, Nov. 24, 1927, *TTT*). "Men good, bad or indifferent or perfect are to be judged by their attitude to my *reading* of Revelation. So they can have the blessings of vs. 1–6 of Rev. 22; or the cursing of vs. 18–19" (to Baesslers, April 18, 1928, *TTT*).

In 1946, only one year before his death, it was revealed to Irvine that he was to be the King and Judge who would judge the sheep and goats and hand out the rewards and punishments of Matthew 25 (to Pages, March 28, 1946, *TTT*; to McCaskills, March 23, 1946, *TTT*).

~~~~~

It would be a colossal understatement to say that Irvine's new insight and "revelations" were not well received by the Senior Workers. In 1919, Jack Carroll sent two letters to his California flock warning about Irvine's delusions and announcing that Irvine had departed from the faith.

> It is just four and one-half years ago since the older Workers in Old Country told William Irvine that they could no longer recognize him as leader, or again as being in the ministry, unless there was a complete change in his manner of life ... His teaching on other matters is equally false and misleading, and it is with much sorrow of heart that I have to add that my sister, May, Willie Edwards and wife have recently come again under the influence of William Irvine's hypnotic personality and for the time being, at least, are deceived. (to My Dear Brother or Sister, April 16, 1919, *TTT*)

1918–1919: Nebraska Schism. Willie Edwards (born in 1878 in Ballinamallard, Co. Fermanagh, Ireland) possibly spearheaded a schism in the 2x2 Sect in Nebraska, protesting Irvine's demotion. At least four younger Brother Workers (two Simpsons and two Waldrons), along with some Friends, including about half of the large Baker family, the Waldrons (owners of the York, Nebraska Convention) and others disassociated from the sect. Some families were divided by the Irvine schism. There were also several in California who departed in sympathy with Irvine, including early Workers Matt and Letitia Wilson, Robert and Minnie Skerritt and the Ritzmans (owners of Fillmore, California Convention).

Off to Jerusalem

After WWI was officially over on November 11, 1918, Irvine fixed his compass on Jerusalem, where he believed the Two Witnesses in Revelation 11 would appear. He wanted to be present for Jesus' return.

Irvine's retreat to Jerusalem, Palestine, likely came as a relief to the Workers; it placed him far away from their fields and converts. Little did they know how much grief he could and would make for them through the copious letters he produced over the next 28 years. Distance did not hinder Irvine from corresponding, recruiting and retaining many followers who supported him financially.

In March 1919, Irvine was ready, willing and eager to leave America for the "promised land." While waiting for some passport difficulties to be resolved, he made his last trip up the California coast. Irvine recollected, "From March 30th to June 15th, 1919, I called all who were or professed to be my friends and delivered to them what I then had of the man and Message. Willie Edwards, Rose and Minnie [Skerritt] were with me all that time, while others only had odd hours till I left" (to Edwards, Aug. 19, 1938, in author's possession).

Irvine, age 56, left New York for Liverpool, England, aboard the SS *Vasari* on June 28, 1919, giving his occupation as preacher. He visited his hometown, family and friends in Kilsyth, Scotland, for about four months. He then boarded a ship (name unknown) at Liverpool, England, on November 2, 1919, and headed for British-occupied Palestine, arriving in Jerusalem on November 27.

He recalled, "It's 27 years tomorrow since I arrived in Jerusalem to learn much of who I was and what I had been doing for 22 years before 1914 when the Alpha Gospel finished, and Judgment had begun. Revelation only began to open up in 1918 when the War finished" (to Dunbars, Nov. 26, 1945, *TTT*).

In December 1919, soon after his arrival, Irvine appeared to be enjoying Jerusalem, "Sharing an old man's room and being a help to the old chap who is 73 ... I am cooking my Sunday breakfast/dinner and tea under the table as I write. It's a little charcoal stove ... made of clay and straw; it keeps my feet warm" (to Dunbars, Dec. 20, 1919, *TTT*).

Of his daily life, health and activities while living in Palestine, Irvine reported very little. He moved back and forth between Jaffa and Jerusalem and was sometimes a travel guide of the Bible lands. He never married, confiding, "What a tragedy it would have been for me to have married and dragged the woman I loved through all the conflict of these 34 years" (to Lauchlins, Feb. 23, 1927, *TTT*).

He never left Palestine, "You can be quite sure I will never be in California or out of Palestine till I go up with John when my work is finished as in Revelation 11" (to Mrs. Weis, Dec. 14, 1934, in author's possession). Nor did he ever again hold a regular job, "I am no man's hireling, but have lived by the gospel as Jesus did and all the true apostles and never asked or needed to ask anyone for money or a meal in 42 years" (to Symington, Jan. 19, 1935, *TTT*).

He usually went to bed at 2:00 a.m. and rose around 9:00 a.m. He lived very frugally, did all his own chores, preserved and stored some of his food. He walked eight to ten miles a day, was keenly interested in healthy habits. Regarding his appearance, he was five feet eight inches tall, had gray eyes, curly brown hair, wore a size 16-1/2 shirt, spent about $10 a year on clothing, and "found it hard to keep on the underside of 200 pounds." His pets were both cats and dogs.

Described by a friend, J. S. Ritchie, "In countenance, temperament and manner of speech, he was characteristically Scots ... he seldom dressed in anything more than an open-neck shirt, shorts and sandals, and invariably carried a walking stick. His shock of white hair was always uncovered ... His room was clean and simply furnished, some of which furnishings he made with his own capable hands" (to Meachen, June 8, 1947, *TTT*).

William Irvine at Jesus' Burial Tomb in Jerusalem

Loyal Workers. Some of Irvine's acolytes who were formerly Alpha Workers were: William (Willie) and Rose Edwards, Robert (Bob) and Nan Skerritt, Bob's sister Minnie Skerritt, Minnie Gerow, Walter Hooe (married to Ruth Gerow), Percy Abbott, Alex Waddell, Sandy Hinds, Sam McMullen, James and Elizabeth Gordon and Joe Kerr (NOT the Joe Kerr responsible for the Living Witness Doctrine).

Loyal Friends. Irvine rejoiced over each old and new contact who reached out to him. His friends who stood with him were very much appreciated. Irvine revealed, "These six years have been the best and the worst ... I had always had a few friends who stuck to me like glue, in spite of all the enemies who tried to wipe me out and make every effort fruitless" (to Dunbars, Oct. 13, 1920, *TTT*). "There are a few at my hometown [Kilsyth, Scotland], New Zealand and California who have been loyal under very trying conditions" (to Bob Skerritt, June 23, 1922, *TTT*).

Loyal devotees from all over the world wrote to him regularly. His replies frequently acknowledged receipt of photographs and gifts, such as money orders, bills, socks, coat, sweater, cakes, cheese and nuts. Some even named their children after him: Irvina Kerr, Irvina Fladung, John Irvine Barnes, William Irvine Loitz, Irvine Noble, William Irvine Hill, John Irvine West and Philip Irvine Edwards.

Some Friends who left the Alpha for the Omega were: Arthur Dunbar, William and Mary Loitz, Sam and Susie Hooe, Susie's mother, Melinda Reed, John Fladung Sr. and Jr., Bob Lauchlin, Claude Billings, sisters Mrs. Moon and Mrs. Hull, brothers Orin and Ira Baker, Neomi Gerow, George Linn and Joe, Sarah and George Kerr.

The owners of the Filmore, California Convention grounds, Emil Ritzman and his wife, became followers of the Omega Message. James Bone stated, "In the summer of 1919, Eddie Cornock and Wilfred Alington had a tent mission in East Bakersfield ... The Workers had to close early because they had to prepare for Convention at Orcutt that year and had to move the equipment from Filmore. Ritchmonds [Ritzmans], where the Convention had been, were no longer in our Fellowship" (1975, *TTT*).

Irvine's Correspondence. Irvine shared his readings and interpretations to his old friends and new followers via correspondence. He was a prolific letter writer. Using a fountain pen, he wrote short to very lengthy letters worldwide, which his followers typed and circulated.

He claimed, "There is not much illness in a man, when he can get 1,000 words out of his pen a day and never less than 500 any [other] day." He sent many letters to children. At times, he dispensed family, medical or financial advice and grief counseling. His letters expounding his Omega Message doctrine provided the Workers with further proof that he "preached false doctrine."

In his letters, Irvine usually referred to the 2x2 Sect as *The Testimony* or *The Testy*. Those who accepted and followed his Omega Message, he called *Little Ones* or *those who have ears to hear*. Current followers of Irvine take no official name and refer to themselves as *Message People* and *The Witnesses*. In this book, they are called *Irvinites*.

So far, the oldest known letter by Irvine is dated January 23, 1911, to Jack (probably Carroll). The next oldest is dated January 17, 1919, to Hon. Lord Northcliffe. According to Alfred Magowan, "William Irvine's first letter from Jerusalem written the day after his arrival there (November 28, 1919) was written to me." A handwritten letter to Walter and Neomi Noble is included in Appendix C. His last known letter was to Elmer and Alma Ackerson in Vallejo, California, dated June 13, 1946, about six months before his death in 1947, aged 84.

William Irvine's Signature

Elmer and Alma Ackerson received   Llewellyn "Lew" Fountain
the last letter Irvine wrote (1947)   (1921–2011), Ex-Irvinite follower

Irvine's letters have been passed down through several generations of followers. Most current Irvinites possess a private collection of his letters, often filling several notebooks. There is no central bank containing *all* Irvine's letters; nor are they all found on a website. No Irvinite has copies of *all* his letters.

Other than his letters, the Irvinites have no printed material or hymnal. Around the 1960s, an Irvinite printer by trade, Orris Mills, duplicated by mimeograph several of Irvine's letters and bound them into what was called *The Mimeographs* and *The Beginner Book*. Some Irvinites used these as primers or hand-outs to help "bring along" or establish recruits. Some Irvinites and former followers have graciously shared their collections, resulting in over 1,000 of Irvine's letters being posted on the website *TellingTheTruth.info* in Founder, Irvine's Letter Collection.

The Beginner Book contained mostly letters written from 1942 to 1946; it was assumed that Irvine had received most or all of his Revelation Program by then. His insight did not come all at once. Over time, Irvine modified, added and expanded his views and prophecies. They evolved. Some saw this as inconsistent, others as progressive. No single letter contains his complete interpretation or "revelation."

Life of Omega Message Followers. Around 1927, Mr. and Mrs. Frank Fountain, their two daughters and son, Llewellyn "Lew," from Saskatchewan, Canada, were converted by Irvine and began receiving personal letters from him. Irvine exclaimed, "It's a joy to find people who have heart or ear for Jesus truly, as Alpha and more as Omega" (to Fountains, May 15, 1928, in author's possession). Lew remembered:

> We had joined with Irvine and were trying so hard to faithfully follow him with all our heart ... At the same time ... all these letters received ... with all his prophecy of gloom and doom. We were all kept sitting on the edge of our chair, wondering what 'this wonderful prophet' was going to have revealed to him next ...

> Keep in mind, these were terrifying words, falling on the ears of a young lad 7 to 17 years old, who had no other yardstick to measure it by ... the only way we would be able to 'get inside the door' or be saved was to read these letters of his, obey everything he said ... and if we followed him closely, did this and much more, maybe just maybe, we would make it, or be saved from the wrath to come. I can remember ... suffering great anguish, about whether I would have a chance ...

> All the time ... I only had a vague idea what his 'Omega Message' was all about. We were all so concerned about pleasing him (W.I.) ... We all gained or lost his 'well done' by how well each of us could feign keen interest in every word he wrote! We were like 'puppets on a string' ... This is the way I spent my early years—from about 1927—1945 ... Father and Mother—well they were just like putty in W.I.'s hands. He had convinced (brainwashed them) them that he was 'This Great Prophet,' and he could do no wrong. (to Dear Friends, July 5, 1998, *TTT*)

Omega followers lived in fearful uncertainty about the future. Fountain called it "*The Everlasting Frenzy*." They believed that God's Day of Wrath could arrive any day. Fountain affirmed, "Irvine kept it at fever pitch. It was going to happen soon. 'The first *WOE* has sounded—the second and the third are about to ... The days of trimming our lamps is over and the great judgment is about to begin,' and on it went. The squirrel wheel that never stopped turning" (to Dear Friends, July 5, 1998, *TTT*). Believing time was fast running out, they feverishly witnessed to others, walking the streets and parks in evenings and on weekends.

November 11, 1918: Armistice Day—the day World War I ended. The anniversary date of November 11 figured prominently in Irvine's prophecies. He and his followers looked forward to November 11 each year with great anticipation. Fountain remarked, "My Mother was always holding her breath or expecting some great thing to happen when November 11th rolled around." They felt the Apostle John might return at any moment, possibly on November 11 that year. Every tick of the clock brought John nearer.

Some chose not to have children, because Irvine expressed a very dim view of marriage and family life: "Sons of God and fair women and nice families, eating, drinking, marrying and giving in marriage is all vanity" (to Pincetl, Dec. 27, 1944, *TTT*). Therefore, his followers did not multiply significantly and have nearly all died out.

Irvine's ideas affected peoples' lives irrevocably. His advice regarding financial matters turned into catastrophes for some followers. They lived on edge watching for John's imminent arrival and did not plan far ahead. Thinking they would not need it, most Omega followers did not seek higher education or provide for their old age.

Omega Burials. Mrs. Skerritt's burial was an example of the procedure used by Omega followers (Irvine's funeral excepted). "There was no undertaker ... ordered the casket and said it was going to be a private funeral and no ceremony of any kind to take place at a certain time ... We had no speaking, singing or prayer at either the house or cemetery" (W. Edwards to Fountains, June 27, 1937, in author's possession).

Failed Prophecies. Fountain pointed out in 1998 that some events had not yet happened; things that Irvine had prophesied many years ago that "would take place soon." He predicted a worldwide drought and famine would come on August 1, 1919, and this prophecy failed (to Edwards, March 31, 1919, *TTT).* Other failed prophecies were, "For this time next year, when John will have come" (to Fountains, Aug. 2, 1930, *TTT*); and "Seven years will bring us to his coming with Jesus to reign" (to Gordons, June 21, 1945, *TTT*). *See* Appendix C for Irvine's failed prophecies.

According to Fountain, when Irvine's prophecies did not come to pass on the dates he predicted, his followers viewed it as a test of their faith to overlook the inconsistencies. They reasoned that his 'human side' became overzealous wanting God's plan to work.

~~~~~~

Willie and Rose Edwards. In late December 1937, Irvine, age 75, devised a new system for distributing his correspondence. He began sending a letter to "Edwards & Co." every seven to ten days, explaining, "In 1938, I felt it was better to write one letter for all and entrusted Willie Edwards to circulate it, which proved useful in one sense, for it saved me; for it was hard at 75 to do what I had been doing" (to Madeline Dunbar, Nov. 26, 1945, *TTT*).

Willie Edwards had someone type Irvine's handwritten letters with several carbon copies. He then circulated the copies with a personal cover letter sometimes addressed to "Our Dear Friends in William

Irvine." Frequently, he reverently referred to Irvine as "Our Leader," stating, for instance, "Surely it would make us tremble if we didn't have a Leader and Commander whose every word is our law and guide."

Edwards encouraged followers to give Irvine's letters far more than a cursory reading. "For if we believe he [Irvine] has the mind of God, then it is only right that we take his words as a *voice from Heaven*" (to Minnie Skerritt, Sept. 4, 1942, in author's possession). The two wisest men in history were Solomon and Irvine, according to the Irvinites.

In 1938, at Irvine's suggestion, Willie and Rose Edwards began traveling to meet with other Irvinites in the US and Canada, interpreting Irvine's letters to his followers. Irvine was pleased, "My heart is glad today to see that they [Edwards] are able to supply what I often felt was beyond the power of my pen" (to Ritzmans, Feb. 13, 1940, in author's possession).

Accepted as Irvine's right-hand man, the Irvinites looked up to and appreciated the Edwards. A grateful follower expressed, "Even after Mr. Irvine's letters, we wouldn't of understood without Edwards to show us." Much obliged, another exclaimed, "So we are more and more thankful for Willie and Rose's life to help us and being able and willing to guide us in all that was so utterly impossible to understand by our own reading of Book and letters."

Both Willie and Rose Edwards were Alpha Workers who married in 1916 and left the Work. They resided in Berkeley, California, and were in the grocery business. In April 1919, the Edwards visited Irvine in Los Angeles and heard for the first time his Omega Message in person. For believing and accepting it, there were serious repercussions; Jack Carroll excommunicated them. In turn, they were some of Irvine's earliest, most faithful, ardent witnesses of his Omega Message—until Irvine cut them off. Rose died from cancer on October 19, 1941, and was buried in Napa, California.

From what can be gleaned from Irvine's letters, in mid-1945, Willie Edwards started writing and distributing his own letters, arranging marriages and divorces and perhaps attempting to become the American leader of the Omega Message. When this came to Irvine's attention, he sent some scathing letters to Edwards, notified others that Edwards no longer had his approval and ceased corresponding with him. For the two remaining years of his life, Irvine returned to writing individual letters to correspondents.

The 1940 Census shows Edwards, age 61, with two of his three children, Anna and John, living in Maricopa, Arizona. He died December 15, 1973, in Prescott, Arizona. Nothing further is known about Edwards' life or activities after he and Irvine parted ways.

1924, March 3: William Irvine Was Officially Excommunicated. *Reportedly,* ten years after Irvine was forced to step down, their tolerance pushed to its limits, Edward Cooney, George Walker, Jack Carroll and Willie Gill were ready to totally sever their association with their erring Brother. They composed a letter to him in 1924, outlining their reasons:

> This deadly doctrine of yours must be completely stamped out that the whole family of God's faithful people perish not as the result of the awful leaven permeating the whole body ... seeing ... that things have reached such a crisis, we consider it incumbent upon us ... our duty in the sight of God, as faithful stewards over His household, to protect the sheep of his pasture; so we regret to say, even weeping, that we must give you in charge, on the ground that you are a lawbreaker and a mover of sedition amongst the people; also that you use witchcraft, sorcery, hypnotism, etc., in order to put people out of their minds; some call it mesmerism ...
>
> Now dear Brother, we hope you will not have any hard feelings towards us, as we still have your welfare at heart ... If you should care to make any statements to us we would be only too glad to hear you, or in the event of your being willing to repent and take your place with us (not over us) again, we might consider extending to you the right-hand of fellowship ... if you come back again to the Father's house we will have the fatted calf ready for you to eat and to make merry with His dear sons and daughters ... We greatly desire to see you back with us again. (to Ethel McFarland, March 3, 1924, *TTT*)

From Irvine's response to Cooney, it appears that McFarland hand copied a letter purportedly written by Cooney and mailed it to Irvine. Irvine questioned its credibility because the letter was not in Cooney's handwriting, nor was it sent directly to Irvine. He replied, "My dear Edward: I had, **what is said to be**, a copy of a letter sent to Ethel McFarland without date or address. If such a letter exists in your handwriting, it must come on to me. I don't object to the whole Testimony having such a valuable document" (July 8, 1924, *TTT*).

Irvine scoffed at their offer for him to "take his place among them." He emphatically declared to Cooney that he was the **Father** (founder) of the 2x2 Sect—**not a Brother.** "The Testimony [2x2 Sect] was the Seal of God and proof of my anointing. **And if I was not the Father, certainly I was not the Brother of any. God never gathered brethren but by a father ...** *No William, no Testimony*" (March 2, 1923, *TTT*).

1936: Irvine's Australian Visitors. Irvine escorted John Hardie and Fred Quick around Palestine, "John [Hardie] says they all feel the need of the head they lost in me ... William Gill is praying that God would raise up a man to be head and leader, and John was anxious that I should come back ... He told of many with heart for me and praying night and day for my return" (to Edwards, Dec. 8, 1936, *TTT*).

1938: Irvine's Irish Visitors. In 1938, Alfred Magowan and Robert Irwin, a 2x2 man from Enniskillen, visited Irvine on their way to Australia. During their 19-day visit, Irvine made his famous statement to Magowan, "**It was a great experiment.**" To which Magowan replied, "**It was a great experience**" (1956, 5, *TTT*).

1937–1938: Irvine's American Visitors. George Linn and Percy Abbott, former 2x2 Sect Workers, became Omega Message followers and corresponded with William Irvine. Linn lived in Vancouver, BC, Canada, and Abbott was a chiropractor from Eureka, California, US. Early in 1937, George Linn decided God had selected him to be the "Apostle John," one of the Two Witnesses, whose arrival Irvine expected at any moment.

Upon learning of the two men's plans to travel to Palestine, Irvine expressed his displeasure, "George Linn writes me about coming here to be my companion, John. Surely, he has fallen into the soup, for he or any other man on the Earth to either to aspire or presume to be John from Heaven, could only have such inspiration from the old Serpent the Devil and Satan. John is the most honored man in Heaven" (to Fladungs, Sept. 30, 1937, *TTT*).

On their way, the two men visited Irvine's sisters in Scotland, who gave them some family photographs to deliver to their brother whom they had not seen or heard from for some time and had feared was dead. They also met with George Walker in Kilsyth. On August 27, 1938, Linn and Abbott arrived in Jerusalem. Having no physical address for Irvine, they waited at the post office for him to pick up his mail. When they met, Irvine would have nothing to do with them.

He recounted their encounter with disgust: "George came up and put his arm around me and said, 'You are William Irvine; I am George Linn.' I said, 'You have made an awful mistake ... let me alone and not to trouble me.' Then he wanted to give me my sisters' photos and I refused it; so then he said they thought I was dead ... Next time George ... followed me out of the post office ... I sent him to Hell and called him a damned fool and turned off ... I advised him to go home" (to Edwards, Jan. 5, 1939, in author's possession).

Abbott went home, but Linn stayed, for he had no home to go to; he had deeded his home to his daughter before he left the US. He also had a heart disease and was living on borrowed time. About four months after arriving in Jerusalem, he died in a hospital and was buried in Mt. Zion Cemetery on December 30, 1938.

1946, January: Visitor Irvine Noble. An English soldier, Irvine Noble, was stationed in Palestine in 1946. His parents were Omega followers Walter and Ruth (Gerow) Noble. Noble was the last known Omega Message person to see Irvine alive. He noted, "I had Irvine Noble for half a day with a companion and enjoyed them" (to Everitts, Jan. 6, 1946, *TTT*).

1940–1941: Irvine Diagnosed with Cancer. Although he gave no indication in any of his countless letters to his followers, Irvine was diagnosed with cancer about this time. *See* Chapter 30.

A DIFFERENT GOSPEL

An Examination of the Teaching

OF

The Cooneyites

BY

LEONARD ASHBY, M.A.

Late Vicar of Holme Eden, Cumberland.
Author of "Keswick and its Message."

PICKERING & INGLIS LTD.

14 Paternoster Row - - - London, E.C.4.
229 Bothwell Street, - - - Glasgow, C.2
MANCHESTER LIVERPOOL EDINBURGH NEWCASTLE-ON-TYNE

5 for 1/ post free.   TWOPENCE

A Different Gospel

MORE than thirty years ago, Mr. William Weir Irvine (or Erwin) and Mr. Edward Cooney began preaching their interpretation of the Gospel message in Ireland. Their followers call their message "**The Jesus Way.**" Owing to the emphasis they place on the words "**Go Tell,**" they are sometimes called "**Go-Preachers,**" but they are generally spoken of as **Cooneyites.** Like other very small sects, they claim that theirs is the only true way. All other ministers and preachers are denounced as hypocrites and imposters. Their position is based on a misunderstanding of the significance of two incidents during our Lord's ministry, due to their failure to perceive the gradual revelation and unfolding of God's purposes of mercy and grace.

"A Different Gospel, an Examination of the Teaching of the Cooneyites"
by Leonard Ashby, Church of England Vicar (1939)

26

1914–1935 – New Era Dawns – On with the Work

Irvine's Mantle. After the takeover, no one person replaced Irvine as the international all-in-all supreme leader and commander who enforced unity and conformity and served as the official authority and interpreter of Scripture. Instead, they formed an international alliance. Irvine's right-hand men, the Senior Workers, became the self-governing administrators of their respective territories. Matters crossing state or country boundaries were resolved on a consensual basis. It was a new era. The Friends were largely unaware that Irvine, the founding father of their ministry and church, was no longer at the helm.

As Irvine correctly observed, "Nobody seems to get my mantle—though many may have tried my shoes, sat in my seat, slept in my bed, ate my meals and have enjoyed the rise to power and prominence" (to Bill Carroll, June 29, 1920, *TTT*).

George Walker was responsible for Eastern US and Jack Carroll for Western US. In Australia, John Hardie, Bill Carroll, Thomas Turner and Sam Jones had the oversight; Willie Gill in the British Isles; Wilson McClung in New Zealand and so on throughout the world. These larger territories were then subdivided into smaller areas under the leadership of these Senior Overseers.

Over the years, various Senior Workers held international Workers Meetings to deliberate issues, work out strategies and determine the path forward. As examples: the post-WWI 1921 Dimsdale Hall, Staffordshire, England Meeting (possibly to discuss Cooney being out of step and moving forward after Irvine's dismissal and WWI); the 1928 Lurgan, Ireland Meeting (to excommunicate Edward Cooney); the 1930 West Hanney, England Meeting (to resolve the Jack Carroll/Walker feud); and the 1938 English Meeting (to rule on divorce and remarriage). Usually at the conclusion of the Meeting, about 12 Senior Workers signed a summary outlining their decisions and conditions. Less important or local decisions were usually settled among fewer Overseers.

1917–1920: The Princess Victoria Connection. Born on July 6, 1868, at Marlborough House, England, Princess Victoria Alexandra Olga Mary was the fourth child of Edward VII (then Prince of Wales and later King of England) and Princess Alexandra of Denmark, who were married on March 10, 1863. Princess Victoria passed away on December 3, 1935, aged 67, having never married.

Princess Victoria of the United Kingdom (1868–1935)
(Public domain via Wikimedia Commons)

It has been claimed that Princess Victoria professed, due to three written accounts and some letters she allegedly penned, although she never physically attended any Meetings or Conventions. According to Brother Worker John Pattison's account about the princess and her connection with the 2x2 Sect, "The essence of these letters ... show that ... Princess Victoria had a clear revelation of Truth; that she was very close to and influential to her mother, as were also the professing girls who were in service to the household" (J. Pattison 1917–1920, Princess Victoria, *TTT*).

Reportedly in 1917, when the princess was 49 years old, she connected with Daisy Bassett, a 2x2 maid who worked in the royal palace in London. From Ruth (Jordan) Aiken's account, "Daisy was in attendance to Lady Keppel, Lady-in-Waiting to Princess Victoria ... Daisy passed on her testimony to Lady Keppel, and from then on Princess Victoria was constantly asking questions and showing her interest ... It was during those free three years [1917–1920] that Princess Victoria made her choice" (J. Pattison 1917–1920, Princess Victoria, *TTT*). Note: no corroboration has been found for a Lady Keppel serving as a royal Lady-in-Waiting during 1916–1918 for Queen Mary or Queen Alexandra; normally, princesses did not have ladies-in-waiting.

It is said that the princess gave Daisy a letter for Edward Cooney, addressed to "the man of God," and for three years, corresponded with Sister Workers Maggie Patton and Emily Ruddell. She substituted symbols for names in her letters and signed her letters "V. W." Seventeen of these purported letters have been preserved.

"When Victoria wrote the last of these letters, she was leaving the palace to live at The Coppins, Iver, Buckinghamshire," wrote Peter Svinth in his account. "She wrote letters from there, but they appear to be lost. Daisy left the palace at the same time. These letters were written to Maggie Patton, a girl from Ireland that had been in the Work some 12 years or so ... Victoria's mother, Alexandra, who was known for her kindness, gave Victoria permission to go to Meetings, and she was expected to [attend] a Convention in Ireland in 1919, which Lord Stamfordham put a stop to" (J. Pattison 1917–1920, Princess Victoria, *TTT*).

Hyde Park. Allegedly, Princess Victoria occasionally went to Speakers' Corner in Hyde Park, London, in a carriage with drawn drapes. There she heard Cooney preaching in 1917; his Co-worker was John Pattison. Opening in 1637, Hyde Park was London's first public park and largest open space, containing 630 acres. In July 2004, my husband and I walked around Hyde Park and photographed Speakers' Corner, a site used for public open-air speeches and debates since the mid-1800s.

A single light post stands in the center of a large, bare, ground-level area; no raised platform or loudspeaker system is present. Speakers usually stand on a small ladder or wooden box, often a soapbox, literally *getting on/off their soapbox.* In the 1910s, there could be as many as 15–20 speakers in the area, all speaking at the top of their voices. If one speaker did not appeal, the listener moved to another, similar to clicking television channels.

Speakers' Corner, Hyde Park, London, England (2004)

Anyone can turn up unannounced to speak on any subject, provided the speeches are lawful. Noted people such as Karl Marx, Vladimir Lenin, George Orwell and William Morris have spoken there. Currently, every Sunday from about midday till long after dark, crowds gather there to listen to enthusiasts expounding their views. Everyone is welcome to join in the debates and discussions.

Willie Gill, Ed Cooney and other Workers used Speakers' Corner to broadcast their Gospel Message. It was said of Cooney, "He can pitch his voice without shouting; he can reason; he can enforce his argument with chapter and verse; and therefore he is listened to, and his reasoning has power and force."

Reportedly, Willie Gill, Overseer of England, was a great passionate orator who could capture and hold the attention of audiences. To get his point across, he "was not shy of using words to enhance his message that some would consider rude and insulting." He went early so he could be in the most prominent place with the least amount of noise situated where the most people could hear him. His preferred spot was at the north end where those in the park could sit and hear him, e.g. the servants, nannies and maids.

Speakers' Corner was an excellent venue for the Workers with maximum exposure. Consequently, many embraced the Workers' message heard there. Some entered the Work, and in a short time, there was a large number of converts with open homes in London, the capital of England. In 1917, Wilson McClung, Overseer of New Zealand, stated to the Military Service Board that there were 5,000 members and 70 ministers in England (*The Dominion*, July 26, 1917, 9, *TTT*).

Open-Air Meetings. In the days before radio or television, many towns had a recognized speaking place, where people congregated for speeches, announcements, preaching and entertainment. The Workers held many open-air Meetings throughout the country—on the Diamond in Enniskillen, on the Square in Newtownards and Conway, at the Custom House in Belfast, as well as Speakers' Corner in Hyde Park and in Tower Hill in London.

~~~~~

1918 Spanish Flu Pandemic. During WWI, a new influenza virus emerged in 1918. The conditions of WWI (overcrowding and global troop movement) contributed to its spread. Poor health and sanitation standards, lack of a flu vaccine and treatments created a major public health crisis, causing at least 50 million deaths worldwide.

1919: Alfred Magowan Excommunicated. At the Illinois Convention grounds on September 27, 1919, Alfred Magowan was expelled, not only from the Work, but also from the 2x2 Sect, by Jack Carroll, George Walker and James Jardine. He was pronounced "unregenerate."

Alfred's son, David Magowan, observed that his father was on his way out long before his excommunication in 1919. "Cooney said he 'went wrong' in 1910 [only 3 years after he entered the Work]. Father said then that he would be guided by the Holy Spirit in what he preached and not by Cooney or any other of those who considered themselves leaders. He never believed in a hierarchy anyway. Not conforming therefore was the reason they put him out; also refusing to accept them as the only Christians. John Long said they unChristianised other Christians. Father traced their decline to that development of a hierarchy, or one above the other."

The final straw was Magowan's communication with Ex-worker, Willie Edwards, who had accepted Irvine's later Omega Message and left the 2x2 Sect. According to Edwards, when Magowan was *on trial*, he asked if he might read a letter from Edwards. Carroll asked if he had corresponded with Edwards. After Magowan confirmed that he had, Carroll responded, "Well then, we need no further witness as that is enough" (to Caseys, Dec. 20, 1942, *TTT*).

Alfred and Harriett Magowan, Irish siblings in the US Work

Magowan shared, "Our only sendoff in the dusk of that early morning … was the slipping of some dollars into our hand by my sister Harriet who looked broken-hearted … She was killed at a railway crossing in Illinois in the year 1936 with her companion and the driver of the truck in which they were riding (to Alex Waddell, Nov 18, 1954, in author's possession).

Magowan relayed to Cooney that he had been excommunicated "on the ground of 'incompatibility of spirit.' I have never been born again!" From there, as Alfred put it, he "went into the wilderness." He described to Cooney the treatment he received after leaving the Work.

> We have not known persecution in its time-glorified forms; and what we have suffered would hardly be worth mentioning in the light of the greater sufferings of others; but for myself I must confess that there were times when I could have borne very little more. What with slurs and insults, hints and insinuations, misunderstandings and prejudices, dark looks and averted faces, where formerly there had been smiles and

friendly greetings; and what I considered my good, hatefully evil spoken of ... My letters have been misread and things found in them that were never in my mind. (Nov. 7, 1953, *TTT*)

Irvine's first letter from Jerusalem was written to Magowan, the day after he arrived there on November 28, 1919. Magowan reminisced, "And giving my testimony, I would say that I have lived abundantly. The 'great experiment' W. Irvine spoke of in Jerusalem was transmuted for me into a great experience, to the enrichment of my life beyond anything I could have anticipated or imagined had it followed any other course" (to Doug Parker, Dec. 6, 1954, in author's possession)

A prodigious writer, Magowan wrote countless letters, poetry and books, including a hymnbook after he disassociated from the 2x2 Sect. He made good use of a typewriter a friend gave him. From 1939 to 1949, he retained copies of his writings (excluding his letters). These were typewritten poems and essays, which he bound into 17 books, with 2,728 pages; about 1,000 pages are in verse. Most of his essays are comments on world affairs, beginning in 1942. Several books followed: *If our Civilization had been Christian, Echoes of World Voices; Purpose and Design,* and more.

After a heart attack in 1951 at age 68, he began making carbon copies of his typed letters, amounting to thousands of pages. I am greatly indebted to Alfred Magowan's valuable insight and information, kindly shared by his sons David and Stephen, and grandson, Daniel Magowan. In a profound statement, Magowan explained his writings to Walker, "A man must express what is given him for that purpose or be like the man who hid his talent in the Earth—miss the purpose of it and lose it into the bargain ... When a man speaks, he speaks to one generation; but when he writes, he may be a benefactor to all coming generations, as Paul was" (Feb. 21, 1954, *TTT*).

Dimsdale, Staffordshire, England Workers' Convention (1921)

1921: Workers' Convention at Staffordshire, England. The familiar old photograph of 208 Workers attending this Convention shows many 2x2 Worker luminaries, such as Edward Cooney (No. 69), George Walker (No. 17), James Jardine (No. 12), Willie Gill (No. 49), Jack Carroll (No. 93), Bill Carroll (No. 91), John Hardie (No. 71), Wilson McClung (92), Wilson Reid (No. 9), Andy Robb (No. 19), Otto Smith (Schmidt, No. 51) and others. *See* website *TellingTheTruth.info* Photo Gallery in Convention Album, British Isles, England, Conventions.

Otto Schmidt's parents were Moravian Brethren who emigrated from Germany to Bethel, South Australia, for religious freedom in 1855–1856. Along with several other families, the Schmidts professed in Sam Jones' 1910 Bethel Mission. *See* Chapter 41.

In what could not be worse timing, Schmidt and James Jardine pioneered the Work in Germany in 1913–1914. When WWI broke out, they fled to England. Schmidt and Sam Dallas held a mission in Staffordshire, where a widow, Annie Heath, and her seven children resided; their father, George, had died in 1901. Annie and her children George, Joseph, Sarah Jane "Jennie" and perhaps more of the Heath family professed.

Schmidt and Jardine returned to preach in Germany after the War. Otto's health deteriorated; he spent about six months in a German hospital. He then recuperated at the Heath's home, where he was instrumental in arranging the first large-scale English Convention in 1921 on the Heath's property at Dimsdale Hall, Staffordshire, a suburb of Newcastle-under-Lyme. In 1927, Schmidt (1888–1976) and Sara Jane Heath (1897–1967) married. They had one child, Mervyn, resided in Mildura, Australia, and were buried there.

The Staffordshire Convention was moved to Heath's property at Stocks Farm in Bramshall, Uttoxeter. Some Workers were buried in the Church of St. Lawrence graveyard in nearby Bramshall. When the Heath brothers died in the 1960s, the Davies bought Stocks Farm. As of 2020, the annual Convention has continued there.

1921: Irish War of Independence. Ireland was ruled by England, in one form or another, from 1175–1921. During that period, most of the native Irish were heavily oppressed. World War I had barely ended when the Irish War of Independence commenced in January 1919. During this War, Britain sent two reinforcement groups to Ireland; *The Auxiliaries,* who were part-time soldiers and the *Black and Tans,* who wore khaki tunics and trousers and dark green (nearly black) caps.

Perhaps of all British troops sent to Ireland, the Black and Tans were the most despised by the Irish people. Regarded by many as "the scum of the Earth," these troops were non-regular soldiers of fortune, many of whom were allowed out of British prisons on the condition that, for a minimal payment, they would go to Ireland and ruthlessly suppress the rebellion. They executed their orders indiscriminately burning, looting, murdering and pillaging all sections of the population. This triggered "tit-for-tat" killings and atrocities by the Irish Republican Army (aka IRA). The IRA regarded anyone even remotely suspected of being sympathetic to the British occupying forces as a legitimate target.

1921: Coolacrease Tragedy. Around 1911, William Pearson, Sr. and his wife Susan (Pratt) purchased Coolacrease, a 340-acre farm in Co. Offaly, Ireland, and moved there with their seven children. They were a 2x2 family. "It was here at Coolacrease that on the 30th June 1921," related Alan Stanley, "a band of 30, perhaps 40 armed and masked men descended on the house, torched it, then in the courtyard shot the two eldest sons of the household, aged 19 and 24. The shooting took place in the presence of the mother, three sisters and a younger brother" (Stanley 2005, 13).

The brothers executed by the IRA were Richard "Dick" and Abraham "Abe" Pearson. When the killings took place, their father and a younger brother were attending a Convention about 35 miles away. The reason for the murders has never been determined with certainty. Similar atrocities were carried out by both sides in the conflict during this period.

About a month after the murders, a truce was signed in July 1921 ending British rule in all Ireland, except the six northernmost counties that remained within the UK, called *Northern Ireland*. The independent portion of Ireland is referred to as the *Republic of Ireland*, or simply, *Ireland.*

After receiving compensation for their land, the Pearson family moved to Australia in 1930. The ruins of Coolacrease House are located one mile northeast of the hamlet of Cadamstown in Co. Offaly (formerly King's Co.), Ireland. *See* details on the website *TellingTheTruth.info* in History Articles, Coolacrease.

In 2005, Alan Stanley published a book titled *I Met Murder on the Way: The Story of the Pearsons of Coolacrease.* His book gave rise to the documentary *The Killings at Coolacrease,* which was a segment of the Irish RTE television series *Hidden History of Ireland* broadcast on October 23, 2007.

North American Workers Increase. By 1922, the Workers had ventured into all but 15 of the then 48 states. For the years 1922–1923 through 1928–1929, the "Workers Lists for North and South America" showed the Worker population as follows:

Years	Total	Canada	US	Foreign Work	Married Couples
1922–1923	475	93	371	11	6
1923–1924	529	106	372	51	9
1924–1925	554	111	425	17	9
1925–1926	612	114	443	55	7
1926–1927	622	119	465	38	12
1927–1928 (Partial List)	592	152	405	35	12
1928–1929	687	113	525	49	13

See website *TellingTheTruth.info* in Workers Lists.

1923: Marriage of David Christie and Emily Wilson. From the platform of the Milltown, Washington, US Convention, Western US Overseer Jack Carroll announced his approval of the marriage of two Workers, his cousin Dave Christie to Emily Wilson.

> Two Workers came to this Convention married and wish me to make the fact known. I refer to David Christie and Emily Wilson. And while we may seriously question the wisdom of this step and recognize that it means greater difficulties in their lives and less liberty in the Gospel, we cannot make dishonorable what God has made 'honorable'; and for this reason, we speak no word of condemnation and attach no penalty. If there is to be condemnation or penalty, we leave this in the Lord's hands … They are willing to be guided by us with regard to the future. They desire to continue in the Work … and have volunteered to go to the Hawaiian Islands. (1923, *TTT*)

1923–1924: William Murray Rule, a trustee of the Bible Book and Tract Depot in Sydney, NSW Australia, investigated and wrote a critique titled "The Cooneyites or Go-Preachers — A Warning" that was published in the periodical *Our Hope* (Gaebelein 1923–1924, TTT).

1929: Subsequently, in 1929, Rule's report was reprinted as a small tract titled *The Cooneyites or Go-Preachers and Their Doctrine* and distributed to ministers and Christians around the world. By cautioning the public to be on guard for itinerant Cooneyite ministers coming among them, the tract hindered the Workers from spreading their message and gaining converts. *Read* Rule's tract on website *TellingTheTruth.info* in Publications.

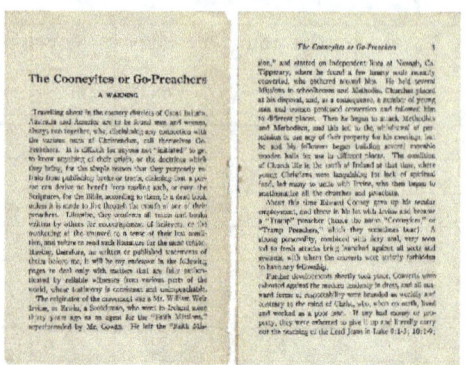

"The Cooneyites or Go-Preachers – A Warning"

John Hardie, of NSW Australia, and Jack Carroll, from the US, vigorously protested against the tract. Hardie met with the publisher in person requesting the tract be removed from circulation, claiming it contained 20 errors and 14 lies. Jack Carroll corresponded with the publishers and author for two years, disagreeing with many points in the tract.

Dear Sirs:

     With regard to my letter of yesterday's date, will add a brief summary of doctrines "most surely believed " and taught by us:-

     We unhesitatingly affirm our belief in the Old and New Testament Scriptures as the very Word of God, the only infallible rule of faith and practice; the Deity of Jesus Christ; His Virgin birth; His substitutionary atonement; His resurrection from the dead; His ascension to the right hand of God; and the glorious hope of His coming again.

     We believe and teach that the New Birth is an absolute necessity and that this is brought about by the Word of God and the ministry of the Holy Spirit; that the call of Jesus to His ministers to follow Him in the way of self denying, self sacrificing service, is for to-day; in Baptism by immersion; in coming together on first day of week to break bread; that the New Testament Church as a Church owned no Church property, took no name but His; that the New Testament saints met together on first day of week for worship and Breaking of Bread in small groups in homes consecrated to God.

     As ministers (preachers) we absolutely and literally "forsake all", own no property of any kind, have no salary, do not lift collections, make no appeals for money to any outside or inside our fellowship - believing as we faithfully "seek first the Kingdom of God" He will in His own way take care of our every need. We have no headquarters, secretary, treasurer, or central fund."

Excerpt from Jack Carroll's letter (April 17, 1930)

Objecting strongly to the name *Cooneyites*, the Workers also denied the tract's claims that preachers were forbidden to marry, and that there was a common fund for supporting their ministers. Carroll was unable to provide any publications to support his position (only letters from several friends and copies of some hymns), while the author had a number of independent individuals confirming the veracity of his writings (corroborating correspondence in author's possession). Ultimately, the tract was not quashed, but some modifications were included in later editions.

Leonard Ashby, Church of England Vicar of Holme Eden, Cumberland, compiled a tract in 1939 titled *A Different Gospel, an Examination of the Teaching of the Cooneyites,* published by Pickering & Inglis, London. The preface states his purpose for publishing his tract. "As the Cooneyites or "Go-Preachers," on principle, avoid publishing books and tracts, it is difficult to find anything that gives a true and full account of their teaching...and to write very plainly and simply about these false teachers."

1928: Colonel Charles Goodnight (1836–1929), a renowned cowman, plainsman and trailblazer from West Texas, was one of the original five men voted into the National Cowboy Hall of Fame in Oklahoma City, an institution honoring men and women who settled the American West. Encouraged by his new wife, Col. Goodnight professed shortly before his death. When someone asked him the name of the church he joined, "he answered, characteristically, 'I don't know, but it's a damned good one' " (Haley 1983, 462).

1929: The Great Depression. The widespread prosperity of the 1920s ended abruptly with the US Wall Street stock market crash that wiped out millions of investors in October 1929. The Great Depression followed, the worst economic downturn in the history of the industrialized world. It brought hardship, homelessness and hunger to millions. Many banks failed. Lasting a decade, until 1939, it was the longest, deepest, most widespread depression of the twentieth century, affecting virtually every country worldwide.

1921: *Heresies Exposed.* The first counter-cult book ever printed was *Timely Warnings* published in 1917. It was compiled by missionary W. C. (William Carleton) Irvine (no relation to the 2x2 founder, William Irvine). A second edition was titled *Modern Heresies Exposed.* The title of the third edition (1921) was shortened to *Heresies Exposed* and remained so in several editions and printings thereafter. Published by Loizeaux Brothers in the US, and by Inland Printing Works in India, the book is now out of print (1929, *TTT*).

Heresies Exposed was one of the first books to critically review new religious movements, e.g. the **Cooneyites,** Christadelphians, Christian Scientists, Jehovah's Witnesses, Seventh-day Adventists, Pentecostals and other non-mainstream groups who had become increasingly prominent. Rule's tract "The Cooneyites or Go-Preachers and Their Doctrine" (abridged) was included as a chapter in *Heresies Exposed,* at least by the 1929 printing. The eighth edition (1935) added a correction from John Long regarding the sect's origins, e.g. the correct name of the 2x2 sect's originator, place and date.

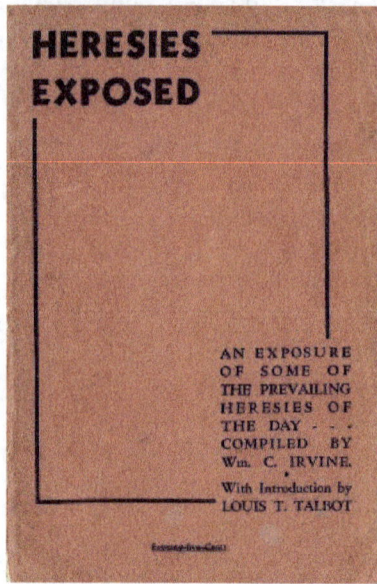

THE COONEYITES

or Go-Preachers and their Doctrines

By W. M. R.

(Abridged)

The originator of this new cult was a Mr. William Weir Irvine,* a Scotchman, who went to Ireland about fifty years ago as a preacher in connection with the **Origin** Faith Mission. He subsequently left them and started an independent Mission on his own lines at a town called Nenagh, Co. Tipperary, where he found a few hearty people who had been but recently converted. These he succeeded in gathering round himself and they became the nucleus of this new sect.

He commenced by holding missions in school-houses and Methodist churches, which had in good faith been placed at his disposal; and in course of time, a number of young men and women professed conversion to his views and followed him from place to place.

The condition of church life in the south of Ireland at that time was such that there were young Christians who were languishing for lack of spiritual food, and were grieving over the want of ardor in the gospel among them. Such were attracted to these preachings, and mistook the vigorous denunciations and excitable preaching of the missioner

*Mr. John Long has written us that he was the man who obtained for William Irvine "the first opening for a mission in Nenagh, August, 1897." That "William Irvine is the name of the original leader of the Go-Preachers. Irvine Weir was one of the first staff of preachers who emigrated to America; these two names seem to have got mixed up." He declares that the movement dates from 1897.

"Heresies Exposed," Cooneyite Chapter (published 1935)

27

1928 – Edward Cooney Cast Out

Edward Cooney's Issues. Edward Cooney had mixed feelings. He had brooded and grieved through the years as he saw their ideal ministry and church go downhill to something he could not endorse. Gradually, the Two by Two Sect had adopted various beliefs and practices with which he disagreed, and it saddened him. He did not, however, believe the whole mission was a mistake; he continued to believe William Irvine's original idea to follow Matthew 10 was a revelation from God.

After Irvine was rejected, Cooney mounted a campaign for the Workers to return to their original model, the way they were in the first four years he and Irvine preached together. Cooney stressed, "Undoubtedly God called us and separated us to be his people at the beginning, and most prominent and most used in this calling out a people for God's name was William Irvine, who, at the time of his being sent forth to be a prophet, saw more clearly than any of us [that] the revelation of the Father to each individual child of His is the Rock alone on which Jesus Christ alone would build His church ... Our only hope is to get back to the simplicity and childlikeness of the beginning, especially those of us who have the oversight" (to My Dear Sister, May 1930, Appendix D).

Cooney believed it was unscriptural to organize religion. He longed to go back to the freedom the Workers enjoyed in the sect's golden years when they were controlled solely by the Holy Spirit. Like Irvine, Cooney, as second-in-command, claimed no particular field and recognized no boundaries. The two roamed the world preaching wherever they felt led to do so. Now, the Workers wanted Cooney to restrict his movements and obtain permission before preaching in areas where other Workers had the oversight.

Cooney struggled to persuade the Senior Workers to discard the hierarchy and organization that divided the movement among geographical fields and the membership into classes of Overseers, Workers and Friends. He felt the Workers should all be servants—not rulers over other Workers or the Friends. He endeavored to show the

Senior Workers how they had set themselves up over the laity, similar to the way Irvine had been set up over the Workers.

Cooney firmly believed the Workers should have freedom to express whatever God revealed to them. To do otherwise he felt was to usurp the role of the Holy Spirit, and this was unfathomable. He explained, "At the beginning we were all free to express the revelation God made clear to our hearts" (to My Dear Sister, 1930, Appendix D). "William Irvine and I were drawn together as Brothers in Christ, each of us claiming liberty to follow Jesus as we received progressive light from God by the Spirit" (to Alice Flett, 1930, Appendix D).

In sharp contrast, the Workers did not want Cooney expressing any of his *revelations* in their fields—unless they agreed with them. Wilson Reid remarked, "Eddie ... had begun teaching things on his own without consulting any of the Brothers" (to Brothers and Sisters in Christ, Dec. 13, 1928, *TTT*). Cooney exasperated the Workers. They never knew what might come out of his mouth, and they had to deal with "the fallout" after he left their fields. His free speech and freedom of movement upset their organizational order.

In Cooney's opinion, the Living Witness Doctrine (LWD) was a heresy that had crept in and permeated the sect, that had cost the Friends and Workers their liberty in Christ. Cooney believed God had children everywhere, and that the LWD should be jettisoned. He viewed Irvine's downfall as a sign that God wanted the Workers to revoke and renounce it. He urged, "Let's return to the Lord and He will return unto us." With Irvine out of the picture, he saw it as a good opportunity for the Senior Workers to renounce and repent of the LWD and go back to the way Cooney and Irvine had preached during the four golden years (1901–1905) before the introduction of the Living Witness Doctrine.

The downside of Cooney's proposal was that removing the LWD concept would seriously compromise the Workers' strongest, most powerful tool of persuasion in motivating outsiders to join their sect; a concept that also bolstered member retention. No longer unique, their sect would be reduced to a church among other churches started by a man. In turn, this would mean people could be saved outside of the 2x2 Church, and that there was no such thing as "God's one right/true way" except Jesus. Cooney also:

- Disapproved of the Workers assuming the name *The Testimony of Jesus* in Great Britain during World War I. It was not just taking a name that troubled him—it was also the name itself. He objected that while they could *give* the testimony of Jesus—they could not *be* the testimony of Jesus.

- Disapproved of the movable halls used for missions and living quarters—they showed a lack of faith. He believed Workers should stay overnight in homes, not in beds in wooden huts. He instructed the other Workers, "I'll have fellowship with you if you use them, but don't ask me to use them."

- Disapproved of holding annual Conventions that had no scriptural basis. Critical of the vast amount of time, organization, money and coordination required to prepare and hold the Conventions, he also objected to Workers going on prearranged Convention tours, instead of going wherever the Spirit led them to save souls.

- Disapproved of quenching the Holy Spirit in others (1 Thess. 5:19).

1914: Cooney's Renunciation. Cooney made a wholehearted, valiant, but ultimately unsuccessful, effort to turn the leading Workers away from the errors he believed had infiltrated the sect over the years. The Workers refused to surrender the Living Witness Doctrine, choosing instead to retain the status quo, and this man-made Doctrine has continued to be an integral part of their beliefs and teachings since 1905–1907.

Therefore, in 1914, Cooney took his stand and openly renounced the Living Witness Doctrine for himself, declaring he had, "returned to the true Gospel William Irvine and I with others preached for some four years before these heresies were introduced" (to Alice Flett, 1930, Appendix D).

While Cooney believed all religious systems, institutions and organizations were unscriptural, he still believed there were people in them who were born again (Roberts 1990, 125, *TTT*). This was radically different from the Living Witness Doctrine the Workers still believed and taught: "A person can be born again by a living witness—without one never." In 1914, Cooney also reclaimed his original conversion to Christ that took place in his heart in 1884 by his bedside when he was 17—long before he met Irvine.

At the time, Wilson Reid was the Overseer of Ireland, Cooney's native home and base. He vilified Cooney in a letter to Brothers and Sisters. "As regards the cause of the trouble, it is not a thing of today or yesterday but a matter of years," Reid recollected. "The first I clearly saw of it was in 1916, although others can trace it back much further. About this time Eddie began to change his testimony and went back to claim he was saved at 17 years old, which was many years before he began walking in The Truth" (Dec. 13, 1928, *TTT*).

Cooney repossessed the belief they held in the early days that people could come to Christ through various means, e.g. nature, Scripture, revelation, individuals, preachers, etc., and that there were people saved outside their sect. This meant he no longer considered the 2x2 Sect to be God's only right/true way. Instead, he believed and preached "God has his children everywhere, even among the heathen."

1914–1921: Cooney refused to be muzzled and continued preaching whatever and wherever he felt led to do so in Great Britain and Ireland. For seven years, the gulf between Cooney and the Senior Workers widened as he disregarded their generally accepted order and administration. Meanwhile, most of the Friends were unaware of the conflict.

1921–1928: Cooney Sent Abroad. After the 1921 Workers Meeting at Staffordshire, England, Cooney was urged to travel abroad with the hope that by mingling with other Senior Workers, he would fall in line, give up his liberty and be willing to submit to their order, rules and control. Perhaps his prolonged absence would also lessen his influence in the British Isles.

On August 4, 1921, Cooney, age 54, boarded the SS *Empress of France* in Liverpool, England, headed for Quebec, Canada, along with George Walker, Willie Gill and Jack Carroll. For the next seven years Cooney traveled in the US, Canada, New Zealand and Australia. The Workers' solution, however, did not have its desired effect on Cooney; if anything, it accentuated their differences.

George Walker, Willie Gill, Jack Carroll, Ed Cooney (circa 1921)
Visual confirmation of Cooney's association with the 2x2 Church

Banned in New Zealand. In 1921, Cooney spoke in the New Zealand Special Meetings. Far from falling into lockstep with the other Workers, he soon managed to antagonize the New Zealand Workers to the point they banned him from their Meetings. Reportedly, the final straw was Cooney's attempt and failure to heal a young woman.

Edward Cooney's brother, Fred, had immigrated with his family to New Zealand in 1924. He protested to the Overseer of New Zealand,

Wilson McClung, "You waited until he had sailed from New Zealand before you set the ball rolling. Furthermore, you forbade fellowship with those who declared belief in Eddie as a Servant of God; so, Brother denied Brother and Satan smiled as Isaiah 9:20–21 was being fulfilled among us ... As regards the doctrine that only through the lips of a true preacher can salvation come to a human soul, I do not believe it; and I refuse to add conditions not found in God's Word" (June 1, 1930, *TTT*). Fred left the sect. Those loyal to Cooney began holding separate Meetings.

Disturbing Australia. Cooney left New Zealand for Australia, where he stayed until early 1925. Bill Carroll, Overseer of Victoria, concluded that Cooney's problem was, "We preach not ourselves. We do not wish to exalt ourselves or our own name. That was the lamentable and dreadful sin of Edward Cooney. We had to come to the definite belief after many years of patience that he preached himself. His message was to exalt his own name, which has been put upon God's people and which God's people reject and resent" (Sermon, Dec. 16, 1950, *TTT*).

Wilson Reid asserted that Cooney "got worse until in 1925 some of the Brothers in Australia and New Zealand sent home quite a few letters showing that *the trouble with Eddie* had become very serious" (to Brothers and Sisters, Dec. 13, 1928, *TTT*).

After disturbing the Australian Workers for four years, Cooney (age 58) left Sydney on April 3, 1925, aboard the SS *Aorangi* for Vancouver, Canada, headed for the US.

Banned by Jack Carroll in Western US and Canada. The saga continued. Overseer Jack Carroll asked Cooney not to preach in areas where Carroll had previously ministered. Believing God had led him to Seattle, in typical Cooney style, Cooney ignored Carroll's request and held a mission there; at least one man professed. Carroll instructed the Friends to boycott Cooney's mission and to withhold their support and shelter. For the next three years, Cooney was forced to work in his former trade, the clothing business, to support himself (Roberts 1990, 140, *TTT*).

George Walker, James Jardine and some other Workers went to Seattle hoping to settle the rift between Carroll and Cooney and to make it possible for Cooney to remain in fellowship. Since their conditions required him to leave Seattle where he felt God had led him, Cooney refused.

Banned by George Walker in Eastern US. Three years later in 1928, Walker, Overseer of the Eastern US, told Cooney in Edgar Hawkins' home in Detroit, Michigan, that he was not welcome in Walker's territory; nor was Cooney welcome in Jardine's territory, which included the North Central States of Wisconsin, Minnesota and North Dakota.

Blacklisted in Ireland. Before Cooney arrived back in the British Isles, the Workers had begun warning the Irish Friends that there was "trouble with Cooney"; that Cooney had changed, something had gone wrong with him, and he was out of step with the other Workers. He was portrayed as not being born again, a deceiver, a preacher of false doctrine, a false shepherd guilty of committing "awful crimes." Alfred Magowan heard that Cooney's dismissal was due to "a little subtle form of pride which shewed itself in an inordinate love for the spotlight and audience admiration" (to Cooney, Nov. 7, 1953, *TTT*).

Being a native of Northern Ireland, Cooney had many 2x2 converts there. Two of his staunchest supporters were brothers, John and William West, and their families, from Ballinamallard, both of whom hosted Conventions on their properties. The West brothers and Cooney were long-time close friends who had enjoyed Bible studies together in Enniskillen long before Irvine and the other Workers came along.

Reid, who often visited the home of John and Sara West, informed them Cooney would soon be returning from America where he had been causing trouble and warned them not to have fellowship with him.

1928, October: Senior Workers Meeting. Cooney arrived in Belfast, Ireland, on Saturday, October 6, 1928, from Montreal, Canada, aboard the SS *Andania*. Plans had been made secretly to give Cooney a last-chance ultimatum. Several Senior Workers from around the world were en route, if not already in Ireland, to attend the Meeting.

A week after he arrived on October 12, 1928, several Senior Workers squared off against Cooney in the home of Andrew Knox in Clankilvoragh, Lurgan, Ireland. They were Jack Carroll, William Weir, Willie Gill, Wilson Reid, James Jardine, Joe Twamley, Andrew Robb, Nat Dickson, Robert Miller, Ben Boles and Thomas Elliott. Carroll appeared to be the Worker in charge of the Meeting. No representatives from Australia or New Zealand were present, nor was Walker, who arrived a week later, on October 19, 1928, aboard the SS *Olympic.*

The purpose of the Meeting was a final attempt to persuade Cooney to agree to restrict his ministry. The conditions necessary for the Basis for Fellowship had been hammered out earlier in a Solemn Agreement they presented to him:

1.   That no Worker would teach or preach anything contrary to what the Worker in whose field he was labouring believed without his permission.

2. That if a Worker desired to preach anything which the Workers as a whole did not agree with, he was to go to a part where the Workers had never been in order to do so (Meeting 1928).

Cooney was unmoved and refused to agree to these conditions, resolutely declaring he would retain the liberty God gave him when he first started preaching. "If I had agreed to abide by these decrees, I would henceforth have been subject to rules which we in public denied existed in this Fellowship" (Roberts 1990, 14, 3, *TTT*).

When the impasse appeared insurmountable, Carroll declared he would have no more fellowship with Cooney and left the room. Of the remaining ten Workers, nine followed suit, except for Elliott, who left with Cooney. In their early days, Elliott had conducted most of the baptisms of new converts, which generated for him the nickname "Tom the Baptist." Ironically, it was Elliott who had baptized the Workers who excommunicated them. Afterwards, Cooney posed the question, "The baptism of Tom—was it of man or of God?"

Cooney's narrative of the Lurgan Meeting reads:

> This is a true description of what took place on that memorable occasion; and as the untruth has been spread that I went out of fellowship from my brethren and thereby caused a division, I write to let you know that I earnestly desired, and still earnestly desire, to remain in the fellowship of my brethren on the same condition as we had from the beginning, viz., that 'the truth as it is in Jesus' be the only test by which His disciples are to be disciplined, and that the Scriptures are to be the only written revelation accepted as declaring the truth.
>
> It seems to be unknown by many of God's children and unrealized by most that on October 12th, 1928, at Clankilvoragh, Lurgan, Ireland, at a Meeting of those who might be called the apostles amongst the people of God—indeed there happened to be twelve present—a verbal Agreement was submitted by the summer-up, James Jardine, expressed by John Carroll, called by the latter [at] different times a 'Solemn Agreement,' binding all the Workers not to express individual revelation even though true, if the Worker in whose field they were had not yet seen it. This verbal agreement was, as declared at that historic Meeting and apostolic council, a 'Basis of Fellowship for all Workers.' (Meeting 1928). *See* details in Appendix D.

James Bothwell, the Wests and some others decided to keep an open mind until they heard Cooney's side. After a Meeting held at Bothwell's home, Bothwell explained to Reid, "I did everything I could to have all present, thinking there might be something wrong with Eddie. But when all was told, I found nothing to condemn Eddie for, no evidence, but only untrue reports written and carried across the country by false and jealous brethren ... I also opened my home to Eddie for him to explain the awful 'crimes' he was being accused of by you and George Walker. If the 'crimes' were so terrible, why did you state here that if Eddie would consent and fall in line with all the others, you would all be one in the morning?" (Dec. 28, 1928, *TTT*).

"We thought it very strange," explained Sara West, "to hear that Edward would change and preach false doctrine inside a few years because we knew that God had used him in a great measure in different parts of England and Ireland. Wilson Reid and many in fellowship with us never came back to our home after making the decision to hear Edward Cooney's side ... When Edward Cooney did come back, we could not see any change in him; he was as sincere and ardent as ever, preaching the same simple Gospel as we heard at the beginning" (S. West 1954, *TTT*).

William West reminded Walker, "You said when you were here that it would be no harm for anybody who felt so inclined to go and hear Eddie; and above all, you said there could be no separation, excommunication or division in the family of God ... Fortified by this assurance, I like many others, went to hear Eddie" (Oct. 1929, *TTT*).

Instead of things happening as Walker promised West, two Workers (Sam McClements and Hugh Breen) went around directing those who met in the West's home for Fellowship Meetings not to go there anymore; half the church turned against them. He and his wife were judged and treated as if they were enemies of God. Incredibly, they suddenly found themselves the victims of bitter hatred and prejudice from the very ones with whom they had worshiped for 25 years.

Cooney was 61 years old when he was cast out in 1928; he had been preaching in the Cooneyite Sect for 27 years. He declared, "I have been excommunicated by my fellow Workers and hundreds of Saints and eight Workers have been put outside the camp with me." He lamented "that I accepted ... that previous to meeting him [Irvine] we were unregenerate ... In 1914, God showed me the pre-eminence William got through this error ... Wilson McClung declared that this, is my chief offence. I am happy to be back at the place we occupied for four years [1901–1905] after God called William Irvine" (to My Dear Sister, May 1930, Appendix D).

Cooneyites Today. A few Cooneyites (Cooney loyalists) still hold Meetings in Ireland, Wales and possibly Australia. Their numbers have dwindled, possibly due to not having any Workers to recruit new converts.   🍀🍀🍀

28

1928 – Aftershocks, Division and Exodus

After the Lurgan Meeting. Wilson Reid, Overseer of Ireland, took charge of the excommunication of Edward Cooney's supporters. George Walker arrived from America a week after the Lurgan Meeting. Reid, Walker and Cooney were all natives of N. Ireland. Reid and Walker arranged Meetings for Workers and Friends announcing that Cooney was out of fellowship, unregenerate, not born again and that anyone who believed Cooney was a Servant of God or opened their homes to him would be disfellowshipped.

Wilson Reid, Overseer of Ireland and South Africa

William West, who professed through Cooney 25 years earlier, explained, "I would rather die than see him cast out. I could do nothing else but stand by him when he was forsaken by his Brother Workers. We brought him to our home and the home was immediately blacklisted and even our lifelong friends, Tom and Mrs. Betty, told us they could not have any more fellowship with us" (Oct. 1929, *TTT*).

One month after the Lurgan Meeting, just prior to the annual Irvinestown, Ireland Special Meeting customarily held on St. Stephen's Day (December 26), Reid, began circulating a letter to the Irish "Brothers and Sisters in Christ," announcing that Cooney was no longer a part of their Fellowship and effectively "poisoning the well" against him.

> We must make it known that we cannot ask Eddie or his companion to take part in any Meetings we are responsible for, nor encourage any Saint or Worker to attend theirs. We feel we must henceforth advise them to stay away. We can't accept any responsibility for those who decide to go with Eddie nor for those who profess in his Meetings now that he is out of fellowship and on his own … if it takes from us only those not 'born of God' we shall see in the end it has been a blessing … We can't bind him down or stop him in any way in this country where he worked many years and has many friends; but we can tell them where he stands. (Dec. 13, 1928, *TTT*)

Division of 1928: Second Exodus. As usual, James Bothwell made the necessary arrangements for the annual Christmas Special Meeting in the Orange Hall at Irvinestown. Several hundred Friends arrived for the Meeting, along with Cooney, but Reid, the scheduled main speaker, never appeared.

Later, Bothwell sent Reid an explanatory letter. "I did not get your note until 4:00 o'clock in the afternoon *after* the Meeting was over. I had written to you that all arrangements would be made for the Meeting … We waited after the time the Meeting was supposed to commence not knowing you would not come. Then I stood up and said: 'Seeing that our Brothers … (you and your companion) have failed to come to take charge, I will now ask our Brother Edward Cooney to take the Meeting' " (Dec. 28, 1928, *TTT*).

Reid's failure to appear caused the Friends to take sides when Cooney took the platform. A large number of the Friends rose up and left while a greater number remained. This forced a division among the Friends. With Cooney loyalists continuing to side with him, the large Second Exodus of the 2x2 Sect ensued; it became known as the *Division of 1928*.

The Purge. By the end of 1928, the news had circulated around the world that Edward Cooney was no longer a 2x2 Sect minister or church member, and the Friends were instructed to have no further dealings with him. If asked, young Workers were to say they were "not allowed to discuss the matter." To continue to communicate with Cooney or to keep one's home open to him was considered taking his side. Those who failed to shun Cooney or aligned themselves with him and Thomas Elliott were cast out or persecuted until they left. They became the shunned Outcasts.

Damnatio Memoriae. After Cooney was ostracized, the Workers reverted to the tactics they had used 14 years earlier when they ousted Irvine. They purged the sect of Cooney's loyal friends and followers. They redacted the sect's history; they edited, obscured, or removed certain information. They began claiming their church had no connection with the Cooneyites, a moniker that testified to their origins. The eponymous nickname *Cooneyites* especially irritated Reid, Bill Carroll and others. Reid relayed to John West that he hoped the banning of Cooney would "clear what is left of the name that has stuck to us like glue all along."

Cooney's name was omitted as the author of the five hymns he wrote in *Hymns Old and New. See* Chapter 37. Even though her brother, Willie, had professed through Cooney in 1905, when a man accused Sister Worker Elisabeth Jamieson of being a Cooneyite, she pretended she didn't know what he meant, saying, "the only *coney* I knew about was the little animal spoken about in the book of Proverbs" (1969, *TTT*).

> First of all let me say, on behalf of those in this fellowship, that we are not now and never have been "Cooneyites". Owing to the fact that we take no denominational name, this name "Cooneyite" was given maliciously by those unduly prejudiced and out of sympathy. While it is true a Mr. Cooney was associated with this movement, it is equally true that at no time in its history was he looked upon either as the leader or pioneer the pamphlet suggests and at no time was the name "Cooneyite" assumed by any. Mr. Cooney's personal friends are comparatively few in number, and these, with few exceptions, in the British Isles.

Excerpt from Jack Carroll's letter (May 27, 1929)

Price of Allegiance – The Outcasts. According to Cooney, hundreds of Saints and eight Workers were excommunicated with him (1930, Appendix D). Some of the eight Workers were: Tom Elliott and his wife, Ellen, Fred Wood, Alex Buchan and perhaps Andy and Sam Boyd. Alfred and Sarah Magowan had become Outcasts in 1919 before the 1928 Division. Wood was a convert of Cooney, and Buchanan was a convert of the Elliotts.

Taking Cooney's side In the Division of 1928 were John and Sara West, former owners of the Crocknacrieve Convention grounds, and John's brother William West, owner of the Mullaghmeen Convention grounds. Cooney's loyalists continued to assemble for Fellowship Meetings at John West's home in Rossahilly.

"My father" [John West], recollected Ida West, "and any who continued to receive them as God's Servants were also cut off from fellowship by Wilson Reid, ... Jack Carroll, Willie Gill, Andy Robb, James Jardine, Ben Boles and some others including George Walker. The most serious statement made to me was that I was doing the Devil's work in standing by Edward Cooney. But God by His Holy Spirit and through Scripture revealed otherwise. We Outcasts learned that man cutting us off was no proof that God had" (1954, *TTT*).

"To the sorrow of many," observed Sara West, "those who kept their homes open to Edward Cooney became outcast from their brethren, and in that way the Division started ... Wilson Reid and many in fellowship with us never came back to our home after ... [we made] the decision to hear Edward Cooney's side" (1954, *TTT*).

William West begged Walker to come help sort out the situation in Ireland in person and expressed how sorely his faith had been tested:

> The charges Wilson Reid brought against him [Cooney] were so easily refuted, and of such trivial character ... there was nothing in them ... And when I looked at this poor rejected man whose zeal and earnestness for God had put so many of us to shame, I could hardly believe that his brethren who used to love him and had 27 years of fellowship with him in the Gospel could turn so bitterly against him for the few trifling faults you and others told us of.
>
> Churches were visited ... Several of them were actually closed. Then individuals were tested privately as to what they thought about Eddie. And if they had any softness in their hearts towards him, they were cast out and refused further fellowship ... In my case, a new church was formed at Reids of Gortaloughan (my brother-in-law) and now half the church meet there. The other half continue to meet at my home ... Where is the scriptural authority for all this? ... Our faith has been tested as never before ... We are cast out. We did not go out. We were put out. I was written to not go to the Convention at Pogues (in this county). This all seems unbelievable. (Oct. 1929, *TTT*)

Cooney's Pain and Suffering. One of the most painful things for Cooney was that the Workers undermined the Gospel he had preached to his converts, stole his converts' love for him, and diverted it to themselves. He lamented that his evangelizing Work had been destroyed and his converts stolen. Adding salt to his wounds, countless Saints and Workers who had professed through Cooney had turned against him.

Fred Wood wept as he recalled a hard experience when he and Cooney visited the home of a 2x2 woman in the middle of winter. A

Sister Worker who was present announced at mealtime, "We will give you food as men, but not as Brothers." Cooney refused. That evening they were put out into the snow with no place to go. "As a last gesture, they decided to let us stay in the shed, but without even as much as a blanket." All night long, Cooney and Fred rubbed each other to keep their blood circulating and to keep from freezing to death (Parker 1982, 77).

In sharp contrast, Cooney continued to refer to the Workers as his *brethren* and instructed his loyal followers not to utter any unkind words against them because "They are all my brethren" (W. West, Oct. 1929, *TTT*). He did not disown those who had rejected him. Even with all their faults, he still believed they were God's people, and their problem was that the zeal of God's house had eaten them up (Psalms 69:9).

Cooney counseled his loyalists to keep their hearts and homes open to those who rejected them—while the Workers counseled their members to do the opposite. Cooney revealed, "I earnestly desired, and still earnestly desire to remain in the fellowship of my brethren on the same condition as we had from the beginning" (Meeting 1928, Appendix D).

1929 Conventions. Although the Workers and Friends boycotted the usual July 1929 Mullagheen Convention held on William West's property, there was a large turnout of Outcasts from all over the British Isles. Cooney, Elliott and Alfred Magowan occupied the platform. This was the Outcasts' final Convention and the last Convention where Cooney preached, since he believed Conventions were not scriptural.

Also in 1929, Reid started another Convention for the remaining members at Greenhill, Co. Fermanagh, near Brookeborough on Albert Pogue's place (Wm. West's brother-in-law) where it continued until 1939, when it was relocated to John Reid's property at Gortaloughan, Co. Fermanagh. The locals, including our tour guide in 2004, refer to them as the *Reidites* and to their Convention as the *Reidite Convention*.

On His Own – Cooney's Ministry

After 1928, Cooney's loyal friends around the world continued to reach out and write to him. His large number of correspondents supported him financially, enabling him to travel widely and fellowship with them. He preached at many sites, often in the open-air in towns and villages in the British Isles. He visited factories during lunch hour where he witnessed to employees. On buses and trains, he witnessed to whomever would listen. As before, he made converts and performed baptisms.

The five years following the Division of 1928 were spiritually active ones for the Outcasts. There was a great outpouring of love and zeal among them and a feeling of release that they had been set free from the bondage of human control to experience once again the control of the Holy Spirit. The Outcasts became more active in witnessing to outsiders. They assembled for Special Meetings and Fellowship Meetings in homes. Cooney, age 61 in 1928, spent the years 1928–1933 in the British Isles where he continued to preach, gain converts and establish churches, often with the assistance of Fred Wood, his right-hand man.

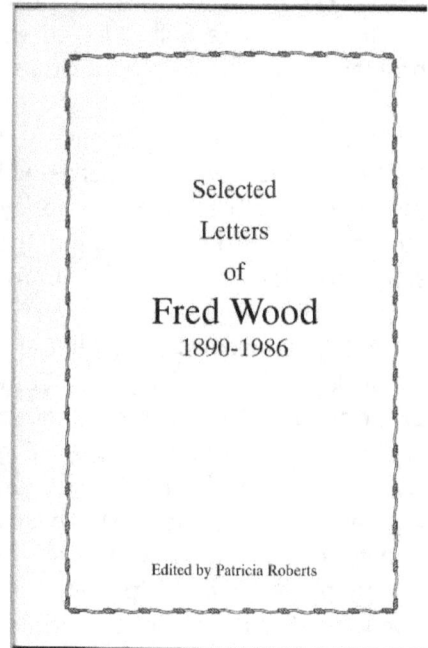

Selected
Letters
of
Fred Wood
1890-1986

Edited by Patricia Roberts

Ed Cooney's right-hand man and successor, Fred Wood, with his wife Sadie and children

"Selected letters of Fred Wood 1890–1986" by Patricia Roberts

Deaths. After her husband, Thomas Elliott, passed away in 1930 in England, Ellen continued to support and encourage Cooney. Mrs. Elliott was a welcome house guest at Cooney's widowed sister, Mary Elizabeth (Cooney) Boyton Smith, in England. After Mary's husband, an Episcopalian rector, died in 1923, she ceased attending an organized church and began meeting with the Cooneyites in England. Mrs. Elliott died in England in 1966.

Cooney's brother, Fred, died April 12, 1940, in New Zealand and his remaining brother, Henry "Harry," died May 31, 1945, in London. He was left with one surviving sibling, his oldest sister, Mary Elizabeth, who predeceased him in 1953, aged 87.

1933–1939: After five years, Cooney felt the Outcasts were on a firm enough foundation that it was safe for him to leave Ireland on a mission trip. He departed on June 17, 1933, aboard the SS *Antonia* for Montreal, Canada. During his preaching tour, he also visited Australia, New Zealand and the US. In 1938–1939, he established a rehabilitation center for alcoholics in Birmingham, Alabama, US (*Arizona Republic*, May 10, 1941, p. 31).

Six years later, in 1939, he returned to his native country, Ireland, where he stayed through WWII until mid-1947. To his dismay, in his absence much had changed for the worse among the Outcasts. He found they had lost much of their zeal and had declined spiritually. Some Elders had become irresponsible, some Outcasts had gone astray, and many who remained were lukewarm. John West was the one most responsible for keeping the Outcasts together. As the Elder of the Fellowship Meeting at Ballinamallard, he was a man of extraordinary discernment and used his influence to bolster many whose faith was failing. When Cooney returned to Co. Fermanagh, as was his custom he stayed at John West's home. Fred Wood became the Belfast church Elder in 1939, and things began to improve spiritually among the Outcasts.

1947–1953: After the war, on May 15, 1947, Cooney, age 80, returned to North America aboard the SS *Marine Falcon*. The Workers had forewarned the Friends not to receive him into their homes, and those who did risked being excommunicated. On his arrival in New York, he was welcomed by Outcasts Earl and Mae Hammond who had professed through him. He traveled thousands of miles crisscrossing America, holding missions and visiting old friends, including Irvine Weir, an excommunicated Irish Worker, who was one of the first three Workers to set foot on American soil in 1903. Friends drove him and/or accompanied him at times on his journeys.

In September 1948, Cooney went to Edmonton, Alberta, Canada, to visit his long-time friends from Enniskillen, Oliver Scott and brothers Sam and Andrew "Andy" Boyd. Long before they ever met Irvine, they had been meeting together in Enniskillen for independent Bible studies. Sam, who entered the Work in 1900, may have gone on the 1899 Bicycle Mission Trip to Scotland. He arrived in Philadelphia in 1907 (age 34), left the Work between 1910 and 1917, married and then resided in Canada.

According to Oliver Scott, who attended the Meeting where Sam Boyd was the Elder, a Worker warned Andy not to receive Cooney in his home. So Sam provided Cooney with accommodations. In mid-winter

1948, "the weather was about 30° below zero; and if Sam had turned the aged Edward away from his door, and he had no other place to go, he could have frozen to death ... they would have been willing that Edward Cooney perish with cold and hunger" (Parker 1982, 78, Fn. 25, 81; Oliver and Elsie Scott, October 1, 1949). For this act of kindness to an old friend, Sam was excommunicated.

The Boyd brothers, Oliver and Elsie Scott and other Friends who were present when the sect was formed in Ireland and remained loyal to Cooney were marginalized, persecuted and cast out. The Friends were forbidden to see or speak to them and risked excommunication if discovered (Parker 1982, 90–91, Fn. 15).

1949: August Gustafson. A 1949 letter by Cooney came to the attention of Gustafson. Cooney had written, "I will forgive you for not forgiving me." He was impressed and contacted Cooney who took Gustafson to be his Co-worker. The pair traveled many miles on mission trips in the US and visited old friends. When he was 25 years old in 1899, Gustafson had become a preacher. Later, he met the Workers, professed, entered the Work and was the first Worker to preach in Sweden. In 1944, at age 70, he was excommunicated, reportedly because he had objected to the harsh treatment a young Worker had received from Senior Workers. Gustafson died in 1970, aged 97.

1954: After they were disfellowshipped, about 20 distressed Australian Friends appealed to Cooney for help. A year had not passed since Cooney, age 87, returned to the UK when, once again, he boarded the RMS *Orontes*, accompanied by Richard Greenaway and Mrs. Elliott, and arrived in Adelaide, Australia, on February 25, 1954. In Mildura, Victoria, where the Greenaways lived, Cooney and Mrs. Elliott held Meetings and visited with numerous Outcasts in several Australian states. *See* Chapter 48, Victorian Division.

Meanwhile, the Workers called a reconciliation meeting, hoping to smooth over problems arising from the purge by Bill Carroll in Victoria in the 1950s. Cooney went, although he was not invited. Tom Turner, the Worker stationed at the entrance, refused to allow Cooney to enter the meeting. When Cooney was rejected, some others also left the meeting. A little over a year later, on February 1, 1955, Cooney left Auckland, New Zealand, for San Francisco aboard the Pan American Clipper Argonaut flight, where he was joined by Gustafson.

1957, July: Edward Cooney, age 90, arrived back in Ireland, where he had planned to spend the rest of his life. He had more friends, fellowship and support there than any other place—but his best-laid plans did not work out.

For many years, Cooney had retained a belief he had not openly disclosed. Knowing his time was short, he felt compelled to share his private conviction with others before he left this world. He believed that God's mercy did not end at the grave, and that there would still be an opportunity for repentance—even after death, for "His mercy endureth forever." This belief parallels post-mortem evangelization, a doctrine adopted by some other sects.

This new belief seriously disturbed many of his followers, and some of his staunchest supporters turned against him; others returned to the 2x2s. It caused a division among the Outcasts. Due to the conflict and confusion, Cooney decided it would be best for him to spend his last days elsewhere in peace. In poor health, at age 92, he sailed from London, England, on April 18, 1959, to Adelaide, Australia, aboard the SS *Orsova,* accompanied by George Greenaway and his mother.

1960, June 20: Edward Cooney Died. After living with Richard and Emily Greenaway in Mildura, Victoria, for a little over a year, Cooney passed away, aged 93. He had been preaching for 59 years total: 27 years before he was excommunicated and 32 years after.

Edward Cooney (1867–1960)

Cooney's hometown newspaper, the *Impartial Reporter,* announced his death with an impressive article, "A Great Figure Passes: One of Enniskillen's most remarkable men, Edward Cooney, who turned his back on wealth to become a wandering preacher and the founder of a new religious sect, the Cooneyites, has died in Australia at the age of 93. The second son of Mr. William Rutherford Cooney … Edward Cooney was a commercial traveller for his father's business. His parents were members of the Church of Ireland and Edward was baptized and brought up in that faith, but … through diligent reading of the

Scriptures, he arrived at variance with the views of the churches" (June 23, 1960, *TTT*).

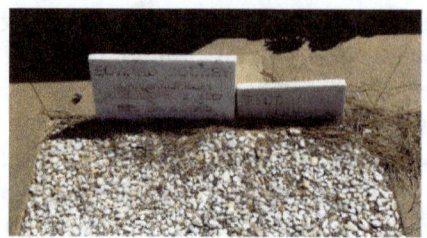

Edward Cooney's Grave – Mildura, Australia

More information about Edward Cooney is found in four biographical books by Dr. Patricia Roberts listed in References. Since Dr. Roberts' family became Cooneyites when she was a child, she was well placed to write a definitive account of his life. Dr. Roberts was the daughter of William Roberts and Emily West, sister of John and William West. She met Cooney in person in 1950 in London. He baptized her in 1953 and officiated at her father's funeral. She retired in Ballinamallard, Co. Fermanagh in 1984.

Cherie Kropp-Ehrig with Author Patricia Roberts (2004)

When visiting Enniskillen, Dr. Roberts graciously invited my husband and me to her home for a very enjoyable tea in 2004, along with her friends, Myrtle Doherty, and Fred Wood's daughter, Elizabeth McCord (mentioned in the acknowledgements of all Dr. Roberts' books). The number of worshippers who met in her home had dwindled to six by 2008. Periodically, they met with others like-minded in nearby towns. *See also* Chapters 7, 14 and Appendix D.

Cooney's Mantle. After his death, Cooney's followers looked to Frederick "Fred" Wood as their authority figure. Wood was a convert of Cooney in 1916 when he was 26 years old and was a Worker for 20 years before marrying one of his converts, Sarah "Sadie" Greenaway, in 1938. They made their home in Belfast, N. Ireland, where they hosted the weekly Fellowship Meeting. They had four daughters: Elizabeth, Mary, Anne and Joanna. Fred retired from his job in 1960, at age 70, the same year Cooney died, and the Woods began shepherding the Outcasts in Ireland. They made missionary trips to England, Scotland, Canada, US and Norway. Fred was born on May 6, 1890, and died on September 11, 1986, aged 96. Sadie died on November 27, 1985, aged 69.

Three Sects Founded by William Irvine

By 1928, Irvine's original movement had split into three separate groups (Irvinites, Cooneyites and Two by Twos), all sharing a common beginning and founder with none acknowledging an official name. While the three sects do not provide public membership statistics, in 2022, worldwide membership is estimated to be 75,000 2x2s and fewer than 100 Irvinites and Cooneyites.

Today, Cooney's remaining followers are sometimes referred to as *Cooneyites*, while they refer to themselves as *Christians* or the *Outcasts*. They continue to meet for fellowship in homes, take no official name and use the 1951 edition of *Hymns Old and New.* Author Dr. Patricia Roberts was one of the Outcasts. Ironically, even though Cooney strongly opposed the sect taking a name in World War I, his surname became the eponym for the sect.

Confusion may arise because the term *Cooneyites* is sometimes used for both the original group (2x2 Sect) and the loyal Cooney supporters (Outcasts). The UK public and press had been referring to the original sect as *Cooneyites* long before it divided. Today, the original group is still referred to as *Cooneyites* in several books, encyclopedias, newspapers, *Wikipedia* and websites.

Edward Cooney's influence has lived on through his much-loved hymns: "As We Gather," "Lord, We Are Met Together," "Our God, Our Father," "Here We Come," and "Jesus Died for Sinners."

See Appendix H for comparison of beliefs of the three sects founded by Irvine. Fred Wood's daughter, Mary Rogers, graciously provided the information for Cooneyites.

Western United States

Western Region shaded in gray

Eastern United States

Minnesota

Wisconsin

Michigan

Iowa

Ohio

Illinois

Indiana

Missouri

Kentucky

West Virginia

Virginia

Arkansas

Tennessee

North Carolina

South Carolina

Mississippi

Alabama

Georgia

Texas

Louisiana

Florida

Maine

New York

Pennsylvania

1. Vermont
2. New Hampshire
3. Massachusetts
4. Connecticut
5. Rhode Island
6. New Jersey
7. Delaware
8. Maryland
★ Washington DC

WESTERN STATES

Alaska
  JUNEAU
  WASILLA

Arizona
  CASA GRANDE

California
  BUTTONWILLOW
  GILROY
  ORICK
  SANTEE

Idaho
  BONNERS FERRY
  PARMA
  POST FALLS

Montana
  DAGMAR
  DEVON
  MANHATTAN
  RONAN

Oregon
  BORING
  SAGINAW

Washington
  CHELAN
  MILLTOWN
  OLYMPIA
  WALLA WALLA

Wyoming
  CODY

CHRISTIAN CONVENTIONS

Representing Assemblies of Christians

and

Christian Missionaries

CANADIAN NORTHWEST

Alberta
  DIDSBURY
  GREENSHIELDS
  HYTHE
  MELLOWDALE

British Columbia
  DUNCAN
  GLEN VALLEY
  PRINCE GEORGE
  SALMON ARM

Manitoba
  BOWSMAN
  PORTAGE LA PRAIRIE

New Ontario
  EMO

Saskatchewan
  AYLESBURY
  SMEATON
  THEODORE

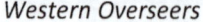

Western Overseers   *Eastern Overseers*

29

US Leader Differences – Divorce & Remarriage

Contention Between US Overseers. Not long after their arrival in 1903–1904, two young Irish Workers in their mid-twenties assumed the responsibility over the Workers and the flock in North America. They were Jack Carroll and George Walker.

In the Two by Two Sect, North America is divided into two jurisdictions, East and West. The Western region includes the area west of the Rocky Mountain range (excluding Utah), including California, Nevada, Arizona, Pacific Islands, Baja California, Northwest Mexico, Washington, Alaska, Oregon, Idaho, Montana and Wyoming; along with the Canadian provinces of British Columbia, Alberta, Saskatchewan, Manitoba and Western Ontario. The Eastern region is comprised of the remainder of the US and Canada. The Western region is shaded in gray on the foregoing map.

The Overseers of the Western US were Jack Carroll (to 1957), followed by Willie Jamieson (to 1974). The oversight was then assumed jointly by a group of Workers:

- From Washington, Tharold Sylvester (died 1994), replaced by Sydney Holt and currently Mark Huddle.
- From California, Eldon Tenniswood (died 2003), replaced by Dick Middleton, replaced by Dale Shultz and currently, Robert Newman.
- From Oregon, Howard Mooney (died 1999), replaced by Ralph Sines, Harold Bennett, Dale Shultz and currently Dean Bruer.
- From Montana/Wyoming, Howard Mooney, Ralph Sines, Everett Swanson, Jack Price, Dean Bruer, and currently Scott Rauscher.
- From B.C. Canada, Ernest Nelson (died 2001) replaced by Paul Sharp, then Walter Burkinshaw and currently, Merlin Affleck.

The Eastern US Overseers have been George Walker (died 1981, aged 104), Andrew Abernethy (died 1988), Taylor Wood (died 2008), and currently, Barry Barkley (1939—); possibly in transition to a successor.

Disclaimer: This list of Overseers was compiled to the best of my ability; even so, it possibly contains errors or omissions.

In the early years between 1910 and 1920, there was a fair amount of Worker movement from East to West. Workers in one area were invited to be speakers at Conventions and Special Meetings in the other area; Workers also exchanged fields from one area to the other.

Until around 1924, there appeared to be harmony between the two Regional Overseers. A 1916 Convention photo at Dalton, Idaho, showed Carroll and Walker standing side by side; a 1924 Convention photo of New Norway, Alberta, Canada, included both men.

Contention arose between the two Overseers in the mid-1920s; the root cause is not clear. Over time, these two men came to be at serious odds with one another. Tensions mounted and produced a gulf between the two.

It has been surmised that the scheduling of Conventions was the proverbial "straw that broke the camel's back." According to Willie Smiley, a Western Canadian Worker under Carroll's oversight, Convention planning was one of the first rebel manifestations of factionalism. As late as 1921, there was still a combined Convention schedule for North America. Around 1922, the Workers in Western North America decided, in Smiley's words, to "make our own wee list." Some speculate that the separate Convention lists, one for the West and another for the East, was the beginning of "when the West broke away from the East."

Dividing the Convention lists had the impact of limiting the visiting guest speakers to their respective territories. After the division in the 1920s, Worker exchanges and traveling between the two territories were rare. Regardless, both Overseers continued to attend the Senior Workers Meetings.

Another issue that possibly added to the fracture concerned the use of radios. During the Pacific War Theater, there were five Workers imprisoned in the Philippines, three from the West Coast. *See* Chapter 38.

Seeking to stay informed of current events relating to these Workers, the West Coast Friends and Workers listened to the radio. However, on the East Coast, Walker prohibited radios in Friends' homes and vehicles. This prohibition was enforced to the point that some Workers broke antennas off vehicles parked at Eastern Conventions. The same prohibition was applied in some other countries.

During the WWII era, significant polarization arose in the rulings made by the two North American Overseers regarding whether the drafted male Friends should apply for the status of conscientious objectors. In the West, Carroll gave the 2x2 men freedom of choice; this was documented in two statements (J. Carroll 1940 and 1942 Statements, *TTT*). In the East, Walker instructed 2x2 men to register as conscientious objectors, and most did so. *See* Chapter 38.

It is also speculated that some antagonism may have been due to Walker's dissatisfaction with the lifestyle of Jack's brother, Bill Carroll. Bill married in 1901; he and his wife entered the Work in 1903. Since 1913, Bill had been the Overseer of Victoria and Tasmania, Australia. Reportedly, Walker disapproved of the Carroll brothers' desire for female companionship. Walker believed in Workers living as they claimed: poor, homeless and celibate.

Allegedly, Walker felt the Carroll brothers misused their positions and funds as Overseers. He disapproved of the lavish way they handled the "blood bought money of the Friends" for their personal use. In the 1950s, the 2x2 Sect in Victoria under Bill Carroll's oversight, split into three factions, during which Jack Carroll and Walker took opposite sides, with Walker working toward Bill Carroll being removed from his role as Overseer.

1930: Senior Workers Meeting. During July 19–21, 1930, a worldwide Senior Workers Meeting was held at the West Hanney, Oxfordshire England Convention grounds on J. Humphries' property. Sixteen Senior Workers were present; all had entered the Work between 1899 and 1905. One item, possibly the main item, discussed was the strained relationship between George Walker and Jack Carroll. Following is a meeting summary from a documented statement:

> For a number of years past, difficulties have existed in the USA between some of the Elder Workers, which in recent years became more acute … it was decided that a number of the Elder Workers from various countries should come together …

> During the days we … were gathered together, full opportunity was given to all to express their minds and to offer any suggestions that would be helpful. After considering the matter from every viewpoint, we are happy to say that those who were most concerned in this trouble expressed their deep regret for any offence at which they had been guilty and apologised to each other and undertook to do all in their power to dispel the existing difficulties and promote the spirit of unity and fellowship amongst the Lord's people …

> **It was unanimously agreed by all present that the past should be buried**, and that in the future, all would use their influence to discourage anything that would disturb the peace in God's family, adhering to the teaching and example of Jesus. [Signed by: W. J. Gill, G.

Walker, J. T. Carroll, J. Hardie, A. Dougal, H. R. Matthews, J. Twamley, J. Doak, W. Jamieson, A. Scott, J. Jardine, J. S. Jackson, A. Pearce, W. Weir, W. Reid, J. Forbes] (Meeting 1930, *TTT*). NOTE: Bill Carroll was not present nor were any Australian representatives.

CLARIFICATION. The often repeated **bolded** line in the above Statement *"It was unanimously agreed by all present that the past should be buried"* has sometimes been taken out of context to mean that the Workers made a pact of silence and agreed to bury the sect's history and Irvine's role in founding the 2x2 movement.

A careful reading of this statement shows that one of the purposes of the meeting was to reconcile the acute *difficulties* involving antagonism between two Elder US Workers, namely Overseers, Jack Carroll and George Walker. *The past* the Workers agreed to bury was the offenses that existed between the two. They *buried the hatchet*, so to speak—NOT the origin, founder and history of the 2x2 Sect, as is sometimes erroneously asserted.

Despite their agreement, over the next two decades, the conflict continued. In 1935, Irvine Weir discovered the seriousness of the enmity between Walker and Carroll, when he asked Walker, his Overseer, to approve his plan to return to California. To his amazement, Walker replied, *"I would not like you to go to California now. I am sorry but I may have to cut the West off"* (Parker 1982, 85).

1942: On occasion, the two North American Overseers transcended their differences and worked toward a common goal. On or before 1942, they apparently agreed to use the name of *Christian Conventions Representing Assemblies of Christians Assuming This Name Only* in North America for their church. Identical letterheads were printed for both East and West; the only difference being the Convention locations shown. This lengthy name was intended to convey the idea that the sect consisted of Conventions that represented local groups (Fellowship Meetings) of Christians who took no name except *Christian*. Subsequently, some began to refer to the sect by the shorter name *Christian Convention Church*, abbreviated *CCC*.

Walker used the Eastern CCC letterhead in 1942 to correspond with the US Selective Service in connection with his requests for exemptions from US military service for the Workers and for non-combatant status for the male members (1942, *TTT*, RIS). Likewise, Jack Carroll composed some letters on the Western CCC letterhead promoting the Red Cross and loyalty to America and its flag (1942, *TTT*).

New Policy for Overseers. Sometime in the early 1930s, the Senior Workers enacted a new policy: An Overseer could not marry and continue to serve as an Overseer. However, the currently married

Overseers in the Work were grandfathered in and allowed to remain as Overseers. This decision may have been reached at the July 19–21, 1930, Senior Workers Meeting.

Bill Carroll, Overseer of Victoria and Tasmania, Australia, sent two Sister Workers, Heyes (28) and Grace Prideaux (34), to work under Jack Carroll's oversight. Heyes, of Evandale, Tasmania, entered the Work in 1913. From Victoria, Prideaux entered the Work in 1915. They arrived in Vancouver, B.C., Canada, on the SS *Niagara* on September 30, 1919. Grace Prideaux married Brother Worker Joe Brown around 1926; the Christies invited them to preach as a married couple in Hawaii.

Reportedly, sometime between 1932 and 1937, Jack Carroll let the Senior Workers know that he and Sister Worker Linda Heyes desired to marry. Carroll wanted an exception made to the new policy so they could marry, and he could remain an Overseer. Instead, the Overseers held fast; they ruled that Carroll could no longer be an Overseer if they married, but they could continue preaching as a married Worker couple. Although it has been reported that Carroll and Heyes were secretly married, no form of marriage documentation has been found.

Sister Worker Linda Heyes (1892–1943)

Linda Heyes passed away July 27, 1943. A reportedly inconsolable Jack accompanied Heyes' body to Milltown, where he was too overcome to speak at her funeral. It was rumored that he wished to be buried next to Heyes' grave. His wishes were disregarded. While they are both buried in the same plot containing eight graves, their graves are not adjacent to each other; however, the corners touch. On either side of Heyes' grave, there were vacant plots until 1989 and 2002. Jack Carroll remained the Western Overseer until his death on March 26, 1957, aged 78.

Linda Heyes was the first person to be buried in a plot of eight graves in the Fir-Conway Lutheran Cemetery, Mt. Vernon, Washington, located one-half mile from the Milltown Convention grounds. It is said that this cemetery possibly contains more Workers' graves than any other cemetery in the world.

~~~~~

1931: *Outline of the History of a Peculiar People from 1900–1931*. In uncomplicated but striking detail, excommunicated Ex-worker Alfred Magowan published a fictional play inspired by actual events that occurred in the 2x2 Sect (1931, *TTT*).

1931: Tom Lyness Shot. Handsome Brother Worker Tom Lyness, age 48, was shot twice in the head in a hotel lobby in Bozeman, Montana, US, on December 10, 1931. Against all expectation, Lyness lived and continued to preach 39 more years until his death in 1970, aged 87.

Tom Lyness (1883 – 1970)

The Great Falls Tribune (Montana) reported: "Tom Lyness, 40 (*sic*: should be 48), an evangelist with missions at Belgrade and Manhattan, was shot and seriously wounded Thursday by William Sumner, 55, a barber of Pony" (Dec. 11, 1931, *TTT*). "Sumner blamed the preacher's influence for his failure to induce his wife to move with him to Pony, where he has a barber shop. The proposed baptism of his oldest daughter brought matters to a crisis, he said" (Dec. 12, 1931, *TTT*). Sumner was sentenced to serve 12 years in the state prison.

1938: Disturbance in Colorado. When Irvine Weir traveled through Colorado in the 1930s where Eddie Cornock was Overseer, he found the Friends and Workers in Denver had declared their support either for Jack Carroll or for George Walker. Each Overseer forbade visits or contact with preachers who were loyal to the other (Parker 1982, 85), which "brought great pain and confusion amongst the people of the Lord."

To resolve this matter, a Workers' Meeting was held in Denver on December 1, 1938, in which Walker "assume[d] responsibility and blame for his unwise attitude and action. He asked for forgiveness for his part and those with him who took part in "this sad disturbance." He agreed to "do all in his power to right this wrong ... and to correct wrong impressions."

On behalf of the Colorado Workers, Cornock "accepts some blame for the part he has had in this and asks forgiveness where in any way the Colorado Workers have failed to keep as closely in line with other Workers as they should." The meeting results were summarized in a statement signed by seven Senior Workers: John Hardie, James Jardine, John S. Jackson, George Walker, Eddie Cornock, William Wilkie and Hugh Matthews; there was no signature by Jack Carroll (Meeting 1938b, *TTT*).

1938: US Workers Convention. Reportedly, in or around 1938, before World War II, a large-scale Workers Meeting was held in Baltimore, Maryland. George Walker, Andrew Abernethy and Horace Burgess were among the approximately 150 Workers present.

Divorce and Remarriage Controversy.

1938: Workers' Council. An international meeting was held in July 1938, at West Hanney, England, where divorce and remarriage (D&R) were discussed. Sixteen of the most Senior Overseers in the world were present.

The passenger lists for ships traveling to England in June and July 1938 showed the following ten Workers: John "Jack" Carroll, Robert Chambers, John Doak, Alex Dougal, John Hardie, John "Jack" Jackson, Samuel Jones, Hugh Matthews, Alexander Pearce and George Walker. Some other Overseers possibly present at the meeting, but for whom no travel arrangements were located, were Joe Twamley (Scotland), Wilson Reid (Ireland), Willie Gill (England), James Jardine (Europe) and Sid Maynard (India).

The council deemed remarriage after a legal divorce to be "living in adultery/sin," a phrase not found in Scripture. Based on their opinions, the Workers formulated a new protocol for judging D&R couples and assigning their status in their Church. Since then, many, but not all, countries have followed the general 1938 Council ruling. Even so, worldwide, their methods of administering the protocols have not been uniform and have changed over time.

Regardless of the cause of the divorce, no exceptions were provided for innocent victims of desertion and spousal adultery (Matt. 5:32). Generally, remarried couples were expelled or silenced, which effectively relegated them to the status of "the least of these my brethren." Where is any Scriptural example corresponding to the man-made practice of withholding communion and participation in worship gatherings?

Future church participation of the couple may be dependent upon the country, the Overseer, and the timing of their remarriage. Couples are judged by their "previous knowledge." How complete was their earlier understanding of the Workers' rules? Were they sincere in their profession? An earlier baptism or growing up in a 2x2 home (sometimes even if they never professed) was sometimes considered evidence of "previous knowledge." Rules vary considerably for divorcees who:

A. Remarried *before* professing with no previous knowledge (outsiders).
B. Remarried *after* professing with no previous knowledge.
C. Remarried *after* professing, both having previous knowledge.
D. Remarried with one spouse having and the other not having previous knowledge.

Various verdicts have been applied and enforced by Workers for D&R couples regarding their participation in Meetings. Some D&R couples may:

1. silently attend but not participate in Meetings or communion (may choose a hymn); sometimes for an unspecified time period, after which full participation is allowed.
2. not attend any Fellowship Meetings, i.e. excommunicated, banished.
3. separate or divorce, remain single and fully participate.
4. continue in their current marriage after they profess and fully participate.
5. not be allowed to profess or attend Meetings (e.g. UK, Ireland, South Africa, Colombia, B.C. Canada, etc.).
6. be allowed to remarry after divorce and fully participate.
7. be allowed to participate if they have a spouse without previous knowledge; and not be allowed to participate if they have a spouse with previous knowledge.

Up until around 1975, the North American Overseers generally followed Nos. 1–4. Depending on the locality, some Workers refuse to spend the night in the home of a divorced and remarried couple or accept their monetary gifts.

1975: Divorce and Remarriage Meeting. A meeting of eight Senior North American Overseers was held in 1975 in Minneapolis, Minnesota, to reassess the remarriage after divorce policy.

Tharold Sylvester represented Western North America and Andrew Abernethy, Eastern North America, in lieu of George Walker, then 98 years old. Additional Western Overseers present were Eldon Tenniswood, Howard Mooney and Ernest Nelson. Eastern Overseers Taylor Wood, Garrett Hughes and Murray Keene were also present.

It was decided that D&R decisions would be judged on a case-by-case basis, and remarriage after divorce would only be considered in cases where fornication/adultery were involved.

They were unable to agree on the interpretation of 1 Cor. 7:15; that when "the unbelieving depart, let him depart. A brother or a sister is not under bondage in such cases." The East contended this meant the deserted, abandoned spouse was free to remarry and have full participation privileges. The West did not agree. The meeting came to a stalemate. Workers agreed to disagree. (Meeting 1975, *TTT*). Many Friends are unaware the Workers hold divergent views and policies worldwide.

Western D&R Protocol. According to Tharold Sylvester, during the 12 years following the 1975 Meeting, 20 Western remarried couples "made it right" by leaving their spouses and were welcomed back to the Fellowship as prodigals.

In the 1970s, perhaps after Eldon Tenniswood became Overseer of California in 1974–1975, the Western Workers (except for Howard Mooney) began taking a stricter stand against remarriage. Professing divorced and remarried couples (no matter when the divorce or remarriage occurred or why) were advised that unless they separated from their second spouse, they were jeopardizing their opportunity to enter Heaven. A number of D&R couples were asked not to attend any Meetings or only attend Gospel Meetings. Families were destroyed. The East did not agree with this practice. Howard Mooney did not separate D&R couples in Oregon.

After Dale Shultz became a Western US Overseer in 2005, he began "cleaning house." In 2013, he "reached out" to some D&R wives about separating from their husbands. He held up as examples three 2x2 women who chose to "make it right" by separating. Further, he mentioned that "God took care of it" for a fourth D&R wife whose husband died suddenly before they separated, perhaps inferring a warning that D&Rs who do not separate may experience dire consequences.

Reportedly, around 2010, former Overseer of BC Canada, Walter Burkinshaw, barred two couples from even attending a Fellowship Meeting after they remarried. As recently as 2019, in Nebraska, US, where Richard Gasser is Overseer, Workers required divorced and remarried couples to divorce and remain single in order to participate in Meetings.

Eastern D&R Protocol. For some years prior to the 1975 Meeting, many D&R situations had been left to the discretion of individual Workers on a case-by-case basis, and there had been a gradual loosening of restrictions. Sometime after the 1975 Meeting, Eastern Overseers of Colorado, Texas, Minnesota, North Dakota, Ohio, etc. began allowing some divorcees to remarry, some without a period of silence in Meetings, and also granting full privileges to D&R couples.

Possibly, the earliest significant advocate for permitting remarried couples in the East to participate and for allowing some divorcees to remarry was Overseer William Lewis. Excerpts follow from Lewis' statement about his convictions:

> It is most awesome being charged to obtain the guidance of the Holy Ghost so that judgment we give would be equitable and merciful, acceptable to and binding in Heaven, following this with the answer to Peter's question about forgiveness [70 times 7] emphasizing compassion and reminding us all of our utter dependence on the merciful and forgiving God, so that we would not deny to another what we must have ourselves ... Justice demands that the guilty bear punishment and not the innocent ... Jesus came to abolish the death penalty of the law and bring life and immortality ... to forgive repentant sins, except one, which was not fornication or adultery.

> The clear intent of the teaching every place is that the innocent victim of divorce for that cause [adultery] is free from the law of husband and wife because an adulterous mate is no longer husband or wife. It was never possible for me to accept that the Law offer a more equitable solution to the problem than our Lord? [Under the Law] the penalty for the guilty was death; harsh, but just; leaving the innocent free and not in an untenable position through a compelling human desire and God-given inclination to seek the love and compassion of a true mate."

> Jesus put it upon the individual's own ability to do so and so did Paul, 'but if they cannot contain, let them marry' ... It seems very clear that in all the Bible, God expected most men and women to seek a mate and enjoy the love and companionship that its union affords; the closest human tie as the most sacred. It is, in its purity, representing the relationship intended between Christ and His church. (Appendix N)

After Leslie White became Overseer of Colorado in 1989, he initiated a revolutionary new practice of allowing remarried couples to follow their personal convictions as to their participation in Fellowship Meetings and communion. The decision was left up to the couple and Holy Spirit—rather than the Workers. Some remarried couples moved to Colorado, specifically for the freedom, tolerance, compassion and mercy existing there regarding their marital status.

Gradually, beginning about 1989–1990, more Eastern US states (and countries under their authority) followed suit and began allowing divorcees to remarry and most divorced and remarried couples to fully participate. However, upon moving from the East to the West US, some remarried couples have been instructed not to take part in Western Meetings. Meanwhile, Western 2x2s view the Eastern as "confused."

Foreign D&R Protocols. In foreign countries, for a time, there appeared to be uniformity among the responsible Overseers in applying the 1938 ruling, but that is no longer the case. Overseers of countries have been adopting various protocols which has been causing confusion, inconsistency and divisions.

Australia and New Zealand follow the 1938 Council rules allowing the remarried to silently attend Fellowship Meetings; if separated, they have full privileges. South Africa, Ireland and the UK forbid remarried couples to even attend Fellowship Meetings. Latin American countries with Scottish Overseers also impose this rule.

Latin American countries all have foreign Overseers, except Brazil, and no uniform protocol exists concerning divorce and remarriage. Workers were unable to agree at two meetings held in Brazil around 2015–2016. Currently, the country Overseer establishes the conduct rules, usually the same as is imposed by his country of origin.

In Venezuela, Brazil and Colombia, divorced and remarried Friends are not allowed to continue attending Fellowship Meetings (even when the couple remarried before they professed) unless they separate. Meanwhile, in Ecuador, and to some degree in Argentina and Chile, members who are divorced and remarried may attend or participate in Meetings and take communion.

The differing D&R persuasions and opinions in the US have caused divisions. Over the years, some have observed that the two opposing divorce and remarriage policies are upheld with equal conviction by the respective "Spirit led" leadership in "God's only right/true way" that "changes not."

See also Chapter 35.

Marriage, Divorce and Remarriage in Jesus' Time

Jewish Marriages. In Jesus' lifetime, in Jewish culture, after their betrothal, the families of the future bride and groom negotiated a formal (conditional) Marriage Covenant (Hebrew: *ketubbah)*, similar to a contemporary prenuptial agreement. Their Marriage Covenant was conditional upon the fidelity of both parties.

The husband's basic obligations to his wife during their marriage were to provide food, clothing, conjugal relations, and a pre-specified cash settlement for the wife should he divorce her, disappear or die. The bride's father provided her with a dowry (assets). The purpose of her dowry (she retained ownership) was to provide her financial security in the event of divorce or death of her husband.

Jewish Divorces. It was not at all uncommon for Jews to divorce and remarry in Jesus' day. The Old Testament law clearly stated that a lawful divorce carried with it the right to remarry. There was no question that remarriage was permissible after a lawful divorce. The law provided "And when she is departed out of his house, **she may go and be another man's wife**" (Deut. 24:1–4).

Divorce Process. To legally dissolve a Jewish marriage, the husband and wife went before a rabbinic court. In the presence of witnesses, the husband delivered to the wife a Bill of Divorcement (Greek *apostasion, Strong's* No. 647), along with the settlement previously agreed upon in their Marriage Covenant. The court acknowledged the document. The wife was then put/sent away from the home with her dowry assets and was legally free to remarry. Mothers received custody of all children under six and of all daughters; and fathers received custody of all sons when they turned six.

This book uses *Strong's* standard reference numbers assigned to Hebrew and Greek words. *Strong's Concordance** is the most complete, well-respected and widely-used Bible concordance ever compiled for the KJV. For over 130 years, it has been invaluable in interpreting and understanding Scripture.

In Jewish history, there was a controversy known as the Hillel-Shammai debate. Hillel and Shammai were Jewish elders, heads of two schools of thought and were president and vice-president, respectively, of the Sanhedrin (the Jewish Supreme Court). The popular view was that of Hillel, who taught that a man could divorce his wife "for every cause" whatsoever, even something so trivial as burning a meal. Shammai held that divorce was lawful *only* for the cause of *fornication* (Greek *porneia, Strong's* 4202, which covered all forms of sexual immorality).

Their debate was *not* about remarriage—it was about the cause or grounds for a *lawful* divorce (which allowed remarriage). Throughout Palestine, the practice of husbands' *"putting away"* their wives for "every cause," (any reason whatsoever) with and without divorcing them was widespread (Hillel's teaching). The Pharisees came to Jesus to learn where Jesus stood on this dispute. Jesus asked them, "What did Moses command you?" The Mosaic law stated:

"When a man hath taken a wife, and married her, and it come to pass that she find no favour in his eyes, because he hath found **some uncleanness** in her: then let him write her a **bill of divorcement**, and give it in her hand, and **send her out of his house.** And when she is departed out of his house, **she may go and be another man's wife.** And if the latter **husband hate her,** and write her a bill of divorcement, and giveth it in her hand, and sendeth her out of his house; or if the latter husband die, which took her to be his wife; Her former husband, which sent her away, may not take her again to be his wife, after that she is defiled; for that is abomination before the Lord: and thou shalt not cause the land to sin, which the Lord thy God giveth thee for an inheritance." (Deut. 24:1–2).

Jesus replied by taking them back to the Mosaic law above under which they were then living. He addressed the practice of "putting away" wives and lawful cause/grounds for divorce. He clarified that the *lawful* cause/grounds for divorce in Moses' law (that of "some uncleaness" in Deut. 24:1) was "fornication" (Matt. 5:32). This meant divorce "for every cause" (Matt. 19:3) was *unlawful;* divorce for fornication was *lawful.* He confirmed that Shammai's position was God's plan. According to Jesus, infidelity was the only lawful cause/grounds for divorcing a wife (Matt. 5:32).

Spousal Abuse of *Putting Away.* Some Jewish husbands were "putting away" their wives **without** providing a formal divorce or paying the settlement in the Marriage Covenant. The Greek term for "putting away" is *apoluo, Strong's* No. 630. It means to put, send, cast away or out; to forsake, depart.

In those days, there were types of *putting away* a spouse. There was a **lawful** *putting away* and an **unlawful** *putting away.* When a wife was *sent/put away* **with a Bill of Divorcement** according to Deuteronomy 24:3, the separation was a permanent *lawful* divorce provided by God as a resolution for the hardness of some men's hearts. But if the husband *put away* his wife **without a Bill of Divorcement,** their separation was *unlawful* and hated by God; the wife remained married (chained) to him, and neither of them could lawfully remarry. Those who remarried were committing adultery.

Putting away a wife, that is, forcing her out of the home *without* giving her a Bill of Divorcement was a treacherous, heartless and cruel action that God hated. "Therefore, take heed to your spirit, and let none deal treacherously against the wife of his youth for the Lord, the God of Israel saith that **he hateth *putting away***" (Mal. 2:16).

The Word "Divorced." ONE word in Matthew 5:32 has created immeasurable grief, heartache and tragedy for many Christians. That is the **mistranslated word** *divorced* in the phrase "marry her that is **divorced.**"

Matt. 5:31: "It hath been said, Whosoever shall **put away (*Strong's* No. 630** *apoluo*) his wife, let him give her a writing of divorcement (***Strong's* No. 647**, *apostasion)*: vs 32: But I say unto you, That whosoever shall **put away (*Strong's* No. 630** *apoluo*) his wife, saving for the cause of fornication, causeth her to commit adultery: and whosoever shall marry her that is **divorced (*Strong's* No. 630** *apoluo*) committeth adultery." (From Jesus' Sermon on the Mount)

How do we know the translation of *divorced* is incorrect? Should it not have been consistently translated the same (*put away*) as the two preceding times in this passage? What should it have been?

Are the terms *divorced* and *put away* interchangeable? The short answer is NO, they are not, nor are they synonymous. Consistently, all three should have been translated as "put away" (Greek *apoluo*, *Strong's* No. 630). If "divorced" were the correct translation, the original Greek word would have been *apostasion* (*Strong's* No. 647), and it is not. It should read:

"It hath been said, Whosoever shall **put away** his wife, let him give her a writing of divorcement: vs 32: But I say unto you, That whosoever shall **put away** his wife, saving for the cause of fornication, causeth her to commit adultery: and whosoever shall marry her that is **put away** committeth adultery."

When the word *divorced* in Matthew 5:32 *(apoluo, Strong's No. 630)* is consistently translated all three times in this passage (Matt. 5:31–32) as *put away*, it harmonizes perfectly. Further scriptural support that the word *divorced* should have been translated *put away* (rather than *divorced*) is found in three follow-up accounts about "putting away" and "for every cause."

Jesus' response in all three accounts harmonized with each other: Matthew 19:8–9 when the Pharisees tempted him; Mark 10:11–12, "his disciples asked him again of the same matter"; and Luke 16:18 in response to the Pharisees' derision. The questions put to Jesus were never about the lawfulness of divorce and remarriage or multiple remarriages. They were about *putting away)* "for every cause" (Matt. 19:3) and **without** a lawful Bill of Divorcement (Mark 10:2); both were deemed unlawful.

The following Bibles correctly translate Matthew 5:31–32: *The American Standard Version* (1901), *Darby Bible* (1890), *Young's Literal Translation* (1862), *Wesley's New Testament* (1755) and *Douay-Rheims Bible (1582)*. The American Standard Version's consistent translation reads:

"It was said also, Whosoever shall **put away** his wife, let him give her a writing of divorcement: but I say unto you, that every one that **putteth away** his wife, saving for the cause of fornication, maketh her an adulteress: and whosoever shall marry her when she is **put away** committeth adultery" (Matt. 5:31–32).

Abandonment, desertion, putting away, and heartless forsaking of a spouse without delivering a *lawful* divorce before *putting her away* was and is forbidden by Jesus. He made no changes to Deuteronomy 24:1–4 and fully upheld the lawfulness of divorce, remarriage and multiple remarriages (Matt. 5:17–19). Jesus made clear his mission on Earth was not to change or destroy the current law: "Think not that I am come to destroy the law, or the prophets: **I am not come to destroy, but to fulfil**. For verily I say unto you, Till heaven and earth pass, one jot or one tittle shall in no wise pass from the law, till all be fulfilled" (Matt. 5:17).

Marital Limbo. The Jewish term, *Agunah* (literally, *one who is chained, anchored or tied down),* denotes a Jewish woman who remains chained to a husband who refuses to give her a divorce, or who has disappeared, e.g. deserted or whose death is unconfirmed. An *Agunah* cannot lawfully remarry without a Bill of Divorcement, or she would be committing adultery, (Mark 10:11, Matt. 19:9), a crime punishable by death (Lev. 20:10).

Back then, Jewish wives had little to no recourse in court. With very few exceptions, they could not initiate a divorce; they could only accept one from their husbands. Even today, Jewish women continue to suffer spousal abuse from their husbands' refusals to lawfully divorce them, which prevents them from remarrying. Similarly, current secular laws prohibit a *separated* married person who is not legally divorced from remarrying another person. To simultaneously be married to two people at the same time is a criminal offence called *bigamy.* Regrettably, *Agunahs* are not uncommon in the Jewish community today.

The consequences could be very dire for an *Agunah* who was driven out of her home, sometimes with young children. Many Jewish women did not work out of the home and relied solely on their husbands to support them. Their marriage settlements that their husbands were withholding were intended to protect and provide for them financially. Some Agunahs became homeless, destitute and prostitutes.

Closing Notes

Marriage Vow. Scripture contains no marriage vows. Marriage was a covenant, conditional upon the fidelity of both parties.

Remarriage. Scripture permits remarriage of Jews and Christians after a *lawful* divorce, and this right will continue to be available *till Heaven and Earth pass* (Matt. 5:17–20; Deut. 24:1–4).

Living in sin/adultery. *Merriam-Webster* defines *living in sin* as: "to live together and have sex without being married." The Bible does not contain the term "living in sin." A lawful remarriage is not *living in sin* and is not adultery according to both Mosaic law (Deut. 24:1-4) and Jesus (Matt. 19:9; Mark 10:11–12; Luke 16:18; Matt. 5:31–32 ASV). There is only one unforgiveable sin, and it is not remarriage.

Fornication. The Greek word *fornication (porneia, Strong's* 4202) refers to all kinds of sexual immorality, including adultery, incest, etc.— not just the modern definition of premarital sex.

Forbidding to Marry. When there has been a lawful divorce, forbidding divorcees to remarry goes *against* Scripture in both the Old and New Testaments. It is also possible that a church that believes a remarried person will lose their salvation unless they divorce (until their previous spouse dies), may have implemented a *doctrine of devils*. "Now the Spirit speaketh expressly, that in the latter times some shall depart from the faith, giving heed to seducing spirits, and **doctrines of devils**; Speaking lies in hypocrisy; having their conscience seared with a hot iron; **Forbidding to marry...**" (1 Tim. 4:1–3).

No going back. Returning to the original spouse after divorcing and remarrying is forbidden in Scripture and is described as "an abomination before the Lord" (Deut. 24:4). This law of God is still in effect.

Confessed sin carries the promise of forgiveness from and peace with God. "If we confess our sins, he is faithful and just to forgive us our sins, and to cleanse us from all unrighteousness" (1 John 1:9). It does not add, *except for remarriage after divorce*. God's grace is able to accept a person's repentance and carry on from where they are—without insisting on separation after remarriage as a condition of salvation and fellowship.

Currently, there are many Agunahs (separated spouses unable to remarry) in the 2x2 Church, due to some Workers' incorrect, unmerciful interpretation of Scripture. Further, even today, some Workers are strongly encouraging remarried members to divorce/separate, insinuating they are in danger of losing their salvation if they do not.

Divisions in the 2x2 Church and much suffering, misery and pseudo-guilt among the Friends could have been avoided had the Workers studied, understood and applied the distinction between **put away** and *divorced* in their original Biblical context. Unfortunately, many manmade cruel harsh practices were instituted based on a single mistranslated word.

Is it up to the Workers to decide the limits of God's forgiveness? Do they have the God-given authority to punish and penalize people who remarry after they are divorced? Where will they stand if they have marginalized and penalized those whom God has forgiven? (Acts 10:15, 47). The cruel, abominable practice of *putting away* wives and creating Agunahs may have been in Jesus' mind when he delivered his "Woe unto you scribes and Pharisees" sermon condemning them for "omitting the weightier matters of the law, judgment, mercy and faith" (Matt. 23:23).

Whether we are or have been observers, participants, or enforcers of this cruel hard-hearted practice,

"Let us therefore come boldly unto the throne of grace, that we may obtain mercy, and find grace to help in time of need" (Heb. 4:16).

See Appendix N - Marriage, Divorce and Remarriage. *See also,* website *Expressions by Ex-2x2s,* The Gift of Marriage, Divorce and Remarriage (*Ex2x2.info*).

References

*James Strong. In 1890, an American Bible scholar, James Strong (1822–1894), published a monumental concordance for the King James Bible. The KJV was translated into English in 1611 from various ancient Bible texts written in Hebrew (Old Testament) and Greek (New Testament). Therefore, every English word was derived from a Hebrew/Greek word. Strong assigned a number to each underlying Hebrew/Greek word, and these numbers have become a reference standard. Countless books use Strong's standardized reference numbers. Over time, *Strong's Concordance* has been revised and reprinted. The latest version, *The New Strong's Expanded Exhaustive Concordance of the Bible, was* published in 2010 by Thomas Nelson Publishers.

Vine's Expository Dictionary of Biblical Words was published in 1985 by Thomas Nelson Publishers. This Dictionary facilitates the study of Biblical word meanings, presenting the English equivalents for the Greek/Hebrew words from which they have been translated, using *Strong's Concordance* Reference Numbers.

William Irvine's Tombstone (1863–1947, aged 84)

Archibald G. Irvine's Tombstone (1886–1952, aged 66)

30

William and Archibald Irvine's Deaths

William Irvine's mother, Elizabeth (Grassam) Irvine, died on November 25, 1897, aged 64. He reminisced, "My mother broke her heart in trying to hinder me from doing what I did ... But both Mother and Father on their deathbed said I was right, and the best son they had" (to M. Canada, Aug. 23, 1933, *TTT*).

Irvine's father died August 12, 1913, aged 80, from chronic bronchitis and cardiac dilatation. Five immediate Irvine family members predeceased him: two infant sons, two daughters and his wife. His surviving children were William, two sons and four daughters.

Irvine lamented, "I did not know what a good dad I had ... till I looked on his face in the coffin ... The night before he died, he said I was the best son he had. The night after he was buried, I knew that I was the most wicked son he had. I had violated the Spirit of Christ and God toward him and caused him to suffer much through my attitude toward tobacco and rum" (to Alfred Magowan, Dec. 13, 1920, *TTT*; Irvine's father smoked and drank rum).

"Every step I have taken has been in opposition to those I loved most dearly. But Father and Mother on their deathbeds left clear witness that they could see that I had done the best thing for all; so that was great comfort and cheer to me after many lonely years when ... they were not in sympathy with my work ... I hurt them badly. Most of my relatives were interested till 1914, when I began to see what's my work today," remarked Irvine (to William Pollock, April 13, 1927, *TTT*).

The first of William Irvine's eight surviving siblings to pass away was his oldest sister, Margaret, in 1886, aged 25, followed by Elizabeth, aged 15, a year later in 1887 (*see* Chapter 2). Next was his oldest brother, John, on May 6, 1918, aged 59, and then James on March 11, 1928, aged 63.

His sister, Jane "Jeanie" (Irvine) Comrie, died on April 28, 1937, aged 63. Irvine explained, "I have been more mixed in her life than any of the others these past 50 years. She was a good sister, wife and mother, though never so robust as the others" (to Hulls, May 1, 1937, in author's possession).

His sister Agnes (Irvine) Freebairn, mother of 12 children, died December 7, 1938, aged 72. The two youngest sisters, Helen "Nellie" Clelland died on November 23, 1952, aged 76, and lastly, Janet "Jennie" Clelland died in June 1963, aged 83. Two infants named Henry died in 1868 and 1872.

1947, March 9: William Irvine Died. Irvine was diagnosed with cancer of the mouth circa 1940, a fact he did not share with his followers. On January 27, 1947, about six weeks before his death, Irvine signed his Last Will and Testament, properly drawn up and witnessed. He died in the Almasie Suisse Pension (a boarding house) in Jerusalem, aged 84, from cancer of the mouth. *See* Appendix B for his obituary in *the Palestine Post,* March 10, 1947. He was survived by his two youngest sisters, Helen "Nellie" Clelland and Janet "Jennie" Clelland.

1946, January: Last Visit. An English soldier, Irvine Noble, was stationed in Palestine in 1946. His parents were Omega followers Walter and Ruth (Gerow) Noble. Noble was the last known Omega Message person to see Irvine alive. Former Omega follower Lew Fountain affirmed, "[Wm. Irvine] at that time, knowing that the cancer ... was terminal made the young soldier swear that he would tell no one ... of his condition and approaching death. Now this information all came to us shortly after William Irvine's death" (July 5, 1998, *TTT*).

An article regarding Irvine's death, purportedly written by Noble, was published in *the Sunday Post* (of Palestine; now *the Jerusalem Post*) on March 16, 1947, reprinted in the *Impartial Reporter*. *See* Appendix B.

The last known letter Irvine wrote was dated June 13, 1946, addressed to Elmer and Alma Akerson. After not hearing from Irvine for some time, Omega follower Orris Mills sent a telegram to the Jerusalem police. Thomas Coussin, a civil servant employed at the Jerusalem Police Headquarters who had known Irvine for 20 years, conveyed the news of Irvine's death to two of his followers:

> I am indeed sorry to have to convey to you the sad news that Mr. William Irvine passed away on Sunday, 9th March 1947. You were no doubt aware that he had been ailing for the past six years. He had nevertheless been able to get about in the ordinary way, and it was only in recent months that his condition worsened, and he was not able to leave his hotel. He took to his bed towards the end of February, where he remained until he left us peacefully, at approximately 11:50 hours a week ago yesterday ... At the beginning of November, when he began to feel really ill, he sent for me, since then I had been with him almost every day until he passed away ... I am enclosing a list of the addresses of letters to the USA that have so far been returned, and I would ask you Mr. Mills to pass the news around. (to Orris Mills, March 17, 1947, *TTT*)

Mr. Irvine had cancer of the mouth, which had been slowly working on him for about six years, and for which he took treatment at the Hadassah University Hospital, Jerusalem ... They even offered to take him and make him comfortable during his last days, but he steadfastly refused and told me that his trysting place was where he resided. His illness progressed rapidly in the last two or three weeks, and this coupled with his venerable 84 years, took him away from us on Sunday the 9th March 1947. (to Mrs. Westlund, May 28, 1947, *TTT*)

Irvine's Funeral and Burial. The day following his death, Irvine was buried in the Mount Zion Cemetery (Protestant section) in Jerusalem, Israel. Coussin arranged his service. "William entrusted me with the last rites ... it may give you peace to learn that his coffin draped with the Union Jack was conveyed to Mount Zion in one of our police tenders with six stalwart British Constables acting as pallbearers. It was indeed an impressive cortege with all the honors he so richly deserved ... The funeral took place at 2 p.m. on the 10th March 1947, on a bright warm Sunday afternoon (to Mills, April 22, 1947, *TTT*).

According to Doug Parker, Irvine's son, Archibald Irvine, was informed of his father's death by a New Zealand Worker, Mr. Beattie (perhaps Ralph Beattie), and by Mrs. Slater from Kilsyth (perhaps Margaret Clelland Slater, Irvine's niece).

William Irvine (1863–1947, aged 84)

Disbursement of Irvine's Possessions. In his will, Irvine designated funds be given to certain hospitals, charities, individuals and to the poor. Monetary bequests were made to his two surviving sisters: Mrs. Nellie Clelland, Kirkintilloch, Scotland, and Mrs. Jennie Clelland, Victoria, Monmouthshire, S. Wales. He left nothing to his son. The total monetary value of Irvine's estate amounted to £1,410.5.11. *See* Irvine's will on website *TellingTheTruth.info,* in Founder, Irvine's Death, Will.

Irvine's sister consented for Orris Mills to receive some small personal articles belonging to her brother. Various California Omega followers have passed the memorabilia down in their families. Coussin clarified, "The main package will be enclosed in an old cigar box that William used to keep his unanswered letters in, as well as some snapshots. In the bottom you will find his own original list of correspondents and some photographs and snaps of himself and some of his friends ... The contents of the box apart from the snaps are: cigarette holder (filigree); magnifying glass, small (in case); magnifying glass (composite handle); fountain pens (two); watch pocket (Genie metal); whistle blast; change purse (old); note wallet (new). The two other packages will comprise the Bibles, one together with a book on *Life Chemistry*" (July 11, 1947, *TTT*).

Aftermath of William Irvine's Death

It would be a mammoth understatement to say that Irvine's "premature" death in 1947 came as a shock to his faithful followers. Baffled and bewildered, they mourned in confusion, "He was *not* supposed to die." They were expecting the Apostle John to come from Heaven, at which time an earthquake would split the Mount of Olives in half and a waterway would be opened to the Dead Sea that would replenish the land, causing the desert to bloom as paradise (Zech. 14). This would create a great valley of refuge where all the Omega followers would be miraculously gathered, through no effort of their own, fulfilling Isa. 2:3. They would then return with Jesus for the 1,000-year reign. Except it did not happen—rather than leaving the world spectacularly, Irvine, too, went the way of all men.

With Irvine's death, his Omega followers were forced to re-evaluate their confidence in his claim to be a prophet of God, a Revelation 11 witness and his biblical interpretations. Some lost faith in his Omega Message prophecies and deserted. Others found ways to reconcile his death, retained their confidence in his interpretations and continued in the Omega Message. Some used the argument from silence, "William never said he was *not* going to die." Others reassessed Irvine's death and began believing that Irvine and Apostle John would be resurrected in the future.

For those who continued following his Omega Message after Irvine's death, it was much the same, except, as Fountain explained, "the people were more relaxed. Many young people were getting married and not feeling guilty. Also, they were building their homes. [Some] felt it was all right, now that William Irvine was dead [to sing the old church hymns] ... Many little things gave the signal that the *Trance* was somewhat over ... [In 1998, those] who profess to follow William Irvine very faithfully ... it is only kind of a quasi-sort of following him—not even a shadow of what he would have required over 50 years ago" (to Dear Friends, July 5, 1998, *TTT*).

Daily Life of Omega Message Followers. "How queer," observed Fountain, "in that all the years my parents were in it, not 1% of his followers had met the man [Irvine]. It was only by letters written back and forth." Up until he was 25, Fountain had been a faithful Omega Message follower. His separation cost him a great deal, as the rest of his family did not collectively depart with him. Eventually, his father and one sister left; his mother and another sister remained Omega followers until their deaths.

Some WWII experiences had caused Fountain to do some serious reckoning. "When I officially departed from William Irvine's so-called Omega Message in early 1946, I already had sufficient evidence to establish in my mind that he was nothing more than a first-class, run-of-the-mill, garden variety, false prophet ... I had certainly given him the benefit of the doubt ... I had chosen to not marry, had really lived what he preached ... had not committed fornication, had not what is called a 'checkered past,' had lived quite a frugal life ... Some years have passed now, and I have become well established in what true Christianity is all about. I know where I am going in my spiritual life" (July 5, 1998, *TTT*).

My first contact with Fountain was an exploratory phone call from him to discover if I would be interested in receiving his collection of Irvine's letters. I certainly was! He wanted to donate them to someone who would find them useful. His generous donation also included volumes of correspondence among the Omega followers. Through the courtesy of Lew Fountain, many details have been included in this book that would not otherwise have been available. We enjoyed many conversations, and I am very glad our paths ever crossed.

On March 8, 2011, Llewellyn "Lew" Fountain passed away in his sleep. His funeral was held at the Island Gospel Church, Burns Lake, British Columbia, Canada.

See Appendixes C and H for details about the Omega Message.

1947–1952: Poliomyelitis Epidemic (aka polio, infantile paralysis). At its peak in the 1940s and '50s, polio would paralyze or kill over half a million people worldwide every year. Various governments worldwide announced restrictions. Schools were closed; children under 16 were not to attend any public gathering nor travel on public transport; school lessons were available by correspondence or on the radio. In some areas, the annual 2x2 Conventions were not held, and/or children did not attend them. The polio vaccine became available in 1955.

1952: Death of Rev. Archibald Irvine. William Irvine's son, Archibald Grassam Irvine, passed away on June 14, 1952, aged 66, in Christchurch, New Zealand. His death certificate showed the names of his parents as John and Elizabeth Irvine, who were William Irvine's parents; they had no natural-born son named Archibald. *See* also Chapters 2, 4 and Appendix B.

1982: Death of Mary Irvine. The wife of Rev. Archibald G. Irvine passed away on December 19, 1982, aged 96. Archibald and his wife share a tombstone in Bromley Cemetery, Christchurch, New Zealand. They had no children.

Many, if not most, 2x2 members today have never heard of the name *William Irvine*, the father and founder of their church, to whom they owe their way of life. Despite efforts to erase his name, role and importance from the sect's history, Irvine's legacy is alive today, decades after his death, in three derivative religious groups. His inescapable name is engraved on the Two by Two Sect's history.

❧❧❧

31

1951–1954 – Doug Parker's Exposé

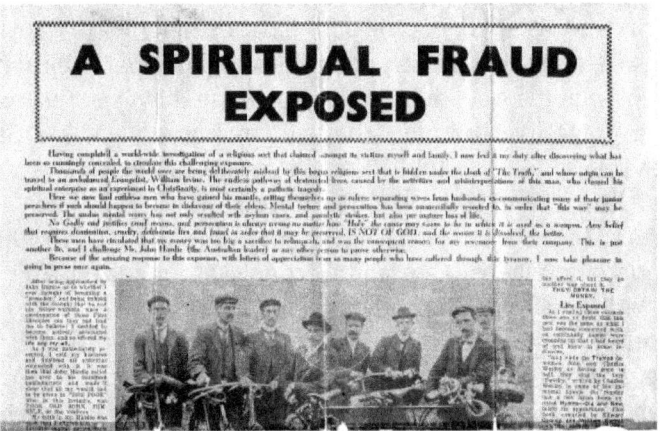

"A Spiritual Fraud Exposed" by Doug Parker (1954)

Doug Parker. In 1954, when he was 24 years old, Doug Parker began researching the faith he was raised in, that of the 2x2 Sect. For years, the story of how and why he discovered its origins remained largely a mystery shrouded in speculation, rumors and misunderstanding of his motives. What moved this young man to go to such great lengths in undertaking such a careful, time-consuming investigation?

Parker Family Background. Doug's mother, Myra (Oldfield) Parker, was born In 1896 in Mudgee, New South Wales, Australia, and grew up in Cudgegong. She met Doug's father, Edmund Ernest Parker, who was working as a station hand on nearby property. They married in 1918 after Ernest returned from World War I. Starting in 1919, they had five children: Eddie, Jean, Gordon, Raymond and Douglas "Doug" Stephen, who was born In 1930 in Padstow, NSW.

The Parker family resided on a farm in Padstow. Mrs. Parker opened a butcher shop and taught all her sons the trade. Doug went to sea as a ship's butcher in his teens; he occasionally spent time with his relatives in Scotland and Ireland on his leaves.

In 1936–1937, the Parker family resided near Sydney at Kogarah, NSW and was active in the Anglican Church. About 20 years earlier, Mrs. Parker had attended a mission conducted by Jack Craig and Jack Annand. When Doug was six–seven years old, these same two Workers knocked on the Parkers' door. Mrs. Parker recognized them. They invited the Parkers to their Gospel Meetings.

"They [the Parkers] were contented in the Church of England [aka Anglican] fellowship and loved their pastor as a true friend," explained Kay Arvig. "But when these stranger preachers came along and invited them to Gospel Meetings ... they fell for their innocent-sounding plea, and with their Church of England pastor's approval, went to the meetings to 'help' these poor, good folks to carry out their mission ... They didn't quit the Church of England because they felt it was wrong ... they quit going to it because they got so busy in the 2x2 Sect" (to Kathleen Lewis, Aug. 21, 1990, in author's possession).

Doug, his parents, his brother Gordon, and his sister Jean all professed. They attended annual Conventions at Guildford or Wattamondara, where Doug and Gordon were baptized. The Sunday Fellowship Meeting was hosted by the Parkers.

Offering for the Work. Later, Doug Parker became the owner of a news agency and a building contractor. He narrowly escaped losing his life when an overloaded brick scaffold collapsed. He was thrown under a wheelbarrow that provided protection as thousands of bricks fell on top of him. Bruised and badly shaken, but uninjured, he viewed it as a miracle and believed God had spared his life for a purpose.

Earlier, John Hardie, the Overseer of New South Wales, had approached Parker and asked if he had ever thought of becoming a Worker. After his near-death experience, he was more than willing to offer for the Work; he was immediately accepted.

Hardie made it clear that all Parker's wealth was to be given to "the poor," (John Hardie or the Workers). Having absolute trust in Hardie, Parker offered him the capital from the future sale of his assets; or the assignment of all his assets into a trust where the income from rents, etc., would be paid to the Workers. The latter appealed to Hardie. It was decided that Parker would wait until after the 1954 Conventions to enter the Work.

Meanwhile, Doug went to visit his Anglican brother on his small farm near Bega. While there, the Anglican minister came to visit, and Doug told him of his plans to enter the Work. He explained that the preachers went out in pairs and church meetings were held in private homes. The minister declared, "You're the Cooneyites." Parker had never heard the term *Cooneyites*. He replied that their church had no name and that it went all the way back to Christ. The minister assured him, "That's what the Cooneyites tell all their people."

Having always believed his nameless church had no founder and had begun with Jesus, Parker was shocked. This news was especially disturbing since he had just sold and disposed of a business he enjoyed and found rewarding.

Later, he asked Hardie if their church had ever been called the *Cooneyites.* Angrily, Hardie exclaimed, "Never!" Perturbed, Hardie cut him off short. Having obviously touched on a very sensitive matter, Parker was bewildered and became suspicious. He searched and was unable to find any information about Cooneyites in the State Library of New South Wales in Sydney (aka Mitchell Library).

Holiday Investigation. After he sold his business and before he was slated to enter the Work, Parker decided to take his parents and uncle on a holiday to the UK at his expense. They had not seen their British relatives since World War I when his father had fought in the Battle of Gallipoli (his tombstone shows a rank of Corporal). His uncle had been a stretcher bearer in the Battle of Somme. Both had long yearned to revisit several sites of WWI battles, and he wanted to make their dreams come true.

When Parker informed Hardie of his plans to visit Britain, Hardie declared adamantly, "You *cannot* go to Ireland. I don't mind if your mother and father go, but *you* can't go. Once you put your hand to the plow, you can never turn back (Luke 9:62). And you cannot go to Ireland." Further, Hardie would seriously reconsider accepting him into the Work if he disobeyed.

Hardie also pressured Parker's parents to keep him from making this trip. He reprimanded his father, "You know our idea about the Trust, and you had no right to think of such a trip without first consulting me. If Doug goes, I'll have to take the Meetings out of your home." Mrs. Parker was beside herself with stress from this threat and nearly had a nervous breakdown.

Eventually fed up with the Workers' harassment, Parker's father told Hardie and Gordon McNab that he no longer wanted the Meeting in his home; did not want to see them at his house again; that there was no compassion in them; and they were not true followers of Christ. The Workers told the Friends the reason Doug did not enter the Work was because he was not willing to sacrifice his money.

Nevertheless, the Parkers left on their journey to Great Britain. They were surprised when professing UK Friends refused to see them (following Workers' instructions). The rumor had been spread that "the serpent has taken charge of Doug and he is a very dangerous man."

After being approached by John Hardie as to whether I ever thought of becoming a "preacher," and being imbued with the thought that he and his fellow-workers were a continuation of those First Disciples (as they had lead me to believe) I decided to become actively associated with them, and so offered my life and my all.

As I was immediately accepted, I sold my business and finalised all activities connected with it. It was then that John Hardie called me over to his Guildford headquarters and made it clear that all my wealth had to be given to "THE POOR" who, in this instance, was POOR OLD JOHN, HIMSELF, or the workers.

My faith in Mr. Hardie was such that I offered him:—
(a) The capital return from the sale and disposal of all my assets:
OR
(b) My signing over of all assets into a TRUST, whereby the income from rents, etc., would be paid, and then circulated amongst the "workers."

The latter appealed to Mr. Hardie, and as it was going to take some time to legally prepare, it was decided between Mr. Hardie and myself that my going out into the work could stand over until after the conventions of 1954.

Feeling indebted to my parents for what I had attained to in life, I was prompted to give them a holiday abroad, and this is where destiny changed for the better, thank God. This is where I saw Godly, saintly men, turn into raving devils, in their endeavour to flog us into submission.

Gordon McNabb threatened my father by saying, "If you don't stop Douglas from going to England, I'll have to take the church out of the home!" John Hardie warned me with, "And if you do go to England, I'll have to seriously reconsider your acceptance into the work." He reprimanded my father with, "You know our idea about the Trust, and you had no right to think of such a trip without first consulting me."

Gordon McNabb brought so much pressure to bear on my mother, by demanding that she stop speaking in all further meetings and mentally persecuting her at every opportunity, that her nerves broke under the strain, and my father ordered both Gordon McNabb and Harry Ellem from the home.

So-called "friends" automatically shunned us, and all channels and connections with workers abroad were closed.

Excerpt from "Spiritual Fraud" by Doug Parker (1954)

Researching the History. After he arrived in Great Britain, Parker quietly, without his parents' knowledge, began investigating the Cooneyites with nothing to go on except the name *Cooneyites*. He searched in vain in British libraries, and finally discovered a pamphlet titled *The Cooneyites or 'Go-Preachers' and Their Doctrines* (Rule 1929, TTT).

An uncle in Glasgow recommended he talk to the principal of the Methodist College, Dr. Norman Snaith, who was scheduled to speak at his uncle's church that Sunday. Parker provided the minister with details about his church without using the name *Cooneyites*. The minister identified the church he described as the Cooneyites. Further, he remarked that he had encountered them many times; that they had started in Ireland. He suggested Parker continue his investigation in Enniskillen, Co. Fermanagh, Ireland.

Following his advice, Parker traveled to the office of the Enniskillen newspaper, then named the *Impartial Reporter and Farmers' Journal*, which had a wide circulation. The owner/editor was William C. Trimble; Mervyn Dane* was a reporter. They allowed him liberal access to their newspaper archives, where there were volumes extending back into the previous century.

Eventually, after tedious hours of scanning through years of newspapers, Parker discovered some articles concerning early Cooneyite Conventions that had been held right there in Co. Fermanagh at a place called *Crocknacrieve* on the property of John and Sara West. For several years, every July, beginning in 1904, the *Impartial Reporter* provided details about this Convention and its preachers who left from that Convention to go preach in Australia, America and other English-speaking foreign lands.

It was quite a shock to Parker to read familiar names of Australian Workers, such as William "Bill" Carroll, John Hardie and Wilson McClung, along with the names of other prominent preachers, such as Edward Cooney, William Irvine, George Walker and Jack Carroll.

Spiritual Fraud. Overwhelmed, Parker wept "when he realized they had been conned and taken in. That this movement did not go back to Christ. That this movement only went back to the beginning of this century when these Conventions just took on like wildfire, and there were thousands of people going to them."

No longer was there any doubt in Parker's mind that the Cooneyites were the same church he had been raised in; that Hardie had hidden the early history from Australians. Now he knew why Hardie was so upset with his plans to visit Ireland. It was because Hardie had led hundreds to believe that his church went right back to Christ—when it was only a little over 50 years old. Parker coined the term *spiritual fraud* for this deception.

During his trip to Britain, Parker met several of the Friends and Workers who had been cast out of the sect or had departed, such as George Beattie, Alfred Magowan, Fred Wood and Ida West. He also learned about the Division of 1928 when Cooney was excommunicated and ostracized.

Traveling to Kilsyth, Scotland, the hometown of Irvine, he visited some of Irvine's relatives. He met Peter Comrie, a widower who had been married to Irvine's sister, Jane. He called on Ex-worker Willie Clelland, a brother to two of Irvine's brothers-in-law, who furnished him with some photos and letters of Irvine and his son.

While in Britain, he learned that Edward Cooney had preached at some Australian Conventions and Hardie had introduced Cooney there. He realized Hardie had lied when he told Parker the sect was *never* called *Cooneyites.* By this time (around 1953), one of Parker's brothers and a sister were still very much involved in the sect, although his brother-in-law had become disenchanted.

Upon his return to Australia, Parker decided to confront Hardie at the Guildford, NSW Convention. On December 28, 1954, Parker, his brother-in-law and a newspaper reporter arrived while the crowd was gathered in the meeting tent; Hardie was on the platform. They took seats and sat quietly until the meeting was over.

As Hardie emerged from the tent, Parker and his entourage confronted him. "You have misled me and my family that this movement went right back to Christ," declared Parker. "And that it had no founder other than Christ. You have also told me that this was never called the *Cooneyites* ... do you recognize this photograph? Is that you alongside of William Irvine?" (Parker 1995, Bellevue Testimony, *TTT*). The photograph was the 1899 Bicycle Mission Trip to Scotland. In recognition, Hardie answered, "Yes," and angrily stormed off as Parker attempted to question him further.

The Aftermath. After the confrontation at Guildford, Parker was immediately vilified to the Friends and Workers; untrue rumors were circulated about him and his family. They were shunned. Friends refused to speak to them and would not allow them inside their homes; others crossed the street when they saw them coming.

According to Kay Arvig, who heard it from the mouths of both Doug and his parents, the Parkers "went back to their Church of England's pastor and apologized, and to their amazement were received back with no condemnation from either the people in the Church of England or the pastor. In fact, the pastor told them he had thought they were still doing a good work helping out a poor little sister church, and he had never been aware of their false accusations about him and the Church of England" (to Kathleen Lewis, Aug. 21, 1990, in author's possession). The Church of England is also known as the *Anglican Church*.

Parker's father, Edmund Ernest Parker, was born in 1891 in Marrickville, NSW, and passed away in 1963, aged 72; his mother Myra (Oilfield) Parker, passed away in 1990, aged 96. They were buried at the Woronora Cemetery in Sutherland, NSW.

1954: The Exposé. Irvine's skeleton remained in the closet until Parker opened Pandora's box. In 1954, he published a pamphlet titled *A Spiritual Fraud Exposed* printed on four 17x13.5-inch pages. In the first paragraph, Doug stated his purpose:

> Having completed a worldwide investigation of a religious sect that claimed amongst its victims myself and family, I now feel it my duty after discovering what has been so cunningly concealed, to circulate this challenging exposure. Thousands of people the world over are being deliberately misled by this bogus religious sect that is hidden under the

cloak of 'the Truth,' and where origin can be traced to an unbalanced evangelist, William Irvine.

The endless pathway of destructed lives, caused by the activities and misinterpretations of this man who classed his spiritual enterprise as an Experiment in Christianity, is most certainly a pathetic tragedy ... These men have circulated that my money was too big a sacrifice to relinquish and was the consequent reason for my severance from their company. This is just another lie, and I challenge Mr. John Hardie (the Australian leader) or any other person to prove otherwise. (Parker 1954, *TTT*)

Parker's exposé contained text, copies of letters, newspaper articles, statements and photographs. It included details about Cooney's hymns and excommunication; of his discovery of the *Impartial Reporter* newspaper articles; of Bill Carroll's purge in Victoria; of Irvine taking up residence in Jerusalem; of the Workers' decision to bury the past; of how the Workers treated the Parker family, his investigation; and more.

Former 2x2 Sect members, Olga Hawkins, Kay Arvig, Ruth Miller and others helped with a carefully planned mass mailing distribution of the pamphlet to thousands of the Friends and Workers worldwide, particularly in the US and Australia. The mailing gave momentum to the Third Exodus already in progress. Suffice to say, the information in Parker's exposé was not welcomed by the Senior Workers. Reportedly, some Workers even intercepted and destroyed the mailed pamphlet addressed to their younger Co-workers.

After the Exposé. With the circulation of the pamphlet, *A Spiritual Fraud Exposed*, the legend began to crumble that the 2x2 Sect had begun on the shores of Galilee; or had been in existence since Jesus sent out his twelve disciples; or began with the foundation of the world and other explanations. Subsequently, when Workers were questioned about Irvine, they frequently obfuscated by using several stock equivocations that discounted the role he played in founding the 2x2 Sect, none of which aligned with documented history.

Some of the Friends were persuaded or inclined to believe the subterfuges, while others shocked to discover "the shores of Galilee" were actually in Ireland! After reading Parker's pamphlet, some Workers left the ministry, while others disassociated from the 2x2 Sect altogether. An avid letter writer, Ex-2x2 Kay Arvig corresponded with many who had left or been pushed out earlier. The recipients circulated Arvig's letters to others. Ex-2x2s from all over the world began connecting. A worldwide loose-knit support network of apostates formed. *See* Chapter 32.

Parker's exposé could not be easily obtained. After the initial mass mailing, there was no further distribution, except person-to-person. It was rare in 1954 for people to make expensive long-distance phone calls; there was no Internet or e-mail communication, just postal letters. A few years after the uprising and upheaval due to Parker's 1954 exposé, the rebellion lost its momentum. Some took a stand against the deception, made their exits from the sect and were soon forgotten.

After *A Spiritual Fraud Exposed* was distributed around the world in 1954, Parker was ready to settle down and grow in his Christian faith. He studied at Moore Theological College from 1956 to 1958, a nearby Anglican college in Sydney, where he first came to an understanding of the gospel of grace. He entered the Anglican ministry in the late 1950s and continued until he retired in 1995. Sometime between 1954 and 1962, he married Helen Marjorie Burgess; they had two sons and a daughter. For several years afterwards, he pursued his new career and life with little contact among the 2x2 Sect members.

Parker, a hospital chaplain, ministered to the sick and the staff, going from patient to patient visiting, listening and attending to their particular needs, regardless of the patient's religion. He was also a minister in various churches in rural areas. In his last parish, he ministered to those incarcerated in a large prison. From 1985 to 1995, he was a chaplain to four hospitals in the Illawarra District, South of Sydney, Australia. When he retired in 1995 at age 65, he and Helen moved to Vincentia, NSW, then to Toowoomba, QLD, for a few years before moving back to Vincentia again.

Doug Parker passed away on April 16, 2014, aged 84. His funeral service was private, with no death notice or obituary. His grave is in a cemetery in Tenterfield, NSW, where his son, Andrew, is also buried. Parker's parents and all his siblings predeceased him.

It is remarkable that Parker was just a young man about 24–25 years old when he personally conducted his investigation in 1954–1955. His assiduous research and efforts are highly respected and appreciated by me and countless others. Subsequently, in 1982, Parker and his wife, Helen, published the most informative book about the 2x2 Sect ever written up to that time. *See* Chapter 33.

Mervyn Dane, retired editor of the *Impartial Reporter* newspaper, gave a splendid tour of Enniskillen to my husband and me in July 2004. Dane had 2x2 relatives and was a cousin to Dr. Patricia Roberts, author of several books about Cooney. He passed away August 15, 2016, aged 87.

❧❧❧

32

1950–1980 – Third Exodus of Apostates

The Exoduses. Several small and local splits have occurred over the course of the 2x2 Sect's history. The first noteworthy exodus took place when William Irvine was forced to step down; the Second Exodus occurred when Edward Cooney was excommunicated. The Third Exodus took place in the 1950s after Doug Parker's exposé, *A Spiritual Fraud Exposed* was circulated.

The Apostates. While visiting Ireland and Britain, Parker was given contact information for some American and Canadian apostates. On his way home to Australia in 1953, he traveled through the US where he listened to and recorded the firsthand experiences of Irvine Weir, Edgar and Olga Hawkins, Ted and Kay Arvig, Dr. Walter Rittenhouse, Will Sweetland, Willie Clelland and others. They provided him with additional information, photographs, documents and letters, including some written by Irvine from Jerusalem.

Following are brief narratives of some Ex-2x2 Sect members Parker visited who became discontented after learning about the short history of the 2x2 Sect, the registration of the official name of *Christian Conventions* with the US government and *The Testimony of Jesus* in Britain, the new policy of not allowing married couples to be Workers, etc. For a time, they worked to promote honesty in the 2x2 Sect and to bring about reform; however, their efforts were mischaracterized and unappreciated. Their reputations sullied, some were shunned and excommunicated.

Irvine Weir, Boston, Massachusetts, US. Reportedly, Irvine Weir met William Irvine through the introduction of the Carrolls from Rathmolyon, Ireland, and went on the 1899 Bicycle Mission Trip to Scotland. In 1900, he was one of the first twelve Workers to go in the Work and was one of the first three Workers to go to America in 1903. Weir's US draft card shows he was working at a steel mill in Pittsburgh, Pennsylvania, US in 1918, indicating that he had left the Work before then. According to the 1930 US Census, he married Mary Elizabeth Lillian Reid from Ballymena, Ireland, in 1921; they had two children. He died accidentally from a fall on October 18, 1957, aged 79.

In 1948, Weir learned that George Walker had registered the name *Christian Conventions* with the US government in 1942. For Weir, this was "a sad departure from the spiritual birth which took place at the beginning of the twentieth century."

After he voiced his strong disapproval, Weir was regarded as an "enemy of the truth." Walker stifled Weir by not allowing him or his family to attend Fellowship Meetings or Conventions. The Friends were notified they, too, would be excommunicated if they maintained contact with the Weir family.

From a letter Cooney received from Weir, "George [Walker] told Irvine that he would instruct the Bishop to close his house to him unless he promised not to speak in the Meetings. Irvine refused, so without any scriptural reason being given, he has been cut off" (Roberts 1991, 56, *TTT*).

When asked about the two men who came with him to America in 1903, Walker replied, "They were Irvine Weir and William Irvine. Sadly, both men got off on the wrong track" (1979, *TTT*).

Edgar and Olga Hawkins, Detroit, Michigan, US. In 1906, Walker knocked on the door of James E. and Annie (Farring) Hawkins, in Brooklyn, Maryland, US. Subsequently, a Convention was held on their farm for 40 years. Six of their seven children went in the Work. One son, Edgar, left the Work, married Olga Iverson, a Sister Worker who had professed in 1911. Olga explained that she and Edgar left the 2x2 Sect in 1944 because she had "an inquiring mind and a refusal to be satisfied with evasive answers to sincere, honest inquiries."

Olga sent a letter dated November 13, 1946, to the US Selective Service in Washington, D.C. requesting information regarding the "Christian Conventions" or "Assemblies of Christians" with "specific reference to the expression of any view regarding conscientious objection."

Olga provided Doug Parker a copy of the reply she received which was accompanied by a copy of Walker's 1942 letter to the US Government (1942, *TTT*). We have Olga to thank for this valuable historical document that has circulated around the world and is posted on the Internet. After she left the sect, Olga "tried in a small way to make known these same facts to others" (to Fred Hanowell, Sept. 17, 1959, *TTT*). She also helped distribute Parker's exposé pamphlet.

Theodore (Ted) and Kay (Curtis) Arvig, Los Angeles, California, US. For five years, Ted was a Worker in Oregon, Idaho, Washington and Montana. One of his Co-workers was Ron Campbell from Adelaide, Australia. After he left the Work, Ted and Kay Curtis married in 1941.

Raised in the 2x2 Sect, they composed their Exit Letter "To our much loved Friends, Saints and Servants of God":

> God gave my husband and me a hunger and thirst for His Word ... As a result, we began questioning the profession and practices of our leaders. We noticed especially that their resultant 'fruit' was not as commendable as that of some of the very churches they condemned. Then the Lord sent across our way several others who had been in the group but left it ... Some lived close enough to fellowship with us occasionally and others corresponded with us by mail, several from overseas who had seen the error from its roots. Thus, we began discovering the truth about 'The Truth.' The day that our leaders knew we knew these things, they excommunicated us ... That was in 1953. My mother was warned not to ever visit me again ... she visited us anyway. As a result, she was excommunicated to the day she died. (1953, *TTT*)

After being married for 26 years, Ted died of cancer in 1968. Kay remarried and shortly after, divorced Tom Downs; she died July 30, 1993, aged 81. Kay also helped to distribute Parker's exposé pamphlet.

Dr. Walter Rittenhouse and William Sweetland, San Diego, California, US. The Arvigs introduced Parker in the early 1950s to these two well-off gentlemen who had been close business friends/partners for many years. They heard the Workers in 1922 and left their respective churches to become a part of the 2x2 Sect, "thinking that the Workers' way was nearest right."

Highly respected by fellow members, they were also close to Jack Carroll, Overseer of the Western US, to whom they provided financial support. According to Kay Arvig, the elder, Dr. Rittenhouse, with Sweetland as his assistant, bought and sold land in the Western US and was wealthy. He lived in a mansion on a hill hidden in acres of fruit trees that was then in the heart of the City of San Diego. Sweetland's home was more modest (to Kathleen Lewis, Sept. 2, 1992, in author's possession). The property and lake of the Hayden Lake Idaho Convention grounds was owned by one or both of these men.

Sweetland's son, Chester, was considered the "biggest catch" of California 2x2 bachelors. He dated Clara DenHerder when Clara and Kay (Curtis) Arvig were single and close friends. By 1942, both Chester and Clara had entered the Work in California. Ten years later, they married on September 3, 1952, in Alpine, California. They were expecting to continue in the Work as a married Worker pair. Kay Arvig pointed out, "Chet and Clara's love for each other won the battle and they married. They were told they couldn't be Workers anymore. This was the first thing that caused Dr. Rittenhouse and William Sweetland to question 'the way' " (to Kathleen Lewis, Sept. 2, 1992, in author's possession).

Rittenhouse and Sweetland were shocked and could not understand Jack Carroll's refusal to allow the pair to remain in the Work. They viewed his denial as neither "scriptural nor reasonable." They strenuously objected, "You have also recently made a ruling relative to Workers who marry and desire to continue in the ministry. You state that to marry is proof of a diminished sacrifice and a limited service and is what you consider to be a change of status not acceptable to Christian Conventions' administration" (to Jack, Willie and Brethren, April 15, 1954, *TTT*).

They reminded Carroll of his earlier comments at the 1923 Milltown Convention endorsing the marriage of David and Emily Christie. *See* Chapter 28. They perceived "inconsistencies between what was being preached and that which was being practiced by our older brethren in particular." Curiously, this same year (1954), Workers Sandy Scott and Eva Idso (from US), who had been laboring in Italy, married on October 28, 1954. Scott stepped down as Overseer of Italy; they continued preaching as long as they were able.

When no progress was made, Rittenhouse and Sweetland composed letters to the Senior Workers imploring them to set matters right. They even "offered to furnish legal counsel ... but it was not accepted."

Rittenhouse and Sweetland declared, "For the past eight years [since 1945], all such organizations by Federal Law have been required to disclose certain information regarding purposes and practices. You men, as administrators of Christian Conventions, are familiar with this law, but refuse to conform to same; with the result you are now in default, and in due course of time, subject to investigation and penalties. As loyal citizens of the US, we cannot be a party to this policy. It is in conflict with the Scriptures, the Government and our own convictions" (to Jack, Willie and Brethren, April 15, 1954, *TTT*).

A month later, the two men announced their departure from the 2x2 Sect, "This law operates in conjunction with the US Revenue Dept. which requires all Religious Organizations to register for the purpose of classification and identification ... so far the records of the Revenue Dept. fail to disclose any registration has been made by you. The indifference to this vital issue compelled us to declare our conviction publicly, so now we are free from further responsibility, either to you, or the US Government ... The responsibility now rests upon the Christian Convention administration or their successors" (to Jack, Willie and Brethren, July 16, 1954, *TTT*).

Deeply disappointed, Dr. Rittenhouse and Sweetland gave up their attempts to correct the errors they perceived in the 2x2 Sect, departed and began visiting orthodox Christian churches. The Hayden Lake Convention held on their property was moved to Post Falls, Idaho.

Dr. Rittenhouse and his wife, Ina, reconciled. Previously, Ina felt her husband was getting "soaked with flattery" by the Workers and insisted on a legal separation with a financial settlement for her and their children. Their son, Eric, lived with his father, professed and married a 2x2 Sect member; his daughter, Patricia, is a California Worker. Dr. Rittenhouse died in 1963 and Ina in 1973. Sweetland died in 1975, his wife, Adina, in 1968, his son Chester in 1985 and Chester's wife Clara in 2020. All were buried in San Diego County, California.

Jack Carroll and Willie Jamieson with Dr. Rittenhouse's Franklin auto (1926)

Fred and Ruth Miller, Kennewick, Washington, US. Among those who were troubled by the history and doctrines were Fred and Ruth Miller. Fred had been a Worker before he married Ruth. They were Elders in south-central Washington with no desire to leave the sect. As many others had done previously, they began asking the leadership questions, hoping for straightforward answers and internal reform.

Disappointed, the Millers connected with Doug Parker, Fred Hanowell, Olga Hawkins, Kay Arvig and other dissenters and began sharing what they had found, including various people who were researching the sect. They were eventually excommunicated, largely over their upholding of the New Testament Gospel of the completed work of Jesus Christ (with dependence upon his righteous life and propitiatory sacrifice), rather than the Workers' Gospel of achieving salvation through acceptance of the ministry and earning worthiness through personal righteousness and self-sacrifice.

Due to their relationship with the Parkers, the Millers, using the business name of Booksellers, USA, became the initial North American distributor of *The Secret Sect* published in 1982. The Miller's efforts, along with others, led to press coverage of the sect. Fred regretted his participation in the Work, and once stated that his goal was to make sure the people who had professed through him had the opportunity of knowing the real truth about the Gospel and the sect.

Convention Grounds Picketed. Cecil Claude McHenry, born in 1921, was one of three professing brothers from Prescott, Arizona, US. He became very upset when he learned in the early 1950s that the 2x2 Sect had assumed the name *Christian Conventions,* and that it had been started by a man at the turn of the 20th century. An elderly Worker confirmed to him this was true. McHenry was excommunicated in 1959 per Tharold Sylvester's orders.

After coming by this knowledge, McHenry made a career of sharing it with 2x2 Sect members. Beginning around 1980, McHenry became infamous for picketing outside California and Arizona Conventions and Special Meetings. At times, he parked across the street and papered his van with posters about the Workers and Irvine. He also handed out tracts he had written and paraded back and forth wearing sandwich boards with messages. One poster read, "Human Sacrifice Practiced Here."

Reportedly, McHenry was sued and taken to court a few times by sect members following the directions of Workers. After a restraining order was issued in 1986, he was prevented from coming near Meetings and Conventions, which brought his picketing to an end.

Even so, Claude McHenry lives on in the memory of many who witnessed his demonstrations. He died July 20, 2006, aged 85, in Scottsdale, Arizona. His biography and some correspondence by the McHenry brothers are posted on the website *Expressions by Ex2x2s.*

~~~~~

1956: *"Testimony of a Witness for the Defence"* was published by Alfred Magowan in rebuttal to Parker's pamphlet *"A Spiritual Fraud Exposed"* (1956, *TTT*).

1957: John "Jack" Thomas Carroll, Western US Overseer, was born on May 9, 1878, at Newtown, Moynalty, Kells, Co. Meath, Ireland and died in Long Beach, California on March 26, 1957, aged 78. He had two funerals, one in Oakland, California (my parents were among the 700 attendees), and another at Milltown, Washington. He was buried in the Fir-Conway Lutheran Cemetery, Mt. Vernon, Washington, located one-half mile from the Milltown Convention grounds. He was survived by three sisters: May Carroll, Frances Carroll and Primrose Perrott.

1958: Religion Analysis Service, Inc. Currently located in Chaska, Minnesota, when this counter-cult agency first became aware of the 2x2 Sect, they printed an article in 1958 titled "Who are the Cooneyites?" in their periodical *"The Discerner"* (Divers 1958, 12–15; RAS.org).

1977: For the next twenty years, except for a few local newspaper articles, no further published information has been found about the 2x2 Sect until 1977, when William "Bill" E. Paul published a booklet titled *"They Go about Two by Two, The History and Doctrine of a Little Known Cult"* (1977, *TTT;* later reprinted and distributed by Religion Analysis Service, Oakdale, Minnesota).

~~~~~

1976: Irish Worker Reveals Sect's Origins in US. Western Overseer Tharold Sylvester arranged for elderly Irish Worker Joshua Gamble to speak at the 1976 West Coast Conventions (WA, OR, CA, AZ) for the express purpose of dispelling the apostolic succession myth that had long circulated about the origins of the 2x2 Sect. From each Convention platform, Gamble informed the listeners that prior to the late 1890s, there was "no continuous unbroken chain" of ministers going two and two. He mentioned by name Irvine and several other early Workers who believed they had received an understanding of a more scriptural way of ministry, had pulled out of their various religious organizations and began preaching accordingly around the turn of the twentieth century. Some were startled at this information, while others took no notice.

1975 – Changing of the Guard

For the first 75 years or so, the direction, teaching and practices of the 2x2 Sect were largely provided by the early original Overseers. Many had come out of various Protestant churches, e.g. Methodist, Presbyterian, Anglican, where they had been indoctrinated with the core doctrines of the Christian faith. Some of these they retained, others they jettisoned while adding yet others to their belief system, as they went along.

By 1975, most of the original Overseers had died out. The next generation of Workers was largely brought up as children in the 2x2 Sect. They were indoctrinated with the understanding that the Workers' ministry and the church in the home were essential for salvation. Over time, the succeeding generations of Workers revised some of their earlier beliefs and practices. Workers are subject to special rules for behavior and appearances which are beyond the scope of this book.

~~~~~

Tragedies. Some 2x2s have been under the impression that God protects them from tragedies, but history shows this is not true. The first Australian Workers to go abroad did not get vaccinated, believing God protected their health. That changed in 1925 after Adam Hutchison died of smallpox in India. Over the years, the Friends and Workers have died various unnatural deaths, e.g. from falls, drowning, lightening, farm, auto and airplane accidents, wars, gunshot, electrocution, snake and spider bites, suicides and weather-related incidents, etc.

Some of the Friends and Workers have even been murdered. The author has personally known four American Friends who were murdered and three 2x2 murderers. Frieda Schwille, a German Sister Worker, died in the gas chamber at Dachau, Germany Nazi concentration camp. Two Pearson Brothers were executed at Coolacrease. In 1983, Kenneth Salvesen died in the IRA bombing outside of Harrods in London. In 1987, on their way to the Gilroy, California Convention, two of three Brother Workers died in an auto accident in Pismo Beach, Michael Murray (27) and John Walker (31). "Time and chance happen to them all" (Ecc. 9:11 NIV).

Doug and Helen Parker, authors of "The Secret Sect" (1982)

33

1982–2022 – The Secret Sect – Fourth Exodus

The Secret Sect. Over the years, Doug Parker was encouraged by some to expand his *Spiritual Fraud Exposed* pamphlet and publish a book. Parker told the story of his investigation to Dr. James I. Packer (1926–2020), considered by some as one of the twentieth century's most influential evangelical theologians. The author of many books, Dr. Packer is perhaps best known for his book *Knowing God,* a discourse on God's attributes. Fascinated with the story, Dr. Packer insisted Parker write a book and promised to provide assistance, suggestions and the book's Foreword.

Some 25 years after he left the 2x2 Sect, Parker, age 52, took a leave of absence from work. He and his wife, Helen, and perhaps their children, temporarily moved to a rented home in London, England. There they laboriously researched the 2x2 Sect and carefully documented their findings. A librarian by profession, Helen's skills were invaluable. They used various libraries in the UK, interviewed people, recorded their statements, obtained copies of documents, newspapers, photographs, etc. Together, the Parkers wrote a book they titled *The Secret Sect,* published in 1982 by Macarthur Press (Books) Pty. Ltd., of Sydney, Australia.

Another person who was very helpful to Parker in compiling his book was Bryan R. Wilson (1926–2004), one of the world's leading sociologists of religion, whose studies and writings on secularism and religious sects are considered classics (Parker 1995, Testimony, *TTT*).

Booksellers USA, Richland, Washington. Formed in 1983 for the purpose of distributing Parkers' book in North America, Booksellers USA, was operated by Fred and Ruth Miller. Sales were marketed by placing several brief advertisements with the weekly statewide classified advertising program in newspapers throughout the US and Canada. The ads employed easily recognized 2x2 jargon such as: *Workers, Nameless House Sect/Church, 2x2s and Cooneyites.* Orders for the book came from far and wide, including Workers.

US Media Spotlights the 2x2 Sect. The 2x2 Sect had maintained a fairly low profile in the US. Only a few newspaper articles had focused on the sect, written by curious reporters who met some Workers or ventured onto a Convention ground.

1982: Their seclusion was suddenly broken in 1982, when reporters spotlighted the sect. In quick succession, two newspapers published four articles about two Washington US Conventions. The *Skagit Valley Herald* of Spokane focused on the Milltown Convention; and the *Union Bulletin* reported about the Walla Walla Convention.

1983: The following year, *The Secret Sect* made its first US public debut in four newspapers while the Idaho and Washington Conventions were taking place.

A reporter who attended the Post Falls, Idaho Convention in June 1983 wrote two articles covering his experiences at this Convention. He supplied critics' viewpoints and compared 2x2 interview responses with information contained in *The Secret Sect*. "Several former members said they had been led to believe the group went back to the time of Christ. They said, 'We're the original church. We follow the Jesus Way,' one ex-member recalled. Several former members report that discovering otherwise was the key blow to their faith in the Two by Twos. They point to a book that traced the group back only as far as 1897, to a movement founded in Ireland by William Irvine" (*Spokesman-Review,* Preecs, June 5, 1983, 1; the book was *The Secret Sect*).

The articles also mentioned a local retail store where *The Secret Sect* could be purchased. "Walter Pollock, a 'worker' or minister, said he was disappointed to learn the Spokane articles were published simultaneously with an advertisement for a book by ex-member Doug Parker, *The Secret Sect*, a historical account of the group's origins and an exploration of its theological positions that members consider unflattering" (*Skagit Valley Herald*, Hosfeld, 1983a).

Word spread on the Convention grounds about the newspaper articles, resulting in the newspapers being sold out and books being purchased. Soon, Workers began warning the Friends not to read *the black book* (the cover of *The Secret Sect* is black).

The Sect's annual Conventions were further thrust into public view that year when more newspapers carried articles about the US West Coast Conventions, laced with comments from Workers. Following are excerpts:

> Hidden from the glare of public scrutiny for 100 years, the group today is being forced into the open in reaction to charges by ex-members that its leaders have systematically withheld the truth of its origin from its members. 'This group is unique in that it has no ... printed matter,' says Ben Johnson, University of Oregon, Professor of Sociology of Religion. 'Their theology is not particularly way-out. They're not dangerous

politically. They don't brainwash or kidnap ... What is unusual is their low profile and what looks now like a deception the leaders are practicing on the members.' (*Bellingham Herald*, Anderson, 1983, 4A; regarding Milltown, Washington Conv.)

The origins of the church are another source of criticism say ex-members ... [who] contend they were led to believe the church is the continuation of the New Testament church, begun at the time of Christ's death. (*Skagit Valley Herald*, Hosfeld, 1983b; regarding Milltown, Washington Conv.)

A top reporter for *the Los Angeles Times,* Russell Chandler, pushed the 2x2 Sect further into public limelight in 1983 with a front-page article after he visited the Santee California Convention. The sect's practices, beliefs and opinions from both current and former members were reviewed. He noted, "Historical information, however, identifies the Two by Twos with a Scottish coal miner named William Irvine, who around 1899 founded a movement nicknamed the 'Tramp Preachers' or 'the Damnation Army' (his followers preached that members of all other churches were going to Hell)."

1984: The following year, reporters for the *Coeur d'Alene Press* attended the Post Falls Idaho Convention. The June 8, 1984, newspaper was printed while the Convention ongoing. It contained two articles of reporters' experiences while visiting the Convention, as well as critics' viewpoints, interviews and comparisons to information contained in *The Secret Sect.*

Brother Worker, Walter Pollock was quoted, "The church was formed at the turn of the century in Great Britain ... A number of people in England, Scotland, Ireland discovered they were 'missing something spiritually ... The Lord brought them together and they found they saw eye to eye on the ministry' " (Toft, 1984, 1).

Reportedly, when the US Workers heard *The Secret Sect* had been published and before they had seen or read it, they decided their first line of defense would be to deny the book was about them; to claim it was about some other similar group. However, photos in the book of Friends, Workers and familiar places put that defense to shame.

Over the next ten years, news of the Parkers' book slowly trickled to the US East coast. Some Friends heard that a book existed but were unable to locate it, largely because it was privately published, and the book title was unknown.

Fourth Exodus. After *The Secret Sect* was published in 1982, the Fourth Exodus began and since then, the number of 2x2s leaving the sect has been steadily increasing. Some members have mailed out explanatory exit letters, vilified by some as *hate mail;* the recipients were urged to destroy or burn the envelopes, unopened.

Reactions to *The Secret Sect*. Hidden for many years, the truth about the 2x2 Sect's origins and its founder were exhumed with the publication of *The Secret Sect*. Not everyone welcomed the information it revealed. An Ex-worker claimed, "That ugly serpent raises its head every so often." Newspapers printed various reactions:

> Parker last year published his findings in *The Secret Sect*, a book available at area bookstores. The book and the publicity about the group that has followed its publication threatens a crisis within the group that may alter it forever ... Parker charges leaders have worked since the early 1930s to conceal the group's origins, substituting a version more to their liking. (*Bellingham Herald*, Anderson, 1983, 4A)

> 'We don't deny that,' said Tharold Sylvester, Washington Overseer, when asked if the historical account was true. He refused, however, to discuss why ex-members had a different impression ... 'Jesus Himself set us up ... Whether it was planted in the first century, the tenth century or the twentieth century, the message is the same, it produces the same thing.' (*Skagit Valley Herald*, Hosfeld, 1983b)

> Richard Wulf, 27, a Two by Two worker in Mexico for two years, was asked about this apparent suppression of the sect's origins. 'Near the turn of the century God raised up godly men in Ireland and Scotland ... We respect them and what they established. But we don't hold to that history and line of succession.' (*Los Angeles Times*, Chandler, 1983, 3)

> The following quote by Walter Pollock was printed in an article titled "Two by Twos" in the *Spokesman-Review* (Spokane, Washington US) on June 5, 1983, by reporter Bart Preecs:

> > Pollock said he doesn't understand why the question of the group's history should be traumatic for ex-members.
> > "I don't know how they could have come up with that," said Pollock, who denied that the fellowship makes unsubstantiated claims about its origins. "We know that it began with a group of men in the British Isles around the turn of the century. That's as far as we've been able to trace it."

Reportedly, in some places, to prevent others from reading Parkers' book, the Friends and Workers purchased all the books available in Christian bookshops and burned them.

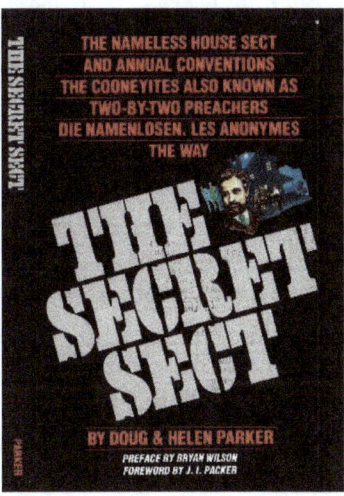

SECRET SECT THREAT TO PERSON'S RIGHTS

Doug and Helen Parker (at right), of Pendle Hill, Sydney, arrived in Toowoomba with some new facts about a nameless religious movement originally called the Cooneyites.

They have spent several years compiling a 125-page book called The Secret Sect.

Mr Parker is an Anglican minister.

"We felt we had to write the book because the history of the movement was so obscure," Mr Parker said.

"Even its own members don't know all the background."

Mr Parker said the sect, which originated in Northern Ireland in 1899, is now active right across the world.

"My own family in Sydney were involved some 30 year ago," he said.

"They were led to believe that the sect went back to the time of Christ.

"Our research has proved this to be wrong.

"The Cooneyites name was never acknowledged by the sect which is now known as non-denominational Christian conventions.

"Meetings are held in private homes, mid-week and on Sundays.

"Large annual conventions are held regionally on private properties."

Mr Parker said the conventioners were Christians belonging to a church that had no name, no permanent church buildings, no offering plate and ministers with no formal title or theological training.

He said the Christian conventions attracted Christians from all denominations.

"The object appeared to be to win them into a movement whose leaders preached that they were the only true stream of the primitive Christian church.

In Queensland, the sect was pioneered by a school teacher from Tipperary, Tom Turner, in about 1905.

The new book carries a warning to people contemplating joining the sect to consider whether or not they are losing all their rights and entering a full-time commitment.

Those who take on the ministry could also lose their finances.

Mr Parker said research had indicated a loss of Christian freedom throughout membership of the 'closed' sect.

He and Mrs Parker said they have received numerous letters from people who had read the book.

A typical comment was "My parents are more settled within themselves since reading the book I sent them. I only wish their parents were alive so they could read it too."

The Secret Sect sells for $5.95 and is available through Christian book shops.

"The Secret Sect"
MacArthur Press (1982)

"The Chronicle," Toowoomba,
Australia (May 17, 1983)

Some have been quite vocal against the Parkers' book, including many who were warned against it, but have never read it. Parkers' motives for writing the book are variously purported to make money, to hurt the church, to hinder others from believing the church is God's one right/true way, and to disrupt or overthrow those with weak faith. Parker has been described as: an enemy of truth, an unwilling, bitter man, an irritated Ex-worker who was put out of the Work when he was unable to control it. Some have described the book as being full of lies, garbage, filth and merely one man's opinion. In a letter to me, Parker recalled:

> People write to me about these stories that are being spread to either discredit the book or myself. I can assure you the book records without

malice a truthful account of the origin and history of the sect. None of
the sect's leaders or Workers has ever written to refute this work; and
indeed, I have never heard from any of them since either the book was
published or my previous pamphlet *A Spiritual Fraud Exposed* circulated
many years ago. I do hear from quite a few people who have found
release from the mental and spiritual bondage of the sect's deception
through reading the book. (Oct. 16, 1993, in author's possession)

The Parkers wrote their book to expose some concealed historical
facts. Their purpose was to record the founding and development of the
2x2 Sect at a time when its history had almost disappeared. Their book
presents the historical details in a well-documented manner from
factual evidence, eyewitness accounts, letters and testimonials, with
verifiable supporting references.

Many have expressed strong feelings about the Parkers' book—both
positive and negative. Some like myself, have read the book and
wondered if it was a truthful, accurate portrayal of the 2x2 history. I set
out on a quest to prove or disprove its accuracy and to discover if it was
true the 2x2 Church began with Irvine. This book is a product of my
investigation and presents my conclusions.

Readers may also investigate for themselves without going to the UK
or Ireland, simply by checking out the references, acquiring information
directly from sources, verifying newspaper accounts online or by post
and obtaining certified copies, inter-library loan, etc.

Truth is truth, no matter who states it. Discounting, undermining and
slandering the character of an author does not change or erase history,
nor does it refute facts presented in a book. If the facts are true, Parkers'
motives and spiritual disposition are irrelevant. To arrive at truth, the
recorded facts and historical documents must be proven or disproven,
credited or discredited *on their own merits*. Attack the message—not
the messenger. Separation from a group does not change historical
facts. No one can intelligently discredit a book he has not read. "He that
answereth a matter before he heareth it, it is folly and shame unto him"
(Prov. 18:13). *Condemnation without investigation is ignorance.*

Some honest Workers have read Parkers' book and have conceded
that as far as they know, the book is historically accurate except for a
few minor details. This is also my conclusion after thoroughly
investigating and verifying all possible sources in Parkers' book. The few
errors I found involved incorrect newspaper dates, an incorrect spelling
of a Worker's surname, an incorrect caption of a photo, incorrectly
calling Willie Clelland a cousin, and referring to the "home of W. Haney"
(should be village of West Hanney).

None of these insignificant errors jeopardize the accuracy or affect the integrity of the historical facts in Parkers' book; they were not deliberate falsehoods intended to deceive. The claim that Parkers' book is "full of lies" is unfair and grossly untrue.

Unfortunately, by 2017, all copies of *The Secret Sect* were sold; the book is out of print, yet still available via inter-library loan. This book, *Preserving the Truth,* covers most of the content of Parkers' book, plus much additional information discovered after Parkers' book was printed in 1982.

Worldwide, *The Secret Sect* has had an immeasurable impact on countless lives, including mine. Along with many others, I feel greatly indebted to the Parkers for their dedication and perseverance in revealing the 2x2 Sect's history. Their protracted research, documentation and copious footnotes have provided irrefutable evidence for future generations about the founding and development of the Two by Two ministry and the Church without a Name. Making the effort to locate and read Parkers' fact-filled informative 125-page book would be time well spent.

See Appendix M, Resources for Two by Two Material, including agencies, books and websites that contain or have distributed relevant material.

Current Status 2022

Unlike most Christian churches, the 2x2 Sect has never published any books or literature for public or congregational consumption, except a hymnal; nor do they have a *written* creed, mission statement, list of rules or official Internet presence. Purportedly, they acknowledge no official name, have no headquarters, own no property, have no media center and no staff of paid preachers, consultants or counselors.

The Bible is their standard, their creed, the underpinning of their faith. They believe the Bible contains God's will, way and "the words of eternal life" (John 6:68). They do not advertise on radio or television. Recruiting is largely through word-of-mouth, in keeping with methods of first-century Christians. While they formerly canvassed door to door, proselytizing is now mostly by invitation and small newspaper announcements of upcoming Gospel Missions.

Although worldwide, few outsiders have heard of it. The 2x2 Sect intentionally keeps a low profile, avoids publicity and promotes minimal social engagement with the world. The slogan "*In the world, but not of the world*" fits with their worldview. They are not associated with any other Christian church, missionary society or parachurch movement, all of which its leadership considers apostate.

Now, over 120 years later, the Two by Two Sect continues to directly influence and shape the lives of thousands of individuals worldwide. While the 2x2 Sect does not provide membership statistics, researchers, reporters and others have come up with a wide range of figures. According to the *Wikipedia* page, membership for "Two by Twos" ranges from 300,000 to 4 million worldwide. In 2022, however, a more probable rough estimate is 75,000 current members worldwide, with the most residing in the US and Canada, followed by Australia. Roughly, the membership has declined by about 50 percent since its peak membership in the early 1980s.

Contrary to what some 2x2s have expressed, those leaving the 2x2 Sect do not constitute the "falling away" described in 2 Thessalonians 2:3. That Scripture refers to the latter-day state of professing Christendom (the body of Christ made up of all true believers), not the membership of a small declining historically recent sect. *See* Chapter 50, The Law of Cause and Effect.

Are you feeling tired of life, depressed or disappointed with religion? if so...

COME TO OUR BIBLE SERVICES

Now being held in
Blacksessiagh Orange Hall,
Lough Muck Road,
Omagh

Every Sunday
7.00pm - 8.00pm

Services are being
conducted by...
THE PRESENT DAY
2 BY 2 APOSTLES
(St Luke's Gospel 10 verse 1)

We have a message from
GOD for you • All welcome

Tel: 07592 123 485
T.Gamble
H. McKnight

Tommy Gamble (Overseer of Ireland) and Harold McKnight,
"Tyrone Constitution," N. Ireland (October 28, 2010)

Convention dining tent, Findochty, Scotland, UK

Findochty meeting hall

Typical Convention meeting tent

Section B – Doctrine and Traditions

Howbeit in vain do they worship me,
teaching for doctrines the commandments of men.
For laying aside the commandment of God,
ye hold the tradition of men ...
(Mark 7:7–8)

For the Lord seeth not as man seeth;
for man looketh on the outward appearance,
but the Lord looketh on the heart.

(1 Samuel 16:7)

"For it is by grace you have been saved,
through faith—and this not from yourselves,
it is the gift of God—not by works,
so that no one can boast."

(Ephesians 2:8–9 NIV)

Queen Victoria, wearing the Robes of State

Portrait By Franz Winterhalter (1859)

34

2x2 Traditions – The Unwritten Rules

It was in July 1903 that William Irvine, for the first time, articulated the core foundational beliefs and methods of his new fledgling sect to a group of about 70 young Workers at the inaugural Rathmolyon Ireland Convention. All groups need some rules of order and standards to avoid confusion. Every group makes decisions about what will and will not be tolerated; what will be discarded and added.

Although not formally written, Irvine clearly established and delivered the basics tenets of his new sect. Having received their orientation instructions, there was no doubt as to the principles, standards, and procedures the Workers were expected to follow. The loose-knit group of Workers were united into a new sect led by William Irvine. *See* Chapters 11 and 16.

Unlike when God gave specific instructions to Moses for constructing the tabernacle; to David for the temple; and to Noah for the ark, Irvine did not receive from God a clear complete master plan for assembling a ministry and church. It would evolve and develop over the years.

Commandments of God and Traditions of Men

Some do not understand that there is a clear distinction between "commandments of God" and "traditions of men." The first is essential—the second is not. To a greater or lesser degree, all Christian churches follow both.

Christianity has traditionally held the commandments of God as non-negotiable instructions and laws. They are globally applicable. East to West, North to South, they remain fixed and constant—not subject to change or modification. According to the Apostle Peter, God's commandments are to be given priority, "We ought to obey God rather than men" (Acts 5:29).

Two by Two Sect members respect and follow two authorities: the New Testament and the Workers. They believe the New Testament contains God's will, way and "the words of eternal life" (John 6:68). The Workers' interpretation of the Bible is their doctrine and is considered superior to that of its lay members.

Nevertheless, many gray areas exist where the Bible is silent. Some ministers and churches impose extra-biblical rules, traditions and doctrinal interpretations in gray areas; others allow members the liberty to choose for themselves, i.e. "... where the Spirit of the Lord is, there is liberty" (2 Cor. 3:17).

"Traditions of men" refers to nonessential practices the Bible does not explicitly command, endorse, or forbid. Traditions are man-made, extra-biblical rules that usually pertain to a particular group, culture, place and time. Traditions have no eternal consequences; they are choices, such as what one consumes, does, practices, or abstains from within their culture.

Many Jewish traditions were orally transmitted. Some Jews gave the traditions of their elders equal importance to—or even precedence over—God's commandments. Jesus harshly rebuked the Pharisees for doing this, pointing out situations where the traditions of men had usurped God's commands, e.g. cleansing rituals, Corban (Mark 7:9–13), and "work" on the Sabbath ("The Sabbath was made for man, and not man for the Sabbath," Mark 2:27).

What is Legalism?

Jesus defined and despised legalism, "Why do ye also transgress the commandment of God by your tradition? ... Thus, have ye made the commandment of God of none effect by your tradition ... But in vain they do worship me, teaching for doctrines the commandments of men" (Matthew 15:3–9, Mark 7:6–13).

The term *legalism* means teaching or following men's commandments or rules as if they were commandments of God. Christians use the term *legalism* to refer to the concept that salvation is earned through good deeds/works and by following certain behaviors, methods and traditions. Legalism is the belief that salvation comes through Jesus' sacrifice plus human effort and obedience to extra-biblical traditions and rules. Legalism usurps the Holy Spirit's role as the believer's inner guide to truth and replaces it with rules of men. "Howbeit when he, the Spirit of truth, is come, **he will guide you into all truth**" (John 16:13).

By contrast, in the New Testament, the term *grace* means "gift of God." The alternative to legalism is the concept of grace; that a believer's standing before God is not based on merit or good works, but rather by accepting the gift of God (grace) through faith in Jesus Christ. As the Apostle Paul expressed, "For it is by grace you have been saved, through faith—and this not from yourselves, it is the gift of God—not by works" (Eph. 2:8–9 NIV). The grace concept is briefly summarized with the phrase "saved by grace through faith." Good works earn heavenly rewards—not salvation (Matt. 16:27).

The Apostle Paul warned against legalism: "Why ... are ye subject to ordinances, (touch not; taste not; handle not; which all are to perish with the using;) after the commandments and doctrines of men?" (Col. 2:20–23).

Extra-Biblical Traditions. The term *extra-biblical* refers to any form of knowledge or experience not clearly specified in the Bible, concerning God, His work, will and teachings. Commandments of God are biblical, whereas man-made traditions are extra-biblical rules of behavior the Bible does not mention and do not deserve the same allegiance, respect and obedience as Scripture. In some instances, rather than simply illustrating how Biblical guidance might be applied to a certain situation, such interpretation can have the effect of adding to, or taking away from Scripture.

Some examples of legalistic extra-biblical practices not commanded by God are withholding of participation and communion in Meetings; not allowing Workers to marry; teetotalism; restrictions on entertainment; and the 2x2 women's dress codes of wearing upswept long hair, no makeup, jewelry or slacks.

Perhaps the most significant extra-biblical doctrine introduced by Workers after the 2x2 Sect started was the Living Witness Doctrine. This is the belief that the Two by Two Church and Ministry are God's only right/true way on Earth and all other churches are false. Currently, most 2x2s believe this. It is one of the sect's core, fundamental beliefs, and over the years, some have been excommunicated for not embracing it. Summarized, it means that the only way to be saved and have eternal life is to come to Christ or profess through the Workers. *See* Chapter 19.

Unwritten Rules – Discipline. It is sometimes claimed that the 2x2 Sect has no rules. It is true they have no *written* doctrines, mission statement or rule book to guide them. However, the consequences of disobedience clearly reveal the existence of a considerable collection of unwritten rules. Warnings, chastisement, withdrawal of privileges and even excommunication by Workers indicate rules have been broken or boundaries exceeded. There is no discipline where there are no laws or rules.

Traditions of Men

Since the examples and perspective in this and the following chapter are primarily relative to the United States, some details may not represent a worldwide view. Also, bear in mind that typically groups, including the 2x2s, are made up of liberals and conservatives.

Therefore, the degree of their submission and observance to group rules will vary.

Through the years, 2x2 traditions have been in a continual, slow state of flux from generation to generation, place to place and Overseer to Overseer. They have been handed down verbally from Worker to convert and by parents, Elders, Friends and peers. Some 2x2 traditions originated with Workers' private interpretation of Scripture, while others were publicly communicated preferences, opinions or judgment calls. A few of Irvine's original traditions have been followed continuously, while many others have disappeared or been modified over the years.

This chapter and the next explore how many 2x2s appear outwardly and conduct their lives as they practice their faith. Their ideal is for the inner beliefs they hold dear to be apparent outwardly. The following provides historical background and examples of some extra-biblical "traditions of men," that have evolved through the years.

The Victorian Era

Are they *Commandments of God* ... or are they Victorian?

The reign of Queen Victoria (1837–1901) over the United Kingdom of Great Britain and Ireland for 63 years is called the *Victorian Era;* her subjects were *Victorians.* The social classes in this era included gentry/upper, upper and lower middle, and working/lower. Dress styles differed for each class. The upper and middle classes were considered the respectable Victorians. At that time, most Workers and Friends were from the middle and working classes.

Victorian Dress Styles. The reigning king or queen set the styles through their ability to dictate the standard of what was acceptable at court. This heavily influenced fashions in the UK and throughout the British Empire Dominions.

The Victorian Era focused on natural beauty and modesty. Taking cues from their queen, the respectable Victorian woman's dress was subdued and dictated by propriety. They wore their long hair in upswept coiffures. Skirts fell naturally from their waists close to the body and swirled around their feet. Hats were small, necklines were high, and sleeves were long; there was very little skin showing. For working women, stockings were thick and black with no leg visible, at least until the early 1900s. It was considered vulgar for a woman to wear trousers or slacks, except for ankle-length split skirts when riding horses.

Victorian men dressed according to their status and duties within society. Most respectable men sported facial hair and wore their hair short. They wore close-fitting shirts with collars and cuffs, topped with a necktie, waistcoat or vest and trousers in muted colors, often with suspenders, leather boots and some type of hat, such as an ivy cap (newsboy cap), fedora or derby.

Early 2x2 Dress Styles. The early 2x2 female converts mirrored the appearance of Victorian women, ranging from plain to severe. The Sister Workers usually wore long-sleeve dark suits, blouses in sober shades, high necklines, black cotton stockings under floor-length skirts, court shoes and demure sailor hats, much like the Faith Mission Sisters. "The ladies affect severity of attire ... it has gone so far that feathers are discarded, and a straw sailor hat is the regulation head covering" (*Impartial Reporter*, Jan. 29, 1903, *TTT*). They did not wear makeup or jewelry, not even a wedding band.

The public had good reason for nicknaming the early Brother Workers *Tramp Preachers*. While they were tramping for the Lord, they only had one set of clothing, the one on their backs. Brown undershirts caused their white shirts to appear unclean. Early newspapers reported that most 2x2 men wore very plain tweeds, rubber collars, flat caps, boots, facial hair and shirts without ties or cuffs.

When the pioneering Workers ventured abroad, they imposed their Victorian traditions and dress codes on their converts. Clues as to the date of origin of a sect can be gathered from dress styles in their early photos, from dates of hymns written by members (*see* Chapter 37) and from its nomenclature (*see* Chapter 11).

2x2 Dress Code Evolution. Fashion is a style temporarily adopted by much of society for a certain time and situation. Within the 2x2 Sect, the Workers dictate and set dress styles, with little regard for worldly fashion. Generally, the Workers have resisted most changes to fashion long after a new trend or fad has become the norm. The "middle of the road" approach Workers promote often lags decades behind, sometimes causing 2x2 women to appear conspicuously old fashioned.

Women and children are expected to be walking advertisements to the world for their church. Many 2x2 traditions enable their women to "deny themselves," "die daily," "take up their cross"—or in other words, to suffer, submit, sacrifice and suppress their natural desire and appreciation for beauty. Some Workers consider these opportunities a cause for rejoicing, believing "suffering *must* precede the glory."

The word *peculiar* in 1 Peter 2:9 ("But ye are ... a peculiar people") has been interpreted by some Workers as unusual, strange, odd or out of the ordinary. When this Scripture was originally penned, it did not hold this connotation. Most Bible versions translate the Greek word *peculiar* (*peripoiesis; New Strong's Exhaustive Concordance* No. 4047) as "a people for God's own possession" or "God's special possession" (NIV). A similar verse is found in Deuteronomy 7:6. Neither verse indicates God's people are to be *peculiar* in a strange or odd *outward* manner. (*Vine's Expository Dictionary,* 465, 477). Some modern translations use the word *particular*—rather than *peculiar*.

Their practice of disdaining worldly fads, fashions, entertainment and recreational activities has sometimes led to the Friends being labeled misfits, oddballs, dorks, nonconformists, old-fashioned and eccentrics. The women are also mistaken for Pentecostals, fundamentalist Mormons and other high-demand sect members who affect similar anachronistic styles.

Is there any Scripture where Jesus suggested his followers should create persecution for themselves by outwardly appearing odd? The New Testament's emphasis is on the heart, the inner man—not the outer man.

There are no similar 2x2 traditions or opportunities that enable men to be *peculiar* witnesses outwardly. Over the years, 2x2 men's dress codes have remained very little different from men of the world. Although worn by many early Workers, facial hair on 2x2 men was later viewed as rebellion. According to history, men in the New Testament days had long hair. An exception where 2x2 men choose to be outwardly different and have suffered persecution for it is by becoming Conscientious Objectors.

Disregarding Leviticus 19:27 (NASB) "You shall not round off the hairline of your heads, nor trim the edges of your beard," Brother Worker Morris Grovum declared at the 2009 Penang, Malaysia Convention, "The mark of a rebel for a man was when he lets his hair grow long. If a woman is rebelling, she starts chopping off her hair." In 2020, some recent Convention photos indicate a gradual return to the styles of the early 2x2 days, with even a few Brother Workers sporting short beards.

In the past, pressure was applied to the Friends to be an example by appearing different and not adopting the world's trends or fads. That era seems to be slowly passing away.

Worldly Hemlines. During World War I (1914–1918), women's fashion changed to accommodate the needs of manual work as they entered the workforce to replace men in factories, farms, offices, post offices, etc. For some of these tasks, women needed more functional work clothing, such as uniforms and trousers. Pockets became the norm. To meet their needs, the skirt hemline rose, revealing ankles for the first time. With the shorter skirts, tan-colored stockings were introduced.

Fabric rationing also influenced women's fashions, which became shorter and looser. A more practical form of dress, the shirtwaist blouse and skirt, replaced the ruffled tea gown. From 1900 to 1930, hemlines rose steadily to their shortest length ever, just below knees. After the 1930s, hemlines wavered between the ankle and knee. In the early 1960s, the mini-skirt raised hemlines to mid-thigh, an all-time high. In the early 1970s, hemlines hit the floor again. From that time forward, almost any hem length has been acceptable in the fashion world.

2x2 Hemlines. In their early days, the 2x2 women's hemlines were the same as worldly women, floor-length. In 1928, when hemlines had risen to below the knees, the Sister Workers' hemlines had only risen about five to six inches above their ankles. A later 1942 photograph shows West Coast Sister Workers' hemlines had risen to about four to five inches below their knees. During the 1960s, the mini-skirt era, the acceptable hemline for 2x2 females was for their knees to be covered when sitting. Frequently, the Sister Workers vintage manner of dress was upheld as a paradigm for female 2x2s. Hemlines shorter than those worn by the Sister Workers were skirting close to immodesty.

Although extremely modest, maxi skirts were initially considered too fashionable. After a while, objections ceased or were ignored. Many 2x2 women preferred maxi skirts which made hosiery unnecessary. Currently, some 2x2 Millennials wear stylish tunics with leggings even to Meetings.

Victorian Hair Dressing. The hair of Victorian women was considered their crowning glory. Ladies grew their hair long, sometimes reaching the floor and beyond. It was unthinkable for an upper- or middle-class lady to voluntarily cut her hair short, although some cut bangs (fringes) and trimmed the ends. For the poor working-class women, long hair was often impractical. Short of money, some cut and sold their hair to hairdressers or wigmakers. Long hair worn down and loose in public was viewed as vulgar and a sign of a "loose" woman.

Like their queen, Victorian women kept their hair healthy, glossy and smooth, with every hair in place. Respectable ladies often emulated their queen by parting their long hair in the center and arranging it in a variety of simple, dignified, upswept styles, chignons, plaited, heavy coils wrapped around their heads or long curled ringlets cascading down the back of their heads, sometimes accessorized with ornate combs, jewels or feathers. Little girls and adolescents usually wore their hair down loose in ringlets, braided or tied up with a ribbon. Young ladies were expected to begin wearing long frocks and pinning their hair up when they reached 15–16 years.

Victorian men kept their hair short, neat and styled with oil, often parted in the middle. Most wore a mustache, beard or sideburns. Having a clean-shaven face returned to popularity in the early 1900s after Gillette patented the first disposable razor blade.

2x2 Hair Dressing. Ever since the 2x2 Sect began, professing women have worn their hair long, as was the Victorian Era custom. The Workers teach that long hair on women and short hair on men is mandated in 1 Corinthians 11. Some Workers considered hair shorter than that worn by the Sister Workers to be short hair; likewise, men's hair or sideburns worn longer than the Brother Workers was considered long hair.

When questioned about the necessity for long hair, Workers' explanations are not consistent. Some reasons given are: it shows a woman is willing to submit and fit into God's order of creation; it is God's way to differentiate between men and women; it shows respect to one's husband; it is a sign of submission; it is a glory to the woman; it is "because of the angels." It is also claimed that cutting hair hinders prayers, is displeasing to God and limits their service to Him.

In some areas, Workers have taught that 2x2 women's hair should grow as long as it will grow and never even be trimmed, while other 2x2 women never heard of this rule and trimmed their hair to a manageable length. One Brother Worker explained, "What is the difference between trim and cut? Scissors are used for both, and then hair is no longer the length that God wants it to be." In the words of Overseer Joe Crane, "Shame on a woman who would put a scissor to her hair."

Some 2x2 women's hair grew so long they could walk on it, causing headaches, neck and shoulder strain. In the 1 Corinthians 11 passage regarding long hair, the Apostle Paul was writing to specific people (the Corinthians) about a controversial topic in a specific time period (first century), addressing particular issues (showing respect and refraining from shaming) in a particular setting (worship). Many of these concerns have not been issues in the culture of the twentieth and twenty-first centuries, nor throughout most of church history.

There are three different Greek words used for *cover* and *covering* in 1 Corinthians 11:1–16 listed in *New Strong's Exhaustive Concordance* of the Bible. They are *kata* (having something down over, *Strong's* No. 2596, vs 4); *katakalupto* (to place something on, over, or in front of, so as to wholly cover or conceal, *Strong's* No. 2619; vs 6–7); and *peribolaion* (something thrown around, suggesting a veil or mantle thrown around the body, *Strong's* No. 4018, vs 15).

Yet all three Greek words are translated in the King James Version Bible with a form of the same English word *cover* or *covering.* Each Greek word has an entirely different meaning every time it is used in this passage. The translation of three distinctly different Greek words with a single English word has generated much confusion in the 2x2 Sect, led to faulty "private interpretations," and resulted in needless, heavy burdens being placed upon female members for over a century.

2x2 Women Wearing Hair Pinned Up. For over a century, 2x2 females have been expected to follow the Victorian custom of wearing their long hair in updos, which spawned the nickname *Bunheads*. To this day, the Workers' ideal is for 2x2 women to arrange their long tresses in a simple knot neatly up on their heads, without bangs or fringes.

Some Workers have stated that hair is supposed to be a covering for the woman's head—not her back, and for this reason, it should be worn up on her head. Others hold that long hair worn down incites lust. Scripture says a woman's hair "is a glory to her" (1 Cor. 11:15). How can restricting women's hairstyle to a bundle of hair wadded up on their heads be viewed as "glorious?" For a time, some Workers ruled that a bun must be worn on the back of the head where it could not be seen in front.

Women's hair length and style remain highly controversial in the 2x2 Sect, frequently generating questions for the Workers, such as how long is long? Is it a sin to trim hair or to cut bangs/fringes? What to do when a woman's heavy long hair causes severe headaches?

The Apostle Paul's instructions in 1 Corinthians 11 applied to the particular time when a woman was praying in a worship service; he also said the churches of God had no such custom. Since there is no Scripture commanding women to wear their hair long or pinned up on their heads, this appears to be an extra-biblical tradition of men held over from the Victorian Era.

Around the turn of the Millennium, the fashionable length for women's hair became long, straight, and loose, sometimes finger combed into messy buns and ponytails. Many 2x2 women, especially the younger generation, began wearing their hair down in public and to Meetings. Possibly, the 2x2 tradition of women wearing their hair long, uncut and upswept will soon become a thing of the past, similar to black stockings. *See* Chapter 36.

Bobbed Hair Revolution. The post-war 1920s era was notorious for women making "scandalous" changes, such as driving automobiles, showing their knees, smoking in public, voting and holding public offices. During WWI, long hair for women fell out of favor, partly because it was dangerous and cumbersome for some women in their employment.

Reportedly, ballroom dancer Irene Castle was responsible for starting the Bobbed Hair Revolution in May 1914, which ushered in short hair for women. Castle cut her long hair into a short bob in preparation for a long recovery after surgery. Later, she resumed her professional career with her short haircut, dubbed the *Castle Bob*, and became the fashion story of the year. Women began cropping their locks and appearing in short, bobbed and waved coiffures. By the mid-1920s, bobbed hair was the dominant female hairstyle in the Western world.

2x2s and Bobbed Hair. When women began adopting short hairstyles, some 2x2 women followed suit. The Workers took exception and the professing women with short hair were not allowed to participate in Meetings until their hair grew back. Interestingly, the only person in the Bible who was restricted due to a haircut was a man, Samson. Workers reaffirmed their traditional ruling that it was scriptural for a "woman professing godliness" to wear her hair long and styled in an updo, just as they had been doing for centuries.

Makeup Revolution. Queen Victoria disapproved of women wearing cosmetics and encouraged a natural, healthy look. During her reign, it was considered proper for women in the British Empire to use makeup sparingly, if at all. Any visible tampering with one's natural skin color was disdained, the most disgraceful being lip and cheek coloring. Using cosmetics was also controversial in many Christian denominations; some banned them as vain, immoral "tools of the Devil."

The Makeup Revolution began during the 1910s when doctors teamed with cosmetic companies to manufacture safer cosmetics. Beauty became a booming business. Cosmetic counters arrived in many stores after the invention of the swivel lipstick container, pressed powder, rouge compacts and mascara, followed by liquid nail polish, foundation base and eyelash curlers. By the 1920s, many respectable women used facial makeup, and few ventured into public without at least light makeup.

2x2 Makeup or Cosmetics. Thanks to Queen Victoria, the early Workers were accustomed to females with natural, unadorned faces. They believed a godly woman should be satisfied with her God-given natural plain-faced appearance without improving upon it as the world did. To support their opinion in this gray area, they provided scripture that "beauty is vain" (Prov. 31:30), and "Let us not be desirous of vain glory" (Gal. 5:26). Some pointed to wicked Queen Jezebel who painted her face (2 Kings 9:30). Workers cautioned women against using cosmetics "so others will admire them and feed their vanity," and for appearing "alluring," lest they tempt men.

By contrast, the Bible makes it clear that God does not judge a person by their appearance. "The Lord seeth not as man seeth; for man looketh on the outward appearance, but the Lord looketh on the heart" (1 Sam. 16:7). There is no biblical directive regarding Christian women's outer appearance, other than modesty.

For nearly a century, makeup has been used by respectable women and has long passed the fad stage. Yet the Workers are still upholding the "natural" extra-biblical tradition as though it were a commandment of God, when it was actually a new standard introduced by Queen Victoria and was the fashion when the 2x2 Sect first started.

Bifurcated Garments (aka slacks, trousers, pants, britches, jeans, capris, shorts, etc. with two holes for legs). In earlier centuries and in Jesus' lifetime, both men and women wore draped or unshaped garments and tunics. With the evolution of tailoring in the fourteenth century, bifurcated garments gradually became associated with men's dress and masculinity. Since then, garments covering the lower half of bodies have traditionally had one hole for women's legs and two holes for men's legs. While some women wore slacks for activities such as gardening, climbing ladders, camping, boating, riding horses or bicycles, etc., women wearing slacks *in public* was most unusual in the Western world until the World Wars when some occupations required it.

In 1944, sales of women's slacks increased five times over the previous year. In the 1960s, slacks for women became a fashion item. By the 1970s, women's pant suits (slacks and a coordinating jacket) paved the way to slacks becoming respectable decorum for women in public for work, dress or play. The first American First Lady to wear slacks was Pat Nixon in a magazine photo shoot in 1972. By the Millennium, women wore slacks and jeans far more than skirts and dresses for both casual and dress.

The acceptance of slacks in public was greatly assisted in 1972 with the passage of the US Education Amendment Title IX that made it no longer compulsory for American girls to wear skirts and dresses to school. It was not until 2017, that some Australian states finally lifted their ban and allowed girls to wear slacks to school. Currently, many New Zealand schools permit girls to wear slacks.

2x2 Women's Slacks Traditions. The Workers argued against their female members wearing slacks, which they viewed as solely men's apparel, citing, "The woman shall not wear that which pertaineth unto a man" (Deut. 22:5). This Old Testament law concerned cross-dressing—not clothing specifically manufactured to fit a female body.

Ignoring other laws in the same passage, the Workers took this one item from a list of commands in the Old Covenant for the Jewish nation and misapplied it, as though it was God's universal commandment for all time for New Covenant non-Jewish believers (for whom the law was not written). Today, it is not difficult to distinguish between men and women who are wearing slacks. Likewise, men could be more easily distinguished if they followed Leviticus 19:27 (NASB), "You shall not round off the hairline of your heads, nor trim the edges of your beard."

Some Workers have asserted that if an activity requires slacks to preserve modesty, then 2x2 women should "deny themselves that pleasure." Sadly, that was not an option for many 2x2 teenage girls who were required to take a physical education class in school. Some were humiliated daily when their parents forced them to work out wearing their normal dresses or skirts (often immodest) or to wear shorts under their skirts.

For well over 75 years in the Western world, slacks have been acceptable—even respectable—attire for women. Around the Millennium, many 2x2 females began ignoring the Workers' prohibition against slacks. Currently, there are many photographs on Facebook of the younger generation pushing the 2x2 boundaries by wearing jeans, makeup, some jewelry, with their hair down and trimmed. Perhaps the antiquated extra-biblical 2x2 traditions are on their way toward becoming a thing of the past.

Adornment – Jewelry. Another 2x2 taboo is jewelry, with a few inconsistent exceptions. This prohibition began in the very early days of the 2x2 Sect, with the Workers citing "Whose adorning let it not be that outward adorning of plaiting the hair, and of wearing of gold, or of putting on of apparel; But let it be the hidden man of the heart, in that which is not corruptible, even the ornament of a meek and quiet spirit, which is in the sight of God of great price" (1 Peter 3:3–4).

In this passage, the Apostle Peter minimized one thing while emphasizing another. He placed the emphasis on the inner man as being far more important than the outer. This same type of idiom was used in 1 John 3:18.

Today we might express this parallelism using "not only ... but also"; as in, "Let not a woman's adorning be [only] that of outward things, such as fixing her hair, wearing gold, pearls or apparel, but let it [also] be the inward adorning of a kind heart and tender spirit." Failing to take into consideration the idiom expressions used in Bible days has led to this unnecessary, extra-biblical rule.

Without exploring deeper, the King James language in this passage could be erroneously employed to forbid women from putting on clothing and wearing braids or buns. The Workers' interpretation disregards the idiom, while focusing on a single item in Peter's list.

The 2x2 jewelry taboo was not limited to gold, pearls and costly gems, but also included inexpensive costume jewelry accessories, silver and gemstones. Some items not permitted are necklaces, bracelets, anklets or finger, ear, toe, school or engagement rings. (Wedding rings will be discussed later.) Men's cuff links, modest tie pins and wristwatches were acceptable in some areas, as well as women's wristwatches, sweater clips and brooches, as they served useful functions and were not necessarily solely for decoration.

In the late twentieth century, various pretty shiny objects (hair jewelry) appeared in many 2x2 women's hairdos. Some of the professing younger generation are ignoring the jewelry taboo, openly wearing engagement rings and wedding bands with gemstones. George Walker, Overseer of Eastern US, pointed out:

> There are other parts of a woman's attire that it may be needful to mention. Is the wearing of a dress that does not come to a reasonable length below the knees when she is seated becoming to a 'woman professing godliness?' The Scriptures speak expressly about outward adorning, wearing of gold, plaiting of hair. We are sometime grieved to see some of our sisters wearing large showy brooches, and we fear the wristwatch, when worn as an adornment, especially a gold one with gold band, is not in keeping with the instructions given in Peter's Epistle.
>
> We fear the tendency some of our sisters have to follow the latest fads in arranging their hair does not add weight to their testimony ... Seeing that the Holy Spirit inspired Paul and Peter to mention these things, we should not consider the outward unimportant. Our unwillingness to obey in this may indicate a rebellious spirit that prevents the Lord working in us and us having the condition of heart and spirit that in the 'sight of God' is of great price. (*See* Appendix I)

35

2x2 Traditions – The Unwritten Rules (continued)

The Same the World Over. For many 2x2s, the worldwide inconsistency in 2x2 traditions and rules has generated confusion and cognitive dissonance, especially so among those who were taught from birth that their church is "the same all over the world." While the spirit may be the same, as they claim, yet many other customs vary considerably.

As background, many grew up not understanding that there are "differences in administrations" and "diversities of operations" (1 Cor. 12:5-6), depending on the location, the local Worker and the area Overseer. They also did not realize that rules have changed over time. This chapter continues the comparison of various 2x2 traditions with God's commandments in the Scriptures.

Social Environment

Homes and Homelife. Usually, the 2x2s who have "open homes" are very hospitable and welcome guests and Workers to their home for meals and accommodations. Most have guest rooms. Some couples have moved to areas or countries where there are no 2x2s, for the purpose of providing an open home where Workers can reside while conducting Gospel Missions.

Most do not use the phrases, "Bless you," "Have a blessed day," "Praise the Lord," or "Hallelujah." Bible verses on anything (pictures, cups, greeting cards, T-shirts, etc.) are disdained. They do not display crosses, fish, doves or pictures of angels or Jesus, since "no one really knows what they look like."

Children of 2x2 parents attend public and private schools and some are home schooled. For a time, home schooling was not approved by Workers (Oregon). Still others attend private schools, including religious/church schools. In Rathmolyon, Ireland, where there was no public high school, some 2x2 parents sent their sons to a Roman Catholic school that was nearer than a private secular school.

The Baldwin Babies. Dr. Wallace "Wally" Emmett Baldwin (1913–2004) was a family physician in the Eugene/Springfield, Oregon area. Dr.

Baldwin was born into a 2x2 home, was married with two children and had a Meeting in his home. Appropriately, his obituary stated: His interests included **assisting in the adoption of children.**

Dr. Baldwin enabled many newborn infants to be legally adopted by 2x2 parents. The babies came from outsiders and unwed 2x2 women, both Friends and Workers. Dr. Baldwin began facilitating adoptions at least by the late 1960s and was held in high regard for his kindness in assisting numerous babies to have the opportunity of being raised in 2x2 homes. Reports vary as to the number of babies (200 to 300?) that he placed in his lifetime. These children were known as the "Baldwin Babies."

Radios. The Golden Age of the American Radio began in the 1930s and rapidly became the dominant home entertainment medium for the next 50 years, until it was usurped by television. Sixty percent of American families purchased radios between 1923 and 1930.

In some areas, including the Eastern US, the radio was banned from 2x2 homes and autos, yet permissible in others. It is speculated there was no ban on radios in the Western US under Jack Carroll's oversight because radio enabled them to keep abreast of events in the Pacific War Theater in WWII where five Workers, including three from the West Coast, were imprisoned in the Philippines. *See* Chapter 38.

Television. Between 1947 and 1957, television entered many US homes. It was marketed as a modern innovation that "brought the world into your home" (Horrors!). Referred to as "hellivision" by some Workers, television was considered an "idol" that opened the door to the world, temptation and sin. Overseer Garrett Hughes proclaimed, "Television is the Devil's masterpiece."

The decision was reached at a Western US Workers Meeting that there would be zero tolerance for televisions. For a time, if a 2x2 was discovered owning one, they were excommunicated or instructed not to participate in Meetings until they disposed of it. Usually, Workers do not (knowingly) place a Fellowship Meeting in a home with a television. This may be changing.

Even so, many of the Friends owned a TV and kept it hidden. When new converts voluntarily disposed of their televisions without pressure, the Workers claimed the Holy Spirit induced them to do so. For some, it was not easy; one new convert confessed that during the few years he professed, he bought and disposed of seven televisions.

Around the Millennium, it became more common for the Friends to own and openly display their TVs. Reportedly, some male Workers have asked to watch sports on the Friends' TV. While US Workers do not currently openly condone television, it appears most Workers are no longer disciplining 2x2s for owning one. Permitted electronic devices allowing TV content have circumvented the TV prohibition.

Automobiles. Released October 1, 1908, the Model-T automobile began to be mass produced. The 10,000 autos produced were priced around $950 each. When customers inquired about color choices for the Model-T, Henry Ford's famous retort was, "You can have any color as long as it's black."

Slow to change, 2x2s continued to purchase black autos long after other colors became available. Normally, 2x2s drove economical autos with a minimum of "worldly" chrome trim; some painted the chrome black and turned whitewall tires to the inside. Those who drove more expensive autos were considered vain and proud, and their sincerity was suspect.

Radios were first installed in autos in 1930. When a 2x2 bought a car containing a radio, they were expected to remove it and the antenna. At some Conventions, some Workers broke off (vandalized) the antennas from parked cars, without regard to the owner's member status. This was not uncommon up until the 1960–1970 Conventions. In some areas, record players, stereos, tape recorders and video cameras were taboo for 2x2s, yet permissible in other regions.

Computers. The IBM personal computer (PC) was introduced in 1981. By 1989, an estimated 54 million PCs were in use in the US. Electronic mail (e-mail) became available around 1993. The Internet was in everyday use around 1993–1994. Soon PCs were considered essential in many homes and businesses.

At first, the Workers viewed PCs as glorified typewriters. PCs had gained a firm foothold before the Workers learned there was such a thing as the Internet. In 1997, Eldon Tenniswood affirmed that if he had known about the Internet, he would have banned computers from the beginning, but once they were in the Friends' homes it was impossible to take them away. Some Workers spoke against PCs at Conventions— to no avail. Currently, many Workers use personal laptops, cell phones, e-mail accounts and the Internet.

Fifth Exodus. In 1994, the first Internet website relating to William Irvine and the early history of the 2x2 Sect was launched by *Research and Information Services (RIS)*. In 1996, the original *Veterans of the Truth* (VOT) website was created; in 1997, the website associated with this book was created, *Telling The Truth (TTT)*. Workers began cautioning the Friends against visiting the "hate sites" on the Internet. In the wake of the Internet, the Fifth Exodus of Friends began and remains ongoing.

Alcohol and Tobacco. From their start, Irvine prohibited the use of tobacco and alcohol in the British Isles. His reason may have been to pre-empt objections from the Temperance Movement, then influential in many quarters of society. The Workers who ventured across the ocean to the United States and countries within the British Empire continued these prohibitions; their converts became non-smoking teetotalers. Andrew Abernethy, Eastern US Overseer, declared, "Anyone who lets alcohol touch their lips is none of us." Jim Brown, a US Worker, instructed the Friends not to eat in restaurants serving alcohol.

In sharp contrast, the early UK Workers who ventured across the English Channel to Europe allowed their converts to continue drinking alcoholic beverages as usual, both wine and beer. Wine was served with the noon meal at Special Meetings in Italy. Beer is consumed by members in Germany.

A Canadian Ex-worker who visited some 2x2 homes in Europe, remarked that "the same God obviously had given completely different guidelines to different messengers in different lands ... After all, had I not sat around tables in France, in Italy, or in Germany and Greece while the Workers uncorked the bottles of wine and, after helping themselves to a sip or two, passed them around in order that the rest of us could fill our goblets as well? I had" (Young 2000, 9:260–261, *TTT*).

Wine is described in the Bible as a symbol of joy and happiness (Ps. 4:7, 104:15; Eccl. 9:7, 10:19; Joel 2:19, 24, Amos 9:13, Isa. 25:6). Wine is also mentioned in the context of a blessing and gift from God (Deut. 7:13, 33:28; Hos. 2:8; Isa. 55:1). A shortage of wine was associated with disobedience to God (Deut. 28:39; Jer. 48:33). During the Old Covenant, God-ordained drink (wine) offerings were poured out into the altar fire with the offerings in sacrifices (Ex. 29:40). Jesus turned water into a superior wine at a wedding where it was running low (John 2:1–11).

Scripture does not condemn the moderate intake of alcoholic beverages. The Apostle Paul did not forbid the Ephesians from drinking wine, but rather encouraged them to, "be not *drunk* with wine, wherein is excess; but be filled with the Spirit" (Eph. 5:18). This is similar to the instruction that believers should be "moderate" (Phil. 4:5) and "temperate in all things" (1 Cor. 9:25). The potential for abuse does not invalidate moderate usage of alcohol, any more than the existence of traffic accidents invalidates the use of automobiles.

The inconsistency in regional applications regarding consumption of alcohol has led some 2x2s to study Scripture and conclude that total abstinence is not a biblical mandate, but rather a man-made 2x2 tradition. Reportedly, some 2x2s have begun to drink in moderation.

Entertainment and Recreation. The following have been taboo for 2x2s at various times, but may not be so universally at present: gambling, dancing, bowling, skating, team sports, swimming in mixed-sex company, attending sports games, concerts, races, plays, movies/theatre, parties or fairs. To avoid the "appearance of evil" (1 Thess. 5:22), some 2x2s do not play games involving dice or cards. For a time, the Workers discouraged reading books except for textbooks and the Bible; the *Reader's Digest* and *National Geographic* were somewhat permissible.

These restrictions were rationalized using the Scripture: "Love not the world, neither the things that are in the world. If any man love the world, the love of the Father is not in him. For all that is in the world, the lust of the flesh, and the lust of the eyes, and the pride of life, is not of the Father, but is of the world" (1 John 2:15–16).

Dancing is considered "indulging in worldliness," and taboo because of "what it might lead to." Few 2x2 teenagers were allowed to participate in school proms, banquets, dances and many other school social functions or offices. This tradition has no biblical support. On the contrary, the Bible states there is "a time to dance," and contains several references to dancing, some of which are associated with praising and giving glory to God.

Music. Workers approve of piano playing; this skill was useful in Gospel Missions. Some were warned against playing secular music ("Devil's music") and believed 2x2s should *only* play or listen to hymns. Even so, many 2x2 children took lessons, learned to play secular tunes and performed in piano recitals. Again, this is in stark contrast to the Bible's record of all sorts of instruments being used in producing "joyful noise" and the lack of any prohibition against non-sacral music. Occupations in music are not encouraged, other than teachers.

Marriage, Divorce, Remarriage

Dating – Courting. Given that their ideal occupation (the highest possible calling) for young 2x2s is to enter the Work, some Workers have taken a dim view of dating and marriage, even though without marriage, Workers would have few open homes, meals or wheels. For many years, Workers, especially those in the US Southern states, discouraged young people from even getting acquainted. Those who do not find a marriage partner within the sect are expected to remain single all their lives, as the Apostle Paul recommended (1 Cor. 7:7–8, 32–34).

For a long time, Conventions were the main place where 2x2 youth could meet potential mates. Some Workers felt strongly that

"Convention is not a place for courting," and prevented young boys and girls from talking or sitting together at Conventions. Before e-mail, many young 2x2 couples exchanged letters after Convention; some eventually married after having very few dates. For example, my parents met briefly at a Sunday Fellowship Meeting, wrote letters during WWII and visited once after the War. They married the third time they saw each other.

Outsiders. It is expected that 2x2s will not marry outside the sect, based on 2 Corinthians 6:14, "Be ye not unequally yoked together with unbelievers." However, a new convert may remain in a marriage with a Non-2x2 and have full participation privileges. A home where a 2x2 is married to a Non-2x2 (outsider) is called a *divided home* (1 Cor. 7:10–17).

Workers strongly discourage 2x2s from dating "a worldly person" (an outsider), although in some foreign countries the Workers accept the Friends marrying outsiders due to the lack of suitable partners within the sect. In some cases, a 2x2 dating an outsider is not allowed to participate in Meetings. A 2x2 who marries an outsider may be temporarily disciplined by not being allowed to participate or take communion in Fellowship Meetings. Australia lifted this restriction in 2020.

Withholding communion from a believer has no scriptural basis. According to the Apostle Paul, taking communion is to be left up to the individual's discretion and is not the Workers' place (in 1 Cor. 11:27–29). Since the Millennium, it has become more common for 2x2s to marry outsiders and even for Workers to attend such mixed weddings.

Marriage Ceremonies. Some Workers considered the decision to marry—rather than going in the Work—as a disappointing second-best choice and not something to be celebrated. Workers do not perform marriage ceremonies, stating there is no precedent where Jesus or His apostles did so. For many years, most 2x2 marriages were performed at the courthouse by a Judge or Justice of Peace. Workers rarely attended.

In the 1940s, when my parents married, weddings were held with little fanfare and a minimum of guests. The Workers cautioned, "Keep it quiet and simple," and some brides were pressured to have a "professing wedding." For many years, Workers severely curtailed the number of guests at a wedding or reception. The most respected 2x2 weddings were very small, held in a home or outdoors with very few guests. Couples were discouraged from holding marriage ceremonies "like the worldly people's weddings."

The format for 2x2 weddings has not been consistent worldwide and has changed considerably over time. Around the 1980s, the US Friends began holding more elaborate weddings. Since then, marriages have varied in size and pomp and have been conducted in homes, outdoors, gardens, hotels, country clubs, event centers, etc. They are almost never performed by a "worldly" minister or in a church building, except in Belgium. In the late twentieth century, Workers began attending weddings, making short speeches and/or praying.

Wedding Apparel. Prior to the Victorian Era, a bride was married in any color, even black. White became a popular option for wedding gowns in 1840, after the marriage of Queen Victoria, who was the first *royal* bride to wear a white gown. Illustrations of her wedding were widely published, and many UK brides began following their queen's color choice.

Since mid-twentieth century, traditionally, most worldly Western wedding dresses have been white, eggshell, ecru or ivory, adapted to the styles of the day. Then in the late 1960s, wedding dresses reverted to long, full-skirted designs reminiscent of the Victorian Era.

In earlier years, professing brides were not supposed to wear "worldly" white wedding gowns, veils, corsages or carry bouquets. Brides were expected to wear an outfit suitable for Sunday Meeting. Grooms usually wore a suit and tie. However, in the 1970s, brides began abandoning the Workers' imposed restrictions for apparel and weddings. Since then, many professing brides have worn traditional, strapless or off-the-shoulder floor-length white gowns with bridal headpieces, veils and bouquets; many grooms have worn tuxedos.

With This Ring. As early as 1908, reporters mentioned 2x2 married women "casting aside the symbol of marriage," and new brides not wearing wedding bands (*Impartial Reporter* Aug. 27, 1908, *TTT*). In the early 1900s in New Zealand, the 2x2 women were encouraged to cast their wedding bands into a pond at a South Island Convention (wearing gold was "not of God").

By not wearing a wedding ring, some 2x2 women suffered uncomfortable moments. Around 1950, a motel clerk refused to rent my parents a room because my mother was not wearing a wedding ring, and they "weren't that kind of place." Soon after that embarrassing experience, my parents purchased Mom a very slim gold wedding band for $8.00 at Montgomery Wards.

An engagement ring is an external symbol of a promise by two people to marry each other. Workers have long considered engagement rings to be worldly. At least by the early 1960s in some areas, it was fairly customary for a 2x2 man to give his 2x2 fiancée an engagement wristwatch; normally the watch was not gold or adorned with gemstones. After the Millennium, it became more common for North American 2x2 brides to wear engagement and wedding rings with diamonds, though this is not yet a worldwide norm.

Eventually, most all 2x2 married women wore wedding bands. At first, the bands were simple, narrow, plain and without gemstones. Worldly men began wearing wedding bands in the mid-twentieth century. By the mid-to-late 1960s, it became permissible for 2x2 men to wear a wedding band in some areas; in Australia, it was not allowed until the 1980s.

Divorce. 2x2s are discouraged from divorcing, but when it occurs, it is generally accepted, provided the divorcee remains single and celibate. After the death of their ex-spouse, they are free to remarry. Worldwide, the Workers are not united regarding the interpretation of Scripture and treatment of remarriage by 2x2s after divorce. *See* details in Chapter 29.

Education and Occupations

Education. For a long time, Workers viewed higher education as a worldly and dangerous environment that could lead young 2x2s to be seduced by the world and jeopardize their faith in God and/or the 2x2 Sect. This attitude may have started with Irvine, who remarked, "I always could see that school (especially high school) life was dangerous for the children, as well as for the home life" (to Fladungs, June 12, 1920, in author's possession).

Ex-2x2 Marti Knight from Pennsylvania recalled, "I felt cold fury over being prevented from using my scholarships—based on Worker preachments and hearty member acceptance that 'worldly knowledge' was worse than useless, it was corrupting. In fact, intelligence was suspect. 'Look what happened to Solomon' was a mantra I heard often."

As late as the 1970s in some Eastern US states, young 2x2 men obtaining higher education were looked down on, e.g. Indiana. Some Workers discounted education, asserting, "It's heart-u-cation that's important—not head-u-cation."

Impact of the American G.I. Bill. Many Baby Boomer men served in the Vietnam War that ended in April 1975. In the US, the G.I. bill was enacted in 1966 to help veterans readjust to civilian life following active service to their country. Higher education became affordable for the average veteran and useful for career advancement. Of the returning Vietnam War veterans, 72% used the G.I. Bill, resulting in a massive influx of veterans into the educational system.

During the Vietnam War, many 2x2 men were drafted into the US Army for a two-year term. Over 250 (all conscientious objectors) passed through Ft. Sam Houston, San Antonio, Texas, where the Army trained medics.

During 1960–1970, after their discharge, many 2x2 veterans took advantage of the G.I. Bill subsidy to further their education. Obtaining a university degree became acceptable for 2x2s. Thanks to the military, the 2x2 stigma against tertiary education has all but disappeared. *See* Chapter 38.

Occupations. To become a Worker is considered the highest and best lifetime occupation. After Workers, the higher 2x2 status roles are held by the Friends hosting an annual Convention on their property, hosting a Fellowship Meeting in their home, operating residential facilities for Workers unable for the Work, providing Workers with a vehicle ("field car"), making large donations and having open homes.

Until the 1970s, in many areas, young 2x2 women were expected to go into the Work, remain single, or marry a 2x2 man and become a "keeper of the home." A 2x2 woman's employment was viewed as a stopgap until she married, started a family and became a stay-at-home mother. Higher education was generally considered a waste for women, although teaching, nursing and secretarial careers were acceptable. The expectation for women to stay at home lightened around the 1980s when economic pressures necessitated two incomes to support a family.

Jobs that restrict a 2x2's ability to regularly attend Fellowship Meetings are discouraged. Early in the US, occupations were promoted where men worked with their hands—rather than their brains. Careers are not encouraged in politics, law, sports, music, arts, the entertainment industry or any job that requires bearing a weapon, such as law enforcement and the military. Even so, in the last two decades, some 2x2 men have chosen law enforcement and military careers; some also have become attorneys, judges and doctors.

Celebrations – Holidays

Christmas. When the 2x2 Sect started, the Workers did not prohibit customary Christmas festivities. They did, however, disassociate the commemoration of Jesus' birth from this holiday. The reason given is because the precise day Jesus was born is unknown, and there is no biblical command to observe the day. For some, Christmas Day is no different from any other work holiday. For others, there may be a family dinner and a gift exchange. It is a rare 2x2 parent in America who teaches their children to believe in Santa Claus and associated myths.

It appears the early Workers who came to North America allowed new converts to celebrate with Christmas trees, as was the British and Irish custom. Currently in Australia, New Zealand, Ireland and the UK, Friends observe a secular Christmas with its customary traditions and seasonal home decorations, including gifts for the family and for the Workers. A Christmas tree may even be situated in the room where the Fellowship Meeting is held.

Christmas Tree Purge. Sometime during 1950–1960, a new ruling was made in North American fields, and Christmas trees were purged from 2x2 homes, lest they be found emulating the "pagan custom" of decorating trees and worshiping them (Jer. 10:1–5). During this time, Howard Mooney's essay, "The Origin of Christmas," was widely circulated. *Read* document on website *thetrutharchive.blogspot.com*.

It is not uncommon for 2x2 parents of young children to bend the rules concerning Christmas trees and gifts. Children of parents who strictly followed the Christmas taboo report being filled with dread when they returned to school and were asked, "What did you get for Christmas?" On the other hand, some Convention grounds in British Columbia and Alberta, Canada, and Idaho, US, are or were Christmas tree farms.

Easter. The 2x2s do not celebrate the Easter holiday commemorating Jesus' resurrection, considered the most important event in Christianity and the foundation of the Christian faith. The 2x2s assert they remember the resurrection every Sunday—not just once a year and that no one knows for certain the date of His death. In some countries, Easter egg hunts and Easter baskets full of treats are not uncommon for 2x2 children.

Disagreements and Discipline

Some disciplinary methods Workers use when 2x2 traditions or rules are broken include public or private rebukes, shaming, humiliation and withdrawal of Meeting participation privileges including communion, refusal or return of money offered to Workers, limited or no daytime or overnight visits from Workers, denial of baptism, withdrawal of Eldership, removal of Fellowship Meetings and the most severe of all, excommunication.

There is no appeal system for disagreements within the 2x2 Sect. The valid concerns of many questioning and disgruntled 2x2s have been ignored, quashed, papered over, swept under the rug and otherwise hidden, sometimes with implied threats. Church discipline or resolution is rarely handled according to the method Jesus set out in Matthew 18:15–20.

The government style of the 2x2 Church is authoritarian, as in a dictatorship. Overseers have absolute authority over the Friends and Workers under them. It is expected that Workers' interpretations and decrees be observed without question, even when they are unable to provide Scripture to support them. Workers stress the Friends cannot go wrong by unconditionally respecting, submitting and obeying those in authority—even if the Workers are wrong.

Unwed 2x2 Mothers. In Wyoming where Stanley Sullivan was Overseer, as recently as 1995, when a daughter of 2x2 parents became pregnant out of wedlock, the Workers excommunicated her. "Multiple meetings with the Workers, and it was made clear to me that **I had to choose between my child or my soul.** I chose my child. It was the most traumatic experience of my life. Consequently, I suffered much anxiety and years of therapy."

Another 2x2 unwed mother was told, "I could never profess again if I was a single mom—and since I was a true believer and trusted the Workers, **I actually believed I was trading my soul for my son**" when she chose to keep her child. Some couples who married after a child was on the way were told not to take part in meetings until after their baby was born. These events beg the questions: How many other 2x2 unwed mothers did the Workers coerce into giving up their babies? How many were told they could never profess again or take the emblems unless they did so?

Many who leave the sect soon discover their reputations among the membership have been discredited. They have been labelled bitter, unwilling, offended, rebellious, lovers of the world, lost their vision, confused, believed the lies on the Internet, were seduced by Satan, never received the revelation nor had a good understanding, have mental issues, etc. Smear campaigns, character assassinations and shunning are not uncommon.

Generally, Workers advise 2x2s not to go to the law, Brother against Brother. That is, not to take legal action over a dispute with another 2x2, citing 1 Cor. 6:1–8. Lawsuits against outsiders are permissible, e.g. for unfair treatment at work. From 1906 to 1913, the Friends and Workers filed eight cases for slander in Ireland and England against an outsider's accusations that they were involved in white-slave trafficking of Sister Workers; most of the cases were settled in their favor. *See* Chapter 22 and website *TellingTheTruth.info* in History Articles, Court Cases.

In the past, Workers have strongly discouraged victims of sexual abuse from taking legal action against a 2x2 perpetrator. This has changed in some but not all areas, due in part to outside pressure from the WINGS website (launched in 2009), and also because of the world's growing awareness of child sexual abuse, legally mandated reporting and the enactment and strict enforcement of new laws. *See* wingsfortruth.info.

As can be seen from the above, it appears that over time within the 2x2 belief system, there has been a variation of thoughts and approaches on many subjects, traditions and methods, which have evolved worldwide under various Overseers. To say the 2x2 Sect as a whole believes or acts in a certain manner would be a mistake and misleading. The only beliefs about which we have a *thorough* knowledge are our own.

Church Procedures

Sunday. The first day of the week is to be a "day of rest" for 2x2s, a concept taken from one of the Ten Commandments: "Remember the Sabbath day, to keep it holy." Members are encouraged not to engage in work or pleasure on Sunday, including performing yard work, washing vehicles, hair or laundry, making non-emergency car/home repairs or maintenance, boating, fishing, sewing, needlework, sports, housework—and in some areas, no purchasing. Cooking, driving, visiting and writing letters to the Friends and Workers are approved Sunday pastimes. Workers cautioned, "Don't make Sunday a fun day." Jesus repeatedly rebuked those who tried to dictate what could be considered "work" on the Sabbath according to their traditions, e.g. "The Sabbath was made for man and not man for the Sabbath" (Mark 2:27). Parents and all their children attend Meetings—there is no nursery, Sunday school or children's classes.

Communion – Emblems (Lord's Supper, Eucharist) . When 2x2 home Meetings were first established in Ireland around 1902–1903, leavened bread and real wine were served for communion in both Conventions and Fellowship Meetings. "Communion wine" was shown on a list of "Receipts and Expenditures" for the 1913 Crocknacrieve Convention (in author's possession).

From its first Sunday gathering, the standard policy at the end of every Fellowship Meeting was for a common cup containing the "fruit of the vine" (unfermented grape juice in the US), followed by a slice of white bread, to be handed from person-to-person, with each member taking a sip or pinch.

The type of grapes required for preserved non-alcoholic grape juice was first bred in 1849. In 1869, Thomas B. Welch successfully developed a pasteurization method that allowed for the storage of juice, without the juice fermenting into alcohol. (Raw grape juice stored at room temperature naturally ferments into wine.) Prior to 1869, *"unfermented wine"* was unheard of. Subsequently, Welch's Grape Juice made its debut at the 1893 Chicago World's Fair. This being the case, in Bible times, wine and fruit of the vine would have been fermented.

When the first Workers came to the US in 1903, alcohol was legal, except during the Prohibition years 1920–1933, during which *alcohol used for sacramental purposes was exempted.* It is very possible the Workers continued their UK practice of serving wine in the US Sunday Meetings. It is not known why or when the Workers chose to deviate from Jesus' example regarding communion and started using purple grape juice rather than wine.

Reportedly, genuine wine is used in Fellowship Meetings in Australia, New Zealand, South Africa, Netherlands, Belgium, Germany, Italy, Greece, Romania, England, Ireland, France and possibly all of Europe. No 2x2 Sunday Meetings have been reported that served unleavened bread or performed foot washing per Jesus' example at the Last Supper.

On the other hand, in Australian Conventions, communion has always been served to hundreds of attendees on Sunday morning. New Zealand stopped serving communion at Conventions in the late 1960s–'70s. In North America and New Zealand this practice is considered unscriptural, as those Workers believe communion should only be taken in a Sunday morning Fellowship Meeting in a home. The rationale is that communion is equivalent to partaking of the Passover lamb in the home of each Israelite family. The Australians serve the emblems at Conventions, their home away from home. This is another instance where the 2x2 traditions are not the same the world over as is claimed.

Baptism. After a person has professed through a Worker, the 2x2 Sect believes baptism by full immersion is necessary for salvation (Mark 16:16), and that God only accepts baptisms performed by 2x2 Workers. A baptismal service is often held during a Convention in a nearby pond, lake, river, creek or ocean for candidates with prior approval of Workers. The convert is dipped under the water by a Brother Worker while he repeats the words, "I baptize you in the name of the Father, the Son and the Holy Ghost/Spirit." They do not practice infant baptism, christening, dedication or designate Godparents.

In their early days, 2x2 converts were baptized very soon after they professed, as was the practice of the New Testament church (Acts 8:36– 38, 16:15). This has also changed. Often before baptism, there is a waiting period to ensure the new convert understands and adheres to the expected external 2x2 traditions. While new converts may immediately begin to participate in Fellowship Meetings, they usually do not take communion until after their baptism (or rebaptism) by a Worker.

Some 2x2s are allowed baptism upon request; for others, baptism may be withheld until they fulfil certain conditions or show "fruits meet for repentance" (Matt. 3:8). At times, baptism has been conditional upon not using tobacco, alcohol or owning a television. A female may be required to grow out her hair, bangs/fringes, discontinue wearing slacks, makeup, jewelry or immodest apparel, etc. For a male, baptism has been at times conditional on the length of his hair, not wearing facial hair or jeans. Failure to submit to these traditional restrictions may be viewed as evidence of a lack of understanding, growth or rebellion.

Since the Millennium, while the Workers have not publicly announced changes in rules, there has been a noticeable lack of discipline regarding items previously forbidden. Rules appear to be relaxing somewhat in several areas, due to 2x2 youths pushing against boundaries. Historically, when the Friends disregarded certain taboos, the rules changed, such as with higher education, women's appearance, black stockings, televisions and radios. In sharp contrast to past policies, it has recently been reported that some West Coast Workers have taken the position that they are not 2x2 "police."

Funerals. For many years, only Brother Workers officiated at 2x2 funerals. Around the Millennium, this changed, and Sister Workers began having speaking parts. Funerals for 2x2s are usually held in a funeral parlor and/or at the graveside. To accommodate large crowds, some funerals have been held in rented facilities or on Convention premises.

Funerals were held in church buildings for Paul Sharpe (2011), former Overseer of Asia, Alberta and British Columbia, Canada, and for Joe Hobbs (2019), Overseer of South Dakota. Some Workers' funerals have been noticeably large, arresting reporters' attention. In 1957, at Jack Carroll's service, 700 attended; 2,500 attended Willie Jamieson's funeral in 1974. In North America, the majority of 2x2s are buried in cemeteries, rather than being cremated. This, too, is changing.

Trinity. Early in the fourth century in the early Christian church, the question of the exact relationship between the Father and His Son, Jesus, was a major religious controversy between Arius, who preached that Jesus, though uniquely holy, is less than God, and Athanasius, who argued that Jesus is God himself in human form. The debate over the degree of Jesus' divinity is ongoing today in Christendom.

The Workers have rarely spoken with clarity or in depth on the topics of the Godhead or Trinity. Therefore, beliefs of the members vary considerably concerning the relationship of God and Jesus. Some 2x2s believe God is the proper name for the Father and that God is the Father only. Further, that God and Jesus' relationship is literally parallel to that of a human father and son; that Jesus had the same divine attributes as His Father (God) and was subordinate to Him, united in purpose and spirit.

Others believe Jesus was *just a man*, a human being like us, who lived a perfect, obedient life and died on the cross; that God exalted/crowned Him with the title and glory of *Christ* (Phil. 2:5–11; Heb. 5:8–9).

Still others believe the one God is made up of three persons (Father, Son and Holy Spirit); that Jesus and the Holy Spirit are the same being, or the same in essence with God the Father; they use the terms *God the Son*, the *Triune God* and believe that Jesus and the Holy Spirit are also God, co-equal and co-eternal. Most Christians hold this belief.

Historically, Irvine and his early Workers believed and taught the concept of the Trinity. In their beginning, according to John Long, Irvine was sound "concerning the principals of the Doctrine of Christ ... He believed ... in the Trinity, in the Divinity of our Lord ... that every saved soul is indwelt by the Spirit of Christ" (March 1898, *TTT*).

The early Workers articulated their belief in the Trinity in their sermons and hymns. A line in the *Go-Preachers' Hymn Book* was "All praise to God, the Three in One; the One in Thee (No. 71.) A favorite hymn "Cease Not," written by early Worker, James Fawcett (1886–1958) who entered the Work in 1904, was not included in the latest *Hymns Old and New* edition (1987). It contained the phrase: "Cease Not to Worship the Father and Son, The Holy Spirit and these Three are One ... my Saviour and my God" (No. 239, 1951 ed.).

In later hymnal editions, some wording has been altered that formerly referenced the Trinity and Jesus being God. The hymn "Our Blest Redeemer" omits verse six: "O Praise the Father, Praise the Son, Blest Spirit, praise to Thee; All praise to God, the Three in One, The one in Three." The well-known hymn "When I Survey the Wondrous Cross" by Isaac Watts contains the words, "Save in the cross of Christ *my God.*" The latest 2x2 hymnal has: "Save in the death of Christ *my Lord.*"

Some who strongly believe in the Doctrine of the Trinity have left the 2x2 Sect because, in their experience and opinion, the 2x2 leaders are not teaching it correctly and have substituted false doctrine in its place.

Black stockings (1927)

36

Black Stocking Church

At the turn of the twentieth century, black stockings were almost universal daytime leg wear for all women (Buck 1984, 142; Cunnington 1970, 567). Made of thick, black, lisle cotton, they were nothing like today's transparent black nylon hosiery. While hemlines were street length, stockings were rarely visible. The early Sister Workers and the female converts dressed likewise and continued the practice among their female converts in other countries.

Due to fabric shortages during WWI and women replacing men in the working world, skirts were shortened. As ankles and legs became visible, stocking styles, colors and materials changed. Long after skin tones in hosiery became the norm, 2x2 women continued wearing thick black cotton stockings. Brother Workers believed it was unbecoming for the legs of "women professing godliness" to be viewed in a flesh color. Wearing black stockings was viewed as a sign of spiritual submission, self-denial and maturity.

Black stockings worn by 2x2 women
Center: Workers Lilly Noren and Hilda Blaue (1944)

Black Stocking Religion. The first Sister Workers my maternal grandmother met in Mississippi in 1931 were still wearing black stockings. So it was that Grandmother donned them when she converted. As time marched on, black stocking clad 2x2 women became highly conspicuous—not dissimilar to nuns with their habits, and Amish and Mennonite women with their peculiar apparel. "Some people thought we wore uniforms," disclosed my mother, Dorothy "Dot" Berry. "Our faith couldn't be identified by a name, but we sure were identified by what we wore" (2008, *EXP*). "Because as members of The Truth Church we had to wear black stockings, we became known as ... the Two by Twos and the Black Socks of Boscobel" (Oman 1992, 59).

US West Coast Workers Minnie Christie and May Carroll,
with and without black stockings (1931)

This highly visible peculiarity led to church monikers, such as the *Black Stocking Church, Black Stocking Religion, Black Stocking Brigade* and *Black Socks*. When the FBI investigated the sect in WWII, they reported "they are many times referred to as members of the 'Black Stocking Church' " (FBI, 1943, *TTT*).

Professing shortly before her 15th birthday in 1938, my mother sadly recalled, "How much I dreaded changing over to those hideous black stockings. I believed it was a necessary step I had to take in order to be accepted by God. I viewed the day I would ... put on black stockings as the day that would mark the beginning of a process of salvation in my life. I wanted above all else to please God and receive eternal life ... I waited until after I graduated from high school when I was 17, to don the color black. *It was a very black day for me*" (Berry 2008, *EXP*).

During WWII, some 2x2 soldiers and their wives from the Western US were stationed in the East where they attended Meetings and Conventions. Many Western wives were wearing tan-colored hose, whereas the Eastern professing women were still wearing black stockings. In a faith that claimed to be the same worldwide, and sang hymn No. 335, "In Christ there is no east or west, In Him no south or north; 'Tis one, the Shepherd's sacred flock, Though scattered o'er the Earth," this obvious difference generated questions and discontent. My mother said, "It took WWII to end the Black Stocking Curse."

Demise of Black Stockings. Soon after WWII, women's nylon stockings supplanted all other types. Manufacturers stopped manufacturing black stockings; the supply ran out. Even so, the two North American Overseers did not lift the black stocking requirement simultaneously. The West discontinued the practice around 1930, much earlier than the East, where they managed to continue the tradition by dying their stockings black.

According to one report, US Sister Worker May Carroll was responsible for influencing her Overseer brothers, Jack and Bill Carroll, in the removal of the grievous burden of black stockings in Western US and in Victoria, Australia; or perhaps she simply refused to wear them any longer. By 1931, May was wearing tan stockings in photographs.

In Australia, black stockings were discontinued around 1935 after May Carroll visited some Australian Conventions wearing tan stockings. Also present was US Brother Worker, Robert Chambers, who pointed out from the platform that black stockings had become a recognized identifier of the sect, much the same as Salvation Army uniforms had come to identify the Salvationists.

Jack Carroll announced, "We don't like to see any wearing stockings so closely like having no stockings on at all, and we feel perfectly sure that when you buy your next pair if you remember ... the word modesty, you will be more careful not only with regard to material but also with regard to color" (n.d. Black Stocking Letter, Appendix I).

In England after WWII, fashion rapidly changed. From the Staffordshire Convention platform, Jack Forbes, the English Overseer, addressed women's hair and dark clothing. Their black stockings, austere hairstyles and dark clothing was causing them to stand out and look different. His comments created a stir and some jubilation. Black stockings became a thing of the past. Hair styles became looser and varied, dress styles and colors changed, lace-up boots disappeared, and heels became higher.

Reportedly, at a Workers Meeting around 1945, George Walker announced he was allowing "the change" to take place. "I favored black because it was furthermost from the flesh color that many of us believed was unbecoming to 'women professing godliness.' At no time did I say black was the only modest color. I spoke against the wearing of it being a condition of fellowship" (Black Stocking Letter, n.d. Appendix I).

The Change. The welcome news about "the change" spread rapidly as 2x2 women happily donned the newly approved stocking colors of gun-metal gray, tan, beige and taupe. "I can still recall so vividly the outpourings of relief from those who were so desperate for the change," disclosed Ex-worker Willis Young in his book *In Vain Do They Worship*, "and the equal protestations from women like my grandmothers who saw it as the end of the faith as they knew it" (2000, 36, *TTT*).

My mother reminisced, "I never got used to wearing black stockings in public, and I hated them right up until the day I took them off ... I remember the day I changed over! There are no words to describe what freedom I felt when I donned my first pair of gun-metal gray hose and saw my legs in the mirror ... The nightmare was finally over! ... the total years I actually wore black stockings was only five years, but ... the effect it had was to rob me of ... an important part of my youth" (Berry 2008, *EXP*).

Shame, Suffering and Discrimination. The requirement to wear black stockings had long-lasting emotional effects on many women and children. Being the object of scorn and ridicule due to wearing black stockings produced extreme self-consciousness, shyness, low self-esteem and introversion in some. For 50 years, black stockings were the dark robber of many girls' youth, causing untold grief and misery to countless 2x2 women.

"You cannot imagine," described my mother, "the remarks, the rejection, the questions, the slights, snubs, etc., we endured from 'those of the world' due to our wearing black stockings ... Shopping took a lot of courage because we were often questioned and usually were gawked at as though we were some sort of freaks. Some people actually turned around to stare at us, whispered behind their hands and snickered as we passed on the street" (Berry 2008, *EXP*).

Workers instructed Sister Worker Hilda Blaue to stop wearing black stockings in the 1970s. Explaining that she had made a vow to God in the 1920s that she would wear black stockings without complaining until the day she died, Hilda protested she could not break her vow to God. She was forced to leave the Work. *See* Hilda Blaue's photo at the beginning of this Chapter.

Is History Repeating Itself? Upholding the black stocking tradition some 30–40 years after styles had changed hindered the sect's growth and was responsible for many dropouts. Rather than attracting others to the sect, they distracted and detracted. The Workers did not lift the rule soon enough, nor did they allow the Holy Spirit to guide women in their apparel.

Is it possible that today there are unnecessary hardships in the 2x2 Sect similar to the black stocking debacle? Requirements that are traditions of men rather than commandments of God? Rules that lack biblical foundation and make peculiar spectacles of women? Some possibilities are 2x2 women not being allowed to trim/cut their hair, wear their hair down, wear cosmetics, slacks or jewelry.

It is now 30–40 years since it has become respectable for women to wear slacks in public and for dress, yet Workers have not yet officially lifted that ban. It appears lessons regarding women's apparel were not learned from earlier mistakes, and history is repeating itself once again.

See additional details on website *TellingTheTruth.info* in History, History of 2x2 Traditions-Rules.

Sam Jones, most prolific hymn author (112) in "Hymns Old and New"

37

Hymns Old and New

For about two thousand years, Christians have used music in their worship services. The Apostle Paul encouraged believers "Speaking to yourselves with psalms and hymns and spiritual songs" (Eph. 5:19, Col. 3:16). For hundreds of years, English Protestants sang only paraphrased Old Testament Psalms in public worship, which did not mention Jesus.

Isaac Watts (1674–1748) believed strongly that Christians should be able to sing about their Lord Jesus Christ. Motivated to make this happen, he became a prolific hymn writer who created hundreds of new hymns. Watts is credited with writing the first English hymn that was not a direct paraphrase of Scripture. He transformed congregational singing from singing only Old Testament Psalms to singing hymns based on New Testament passages that glorified the power, wisdom and goodness of God and Jesus. Described as "the liberator of English hymnody," Watts published his hymnal *Hymns and Spiritual Songs* in 1707.

In 1450 in Mainz, Germany, Johannes Gutenberg invented the printing press which started the Printing Revolution. Before this, books were scarce; it could take months, sometimes years, to write or copy a new book by hand. The first book printed by the printing press was the Gutenberg Bible in 1455. Before long, hymnals were being mass produced. Up to that time, in some congregations, hymns were traditionally sung or chanted by "lining out," where the worshippers repeated a line of a hymn after the hymn leader read it out loud.

Bound collections of hymns are called *hymnals* or *hymnbooks*. In 1524, the Lutherans published in Germany what is reputed to be the first Protestant collection of hymns, the *Achtliederbuch*. Also claiming to be the first Protestant hymnal was the *Ein New Gesengbuchlen* published in 1532 by the Moravians in Bohemia. The first Catholic hymnbook (in German) appeared in Leipzig in 1537, *Ein New Gesangbuechlein Geystlicher Lieder by* Michael Vehe. Calvin's *Genevan Psalter* was published in 1539.

In 1535, *Goostly Psalmes and Spirituall Songes* by Miles Coverdale was published and is regarded as the first English hymnal; the second being Sternhold and Hopkins's *Whole Book of Psalm*. In 1612 in Holland, Henry Ainsworth prepared the *Ainsworth Psalter* for the Puritans. The Pilgrims brought it to America, and in 1640, Cambridge published it as the *Bay Psalm Book*. This was the first book and the first hymnbook to be printed in North America. Nearly 400 years later, in 1913, R. L. Allan published the first *Hymns Old and New* in Scotland for the 2x2 Sect.

~~~~~

Go-Preacher's Hymn Book. In Great Britain, at least by 1907, the 2x2 Sect printed and began singing from a words-only small booklet titled *Go-Preacher's Hymn Book*. Of its 130 hymns, only 13 (10 percent) were written by 2x2s (12 by Edward Cooney and 1 by Sam Jones).

History of 2x2 Hymnbooks. During their formative years, the 2x2 Sect sang hymns found in various non-denominational hymnals, such as *Redemption Songs* and *Songs of Victory*—the hymnal used by Faith Mission (FM) (*Impartial Reporter* June 2, 1904, *TTT*). In their early days, it was not unusual for converts to "march through the town singing hymns. Crowds of people lined the streets as this unique procession passed along" (*Anglo-Celt,* Dec. 30, 1905, *TTT*).

A reporter observed, "While the Tramps denounce John and Charles Wesley as having gone to Hell, they sing the very 'devilry' written by Charles Wesley in some of his immortal hymns" (Aug. 27, 1908, *TTT*). The Wesley brothers, born in the early 1700s, were leaders of the English Methodist movement; Charles composed about 6,500 hymns.

A *Lloyd's Weekly* newspaper reporter explained "In the 10th chapter… Matthew—which is the mission's charter—occurs the phrase: 'And as ye go, preach, saying, The kingdom of heaven is at hand.' Hence the name *Go-Preachers*, and as missioners use a hymn book called the *Go-Preacher's Hymn Book*, this is perhaps the most characteristic and comprehensive title. It has besides, the sanction of the Workers, who sometimes vary the name by calling themselves 'Tramp Preachers' " (Feb. 3, 1907, *TTT*).

1913: New 2x2 Hymnbook. In 1913, the sect's first hymnal containing 218 hymns was printed, which did not go unnoticed by reporters visiting Crocknacrieve Convention. "On Sunday last a new hymnbook entitled *Hymns Old and New*, made its appearance. This book, compiled by Edward Cooney and William Carroll, consists entirely of hymns taken from such collections as *Songs of Victory, Redemption Songs,* and *Songs and Solos*. The *Go-Preacher's Hymn Book* is no longer used" (*Impartial Reporter* July 3, 1913, *TTT*).

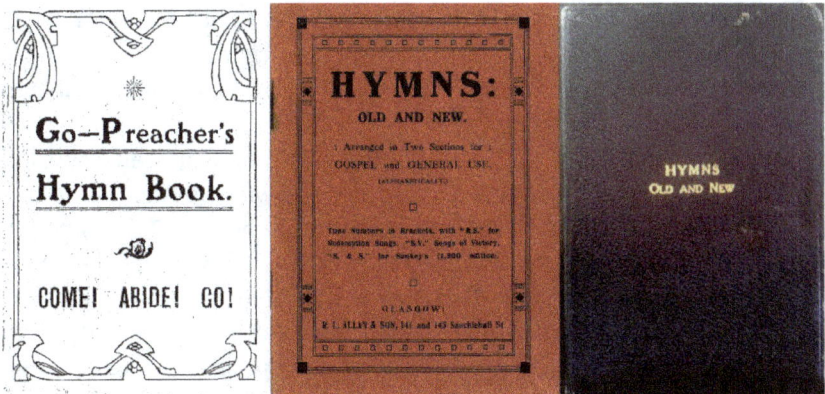

"Go-Preacher's Hymn Book" (first hymnal); "Hymns Old and New" (1913); "Hymns Old and New" (1951)

Hymns Old and New is an English language hymnbook published exclusively for use by the Friends and Workers. These hymns are valued highly by them and are an important part of their spiritual lives. They sing, hum, quote, study, preach, speak, are touched and moved to tears by these hymns. Singing at 2x2 Fellowship Meetings and Conventions has always been *a capella*; organ or piano accompaniment is sometimes used at Gospel Meetings.

Since 1913, the 2x2 Sect has been singing from various editions of *Hymns Old and New,* their official hymnbook. It is the only widely disseminated publication reflecting their beliefs, produced under the direction of sect leaders. The 1987 edition is currently being used in all English-speaking countries. An unusual feature of their hymnbook is that no hymns associated with Christmas are included. Since its first printing, the title of their hymnal has not changed in English-speaking countries. A simple method for identifying this nameless sect is to learn the title of their hymnal.

R. L. Allan & Son, Publishers Ltd. In 1863, Robert Allan established a publishing company in Glasgow, Scotland. They published the first edition of *Hymns Old and New* in 1913 and subsequent editions in 1919, 1928, 1951 and 1987, with a supplemental section added onto the back of some editions between publications.

Reportedly, there was a fire in the 1920s or '30s that destroyed Allan's early records and stock. They retained no archive of out of print titles, nor do they have copies of the 1919 or 1928 editions.

Nicholas Gray, Director of R. L. Allan, supplied the following explanation: "Pickering & Inglis bought the business [R. L. Allan] from the owner, Mr. Smith, in 1970 ... Allan publishes a hymnbook called *Hymns Old and New* in English and German and specially bound *King*

James Version Bibles for this group" (to Kropp April 19, 1994, *TTT*). *John Gray* of Pickering & Inglis Ltd. licensed the rights to two hymnbooks from R. L. Allan & Son, which was the start of Gray's relationship with Allan.

Subsequently, the R. L. Allan & Son business was passed down in the Gray family and is currently managed or owned by Ian Metcalfe. In 2013, they moved the company to Surrey, England. The compilation copyright was registered in US by Pocock & Martin, under the name of Trustees for the Christian Church in England, in 1987. *See* Allan link at Bibles-Direct.co.uk (password is allan, all lower case). *See* letters from R. L. Allan & Son on website *TellingTheTruth.info* in Photo Gallery, Hymn Album.

Hymnbook Editions. Over the years, *Hymns Old and New* has been revised and republished several times by the same publisher in English, German and recently in Spanish (2016). Many editions do not show the date of publication. For identification purposes, the following list shows the total number of hymns and the titles of the first and last hymn in each English edition published by R. L. Allan & Son.

Year	No. of Hymns	First Hymn	Last Hymn	Comment
1913	218	*Are you sowing the seed*	*Within Thy Tabernacle Lord*	Words-only edition
1914	256	*As We Gather*	256 *Bow Down Thine Ear* as an alternative tune for No. 64	The Words-only edition ended with No. 255, *Lord in Our Need*
1919	208	*Don't you hear Him Knocking*	*We Thank Thee Lord for Weary Days*	
1922	256	*As We Gather*	*Bow Down Thine Ear* as an alternative tune for No. 64	Appendix of 27 hymns was added to 1914 edition
1928	301	*As We Gather*	*The Saviour now is seeking*	Plus Appendix of 12 hymns
1935	374	*As We Gather*	*Called Home to Rest*	Supplement of 73 hymns added to 1928 edition, plus Appendix of 12 hymns
1951	335	*Tell Me the Story of Jesus*	*Called Home to Rest*	
1987	412	*Tell Me the Story of Jesus*	*When Life Is Ended*	

The 1987 edition states on the copyright page: *"Previous compilations entitled "Hymns Old and New" were published in 1919, 1928 and 1951."* (This statement omits the 1913, 1914 and editions reprinted with supplements in 1922 and 1935.) In New South Wales, Australia, editions were published in 1917, 1918 and 1921. The US *Gospel Hymnbook*, a shortened hymnal version, contained 122 hymns. For many years, the Workers provided copies for attendees' use during Gospel Missions.

1951 Edition of *Hymns Old and New*. A document titled "A Review of *Hymns Old and New*" compiled by Brother Worker Bert Pattison was a widely distributed accompaniment to the 1951 edition. While providing many interesting details about the authors and composers (some incorrect), it divided the authors into two groups: "those written by our Friends and those by writers unknown to us" (outsiders) (1951, *TTT*).

Pattison explained that the 1935 hymnbook was republished in 1951 because "the type had become so worn and the book so bulky; this necessitated many old favorites being left out so that room might be found for new ones ... We were unable to obtain some tunes because of copyright difficulties" (1951, *TTT*).

1987 Edition of *Hymns Old and New*. In 1985, a committee of Workers from around the world met in Lakewood, California, and began revising the 1951 hymnbook. The resulting 1987 edition includes 412 hymns. Of the 110 "new" hymns, the authors of 13 were outsiders; 66 were brought back from previous hymnbook editions or leaflets; and 33 hymns from the 1951 edition were excluded. Some changes were made to both words and tunes, and a new topical index was included. Upon receiving their new hymnbooks, some Workers instructed the Friends to burn their old ones, lest they fall into "the wrong hands." Some obeyed; others did not.

Authors of Hymns. Many 2x2s have been under the impression that all the hymns in *Hymns Old and New* were written by the Friends or Workers. On the contrary, this hymnal is a composite, drawing from many sources. Many hymns and/or tunes included were taken from outside hymnals. It contains at least one hymn written by a Catholic Saint, fourteen by Anglicans, five by Baptists, sixteen by Methodists, ten by Presbyterians and five by Salvation Army members.

Consequently, some 2x2s have been astonished upon discovering that other church hymnals contain some of the same familiar hymns included in *Hymns Old and New*. Some examples are "Just As I Am" (No. 158); "Tell Me The Story Of Jesus" (No. 1); "Wash Me from Sin" (No. 17); "When I Survey" (No. 6); "Nearer, Still Nearer" (No. 125); "Moments of Blessing" (No. 228); "Have Thine Own Way, Lord" (No. 58); "A Tender

Heart" (No. 215); "Abide with Me" (No. 170); "From Every Stain" (No. 24); "Was It for me" (No. 8), etc.

The earlier editions of *Hymns Old and New* contained more hymns written by Non-2x2s than by 2x2s. The percentage of hymns written by 2x2s in *Hymns Old and New* in the four editions printed between 1919 and 1987 increased from 45% to 74%. The currently used 1987 edition contains 412 hymns of which 26% (or 109) were written by Non-2x2s.

	Authors	
Hymnal	**2x2**	**Non-2x2**
1909 *Go-Preacher's Hymn Book*	10%	90%
1917 *Hymns Old and New*	35%	65%
1919 *Hymns Old and New*	46%	54%
1928 *Hymns Old and New*	59%	41%
1935 *Hymns Old and New*	64%	36%
1951 *Hymns Old and New*	64%	36%
1987 *Hymns Old and New*	74%	26%

See *Hymns Old and New – An Unofficial Compendium* at www.hymnsoldandnew.info/home/sources-of-hymns

Identifying Authors in *Hymns Old and New*. According to R. L. Allan, the authors' names were omitted because "part of the agreement concerning the new hymnbook [1987] was that the authors were to be kept anonymous to avoid unhealthy pride, etc." (Allan 1988, *TTT*). However, hymns written by 2x2s are designated with the notation "Words: ©*." Also, various supplemental booklets pertaining to the hymnbook show names of 2x2s in uppercase (capital) letters.

In the 1987 edition, Western Australian Overseer Sam Jones wrote the most hymns—112 and composed the tunes to four of them. Alexander "Sandy" Scott and James Jardine each wrote 18 hymns; May (Carroll) Schultz and Elma Wiebe-Milton both wrote 10 hymns; Jack Annand, Ken Paginton and Glenn Smith each wrote 9 hymns.

Oldest Hymns. While some hymns in *Hymns Old and New* were written before 1900, **none of these were written by a Worker or Friend**. Learning this has come as a surprise to many 2x2s. The five 2x2 hymn authors who entered the Work the earliest are John Sullivan and Tom Turner in 1900; Sam Jones in 1902; and William "Bill" Carroll and William Weir in 1903.

The oldest 2x2 hymn authors according to their birth years were Edward Cooney (1867); Charles Hultgren (1869); James Patrick (1872); Adam Hutchison (1873); John Sullivan and Robert Blair, (1874); Robert

Skerritt and Charles Morgan (1875). None of these men entered the Work before 1900.

Edward Cooney – the Unacknowledged Hymn Author. Four very familiar, often-sung hymns by Edward Cooney are printed in the currently used *Hymns Old and New,* 1987 edition. They are "As We Gather" (No. 179); "Lord, We Are Met Together" (No. 182); "Our God, Our Father" (No. 183); and "Here We Come" (No. 184).

Cooney's initials "E. C." appeared in *some* of the older hymnbooks, but never his surname. Further, on the accompanying "List of Hymn Authors" to the last two editions of *Hymns Old and New* (1951 and 1987), the author's name is left blank for his hymns.

English Brother Worker, Ken Paginton, handled copyright matters for the 1987 edition hymnbook. He acknowledged, "With regard to the four hymns—179, 182, 183 and 184, these were written by E. Cooney in the early part of this century." Concerning the omission of Cooney's name in the hymn author supplement, he stated, "For various private reasons, the name is not given for those four hymns, and this should be respected" (to Cherie Kropp, Feb. 24, 1992, *TTT*; *See* letter in *TellingTheTruth.info* Photo Gallery, Hymn Album).

After attention was called to this omission on the Internet, a revised 2004 author list was printed in which Cooney was finally given *some* credit for the hymns he wrote. His name is shown in lowercase type (code for indicating the author was not a 2x2 Sect member). The revised and expanded *Hymns Old and New – Concordance – Theme and Subject Index – Authors, 2004 edition* includes the partially true statement, "Edward Cooney (1867–1960); the author was an independent evangelist."

When Cooney wrote the four hymns, he was a renowned Worker, second-in-command to William Irvine, in good standing. The four hymns have been included in each hymnbook edition at least since 1917. After the Workers excommunicated Cooney in 1928, they continued including his hymns in their hymnbook but withheld authorship credit to him.

It is obvious that even as recently as 2004, Workers continued their attempts to purge Cooney's name from the 2x2 Sect's history by calling him "an independent evangelist," by obscuring his pioneering role, and obfuscating his 27 years as a prominent leader and major soul winner in the 2x2 Sect. However, it is a losing battle for them since Cooney's role and name are so well known. In fact, *Cooneyites* is the second most commonly used name for the Two by Two Sect in various books, encyclopedias, newspapers, websites and *Wikipedia*.

Non-2x2 Hymn Authors. Listed in order by their birth year, the five oldest Non-2x2 hymn authors are St. Bernard of Clairvaux (1090) Catholic; William Whittingham (1524) religious association unknown; Paul Gerhardt (1607) Lutheran; Rev. Isaac Watts (1674) English Congregationalist; and Gerhard Tersteegen (1697) German Revivalist.

St. Bernard of Clairvaux, born in France, was the author of the Latin texts that were later translated to English and then became the hymns "Jesus, the Very Thought of Thee" (No. 13) and "Jesus, Thou Joy of Loving Hearts," (No. 204, 1951 ed.; not in 1987 ed.). In spite of the 2x2's very negative views regarding Catholicism, the Workers included these two hymns based on texts by a highly revered Catholic Saint in *Hymns Old and New*.

My husband and I visited the St. Bernard of Clairvaux Catholic Church in Tulsa, Oklahoma, where we were given a pamphlet, "Who was Saint Bernard of Clairvaux? He was born in 1090 near Dijon, France, and entered the order of Cistercian monks at the age of 21 ... Because of his success, his monastery became known as the Valley of Light ... or Clairvaux ... [he] influenced the Church's thinking for centuries ... He died on August 20, 1153, and was canonized [made a saint] by Pope Alexander III in 1174 ... he is often called the *Last of the Fathers of the Church*."

Second Oldest Hymn Author. William Whittingham (1524–1579) paraphrased Psalms 23, "The Lord's My Shepherd" (Hymn No. 308), originally written by King David (1000 BC).

Third Oldest Hymn Author. Paul Gerhardt (1607–1676), born in Germany, was the author of "God in Heaven Has a Treasure" (No. 351), translated from German into English; and "A Homeless Stranger" (No. 209 in 1951 ed.; not in 1987 ed.). Gerhardt wrote 123 well-known hymns. An ordained Lutheran minister, he was called the *Sweet Singer of Lutheranism*.

Fourth Oldest Hymn Author. Rev. Isaac Watts (1674–1748) was an English Congregationalist who is credited with writing some 750 hymns, earning him the title *Father of English Hymnody*. He was the author of "When I Survey" (No. 6). He also paraphrased the Psalms in Nos. 238 and 378. A monument was erected in his honor in Westminster Abbey, England.

Watts's original "When I Survey," (Hymn No. 15, Vs. 2 in 1951 ed. *Hymns Old and New*) contained the words "Save in the death of Christ *my God*." This phrase was changed to "Christ *my Lord*" in Hymn No. 6 the 1987 ed., which is more in line with the generally held 2x2 view of Jesus and God's relationship.

Fifth Oldest Hymn Author. Gerhard Tersteegen (1697–1769), was one of the two most famous eighteenth century German hymn writers. He grew up in poverty, could not afford an education, studied theological books at home and became an outstanding lay theologian and lay pastor in the Protestant Pietist movement. He was the author of Hymn Nos. 95, 247, 263, 304 and 305, translated from German into English.

Notable Author. Charlotte Elliott (1789–1871), born in England, became an invalid in her early thirties. A minister asked her if she had peace with God and invited her to "Come just as you are." Ms. Elliott did so, became an Anglican and later wrote the hymn, "Just as I am" (No. 158). This touching hymn has been called *the world's greatest soul-winning hymn* and has influenced countless people, including many 2x2s, to respond to Jesus' invitation to "come to Him, just as you are."

Notable Author. Frances "Fanny" Jane Crosby (1820–1915) was a blind author born in New York, a Methodist. She composed more than 8,000 hymns, the exact count obscured by her numerous pseudonyms, earning her the title *Queen of Gospel Song Writers.* Nine of her hymns are included in *Hymns Old and New,* including the beloved oft sung No. 1, "Tell Me the Story of Jesus." Her tombstone contains the first verse of her most famous hymn, "Blessed Assurance." This hymn has never been included in *Hymns Old and New;* the 2x2s reject the doctrine that in this life one may be assured of their salvation.

Many Christian bookstores stock books containing interesting stories telling how various hymns came to be written by Non-2x2s. The stories behind the hymns are often moving and intense. Some of the best-loved hymns came out of tragic circumstances.

Foreign Language Hymnbooks. Hymnbooks for 2x2s similar to *Hymns Old and New* are printed in several languages: German, Spanish, French, Portuguese, Dutch, Afrikaans, Norwegian, Swedish, Finnish, Italian, Korean, Tagalog, Malagasy, Icelandic, Vietnamese and perhaps Greek, Japanese and others.

Leaflets or Supplements. For up to 50 years, some countries also sang from leaflets, or supplements containing additional hymns. They were used in Western US but not in the East under Overseer George Walker. After the 1987 edition of *Hymns Old and New* was published, they were discontinued.

Table Graces. In private, before eating a meal, 2x2s bow their heads and pray. The 2x2 head of the home may pray aloud an impromptu thanksgiving for their provisions or ask someone else to do so, including children. The group may be standing or seated; they do not hold hands.

In public, individuals usually bow their heads and silently give thanks (grace) before meals.

Before a meal when a group of 2x2s are gathered, they sometimes sing together a table grace *a capella*; this is customary when large groups of 2x2s are gathered, e.g. Conventions and Special Meetings. Table graces have been printed on cardstock and distributed to members. *See* website *TellingTheTruth.info* in Photo Gallery, Hymn Album.

Sam Jones' artistic cover to booklet of his hymns and poems
Notable and prolific 2x2 hymn author

38

Military Service

World War I (July 28, 1914–November 11, 1918). At the beginning of the twentieth century, the British Empire covered more than 13 million square miles, making it the largest empire ever known. When the War trumpet sounded in Britain, the echoes carried to all corners of the British Empire.

The spark that set off World War I came on June 28, 1914, when a young Serbian patriot assassinated the heir to the Austro-Hungarian Empire (Austria), Archduke Franz Ferdinand and his wife. A month later (July 28, 1914) Austria-Hungary declared war on Serbia. On August 3, 1914, Germany declared war on France and invaded Belgium. This led to Britain declaring war on Germany on August 4, 1914, which involved the entire British Empire, including Canada, New Zealand, Australia, South Africa, etc.

Since ancient times, when larger military forces were needed than were voluntarily provided, governments have conscripted men to serve in their armed forces. Required military service is called *conscription* or *the draft*. In January 1916 the UK Military Service Act was passed, and all single British men between 18 and 41 were immediately required to register; clergymen and teachers were exempted.

UK Military service was divided into combatant and non-combatant service. The choices were to: (1) serve as an armed combatant soldier; (2) serve in non-combatant military service without bearing arms (a conscientious objector); or (3) refuse to serve In the military in any capacity (an absolutist).

World War I was the first time the Workers encountered war and military service. Conscription presented the Senior Workers with some serious questions. They were forced to make decisions. Pacifism is the principled opposition to war and violence as a means of settling disputes. The UK Overseers' response was to adopt the pacifist stand; the male Workers would apply for exemptions as Ministers of Religion, and male Friends would seek non-combatant service roles (conscientious objectors).

To become a Conscientious Objector, men had to attend a Tribunal hearing to register their objection to participating in combat. The exemption was available only for men associated with "a recognized religious body" whose principles forbade bearing a weapon of war. This was a problem, since the 2x2 Church had no official name.

Taking a Name. The Overseers worldwide did not all use the same name for their Church, nor did they do so in WWII. Cooney reminisced, "In 1914 when all of military age were required to register ... Willie Gill ... said 'Let us take the name we call ourselves by, *The Testimony of Jesus.*' At that time, I am sorry to say, I used to go contrary to my conscience to avoid differing from my fellow Workers. I gave in to Willie in this respect and so erred but have confessed my sin to God, and God has forgiven me. We have committed the same sin in the USA in calling ourselves *Christian Conventions.* We should repent and take the consequences" (1947 Testimony, Appendix D).

Perhaps this name was derived from Revelation 19:10 "brethren that have *the testimony of Jesus.*" *See also* Rev. 1:2, 9 and 12:17. Reportedly, in 1914, the Overseer of England, Willie Gill "officially took the name of *Testimony of Jesus* and was duly listed as such with the Conscientious Objectors Board." Cooney was unsuccessful in obtaining conscientious objector exemption for the male Friends, some of whom went to prison (Roberts 1990, 119, *TTT*).

Some Brother Workers were exempted from military service. The *London Daily Mail* reported about a hearing for John Baillie to determine "whether the defendant was a regular minister of an established religious denomination." A large number of his friends were present. A member of the Bar in London "submitted that the defendant was one of the 70 ministers of a denomination which claimed to have a following in the United Kingdom of 5,000 members. They took the Bible as their sole guide and modelled themselves on the lines of the Primitive Church" (March 23, 1917, *TTT*). Evidence was given ... to prove that the followers of the defendant, known in their Irish constituencies as 'the Dippers,' were a recognized religious body." Baillie was exempted (March 23, 1917, *TTT).*

Conscientious Objection. The term *conscientious objector* (abbreviated C.O.) refers to a person who refuses on moral or religious grounds to conform to the government's requirements to bear arms in a military conflict or to serve in the armed forces. In wartimes, each country individually enacts new regulations regarding C.O.s. Some countries allowed C.O.s, while others imprisoned or executed them. These are discussed in later chapters related to Canada, Australia and New Zealand.

Worldwide, the Regional Overseers were not consistent in their instructions for 2x2 men regarding military service. At least one encouraged them to follow their consciences (US in Jack Carroll's territory); some advised them to be absolutists (New Zealand). Still others instructed them to serve as non-combatant C.O.s (Walker's Eastern US territory, Great Britain, Australia, Canada).

Why 2x2 Men Became Conscientious Objectors. The 2x2s consider their church to be a worldwide family of individuals united around common beliefs and practices. As a peace-loving sect, they oppose violence and killing. A tenet of their faith is to love their Brothers and Sisters in Christ, regardless of their nationality. As a combatant soldier bearing arms, it is conceivable that some 2x2 men could kill their 2x2 Brothers serving in opposing armies. Professing to love their Brothers, some could not in good conscience bear weapons of war opposing them. The following Scriptures have been cited as reasons:

(1) "Thou shalt not kill" (Matt. 5:21).

(2) "Vengeance is mine, saith the Lord, I will repay" (Rom. 12:19).

(3) Christ's teaching to turn the other cheek (Matt. 5:39).

(4) Christ's admonition to Peter to put up his sword (John 18:11).

(5) "If my kingdom were of this world, then would my servants fight" (John 18:36).

1917: US Entered WWI. The United States, led by President Woodrow Wilson, did not join WWI until April 6, 1917, which ended one year and seven months later. The draft was introduced on May 18, 1917; all American men between the ages of 18 and 45 years were required to register.

The US Selective Service Act of 1917 allowed only those who were members of a "well-recognized religious sect or organization" whose creeds forbade participation in war, to perform alternative, non-combatant service. No evidence has been found to date showing the US Government acknowledged the 2x2 Sect as a "well-recognized religious sect" during WWI.

Earl Huckleberry, an American 2x2 C.O., refused a uniform and gun and was sent to prison in Ft. Leavenworth, Kansas, where he made tents. Lewis Murray recalled in his memoirs, "At that time, there were no provisions made for conscientious objectors ... and it wasn't clear what a person should do when they were drafted. I finally said I would go and accept the equipment, all except the gun, and would take my stand as a C.O." Lewis suffered considerably. Attempting to force him to bear arms, he was beaten several times. Finally, he was given the job of caring for the horses. After his discharge, he entered the Work.

Another 2x2 man with medical experience, Oliver Taylor, became a medic.

The *Indianapolis News* reported that George Walker, Overseer of Eastern US, declared that they teach "that a citizen must perform his duty to his country. Consequently, when the United States entered the World War [One], members who were drafted wore the uniform, but obtained transfers to non-combatant units. They would not bear arms because they did not believe they should kill any man ... but they aided all they could in other ways. Preachers of this belief are officially designated as such, but they bear no ordination papers, and hence in the War period, some local Draft Boards did not recognize them as preachers, and some were drafted" (Sept. 26, 1921, 11).

Of the 2,810,296 men inducted into the US armed forces in WWI, approximately 4,000 were C.O.s. Some believed going to prison was less damaging to their souls than killing others and considered their refusal to serve as "holy disobedience." Some absolutists refused to work while in prison, believing the work assigned to them amounted to the non-combatant service they had refused, since it relieved other men to do the work they conscientiously opposed. Absolutists were sent to one of the three US federal military prisons located at Ft. Leavenworth, Kansas, Governor's Island, New York, and Alcatraz Island, San Francisco Bay, California.

Lewis Murray. After his discharge in 1919,
he entered the Work and pioneered Mexico (1933)

1919: The Armistice was signed between the Allies of World War I and Germany at Compiègne, France, for the cessation of hostilities on the "eleventh hour of the eleventh day of the eleventh month" of 1918 (November 11, 1918). The date of the Armistice has been declared a national holiday in many Allied nations. This holiday is now called *Veterans Day* in the US.

1939: World War II. On September 1, 1939, Adolph Hitler invaded Poland and France. Great Britain declared war on Germany two days later, and WWII began. Soon, more than 30 countries were involved. Britain began conscription in 1939 and established a register for C.O.s. The British regulations for C.O.s were the most humanitarian in the world; objection could be for any reason.

US in World War II. From 1939 until 1945, World War II was fought under two presidents, Franklin Roosevelt and Harry Truman. On September 16, 1940, the US enacted the Selective Training and Service Act of 1940 requiring all men between the ages of 21 and 45 to register for the draft. There were no educational deferments. The new Act of 1940 was an improvement over the Act of 1917, in that the requirement for C.O.s was broadened to include any who "by reason of religious training and belief" believed they should not serve or bear arms. No longer was it required that they be a member of a registered religious body.

Requests for classification as a C.O. went before autonomous local Selective Service Boards. These requests were approved almost routinely by some boards and routinely denied by others. Difficulties in obtaining non-combatant classification were encountered by some 2x2 soldiers, e.g. their papers were ignored or "lost," etc. *See* Appendix K.

The US fought in WWII from December 7, 1941, through December 31, 1946, inclusive. For nearly four years, the US fought on four of the seven continents and on all the seas. Over ten million American men were inducted. Of the approximately 43,000 C.O.s, most were Mennonites, Church of the Brethren, Quakers, Roman Catholics, Christadelphians, with Seventh-day Adventists being the largest group. The Jehovah's Witnesses (absolutists) were the largest group to be imprisoned.

The non-combatant status of C.O.s was often unknown by fellow soldiers as they were not distinguishable from combatants. As regular Army members, they were not required to carry arms or be trained in their use. They wore the Army uniform, received Army pay and dependency allowances, were under Army discipline and received the usual military awards. On January 25, 1943, the Secretary of War declared that all non-combatants would be assigned to medical units, unless requested otherwise. They were not kept from the front lines and faced all the dangers of ordinary soldiers.

An anonymous non-combatant medic articulated: "So instead of having a state-of-the-art weapon to defend yourself, you got this really neat red cross target on your helmet and a conspicuous white arm band with a red cross, as well. These made sure that the enemy would know for certain that here were targets that had no means of defending themselves and might have supplies that would be useful. But to the wounded, you were like a god. And over time, you learned a lot of tricks that did help get people back home."

During WWII, 2x2 Conventions in European countries were discontinued as they could be seen from the air by enemy aircraft. In some places, smaller Special Meetings were held instead (Sanderson 2001, *EXP*).

Assuming a Name in the US. Around the beginning of World War II, laws were enacted in the US and Canada requiring all religious gatherings of more than five to seven people to register with the government. Overseer of Western US, Jack Carroll, provided the government with the 2x2 membership statistics. "There are in the USA approximately: 3,000 Assemblies of Christians meeting for worship and breaking of bread in homes of members; 900 Ministers—men and women devoting all their time to evangelistic and other church work; 100 Christian Conventions of four-days duration each year with an average attendance of from 350–500. I submit to you that as a body of Christians we are entitled to recognition" (Rittenhouse and Sweetland, April 15, 1954, *TTT*).

In 1942, the name *Christian Conventions* became a recognized religious body in the US. This was confirmed by Major Neal M. Wherry of the National Headquarters for the US Selective Service System, Washington D.C. He stated, "This Headquarters has issued a predetermination that *Christian Conventions* is a recognized church, religious sect, or a religious organization, within the meaning of Section 622.44 of the Selective Service Regulations. This predetermination was based upon information procured directly from officials of the church; namely George Walker (Overseer), 2350 East Susquehanna Avenue, Philadelphia, Pennsylvania, and others" (Nov. 22, 1946, *TTT*).

US Ministers of Religion Exemption. In World War II, ministers in the US were entitled to complete exemption and were not required to serve in the military. An undated, unsigned letter (probably written by Carroll) explained the nature of the work of the Brother Workers, who were "Ordained Ministers" applying for a ministerial exemption: "The Ministers of this body of Christians and representative members of each local group assemble annually in Conventions ... At these annual Conventions, young men desiring to enter the ministry and devote their lives to the preaching of the Gospel have their qualifications considered; and if counted worthy of a place in the ministry, are ordained, given a definite field of labor, in fellowship with, and under the guidance and instruction of an older minister. Ministers are supported by the freewill offerings of the members of these Assemblies of Christians" (n.d., Minister Statement, *TTT*).

In 1942, Walker, Overseer of the Eastern US, wrote a three-page statement on Christian Convention letterhead to the US Selective Service System "for the purpose of enabling the local Draft Boards to correctly classify *ministers* of this church throughout the United States who are subject to the Selective Service Laws" (1942, *TTT*, RIS).

To facilitate applications for conscientious objection classification by 2x2 men, the Workers prepared a Certificate of Membership (a form letter) on their official letterhead titled *Christian Conventions – Assemblies of Christians Assuming This Name Only.* It certified that the named 2x2 male "was a sincere member in good standing," and was signed by a Senior Brother Worker. *See* example signed by Samuel Charlton on website *TellingTheTruth.info* in Photo Gallery, Correspondence Album, Christian Convention Stationery.

It appears that most 2x2 men from the East under Walker's oversight elected to be C.O.s and were under the impression it was a nationwide and worldwide tenet of their church to do so. This was not so. My father, Raymond Berry, from Texas, was a C.O.; while my husband's father, Adolph Ehrig, from California, was not.

In the West, Carroll announced, "We encourage all ... to loyally serve their country and government in some way at this time. All are individually responsible for deciding the form of service they will render. Liberty of conscience is given to each and all. The form of service rendered is a personal and individual matter, and whether called to serve in the non-combatant or combatant capacity, no difference is made in our relationship or fellowship as brethren in Christ" (Sept. 4–7, 1942, *TTT*).

1945: The War in the European Theater ended May 7, 1945, when the Germans surrendered to the Allies. The Pacific Theater War ended with the surrender of the Japanese on August 15, 1945. WWII was the most devastating war in history, claiming millions of lives. Technology helped to make the twentieth century the bloodiest in history: World War I, which introduced the machine gun, the tank and poison gas; and World War II, with its firebombs and nuclear weapons, killed untold millions.

US Prisoners of World War II. Adrian Oldham, Phillip Parrish and Marcelo G. Jomok were 2x2 American servicemen stationed in the Philippines in WWII who survived the Bataan Death March. A few 2x2s died in this War, including the brother of William Lewis, Overseer of Texas.

On July 8, 1941, four Brother Workers laboring in the Philippines, along with many other American missionaries, priests and nuns were imprisoned in the Los Baños Internment Camp about 40 miles south of Manila. Three were from the California staff: Willie Jamieson, Leo Stancliff and Herman Beaber. Also taken captive were Cecil Barrett, who had immigrated to New Zealand, and Ernest Stanley from England.

Stanley remained at Santo Tomás Internment Camp. Previously, he had been preaching in Japan; he became an interpreter for the Japanese and was able to aid the other imprisoned Workers. While Beaber's diary does not record that any of the four Workers imprisoned were tortured physically, all of them were anemic, near starvation and had beriberi when released. Cecil Barrett recounted, "One evening after three years had elapsed ... Willie got us together and said, 'Today a verse has been going through my mind: *Be still and know that I am God*.' "

The very next morning, on February 23, 1945, in a daring guerilla and paratrooper rescue, just one day before the Japanese planned to execute all the internees, American soldiers liberated over 2,000 Allied civilian and military internees from Los Baños.

Worker Ernest Stanley [as interpreter] leading Japanese across Manila,
from "Life Magazine" (March 5, 1945)

From Beaber's diary, "At 7:00 a.m. sharp, we heard and saw nine large transport planes flying low and passing close to the camp... we saw doors open and paratroopers came tumbling out. OH! WHAT A SIGHT! ... about 150 parachutes open[ed] ... We knew help had come ... It was guerillas with American Officers ... [the guerillas] defeated the Japs ... It was over in less than an hour. All the Japanese guards were killed ... **Deliverance—It has come!** Accounts by and about these five Workers are posted on the website, *Diary of a POW: Deliverance has Come!* owned by Herman Beaber's son, John. The March 1945 issue of *Life Magazine* contained a story titled "Santo Tomás is Delivered" with photos of Stanley, described as "a missionary who worked as an interpreter during the talks between Colonel Brady and the Japanese" (Carl Mydans 1945, 25–29).

After their release, all the internee Workers returned to the Work, except Ernest Stanley. Herman Beaber (1907–2001) continued to preach in the Philippines, left the Work in 1951, married Blanche Berry (my paternal aunt) from Henderson, Texas, and adopted two children.

WESTERN STATES

WASHINGTON
OLYMPIA
WALLA WALLA
CHELAN
HILLTOWN

OREGON
DORING
SAGINAW

CALIFORNIA
BAKERSFIELD
LOS GATOS
ORICK

IDAHO
PAYETTE
HAYDEN LAKE
BONNERS FERRY

MONTANA
MANHATTAN
GERALDINE
DAGMAR

WYOMING
POWELL

ARIZONA
RANDOLPH

CANADIAN NORTHWEST

BRITISH COLUMBIA
VANCOUVER
SALMON ARM
PRINCE GEORGE

ALBERTA
LACOMBE
CARSTAIRS
GREEN SHIELDS
STONY PLAINS
NAMPA

SASKATCHEWAN
THEODORE
ANTLER
AYLESBURY

MANITOBA
SIDNEY

NEW ONTARIO
EMO

CHRISTIAN CONVENTIONS

Representing Assemblies of Christians
Assuming This Name Only

2010 Rainier Avenue
Everett, Washington
March 19, 1947

TO WHOM IT MAY CONCERN:

Mr. Herman Beaber
738 Maud Avenue
San Leandro, California

is an ordained Minister (Missionary) of the Gospel in fellowship with Assemblies of Christians in the United States of America.

Mr. Beaber has labored in this Christian Fellowship in Pacific Northwest States from 1929 to 1939 and in the Philippine Islands from 1940 to 1946. Mr. Beaber is now desirous of returning to the Philippine Islands in order to resume his pastoral and evangelistic work there.

Mr. Beaber will be supported by the Ministers and Members of this Christian Fellowship while laboring in the Philippine Islands.

John T. Carroll
Overseer for
Pacific Coast States,
U. S. A.

Christian Convention Letterhead (1947)

Willie Jamieson (1881–1974) succeeded Jack Carroll in 1957 as the US West Coast Overseer/Patriarch. According to the October 17, 1974, *Whittier Daily News*, 2,500 people attended Carroll's funeral. Leo Stancliff (1912–2005) continued preaching in the Philippines, Guam and other South Pacific Islands before returning to California and Nevada. Cecil Barrett (1902–1968) preached in Japan until 1964, when he returned to New Zealand.

Stanley, an Englishman born in 1901, was in the Work in England and California before going to Japan a few years before the War. By the time war had broken out, he had become quite fluent in Japanese. Stanley married a Japanese singer who professed for a short time, adopted a son and resided in Japan. A 2x2 to the end of his life, he and his wife both died in 1990.

Workers Cecil Barrett, Herman Beaber, Leo Stancliff, Willie Jamieson;
photo taken 10 days after their rescue from the
Japanese Los Baños Internment Camp, Philippines (February 23, 1945)

European Countries. In both World Wars and up until the 1960s, France, Germany and Belgium had no legal provision for C.O.s. "It is remarkable that hardly any provisions for conscientious objectors existed in the laws of Continental Europe's major nations ... However, by the beginning of WWII, formal recognition of the objection on the Continent [Europe] seems to have been confined to Scandinavia and the Netherlands" (Sibley and Jacob 1952, 16).

Considered deserters or traitors, some C.O.s were imprisoned or faced the firing squad. Therefore, Orin Taylor, Overseer of France during WWII, reportedly advised 2x2 men to take up arms and fire into the air over the enemy's heads.

Some German Workers and members were imprisoned. In 1942, Fritz Schwille, a German Brother Worker, was sentenced to death for refusing to bear arms, but the sentence was commuted to military service on the Russian front as a stretcher bearer. He was captured by the Soviet Army on the Eastern Front in 1942 and sent to a POW hard labor camp in Siberia, where he died in 1943. His sister Frieda, also a Worker, was killed in the gas chamber at Dachau in 1944 (Laderer, WWII Experiences, *TTT*). The Laderer sisters, Pauline Schnitzer, Erich Lischik, Gustav Ege, Werner Gebhardt and some of the Friends all spent time in concentration camps (Schnitzer WWII Experiences, *TTT*).

Other Wars. During the first Civil War in Liberia (1989–1996), John Johnston (from Ireland), who became Overseer of Romania, and Wyngrove Carter (from Barbados) were held captive several months by rebel forces and were frequently threatened with death. Several of the Friends were killed in this War.

During the Cenepa War (January 26–February 28, 1995) between Peru and Ecuador War, Brother Workers Aníbal Zárate and Rojano González were accused of being Peruvian spies and imprisoned in Ecuador. Allegedly, they were tortured severely in attempts to get them to sign confessions.

1950–1953: Korean Conflict. Communist-ruled North Korean troops began invading South Korea on June 25, 1950. Fourteen United Nation countries sent troops and 41 countries sent military equipment and supplies to South Korea, with the US providing more than 90% of both. The Korean Conflict ended on July 27, 1953. At least one professing man, the late Robert E. Neely, went to prison in the Korean conflict, due to issues with his non-combatant status. (*World War II Reunion Memory Book, Charleston, SC April 19–21, 1995*, 58).

1959–1975: Vietnam War. In 1954, Vietnam was divided into North and South Vietnam. The Communists ruled the North, supported by the Soviet Union, China and other Communist Allies. South Vietnam was supported by the US, Australia, South Korea, the Philippines and other anti-Communist Allies. On November 1, 1955, the North Vietnamese and their sympathizers in the South (the Viet Cong) began an insurgency against South Vietnam. In 1965, the US became more directly involved in the War and participated until 1973.

In 1957, the first two Workers arrived in Vietnam, Fred Allen (from Australia) and Maurice Archer (from New Zealand), followed by other foreign Workers. Many foreign 2x2 soldiers stationed in Vietnam visited Allen and his Co-worker in Saigon; some attended Saigon Fellowship Meetings and Conventions.

In 1973, after the US removed its troops, the Communists soon launched another offensive against South Vietnam, and in April 1975, Saigon fell to the Communists. All the foreign Workers evacuated, leaving in charge the two native Vietnamese Brother Workers, Nguyễn Thanh Hoa and Vu Ngoc Châu.

During the Vietnam War, the US required all men between the ages of 18 and 26 to register. Many were drafted to serve a mandatory two-year term in the US Army. Other branches of the military relied exclusively on enlistees, and did not accept C.O.s.

When the US entered the Vietnam War, the US Overseers, apparently in nationwide agreement during this War, encouraged drafted American 2x2 young men to become C.O.s, and most did so. There was strong social pressure to seek C.O. status, and failure to do so was dimly viewed by many of the 2x2 Army soldiers, Friends and Workers. Vietnam Veteran Frank Kelly explained, "Why did the vast majority of Friends entering the draft seek C.O. status? I sought such status in the belief I was obeying a tenet of a system of universal truth, which, by definition, was a requirement for all people" (J. Daniel, 1996, 164).

Most C.O.s were initially sent to Fort Sam Houston (commonly called *Ft. Sam*), in San Antonio, Texas, for basic and medical training. This included over 250 young professing 2x2 men who enjoyed fellowship and good times with other young men of like faith and resulted in many lifelong friendships. Some roomed together off base. Several local Elders and Friends welcomed the soldiers into their homes when they could get away. The Fellowship Meetings swelled; at one time, there were 165 professing soldiers based at Ft. Sam. At least 14 Brother Workers went through Ft. Sam. In 1992 and 2001, reunions were held in San Antonio, Texas, for 2x2 soldiers stationed there between 1965 and 1972.

During the Vietnam War era, at least two young 2x2 men were noticed by news reporters. In 1967, newspapers reported that Dominic "Nick" Enrietta was denied a ministerial exemption in a hearing in Denver, Colorado. Enrietta professed in 1962, graduated high school in 1963 and entered the Work in 1964. He had been a Worker for three years when he was drafted at age 22. He returned to the Work after his discharge from the Army (*Denver Post*, July 12, 15, 1967).

Another 2x2 soldier featured in newspapers was David Kropp of Caddo, Oklahoma. Tom Tiede, a nationally syndicated newspaper reporter, interviewed Kropp in Cu Chi, Vietnam, focusing on his C.O. status while serving as a front-line combat medic for the 25th Infantry. The resulting article titled, " 'Fink' Objector Now Hero: Sooner Saves Two Fellow Soldiers," was published in numerous US newspapers during 1966–1967, including the front page of the *Oklahoma Journal* serving his home state capital city on January 13, 1967. Kropp received two bronze stars and two purple hearts. He and his wife left the 2x2 Sect in 1990.

Five US professing men died in the Vietnam War. The first was Timothy E. Workman, aged 22, from Washington on January 18, 1967; followed by Ronald C. Stallings, Kentucky; Ronald A. Slane, Oregon; Allan E. Schwartz, Nebraska; and Donald W. Sperl, Alaska. No 2x2 soldiers were imprisoned.

Since 1980, there has been no draft in the US. Some American 2x2 young men have voluntarily enlisted in the military, possibly because jobs were scarce or to receive military funding for higher education. Individuals who enlist voluntarily cannot be non-combatants (C.O.s); if called to serve in a war, they are classified as combatants and bear arms.

American Soldiers after meeting while stationed in Vietnam in 1965-66

2x2 Veteran Reunions. Over the years, several reunions have been held for 2x2 veterans of various wars, accompanied by memory booklets with a page and photograph for each attendee.

See Appendix K.

Section C – International Development

Go ye therefore, and teach all nations,
baptizing them in the name of the Father,
and of the Son, and of the Holy Ghost:
Teaching them to observe all things
whatsoever I have commanded you:
and, lo, I am with you always,
even unto the end of the world. Amen.
(Matthew 28:19-20)

The harvest indeed is plenteous,
but the laborers are few...
(Luke 10:2)

Ireland is the only country where Workers weren't
imported, but rather exported.
(Sydney Holt, Western US Overseer, June 27, 1985, TTT).

Disclaimer. The information in the following chapters relating to foreign countries was compiled to the best of my ability. Any errors or omissions are unintentional.

Ray Bonds (US, labored in France) with Hans Gisin (a Swiss Worker)

It Is not that I hate thee, dear homeland,
That I crossed o'er the seas to toil,
To offer the evening sacrifice and sow on virgin soil,
Oh, no! I could never forget thee,
For fairer land never was found,
But we owe a debt also to other lands,
Since we with rich blessings are crowned.
Au revoir, —not goodbye, now I bid you—
Ere settles the shades of night;
I left without fears, but not without tears,
As I watched as you sank out of sight.
(Ray Bonds, Corsica, 1971)

Workers leaving for overseas

39

The Pioneers

The British government encouraged missionary outreach to their colonial empire as a means of building a framework of acculturated native people who could be useful in helping run the colonies. In 1804 the British and Foreign Bible Society was formed to translate the Bible into the world's dialects. Protestant missionaries distributed many copies of the translated Bibles as they carried the Great Commission to the world.

Up until 1949, citizens of any colony or dominion in the British Empire were automatically considered British subjects. The British Workers followed their flag and rapidly spread to the English-speaking countries of Canada, Australia, New Zealand and South Africa. Subsequently, those countries exported Workers to other countries with foreign languages and supported them.

The first missionary to go evangelize in an area or country where Christianity had not then been established is called a *pioneer*. Some missionaries volunteer to go preach in areas where they have connections, ancestors or relatives; others enter a country as total strangers and foreigners. Some missionaries have sponsors and receive financial support; others are faith missionaries who rely on God to supply their needs.

Workers had only pioneered a few European countries, e.g. France, Norway, Switzerland, Germany, Sweden, etc., when World War I began; most Workers evacuated. Usually, after each war, the country who sent the first Workers to a foreign country arranged for the same or some other Workers to return, re-establish and pioneer it further.

Between the two World Wars, some pioneering Workers returned to their foreign fields. Other countries resumed sending volunteer Workers to pioneer foreign lands (Austria, Denmark, Greece, Hungary, Italy, Japan, Philippines, Poland, etc.). Some US Workers pioneered China and Latin America, whereas Australia and New Zealand Workers tended to pioneer Asian and Pacific countries (India, Burma, Indonesia,

Malaysia, Singapore, etc.). South Africa sent the first Sister Workers to India. *See* details in Appendix L, Pioneers to Various Countries.

Initially, many Workers found it very difficult to pioneer a foreign country. Imagine leaving your home and going to the other side of the world to a place where you do not have a single friend. When the little money you brought with you runs out, you have no one to turn to, no place to sleep, no food to eat, no transportation, all made worse if you did not speak their language. "Paying for lodgings for two, and also for a hall in a town where we were only strangers was no small matter of faith," disclosed John Long.

Some arrived on foot while others shipped their bicycles and a supply of hymnbooks with them. Some went hungry, were wet and cold and slept outdoors, having no money for lodging. Some accepted money from outsiders; others occasionally worked miscellaneous jobs. While some areas were reasonably productive with new converts, many pioneering Workers saw very little fruit from their labor. *See* examples of hardships in Chapter 20.

In pioneering countries, there were no examples for newly-made Saints to model their behavior. Many converts were not accustomed to having house guests and did not know how to be hospitable. Their expectations were not what the Workers were used to in the Old Country they hailed from. Some mistakenly expected the Workers to live up to the title they gave themselves ("Servant") and to be their servants in mundane matters. The Workers often pitched in and helped the Friends with their work, whatever it was. They could not very well tell the new converts what service they expected them to provide. Enter William Irvine. According to Alfred Magowan,

> Irvine went from convention to convention thundering against 'Saints' who took advantage of Workers put at their mercy in the matter of homes. There was one notorious case in the coal fields of Western Indiana—which drew his lightnings and thunderings in unusual vehemence. 'Saints' there saved up their washings for the coming of the Sister Workers needing rest; and washings in coal mining regions are heavy burdens to bear ... Necessity was laid upon William to roar about the great and special Christian virtues of feeding hungry preachers; clothing naked preachers; visiting or ministering to sick preachers; opening homes to stranger preachers; and it struck such fear into advantage-taking Saints' calloused hearts, that until the following year the 'Servants' could nearly be sure of good treatment at their hands and under their roofs.

This was a service William did for them [Workers] that propriety and modesty would hardly have let them do for themselves. But when he was removed, they had to devise other means of ensuring that they would get their serving due, so they went in for preaching about their homelessness ... As clergymen have to make special appeals for money support at home and abroad, these 'homeless' preachers had to resort to proclaiming their own special 'virtues' as sacrificers, renouncers, and sufferers. (to Cooney, Nov. 7, 1953, in author's possession)

The Workers had to provide basic training for their new converts; there were no experienced members to be examples. Upon professing, the Saints did not automatically know how to conduct themselves or participate in meetings. Reportedly, some hurtful "hitting out" happened in some Fellowship Meetings; wounded feelings and pettiness were not uncommon.

Although some Workers easily learned new languages, it was a difficult struggle for others. The poor living conditions, lack of response, adjusting to a new culture and infrequent home visits provided many challenges. However, many Workers came to love their adopted country and its people. The exported Workers generally remained there for the rest of their active years in the Work except for health or safety issues (wartimes). Some Workers chose to die and be buried in their adopted country, rather than in their homelands. Currently, most overseas Workers have home visits every five–seven years.

Currently, all the UK countries have Overseers from Ireland. Most foreign countries continue to have Overseers from English-speaking countries, long after there are experienced local native Workers, which has created significant problems at times. The Vietnamese schism seems to have occurred in part from Canadian Overseers not being sensitive to local customs. *See* Chapter 48.

Traditionally, when US Workers departed on ships from the West Coast to foreign countries, a crowd of 2x2s went to the harbor to send them off and show their support. As the ship drifted away, Workers and Friends waved and sang "I've a Friend Who Meets my Every Need" to the tune of "Aloha Oe" (Author Willie Jamieson).

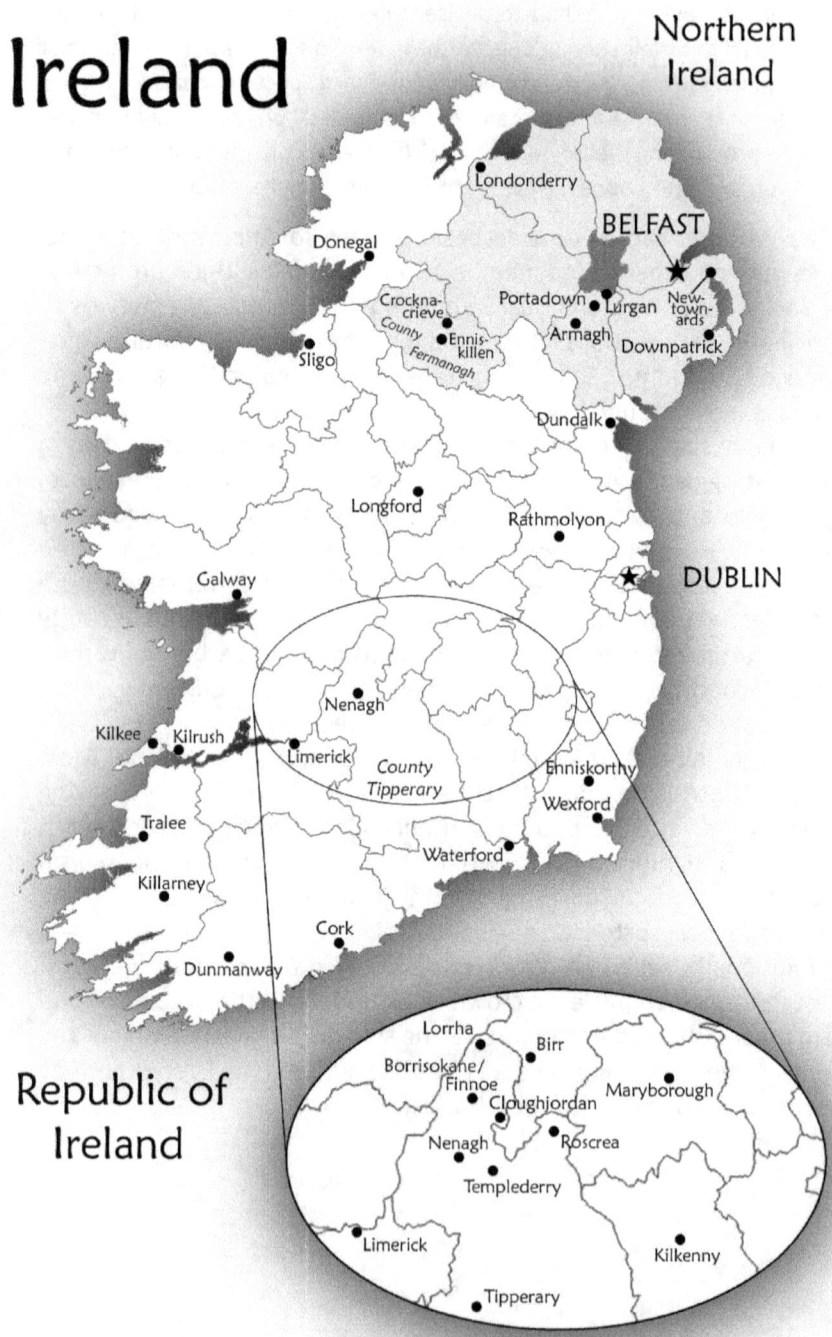

Ireland – The Emerald Isle

Beginning at the Nenagh Revival Mission held by a young "red-hot evangelist" (William Irvine), the new sect spread like wildfire in Ireland. Details are included in Section A in this book.

Entire families were converted, and many young men and women entered the Work. Passionate young Workers were eager to spread the *good news*. Between 1899 and 1903, 192 Workers entered the Work. Soon, there were far too many Workers for the small island of Ireland, so the Workers went abroad to preach in other countries.

> *Ireland is the only country where Workers weren't imported,*
> *but rather exported.*
> **(Sydney Holt, Western US Overseer, June 27, 1985, *TTT*)**

Many children in some large families became Workers, e.g. eight from the Morgan family in Ireland; six Todhunters from Scotland; six Hollands from Ireland. Many other families had four–five siblings in the Work.

Early Irish Workers who became Overseers
L-R, Back: Jack Carroll (Western US), George Walker (Eastern US);
Front: Willie Gill (England), Bill Carroll (Victoria, Australia)

Some Irish Overseers may have been Wilson Reid, Hugh Breen with Irvine Pearson; a triumvirate of Bertie Anderson, Willie Wilkin and Sam Dewart and Joshua Gamble; currently, Thomas Gamble. Conventions are held in Cork, Antrim and Down counties; Carrick, Co. Laois; and Gortaloughan, Enniskillen, Co. Fermanagh.

The two most comprehensive historical accounts central to Ireland are written by Irishmen Goodhand Pattison, an early convert, and Ex-worker John Long. You are encouraged to read these fascinating documents posted on the website *TellingTheTruth.info* in Publications.

Scotland

While Irvine's new sect spread rapidly in Ireland, growth was slower in Scotland, England and Wales. Prominent places in early 2x2 Scotland history include Duns, Kilsyth and Bathgate. Since Chapters 1–4 cover events that took place in Scotland, this summary of Scotland is concise. Kilsyth, Stirlingshire, was where William Irvine was born, grew up and worked.

Irvine and John Long (an independent evangelist since January 1, 1899) had attended the Faith Mission Convention in Rothesay, Scotland, held the last week of September 1899. Afterwards, Irvine invited Long to his sister's home in Queenzieburn, Kilsyth, while "he went to meet some young men that came over from Ireland, with the intention of going fully on the Lord's work" (Oct. 1899, *TTT*).

In October 1899, Irvine led this group of eight or nine young men on a bicycle mission tour in Scotland, putting into practice Matthew 10 as far as they could. This became known as the "1899 Bicycle Mission Trip to Scotland." Having proved *Faith Lines* worked, they returned to the Emerald Isle, pleased to have helped some get right with God and considered their trip a success. All but two would enter the Work full time.

One of the men, Irvine Weir, declared, "This in my mind was the start of the work of William Irvine outside the Faith Mission" (Parker 1982, 37, Fn. 23). Prior to this, Faith Mission records show William Irvine preaching in Scotland and going to and from Ireland at various times. The Bicycle Mission was different—it was not carried out under the auspices of FM.

In Irvine's absence, Long assisted a Faith Mission Pilgrim in a Kilsyth Mission where more than 100 decided for Christ. Irvine returned in November as Long was starting a mission in Condorrat and left Irvine Weir with him. Not long after, Sam Boyd (also on the Scotland trip) replaced Weir. Long continued holding missions in Scotland the following year (1900); Irvine continued sending him Co-workers.

The 1901 Scotland Census showed John Kelly and Harry Sherratt as "Tramp Preachers," lodging in Duns, Berwickshire, with Janet Buckham. Possibly, these were the two Brother Workers Mary Moodie wrote about who held a mission for a few weeks in her district of Sauchie, Clackmannanshire, in January 1901.

In January 1902, Mary Moodie attended a Convention held in Kilsyth. She left her home in Scotland in June 1902 to attend the Irish Portadown Convention. From there she returned to Perthshire, Scotland, with Dora Holland, who had entered the Work in May 1902, where they commenced mission Work (Moodie, n.d. 1913, *TTT*).

The 2x2 Church at Kilsyth asked Irvine to make it his headquarters. He refused. According to Irvine, "In September 1903 I was put out of [the] church I had formed in my native town [Kilsyth] because I would not make it the head of the work I was doing" (to Dunbars, Oct. 13, 1920, *TTT*). He left for America shortly thereafter, taking with him Irvine Weir and George Walker.

By 1904, there were 30 Workers in Scotland (*Freeman's Journal*, Oct. 14, 1904, *TTT*). At least 60 Workers on the 1905 Workers List were Scots, including John Hardie, Adam and Aggie Hutchison, James Jardine, Willie, Elisabeth and Violet Jamieson, Joe and Bella Kerr, Rob Darling, etc. The *Kilsyth Chronicle* for May 5, 1905, reported a baptism of 18 people held at Banton Loch attended by several hundred spectators.

Crovie, Scotland, is a small seaside village that clings to a ledge between the bottom of a cliff and the sea, with no road access to many houses. In the early 1900s, Workers held Meetings there and the majority of the village professed. Several Sunday Fellowship Meetings were held in this tiny village of only 40 houses. Converts lived in more than every second house; now most houses are just holiday homes.

The first Convention in Scotland may have been held in Chirnside in 1911; or at Avonbridge (Falkirk, Stirlingshire), date unknown. Over the years, others convened at Banffshire, Caithness, Dunbartonshire, Fifeshire, Findochty, Maud, Pittenweem and St. Monance/Monans. In 2022, two Conventions are scheduled at Gartocharn, Dunbartonshire and one at Aberdeenshire. Scots also attend the Wigton, Cumbria Convention in North England.

Edgar Lowe, the current Overseer of Scotland, is from Ireland. Previous Overseers may have been Ben Boles, Wilson Reid, Joe Twamley, Willie Ross, Archie Turner, Horace Todhunter, Frank Simpson, Alan Beggs, Bob Kerr. Six of the nine Todhunter children entered the Work. *See* also website *TellingTheTruth.info* in History, Pioneering Missions, UK-Scotland.

Wales

There has never been a separate staff of Workers in Wales. Possibly the first mission was held in January 1905 by John Long and Sam Jones in Holyhead; the second was in Bangor. They happened to arrive when the Welsh Revival was taking place. However, the enthusiasm did not extend to the Workers' Gospel Message. Long reported, "the truth as it is in Jesus in the practical sense seemed to be not popular. No one ministered to our necessities in that town, and the few shillings we had in our pocket ran out." The 1904–1905 Welsh Revival was the largest Christian revival in Wales during the twentieth century.

England

Events relative to the Work in England are scattered throughout Section A. Therefore, only a few high points are provided here. From what little information is available, it appears that William Irvine may have been the first to hold a mission in England sometime before August 1900, for he asked John Long to go to Darlington, Durham Co., and use a new wooden hall "newly built by him [Irvine] for the Darlington city mission." When Long arrived in August 1900, he found the new hall being used by someone else.

Expecting the English to respond as they had in Ireland and Scotland, Long was astonished when only one person came to his first Gospel Meeting. "That was my first English experience, which was rather painful" (Aug. 1900, *TTT*). On foot, with no friends or Co-worker and little money, he started walking north, preaching in every town and village. By the time he reached Morpheth, he was "tired, weary, languid and discouraged. He disclosed, "From the time I started on *Faith Lines* until the experience in England, I had no financial straits; but from that time until February 1905, I had repeatedly some severe trials" Oct. 1900, *TTT).*

After the 1904 Crocknacrieve Convention, the first group of Workers headed for England in 1904, including Willie Gill, Wilson Reid, Andy Robb, Mr. and Mrs. McClung, Alice Pipe, May Carroll, Annie Smith and Lizzie Sargent. By 1904, there were 50 Workers in England (*Freeman's Journal*, Oct. 14, 1904, *TTT*).

Long and John Fawcett also crossed to Liverpool, England in 1904. In Long's opinion, "It would have been better not to have a companion man while doing pioneer Work in a strange place among unsympathetic people, until an opening was first made; as lodging the expenses were great, and no income until the word of truth produced enough Friends and money to go ahead." They ventured to Prescot and St. Helens where they rented halls for Meetings, but people did not come. So they began street preaching in the open-air until the police removed them. (Nov. 1904, *TTT*)

"Our financial weakness was at that time a great cause of humility and faith and prayer; not at all pleasant to the flesh." Fawcett left due to his father's death, and Long "was hard put to it; my last copper went to a beggar on the Street. Next day ... resulted in a gift of six pence that preserved me for a night; next day I walked six miles looking for work. I found none but a woman gave me one shilling which did another day and night. On hearing that some Go-Preachers were leaving Liverpool to go to America, I walked into the city and saw them off; one of them gave me ten shillings and the present of a bicycle; another gave me half a crown, and looking thin in appearance, a Sister gave me a bottle of Bovril" (Nov. 1904, *TTT*).

Back in Ireland, Long reconnected with Fawcett and held some missions. Then, Irvine directed Long to "go back again to England and get the victory," so on January 7, 1905, he returned with Sam Jones (Feb. 1905, *TTT*).

Meanwhile, in Warrington, England, an assembly of Christians (called the *Free Gospel Assembly*) were meeting in the Academy Street Chapel. On hearing of the Welsh Revival, they began praying for a visitation in Warrington, and were prepared to receive whoever God sent. It was fortunate that John Long and Sam Jones happened along in March 1905—they were received as angels sent from God!

The chapel was owned and worked by three English brothers, William, Edward and Joseph Twiss, who were church elders. "They were Arminians in doctrine, of a Primitive Methodist type, whose ancestors received John Wesley when he preached in Warrington. Besides their occupation as house builders, they spent much spare time and expense to spread the gospel.

> Except on the doctrine of believers' immersion alone, they were receptive of all the truth that we believed. Brother William [Twiss] could not see his way in changing his mind regarding infant sprinkling. Where he saw otherwise, I did not think it to be the will of God to guess the conscience or make it a bar to fellowship at a time when God's Spirit was at work. As an unsectarian evangelist, I often found myself in such a position ... that the four laws observed by Paul had to be carried out, if by any means I might save some; and some were saved in that Chapel. The law of expediency, 1 Cor. 6:12; the law of profitableness, Acts 20:20; the law of charity, 1 Cor. 14:1; and the law of liberty of conscience on minor points, Rom. 14. (March 1905, *TTT*)

In a nine-week Gospel Mission in that chapel, "many persons decided for Christ; others got restored, stirred up and blessed. The meetings were well attended, persons came from all parts of the town and from every sect. We can never forget the warm Christian fellowship; and the active part ... [of] the three brothers ... We felt the presence of God was very manifest, the ministry of prayer, praise and preaching was glorious; there was a shout of triumph and a ring of praise which was magnificent. Those were days of refreshing never to be forgotten. Besides the revival meetings, we had some street preaching and house-to-house visitation and tract distribution" (March 1905, *TTT*).

At the close of that mission, the brethren sent us away after a godly sort with a new suit of clothes each, and the present of a bicycle. From that time, I always had an open door to preach the Gospel in England." Their friendship would endure for all their lives (Feb.–March 1905, *TTT*).

The first annual English Convention assembled in 1909 at Debenham, Suffolk Co. and continued until 2007. In 1915 a Convention began at West Hanney where it continued (in two locations) until 2012. In 1921, a Workers' Convention was held at Dimsdale, Staffordshire, England; about 208 Workers attended. *See* photograph in Chapter 26.

Early English Conventions were held at Debenham, Suffolk Co. (started in 1909); Coppull, Lancashire; Thorpe-on-the-Hill, Lincolnshire; Bruton, Somerset Co.; Spilsby, Lincolnshire; West Hanney, Berkshire. In 2022, Conventions are scheduled for Uttoxeter, Staffordshire; Preston, Lancashire; and two at Yorkley, Gloucestershire (none in Wales). The Convention at Wigton, Cumbria in Northern England is attended by Scottish Friends.

By 1917, there were 5,000 members and 70 ministers in England. (*Dominion*, July 26, 1917, 9, *TTT*). Reportedly, Willie Gill registered the name *The Testimony of Jesus* with the UK government during WWI. Allegedly, in 1917, Princess Victoria listened to Cooney preach from her carriage at Speakers' Corner in Hyde Park, London. Other Workers, including Willie Gill used this site for open-air preaching.

The first Overseer was Willie Gill; then Jack Forbes; others may have been Percy Fletcher, Norman Henderson, Ken Paginton, Dennis Fenton with Ben Crompton; and currently, Ben Crompton assisted by David Delaney. *See also* Chapters 22, 28 and website *TellingTheTruth.info* in History, Pioneering Missions, UK England.

Canada

YUKON

Whitehorse

NORTHWEST
TERRITORIES

Yellowknife

NUNAVUT

Iqaluit

NEWFOUNDLAND
AND LABRADOR

St. John's

BRITISH
COLUMBIA

ALBERTA

Edmonton

SASKAT-
CHEWAN

MANITOBA

Winnipeg

ONTARIO

QUÉBEC

Québec

Montréal

Ottawa

Victoria

Regina

Toronto

Western Region shaded in gray

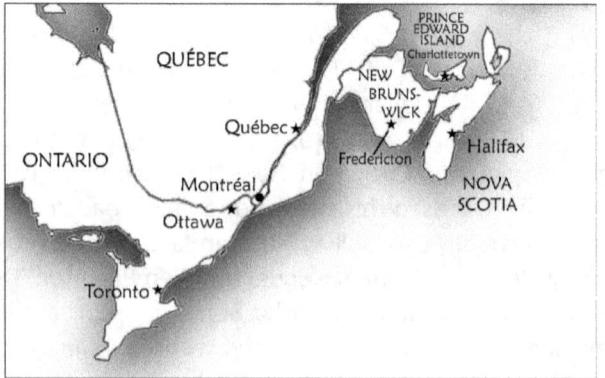

QUÉBEC

ONTARIO

Québec

Montréal

Ottawa

Toronto

PRINCE
EDWARD
ISLAND

Charlottetown

NEW
BRUNS-
WICK

Fredericton

Halifax

NOVA
SCOTIA

40

Canada

Canada, the world's second-largest country in landmass, contains ten provinces and three territories, covering 3.85 million square miles (9.98 million square km), with an approximate population of 38 million in 2021. Ottawa, Ontario, is the capital; the largest metropolitan areas are Toronto, Montreal and Vancouver

First Workers. Very little historical material has surfaced about the early days of the 2x2 Sect in Canada. During 1904–1908, at least 50 Workers arrived in Canada.

1904: After the 1904 Crocknacrieve Convention, the first four young Workers, all in their mid-twenties, headed for Canada. Harry Oliver (23), Tom Craig (22), George Buttimer (21) and John Doak (25) departed from Liverpool, England, on the SS *Parisian* and arrived in Montreal, Quebec, on August 13, 1904.

Their destination was Souris, Manitoba, where Dora Holland's relatives resided. "When we four boys came up the St. Lawrence [River] in 1904," recalled John Doak, "there was not a person professing here on the prairies. Just four little corns of grain going into the ground and look at the harvest" (1945, Sermon). They had all been in the Work for one year.

1905: The following year, 18 young Workers departed from Londonderry, Ireland, for Canada aboard the SS *Virginian.* On August 10, 1905, some Workers disembarked at Quebec City and others at Montreal. The 12 Brother Workers aboard were William Jackson (25), Thomas Lynn (32), Ralph Bullick (22), Noble Stinson (26), Hugh Doak (23), Tom Patterson (23), Robert S. Skerritt (misspelled Kinitt; 29), Edward Armstrong (24), Richard "Dick" Watchorn (25), Robert Johnston (25), Tom Purves (19), and reportedly Tom Boyd (25) was on board although the passenger list does not show him. The six Sister Workers aboard were Martha Cooper (30), Dora Holland (29), Ann Irwin (24), Martha "Mattie" McGivern (30), Mable Reid (22) and Ann Skerritt (misspelled Kerritt; 24).

Later that year, on December 24, 1905, eight more UK Brother Workers arrived at Halifax, Nova Scotia, aboard the SS *Parisian,* headed for Winnipeg and Toronto. They were George Nelson, Robert Darling, Crawford Crooke, John McNeill, William Armstrong, William Snedden, George Manning and William McIlwrath (who would later marry and remain in the Work).

1906: William Irvine Arrived in Canada. Aboard the SS *Moana* from Sydney, New South Wales, Australia, Irvine, age 43, arrived in Vancouver, British Columbia (BC), Canada, on April 11, 1906. Less than a week later, he sailed from Victoria, BC, aboard the SS *City of Topeka* to San Francisco. Arriving on April 16, 1906, he was just in time to experience the great San Francisco earthquake; fortunately, he was unharmed (to Lauchlins, April 24, 1945, *TTT*).

1906: Six UK Workers departed from Liverpool, England, aboard the SS *Siberian* and arrived in Halifax, Nova Scotia (NS), Canada, on September 4, 1906. They were Albert Quinn (29), Jimmie Patrick (33), Willie McAllister (25), Alex Gibson (24), Mary Cook (40) and Annie Dodds (22).

In August 1907, five UK Workers arrived in Halifax, NS aboard the SS *Carthaginian*, and in August 1908, eleven more disembarked from the same ship, including Irvine, age 45. This was Irvine's fourth annual trip abroad. There were at least 50 British Workers laboring in Canada by 1908. The 1913 Workers List showed at least 80 Canadian Workers.

1906: First Three Canadian Conventions. The very first Convention in North America was held at Toronto, Ontario, in a rented house and tent in June 1906. William Irvine was there. The "List of Workers at the 1906 Toronto Convention" shows 62 Workers present, 37 men and 25 women, including one married pair, Matt and Letitia Wilson, possibly the first set of married Workers to enter North America.

In November 1906, a second Canadian Convention was held at Minnedosa, Manitoba. Another took place in Dartmouth, Nova Scotia, in 1908. "Mr. William Irvine, the leader of the organization, has set sail for [North] America and is to open a Convention in Halifax on Sunday 16th" (*Impartial Reporter*, Aug. 13, 1908, *TTT*).

In 1913, British Sister Workers laboring in foreign fields were asked to provide testimonial letters of their experiences in the Work for Edward Cooney's court case in the UK. Some Sister Workers then preaching in Canada who wrote letters were Kate Adamson, Annie Corcoran, Janet Dougal, Daisy Fee, Helen "Ellen" Harrison, Dora Holland, Annie Irwin, Lizzie Kerr, Minnie McGuirk, Rosetta "Nettie" Millar and Annie Stanley. *See* Chapter 22. *See also* letters posted on website *TellingTheTruth.info* in Workers Early, Sister Workers.

Canadian Province Pioneers, Overseers and First Conventions

Like the US, Canada is divided into East and West regions with Overseers. Shaded in gray on the map, the Western region includes the provinces of British Columbia, Alberta, Saskatchewan, Manitoba and Western Ontario. The remaining provinces are included in the Eastern region.

British Columbia

Irvine arrived in BC in April 1906 and stayed less than a week. In 1907, Jack Carroll and an unknown Co-worker went from the Manitoba Convention to pioneer BC, along with Kate Rankin, Jean Houston, May Carroll and Florence May.

Overseers: Jack Carroll 1907–1956; Ernest Nelson 1956–1989; Paul Sharpe 1990–2008 (also of Asia); Walter Burkinshaw 2008–2016; Merlin Affleck 2017—. The first Conventions were held in Nelson in 1908, and in Vancouver in 1909. The sect in BC was mentioned in the book: *Through Western Canada in a Caravan,* by F. H. Eva Hasell. *See* "Two by Twos," page 244.

Alberta

In 1907, Robert Darling, Noble Stinson, Maggie Rowe and Grace Douglas were the first Workers to arrive and pioneer the Work. Darling died in the Work in Argentina in 1970. Stinson married and resided near Enniskillen, Ireland. The Workers List for 1908 showed Harry Oliver, John Fox, Robert Darling, John McClean, Jim Moore, Maggie Rowe and Lizzie Kerr. The 1909–1910 Workers List included Harry Oliver, John Zogg, Robert Darling, Jim Moore, Sandy Scott, Maggie Rowe and Lizzie Kerr.

Overseers: 1907 [unknown]; Robert Graham to 1929; W. D. "Willie" Fullerton 1932–1956; Stanley Watchorn 1964–1965; Harold Stewart 1974–1983; Willis Propp 1983–2009; Merlin Affleck 2009–2016; Michael Hassett 2017—. The first Conventions were held at Mission Centre in 1908; Leduc in 1909; Calgary in 1910; and Beddington and Fort Saskatchewan in 1911.

Some books featuring the 2x2 Sect in Alberta are *Sect, Cult and Church in Alberta* by William Edward Mann, 1955, out of print (*See* "Cooneyites"). And *Along the Fifth: A History of Stony Plain and District*, by Stony Plain and District Historical Society, 1982, page 375, which includes an article by Carlos Propp's relatives Joe and Minnie (Propp) Kleven, a native Canadian married Worker pair.

Details about the Alberta incorporation, excommunications and purge follow below and are also on the website *TellingTheTruth.info* in History, Divisions.

Saskatchewan

The arrival date of the first Worker is unknown. The first Convention was held in 1911 at Bredenbury.

Overseers: Willie Abercrombie; Willie Smiley 1932–1972; Willis Propp 1976–1983; Stanley Sharpe 1983–1987; Dale Shultz 1988–1990; Jack Price 1991–1995; Dale Shultz 1996–2005; Jim Atcheson 2009–2010. Beginning sometime after 2010–2011, Saskatchewan, Manitoba and NW Ontario were combined on the Workers Lists.

The 2x2 Sect is referenced in the book "*Windthorst Memories, A History of Windthorst and District, 1806–1981,*" by Windthorst History Book Committee, 1983. *See* "The Church in the Home," page 258. Out of print.

Manitoba and Northwest Ontario (a combined field)

The first Workers, Harry Oliver, Tom Craig, John Doak, George Buttimer and Dora Holland arrived in 1905. The first Convention was held in Minnedosa in 1906. The list for the 1909 Sidney Convention photo of Workers and Friends taken by Herb Minty contains 112 names plus 6 Workers not shown.

Dora Holland professed in a mission Irvine held in 1897 in Kilrush, Co. Clare, Ireland. She was his first convert. She entered the Work in May 1902, and in 1905, she came to Sidney, Manitoba, where she had family. Five other Holland siblings became Workers: Harry, Maud, Kathleen, Mable and Muriel. Dora died August 1, 1968; she and her brother, Harry (1877–1967), share the same tombstone in Graceland Cemetery, Madison, South Dakota, US.

Overseers: Mark Craig; Stanley Watchorn 1932; Stanley Lee 1964–1967; Stanley Sharpe 1978–1982; Jack Price 1983–1990; Alton Mose 1991–2010; Jim Atcheson 2010–. Sometime after 2010–2011, the Workers List combined Saskatchewan with Manitoba-NW ON.

East Ontario and West Quebec (a combined field)

The first Workers arrived in Montreal, Quebec, in 1904 and traveled from there to Manitoba. They were Harry Oliver, Tom Craig, John Doak and George Buttimer. The first Conventions were held in Toronto in 1906 and Holland Landing in 1908.

1906–1907: First and Only 2x2 Church Building Erected. Alfred Magowan informed Jack Carroll about the construction of a church/meeting house in Gesto, Ontario, Canada, "At Gesto, Ontario, in the year 1906–1907 ... I saw the church or meeting house put up by a grateful community after a spiritual 'moving of the waters' under the ministry of James Jardine and Willie Edwards ... When William Irvine heard about it, he made that strange pronouncement: *'All public worship is an abomination to God.' "* (April 6, 1954, in author's possession). From that time on, no church buildings were constructed or used for Fellowship Meetings; portable halls continued to be used for Gospel Missions.

Overseers: Jack Jackson; Andrew Blair 1972–1973; Carson Cowan 1978–1997; George Poole 2003–2004; Carson Wallace 2009—. An early history account titled "Southern Quebec Gospel History 1908–1920" is on the website *TellingTheTruth.info* in History, Pioneering Missions, North America, Canada.

East Quebec and Atlantic Provinces of Prince Edward Island, New Brunswick, Newfoundland and Nova Scotia

Harry Dennison (from Ireland) and John Baillie (from England) arrived in Quebec in August 1908 and were the first to preach to the French-speaking Canadians but had no converts. After the Holland Landing Convention in 1908, Dennison returned with Willie Wilson from Scotland; they preached to English-speaking Canadians. The first English Convention was held at Magog in 1917.

The current Richmond Quebec Convention is bilingual; both English and French simultaneous translations are provided. The 2x2 Sect is mentioned in the book *Yesterdays of Brome County, Quebec* by Clifford W. Smith, Brome County Historical Society, 1976, pages 119–120. Out of print.

It is not known who the first Workers were to arrive in the Atlantic Provinces. The Workers, then known in the area as "Go-Preachers," had attracted some notoriety and were mentioned in the press, particularly after violent clashes during 1910–1912. The Workers' missions provided part of the backdrop for the novel *Mistress Pat: A Novel of Silver Bush*, by Lucy Maud Montgomery (author of *Anne of Green Gables*).

Bill Bryant was the Overseer of these provinces collectively for most of the 30 years leading up to his death. They have never had separate Overseers, even though they were traditionally listed separately as provinces on the Workers List until Wayne Hutchison became Overseer around 2009.

Prince Edward Island

In 1907, the first Workers arrived in Prince Edward Island. They were Willie Snedden (from Scotland) and Willie McAllister (from Ireland), arrived in 1907. The first Convention was held in St. Eleanors in 1913. There is an early historical account titled, "Early Days on Prince Edward Island, 1907" on the website *TellingTheTruth.info in* History, Pioneering Missions, North America, Canada.

New Brunswick

The first Worker to arrive was Galen Harris, date unknown. In 1911, the first Convention was held at Smithtown. *See* early historical account, "Napan, New Brunswick – The Go-Preachers, 1912" on the website *TellingTheTruth.info* in History, Pioneering Missions, North America, Canada.

Newfoundland

In 1908, George Johnson, Tom McGivern, Blanche Chappell and Rosetta Miller arrived. The first Convention was held at Paradise in 1915. Early historical accounts are: "Coming of Workers to Newfoundland, 1908"; "Traytown, Newfoundland: Gospel Came in 1912"; "West Point, Newfoundland: Account of the Gospel Coming in 1915." *See* website *TellingTheTruth.info* in History, Pioneering Missions, North America, Canada.

Nova Scotia

It may have been 1908 when the first Workers arrived; the first Convention was held in 1908 at Dartmouth. The early historical account "When the First Workers came to Nova Scotia" is posted on the website *TellingTheTruth.info* in History, Pioneering Missions, North America, Canada.

NW and Yukon Territories: Details unknown.

~~~~~

Married Workers. Seven married Worker couples preached in Canada. They were Joseph "Joe" and Minnie Kleven; Verdun and Anna Jane Batstone; William "Willie" and Mildred "Millie" McIlwrath; Murdo and Dollie MacLeod; George and Margaret "Maggie" Walker, (not to be confused with George Walker, Overseer of Eastern US); Lars and Olga Bye; and Overseer of British Columbia and Alberta, Robert Graham, married to Maude (Pryor), parents of five children. They left the Work.

1926: Springside Saskatchewan Workers Convention. This was the first Canadian Workers Convention. The second was held at Didsbury, Alberta, 81 years later in 2007.

First Canadian Workers Convention, Springside, Saskatchewan (1926)

Alberta Christian Conventions
1930

Drumheller, July 3, 4, 5, and 6.

Stony Plain, July 10, 11, 12, 13.

New Norway, July 17, 18, 19, 20.

All trains will be met the day before meetings commence.

Those attending conventions are requested to bring bed clothing and towels properly marked.

You are encouraged to bring children of understanding age and any friends that you know are interested.

For further information write:

LARS BYE, Box 238, Drumheller

ANDY SCOTT, Box 43, Stony Plain

STANLEY WATCHORN,
Box 59, New Norway

World Wars. When the British Empire entered both WWI and WWII, Canada was automatically entered on the side of Britain. When military conscription was introduced in Canada, the vague wording of the Military Service Act of 1917 did not adequately define the religious basis for conscientious objection to bearing arms. Members of some groups/churches holding pacifist beliefs who were not widely recognized, such as the 2x2s, often had a difficult time demonstrating their eligibility.

Several 2x2 Saskatchewan men refused to bear arms, and were held together in the Regina, SK jail; eventually, they were given non-combatant jobs.

WWI: jailed 2x2 men in Saskatchewan, Canada (circa 1917)
Top Row, L-R: Robert Fraser, Clifford Fleming, Matthew Thompson
Middle Row, L-R: Blake Pierce, Dugald Murdoch, Carl Jensen
Front Row, L-R: Elmer Larson, Jim McChesney, Fred Hardy, Albert Phillips

When Hugh Roberts (from Ireland), an early Canadian Worker, was conscripted, he refused to wear a uniform or bear arms. While confined to a Canadian prison, he wrote the hymn "Strong in the Strength of Gentleness" (No. 283 in *Hymns Old and New*).

World War II. An interesting provision in Canadian conscription laws for WWII was that no one could be conscripted for service *outside* of Canada. "Regulations provided postponement of service for those who conscientiously objected 'by reason of religious training and belief to war in any form and to participation in combatant military service.' " Some served in the medical corps, others in work camps engaged in forestry and road building (Sibley and Jacob 1952, 8–9). *See also* Chapter 38, Military.

Willie Martin. Reportedly, in late 1960–1970, Overseer George Semple excommunicated Martin. Some loyal Workers and Friends also left the sect, including the owners of the Spring Valley (aka Kensington) PEI Convention; the McLeods who owned the Cape Breton Convention;

and the Woods. The group was called the *Willie Martin Gang. See* details in Chapter 48

Alberta Society of Christian Assemblies

Willis Propp was the Overseer of Saskatchewan from 1964 to 1983 and the Overseer of Alberta from 1983 to 2009. Born September 17, 1920, he professed in 1940, entered the Work in 1948 and passed away November 28, 2015, aged 95.

1996: In early 1996, an estate lawyer notified Propp that his client, a Canadian 2x2 woman, had left funds in her will to "the ministers of my church." Propp refused the money in a letter dated July 3, 1996, that he wrote on Christian Convention letterhead. Above Propp's signature was typed: "Alberta Society of Christian Assemblies."

In August 1996, Ex-2x2 John Mitchell fortuitously discovered that the "Alberta Society of Christian Assemblies" had been incorporated in mid-1995, under Certificate of Incorporation No. 50654949 granted by the Government of Alberta. This document was signed by Brother Workers F. Willis Propp, Jim Knipe, Dennis Einboden and witnessed by Rowland Jackson. *See* website *TellingTheTruth.info* in History, Divisions, Alberta.

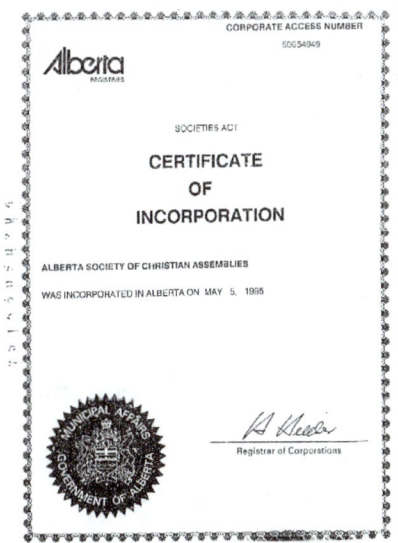 

Alberta Society of Christian Assemblies Incorporation Document (May 5, 1995) and Willis Propp's Letter on Christian Convention Letterhead (July 3, 1996)

By the fall of 1996, copies of the incorporation document had been widely distributed and placed on the Internet. The discovery of this document astonished, shocked and upset many 2x2 Sect members worldwide. While some doubted its authenticity, others found the evidence convincing.

Willis F. Propp (1920–2015)

It was especially troubling to some members that Workers had registered an official name and incorporated their church while they continued to publicly claim that their church was not an organization and took no name. To address the considerable concern and unrest, Propp wrote a letter of explanation:

> To All of Concern ... one of the Workers in Hungary whose Visa was soon to expire was faced with the problem of being refused permission to remain in the country because the 'Group' she was representing was not a registered body in Hungary.

> Our sister who labours there was companion to the girl in question and she appealed urgently to us that we do something ... because any approach they made to the local authorities was to no avail and they needed help badly ... there was a deadline to meet. Hungary would accept our Registration as backing ... we sought a lawyer's aid ...

> We learned to our dismay that to be registered we had to become incorporated as a non-profit Society. While it was solely for the purpose of those in authority, the document gave us a long-handled name. We were hesitant to do it, but for the sake of our Workers in Hungary, we signed the document ... We are in the process now of having the whole document cancelled, since it is not required in Canada ... and we hope the matter will settle down in time. (Nov. 9, 1996, *TTT*)

Anne Court from Scotland was the Sister Worker in distress; her Co-worker was Esther Laslo, an Alberta Worker laboring in Hungary. The incorporation gave the 2x2 Sect a legal identity, along with the means to sponsor and support Workers preaching in foreign countries.

Nine days after his explanation, Propp composed a letter of apology: "To Whom It May Concern: The concept of the Document of Registration that was drawn up and filed in Alberta, Canada, on the 5th day of May 1995, was totally contrary to the basic tenets of our Fellowship, and so was totally wrong. I, Willis Propp, acted unilaterally without due consultation with my seniors in the ministry ... I assume full responsibility for involving in this process my fellow Workers in Alberta ... I have instructed a lawyer on November 8, 1996, to have the said Document completely revoked" (Nov. 18, 1996, *TTT*). The Alberta Society of Christian Assemblies was voluntarily dissolved on December 11, 1996. *See* Certificate of Dissolution on *RIS website* at workersect.org/2x205rb.html.

Soon after, on January 8, 1997, a meeting was held in Calgary, Alberta. Those present included all the Alberta Workers, plus Western Overseers Harold Bennett, Alton Mose, Paul Sharpe, Jack Price, Sydney Holt, Dick Middleton, Charles Preston, Ernest Nelson, Eldon Tenniswood and perhaps more.

Regarding this meeting, Jack Price stated in a letter to Co-workers dated January 23, 1997: "Most of the Alberta Workers ... were interviewed ... resulting in the majority asking that Willis would remain as their Overseer ... Due to the fact that this was a first admonition, and since Willis manifested a true spirit of repentance, in addition to making every effort to get the 'Document' dissolved, it was only reasonable to give him another chance to prove himself in the place where he has had the privilege and responsibility of serving. Should also add that we were satisfied with the apologies from those who co-signed the Document."

Incorporation Precedent. There were at least two precedents for the incorporation of the 2x2 Sect. The charity, Christian Conventions of Victoria, Australia, was registered as early as 1929. Also, the church was incorporated under the name of *Christians in Sweden* in 1992.

~~~~~

In early 1997, the child custody battle of Duncan P. Dorey and Margaret J. Dorey v. Janice L. Steingard began in Alberta Family Court. It involved a 2x2 mother (Steingard), her Non-2x2 ex-husband (Duncan Dorey) and their two young daughters. Dorey's attorney attempted to show that Ms. Steingard was a member of a cult, and therefore, her home was not the best one for the children (*the Alberta Report,* Sept. 1997, in author's possession). Some 2x2s attended the hearing.

During the Dorey-Steingard court proceedings in 1999, Willis Propp was questioned under oath, and some of his personal business activities became public. Even though one child was her stepchild, sole custody of both children was awarded to Ms. Steingard, with Doreys having access. A partial court transcript was printed and bound containing the testimony of Propp and two 2x2 Elders (Dorey Transcript Feb. 8, 1999, in author's possession).

Excommunication of Alberta Friends

During the 1990s, many of the Alberta Elders and Friends were excommunicated, and at least one Worker was expelled from the Work. Ripples from that purge are still felt today. Alberta Overseer Willis Propp was responsible.

Many of the Friends were disturbed when they discovered Propp and some other Alberta Workers had violated certain fundamental core beliefs, such as taking no name and Workers disposing of all their possessions. They observed that money appeared to be highly regarded—even sought after—by various Workers, and that some Workers were not relying totally on faith for their financial support. For example, Workers were applying for and receiving old age pensions that they turned over to their Overseers.

Troubled by various actions they viewed as unscriptural, unethical and immoral, various Elders and members attempted to discuss these and other issues with Senior Workers, including Propp and the Western Overseers. They suspected the Holy Spirit was not leading certain Workers to some of their actions. When questioned, most Workers' views aligned with that of their Overseer, and they indicated they would look into and take care of the issues.

In May 1999 (after the Dorey-Steingard case), a meeting convened of 11 Senior Workers and Overseers and about 50–60 of the Friends, including Elders. The Workers present were Eldon Tenniswood and Dick Middleton (California); Harold Bennett (Oregon); Sydney Holt, (Washington); Paul Sharpe and Ernest Nelson (British Columbia); Dale Shultz (Saskatchewan); Willis Propp, Jim Knipe and Eldon Kendrew (Alberta); Jack Price (Montana) and perhaps others.

Dick Middleton started the meeting by admitting that Propp had "made some mistakes along the way." After some others spoke, the meeting was opened for discussion. Some of the Friends and Elders addressed their concerns relating to Propp and the attempted cover-up of the incorporation; Propp's Visa gold card with a $20,000 credit limit;

Propp's inherited oil and gas mineral interests that he had retained and leased; Propp's substantial bank account in the name of "F. Willis Propp Enterprises" at the Canadian Imperial Bank of Commerce (CIBC), among other issues. *See* website *TellingTheTruth.info* in History, Divisions, Alberta.

Subsequently, Dale Shultz, Overseer of Saskatchewan, informed several Alberta members that it was their place to accept the Workers' decisions, even when they disagreed with them:

> I do know ... that your confidence in the oversight in Alberta has been eroded ... You have hoped and, at times, expected that some change in the oversight would be implemented ... However, as you know, the decision coming out of the meeting last July [1998] was to support the status quo in Alberta. That was not the thinking of everyone there, but it was the decision of the meeting.
>
> We realize that the fact that we are servants of God, or even very responsible servants of God, doesn't make us infallible. However, something that is very much a part of being a child of God is to respect those who are over us in the Lord, to pray for them, to obey them, to esteem them very highly in love for their work's sake. **Their judgement may not always be right, but it is always right for us to respect that judgement and to work with it in the best way that we possibly can ... Whether the decision is right or wrong, the right thing for all of us is to respect it because of those who have made the judgement ... because of where it has come from and to work with it no matter what our own thoughts might be on the subject.** (April 12, 1999, *TTT*)

Purge in Alberta. Subsequently, some members lost their trust and confidence in the 2x2 Ministry and withdrew their support. The Workers considered the members' questioning to be disrespectful and out of line. Exerting their authority and control, the Workers began excommunicating members who resisted and were unwilling to accept the Workers' decisions.

In 1997, Fellowship Meetings were removed from two Elders' homes, when they refused to allow certain Workers into their homes; the Elders were allowed to continue attending Meetings. Confrontations between Workers and questioning members led to more Fellowship Meetings being removed from Elders' homes and to their excommunications. When the excommunicated Friends visited other Fellowship Meetings, those Elders were also expelled. Some Elders continued holding *unsanctioned* (not Worker approved) Meetings in their homes; those who attended were soon cast out also.

At Propp's authorization, ultimatums were delivered by Workers via visits or telephone, with Propp's approval. Propp's right-hand man, Jim Knipe, was his chief henchman. Knipe instructed the Workers in their respective fields to consult with certain Elders and Friends or to accompany him in doing so. After a brief discussion, the Workers usually explained to the 2x2 member the conditions required for their continued membership in the church. Unless they gave their unconditional support, they were excommunicated. "The Question" the Workers usually asked was:

> **"Are you prepared to support the Alberta ministry in all their decisions regarding the Fellowship? Yes, or No?"**

When questioned about these events later, some Workers claimed the expelled members *chose* to leave or to give up their Meetings.

Elders Dale and Marlene Jordan tape recorded their ultimatum telephone conversation and continued to hold unsanctioned Meetings. Their son, three daughters and their husbands attended and were also excommunicated. (*Listen* to Alberta Excommunication Tapes, 1999, *TTT*.)

The chain reaction continued; Elder after Elder was cast out. After Don and Myrna Galloway allowed an excommunicated couple to attend their Meeting, they were visited by Jim Knipe and Scott McChesney. The Galloways were reminded that the ministry is the foundation of the Gospel; that the Friends and Elders have no right to question the Workers; that the Friends must accept without question Workers' decisions; that Friends must "keep in their place"; and that while Elders had control over who they invited into their homes any other time, *only* the 2x2 Workers had control over who could attend Meetings in their homes.

Jim Knipe posed the "The Question" to the Galloways. They were not willing to give their unconditional support. Knipe replied, "Well then, you folks are no longer a part of this Fellowship." He cautioned the local Friends that if they or any others attended a Meeting in the Galloways' home, they would be excommunicated also. *See* details on website *TellingTheTruth.info* in History, Divisions.

In June 1999, the O'Dells, who had been excommunicated earlier, spent the weekend with Fred and Verna Alder of Lethbridge and attended a Meeting in their home. Knipe called Fred Alder and asked him the "The Question." Alder's answer was a definite, "No." The Alders were advised they were no longer a part of the Fellowship. Knipe became quite angry when Alder informed him that he had recorded their conversation. *Listen to* Alberta Excommunication Tapes, 1999, *TTT*.

In 2001, a Saskatchewan Sister Worker Margaret "Marg" Magowan visited some excommunicated Friends and attended an unsanctioned Meeting. On February 16, 2001, her Overseer, Dale Shultz, asked her to promise she would have no further communication with any of the excommunicated Friends. She refused, believing it was her duty as a minister to reach out and care for all who were in need wherever they were. She was put out of the Work. Currently, she is no longer a 2x2 Sect member, is married and resides in Canada.

Purge Totals. Friends and Workers around the world were stunned to learn there were about 24 Alberta Fellowship Meetings where the Elder and his wife were either excommunicated or opted to give up their Meetings. In addition, at least 200 of the Alberta Friends were excommunicated or voluntarily left the 2x2 Sect, and at least one Worker (Marg Magowan) was dismissed from the Work. Two Brother Workers were arbitrarily transferred from the Alberta Workers' staff and one of them, Dan Hofer, left the Work. *See* details on website *TellingTheTruth.info,* History, Divisions.

Update: Eldon Tenniswood, Sydney Holt, Roland Jackson, Dennis Einboden, Willis Propp (2015) and Jack Price (2015) have passed away. Jim Knipe went to labor in Argentina in 2000. Eldon Kendrew left the Work and married.

Workers present at Almonte, Ontario, Canada Convention (2018)

Australia

41

Australia

The Commonwealth of Australia is a sovereign country comprised of the Australian continent mainland, the island of Tasmania and numerous smaller islands. It is the world's sixth largest country by total land area, containing 2,966,152 square miles (7,682,300 sq km); population in 2021 is 25,884,430. Australia has six states: New South Wales (NSW), Queensland (QLD), South Australia (SA), Tasmania (TAS), Victoria (VIC) and Western Australia (WA) and two major mainland territories: the Australian Capital Territory (ACT) and the Northern Territory (NT). Canberra, ACT, is the capital. The 2021 population is around 26 million.

1904: First Two Workers Arrived. The very first two Workers to set foot on Australian soil were John Hardie (34) from Kilsyth, Scotland, and Alex "Sandy" Alexander (28); both men entered the Work in 1900. Their passage fares to Australia came from reimbursement received for the malicious destruction of John Hardie's wooden mission hall in Ireland. They arrived in Melbourne, Victoria, on July 24, 1904, aboard the SS *Medic.* They made no converts and soon left.

First Workers to Pioneer Australian States.

1904 Victoria briefly with no results by John Hardie and Sandy Alexander

1905 Western Australia by Tom Turner, Jim McCreight, Laura Falkiner and Aggie Hughes

1906 Queensland by John Sullivan, Jack Little, Polly Hodgins and Lizzie Sargent

1907 New South Wales by John Hardie and Richard "Dick" McClure

1907 Victoria by Adam Hutchison, Willie Hughes, Charlie Dubman and Archie Murray

1908 South Australia by Adam Hutchison and Jim McCreight

1908 Tasmania by Annie Smith and Fannie Carroll

Aggie Hughes, Edith Sadlier,   John Hardie, Dick McClure (1907) Tom Turner
Laura Falkiner, Alice Begbie

Archie Murray, Willie Hughes, Adam Hutchison, John Sullivan

1905: Arrival of UK Workers. William Irvine and eight UK Workers arrived in Melbourne aboard the SS *Geelong* in October 1905. Soon after, they all departed for New Zealand, except for Irvine who disembarked in Adelaide, SA. Five months later, on March 19, 1906, he departed from Sydney aboard the RMS *Moana* bound for Vancouver, Canada. His activities during this five-month period remain a mystery.

1905: Western Australia. The four UK Workers who pioneered Western Australia were Thomas Turner (26), James McCreight (21), Laura Falkiner (24) and Agnes Hughes (22). They departed from Liverpool, England, on the SS *Oroya* and disembarked at Freemantle on December 1, 1905.

1906: Queensland. About two months later, on January 19, 1906, two Workers also aboard the SS *Oroya*, John Sullivan (31) and John "Jack" Little (27), disembarked in Brisbane. They made no converts that year.

Later that year, UK Sister Workers, Mary Elizabeth "Polly" Hodgins (25) and Elizabeth "Lizzie" Sargent (24), departed from London and arrived in Brisbane, QLD, on November 16, 1906, aboard the SS *Ortona*.

These Sister Workers were responsible for the first Queensland converts in 1907. Reportedly, John Hardie "visited Queensland late in 1907 and baptised Queensland's first fruits in the creek at Enoggera."

1907–1908: Victoria and New South Wales. Departing from New Zealand, six Brother Workers arrived on March 16, 1907, in Melbourne, VIC, aboard the SS *Moeraki* (John Hardie, 1982, *TTT*). Adam Hutchison, Willie Hughes, Charlie Dubman and Archie Murray pioneered Victoria. Their first convert was Ada Cousins. John Hardie and Dick McClure pioneered New South Wales, where Ruth and Ethel Harrison were the first converts.

1908: Sam Jones and Robert "Bob" Bashford departed from London on December 27, 1907, aboard the RMS *Orontes.* After taking in the very first Australian Convention in Northcote, VIC, they arrived in Freemantle, Western Australia in April 1908. Sandy Hinds and Sam McMullen also arrived in Australia in 1908.

1908: South Australia. Adam Hutchison and Jim McCreight arrived in Adelaide in 1908 and began pioneering South Australia. Shortly after they arrived, McCreight gave up and was replaced by Jim Vallance, a convert from New Zealand. They held their first Gospel Mission at Woodside in March 1909, where the first Sunday Fellowship Meeting was established in the Wuttke's home. During the first South Australia Convention held in Woodside in 1909 at Mrs. Alf Harris' home, the local residents were very hostile; hoodlums threw rotten eggs. Subsequent Conventions (1910–1926) were moved to Wuttke's rural farm at Woodside.

1908–1910: Tasmania. Annie Smith and Fannie Carroll pioneered Tasmania; Adam Hutchison was the Overseer of South Australia and Tasmania.

Pioneering Workers. In 1905, some of the Senior Workers were over 30 years old and only a few Workers worldwide were over 40. By 1910, there were Workers preaching in all Australian states. The early Sister Workers from the British Isles numbered about the same as the Brother Workers.

First Conventions

*Victoria 1908 March: Northcote, the first Convention to be held in Australia, was attended by 26 Workers from Australia and New Zealand. Afterwards, at least four new Workers joined the Work, including Sidney Maynard, Ethel Harrison, Flora Finch and Ada Cousins. Subsequent Victorian Conventions were held in Warrandyte 1911–1912; Clayton 1913–1915; Dandenong 1916–1974.

Tasmania 1909: Evandale 1909–1911; Springfield 1912–1913; Scottsdale 1914–1916.

South Australia 1909: Woodside at Mrs. Alf Harris's place; 1910–1926: Wuttke's farm at Woodside (except for 1918–1920); Islington at Vogts 1918; Bethel at Schmidts 1918–1920; Strathalbyn at Thrings 1919–1951.

Queensland 1910: Mt. Gravatt 1910–1917. Coopers Plains 1918; Rochedale 1929.

Western Australia 1915: Between Radford's and Jacob's homes in Bassendean, then known as West Guildford 1915–1916; Butcher shop in Bassendean 1917; Radford's home in Canea, Gosnells 1918–1930; Radford's property Canea, Helena Valley 1931–1982; Williams 1983—.

*New South Wales 1908–1923: Major Pinchin's, Chetwynd Road, Guildford (except for 1912 at Rooty Hill, Granny Marshalls); Rodwells in Shadforth 1918; No Convention in 1919 due to flu. In 1920, three Conventions held at Shadforth, Granville and Scone; Pritchards in Guildford 1922–1964; Wattamondara in 1921; Dawsons at Dumaresque in 1923.

*Children's Meetings were held at these Conventions.

Australian State Overseers

Some of the first pioneer Workers from the British Isles who arrived in Australia between 1904 and 1908 became Overseers of various states.

NSW: John Hardie 1907–1961; Joe Williamson 1961–1963; Gordon McNab 1963–1991; Dan McNab 1991–1995; Clyde McKay 1995–2016; Allan Kitto 2016–2019; Graham Snow 2020–2021; Graham Dalton 2021—.

QLD: John Sullivan 1906–1924; Thomas Turner 1924–1959; no one 1959–1961; Archie Turner 1962–1971; Albert Barnes 1972–2002; Ray Corbett 2002–2014; Malcolm Clapham 2014—.

SA: Adam Hutchison 1908–1922; Willie Hughes 1922–1940; John C. Baartz 1941–1964; Robert Barbour 1964–1994; Stan Cornthwaite 1994–2009; Allan Kitto 2009–2015; Wayne Dean 2015–2019; Graham Dalton 2020–2021; Trevor Joll 2022—. Baartz was the first Australian native to become a state Overseer; Up to that time all the state elderships were held by the "originals" from the British Isles.

TAS: Adam Hutchison 1914–1922; Sam Jones 1922–1938; Since 1940, the VIC Overseer has also been responsible for TAS. Allan Mitchell 2018—.

VIC: Wilson McClung 1908–1913; Bill Carroll 1913–1953; Chris Williams 1953–1955; Archie Turner 1955–1957; Willie Donaldson 1957–

1985; Herwin Bell and Evan Jones (shared) 1985–2001; John Robinson 2001–2014; David Leitch 2014–2018; Allan Mitchell 2018—.

WA: Thomas Turner 1915–1924; Ted Terry 1924–1928; Nestor Ferguson 1928–1937 (married in 1938); Willie Phyn 1938–1939; Sam Jones 1939–1946; Joe Williamson 1946–1950; Walter Schloss 1950–1955; Bert Cameron 1956–1963; Clem Geue 1964–1980; Bill McCourt 1980–2008; Peter Doecke 2009–2017; Graham Snow 2018–2019; Max Goldsack 2020—.

Disclaimer. Some historical accounts contain conflicting dates for the trips made by the first Workers to Australia and New Zealand. In those cases, dates of ship passenger records from Ancestry.com have been used. *See* website *TellingTheTruth.info,* History, Pioneering Missions, Oceania.

Profiles of First Overseers of Australian States

Victoria and New South Wales. John Hardie and Sandy Alexander arrived in Australia in 1904 and held a two-month tent mission at Oakleigh, near Melbourne, VIC. They lived in one part of their tent and used the other part for Meetings. No one responded. After a storm destroyed their tent, they slept out in the open on the ground on newspapers. One morning Hardie woke up to discover Alexander had left during the night with their money.

After about two hard months in Australia, some of them alone, Hardie traveled to Wellington, New Zealand, to visit his Irish friends, Tom and Emilie Hastings, who had emigrated there from Ireland in 1901. Little is known about Hardie's activities during the following year.

In March 1907, Hardie and Dick McClure traveled from New Zealand to Sydney, Australia, and pioneered New South Wales, where Hardie was Overseer from the time he arrived until he died, the longest held Australian oversight (54 years). He was also the Senior Worker over all Australia until his death. Born May 2, 1871, in Rattray, Perthshire, Scotland, he died on April 26, 1961, aged 89, and was buried in Rookwood Cemetery, Sydney, NSW. Dick McClure left the Work in 1913, married and had five children.

Victoria. Wilson and Annie McClung, from Co. Armagh, Ireland, were a married Worker pair who arrived in VIC Australia in 1908 where Wilson had the oversight until 1913. After that, he became the New Zealand Overseer until his death in 1944. *See* Chapter 42 for McClung's profile.

Annie and Wilson McClung. He was Overseer of Victoria (1908–1913)

Bill Carroll, Overseer of Victoria (1913–1953)
with wife Maggie and daughter May

William "Bill" Charles Carroll succeeded McClung in 1913. Carroll was born August 15, 1876, in Newtown, Moynalty, Kels, Co. Meath, Ireland, the eldest of six children. He and Margaret "Maggie" Elizabeth Hastings, born April 20, 1875, also in Co. Meath, were married on June 6, 1901, in the Rathmolyon Church of Ireland. Five of six Carroll siblings entered the Work; four remained until death. *See* Carroll Family details in Chapter 6.

Bill and Maggie Carroll entered the Work in 1903 as a married Worker pair and first preached in the UK. Earlier, on May 31, 1902, their daughter, May, was born in Ireland. The "Mary Elizabeth (Coles) Waddingham Testimony" incorrectly gave 1899 as the year the Carrolls entered the Work (1899 was two years before they were married in 1901); it also gave an incorrect birthdate for their daughter May (Waddingham, n.d., *TTT*). *See Morning Leader,* June 15, 1906, *TTT*.

Bill, Maggie and May (age 11) Carroll left the UK on October 24, 1913, aboard the SS *Orsova*. Before their departure, reportedly, Bill's mother (1851–1909) had cared for May. In 1913, Carroll assumed the Victorian oversight from Wilson McClung which he held for 40 years, until his death on November 13, 1953, aged 77. He wrote Hymn Nos. 70 and 204 in *Hymns Old and New*, 1987 Ed.

Their daughter, May Carroll, was never in the Work although some group photographs of Workers show her with her parents. In 1926, she married Adolphus "Dolph" Harry Schulz from Queensland, born in 1896 (in the Work for a few years in the early 1920s). They resided in Melbourne, Victoria, and had two sons. Dolph died in 1987 and May in 1991. May was the author of 10 hymns in *Hymns Old and New,* 1987 Ed. (Nos. 69, 195, 209, 223, 258, 279, 315, 370 and 402).

Victoria, South Australia and Tasmania. Adam Dickson Hutchison was born September 10, 1873, in Lauder, Berwickshire, Scotland. A blacksmith before becoming a colporteur with the Faith Mission, he professed in a Gospel Mission held by George Walker and Albert Quinn in 1900 and entered the Work in 1902. He was the author of three hymns in *Hymns Old and New,* 1987 ed. (Nos. 243, 363 and 377). In October 1905, he was among the first group of Workers to venture to New Zealand. In 1907, Hutchison, Jim McCreight, Willie Hughes and Charlie Dubman left New Zealand to pioneer the Work in Victoria.

Sam Jones, Overseer of Tasmania, then Western Australia,
Chris Williams, Overseer of Tasmania and Victoria

Hutchison and Jim McCreight began pioneering South Australia in 1908. Shortly after they arrived, McCreight left the Work. At the Woodside Convention in 1911, four Brothers and one Sister entered the Work. Hutchison brought his sister, Aggie, from Scotland, to be the Sister's Co-worker.

In 1924, Hutchison and Alex Leadbetter were the first Workers to preach in Burma, where Hutchison died from smallpox in January 1925, aged 51. Unfortunately, Hutchison had not been vaccinated for smallpox. He and others believed that God protected the Workers' natural lives, and that they were immune from most human ailments and disease. So his unexpected death came as a great shock to many members. After that, there was no question regarding the necessity of vaccinations for all Workers going abroad.

Hutchison's sister Aggie started in the Work in 1905. At her brother's invitation, she went to South Australia aboard the SS *Wilcannia*, arriving in Sydney, NSW, on December 9, 1911. She preached in South Australia, Tasmania and Queensland. When Adam went to India in 1922, she returned to Scotland in 1922.

Western Australia. Thomas "Tom" McCausland Turner was the Overseer in Western Australia from his arrival in 1906 to 1924. Born September 1, 1877, in Swatragh, Maghera, Co. Londonderry, Ireland, to William and Melisina (Bateman) Turner, he was a schoolteacher when he professed in 1898. In 1899, he was one of the first four converts to commit full-time to the Work.

In January 1906, Tom Turner (26), James McCreight (24), Laura Falkiner (29) and Aggie Hughes (27) sailed from Liverpool, England aboard the SS *Oroya* to Melbourne, Victoria, arriving on January 4, 1906. They pioneered Western Australia for two very hard years with only two converts, Sid Maynard and Mrs. Burgess. In 1924, Turner succeeded John Sullivan as Overseer of Queensland until his demise on April 19, 1959, aged 82. He was buried in Brisbane. Turner wrote three hymns in *Hymns Old and New,* 1987 Ed. (Nos. 306, 365 and 369).

Sid Maynard

Sidney "Sid" Maynard (age 20), who professed in Kanowa through Laura Falkiner and Aggie Hughes in 1906, was the first person to convert on the continent of Australia and in Western Australia; he was also the first native Australian to become a Worker. He preached for 10 years in Western and South Australia and for 29 years in India. After

Adam Hutchison's death in 1925, Maynard took up his torch and was Overseer of India until his death in 1954, aged 68.

The Western Australia Workers attended the Woodside, SA Convention in March 1909. No Workers returned to WA until about 1911, when Annie Smith and Bess Pattison ventured there. In 1912, Grace Snowball and her mother were among the first converts. It appears there were no Brother Workers in this state until 1915, when Tom Turner, Sid Maynard and possibly Oscar Collins arrived.

Samuel "Sam" Jones was Overseer of Western Australia from 1939 to 1946. Born June 11, 1877, in Portadown, Co. Armagh, Ireland, Jones was a landscape gardener before he entered the Work in 1902. He arrived in WA on April 8, 1908, where he spent one year. During their difficult pioneering days there, his Co-worker, Bob Bashford, became so discouraged that Jones gave him what little money he could, and he left.

Jones struggled on alone, sleeping in a dry riverbed and took shelter in an empty house. He became so ill he could not walk and remained there 18 days before some gypsies discovered him half dead. They took care of him, and he recovered. He preached in South Australia until 1914 when he went to Victoria. Sam was often sick and unable for missions (B. Pattison 1951, *TTT*). From 1922 to 1938, Jones was Overseer of Tasmania.

Jones traveled back to Ireland in 1938—he had not been home for 30 years. He returned to Western Australia in 1939 where he had the oversight until his death of heart failure on April 14, 1946, aged 68, in Rockingham. He was the author of the greatest number of hymns included in *Hymns Old and New, 1987 ed.* (112) and has been called *"The Sweet Psalmist of Israel."* The 1910 Bethel Mission in South Australia was the high point of Jones' missions. *See* details below.

By the 1960s, worldwide, there were few workers still active in the Work from the original group of British Workers (pre-1906 from the British Isles). John Hardie, Tom Turner, Bill Carroll and Willie Hughes, internationally recognized as Senior Overseers for most of their lives, had all previously passed on. After the deaths of Joe Williamson and Willie Hughes in 1962–1963, there were no Overseers left in Australia and New Zealand from the *original* group. Beginning in 1963, when Gordon McNab was given the oversight of New South Wales, Overseers have been natives of Australia, until Graham Snow (from New Zealand) was appointed in 2018.

Queensland. John Sullivan, from Dunmanway, Co. Cork, Ireland, was born in 1874 and was a schoolteacher before he entered the Work in 1900. He and John "Jack" Little arrived in Brisbane on January 19, 1906. Their first two years in Australia were very hard, and Little deserted

Sullivan. From the time he arrived in 1906, Sullivan was the Overseer of Queensland until his unexpected death on December 1, 1924, aged 50. He was buried in Lutwyche Cemetery, Brisbane, QLD. He wrote No. 46, "Lord Jesus Lead" in *Hymns Old and New*, 1987 Ed. Thomas Turner succeeded Sullivan until his death in 1959.

Last Coopers Plains, QLD Convention (first one held in 1918)

Arthur McCoy. Shortly before the 1912–1913 Woodside, South Australia Convention, Jim Gordon and Jim Vallance held some open-air Meetings at Wattle Flat and Yankalilla. Arthur McCoy and his mother attended and professed. McCoy was born February 9, 1892, in South Australia, entered the Work in 1914, and preached in Tasmania under Adam Hutchison until 1921, when he was transferred to New South Wales where John Hardie was in charge.

Before the Workers had many converts to support them and provide shelter, those laboring in the rural areas of Australia endured severe hardships. For three years, McCoy and his companion lived in very rough huts, slept on haystacks in barns, drank water from creeks and roadside tanks. Since Workers were forbidden to carry a change of clothing, they were sometimes wet; they washed and dried their one set of clothes as best they could. They often had holes in the soles of their shoes/boots from traveling primarily by walking or biking. Not having ten shillings for a dentist to fix a damaged tooth, McCoy filed it off himself; it later abscessed.

McCoy confessed, "I would go about a whole year without buying a cup of tea or a meal ... In an old bucket we found we made thin apple jam from windfall apples and a little sugar, and we were so thin that our clothes hung on us. Weeks behind with rent for our empty cottage, we cut 22 tons of boiler wood at three shillings and six pence a ton, and packed loads of blue-gum leaves into containers for a friendly old Congregational Church man who ran a eucalyptus distillery" (Parker 1982, 40). When Ed Cooney and Adam Hutchison heard they worked to earn money for food and rent, Cooney said it was a "travesty of

Matthew 10." McCoy pointed out that the Apostle Paul worked in necessity and wrote of it.

Upon feeling severe pain in his right leg, McCoy went to a doctor who sent him immediately to the hospital. That evening the doctor opened his leg from hip to knee to the bone. Eight operations followed, resulting in his hip becoming rigid. The doctor left instructions to feed him well, explaining, "This man is dying because he is starving to death" (Parker 1982, 36–41).

After his hip injury, McCoy was unable to ride a bicycle. McCoy's brother, Keith, furnished a Harley-Davidson motorcycle with a sidecar for him and his Co-worker. McCoy believed he had been crippled due to the unnecessary hardships and poverty he suffered while in the Work under John Hardie's oversight.

Brother Worker Arthur McCoy's sidecar, used after his hip injury

McCoy refused to accept the indifference shown by his Overseers to the shocking needless poverty, living conditions and health challenges suffered by younger Workers. He worked hard to make the Australian Friends and Workers aware of the pitiful, deplorable conditions under which the Workers often labored. *See* Chapter 20.

At several Conventions, McCoy urged Overseers John Hardie and Willie Hughes to review the policy of sending men and women out to preach under conditions that seemed to him to be contrary to the mind of Christ. He disclosed, "In any case the set of commandments given to the apostles at first should not have been taken out of its proper time and situation ... *This way*, as it was popularly called, can be seen to be in effect a parody, a travesty, a clumsy and poor imitation of the Work into which Christ Jesus called the twelve apostles. It should be admitted honestly that many suffered needlessly for not discerning the true time, situation, circumstances and reasons for the set of instructions Christ gave to the apostles" (Parker 1982, 44–45).

Whether McCoy's pleas to the Overseers on behalf of the Workers had any effect or fell on deaf ears is unknown. Optimally, his outcry to this great injustice made a difference and caused changes that eased the needless suffering. God respects those who take up for the oppressed. "Learn to do right; seek justice. Defend the oppressed. Take up the cause of the fatherless; plead the case of the widow" (Isa. 1:17 NIV).

Workers' Bank Accounts. To her neighbor, McCoy's mother described her preachers as being poor, and unlike other church preachers, they had no bank accounts. The neighbor respectfully disagreed. It turned out that two of the neighbor's family members were employed at a bank where there was a trust account in Arthur McCoy's name. McCoy investigated and was astounded to discover a joint bank account at the National Bank of Australasia Ltd titled *John Christian Baartz and Arthur McCoy Trust A/C.* had been opened in 1937 with $20.00 AUD and closed in 1940; the largest deposit was $700.00 AUD and the highest balance was $1,191.00 AUD. John Baartz had succeeded Willie Hughes as the South Australia Overseer.

McCoy was highly indignant. While he had barely survived on a mere pittance, with no change of clothes, often wet, hungry, sick, in pain and sleeping in the open, the Overseer actually had a central fund (Parker 1982, 42) that could have been used to save his health. Possibly discovering the bank account was the proverbial "straw that broke the camel's back."

Overseers Willie Hughes (1922–1940), John C. Baartz (1941–1964)

In 1939, McCoy, age 47, renounced the 2x2 Sect, along with his mother, brother and sister. He announced, "After I protested to the Overseer face to face, I left the Fellowship and preached no more. I regret at least some of my own venture and have the crippled hip because of it" (Parker 1982, 45). Until his death, McCoy openly criticized the handling of funds in the 2x2 Sect and the Workers' method of following Matthew 10.

He married Vera Fanny Mogg in 1943 and died in 1982. McCoy distributed several letters and lengthy statements providing a vivid picture of hardships experienced by the Australian Workers in rural areas between 1913 and 1939 (Parker 1982, 38–45). Regardless of his good intentions to ease the suffering for others, many of his close friends and Co-workers considered McCoy to be bitter, obsessed, eccentric and fanatical. They maligned his reputation, as he nobly attempted to "make his paths straight" (Matt. 3:3).

1910 Bethel Mission, South Australia

The first German settlers came to Australia seeking religious freedom to follow their particular (minority) form of Lutheranism. Some settled in Bethel, South Australia, where a number professed in 1910. The Bethel Mission story has been widely circulated.

Attendance was very good in the Bethel Mission that Sam Jones and his Co-worker, Jim Vallance, were holding in the home of Hermann and Lydia Geue. After a few weeks, a disagreement arose among the Bethel community, with some siding with the Workers and others against them. The pastor of the Bethel Lutheran Church held a special meeting to "expose the imposters." He upbraided the two foreigners, charged them with being hypocrites of the worst kind, wolves in sheep's clothing who had no other purpose than to tear apart the Bethel flock.

Hermann Geue jumped up and walked out, and 23 others voted with their feet and followed him. "That same night he [Sam Jones] gave them opportunity to declare their support of the Gospel that he and Jim had preached to them, and the same 24 raised hands." *Read* full story as told by Clem Geue on website *TellingTheTruth.info* in History, Pioneering, Oceana, Australia, Bethel Mission.

The Workers left to attend the Woodside, SA Convention, accompanied by two of the Bethel men. They returned with William Irvine and Wilson McClung. During Jones' absence, the Bethel families realized that baptism was scriptural, and all had been baptized by a Baptist preacher. Some of the Bethel Mission family names who converted were Geue, Vogt, Schmidt, Matz, Doecke, Loechel, Punke, Schubert, Schilling and Eisen.

Otto Schmidt professed in the 1910 Bethel Mission. At the 1911 Convention, Irvine asked him if he had given any thought to going into the Work. When Schmidt replied that he had, Irvine asked him to be ready in two weeks. According to his son, Mervyn Schmidt, Otto believed he had been born again before he ever met the Workers.

Outreach to Foreign Countries. Otto Schmidt may have been the first Australian Worker to go overseas to a foreign field. In 1913, Schmidt and James Jardine went to Switzerland, then to Germany in 1914. Coming from a Bethel Mission family, Schmidt was of German descent and spoke German.

In the 1920s, more than 100 Workers started in the Work in Australia. A number of those young Workers went overseas to US, Canada, Europe and Asia. Many evacuated during the world wars. After WWII, Workers returned to Southeast Asia countries (Malaysia, Sri Lanka, Thailand, Sarawak, Japan). From 1950 to 1969, over 50 Workers went overseas for the first time.

Married Workers. The earliest married Worker pairs who preached in Australia were the McClungs, Carrolls and Beatties. Others included Ernst and Finny Punke, Frank and Hilda (Vogt) Quick, Mr. and Mrs. Gus Peterson and Les and Evelyn Robinson.

Indigenous Natives. Generally speaking, the Australian Workers have not preached among the aboriginal community, the native population. To their credit, Australian Workers preaching in foreign lands have been involved in numerous indigenous cultures.

In 1958, Cooper Sandosham from Malaysia was the first dark-skinned Worker to visit Australia. He made a favorable, lasting impression at the Conventions he attended. He also preached in Indonesia and North Borneo and died in 1981, aged 64.

Hymnbooks. In 1913, R. L. Allan published *Hymns Old and New* in English in Scotland, which was used worldwide. In New South Wales, Australia, at least three additional hymnal editions were published in 1917, 1918 and 1921 with 226–233 hymns.

The Supplement. In the 1940s, two South Australia Overseers with an appreciation for music, Willie Hughes and John Baartz, introduced a supplementary booklet of hymns called the *Supplement* or *Leaflet*. It contained about 12–18 hymns (more were added in later printings) and was used for nearly 50 years.

In 1941, the Victorian Overseer, Bill Carroll, introduced a leaflet titled *Supplementary Hymns for Field and Fold* that included hymns by Willie Hughes, Sam Jones and Carroll's daughter, May Schulz. It was used in Victoria for about 25 years.

The Secret Sect. In 1982, the publication of a book titled *The Secret Sect* by Australian authors Doug and Helen Parker caused a massive upheaval in the 2x2 Church worldwide. It was the first significant published historical account of the Sect's founder and beginning in Ireland at the turn of the twentieth century.

Military in Australia

When the British Empire entered WWI, Australia entered the War on the side of the British. After the ratification of the Statute of Westminster in 1931, Australia gained complete control over its foreign policy and military. However, it has remained close allies with the UK and with the US since WWII, when Australian and US troops fought together against the Japanese in the Pacific.

During WWI, in hearings applying for military exemption and conscientious objector status, some Australian 2x2 men used the sect's name registered in the UK for their religious body, *"The Testimony of Jesus"* (*Barrier Miner*, Broken Hill Nov. 24, 1916, *TTT*).

In 1917, Wilson McClung stated to the Military Service Board that the body known as *The Testimony of Jesus* had 2,500 adherents in Australia and 74 evangelists (*Dominion* July 26, 1917, 9, *TTT*). Due to his German ancestry, Brother Worker Ernst Punke spent some time incarcerated during the War.

In 1928, another name came into use. Willie Hughes, Overseer of South Australia, certified on letterhead for the *"United Christian Conventions of Australasia and New Zealand"* that Brother Worker Ron Campbell was "an ordained minister of the gospel labouring in fellowship with a body of Christians assuming this name only" (Hughes, April 20, 1928, *TTT*).

During World War II, in Victoria and South Australia, the church name of *Christian Assemblies of Australia* (CAA) was used to obtain petrol coupons (Vogt 2008, *TTT*). There was no Dandenong, VIC Convention held in 1942, as it was taken over by the military and used for a camp.

Newspapers reported that a number of Australian men belonging to the *Christian Assemblies Church of Australia* appealed for conscientious objector status and were granted non-combatant classification and served as civilians. Brother Worker Daniel McNab of NSW applied for an exemption as a Minister of Religion for the church called the *Christian Assemblies of the Commonwealth of Australia*.

Religious Bodies in Australia, 3rd edition, contains an entry for "The Nameless House Church (Two-by-two preachers)" in its section Non-trinitarian, Unclassified (Humphries 1995, 218–219).

In WWII, for over three years, from early January 6, 1942, to February 23, 1945, the Japanese interned Brother Workers Alex Mitchell, Arthur Shearer, Archie Wilson (from New Zealand) and later Bert Cameron (from Tasmania) in Changi Camp and Sime Road Camp, Singapore. Lindsay Stratford (brother of Reg, from South Australia) went to Singapore/Malaya to preach in 1932. While attempting to flee from Singapore in January 1942, the Japanese sank the ship he was aboard; all passengers were presumed drowned. *See* Chapter 38, Military. *See also* website *2x2 History*, Australian Files.

1929, January 1: *Christian Conventions of Victoria* was established as a registered charity in Victoria on January 1, 1929. Ninety years later, it was revoked on November 15, 2019. In the 1990s, it also operated as an incorporated entity. At least from 2016, it operated as a Trust registered with the Australian Charities and Not-for-Profit Commission (ACNC). *See* website acnc.gov.au.

Workers Conventions. In January 1928, the first Australian Workers Convention was held in Sydney, NSW, for two days. All the Australian Workers (about 120) attended. Bill Carroll's brother, Jack, from the US, and Edward Cooney were present. Several changes and transfers were made in all states. In the previous year, there had been 23 new Workers.

Thirty-six years later in January 1964, Jack Jackson led the second Australian Workers Convention, also in Sydney. Several Worker transfers were made between the states. Robert Barbour was appointed to succeed John Baartz as Overseer of South Australia. Clem Geue assumed the oversight of Western Australia.

In January 2020, the third Australian Workers' Convention was held on the Maroota, NSW Convention grounds near Sydney. Approximately 160 Workers attended (120 Australian Workers, including some who returned from their foreign fields and about 40 from New Zealand, Canada, South Africa and one from the US, a Sister Worker). It is not known to what extent child sexual abuse and other issues were addressed; the most visible changes following the Convention were appointments and removals of state Overseers.

2020: *60 Minutes Australia* Program. On Easter Sunday, April 21, 2020, a media bombshell hit the 2x2 Church when a *60 Minutes Australia* television documentary piece was aired nationally exposing mismanagement of child sexual abuse cases within the 2x2 Church in Australia. Victims were interviewed, and names and crimes were exposed of historic sex offenders in the male 2x2 ministry and laity. Brother Worker Allan Kitto was featured in the *60 Minutes* episode.

Ross Bowden, a prominent Ex-2x2 NSW man, was interviewed and described the 2x2 Sect's usual practice of protecting the sect by suppressing dissent and covering up this type of criminal behavior. News of the program went worldwide and countless 2x2 members viewed the episode online. Reactions ranged from outrage that such things happened to denial and assumptions that the victims were lying.

While the first time the 2x2 Sect was exposed on television happened to be in Australia—this issue is by no means unique to that country. It has been an international problem the 2x2 Sect has struggled with for far too long, along with other denominations and the Catholic Church, for an atrocity that should never occur.

Until recently, the Workers' usual mishandling regarding the perpetrator consisted of denial, cover up and moving the perpetrator to another location. Victims were strongly encouraged to let the Workers take care of the matter and not to go to the law. Many victims' reports have been disbelieved, discounted and their characters assassinated. Some have been threatened with excommunication (and their families) if they did not remain silent. Rarely, if ever, have the victims been provided with financial assistance for much needed counseling for their healing or restitution compensation.

An advocate group was formed in 2009 in America who attempted to aid 2x2 Sect victims of child sexual abuse. They have assisted with investigations, some of which resulted in prison sentences and Workers being expelled from the Work. The group is commonly known by the acronym *WINGS*, whereas the full name is *Working to INform Guide and Support Those Who Have Been Sexually Abused Within the Fellowship of Friends and Workers. See WINGS* Website: *wingsfortruth.info/*.

The Australians are to be commended for courageously taking the lead in bringing this to the attention of the media and law, which brought pressure upon the 2x2 Sect to make long needed changes. To their credit, some Senior Workers worldwide have taken some positive steps to address the issue. All Australian states except QLD have rolled out a detailed Child Safety Policy and Worker Code of Conduct. In the US, and possibly elsewhere, Workers have taken Ministry Safe classes. Some Workers have begun advising their members to report such abuse incidents to the law, rather than the Workers. Hopefully, the Workers will soon begin financially providing for the victims' healing and restitution.

~~~~~

Graham Snow, formerly the Overseer of Europe, arrived in Australia in 2018 and since then, new Overseers have been installed in all Australian states except Queensland. Snow, as the de facto national Overseer of Australia, was responsible for the shuffling. Following Allan Kitto's dismissal from the Work in 2021 due to an alleged breach of the Worker Code of Conduct/Child Safety Policy, some new Overseers were appointed. Graham Dalton for NSW, Trevor Joll for South Australia, and Max Goldsack for Western Australia. Graham Snow (in his early 80s in 2022) has recently indicated that he plans to step down from his Overseer roles in 2022.

In 2021, reportedly, some Australian Overseers began allowing members married to outsiders to fully participate in Fellowship Meetings. They also appeared to distance themselves from their long-held claim that they followed Matthew 10, one of the Sect's earliest core tenets. Instead, they shifted the focus to their itinerant ministry being based on the New Testament.

🍀🍀🍀

42

New Zealand

New Zealand is a sovereign island country in the Southwest Pacific Ocean, situated some 1,200 miles (2,000 km) east of Australia. Divided into two main regions, the North Island and the South Island, it includes about 600 smaller islands. Total land area is about 103,500 square miles (268,000 square km; near the size of Oregon or Colorado, US). The South Island is the larger in surface area; the North is the more populous. Auckland is the largest city; Christchurch is the second largest; and Wellington, North Island, is the capital and third largest city. In 2021, population is near five million.

1901: Arrival of First 2x2s. Two Irish 2x2 families who immigrated to the North Island in 1901 opened their homes for accommodations when the Workers arrived to pioneer New Zealand. Tom and Emilie Hastings settled in the south of the North Island in Lower Hutt, Wellington Region. Tom, a builder by trade, built a home on High Street, Petone.

Siblings Tom, Warren and Margaret Hastings. Thomas "Tom" was born in 1872, Warren in 1874 and Margaret in 1875; all were baptized in the Church of Ireland and grew up in Rathmolyon, Ireland. Tom (28) married Emilie Susan Nevitte (26) on December 17, 1900. Newly married, they arrived in Australia on February 14, 1901, and then sailed on to New Zealand. Warren was 25 when he went on William Irvine's Bicycle Mission Trip to Scotland in 1899; in 1901, he married Elizabeth Anne Winter. In 1901, Margaret "Maggie" Hastings married Bill Carroll, who became the Overseer of Victoria, Australia, in 1913.

The other couple, Jack and Dot Lowe, made their home in the north of the North Island at Buckland in the Auckland Region. According to John Hardie, "Jack Lowe and his wife Dot came from Ireland to live near Pukekohe East and had a little farm there. It was the only open home in that part, they were a great help to us all" (1982, Australia, *TTT*).

1904: First Worker Arrived. John Hardie (age 33, from Kilsyth, Scotland) was the very first Worker to set foot on New Zealand soil. Hardie was an engineer before he entered the Work in 1900. After spending about two months in Melbourne, Australia, Hardie arrived in Wellington, New Zealand, where his Friends Tom and Emilie Hastings lived. He had a few Gospel Meetings in Alicetown, Lower Hutt. Sometime later, Alex "Sandy" Alexander turned up in Wellington; before long, both Workers returned to Australia.

1905: More Workers Arrived. Irvine and eight UK Workers arrived in Australia on October 11, 1905, aboard the SS *Geelong* and transferred to ships sailing to various parts of New Zealand.

Annie Smith (28) and Fannie Carroll (24) boarded the SS *Monowai* for Dunedin. They started a mission on the South Island in the Otago region at Berwick where Jack Craig was the first to profess in 1906.

Four Workers, Adam Hutchison (28), Joe Williamson (32), Maggie McDougal (31) and Frances Hodgins (26) boarded the SS *Warrimoo* bound for Wellington, North Island, where they went their separate ways (Gospel in India, 1982, *TTT*). From there, Hutchison and Williamson went to the Canterbury province and worked a large mission at Oxford, a few miles out of Christchurch. Some who professed during that mission later went into the Work. They included Ada Cederman, Jim Vallance and Cissie Taylor.

John Hardie, Adam Hutchison and Joe Williamson, Pioneers to New Zealand

Polly and Frances Hodgins
Frances Hodgins pioneered New
Zealand (1905); Polly pioneered
Australia (1907)

Fannie Carroll and Annie Smith
pioneered South Island, New
Zealand (1905)

Maggie McDougal and Frances Hodgins stayed with the Hastings in Petone. They held a mission at Epuni, a suburb of Lower Hutt, and made quite a few converts in Wellington. The first person to profess was Nellie Fake, age 15, in 1905. Jim McLeod, Will Hooper and several others from the Fake, Lawson and Berryman families also professed.

By November 1905, John Hardie and Sandy Alexander were helping Maggie McDougal and Frances Hodgins in a Gospel Mission at Hutt Valley, near Wellington, where response was good. ("Friends Who Lived in the Hutt Valley" 1901–2006, n.d. *TTT*). Alexander left the Work to preach with the Plymouth Brethren. This was the second time he deserted Hardie.

Meanwhile John Fraser (27) and James "Jim" Hodgins left Sydney on October 18, 1905, for Auckland aboard the SS *Zealandia*. They worked a mission at Pukekohe where about 40 professed; some became Workers, including Teenie Walker, Alice Begbie, Percy Hartland and others. From Ireland, three of the Hodgins' family entered the work in succession: Polly in 1903 (pioneered QLD Australia), Jim in 1904 and Frances in 1905 (both did pioneer Work in New Zealand).

In 1906, James "Jim" Hodgins was diagnosed with tuberculosis. After 10 months, he passed away on May 15, 1907, aged 23, and was buried in Greytown Public Cemetery, Wairarapa. While his Co-worker, Fraser, stayed with Jack and Dot Lowe waiting for another Co-worker, he held a remarkably successful mission in Pukekohe East and others at Glen Murray and Tuakau.

While the pioneering Workers faced many hardships in New Zealand, they also held some highly successful missions; during their first year, about 100 were converted. In the following three years, twenty converts entered the Work; most continued into their old age.

1907: Eight Workers left Liverpool, England, on the SS *Oswestry Grange* on January 19, 1907, and arrived in Wellington on January 30, 1907. They were William "Willie" Hughes (26), Charles Dubman (22), Richard "Dick" McClure (24), Duncan McLachlan (28), George Harvey (21), James "Jim" Corcoran (23), Ida Davis (22) and Sarah Kelly (22). En route to New Zealand, they held Gospel Meetings while the ship was in the ports of Adelaide, Melbourne and Sydney.

1907, February: First North Island Convention. These UK Workers were welcomed at the first New Zealand Convention, held on the North Island at Wellington. From 1919 to 1941, a Convention was held at Te Rapa (near Hamilton) on the Kells' family farm. This site became unsuitable due to noise from the Air Force using the adjacent property for refurbishing and testing running aircraft engines. Currently, Conventions are held at Pukekohe, Masterton and Ngaere.

1907, March: First South Island Convention. A month later, the UK Workers arrived just in time for the first South Island Convention held on Harper Street, Sydenham, Christchurch, on the Linton's property; about 70 attended. Currently, Conventions are held at Winchester.

"My grandmother was among the first converts in New Zealand," relates Colleen Phelps, "and John Hardie was one of the two Workers ... The women all cast their wedding bands into a pond on the South Island Convention grounds, as the wearing of gold was 'not of God' ... the shedding of wedding rings was not uncommon in New Zealand in the early 1900s, and it also happened on the Dandenong, VIC, Australia Convention grounds" (personal communication, March 31, 2000).

1907: First Native Workers. Some New Zealanders entered the Work in 1907 at the first South Island Convention; Alice Begbie, only 19, was one of the youngest. Arthur "Archie" Murray professed in 1907 and left soon after with Adam Hutchison, Willie Hughes and Charlie Dubman to pioneer the Work in Victoria, Australia.

1908, March: Second Christchurch Convention. Irishman Harry McNeary arrived in New Zealand in 1908. After this Convention, eight New Zealanders went into the Work, including Jack Craig.

Circa 1908. The Wix family professed at Purakaunui, near Dunedin, South Island. Siblings George, Lottie and Mabel Wix entered the Work in 1911 and their sister, Alice, in 1914. George went to Germany in 1925. He and Lottie, along with Katie Hay (from Canada) and Edwin Schaer (from US, with Swiss parents) went to Switzerland as pioneers in 1926–1927.

1909: Wellington Convention. The 1909 North Island Convention was held in an empty shop on Adelaide Road, with accommodations in two nearby barns. In 1910, it was held for one year at Berryman's farm between Woodville and the Manawatu Gorge.

1903–1914: Irvine went on annual worldwide tours overseeing the Work. His trips were scheduled so that he was present at various Conventions in English-speaking countries. He visited New Zealand Conventions on most, if not all, of his world tours.

1913: New Zealand Workers List. Irvine attended a 1912 New Zealand Convention. Strangely, no Sister Workers were shown on the 1913 Workers List for New Zealand, whereas the 1912 list included 10. *See* Chapter 23. *See also* New Zealand Workers List on website *TellingTheTruth.info* in Workers, Workers Lists, 1912–1913 New Zealand.

BACK - William Irvine, John Hardie, Alex Walker, George Harvey, Archie Murray, Jack Annand, Jack Craig & Les Robinson
FRONT - Ruth Harrison, Dick McClure, Duncan McLachlan, Oliver Beattie, George Billings, David Matthews, Chris Williams & Queenie Higgins

1913 Workers in New Zealand

Jack Craig, first to profess in New Zealand (1906)

Archie Murray, first native New Zealand Worker (1907)

Alice Begble, youngest to enter New Zealand Work in 1907 (age 19)

New Zealand Overseers (aka Head Workers, Elders). John Fraser 1905–1909; Willie Hughes 1910–1913; Wilson McClung 1914–1940; Willie Hughes 1941–1963; Willie Phyn 1963–1985; Nathan McCarthy 1985–2006; Alan Richardson circa 2004—. In July 2021, it was announced that Alan Richardson would be retiring over a two-year period and will be replaced by Wayne Dean from NSW.

Wilson McClung, Overseer (1913–1944) and Annie McClung
with Willie Hughes who succeeded McClung as Overseer

Profile of John Wilson McClung. Wilson and Anne "Annie" Elizabeth (Kerr), married on March 19, 1897. They professed through Irvine in 1898 in Galway, Ireland, and entered the Work in November 1903 as a married Worker pair. He was born in Killyfaddy, Co. Armagh, Ireland, on December 24, 1867, and died on May 15, 1944, aged 76. Annie was born in 1871 and died on January 29, 1945, aged 73. Childless, both died in Auckland.

Wilson McClung (26) and his wife, Annie (24), along with Hannah Alexander (23, sister of Sandy Alexander) and Eugenia Victoria "Queenie" Higgins (27), both of whom entered the Work in 1905, and James "Jim" Gordon (31) departed from London on October 12, 1908, aboard the SS *Geelong* for Cape Town, South Africa. Perhaps, they visited Wilson's brother, Walter, and his wife, Christina McClung, a married Worker pair laboring in South Africa.

They continued to Sydney, Australia, arriving on January 23, 1909. After attending some 1909 Conventions in Australia and New Zealand, McClung went to Victoria where he assumed the position of Overseer of Victoria and Tasmania from 1909 to 1913.

After the 1914 Victorian Conventions, Wilson and Annie McClung transferred to New Zealand, where he was the Overseer until his death in 1944. At that time, New Zealand was a significantly larger responsibility than any single Australian state.

Profile of William "Willie" John Hughes. Born April 23, 1880, in Rathmolyon, Co. Meath, Ireland, Hughes was a purser in the Navy when he professed in 1898; he entered the Work in 1906. After attending the first Wellington Convention in February 1907, he crossed over to

Victoria, NSW, where he spent three years (1907–1909). He then returned to New Zealand where he was Overseer for three years (1910–1913). During 1913, he visited his home in Ireland, then preached in the Canadian Maritime Provinces for a few years before returning to Australia in late 1917. When Adam Hutchison left to pioneer India, Hughes became Overseer of South Australia from 1922 to 1944.

Hughes spent 1936–1938 in New Zealand assisting Wilson McClung. Following McClung's stroke, Hughes replaced him as Overseer (1941–1963). Hughes was incapacitated in 1963, died October 5, 1966, aged 86, and was buried in Pukekohe Cemetery. Five of his hymns are included in *Hymns Old and New,* 1987 ed. (Nos. 35, 72, 133, 161 and 399). A surge of new Workers offered for the Work during Hughes' oversight.

Profile of Edward William "Willie" Wallis Phyn. Born in 1902 in New Zealand, Phyn started in the Work in 1927, and died on April 15, 1985, aged 83. He preached in Australia, Greece, Cyprus, Egypt and England. He succeeded Willie Hughes as Overseer of New Zealand from 1963 until his death in 1985. Succeeding Willie Hughes from 1963 until his death in 1985, Phyn was the first native New Zealander to become its Overseer.

Profile of Nathan McCarthy. From New Zealand, he started in the Work in 1948 in New Zealand and then preached mostly in Victoria, Australia. He succeeded Willie Phyn in 1985 as Overseer. McCarthy was born April 28, 1921, died June 4, 2006, aged 85.

Profile of Alan Thomas Richardson. The current (as of 2022) New Zealand Overseer was born in 1941 at Palmerston North, NZ, and entered the Work circa 1972–1973. Before succeeding Nathan McCarthy around 2004, he preached in New Zealand and Uruguay. In 2021 he announced his intention to hand over his Overseership to Wayne Dean from Australia over the following two years, since he had reached the age of 80.

1913: No Sister Workers. A curious incident occurred in 1913. Sister Workers were discontinued. Whereas the 1912 Workers List included ten Sister Workers, the 1913 List had none. This was confirmed by Willie Hughes in a 1913 letter to Willie Gill. It was said that the Brother Workers had become concerned that women preachers were not scriptural; there were also concerns that some may be pregnant by William Irvine. Accordingly, after the 1913 Convention, all the NZ Sister Workers were sent away (four to Australia. That year the Brother Workers' missions produced no converts. No Irvine offspring was born. The following year, six reinstated Sister Workers' names were on the 1914 Workers List.

Married Worker Couples. Wilson and Annie McClung were the first pair of married Workers in New Zealand. They were married in Ireland on May 19, 1897, prior to entering the Work in 1903.

Ralph and "Rene" Beattie (nee Amy Constance Irene Lester) were married on April 2, 1907, professed around 1909 and went into the Work in 1911, in Victoria, Australia. During their first year in the Work, Ralph preached with Wilson McClung, and Rene with Annie McClung. After that, they preached together most of the time. In 1920, they transferred permanently to New Zealand under McClung's oversight.

Since Irvine did not allow children of married Worker couples to remain with their parents, Beattie's 18-month-old son, Archie, was raised by Rene's brother, Clyde Lester, and his wife. After Irvine was expelled in 1914, the Beatties had three more children who remained with their parents while they preached in New Zealand. Ralph died in 1958; Rene in 1969. The seven hymns in *Hymns Old and New,* 1987 ed. that Rene composed are Nos. 38, 66, 71, 79, 91, 140 and 282 (Beattie 2001, *TTT*).

Frank and Hilda Quick (Vogt) were another married pair. Frank started in the Work in Victoria in 1917, left and married Hilda in the 1920s. In 1937, they were accepted in the Work and preached together in South Australia and Western Australia. They labored in New Zealand from 1946 to 1972, before returning to South Australia where Frank died in 1975, aged 85; Hilda passed away a year or two later.

Sister Worker Queenie Higgins from Ireland and Brother Worker Alexander Walker left the Work and married in 1920. Both had preached in New Zealand and New South Wales, Australia. They made their home in New Zealand. Their daughter, Florrie, preached in Malaysia for much of her life.

World War I. When the British Empire entered both WWI and WWII, New Zealand was automatically entered in the War on the British side. Conscription started in 1916 for men ages 20–45 for the Expeditionary Force. "The law exempted only those who were members of a religious body having as one of its written tenets the objection to bearing arms; even then, non-combatant service in the Army was required. Altogether, about 400 objectors were sentenced to prison, for terms ranging up to two years" (Sibley and Jacob 1952, 7).

Wilson McClung stated to the Military Service Board that he was the "Overseer" and "principal representative of the body in New Zealand 'known as *The Testimony of Jesus*,' with 700–800 Members and 24 Evangelists or Ministers in New Zealand; 2,500 Members and 74 Evangelists in Australia; and 5,000 Members and 70 Ministers in England. He declared the society had been established for a few years when he joined it some 20 years previously" (*Dominion*, July 26, 1917, 9, *TTT*).

New Zealand newspapers reported that appeals for military exemptions by some 2x2 men affiliated with the church called *The Testimony of Jesus* were dismissed because they were absolutists. All told, 22 professing men refused to wear military uniforms or perform any service in the military, including non-combatant, and were given prison sentences up to two years of hard labor (*Evening Post*, Sept. 18, 1917). *See* Chapter 38. *See also* website *2x2 History*, New Zealand History.

World War II. The names used by most members for their church during WWII were *Christian Assemblies of Australia and New Zealand; Christian Assembly; Fellowship of Christian Assemblies;* and *Christian Assemblies of God* (*Evening Post*, Dec. 12, 1940, 15, *TTT*). Commonly referred to as *Christian Assemblers* (CAs), many 2x2 males were imprisoned.

According to author David Grant, "The Christian Assemblies, a scattered, largely rural-based sect, had the largest number of men in detention from any church group. While nominally free to make up their own minds, the 122 Christian Assembly conscience appellants represented nearly 100% of members who had been called up in the ballot. Of those whose appeals were denied, only two opted for non-combatant service when they had the chance. The rest went to [prison] camp [for the duration of the War]" (1986, 165–66).

According to New Zealand Overseer W. J. Hughes, of the New Zealand 2x2 men of military age, "98 percent found it impossible to take part in warfare in any capacity ... Of the 121 members committed to Defaulter's Detention, 117 remained faithful ... Our Missionaries were labouring in all those countries previous to the War ... have the satisfaction of knowing that we have not made one wife a widow or one child fatherless ... we did not go first with the Gospel, then with weapons of war and then return again with the Gospel" (Statement, Jan. 6, 1945, *TTT*).

On July 8, 1941, Cecil Barrett (emigrated from England to New Zealand) and three other Brother Workers laboring in the Philippines were imprisoned in the Los Banos Internment Camp south of Manila. *See* Chapter 38.

1947–1948: Poliomyelitis Epidemic. For more than two years after World War II, more than 1,000 people in New Zealand were infected with infantile paralysis (polio); around 70 died. Alan Richardson, Overseer of New Zealand, explained, "From the time of the government restrictions announced in newspapers, on Saturday of both 1st

Winchester and 1st Pukekohe Conventions (at the beginning of December 1947), all schools were to be closed, and no child under 16 years of age was to attend any public gathering nor travel on public transport. Children under this age were sent away from those two Conventions to private homes that day, and none of them attended subsequent Conventions that year. Some schools didn't re-open until the second half of April 1948—in the intervening period, school lessons were available by correspondence or on the radio" (Statement, March 14, 2020, *TTT*).

Indigenous Natives. In New Zealand the Maori native people migrated from Polynesia around 1320–1350 AD. A number of Friends have some Maori ancestors. A part-Maori Worker, Isabel Honeycombe, was on New Zealand Workers Lists from 1938 to 1997. She led a mission dedicated to Maori from 1953 to 1955 as she was fluent in Maori language. A hymn book was published, *Himene Maori Tawhito, Hou* (Maori Hymns Old and New), with 55 Maori language hymns.

Outreach. In the 1920s, there were approximately 50 new Workers in New Zealand. Over the years, New Zealand sent abroad and supported a significant number of Kiwi Workers, some of whom were *the first* Workers to go pioneer a foreign country. After WWI, in 1927, New Zealand sent George and Lottie Wix (siblings) and two others to Switzerland. In 1926, Jack Craig went to Eastern Europe where he and Jack Annand were pioneers to several countries. In 1925, Teenie Walker with Gertie Barendilla and Doreen McKenzie were the first Sister Workers to preach in India. In 1957, Maurice Archer and Fred Allen (from Australia) pioneered Vietnam.

Alex Mitchell was born in Scotland, immigrated to New Zealand, professed in 1921 and entered the Work in 1922. After a year in Victoria, Australia, he and Jack Trigg pioneered Ceylon (now Sri Lanka) in 1927. He then went to Singapore in 1936 (possibly the first Worker to go there), where apart from home visits, he spent the rest of his days in the Work. From 1942 to 1945, he was interned in Changi Camp, Singapore. He was the Overseer of Singapore, Malaysia, Borneo, Thailand and Vietnam until 1974, when he returned to New Zealand and died in 1980, aged 84.

Workers Lists from 1905 onward provide evidence of the growth in numbers of Workers, followed by a decline since the 1970s.

New Zealand Local and Overseas Workers 1905-2022

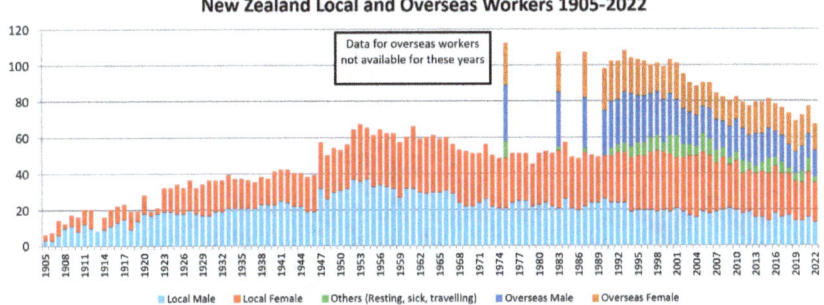

Data for overseas workers not available for these years

Local Male   Local Female   Others (Resting, sick, travelling)   Overseas Male   Overseas Female

New Zealand Local Workers/Million Population 1905 - 2022

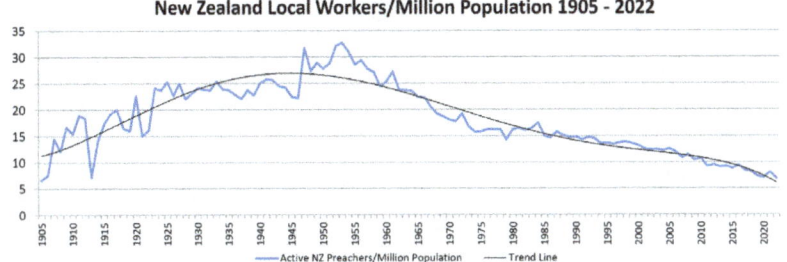

Active NZ Preachers/Million Population   ——— Trend Line

Charts of NZ Worker numbers from website 2x2Church.info

Sources. The above information was taken largely from several non-published historical documents on the website *TellingTheTruth.info*. Since memories are not totally reliable, some of these accounts contained conflicting dates. In such cases, the author used dates provided on ship passenger records on the website Ancestry.com.

Ralph and Rene Beattie with son Archie, 1912

❖❖❖

South America

43

Latin America and the Caribbean

Latin America consists of 20 countries and 14 dependent territories that cover an area stretching from Mexico to Tierra del Fuego, Argentina, and includes much of the Caribbean. It has an area of approximately 7,412,000 square miles (19,197,000 km), almost 13% of Earth's land surface area. As of March 2, 2020, the population of Latin America and the Caribbean was estimated at more than 652 million.

Latin America Pioneering Mission Work

1919 Argentina	Jack Jackson, Glenn Smith, Herbert Vitzthum and Maurice Hawkins
1923 Brazil	Jack Jackson and Robert "Bob" Smith
1921 Chile	Jack Jackson and Maurice Hawkins
1920 Uruguay	Robustiano Ferreira
1933 Mexico	Lewis Murray and Daniel Leighty
1954 Falkland Islands	Jim Boles and Lawrence Blizard
1957 Bolivia	John Pattison and Fred Hogan
1962 Guatemala	Lynn Walker and Wilbur Walker
1962 Paraguay	Jorge Webster and Steven Stivers
1969 Peru	Willie Boles and Norman Campbell
1970 Costa Rica	Lynn Walker and Jack Campbell
1973 El Salvador	Patricia Daniels and Lilian Bateman
1974 Ecuador	Willie Boles and Norman Nash
1977 Honduras	Ronald Elliott and Benigno Morales
1980 Venezuela	Ted Rozema and Lynn Walker
1985 Colombia	Munro MacAngus, William Rosal and David Lockhart
1985 Belize	Jack Campbell, Holmer Bollnger and Willie Pollock
1990 Nicaragua	Carolyn Forsland and Lesvia Dominguiez

Due to a limited collection of early historical Two by Two records for Latin America, I regret only being able to present the few facts below for so great a continent. All the Latin American countries have been pioneered, with Argentina being the first in 1919 and Nicaragua being the last in 1990. Historically, the three smaller South American countries on the Atlantic Ocean coast in the Northeast—Guyana, Suriname and French Guiana—have been ministered by Caribbean Workers.

Spanish is the official language except for Brazil where it is Portuguese. The Bible used by 2x2s in Spanish-speaking countries is the *Reina Valera*, 1960 version. The Workers are called *servants.*

All the Overseers of each Latin American country are foreigners, except for Brazil, where by law there can be no foreign missionaries; missionaries go there as teachers, etc. The Overseer of all South America was Jack Jackson until his death in 1966. Those who assumed his mantle were (possibly) John Tuft (US); Duane Hopkins (US); Colin Sanders; and reportedly, it is presently Lealand "Percy" Broughton who is based in Rio Grande Do Sul Brazil. The origins of the Overseers of South American countries are: Brazil (3), Scotland (3), Australia (1), Western Canada (1), Western US (2) and Eastern US (1).

1919 December 19: Argentina. The first pioneer Workers to carry the 2x2 message to South America were four Brother Workers who sailed from New York to Buenos Aires, Argentina, on December 19, 1919. One was Irishman, John "Jack" Samuel Jackson, who was converted by William Irvine in 1898 at Parsontown, Ireland. He entered the Work in 1901 and went to preach in North America in 1904. The other three were Glenn Smith, Herbert Vitzthum and Maurice Hawkins, all from the US. After their mail was stolen, they took jobs and attended Spanish classes.

South America pioneers arrived in Buenos Aires, Argentina (Dec. 19, 1919) Front Row: Jack Jackson (Ireland and US), Glenn Smith (Nebraska US), Back Row Herbert Vitzthum (Minnesota US), Maurice Hawkins (Maryland US)

Basilio Alvarez First native South American Worker

About a year after the first Workers went there, in November 1920, Ernest Benton (from England) and Willie Sutter arrived in Buenos Aires. By the end of November 1921, eight adults had professed.

In early 1923, John Pattison (son of Goodhand Pattison) and Willie Boles (both from Ireland) arrived in Buenos Aires, along with American Sister Workers Ruby Pellett and Leah Hawkins (sister of Maurice). The first Argentina Convention was held in February 1923, in Dalla Rivas' home. With Robert Darling's arrival from Scotland, there were 11 Workers and about the same number of Friends. (Maurice Hawkins n.d., *TTT*).

Basilio Alvarez, a Spaniard who had immigrated to Argentina at an early age, was a student of Jackson, who had taken a job teaching. Basilio professed, started in the Work in 1924 (age 21) and became the first South American native Worker. After WWII ended, Basilio returned to Spain and spent the rest of his life overseeing the Work there until he died in 1985.

Cándida Rodríguez, a devout Catholic young lady about 30 years old, was very impressed with the words on the tombstone of Brother Worker Reginaldo Edwards in San Rafael: "A Faithful Servant of the Lord." She kneeled at his grave and asked the Lord to help her to have a testimony like the person buried there. Later, she met Basilio and his Co-worker and professed. In 1938, she entered the Work in Argentina. Later, she labored in Spain for 22 years before returning to Argentina where she died in 1990. Fittingly, Cándida was buried in the same grave as Reginaldo Edwards. *See* details on website *TellingTheTruth.info* in History, Pioneering, South America.

Of the original four pioneers to South America, only Jackson remained there until his death. Born in Edenderry, Ireland, on October 20, 1880, he was buried in the British Cemetery in Buenos Aires in 1966. Glenn Smith and Maurice Hawkins left the Work and returned to the US. In 1935, Vitzthum returned to the US and spent most of the rest of his life based in New Mexico as Overseer of the US Spanish Work, as well as all the Spanish-speaking areas of the Southwest US.

Willie Walters and Willie Boles remained in South America until they were very elderly. Robert Darling died in Argentina in 1970, and Millie Griffin died in 1983; they were buried in the same grave as Jackson. Argentina custom permitted burying three bodies in one grave (William Berger, n.d., *TTT*).

In 2022, Argentina, Rio Grande Do Sul Brazil, Uruguay and Paraguay consolidated into one staff with the Overseer being Lealand "Percy" Broughton (from Western Canada, Ontario).

Latin America Church Names. Respecting the law, the Workers have registered names for their church with the government that typically include the base words *Christian Church (Iglesia Cristina).* Each country's name is unique, e.g. Christian Church of San Felipe (Chile), Christian Church of Paraguay, Primitive Christian Church of Peru, etc. Avoiding a common sect name or a regional or global identification preserves their anonymity and makes tracing them difficult. New registrations may become necessary to comply with authorities; the name may change, and board members may change.

1923: Chile. On March 16, 1923, Jackson and Hawkins arrived in Santiago, Chile. In August 1923, Willie Walters (from US) and Ernest Hamon (from Canada) arrived in Valparaiso; John Pattison (from Ireland/Argentina) joined them. The Work in Chile had little response through the 1920s. Some Workers were close to abandoning the country when, in 1928–1929, they found a community of Germans who had recently immigrated to Southern Chile and were interested in hearing them. Fortunately, one pair of Workers spoke German. The first 2x2 Fellowship Meetings established in Chile were conducted in the German language.

The current Overseer is Max Bowman (Idaho, Western US). Official church name is *The Christian Church of San Felipe.*

1923: Brazil. Jackson and Robert "Bob" Smith (born in 1894 from US) pioneered Brazil in August 1923. Smith later married Martha Hogg (from Ireland). Both were young Workers, who went to Brazil where they met and married, possibly around 1938. They pioneered very remote areas of Brazil and were quite successful evangelists. When they were unable to continue in the Work, they returned to Virginia, US, where they died, she in 1987 and he in 1990.

Brazil is divided into three staffs of Workers. In 2022, Rio Grande Do Sul Brazil, Uruguay, Paraguay and Argentina consolidated into one staff with the Overseer being Lealand "Percy" Broughton (from Western Canada, Ontario). Northern Brazil has two staffs under three Overseers, Elpidio Arruda, Wander Albino and Peter Sander (all native Brazilians). The official church name is *Igreja cristã* (Christian Church).

1938: Uruguay. In the 1920s, Robustiano Ferreira, a Uruguayan man, professed through the Workers in Argentina. He and a Co-worker started the Work in Uruguay. Except for Guyana, Uruguay has exported the most Workers in South America. Most of the Worker staff understand both Portuguese and Spanish.

In 2022, Uruguay, Rio Grande Do Sul Brazil, Paraguay and Argentina consolidated into one staff with the Overseer being Lealand "Percy"

Broughton (from Western Canada, Ontario). The official church name is *Igreja cristã* (Christian Church).

1957: Bolivia. John Pattison (from Ireland) and Fred Hogan pioneered the Work in Bolivia. Pattison died there in 1978, aged 85, and was buried in Cochabamba. Beginning in 1922, he labored in South America for over 50 years. At his urging, his father, Goodhand Pattison, of Cloughjordan, Co. Tipperary, Ireland, compiled an "Account of the Early Days," an invaluable resource quoted many times in this book and reprinted on the website *TellingTheTruth.info* in Publications.

The current Overseer is Brett Hammett (California, Western US).

1962: Paraguay. Jorge Webster (from Chile) and Steven Stivers (from Argentina) went to pioneer Paraguay in 1962. The first Sister Workers to arrive in 1968 were Morelia Zapata (from Chile) with Margery Harrison (from US).

In 2022, Paraguay, Rio Grande Do Sul Brazil, Uruguay and Argentina consolidated into one staff with the Overseer being Lealand "Percy" Broughton (from Western Canada, Ontario). The official church name is *The Christian Church of Paraguay* or *Friends in Paraguay*.

1969: Peru. Freedom of worship was granted in May 1967. The first Workers to go to Peru were Norman Campbell and Willie Boles in 1969. A couple from whom they rented a room were their first converts. In the first five years after the Workers arrived, five or six converted.

The current Overseer is Trevor Loechel (South Australia). The official church name is *The Primitive Christian Church of Peru*.

1974: Ecuador. On the Tica Bus from Nicaragua to the US in late 1973, two married Ecuadorian men, Eduardo Pizarro and Antonio Ruilova, met four Workers (two Brothers, Lilian Bateman from Ireland and Patricia Daniel from US). At their destination in El Salvador, the Workers invited the men to spend Saturday night with them. Their host was the Elder of the 2x2 Sunday Meeting; the men attended.

In May 1974, the two men asked the Workers to visit them in their hometown, Guayaquil. Subsequently, two Workers laboring in Peru, Paul Schluep (from Switzerland) and Norman Campbell (from Scotland), spent about a week with them. They returned for two more visits that year.

Beginning early in 1975, Norman Nash and Willie Boles (both from Ireland) held a mission in Guayaquil. Sergio Reyes and his wife professed. In 1976, Boles was replaced with Maurice Pife (from Canada); Pizarro, Ruilova and others professed. On January 12, 1980, the first Sister Workers arrived in Guayaquil: Morelia Zapata (from Chile) and Lilian Bateman. The Brother Workers left to pioneer the capital city Quito, where the Convention is currently held.

During the Cenepa War (January 26–February 28, 1995) between Peru and Ecuador, Brother Workers Aníbal Zárate and Rojano González were accused of being Peruvian spies and were imprisoned in Ecuador for several months. Allegedly, they were severely tortured during attempts to get them to sign confessions.

The current Overseer is Jim Price (New Mexico, Eastern US).

1980: Venezuela. On April 2, 1980, the first two Workers arrived in Venezuela, Ted Rozema and Lynn Walker, both from the US. Previously, Rozema had worked in Brazil and Walker in Central America. Venezuela currently has about 150 baptized members in 13 cities/towns; the majority live in Valencia. There are five pairs of Workers; two Venezuelan men and the rest are foreigners. Rozema died December 19, 2020, aged 101.

The current Overseer is John Newlands (Scotland, UK). The official church name is *Iglesia Cristiana* (Christian Church).

1985: Columbia. An exploratory trip was made in 1985 by Munro MacAngus (Scottish, previously worked in Chile and Venezuela). The Workers began laboring there in 1986 with William Rosal (from Venzuela) and David Lockhart (Irish, previously worked in Bolivia). Julio Gómez was the first Colombian to start in the Work in 2008. The most successful mission was in Ipiales, a town on the Colombia-Ecuador border where perhaps 200 people professed, and five Fellowship Meetings currently assemble there.

The current Overseer is Munro MacAngus (Scotland, UK).

1990: Nicaragua. The last country to be pioneered in Latin America was Nicaragua in 1990 by Carolyn Forsland and Lesvia Dominguiez.

~~~~~

Mexico. Lewis Murray and Dan Leighty went to East Mexico on October 10, 1933. In 1962, after Fidel Castro rose to power and they had to leave Cuba, Roy Lacy and Richard Frederick (from US) were the first Workers to arrive in West Mexico.

East Mexico Overseers have been Clarence Anderson (died in Melbourne, Australia January 17, 1987), Donald Bowen and Alan Anderson (Clarence Anderson's nephew). West Mexico Overseers were Roy Lacy, William Berger and Glen Yung. After Mexico was united into one field in 2004, the Overseers have been Alan Anderson, William Berger and Alan Anderson again.

The first native of Mexico to enter the Work was Manuell Leon in 1942. He was in his 60s and spent 15 years in the Work. Previously a landlord, he burned the deeds to his property, which effectually gifted the property to his tenants. Juventino Valdez was the second native to enter the Work.

The first Convention was held in 1943 in a ranch village, El Venado, Nuevo León, in Northeast Mexico, 10 years after Workers first arrived. About 25 people attended, including George Walker, Overseer of Eastern US.

1947: Old Mexico Workers List. Clarence Anderson, Daniel Leighty, Lewis Murray and Manuel Leon.

The Caribbean – West Indies

Jamaica. Willie Snedden (Scottish) and Frank Stephens (English) arrived in 1922 by ship in Kingston, Jamaica. The 1925–1926 Workers List added W. (Willie) Donaldson, Sam Driver, Lena Brindle and Florrie Elliott. The 1928–1929 Workers List showed seven Brother and four Sister Workers.

Guyana, Suriname and French Guiana. Situated on the Atlantic Ocean coast in Northeast South America, these countries are ministered by the Caribbean Workers. Guyana has exported many Workers to other countries; a number of Guyanese Friends live in New Jersey, US.

The current Overseer is David Newlands (Scotland, UK).

Cuba. Two different years are given for the first Workers' arrival in Cuba. One is 1944 with Roy Lacy, Tom Law and possibly Clarence Anderson. Another is 1949, with Wilbur Walker among the first.

See Appendix L for Pioneers of Various Countries.

Southeast
Asia

44

Asia

Asia and Europe are part of the same land mass, with Europe occupying the western portion and Asia taking up the other three-fourths. Asia is the largest of the world's traditional seven continents, covering approximately 30 percent of Earth's land area. It is also the world's most populous continent, containing roughly 60 percent of the world's total population. Containing approximately 49 countries, Asia is divided into various sub-regions.

This chapter briefly covers the Workers' initial outreach to some countries in Asia prior to 1940. For most countries worldwide, the pioneers' names and dates are shown in Appendix L, Pioneers of Various Countries. As more historic records are digitized, additional information may become available for countries inadequately represented in this book.

Following are the countries who sent the first Workers to Asia. Australia sent the very first Worker to preach on the continent of Asia (India) in 1922 (Adam Hutchison); to Burma (now Myanmar) in 1924 (Adam Hutchison and Alex Leadbetter); to Ceylon (now Sri Lanka) in 1927 (Alex Mitchell and Jack Trigg); and to Singapore/Malaya/Malaysia in 1932 (Lindsay Stratford and Bert Cameron).

Canada sent Bert Middleton and Ernest Davis to pioneer Japan in 1926. This was followed by England sending Ernest Stanley and New Zealand sending Sam Lang to Japan in 1929, and Cecil Barrett in 1937. The US dispatched Workers to China in 1926 (Willie Jamieson and Max Bumpus); to the Philippines in 1936 (Hubert Sylvester and Howard Ioerger); and to Hong Kong in 1938 (Charles Preston with Tom Fowler from New Zealand).

Far East

People's Republic of China (PRC). In 1921, Mao Zedong founded the Chinese Communist Party in China. Brother Workers William "Willie" Jamieson (from Scotland) and Maxwell "Max" Bumpus (from US) arrived in China in 1926. Workers increased to about six from 1926 to 1939, including Tom Fowler and Jim Pascoe (from New Zealand); and Alfred

McLeod, Charles McKeown and Charles Preston (from US). The first Sister Workers arrived at least by 1927.

Standing, Max Bumpus, Ross Steele, Charles Preston, Willie Jamieson, Tom Fowler, Alfred McCloud

In 1927, the Chinese Civil War began. The Nationalist Party leader, Chiang Kai-shek, launched an anti-communist purge. Nationalist forces began firing March 21–25, 1927 in Nanking where Workers were living. Jamieson stated that on March 24, 1927, several soldiers burst into the home where they were staying, demanding money, discharging their rifles and threatening to kill them.

Bumpus was not there, having spent the night at the Y.W.C.A to protect the Sister Workers. The soldiers left after abusing Jamieson and amassing all the loot they could carry. Outside, a Chinese mob enjoyed the scene. Jamieson wrote from Shanghai, "We were cleared out to the last penny and lost all our clothes but those we wore. Max had even his coat and vest taken off his back. The experience none of us will ever forget."

Jamieson continued, "Max … was stopped by a soldier and tied up to a pole and the soldier intended to shoot him. Some other Chinese gathered around, and the soldier was showing them how his gun worked. While this was going on, an officer came along and asked him why he had Max tied to the pole, and he said, 'I am going to shoot him.' The officer said, 'He hasn't done anything to harm you, so you let him go.' So he untied Max and let him go. Max had trouble with his nerves after and wasn't able to continue in the Work" (to Jack Carroll, April 1, 1927, *TTT*).

Jamieson's servants urged him to flee and hoisted him over a wall into a neighbor's yard where he hid behind some barrels for nine hours. A neighbor boy found him and returned with officers who escorted him to safety where other foreigners had collected, including Bumpus.

In self-defense American and British warships fired at Chinese forces and used armed landing parties to evacuate foreign residents into three American, two British and four Japanese gunboats headed for Shanghai. The Workers were on board. Fearing a repetition of Nanking in Shanghai, the Workers were anxious to leave China. By April 1, they had received "remittances" from Carroll and were able to leave the country, a very good move, since the Shanghai Massacre took place shortly thereafter, on April 12, 1927.

Jamieson went to the Philippines nearby. Bumpus (age 36) returned to the US aboard the SS *Empress of Russia*, arriving in January 1928. He married Bertha E. Johansson Lindberg in 1934; they adopted a daughter, Edith Gertrude, born in 1934. He passed away at the Newry, Pennsylvania Convention in 1970. Sadly, his 2x2 widow and daughter were brutally murdered on May 5, 1998, in Pelahatchie, Mississippi, US, by his 2x2 son-in-law, Elbert Walters, (aged 72) who then killed himself. On a personal note, I grieved over this tragedy; for many years, I attended Meetings with the Walters family and have sweet childhood memories of summer days spent on their farm.

Around 1934, the Workers' language teacher in Nanking, Mr. Wong, his son and daughter, professed. Jamieson was the Asian Overseer until 1939.

Hong Kong. Forced to evacuate from China in 1937, Tom Fowler and Charles Preston went to Hong Kong; Jim Pascoe followed in 1938. Fowler and Pascoe were interned at Camp Stanley in Hong Kong from 1942 to 1945 by the Japanese. Preston escaped internment as he was on a home visit to the US. After the War, Pascoe returned to Hong Kong where he remained from 1946 to 1984. The first Convention was held circa 1961. The first native Worker was Grace Law.

Taiwan. In 1956, Dellas Linaman, Charles Preston and Wolfgang Klussmann were among the first to go preach in Taiwan. Preston continued there until after 1990. The first Taiwanese Sister Worker, Hsin Shyu-yueh, began in 1966–1967, followed by her three younger brothers. In 1965, there were six pairs of Workers.

South Korea. Although Willie Jamieson spent a little time in Korea in the 1920s, the first Workers to hold missions in Korea were Sproulie Denio and Don Garland (from US) in 1949. During the Korean War (June 1950–July 1953), they stayed in Japan and returned to Korea after the War in 1955. Additional Workers who arrived in 1957 from Canada were Merlin Howlett, Gordon Winkler, Paul Boyd, Mark Wiseham; and from the US: Dick Owen, Marion Robinson, Isabel Boyd, Alice Ramsden and Jeannette Munn.

The first Overseer was Sproulie Denio, who died suddenly in 1964, aged 54. He was succeeded by Don Garland who died in 2002. The oversight then went to Ernest Robinson from South Africa, who soon turned it over to Kim Jinui. After a short time, Jinui died of cancer in 2006, aged 57. Ernest Robinson became the Overseer in 2013.

Kison Ko was the first native Korean to enter the Work in 1960. The first Convention was held on a Friend's property at Sampori, Youngam, around 1969–1970; the second was held on Wando Island in the early 1970s. In 2006, the ratio of Workers was 85% native and 15% foreign. South Korea has exported many Workers around the world. The first native Worker to venture to another country was Lee Jungho in Taiwan.

North Korea. No Workers have been known to go there. A few Workers born in North Korea fled to the South in the War as children with their parents and met Workers there.

Japan. Comprised of about 6,852 islands, Japan has five main islands. The capital, Tokyo, is on the largest island, Honshu. Containing about 146,000 square miles, Japan is about the size of California. Religion in Japan manifests primarily in Shinto and Buddhism, with some ancestor worship.

Canadian Brother Workers Robert "Bert" Middleton and Ernest Davis pioneered Japan in 1926. Sam Lang was in Japan from 1929 with Ernest Stanley, then he returned in 1937 with Cecil Barrett (also from New Zealand). After three years, Barrett could speak and understand the Japanese language—no small accomplishment. WWII started, and the workers evacuated to the Philippines in December 1940, without making any converts. Sam Lang married Mitsuko, a local, in 1940 and stayed in Japan during the war.

After World War II, Cecil Barrett returned to Japan in 1947 with Ernest Stanley when all missionaries were invited to do so. Later that year, two portable halls and two Workers from Canada arrived. In 1948, the first post-War Gospel Meetings were held in Tokyo and Yokohama; five converts were made. A widow woman offered her home for the first Sunday Meeting, where they squatted on the floor, kneeled to pray and stood up for testimonies.

Tatsuo Asaka was one of the first natives to enter the Work around 1951. In 1957, Cliff Wells and Richard Sullivan pioneered Okinawa, the fifth largest island. In 1965, lists showed three Conventions, thirty-six Workers (five native Sisters and three native Brothers).

Southeast Asia

Thailand. After WWII, Ralph Joll (from New Zealand) arrived in 1954–1956. Reports differ as to who accompanied him: Ray Jamieson (from

US) or Edgar Bell (from Australia). Gwen Pampling (from Australia) went in 1961 as one of the pioneering Sisters. Merle Schulz (from Australia) arrived in 1965. The Thai people have been very slow to accept the Workers' doctrine; most are Buddhists. Alex Mitchell was the Overseer from about 1936–1974.

South Vietnam. The conflict between North and South Vietnam began in 1955. During 1957–1959 Fred Allen (from Australia) and Maurice Archer (from New Zealand) pioneered Vietnam. Their first Gospel Mission was held in their bach (temporary accommodations) in Saigon in 1958. The first two Sister Workers, Bonnie Dahlin and Phyllis Munn (from US), came in late 1959. Edwin Allen (Fred's brother) arrived in 1961. Working under Overseer Alex Mitchell, Fred Allen was responsible for Vietnam from 1957 to 1975.

The first major deployment of US troops, 3,500 Marines, arrived in Da Nang, Vietnam, on March 8, 1965. The US remained fully engaged in the conflict until Saigon fell on April 30, 1975. During the Vietnam War, many 2x2 servicemen visited Allen, the Vietnamese Friends, Fellowship Meetings and Conventions.

The first to profess were two single men, Nguyễn Thanh Hoa and Vu Ngoc Châu, in June 1961 in Saigon; both were 21 years old. In 1967, they were the first natives to enter the Work. In late 1961, Mr. and Mrs. Nguyễn Huu Bau were the first married couple to profess. The first native Sister Worker was Ho Thu Anh in 1973.

When Communist occupation of South Vietnam began in 1975, all the foreign Workers evacuated, and left the two native Vietnamese Brother Workers, Hoa and Châu, in charge for about 20 years.

After the country reopened in the late 1990s, Canadian Workers arrived, took control of the Work, made changes and began implementing Western rules and traditions. This did not go over well with many of the Friends and resulted in a split. Around 2010, preferring the methods and instructions of the first Workers, about half the Vietnam Friends and Brother Worker Hoa began holding separate Meetings and missions, continuing as before, in the Golden Time (1956–1975). They called themselves the *Golden Friends. See* further details on the website *TellingTheTruth.info* in History, Divisions. *See also* Chapter 48.

Malaya – Malaysia. Malaya achieved independence on August 31, 1957. On September 16, 1963, the independent Federation of Malaysia was formed following the merger of the Federation of Malaya, Singapore, Sarawak and North Borneo (Sabah).

In 1932, Lindsay Stratford and Bert Cameron (from Australia) were the first Workers to arrive. Arthur Shearer (from Australia) arrived in

1937 and Archie Wilson (from New Zealand) in 1940. When the Japanese invaded Malaya in January 1942, Lindsay Stratford was in Singapore. He attempted to escape by ship, but unfortunately, the ship was sunk and those on board were presumed drowned.

After WWII, Workers from Australia and New Zealand resumed the Work in Malaya. Edgar Bell, Dan McNab and Norma Loechel arrived in 1946. The following year Archie Wilson, Arthur Lomas and Daphne Bonney arrived. Fred Allen was there from 1954 to 1957.

Singapore. Singapore was a British colony until the Japanese conquered and occupied it from 1942 to 1945. After WWII, Singapore reverted to British control. In 1963, it merged with the Federation of Malaya to form Malaysia. Then on August 9, 1965, Singapore gained its independence.

During 1936–1937, Alex Mitchell (from Scotland/New Zealand) and Arthur Shearer pioneered Singapore. Mitchell spent the rest of his days in the Work there. He was the Overseer of Singapore, Malaysia, Borneo, Thailand and Vietnam from about 1936–1974. Arthur Shearer, Archie Wilson, Alex Mitchell and later Bert Cameron were interned by the Japanese in Changi Camp, Singapore, from 1942 to 1945.

Indonesia (formerly Dutch East Indies). In 1929, the Workers pioneered Java, one of the largest five Indonesian Islands. They were George Absalom (from South Africa) and James Bird (formerly of Dutch East Indies). Willem Boshoff (from South Africa) arrived in 1939. During WWII from April 14, 1942, Boshoff was interned in Java by the Japanese, along with his Co-worker, Bernard Frommolt, two Dutch Sister Workers, Gertie Maree and Esther Loots (and some Friends), until December 31, 1945. Boshoff was able to witness to some prison inmates and some professed.

After the War, Boshoff returned to Indonesia from 1948 to 1963. Joshua Van Ysseldyke (from Holland) preached in Indonesia from 1950 to 1962 when he left due to immigration issues. Later, he returned and was Overseer from 1970 until his death in 1990.

Philippines. The first two Workers, Howard Ioerger and Hubert Sylvester, went to the Philippines in September 1936. They held English Gospel Missions in Cavite City; Dorotea Mangila was their first convert. After about 15 adults had converted, Fellowship Meetings were established in late 1937. The first baptism occurred in 1938.

After a home visit to the US in 1939, Willie Jamieson was refused admission to Shanghai; instead, he travelled to the Philippines. In December 1940, Sam Lang and Cecil Barrett left Japan for the Philippines.

Japan attacked the Philippines on December 8, 1941, the same day as its raid on Pearl Harbor. In 1942, Jamieson, along with Brother Workers Leo Stancliff, Herman Beaber and Cecil Barrett were interned at Los Baños Internment Camp, south of Manila, from January 6, 1942, to February 23, 1945. Ernest Stanley remained as an interpreter at Santo Tomás Internment Camp in Manilla. *Read* each of their accounts and about their spectacular rescue on website *ithascome.bravehost.com.*

After WWII, the first Sister Workers, May Sylvester and Bernice Beaber, arrived in 1946. Dan McNab (from Australia) spent some time in Sabah and the Philippines. Conchita Sansano was the first Filipina Sister to enter the Work in 1950; Simeon Sarmiento was the first Filipino Brother in 1957.

South Asia

In the early 1920s, there was a strong British presence in India with a significant English-speaking Anglo-Indian population. Among these, the first Workers had good response without having to overcome the language barrier.

Syd Maynard and Adam Hutchison
Hutchison pioneered Asia (India). Maynard succeeded him as Overseer

India. In late 1921–1922, Adam Hutchison (age 49) sailed from Australia to Madras, India, the fourth largest country in the world. He was the very first Worker to preach on the continent of Asia. Colin Watt (from Australia) joined him. Later that year, Sandy Maxwell (from Scotland) and Ben Buys (from South Africa) connected with Hutchison and Watt. They went to Allahabad where Maxwell had previously been stationed with his regiment. For about six months in 1923, they held Gospel Missions in various places. Nine people attended their first Meeting and five people professed.

The first Special Meeting in India took place in Allahabad in October 1924 with five Friends and seven Brother Workers. In June 1925, Sydney Maynard, Stanley Berriman and Tom Beattie (from Australia) arrived. In October 1925, the first Sister Workers appeared: Teenie Walker (from

New Zealand), with Gertie Barendilla and Doreen McKenzie (from South Africa).

Pioneers to India: Ben Buys, Willie Clark, Arthur Arnold, Colin Watt

India's first Convention and baptism were held in the Nicoll home at Allahabad in November 1925. Subsequent Conventions were held in Delhi during 1926–1937.

After Adam Hutchison passed away in 1925, aged 51, Syd Maynard took his place as Overseer of India. After Maynard passed away in 1954, the oversight went to two Australians, Reg Stratford over South India and Percy Hill over North India.

After WWII, when the British rule ended on August 15, 1947, India and Pakistan became independent dominions within the Commonwealth. The subcontinent was partitioned along religious lines into two separate countries: The Republic of India, with a majority of Hindus, and the Republic of Pakistan, with a majority of Muslims. After the "Partition," around two million people fled from their homes to areas of Pakistan or India where they would not be a minority. Many immigrated to other countries; violence continued for some time. Some Anglo-Indian Friends escaped to Australia, where the Friends welcomed and aided them. This was a serious setback for the Work and Workers in India.

Sri Lanka (formerly Ceylon). Ceylon gained its independence from Britain in 1948. The name changed to Sri Lanka when it became a republic within the Commonwealth in 1972. The first Brother Workers who entered Ceylon in 1927 were Alex Mitchell (from Scotland/New Zealand) and John "Jack" Trigg (from Australia). Mitchell remained there from 1927 to 1936; Trigg for about 20 years. He was expelled from the Work for child sexual molestation. The first Sister Worker, Alice Morris (from Australia), arrived in 1928 and continued preaching there until her death in 1962. Arthur Shearer (from Australia) preached in Sri Lanka from 1929 to 1937.

Harry Morgan and Clem Geue (from Australia) went to Sri Lanka in 1937. After WWII, Shearer had the oversight from 1946 to 1973, succeeded by Morgan until his death in 1988, followed by John Blair (from New Zealand). Around 2014, Peter Morrison (from Australia) became the Overseer.

The first native to enter the Work was Lucian Garth in 1938. The first Convention was held at Nugegoda from about 1973 to 2013. Since then, Conventions have been held in a rented facility in Arunodhaya, Athurugiriya. Around 2016–2017 a crisis in the church occurred. *See* Chapter 48; *See also* details on website *TellingTheTruth.info* in History, Divisions.

Bangladesh. The War in East Pakistan in 1971 led to the formation of Bangladesh, where the language is Bengali (aka Bangla). In 1990, David Rundle and John Watt (from New Zealand), were the first Workers to go there. The first two Sister Workers arrived in 2000: Adele Jeske (from US) and Fiona Muirhead (from New Zealand). Conventions have been held in a rented facility at Dhaka, the capital, with an estimated 50–60 attendees.

Burma (now Myanmar). Located near India in Southeast Asia, this British colony was part of the British Empire of India from 1824 to 1937. In November 1924, the first Workers, Adam Hutchison and Alex Leadbetter, entered Burma and commenced Gospel Meetings in Insein. Not long after, Hutchison contracted and died of smallpox in January 1925, aged 51. Unfortunately, he had not been vaccinated for smallpox, the sect then believing that God protected the Workers' health.

Alex Leadbetter went to India and then to Burma in 1926 with Stan Berriman (from Australia). When Leadbetter was unable to continue, Nelson Retchford joined Berriman in January 1927. The first Sister Workers, Cora Bailey and Doreen Blair (from Australia), arrived around 1927–1928. In January 1929, Tom Montieth (from New Zealand) and Ron Schilling, Una Hedderman and Muriel Paynter (from Australia) arrived. A small Convention in Burma was held in November 1929. After WWII, in 1947, Berriman with Maurice Bowyer (both from Australia) returned.

During World War II, Burma was an extremely violent theater of conflict. In early 1942, Nelson Retchford and Percy Attwood, the only Workers left in Burma, escaped from the Japanese Armed Forces to India on the last plane out of the country. Many of the Friends evacuated; some immigrated to India and others to Australia.

For over 50 years afterwards, the government would not allow the Workers to stay in Burma permanently. Workers from India and Thailand visited the sizeable group of Friends that remained. A young Burmese lady started in the Work in Cambodia. Around 1980, the political situation changed, and Workers commenced holding Meetings openly. In 2014, the first Convention was held.

Central – Western Asia

Kazakhstan. Formerly part of the USSR, Kazakhstan is a transcontinental country mainly located in Central Asia. It is the ninth largest country in the world, with a population of about 19 million. In 1990, the pioneering Workers, Dale Benjamin (from US, formerly preaching in Korea) and Pahk Chansun, arrived and worked among the large ethnic Korean community there. By 1994, four Sister Workers had arrived. Their first Convention was held in August 1994. An Australian Worker, Ian Rowe, has spent several years there since the early 1990s.

Armenia. Little is known about Armenia. Workers from Romania, Switzerland, UK and the US have worked there. Eric Culbert worked there alone, before Teo Bocancea from Romania joined him. Culbert left Armenia to become Overseer of Greece in 2005.

Middle East

Palestine – Israel. William Irvine arrived in Jerusalem on November 27, 1919. It is not known who the first Worker was to preach in this region. Willie Brown preached in Egypt as early as 1932 and worked some in this region also. Some were converted, including an elderly rabbi in Jerusalem. During 1967–1970, Donald Karnes was in Jerusalem with Eric Thompson and Harold McKnight.

Later, Harry Woodley (from England, who professed in Egypt and worked for years in West Africa) and Hans Müller (from Germany) arrived. They had some converts who went in the Work but did not continue. For several years afterwards, the Work was sporadic until Bernard Manning and a young Greek Brother went there in the 1990s.

Sister Worker Geri Weiner (Jewish by birth, from Ohio, US) and various Co-workers have preached there. While a college student in Israel, Weiner first listened to Workers in the early 1970s; after she returned to the US, she converted. Other American Sister Workers have preached there also.

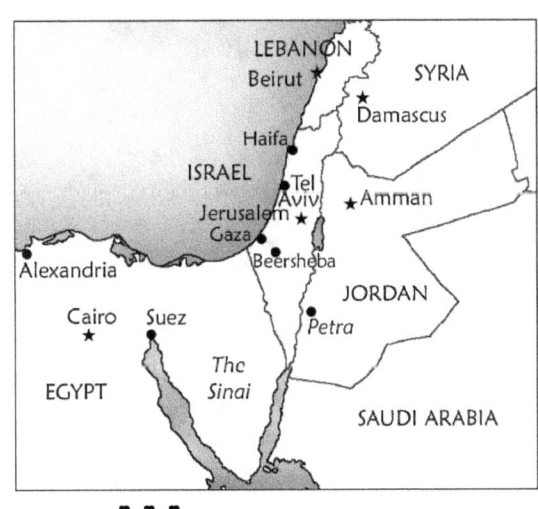

The

Middle

East

Europe

1. Northern Ireland (UK)
2. Slovenia
3. Montenegro
4. Kosovo
5. N. Macedonia
6. Albania
7. Corsica (France)
8. Sardinia (Italy)
9. Sicily (Italy)
10. Crete (Greece)

45

Europe

The continent of Europe covers about 3,930,000 square miles (10,180,000 km), 6.8% of Earth's land area. Politically, Europe is divided into about fifty sovereign states, of which Russia is the largest and most populous. Total population in 2021 was more than 748 million, or about 10% of the world's population.

Regrettably, the pioneering Work in Europe is inadequately covered in this chapter. Many European countries were not overlooked—there just was no available information.

Very few early Workers would have learned a foreign language in school, as attendance was compulsory only for children up to age ten years in 1900. Therefore, the early Workers pioneering missionary trips were made to English-speaking countries. With the language barriers, they were slow to cross the English Channel to Europe and proselytize there; then WWI made it impossible. So it was not until the early 1920s after the War that a few Workers began venturing to Europe.

The following paragraphs briefly address the Workers' initial outreach prior to 1940. *See* Appendix L Pioneers of Various Countries.

European Overseers Meeting in Luxemburg, 2005

FRONT ROW L-R: Tommie Gamble (Ireland), Eldon Knudson (Sweden originally Canada), David Butterworth (Italy originally England), Werner Leonhardt(Germany), Graham Snow (Holland originally New Zealand), Lars Lund (Norway originally Denmark).
MIDDLE ROW L-R: Bob Kerr (Scotland), John Johnston (Rumania originally Ireland), Peter Liddle (France originally England), Dan Sherrick (Ukraine originally USA), Loran Skaw (Poland originally USA), Erik Lund (Denmark), John Gunn (Spain originally Scotland), Eric Culbert (Greece originally England).
BACK ROW L-R: Dale Benjamin (Russia originally USA), Peter Zurcher (Czech/Austria originally Switz), Ben Crompton (England), Stefan Sorrenson (Finland originally USA), Hansruedi Fehr (Switzerland)

In sharp contrast to many countries, the Friends and Workers in Europe drink alcoholic beverages, both wine and beer. In Italy, wine was served with the noon meal at Special Meetings; beer is consumed in Germany. After visiting some Friend's homes in Europe, a Canadian Ex-Worker remarked that "the same God obviously had given completely different guidelines to different messengers in different lands ... After all, had I not sat around tables in France, in Italy, or in Germany and Greece while the Workers uncorked the bottles of wine and, after helping themselves to a sip or two, passed them around in order that the rest of us could fill our goblets as well? I had" (Young 2000, 9:260–261, *TTT*).

Reportedly, the Workers hold an annual international European Workers Meeting; for a time, it was held in Luxembourg. Whether the European Workers are uniform in their handling of divorced and remarried Friends is not known.

Western Europe

France. John Baillie and Harry Dennison from the UK arrived in 1908 but left before WWI. Baillie returned after the War with Ray Bonds (from US) who had been a soldier in France during the War. Kitty Westerby and Dorothy Brown were the first Sister Workers to arrive.

Belgium. The first Workers to hold missions in Belgium were Joe Hogan and Jim Chapman in 1928. Belgium Workers are included with the French staff.

Netherlands (aka Holland). The first two Brother Workers arrived in the Netherlands in 1923. They were Frank van der Merwe (from South Africa) and Willie Smeenk (from US, originally from Holland). Around 1924, G. Gerritsen and his daughter from South Africa came to Apeldoorn to provide an open home for the Workers. Sister Workers, May Lund, Bernice and Eunice Jelliman and Matilda Smeenk, (sister of Willie Smeenk) soon arrived. About 40 attended the first Convention held in Apeldoorn in 1926.

Northern Europe – Scandinavia

Norway. It is unknown when the Workers first went to Norway. Edith Hanson (from Oregon) went to Sweden with her brother J. Henry Hanson in 1920. The earliest Workers List for Norway located thus far (1924–1925) shows 13 Workers in Norway. Edith Hanson and Alma Lee were arrested in Norway on October 14, 1942, and were incarcerated there and in Germany during WWII.

Sweden. August Gustafson (1873–1970), probably of Norwegian descent, was the first. In 1899, when he was 25, he began independently preaching according to Matthew 10. After meeting the Workers, he joined them in the Work. Some other Workers went there in 1910–1911.

The 1912 UK Workers List for Sweden shows August Gustafson, Bob Skerritt, Edgar Carlson/Karlsson, Edith Eklund and Esther Hanson. The expenditure records for the July 1913 Crocknacrieve Convention showed: "Cash to Workers – Sweden £28." After WWI, the 1919–1920 North and South American Workers List showed T. Larson and R. Carlson in Sweden. The 1923–1924 list contained 20 Workers in Scandinavia.

In 1992, the church was incorporated under the name of *Christians in Sweden*. The attendance record of its first board meeting was signed by the Senior Worker in Sweden and other Workers, including Edgar Massey, who stated he had not been present, did not sign the document and had no knowledge of it until much later (Massey, 1992, item 3).

Finland. Possibly Adolph Pearson was the first Worker to arrive in 1920. The earliest Finland Workers List located to date (1924–1925) shows four Workers: Adolph Pearson and August Karlson (both from Sweden); and Edith Hanson and Hilda Halberg (both from US). Emil Kelto (born in US) entered the Canadian Work in 1923 and went to Finland in the late 1920s. As Kelto's parents were from Finland, he was fluent in Finnish.

Denmark. Workers first arrived in 1920. Peter Svinth (from Denmark, professed in England) returned to preach to his countrymen. By 1924–1925, there were four pairs of Workers in Denmark. In 1925–1926, Svinth and Krisoffer Kristiansen (from Norway) pioneered the **Faroe Islands.**

Iceland. It is uncertain when a Worker first went to Iceland; however, Rasmus Prip spent several years there. Through the years, there have been up to three pairs of Workers at a time, then none. Only one native Icelander has professed. A 2x2 Irish couple lived there for a time.

Greenland. When Workers are laboring in Iceland and Greenland, they are shown on the Scandinavian Workers Lists. Rasmus Prip (born in 1896 in Denmark), professed in 1921 in Canada, went into the Work in 1923 in Saskatchewan. He was shown on the Denmark Workers List by 1929 and labored in all the Scandinavian countries except Finland. In WWII, at the time of the German occupation of Denmark, reportedly Prip spent the War years in Greenland and in the Danish dependencies. He was listed during 1964–1967 as laboring in Greenland without a companion.

Central Europe

Germany. Otto Schmidt (of German descent from South Australia) and James "Jim" Jardine (from Scotland/US) went to preach in Switzerland. The expenditure records for the July 1913 Crocknacrieve Convention showed: "Cash to Workers - Swiss £37." After three to four weeks, when the German-speaking part of Switzerland showed no interest in their message, they relocated to Germany. Since Jardine did not speak German, Schmidt did all the preaching in the early months.

The first few Gospel Meetings in Germany were held in February of 1914 in Lustnau, Württemberg. Mrs. Myer was the first convert; also, the Märkle family and several others professed. After about six months, the first Fellowship Meeting was held in Margereth Märkle's home in Lustnau. In May that year, the Brother Workers left to attend the English Conventions. WWI broke out and they did not return until after the War.

Schmidt returned to England where he preached for a few months and the Heath family professed. He helped start the Convention at Dimsdale Hall, Staffordshire, England, on the Heath's property. This was the site of the 1921 photo showing about 200 Workers. *See* Chapter 28. The Convention was later moved to the Stocks Farm also owned by the Heath family.

During WWI, having come from Germany and being of German stock, Schmidt and Jardine were not welcome (or safe) in England. They went to Wisconsin, US, and preached among a German community there.

After WWI, Schmidt and Heinrich Grefe (laboring in the US) went to Germany and preached to Grefe's relatives. James Jardine also returned. In Germany, they discovered the earlier church had faithfully continued. Some months later, Schmidt's health broke down. After about six months in a German hospital, he went to recuperate at the Heath's home in England. He regained his health and married Sarah Jane Heath in 1927. They moved to Mildura, Australia, in 1928.

The Brother Workers in 1922–1923 were: J. Jardine, H. Grefe, F. Hanowell, A. Scharmen, W. Kleme, plus the first two Sisters Workers, Anna Stuhr and Henrietta Schildt (both from US, of German descent). The first native to enter the Work was Ella Gerisch. In South Germany, the first Convention was held in Urach; in North Germany, the Convention was held at Berlin-Borsigwalde. The 1924 German Workers List shows five pairs of Brothers and three pairs of Sisters. From the start, James Jardine was the Overseer. Other Overseers have been Werner Leonhardt followed by Graham Snow.

Poland. After WWI in 1918, Poland regained its independence as the Second Polish Republic. World War II began in Europe on September 1,

1939, when Germany invaded Poland. After WWII from 1945 to 1989, Poland was under Communist rule.

Tom Alexson (born in Ukraine, professed in Canada) and Jack Annand (from Australia) were possibly the first Workers to go there in 1926. Willie Evanov (born in Ukraine, professed in the US) and Carl Leonhardt (from Canada) arrived in 1927.

During Bert Todhunter's years in Austria, there was a relatively large group of Workers. Most of them learned various languages and were able to make rotating visits in and out of the countries then under Communism, including Poland. Outside Workers might visit Poland for a few weeks at a time when they were unable to obtain visas. Shortly after the War started, Mila Gargas (from Poland), started in the Work with a Swiss Co-worker. For the most part, Mila and Brother Worker Eduard Podgorski (from Poland) were the only Workers there for over 20 years during the Communist regime. Podgorski labored in Poland for over 50 years.

Czech Republic. Czechoslovakia existed from 1918 until 1993, when it peacefully split into the Czech Republic and Slovakia. Tom Alexson and Jack Annand (from Australia) arrived there in 1926. During the interwar period, a number of Workers in East Central and Eastern European countries, e.g. Czechoslovakia, Poland, Latvia and Lithuania worked together as a group. Following WWII, some Workers to go there were: Vasyl "Willie" Evanov (born in Ukraine, professed in US); Carl Leonhardt (from Canada); and Willie MacDonald, Frank Patrick, Bert Todhunter, all from Scotland. The Convention is held at Rohozna. Currently, Czech, Austria and Hungary work as one group where Peter Zürcher (from Switzerland) is the Overseer.

Slovakia. During the 1990s, Richard Davis (from US) and Jurjen Pettinga (from Netherlands) preached in Slovakia for several years with no results.

Hungary. Jim Jardine left Germany to pioneer Hungary. Possibly Alex Secker preached there in the interwar years. As children, Alex Secker and his sister Lena (born in Hungary) immigrated to the US with their parents. The two siblings entered the Work in 1926 and 1920, respectively. Reportedly, in 1930, Lena Secker was the first Sister Worker to labor in Hungary. A number of people converted. With the onset of WWII, when her Co-worker had to leave, Lena renewed her citizenship and stayed there until she died in 1957. Hungary, Czech and Austria work as one group where Peter Zürcher (from Switzerland) is the Overseer.

Austria. World War I began in 1914 after the assassination of the Archduke Franz Ferdinand, heir presumptive to the Austro-Hungarian throne, and his wife, Sophie. His murder catapulted into a War across Europe that lasted until 1918.

Arnold Scharmen and Gustav Ege arrived in Austria in 1931. The first Sister Workers were Irene Zahorkia and Bertha Schmidt (from US) in 1935. The first Convention was held in 1935 in St. Johann, Kitzbühel in a knitting factory owned by Sigi Scheiber. After WWII, in 1949, Irene Zahorkia (from Wisconsin) returned to Austria with Alwilda Watkins (from Michigan).

When WWII broke out, Bert Todhunter was in Switzerland where he was trapped for the duration of the War. Afterwards, he was the Austrian Overseer until late in his life when he returned to Britain and died in 2008, aged 102. Loran Skaw took his place. Austria, Czech and Hungary work as one group where Peter Zürcher (from Switzerland) is the Overseer.

Switzerland. The four main languages spoken in Switzerland are Italian, German, French and English. The main language of the Northern half is German; their two Conventions are spoken in German. French is the main language of the Southwestern section. One-eighth of the population speaks Italian. There is an Italian Sunday Fellowship Meeting in Ticino.

The earliest recorded mention of a Worker preaching in Switzerland was Penny Barton. Concerning the speakers at the 1914 Crocknacrieve Convention, the *Impartial Reporter* newspaper noted, "Two preachers, one of whom is Miss Barton, Pettigo, have lately returned from North Italy and Switzerland." Previously, newspaper accounts for July 1908 and 1909 reported Penelope "Penny" Barton was a speaker at the Convention. However, her name did not come up again until 1914 after she had returned from North Italy and Switzerland (July 9, 1914, 8). Possibly she was preaching in Italy and Switzerland from 1910 to 1914. Barton's Co-worker was Maggie Johnston.

After WWI, around 1925–1926, the first Workers to go to Switzerland for an extended mission were Edwin Schaer (from US, of Swiss descent); Katie Hay (from Canada); and George and Lottie Wix (siblings from New Zealand). Both Sister Workers died in Switzerland—Katie in 1955 and Lottie in 1975. George preached in Germany in 1925 and then went back to Switzerland in 1927, where he continued until his death in 1956.

Edwin Schaer was the first Switzerland Overseer until his death in the 1960s He was succeeded by Paul Schluep, Willy Geiser, Graham Snow and Hansruedi Fehr. All were native-born Swiss except for Snow (from New Zealand).

The first Switzerland Convention convened in a school in Bern. After that, Conventions were held for many years in a tiny hamlet called

Hämlismatt, near the village of Biglen, before moving to its current location at Wahlendorf. Later, another Convention was started at Stilli and moved to Villigen, where it is located presently. Both of these Conventions are German-speaking. The French-speaking Convention started at Nyon and moved to Donneloye, where they continue to this day. Some Swiss Workers attend the Conventions in Italy, and some Italian Workers attend the Switzerland Conventions.

Southeastern Europe

Romania. The Romanian Socialist Republic was under Communist rule from 1947 to December 1989. Ceauşescu's regime was from 1965 to 1989. Before WWII, no Workers were known to have preached in Romania.

In 1964, Richard Davis (from US, laboring in the Netherlands) was the first Worker to visit Romania. The first Sister Workers arrived from Austria the following year. They were Maria Hartig (born in Romania, lived in Austria, immigrated to US) and Ruth Christian (from Australia). Davis returned in 1968 with Jim Wood (from US). Other Workers arrived under tourist visas.

The first Workers discovered a family with seven children in Sibiu meeting in their home on Sundays studying the Bible. The father and children embraced the Workers' Gospel Message. Under Communist rule, Romanians were not allowed to have formal meetings. The Workers spread their Gospel message through visits in various places, sometimes in the woods, by a river, etc.

Around 1973, a new Romanian law restricted Romanian citizens from hosting foreigners. Davis discovered the Workers could remain in the country as registered university students. Davis and Loran Skaw were the first Workers granted student visas. Subsequently, several foreign Workers attended university year after year, some stretching out their studies by failing classes or obtaining secondary degrees.

In the summer of 1979, some Friends and Workers took a hike into a remote mountain area on a "camping trip" (a Convention). These summer camps were repeated the following years with more Friends rotating in and out; some were very secretly baptized.

By the time Communism fell in 1989, there was a well-established group of Friends and four foreign Workers. One of the seven children from Sibiu, Teo Bocancea, along with Viorel Carcu and Vergi Handaric were the first Romanians to give up their jobs and become full-time Workers. In recent years, Romania has been sending out a large number of Workers to other countries.

During the Communist years, Romania was under guidance of Bert Todhunter in Austria. Later, Glen Watkins (from US, laboring in Italy) became the first Romanian Overseer. John Johnston succeeded him. Currently, there are two small Conventions held near Sibiu.

Moldova. Attached to the Work in Romania, the two countries share a common language. One Moldovan Sister Worker labors in Romania.

Southern Europe

Greece, Crete, et al. Crete became part of Greece in December 1913. The Work in Greece also includes Armenia, Cyprus, Albania, Lebanon, Israel, Jordan and the republics that were formerly Yugoslavia (Bosnia, Croatia, Macedonia, Montenegro, Serbia and Slovenia). Eric Culbert, who formerly labored in Armenia, became Overseer of Greece in 2005.

John Micheletos was born in Crete around 1880 and immigrated to Canada when he was 17. He professed around 1910–1911 through Annie McBride and Sue Pattison (both from Ireland). McBride professed through Ed Cooney in Belfast and went in the Work in 1904.

Micheletos entered the Work in 1912 and wanted to spend his life preaching to people in his homeland. Because of the total control of the Greek Orthodox Church, it seemed impossible to go without a Greek male Co-worker, but none was available. After WWI, times in Greece were difficult with a lot of internal political turmoil in the country. When he discussed the situation with Annie McBride, she (almost 20 years his senior) offered to marry and accompany him to Greece. Many attempted to discourage them; regardless, they were married in 1917.

After WWI ended, they departed from Canada for Greece in 1920, via Ireland and England. The 2x2 Friends in those countries supported them during the difficult years when there were no converts in Greece. They went to Athens, then to Crete to visit Micheletos' family while Annie learned Greek (E. V. Vaassiliou, Introduction, January 1986, *TTT*). In 1924, Theodosios "Theo" Karvounakis (a Greek from Australia) and Fred Quick (from Australia) joined them.

Around 1964, Micheletos came home to Canada for his first home visit in 44 years. Annie passed away in Hania, Crete, in 1944. While in Canada, he had a heart attack and was cared for by some Friends who were nurses. Micheletos had been in prison many times for proselytizing, and the nurses witnessed his many stripes from beatings he suffered. Micheletos returned to Greece and died in Athens in 1966.

Greece Split. Overseer Nikolas Papadakis was removed in 1985. A division resulted. Papadakis and a few other loyal members formed a splinter group. After Papadakis' death, the fissure was mended, and the Friends and Workers were reunited. *See* details in Chapter 48.

Italy. Upon their return from Italy and Switzerland where they had been pioneering the Work, Penny Barton and Maggie Johnson attended the 1913 Crocknacrieve Convention (*Impartial Reporter,* July 9, 1914, 8). The exact year Brother Workers first went to Italy is unknown. Alexander "Sandy" Scott from Scotland was of the first. He entered the Work in 1909 and preached in Scotland, US and Canada. After WWII, by 1924 at the latest, he and Robert Marshall were preaching in Italy; Scott was the Overseer.

By 1929, the Italian staff had grown to eight Workers: Sandy Scott, Virgil Simpson, Peter McKeever, Sam Dawson, Edwin Mills and Reg Beer; and two Sisters, Sadie Marshall and Florrie List. The first eight Italians to profess lived in Picciano where the first Convention was held and continued for 44 years.

After WWII, Florrie List and Lucy Hiscock returned to Italy and preached there for as long as they were able. In 1948, Sandy Scott and Reg Beer had a mission in the mountain village of Carema, Torino, North Italy, where several women converted. Sister Workers Edna Powell (from Canada) and Virginia Micheletti (of Italian descent from US) arrived to help establish the women. A Convention was held in Carema, Italy.

Reportedly, Scott thought a married missionary couple (rather than two single men) would be more easily accepted in Italian villages. So, on October 28, 1954, Sandy Scott married Eva Idso, an American Sister Worker who went to labor in Italy in 1952. Eva was 40; Sandy was 68. Earlier, Scott had professed in one of Eva's Gospel Missions in Canada. By that time, the rule had been enacted that Overseers could not be married, so Scott stepped down and Sam Dawson became the Italian Overseer.

Spain. In 1933, Sandy Scott and Otto Kemich were the first Workers to pioneer Spain. Scott was probably working both Italy and Spain at the same time. In 1939, the Spanish Civil War broke out and many fled, including the Workers. The Francoist totalitarian dictatorship of Spain began in 1939. After Francisco Franco's death in 1975, Spain transitioned into a democracy.

In the 1950s, some government reforms permitted those of Spanish origin to enter Spain. So, Basilio Alvarez (born in Spain, entered the Work in Argentina in 1924) went there to preach in 1951. He was frequently abused for not being a member of the official state church (Roman Catholic). The first Sister Workers to enter Spain may have been Carmen Meana (from Spain); Cándida Rodríguez and Nélida Romera (both from Argentina) arrived in 1954. There have been a number of native-born Spanish Workers.

The years of persecution during Franco's dictatorship made large gatherings impossible. The Friends and Workers gathered discreetly in parks for fellowship. Barcelona has always been the center of the Work in Spain and the site of the first Convention (sometime after 1985).

Portugal. While Workers from Spain went into Portugal occasionally through the years, no converts were made. In the mid-1980s, Carl Schupbach and Elpídio Arruda arrived from Brazil which was a colony of Portugal before its independence. Portuguese is the chief language of Brazilians. A few other Brazilian Brother Workers also came and had missions with no results. In 1986, Neri Mendonça unexpectedly died there in his sleep, aged 47. Thus, a Worker was already dead and buried in Portugal before any converts were made.

In 1995, Portugal began to be shown on the Workers List with Spain; the two countries are worked as one field. Two pairs of Workers are usually assigned to Portugal; their fields include some border areas of Spain. The first Convention was held at Lisboa in 2005. Overseers have been Sandy Scott, Basilio Alvarez, Omar de Abreu (from Uruguay) and John Gunn.

Eastern Europe

Between the wars, various Workers moved around in the East Central and Eastern European countries of Latvia, Lithuania, Poland and Czechoslovakia as permitted by their visas. Currently, the Work in the former USSR is shared among a group of Workers from all over the world—Netherlands, Italy, Korea, US, Canada, Australia and several other countries. Several natives from these countries have entered the Work. Conventions are held in Latvia, Russia, Belarus and Kazakhstan.

Estonia. The Soviet Union recognized the independence of Estonia on September 6, 1991. It is doubtful there were any Workers there in pre-Communist times. Since it is just a short boat ride across the water, Estonia has been worked mostly from Finland. The Estonian and Finnish languages are closely related. Possibly Larry Stephens (from Montana, US) arrived in 2005.

Latvia. Jack Craig (from New Zealand) and Carl Leonhardt (from Canada, of German descent) were the first Workers to go to Riga, Latvia and then to Russia before WWI. A church was formed in Riga in the interwar years. Some converts continued through the years of Communism and received Worker visits when possible. When there was liberty to do so, the Riga area was used as a base to reach out to the former USSR regions. Most Workers in the former USSR get together each year at the Kegums, Latvia Convention. There are a number of Latvian Friends.

Lithuania. Re-established as a democratic state in 1918, Lithuania remained independent until the onset of WWII, when it was occupied by the Soviet Union. Workers were there during the interwar years. Born there in 1938, Ruta "Ruth" Sprogis and her family were deported to Siberia after the Russian takeover. She returned to Germany, professed in 1959 and went in the Work in 1962. Because she spoke both Lithuanian and Russian, she traveled to the Soviet Union as often as possible during the Communist years visiting the Friends and following new leads. Workers are now free to visit there.

Ukraine. In March 1925, Tom Alexson (a Ukranian who professed in Canada) and Jack Annand (from Australia) went to Zdolbuniv. The Gargas and Szenderovski families and Mr. Kameniuk were the first to convert and form a church. In the 1930s, Willie MacDonald and Bert Todhunter (both from Scotland) went to Western Ukraine under Polish occupation. When WWII broke out, MacDonald was trapped. He continued there alone until his death in 1957. Workers found a few converts from that time still alive when Ukraine reopened in the 1990s.

With the dissolution of the Soviet Union in 1991, Ukraine became an independent country. The returning Workers found a few faithful Friends. Currently, Ukraine has a large group of Workers, mostly American with several Ukrainian Brothers. They have several Conventions throughout the country. Dan Sherick (from US) is the Overseer (2022).

Russia (USSR). In 1917–1927, a radical transformation took place. The Russian Empire became the Soviet Union. Missionary work was punishable with imprisonment. A Russian Brother Worker, Konstantin Petrochuk, professed in Germany in the early 1920s. By the mid-1920s, he had returned to Russia alone where he worked in Leningrad and had some converts. As far we know, he was never able to leave the country again; it is not known if he survived WWII.

During the Communist years, Bernard Manning (from Australia), visited the USSR as often as possible from his field in Italy; he was the first Overseer. Dale Benjamin (from US) took his place.

Russian Far East (Northern Asia). Brother Workers from Japan were the first to go to this area. There are at least two pairs of Workers in the extreme Russian Far East (Vladivostok, Kamchatka, etc.). A Russian Sister Worker (of Korean extraction) is from that area. The Workers sometimes attend the Latvian Convention and usually travel to Japan for Convention. See Appendix L for Pioneers of Various Countries.

Africa

Showing largest countries

46

South Africa and Madagascar

The Republic of South Africa, situated at the southernmost tip of the continent of Africa, contains approximately 471,000 square miles, divided into nine provinces. The 2021 population of more than 60 million uses 11 official languages. It has three official capital cities, though Pretoria is considered the main one since the president and most embassies are there. The Parliament is in Cape Town, the Supreme Court is in Bloemfontein, and Johannesburg is by far the largest city. The Western Cape province is the most popular for tourism. In 1867, diamonds were discovered at Hopetown, Northern Cape, and in 1884, gold was discovered in Witwatersrand; both are still important industries.

By 1833, all slaves within the British Empire and Dominions, including South Africa, had been emancipated. White people were a minority, with the majority of the population being Africans (black people), colored people (mixed race) and Indians (from India). Although the native language of the white population was Dutch, about half spoke English. The Dutch language of South Africa diverged considerably from European Dutch to the point that it was declared a separate language by the government in 1925, called Afrikaans. Over the years, many Dutch Workers ventured to preach in South Africa.

First UK Workers to arrive in South Africa (1905)
Alex Pearce; Joe Kerr, John Sullivan, John Cavanagh; John Cavanagh;
Mary Moodie; Wilson Reid

1905: First Eight Workers Ventured to South Africa. The SS *Geelong* departed on August 25, 1905, from London headed for Australia via

Cape Town and arrived on September 17. The passenger list included Wilson Reid (24), Joe Kerr (24), Martha Skerritt (22) and Barbara Baxter (24) who disembarked at Capetown. Alex Pearce (29) and John Cavanagh (27) went ashore at Port Elizabeth; and Mary Moodie (38) and Lily Reid (26) traveled on to Durban.

Wilson Reid (1881–1968) and his sister, Isabella "Bella" (1884–1937), from Carnteel, Co. Tyrone, Ireland, professed in 1903 through Adam Hutchison. Wilson entered the Work in 1904 and Bella in 1905. After preaching a few years in England, Wilson went to South Africa. Soon after his arrival, he was deserted by his Co-worker (probably John Cavanagh, who returned to blacksmithing in King William's Town, South Africa). At night, Reid slept in the fields; during the day, he preached on street corners to those passing by, sang hymns and held open-air Meetings.

Carnteel schoolhouse where Wilson Reid (1881–1968) and his sister,
Isabella "Bella" (1884–1937), from Carnteel, Co. Tyrone, Ireland,
professed in 1902 through Adam Hutchison and John Breen

On his way home from work, Mr. Muller, an Irish white man of Dutch descent, stopped to listen to Reid and invited him to his home. Within three weeks, his wife, Mrs. Muller, a colored (mixed race) lady married to a white man (mixed marriage), professed; her husband soon followed suit. Mrs. Muller was the first person to profess on the continent of Africa. They hosted the first Fellowship Meeting in Africa in their home.

When the Workers first arrived, a great deal of racial prejudice and discrimination existed. People were strictly classified according to race: white, black, colored, Indians, etc. After a few Gospel Meetings in the Mullers' home, Reid, seeking to be more accommodating to listeners who might be racially prejudiced, suggested that Mrs. Muller refrain from attending his Gospel Meetings. He hoped that after some whites converted, they would gain a better understanding and fully accept Mrs. Muller.

Mr. and Mrs. Muller had one daughter, Nunnie, who had inherited the features and complexion of her white Dutch father. Having a colored mother, she was not fully accepted by whites or coloreds. Around 1950–1960, when Vernard Karstadt's health would not permit him to remain in the Work, Karstadt and Nunnie (age 56) married at Reid's suggestion. She passed away in 1995, aged 93. The couple moved to Freetown in Sierra Leone to provide an open home for the Workers. Unfortunately, an account reportedly written by Nunnie regarding the beginning of the Work in South Africa has not surfaced.

1906: Eight More UK Workers Arrived. Departing from London, England, on August 14, 1906, aboard the SS *Wakool* and arriving in Cape Town, South Africa, were four Brother Workers: Hugh McKay (27), James "Jim" Dunlop (24), Fred Alder (19), and John Golding (18); and four Sister Workers: Jean Allen (22), Nellie Taylor (25), Beatrice "Cissie" Maughan (19), and Edith Easy (20). Easy's father foiled her plans to go preach in America in 1905, due to her being a minor. So she preached in the UK until she turned 21, and then left with this group for South Africa (*Lloyd's Weekly,* Jan. 27, 1907, *TTT*). *See* Chapter 22.

Some UK Workers who arrived in 1906
Fred Alder and Jim Dunlop; Hugh McKay; Nellie Taylor and Jean Allen

1907: More Workers Arrived. Archibald "Archie" Russell and David Gibson departed from London on August 19, 1907, aboard the SS *Geelong* and arrived in Cape Town in September. Born November 4, 1879, in Scotland, Russell entered the Work in 1904 and preached until 1915. Reportedly, when he was a baby, he and his siblings were orphaned in the Tay Bridge disaster near Dundee, Scotland, on December 28, 1879, and were raised by their Grandmother Russell in Philipstown, Scotland.

Joe Kerr, a convert of Eddie Cooney, had arrived with the first batch of Workers in 1905. Born in 1881 in Wanlockhead, Dumfriesshire, Scotland, he grew up in the small village of Philipstown, Scotland, and entered the Work in 1902. The Kerrs lived next door to the Russell household; from their childhood, Archie Russell and Joe Kerr remained lifelong friends.

After his arrival in South Africa, Russell joined Kerr, and the pair traveled around the country preaching. They went to the Diamond Rush area in Kimberley, Northern Cape, thinking it would be a promising mission field.

They held Gospel Meetings in the home of the Koekemoer family who were of Dutch descent; the parents and their three daughters professed. Kerr and Russell spent several years in the area preaching in the open-air and holding in-house Gospel Meetings, and one night in jail for disturbing the peace. Eventually, they moved to Johannesburg, as did the Koekemoers, whose eldest daughter, Gladys, entered the Work and became Barbara Baxter's Co-worker.

After Fred Alder arrived in 1906, he and Reid went to the Kimberley Diamond Mine area and lodged with a miner. To pay their lodgings, they dug each morning till midday; in the afternoons they visited; in the evenings they held Gospel Meetings. Reid only had one pair of trousers. After washing them at 4:00 on Sunday mornings, he hung them on his pick head; within a couple hours, they were dry.

George Absalom, one of first native South Africans to become a Worker

While digging for diamonds, Wilson Reid met George Absalom. Eventually Absalom professed in 1908–1909 and became one of the first native South Africans to enter the Work. In 1910, a Convention was held in East London, South Africa. Alex Pearce and Fred Alder held a very successful Gospel Mission in Butterworth in the Eastern Cape Province during 1909–1910. *See* "Butterworth Mission Account" and photos on website *TellingTheTruth.info* in History, Pioneering, Africa.

Back row: Hugh McKay, Frank van der Merwe, Wilson Reid
Front row: Lottie and Lizzie English, Jean Allen, Minnie Skerritt, Alex Pearce

1912–1913: South African Workers List. After the 1912 Irish Conventions, a worldwide Workers List was prepared that showed the following Workers laboring in South Africa: Walter and Christina "Chrissie" McClung, George Humphries, Sarel Du Toit, Wilson Reid, Ben Baldwin, Fred Alder, Arthur Arnold, Alex Pearce, James Bird, James Dunlop, Hugh McKay, Archie Russell, Joe Kerr, George Absalom and Albert van Lingen; Eddie Barendilla and J. Temane (black); with Sister Workers: Nellie Taylor, Cissie Tregurtha, Mary Moodie, E. Johnson, Barbara Baxter, Gladys Koekemoer, May Lund and Jean Allen; Gertie Barendilla and K. Williams (black).

Overseers: Alex Pearce 1905–1946; Wilson Reid 1946–1968; Willie Clark 1968–1970; Fred Alder?; Jim Johnston 1970–1993; Louis van Dyk 2007–2008; Johan Kotze and Andy Robijn 2008—; and Johan Kotze— (Robijn went to pioneer Ethiopia).

Early Overseers of South Africa (no particular order)
Fred Alder and Wilson Reid; Jim Johnston;
Willie Clark, Alex Pearce and Willie Brown; Wilson Reid

Archie Russell (35) and Gladys Koekemoer (23) were married on February 3, 1915. It is not known whether they married and left the Work or were expelled. Russell worked for the South African Railways as a fitter and turner until he retired. They had three children; Russell died in the mid-1960s.

Joe Kerr and Barbara Baxter also married in 1915; they had three children. Barbara died in 1947, aged 64. Joe died in 1966, aged 85, in Cape Town where he had been Chief of the Traffic Department. Both the Kerrs and Russells joined the Plymouth Brethren Church after separating from the 2x2 Sect. Kerr is credited for being the Worker who first applied the Living Witness Doctrine theory to the 2x2 Ministry circa 1907. *See* Chapter 19.

No details have surfaced for why the Kerrs were expelled from the Work and excommunicated from the 2x2 Church. Possibly they did not seek Workers' approval to marry. Kerr explained to Irvine Weir in a letter: "[The Workers] sent the Saints who owned these things [beds, etc.] and took them from us and left us the floor to sleep on. They forbid any of the Saints to come near us ... the Workers have almost the same power over the so-called Saints as the priests have over their people ... Then I had not any trade and all the unskilled work is done out here by the coloured and native people. I took a Diploma in Motor Engineering and later a Diploma in Fire Engineering and then a Diploma in Traffic Engineering" (c. 1955, *TTT*).

Married Worker Couples in South Africa. Tom and Martha Kilpatrick, an Irish married couple, immigrated to South Africa where they met the Workers. The same year (1915), that the married Kerrs (and possibly the Russells) were put out of the Work and the 2x2 Church, the Kilpatricks were allowed to start in the Work as a married couple. Martha's grandmother raised their daughter, Elna, who was then about three years old. After Tom's death in 1959, Martha continued to preach another 20 years before she passed away in 1979.

Walter McClung (from Ireland) and his wife, Christina "Chrissie" (nee McLennan, from South Africa), were a married couple in the Work in South Africa by 1912–1913 at the latest. Walter was the brother of Wilson McClung, Overseer of South Australia and New Zealand (also a married Worker).

~~~~~

Segregation. Prior to 1948, South Africa enforced racial segregation, except for worship or religious gatherings. Congregations in most churches and religions could mix freely. By contrast, from their early days in South Africa, the Workers practiced racial segregation in their gatherings.

1948–1983: Apartheid – South African Independence. After the white-ruled South African Nationalist Party gained power in 1948, it immediately began enforcing harsh policies of racial segregation under a system of legislation called *apartheid* ("apartness" in Afrikaans). After 1948, attempts at religious separation of the races became a matter of public policy.

The Anglican bishops declared in 1957 that if the law segregated the churches, they would be bound in conscience to disobey (Historian Alan Paton). Several black South African theologians and clergymen came to international prominence for defying the apartheid creed, e.g. Archbishop Desmond Tutu.

~~~~~

Sheila (De Jager) Martin was born on December 14, 1947, in Cape Town to 2x2 parents born in the 1920s. She was colored, her grandparents being East Indian, Dutch, German and South African (colored). She professed at age 15 through Eddie Barendilla and immigrated to Canada in 1971, where she died of cancer in 2005, aged 57.

According to Martin, the Workers told the South African Friends that the law mandated that the white sector must sit apart from the others during Meetings. In truth, the 2x2 Sect was possibly the *only* Christian church in South Africa that openly practiced racism and supported segregation, except for the State Dutch Reformed Church.

The Friends and Workers entered their Convention hall by entry doors marked *Whites* and *Darkies*. Races were segregated by the middle aisle. The Workers were also divided by races. Families did not sit together (sexes were seated separately). The colored Workers stood and spoke from the back; only white Workers were allowed to speak from the platform. This practice continued until the early 1980s, when the colored Workers were finally allowed to speak from the platform, but not to sit on it or lead a Convention Meeting. Seeing the colored Friends on the streets, the white Friends often looked the other way. Martin elaborated further.

> The previous generation, our parents, were so conditioned into believing that this was part of our suffering for Christ, that they encouraged us to look past all this, and that someday the Lord would correct this problem as we all stood before the great white throne. Our parents said we had to put up with it because 'The way was perfect, but the people went wrong.' Jesus would one day make things right. And so, we professed and endured it because we did want to serve the Lord and be with Him one day.

> We were even told from the platform at Convention, that coloured people should be thankful that the white Workers made the sacrifice to save their souls, or else they would have missed salvation. The phrase often used was 'Know your place and keep it.' Our head Worker told someone that Jesus was a white man, and therefore, the authority should go to the white man. The abuse was terrible, but who is to blame? We allowed it to happen to us—for Jesus' sake. (personal communication, Martin 1998)

Eddie Barendilla and his sister, Gertie (colored), went into the Work when they were very young, possibly 17–18 years old. In 1925, Gertie Barendilla and Dora McKenzie (from South Africa) and Teenie Walker (New Zealand) were the first Sister Workers to preach in India.

In the 1950s, Eddie Barendilla vocally opposed segregation so strongly that the Workers shipped him off to the United States. The white Workers dreaded Barendilla's periodic home visits every five years to South Africa when his outspokenness regarding segregation created dissatisfaction and discontent among the black and colored Friends and Workers. The Workers were left with the task of restoring the peace after he departed for the US.

Eddie Barendilla and Ernest Prinsloo

1960s: Revolt of the 2x2 Black and Colored Elders. In the mid-1960s, a 2x2 black Elder personally checked with a government official and was assured that it was ***not*** the law that churches must be segregated. He was provided with a document containing the law then in effect. When he showed the document to the white Workers, none would read it. Reportedly, Brother Worker Fred Alder's reply was, "If people are not prepared to come into the fold on these conditions [segregated], they can stay outside and perish."

It seemed this was the last straw. The black and colored Elders revolted against the white Workers. Confusion reigned. Meetings were removed from some homes. Friends and Elders were excommunicated. For a time, there was utter chaos in the 2x2 churches in South Africa.

Sheila Martin's father was involved in the revolt. She recalled, "When I gave my testimony, people used to close their Bibles because I was born of the wrong spirit … one of the Workers approached me at the death of my father and told me that if my dad had still been involved in the revolt to the end of his life, he could not bury him."

Dimitri Tsafendas

"Rand Daily Mail," Johannesburg, South Africa (Sept. 8, 1966)

It was into this atmosphere that a vagrant arrived in South Africa. Dimitri Tsafendas (aka Demetrius) was born in the capital of Mozambique on January 14, 1918, the illegitimate son of a white Greek man, Michaelatos Tsafandakis, from Crete and Amelia William, a black woman from Mozambique. Sometime later, his father married a European Greek woman who did not want a stepson living with them. When Dimitri was only eight years old, his father gave him a large sum of money and sent him away. He became a stowaway, traveling to many countries by hiding on trains, ships, etc.

In the mid-1960s, Tsafendas arrived at the home of one of the Friends in South Africa. He claimed he had professed and had been baptized by Brother Worker John Micheletos in Greece in 1947. Supposedly, he was looking for a wife. They invited him to stay with them in their duplex residence. Sheila Martin and her sister (both 2x2s) lived in the other half of the duplex.

According to Martin, their first impression of Tsafendas was that he was a mysterious character. She described him as quiet, gentle and restless, but not threatening. He spoke eight languages fluently. He regaled them with interesting stories about his travels. While he attended the same Fellowship Meetings as Martin and read his Bible constantly, he was never quite in tune with 2x2 doctrine. He once prayed the Lord's Prayer aloud at Convention. Without fail, he read the daily newspaper from cover to cover. He somehow acquired a job as a messenger at the House of Parliament.

Prime Minister Assassinated. In 1961, Prime Minister Dr. Hendrik Verwoerd withdrew South Africa from the British Commonwealth. He was a harsh, ruthless, merciless man; some believed he was evil and insane. He planned to pass another very cruel law against the already suffering black population. On September 6, 1966, as he stepped forward to deliver a speech regarding the new law to Parliament, he was stabbed several times and died. The murderer was none other than Dimitri "Demetrius" Tsafendas, age 48.

The assassination appeared well planned. The story was published in South African daily newspapers such as the *Argus* and *Cape Times*, and also internationally, including in the US editions of *Time* and *Newsweek* magazines. Reportedly, Tsafendas told the police he killed Verwoerd because he was disgusted with his racial policies. The September 6, 1966, *Star Newspaper* of Johannesburg reported that Tsafendas claimed a tapeworm had possessed him. At his one-day trial, Tsafendas was ruled insane, detained at Pretoria Central Prison and incarcerated until his death in 1999.

In 2018, a document entitled "Report to the Minister of Justice ... in the Matter of Dr Verwoerd's Assassination" re-evaluated Tsafendas' actions and judged his motive to have been political, and the insanity verdict and tapeworm story to have been a cover story to save the government embarrassment over the security lapse. It remains to be seen if South African history books will acknowledge the findings of this report. *See Wikipedia* "Dimitri Tsafendas."

The background story was also circulated that Tsafendas had taken a job in England in 1959 offered by a British man, Anton Rupert, who owned the Rothmans cigarette factory. In 1960, Rupert learned that Tsafendas had stated he wished for an opportunity to kill the South African Prime Minister. Rupert and some murder-plot members held a meeting in Birmingham in March 1963. They made an agreement with Tsafendas that they would pay him 5,000 rand to assassinate Verwoerd.

This man, Dimitri Tsafendas, who irrevocably changed the course of South Africa's history, died of pneumonia in Johannesburg on October 7, 1999, aged 81. His funeral was held according to Greek Orthodox rites; less than ten people attended. He was buried in an unmarked grave outside Sterkfontein Hospital where he had been detained for 33 years.

End of Apartheid (1948–Early 1990s)

Since most apartheid laws were repealed in 1989, the Fellowship Meetings have been comprised of mixed races. Finally, in 1991, after the better part of 50 years, the country's harsh, institutionalized system of racial segregation came to an end in a series of steps that led to the formation of a democratic government in 1994. Nelson Mandela was elected the first black South African president.

While the 2x2 Sect started in South Africa among English-speaking people, it quickly spread among the Dutch/Afrikaans-speaking people. Currently, the white congregation is divided about equally between English and Afrikaners. Most of the mixed-race people speak Afrikaans. The Fellowship Meetings have long been linguistically mixed, with both languages in the same hymnbook, with Friends free to choose hymns in either language. The Conventions have speakers in both languages. In Conventions at least since 1980, the colored Workers have sat on and spoken from the platform; some have led Meetings; people enter and exit at any door.

Workers at convention, Pretoria, South Africa 1993

Secret Mormonism and Christian Science

In 1927, while living in Salisbury, Rhodesia, Africa (now Harare, Zimbabwe), Amelia A. Atmore, wrote the book *Secret Mormonism and Christian Science.* She dedicated her book "to the many lives blighted and the many homes broken up by these secret Mormon agents, who say they are only just Christians come to preach the true Gospel of Jesus. They are best known as the Gospel Readers, the Evangelists, the Cooneyites, the Go-Preachers or the Disciples." *Read* book on website *TellingTheTruth.info* in Publications.

Atmore believed her young adult daughter had been entrapped by 2x2 Workers. Attempting to get her daughter out from under her parents' control and influence, the Workers hid her and limited contact with her parents. While the Workers were grooming her daughter to become a Worker, Atmore prevented the Workers from transporting her out of the country three times. Mrs. Atmore, a Christian and student of the Bible, saw many parallels between the Workers' practices and beliefs and those of the Mormon and Christian Science cults. She mistakenly assumed the Workers were Mormons from America and/or Christian Scientists in disguise. She wrote her book to expose them and warn others.

Additional References:

Harris Dousemetzis and Gerry Loughran. 2019. *The Man Who Killed Apartheid: The Life of Dimitri Tsafendas*: Jacana Media, South Africa.

Meredith, Martin. 1988. *In the Name of Apartheid: South Africa in the Post War Era*. New York: Harper & Row Publishers Inc.

Madagascar

Situated in the southwest area of the Indian Ocean off the coast of Africa about 250 miles (400 km), Madagascar gained its independence from France in 1960. Kenneth Paginton (from England) went alone to pioneer Madagascar in 1965. There were no Friends there. A Co-worker followed. Six years later, there were eighty Friends at a Convention. Around 1980, a native Madagascan man and a native Sister Worker went in the Work. Currently (2022), annual Conventions are held at Antananarivo and Fianarantsoa.

Ken Paginton from England, sole pioneer of Madagascar in 1965

❧❧❧

Sherdenia Thompson and Debbie Jones   *Fern Duncan and Pat Inniss*

47

US Black History

If ye have respect to persons, ye commit sin. (James 2:9)

In the twenty-first century, the culturally acceptable ethnic terms for dark-skinned people in North America are *black* and *African American*. Some dark-skinned persons prefer to be identified by their country of origin, such as Jamaican, Haitian or Dominican, to name a few. In this chapter, I have respectfully chosen to use the term *black,* which does not address Latinos, American Indians, Asians, Pacific Islanders, South Americans or Europeans.

There are very few black Friends and Workers in the US, and most of these professed before they emigrated from Jamaica, the Caribbean Islands and other countries.

Southern States. A few general remarks will help set the scene. The states in the southeastern corner of the US are referred to as *The South* and the *Deep South.* In this region, also known as the *Bible Belt,* Christian church attendance across the denominations is generally higher than the nation's average.

From Independence Day on July 4, 1776, slavery was legal in all 13 Colonies. By the end of the eighteenth century, most of the Northern states had abolished slavery. In 1808, Congress prohibited the importation of more slaves. However, the Southern states continued as slave states. The rapid expansion of the cotton industry, especially after the invention of the cotton gin, greatly increased the demand for slave labor. Driven by labor demands from cotton plantations, slave trading continued in the Deep South, where the slave population eventually grew to an estimated four million.

American Civil War. When Abraham Lincoln won the 1860 presidential election on a platform of halting the expansion of slavery, the seven southern states holding the greatest number of slaves seceded from the US and formed the Confederate States of America. They were South Carolina, Mississippi, Florida, Alabama, Georgia, Louisiana and Texas, followed by Virginia, Arkansas, North Carolina, Tennessee, Missouri and Kentucky after the war began.

The War Between the States, also called the *Civil War,* began April 12, 1861, when Southern troops fired on Ft. Sumter, a US military post in Charleston, South Carolina. Two days later, President Lincoln called for 75,000 volunteer soldiers to help quell the Southern insurrection. This four-year Civil War ended April 9, 1865.

US Black Population. The 1950 US Census showed the black population at 15 million or 10% of the total population. In 2010, the black citizens numbered 38.9 million or 12.5% of the total population. Over half the black citizens (55%) resided in the Southern states.

First US Black Workers. By 1935, there were a few black Sister Workers. They were Christine Gordon (1935–1989), Elizabeth Robinson (1935–1945) and Olive Steele (1941–1971). In the late 1940s, the first black Brother Worker, Edward "Eddie" Barendilla, arrived in Virginia from South Africa, followed by Ernest Prinsloo, George Koetzee, David Jordan, Hugh Morris and later, Harold Jegels.

Doylestown, Pennsylvania Convention (1954),
succeeded by Quakertown Convention
L-R Back Row: Ernest Prinsloo, South Africa; George Koetzee, South Africa;
Vernandez Harris, Panama;
Front Row: Fern Duncan, Canada; Olive Steele, Jamaica; Christine Gordon,
Virginia US; Mrs. Edith Harris, Panama; Frances Brown, Virginia US

US Black Convention. Eddie Barendilla had a history of disturbing the peace in the 2x2 Fellowship in South Africa by vocally protesting the practice of segregation there. He was sent to the US where he found the situation little improved. Sometime before 1950, he was responsible for starting the Scrabble, Virginia Convention (near the small town of

Culpeper) for black people. This has been the only annual 2x2 Convention specifically for black people in North America.

Barendilla's reason for forming this Convention was so that "the blacks would not have to suffer abuse from the whites." The name of this Convention was later changed to *Boston.* It was discontinued about 50 years later when all US Conventions became integrated in the late 1900s.

Sheila Martin reminisced, "When I came to Toronto in 1971 from South Africa, one of my first desires was to see the greatest country— the United States of America. The champion of democracy and freedom! To my horror, I discovered that apartheid was practiced there! I learned that the black Workers [and Friends] ... were allowed to visit only two Conventions: Scrabble, Virginia, and Quakertown, Pennsylvania" [also Altamont, New York].

"I went to Scrabble in about 1988. A couple of chartered buses brought some New York City Friends. The ratio of black to white was about four to one—about 300 to start with and on up to about 450 on Sunday ... They all intermingled. The cooking was done by black Friends."

US Black Workers. For some time prior to 2000, there were no pairs of black Workers ministering to the black population in the US. For many years before that, the few black Workers in the Eastern states were included on the Virginia Workers List, even though some worked in other states, ranging from Texas to New England. Most years, there were two pairs of black Brother Workers, four pairs of black Sister Workers and a married couple, Vernandez and Edith Harris, who spent many years around Washington, D.C.

Some better known black Sister Workers were Sherdenia Thompson, Deborah "Debbie" Jones, Fern Duncan and Frances Brown. Thompson, from North Carolina, was in the Work for more than 25 years (1967–2006, married in 2008). Her cousin, Debbie Jones, was in the Work from 1969 to 2000 and passed away in 2014, aged 65. Jones spent time in Africa where she is best remembered for her role in leading a witch doctor to profess. Fern Duncan, from Eastern Canada (1963–2017), preached mostly in the US. Frances Brown was in the Work from 1953 to 1961.

During 1970–1980, a few more black Americans entered the Work: Lillie Sweatt (1973–1985) and Pearl Bailey (1977–1983). Denver Hayes (1979–1982) was paired with a white Co-worker in Colorado. In the late 1980s, Michelle Johnson preached with a white Co-worker in Florida.

On the US West Coast, Steve Peirson (born in 1949) started in the Work in 1972 in California; he also preached in Baja California, Mexico, West Africa (five years) and is currently based in Washington, US. In 2022, there appears to be fewer than ten black Workers in the US.

Pat Inniss and Steve Peirson

While white Workers frequently moved from state to state, the black Workers did not come and preach in my home state of Mississippi, where the population was 45% black. A pair of black Sister Workers preached in the neighboring state of Alabama from 1964 to 1971 but did not attend the Jackson, Mississippi Conventions, as most Alabama Friends did.

In the adjacent state of Tennessee, black Sister Workers, Fern Duncan and Sherdenia Thompson, occasionally visited a Friend's black professing domestic. She was the only black person at the Knoxville, Tennessee Convention. In the 1960s in Mississippi, a black domestic professed after listening to Gospel Meetings from the kitchen of her 2x2 employers. During Fellowship Meetings in their home, she sat in the kitchen, and did not attend Conventions.

The Olivers, owners of the Fosters Alabama Convention grounds, were cotton farmers and hired black people to pick their cotton crop, some of whom lived on their property, including a couple named Tom and Velma Lewis. Velma worked as a domestic for the Olivers. She and her son, Ed, professed. During the Alabama Convention, they stayed in the background, sitting in the back row during Meetings or in the dining tent.

Civil Rights Acts of 1964. President Kennedy was assassinated on November 22, 1963. His proposed Civil Rights Act passed on July 2, 1964, and legally ended the discrimination and segregation institutionalized by the Jim Crow laws. However, the road for black people to claim the equality that was theirs by law was far from smooth. It would be a long time before their problems with poverty, unemployment and poor housing improved.

Every dictatorship in history has fallen when the peons refuse to submit any longer. For the black people, this took the form of a wave of civil rights activities that swept through the Deep South in the 1960s. They staged sit-ins at public segregated facilities, freedom rides, boycotts, rallies, marches, and registered at all-white universities.

Integration in all areas did not take place immediately or without resistance. In this time period, white people still had to be careful about mixing with black people. The Ku Klux Klan (aka KKK), a white supremacist hate group, was still actively employing intimidation tactics such as night rides, burning warning crosses in yards, bombings, hangings, murders, etc. A wary, uneasy peace between the races continued for many years. Some went quietly about mixing with the other race. Following are descriptions by Workers and Friends:

"I first heard the Gospel in 1962 [in Minnesota] ... By the time Convention rolled around the second year, I was wondering why there were no black people in all the crowd. Jim Jardine ... was at the Convention, so I asked him, "Where are all my black brothers and sisters?" He answered that there were black churches in the South, as well as Conventions. He also said that they were kept separate because there were whites, who if they knew you were having anything to do with black people, you or your property would be in danger, as well of that of your black brother and sister."

In 1988, a Worker remarked, "Of all the blacks here in Alabama-Mississippi, we have only three professing—all in Alabama; not much interest with those people for the Gospel."

An Ex-worker admitted there is no question the Workers could have done much better on racial issues through the years. While in the Work, he found it difficult to get black people to come and listen to white preachers, even though the Workers were house guests of black Friends during their missions.

US Black 2x2s and Meetings. For a time, there were a few all-black Fellowship Meetings in the South, with at least one or more in North Carolina. In Lorain, Ohio, an all-black Meeting was held in the Beasley home. Their son, Edward, is in the Work in the Dominican Republic.

An Ex-worker recalled, "For many years I had been told there were only two Meetings in all of New York City. Imagine my surprise to find there were many more Meetings there in the 'Big Apple.' Turns out the rest were black Meetings. The black Friends attended the Gospel Meetings of two black Sister Workers in the city who had 'apartheid' services. I was told I would not be welcome to attend them nor to visit in their homes. Although I was discouraged greatly from doing so, I finally made arrangements to meet with the black Sister Workers and discovered that segregation was not their choice."

In 1990, there were nine black Fellowship Meetings in New York City; about 150–200 black people attended Gospel Meetings. Most New York City black members are immigrants from the Caribbean Islands where they were converted. In the New York City/Brooklyn area, the professing black people outnumber the white people.

In the 1990s, Fern Duncan, Deborah Jones and Sherdenia Thompson were transferred to the New York Workers staff, ending the US practice of pairing the black Sister Workers with black Co-workers and working mostly among the black people.

In 2020, and for the past several years, Mark King, of mixed race, has been the Senior Brother Worker in New York City, where the majority of black members reside. It is not possible for all the NYC Fellowship Meetings to be integrated, due to insufficient white members. Currently, the Meeting distribution is geographical—not racial.

As the members moved or passed away, the all-black Meetings were phased out. The Boston (Scrabble), Virginia Convention was integrated for a while and eventually closed. When Meeting changes took place in the Mid-Atlantic states, a special attempt was made so there would not be any all-black or all-white Meetings. In 2020, and for some years previously, there has been no problem in the South or the US in general when black and white people have assembled together for 2x2 Meetings.

BOSTON, VA – AUGUST 20, 1999
1ST OLIVE STEELE, DORRY PENNY, IRIS MURRAY
FERN DUNCAN, LEONIE IRONS, VELLA DAVIS
2ND DEBORAH JONES, JOAN HOWARD, GLEN RICHARDS,
BEN CROMPTON, SHERDENIA THOMPSON,
PRISCILLA FARRING, ETHELINE WARD
3RD JOHN GUY, SAM MCCRACKEN, ALBERT KNAGGS
STEVE PEIRSON, STEVE JAYNE, TIM CHUNG

Boston, VA Convention (1999)
(formerly Scrabble Convention for Blacks)

❧❧❧

48

Divisions, Purges, Rifts and Revolts

Behold how good and how pleasant it is for brethren
to dwell together in unity (Psalm 133:1)

All that the Father giveth me shall come to me; and him that cometh
to me I will in no wise cast out (Jesus Christ, John 6:37)

The unity, uniformity and harmony existing in the Two by Two Church are considered unique and universal attributes by many members. The words of their hymn convey this ideal, "His fellowship of love, where there's peace and love abounding till they reach their home above" (No. 232). Yet, continuous "perfect peace … along the way He trod" (hymn No. 240) has eluded them. Over the years, there have been serious disagreements, divisions, excommunications and purges, usually downplayed and hidden. The following is an overview; some are discussed in more detail in earlier chapters, and on the website *TellingTheTruth.info* in History, Divisions.

1914: The William Irvine Division. The first significant split within the 2x2 Sect occurred in 1914 when the founder, William Irvine, was removed from leadership; some of his loyal acolytes followed him out or were expelled. *See* Chapters 23 and 24.

According to Irvine, "There were over one hundred Workers rejected and as many hundreds Saints these past seven years, and no two alike, and yet the treatment has been the same: unmerciful judging of their brethren, casting and shutting them out of fellowship. For anyone to have my name in honor, or in grateful memory, or to plead my cause, means to be cast out … and nothing pleases them better than when someone can speak more evil of the man to whom they owe all they have" (to Willie Abercrombie, March 2, 1921, *TTT*).

1928: The Edward Cooney Division. The second major split occurred in 1928 when Edward Cooney was excommunicated from the Work and the 2x2 Sect; his loyalists were put out or left voluntarily.

William West's description: "Two Workers … [went] around the little churches and then round to individuals, applying the test of whether or not the people believed in Cooney. Churches were visited on Sunday mornings for the sole purpose of closing them ... Several of them were actually closed. Then individuals were tested privately as to what they thought about Eddie [Cooney]. And if they had any softness in their hearts towards him, they were cast out and refused further fellowship" (Oct. 1929, *TTT*). *See* Chapter 27.

1920s: East-West Conflict in North America. A rift between the US Overseers of the East (George Walker) and West (Jack Carroll) occurred sometime in the 1920s; the cause remains unclear. It is known that contention arose concerning Convention lists and visitors, exchange of Workers across the East/West boundaries, use of radios, and doctrine regarding divorce and remarriage. A mediation meeting took place on July 19–20, 1930, at West Hanney, England, attended by 16 Senior Workers. Regret and apologies were rendered (Meeting 1930, *TTT*).

The East/West Conflict did not die with Carroll and Walker; succeeding Senior Workers in the various areas continued the separation. For many years, there was little to no exchange of Workers, nor were Convention speakers invited to the others' territory. The conflict extends beyond North American boundaries with Overseers enforcing their practices and beliefs in other countries under their jurisdictions. *See* Chapter 29.

1938: Disturbance in Colorado, US. In the late 1930s, In Colorado where Eddie Cornock was the Overseer, some Friends and Workers declared their support for either Carroll or Walker. Each Overseer forbade visits or contact with the Workers who were loyal to the other Overseer (Parker 1982, 85). A Workers' Meeting was held in Denver. A statement signed by seven Senior Workers dated December 1, 1938, was distributed to those affected by the disturbance; apologies and good intentions were made. (Meeting 1938b, *TTT*). *See* Chapter 29.

1960–1980s: South African Revolt. From their start in South Africa, the Workers enforced segregation in their Meetings and Conventions even though the South African law did not require segregation in religious gatherings. In the mid-1960s, a South African government official assured a 2x2 Elder that there was no law against races mixing for religious services. They provided an official document stating the law in effect at that time. The white Workers refused to read it.

After discovering white Workers had deceived them, some colored and black Elders rebelled against the racial barriers that the white Workers had been enforcing. In an attempt to quash the revolt, Workers removed Elders and their Fellowship Meetings and excommunicated some members, leaving chaos and heartbreak in their wake. At least since 1970, segregation has ceased in the 2x2 Sect in South Africa. *See* Chapter 46.

1968–1969: Willie Martin – Canadian Maritimes. Reportedly, in late 1960s, Martin, who entered the Work in 1929, began openly questioning and disagreeing with some 2x2 tenets and traditions; he was expelled by Overseer George Semple. Martin was accused of offending the Friends, teaching false doctrine and drinking. Afterward, Martin lived with various loyal followers and passed away in 1998, aged 90.

The disturbance continued into the 1970s. Brother Worker Martin MacMillan (Willie Martin's nephew) and some other Workers and Friends also left the sect, including the owners of the Spring Valley (aka Kensington) PEI Convention; the McLeods who owned the Cape Breton Convention; and the Woods. The group was called the *Willie Martin Gang,* and the Friends who allowed them in their homes risked excommunication.

1985: Greece Split – Overseer Nikolas Papadakis. About 1984, some Greek Workers became concerned about the mishandling of funds by the Overseer of Greece, Nicolas Papadakis. They appealed to European Overseers to replace him. Pierre "Peter" Bill came from Switzerland to investigate; Papadakis was removed.

A division resulted. Papadakis, Sister Worker Catherine Stavroulakis, a young Brother Worker, Athanassios Kalogeropoulos, along with a few other loyal members left the sect and formed a splinter group. Reportedly, Papadakis absconded with a large sum of money and bought a lavish villa in Athens. He married Stavroulakis and died around 2003–2005. After Papadakis' death, some who had left earlier returned to the fold, including his wife. Eventually, the division in Greece was mended and the Friends and Workers were reunited.

1989–1990: Montana and Alaska Divisions. About 1967, three Brother Workers from Montana, John R. Starkweather, E. Truitt Oyler and Walter J. Oyler, were accused of either teaching and/or believing false or "divisive doctrine" and were dismissed from the Work.

Their doctrinal understanding was basically that Jesus was divine and could not sin or be tempted to sin. This concept was called *Truitt's Doctrine.* Perhaps in 1973, both Starkweather and Truitt Oyler were reinstated in the Work after agreeing they would not teach Truitt's Doctrine. Starkweather was sent to Texas in 1973, where he became the Overseer; Truitt went to Alaska in 1974. Walter Oyler did not return to the Work.

Truitt resumed teaching his doctrine in Alaska. Some Alaska Workers brought Truitt's Doctrine to Washington, causing a division in the ministry. Truitt was then paired with Willis Propp in Alberta to help him see the error of this teaching.

The Workers admonished Truitt several times for continuing to teach the divisive doctrine. In 1990, he was told that he must step aside from the ministry. Likewise, Starkweather had been dismissed in 1986. Neither man was allowed to attend Fellowship Meetings or Conventions. Truitt married a Sister Worker.

Reportedly in the 1980s, at some Meetings and at Manhattan Montana Convention, Brother Worker Everett Swanson asked all the Friends who "accepted the decisions of the Elders of the ministry as just and final" to stand to their feet. Most of Oyler's relatives did not stand; those who did not stand were excommunicated, some with their families.

Around 2016, Truitt and his wife relocated to Northeast Colorado where Jim Price, the Overseer, allowed them to have full participation in Meetings. In 2017, John Starkweather moved from Montana to Colorado, where he was allowed to participate in Meetings for the last few weeks of his life; he passed away on April 27, 2017. *See* more details on website *TellingtheTruth.info* in History, Divisions.

1989: Workers' Revolt against Tharold Sylvester and Bob Ingram. From the mid-1970s through the 1980s, after Overseer Willie Jamieson passed away in 1974, the Western N. America oversight was handled by a quadrumvirate made up of Tharold Sylvester, Eldon Tenniswood, Howard Mooney and Ernest Nelson; all deferred to Sylvester.

In 1965, Sylvester appointed Robert "Bob" Ingram as the Alaska Overseer. In 1989, when Sylvester was up in years, it became known that he had picked Ingram to take his place as Overseer of Washington, Alaska and N. Idaho. This seriously distressed a number of young Sister Workers with whom Ingram had been "taking liberties." The Sisters had attempted to discuss the matter with Sylvester (Ingram's and their Overseer). They found him unapproachable, and the matter was not resolved. For some time, the morale of the staff of Washington-Alaska Workers had been suffering from Sylvester's imperious ways.

Some of Ingram's victims let it be known to other state Overseers that if Ingram should replace Sylvester as Overseer, they would have to either give up the Work or go to another state—they would not work under Ingram. Disheartened, they disclosed details of the liberties Ingram had taken with them and shared their embarrassment and discouragement.

It took a minor revolution before the matter was resolved, involving Workers Meetings, Elders Meetings and Overseers stepping in to hear the complaints against Sylvester and Ingram. After badly bungling the

Ingram situation, Sylvester was demoted in 1989. He remained on the Workers List with a companion through 1991 and died in 1994. He was replaced by Sydney Holt.

A letter to the Friends from the four Overseers explained the change in Ingram's status in 1989 and the need for it. They also compiled a list of reasons Ingram was asked to step aside from the ministry and the Conditions for Fellowship for Ingram. *Read* both on website *TellingTheTruth.info* in History, Divisions, Alaska. Supported by the Friends, Ingram lived in Fairbanks where he attended and fully participated in Fellowship Meetings until his death in 2015.

2009–2014: Vietnam Division. When the Communist took over Vietnam in 1975, all foreign Workers evacuated, leaving in charge for the following 20 years or so, the two native Vietnamese Brother Workers, Nguyễn Thanh Hoa and Vu Ngoc Châu. They were the first to profess in Vietnam in June 1961 in Saigon; both were 21 years old. In 1967, they were the first natives to enter the Work.

In 2000, Canadian Workers Darrel Turner, Morris Grovum and Lyle Shultz went to Vietnam under the guise of being "teachers." The Canadian Workers usurped the leadership of the native Workers (Châu and Hoa). Further, they instructed the rest of the Vietnam Workers that henceforth, they were under the Canadian Workers' oversight. They instituted various changes to long-held procedures.

Further, the Canadian Workers dismissed Châu from the Work based on the false accusation that he owned a home (his brother was the owner). After the house was sold, he was reinstated in the Work in another country in the very lowest Worker position, that of assistant to a younger Worker. Seeing the handwriting on the wall, Hoa left the Work and became an independent missionary, supported by loyal Friends.

Many of the Friends had been happy and satisfied with "God's Way" as it had been for the first 50 years after the first pioneering Workers arrived in Vietnam, a period they refer to as *The Golden Years*. About half the Vietnamese 2x2s left the group controlled by Canadians and are referred to as the *Golden Friends*. An Elder of the Golden Friends was Nguyễn *Huu Bau;* he and his wife were the first couple to profess in Vietnam. Some of the Nguyễn family's issues were:

> It was not these unimportant things that caused the split. The Important thing was their deeds, such as changing this or that, were not done in the Spirit of God. And we didn't see the love among the Workers ... *The two main things that we did not agree with in his* [Lyle Shultz'] *letter were that the Workers 'deserve our highest respect' (it is our Lord's place in our heart, not Workers). And that Uncle Hoa 'is not considered a part*

of the teacher [Worker] staff ' in this country now. Seeing my father disagreed with his letter, Lyle Shultz told him. 'I can't take care of you anymore.' My father replied, 'God will take care of us.' (M. T. Nguyễn 2014, *TTT*)

Along with Hoa, the Golden Friends have continued to hold Fellowship, Gospel and Special Meetings and Conventions. They have also taken day-trip missions to visit Friends and recruit people interested in their faith in remote areas; their numbers have increased. Sympathetic foreigners have provided the Golden Friends with financial support for their ministry. *See* website *TellingTheTruth.info* in Divisions, Vietnam.

2016–2017: Sri Lanka Schism. When some Friends questioned the Sri Lanka Overseer, Peter Morrison, they were excommunicated, Elders and Meetings were removed, and some were deprived of communion. Others left voluntarily. False accusations against professing Trustees of the Snell Trust were made regarding mishandling funds left for mission work by deceased Friends. Peter Morrison informed them, "I am in charge of your salvation."

Some elderly Workers were harassed and marginalized as unfit for the Work. The outcome was that 18–20 out of about 75 total professing Sri Lankans left or were cast out; some are now happily attending other churches. *See* website *TellingTheTruth.info* in History, Divisions.

Controversies in Australia

1951–1952: Purge in South Australia by John Baartz. Information is scarce, and documents are few, leaving gaps and questions. Reportedly, in late January 1951, there was a meeting during preparations for the Strathalbyn SA Convention. It appeared to be prompted by some actions of Brother Worker Ron Campbell and opposition to Bill Carroll's expulsions of Friends in VIC. John Baartz, the SA Overseer, greatly respected and supported Bill Carroll. Tensions ran high, particularly at the Strathalbyn Convention grounds, where the owners, the Doeckes, were sympathetic to Campbell.

Ronald "Ron" Ian Campbell was born on June 16, 1902, in Mannanarie, South Australia to Angus and Mary Ann (Scharber) Campbell. His mother and three of his sisters professed at the 1911 Mannanarie Convention when he was a child. He entered the Work in South Australia in 1926 under Willie Hughes. In 1928, Campbell and Jim Wingfield left for the US to labor under Jack Carroll.

When Campbell learned the Workers had assumed a name for their church in America around 1942, he declared, "I cannot understand the honesty of any preacher out preaching in the name of Jesus and associated with the 'Christian Conventions Assuming This Name Only.' This word *only* rules out all other names, so by right they cannot be honest and use the name of Jesus at all."

After WWII in 1947, Campbell made a home visit to Australia. Upon his return to Idaho, he was shocked to find the Friends and Workers had turned against him. One reason given for Campbell's dismissal was because he had confronted Carroll about his relationship with Sister Worker, Linda Heyes. Reportedly, Howard Mooney told Campbell that Mooney's father thought Carroll and Heyes were secretly married. While Mooney also suspected it was true, he refused to join Campbell in a discussion with Carroll, stating, "If we face him up, you will be sent back to Australia, and I will be sent back to the print shop."

Believing Carroll was a true Brother who had temporarily fallen, Campbell confronted him alone. Suffice to say, Campbell's comments were not well received. Carroll dismissed him from the US Work (Derkland to Malcolm Graham and Willie Jamieson, Sept. 5, 1957, *TTT*).

Campbell returned to Australia in 1949, where for a time, he was allowed to preach on a limited basis without a Co-worker. His relationship with the Workers seriously deteriorated after he began openly criticizing the Work in South Australia.

In 1950, Campbell confronted Willie Hughes, then the New Zealand Overseer (formerly the South Australia Overseer), for sexually harassing Campbell's pretty sister, Adelaide. Shortly after their clash, Hughes returned to New Zealand. Campbell disclosed to George Walker, "Willie Hughes disgraced himself and let some of us down by his conduct, and my own family are amongst those who feel this the keenest" (Campbell 1952, *TTT*).

Ron Campbell was put out of the Work and left the 2x2 Church (circa 1950)

~~~~~

Subsequently, in June 1951, a meeting was held at Ernie Wirth's home in Tusmore, Adelaide, SA, where nine Elders (Wirth, Con Doecke, Walter Vogt, Fred Ashman, Mr. Sharpe, etc.) met with John Baartz and

Ian Reid. They "pleaded for love to reign." Soon after, the nine Elders received letters informing them that they and their families were to cease attending Meetings. About 70 of the Friends were "stood down," including Brother Worker, Clyde Crettenden. Others were given the choice of cutting off all association with those expelled or losing their place.

Several Bethel Mission families were cast out. One noted, "Week after week, numbers were put out including whole churches. No one knew why, and appeals were sent to Senior Workers to come over and help us and give us a hearing." Walter Vogt's excommunication included ten of his immediate family members.

Ken and Dorrie Hacket were still attending Fellowship Meetings in South Australia where Ian Reid was the second-in-command Worker. He informed them if they did not cut off all contact with their two daughters who had married Vogt men, they would not be welcome at any 2x2 Meetings. They chose their daughters, and with that decision they were "put outside the camp."

The affected families included the Vogts, Doeckes, Berritts, Sharpes, Wirths, Harrises, Bruses, Ashmans, Masons, Fergusons, Loechels and others. Only a few who left at that time would return later (Vogt 2008, *TTT*). Campbell proclaimed:

> Never before have [I] seen such a display of human and spiritual corruption in lies being told, false accusations, agreements broken, hate, bitterness, defiance and other unChristlike marks expressed. They are going like a storm hitting the country leaving behind them a trail of broken hearts, homes, churches and relatives, forcing people to submit to them; if not, they tell that they are cut off and doomed, stopping some from holding Meetings if they can, refusing them to attend Convention ... telling them not to have anything to do with this one or that one, to walk off the street and out of the home if this one comes to see them. Christ is a secondary person. Workers are the supreme authority and gone as far as to say that no Saint can receive anything from God unless it comes through the Workers. (Oct. 20, 1952, *TTT*)

The 1951 closure of the Strathalbyn SA Convention owned by the Doeckes was accommodated by holding two annual Conventions at Oak Lodge, Kapunda. A new Convention was established at Wilmington in January 1952.

Although Ron Campbell returned to America in 1951, he was not reinstated in the Work. He returned to his family farm in South Australia where he spent the rest of his life, unmarried. A United Church minister officiated at his funeral. He died on December 14, 1977, aged 75, survived by two unmarried sisters, Adelaide, age 80 and Ellen, age 89.

1950s: Purge in Victoria by Bill Carroll. For reasons unknown, during the 1950s, Bill Carroll, the Overseer of Victoria, commenced a purge and cast out of the Church many Friends, parents, their children and even entire Meetings, many without a hearing.

Mervyn Schmidt, son of Otto Schmidt, remembered, "I professed at 12 years of age. At 13, in the 1950s, I was excommunicated, along with my parents and many others in the states of Victoria and South Australia, as a result of a purge by William Carroll. In my case, my only crime was I was the son of my father."

Separate Fellowship Meetings were established. Some children and teenagers with 2x2 parents attended school together but did not come together for Fellowship Meetings. Mervyn Schmidt recalled, "For approximately four years, about 16 of us met in our home, unofficially … with others who had been put out of Fellowship … We were reinstated again after this with the help of George Walker (US) and Jack Forbes from England" (Why We Left, *EXP*). *See also* Chapter 41.

Bill Carroll's Latter Years. Victoria was self-sufficient regarding Workers and had also sent many Workers overseas. Carroll had visited outside Victoria less and less in his later years. The amount of interchange between Victoria and the other Australian states had lessened to the point that Victoria was all but isolated from the other states.

For about the last ten years of his life, Bill Carroll, a widower and diabetic, lived in a comfortable residence located south of Melbourne owned by his daughter and her husband. His personal letters during this time bear the address: Greenhaven, Rosebud West, Victoria, Australia.

"Two Sister Workers and a Brother stayed with him at Rosebud to look after him, when there were open homes who would gladly receive him and cater for his needs and do the superintending of his meals necessitated by the fact that he was a diabetic. This went on for ten years. These Workers had no Gospel Meetings while at Rosebud" (Appendix J, Item No. 13).

1953: Death of William Charles "Bill" Carroll. For 40 years, Bill Carroll had been the Overseer of Victoria, beginning in 1913 when he arrived in Australia with his wife and daughter. He died November 13, 1953, aged 77. As Alfred Magowan aptly phrased it, "Very soon reverberations of Australian thunders began rolling and crashing over Bill's grave."

Chris Williams, the Overseer of Tasmania, having been appointed by Carroll to be his successor, assumed the Victorian oversight from 1953 to 1955. Originally from Victoria, Williams started in the Work in 1914 in Queensland. From there, he went to Tasmania in 1925 where he was the Overseer from around 1939 to 1953. The Senior Workers in other Australian states registered their "disapproval of certain things that happened in connection with our departed Brother's life." They felt strongly that they should have been consulted regarding the selection of his successor (Appendix J, Item No. 13).

1954: Guildford Meeting. During February 20–24, 1954 (about three months after Carroll's death), the two Senior Overseers of Australia, John Hardie and Tom Turner, held a meeting of all the Overseers of New Zealand and Australia at the Guildford, NSW Convention grounds near Sydney. It was the first time the Overseers of the various Australian states had assembled in many years (Meeting 1954).

Turner led the meeting. Eleven Workers were present: John Hardie, Joe Williamson, Chris Williams, Walter Pickering, Willie Hughes, John Baartz, Les Hawse, Walter Schloss, Alex Mitchell and Harry Morgan. A written report of the meeting was prepared, called the *Guildford Report*.

The major issues addressed were Bill Carroll's successor; the exchange of Workers within Australia; cooperation of Victoria with the other Australian states; dealing with the Outcast Friends in Victoria and South Australia; and Carroll's permanent residence at Rosebud. The Workers "separated at Guildford with high hopes that unity and harmony would prevail, and all would be well." See Guildford Report in Appendix J.

Chris Williams and Walter Pickering returned to Victoria where they held a Victorian Workers Meeting at Dandenong to discuss the Guildford Meeting and Report. The Victorian Workers felt that the purpose of the Guildford Meeting was to make a personal attack on the life and testimony of Bill Carroll and viewed it as an attempt to interfere with the Work in Victoria. They drew up a document expressing their viewpoints, and Chris Williams delivered it to the Fellowship Meetings in Victoria. Some Victorian Conventions were cancelled.

Eventually Williams wrote Hardie that "A breach even greater, seems imminent ... Could it not all be withdrawn?" Over a year later, on April 20, 1955, all the Senior Overseers, including those of Victoria, indicated that they regretted their actions and unconditionally withdrew their statements. Three items they all agreed upon were:

- "Regarding the residence at Rosebud ... we cannot accept such an arrangement as a precedent that could be repeated.

- "When an Overseer in any state or country, through infirmities or other circumstances is unable to personally carry out his responsibilities, he should call to his aid a Brother who has the approval and confidence of his Brethren and who can eventually assume the oversight.
- [They would] "find an impartial Brother from overseas who will supervise and cooperate in the oversight of the Work in Victoria for such time as may be considered necessary" (Meeting 1955).

The divisions within the church remained a serious problem. Some Australian Senior Workers asked Senior Workers from other countries for help. Also, in 1954, at the request of about 20 Outcast Friends, Edward Cooney (then 88 years old) traveled to Mildura, Victoria, to help mend the rupture.

In 1955, Jack Carroll, George Walker and Jack Forbes arrived to assist in reuniting the church. They held Reconciliation Meetings in various locations in Victoria where the outcast Friends could be reinstated as a group without re-professing. When a Reconciliation Meeting was scheduled in Mildura, Edward Cooney went uninvited, along with Jack Schmidt, the disfellowshipped owner of the Mildura, VIC Convention grounds and a few other members. Tom Turner met them at the door and turned Cooney away; his loyal Friends left with him.

In late 1955, Chris Williams was replaced by Archie Turner, a Scotsman. The situation was too much for Turner who returned to Scotland in 1957. Meanwhile, Jack Forbes (from England) acted as the interim Overseer until Willie Donaldson arrived.

1957: New Overseer of Victoria. Willie Donaldson was born in Ireland in 1900. He entered the Work in the 1920s, and in 1928, he pioneered the Work in Barbados, West Indies, where he remained for the next 30 years. In 1957, when he was 57, he assumed the Victorian oversight, and successfully restored harmony to the 2x2 Sect in Victoria, where the Workers and Friends held him in high esteem. After a couple years, the Friends returned to common Conventions. After Donaldson died in the West Indies in 1987, aged 87, Evan Jones and Herwin Bell shared the Victorian oversight.

Shades of the Past. Almost 50 years later, a parallel to the expulsions, purges and divisions in Australia took place in Alberta, Canada, when over 21 churches were closed, and countless Elders and Friends were excommunicated at the direction of Overseer Willis Propp. *See* Chapter 40. A similar *modus operandi* (M.O.) took place previously when Irvine and Cooney were excommunicated.

1997–1999: Alberta, Canada Purge by Willis Propp. From 1997 to 1999, there were around 24 Alberta Fellowship Meetings in which the Elder and his wife were excommunicated or opted to give up their Meeting. In addition, at least 200 Alberta Friends were excommunicated or left the sect. At least one Worker (Marg Magowan) was put out of the Work, and another left the Work. *See* Chapter 40 for details.

2020: The Current Covid-19 Disease Pandemic Schism. On March 11, 2020, the World Health Organization (WHO) declared the Covid-19 (Coronavirus) a global pandemic. Global cooperation was spurred for vaccine research and distribution.

Worldwide, national governments began issuing travel bans on non-citizens entering their countries, stay-at-home orders, capacity limits, and other restrictions. Mass group gatherings (church services, weddings, funerals, graduations, schools, etc.) were severely curtailed, cancelled or closed. Eldercare facilities went into lockdown and residents were sequestered; hospitals refused visitors. Students were educated by virtual learning from home. Only government-defined *essential* businesses remained open. Many worked from home. The pandemic containment measures created a *new normal* of face mask-wearing, social distancing and sanitizing.

In compliance, around March 2020, most in-person 2x2 gatherings (Conventions, Fellowship, Gospel and Special Meetings) were suspended indefinitely. Workers stayed in one place. For years, the Workers were not in favor of listening to Workers speak over electronic devices (even for shut-ins and disabled elderly), claiming the Spirit was ONLY transmitted on a one-to-one basis. By the Millennium, it appeared the Holy Spirit had progressed/evolved to the point it was transmittable via telephone, and those who were unable to attend conventions in person were allowed to listen via a (carefully guarded) call-in number.

Meeting participation continued during the Pandemic using alternate methods to share thoughts, i.e. by text, email, telephone, and it was discovered that the Holy Spirit was not opposed to Zoom meetings. Some participated in hybrid Zoom Meetings, where some were in person and others online with sound and video.

Later, when mass group requirements relaxed, some Meetings and Conventions resumed with social distancing, face masks, no handshaking or hugging. Procedures varied depending on the country, state and Overseer. Many Meetings were limited to ten or fewer people, requiring the formation of additional Meetings. At times, hymns were hummed or sung through masks.

When required to wear masks, some Elders gave up their Meetings and some members did not attend. Others did not attend because masks *were not* required. In some areas, separate Meetings were held for the masked and unmasked. Some were not comfortable resuming in-person gatherings and listened by phone.

Emblems. When in-person Meetings resumed, the emblems were present in some but not all. Some Overseers insisted on continuing with the common cup "because that was how it was done in the Bible." Some masked members drank from the communal cup. This unsanitary practice has long been a concern to some, especially those in medical professions. All were free to abstain.

Other Workers instructed the Elders to prepare individual disposable cups for the fruit of the vine, and to cut the bread into small squares, a method long used in many Christian churches with some also serving *unleavened* bread, as was done at the Last Supper. Separate Meetings were held in some locations where one used a shared cup and another used single (individual) cups.

New Zealand Overseer Alan Richardson supported the claim that "it is always sound practice to use wine that has an alcoholic content of at least 15%," such as Port Wine (self-sterilizing), but also required single use individual cups. He instructed, "Thanks should be given in the Meeting for an emblem...to remember the Lord Jesus," even when the emblems were unavailable (Statement, March 14, 2020, *TTT*).

Some Conventions resumed in person; some were shortened to weekends with no food or on-site accommodations, with masks being required. Many did not attend due to the number of unvaccinated present. Reportedly, there were large Covid-19 outbreaks after the 2021 US Conventions at Ronan, Montana, and McCordsville, Indiana. For some Conventions, Special and Gospel Meetings, a call-in number was provided to listen to the Workers speak. The New Zealand Overseer's instructions for December 2021 meetings included restrictions on sharing the number:

> Obtain from the Workers of the corresponding meeting date above, the online link to give to those in your field who are entitled to it, e.g. only to those who for unvaccinated reasons, health reasons or for limits to numbers attending, cannot be physically in the meeting. We request that, when giving the link to any such person, you tell them that the link is just for their household alone and is not to be forwarded on to other people. We also need to request that no recording be made of any meeting, whether it be in a hall or online. Our concession of online listening will not continue beyond the present Covid-19 situation.

Covid-19 Vaccine. When the vaccine became available in late 2020, some 2x2s eagerly received it right away, while others cautiously refused it, preferring to wait for side effects to be revealed. National pressure was applied to be vaccinated with the goal of achieving herd immunity. Media kept the public abreast of what percentage of the country's population was vaccinated. Some restrictions lifted as more became vaccinated.

Reactions to the vaccine varied considerably. Similar to the world, there were passionate differences of opinions among the 2x2s. Some called it *evil.* Some questioned if the vaccine might be "the mark of the beast" (Rev. 13:17). Some 2x2 Overseers mandated their Worker staff all be vaccinated.

To vaccinate or not vaccinate was a very polarizing issue that appeared to generate irreconcilable divisions among some members. In some places, there were separate Meetings for the vaccinated and unvaccinated; in others, the Meeting room was divided into vaccinated and unvaccinated sections. Some 2x2s refused the vaccine and longed to go back to their normal, pre-Covid in-person Meetings with unmasked singing and single cup communion. Others following recommended precautions preferred not to gather in-person. Some wanted their Meeting to be fully vaccinated. At least one Overseer requested that no one ask another for their vaccination status.

Since the Millennium, increasingly more Friends have started following political trends of the world which has led to strife and division. Not unlike the world, the diametrically opposing viewpoints of the vaccinated and unvaccinated have caused a number of members to question, become discouraged and disheartened. Grievous divisions have separated families and friends. Some have resorted to unkind, scoffing, judging, shunning, labeling, accusing and belittling those with differing opinions, resulting in hurt feelings. Some viewed those who were insistent on the necessity of the vaccine as choosing "fear over faith," and not trusting God. Disappointed that some would not get vaccinated for the sake of others, even if they did not do it for themselves, caused some feel, "These are not my people."

Without a unified management strategy, some Workers are "near breakdown level" dealing with the discord. One Worker stated he doubted the Fellowship would survive the Covid-19 Pandemic. Some Workers are referring to Scripture such as "*in the last days* perilous times shall come" (2 Tim. 3:1) and "*in the latter times* some shall depart from the faith" (1 Tim. 4:1). Although this world is living in the Age of Apostasy (abandoning Christianity), losing faith in the 2x2 church that some consider the "falling away" is not a clear sign that the tribulation and end of the world *are imminent*.

A close study of eschatology (end times) will show a number of events that will precede the seven-year tribulation period, such as the invasion of Israel from the north; the one world government that splits into ten kingdoms; the revealing and rise of the Antichrist; the building of the third Jewish temple in Jerusalem; Israel's signing of the seven-year covenant with the antichrist. The last event is the beginning of the seven-year tribulation. Opinions differ as to when the saints will be "caught up...in the clouds to meet the Lord in the air" in 1 Thes. 4:13–18, called the rapture, e.g. before, during or after the seven-year tribulation (Fruchtenbaum 2020, 91, 106, 126–140).

Departures. Meanwhile, some people following stay-at-home orders have discovered they rather like the break from attending Meetings regularly. When Meetings resumed in person, some have taken the opportunity to announce their decision not to return. Since the Covid-19 Pandemic is still ongoing, it remains to be seen how many Friends will have disassociated from the 2x2 Sect by its end. Yet another reason why some are leaving the 2x2 Church has been added to the list—the Covid-19 Pandemic schism.

2022: Current State of the 2x2 Church – Declining Membership. Many members have and are leaving the sect for various reasons, especially since the Millennium. Some estimates suggest a decline in worldwide membership of up to 40% since 1980. Interestingly, the number of active US Workers in 2021 was about 38% less than in 1980.

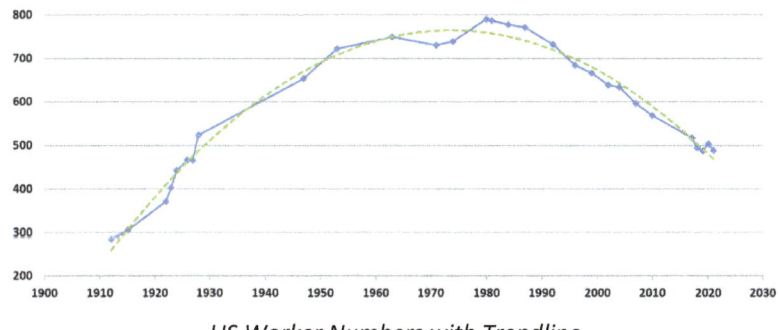

US Worker Numbers with Trendline

> *And if a kingdom be divided against itself, that kingdom cannot stand.*
> *And if a house be divided against itself, that house cannot stand.*
> (Mark 3:24–25)

✤✤✤

Section D – Finale

Truth will always be truth, regardless of lack of understanding, disbelief or ignorance.

(W. Clement Stone)

Truth is not only violated by falsehood;
it may be equally outraged by silence.

(Amien)

There is a principle which is a bar
against all information;
which is proof against all arguments;
and which cannot fail to keep people
in everlasting ignorance.
That principle is Condemnation before Investigation.

(Herbert Spencer)

Truth will out.

(William Shakespeare, Merchant of Venice)

49

Witness and Power of History

It does not pay to underestimate the power of history.

Historians, historiographers and biographers are merely tour guides who research and collect information left behind and present it to readers. They penetrate the guesses and gropings, the perhapses and maybes. They investigate and analyze the counterfeits, substitutes, myths, falsehoods and red herrings. Relentlessly, they research, detect and unearth events and truth buried in the graveyard of the past. Focusing on a particular subject, they arrange events that occurred over time into a narrative, usually in chronological order.

Authors, journalists, researchers, investigators, etc. have generally concluded that a narrative is incomplete unless it answers six questions: who, what, when, where, why and how (commonly referred to as the *Five Ws and One H*). Omitting any one of these questions can leave a gaping hole in a narrative. I have strived to answer all these questions in *Preserving the Truth*.

The words we speak, the words we read, and the sentences we write reverberate with the voices of those who preceded us. Some past events are celebrated; others are concealed, pending discovery by diligent searchers and truth seekers. History proclaims advancements, achievements, successes and triumphs; it also lays bare tragic blunders, foolish missteps, dark secrets and skeletons.

Regrettably, history is often undervalued, overlooked or dismissed. However, without the past, the present cannot be *fully* understood. For example, without knowledge of the Old Testament background and prophecies, one is unable to fully comprehend or appreciate the New Testament and the arrival of Jesus Christ.

The Old Testament records in detail not only the many blemishes, stains, sins and evil deeds of God's people, but also affirmations of God's faithfulness to them. Imagine the loss if the instructive, fascinating histories of Adam and Eve, Noah, Jacob, Moses, David, Solomon, Ruth, Nehemiah and Samuel, to name just a few, had not been included in the Bible.

Early on, Moses relayed God's instructions to the Jews that their history must be kept alive forever. "Only take heed and keep your soul diligently, lest you forget the things your eyes have seen and lest they depart from your heart all the days of your life; make them known to your children and your children's children" (Deut. 4:9; Ex. 13:3–10).

Remembering sustained their survival as a nation, as God's chosen people. When they remembered their history, things went well; when they forgot, they paid dearly. Their memories told them how and who delivered them (God), what to do, when and where. By remembering their yesterday, the Jews discovered the meaning of their today and the goal of their tomorrow. Knowing and passing on their nation's special history was very important. God ordained several commemoration celebrations that Jews continue to observe annually on special days.

If the Two by Two Church leaders had acknowledged the legacy of their past history and founder and passed it down to succeeding generations as the Jews and Luke did (Luke 1:1–4), there would have been no need for this book to be written.

Why Historical Facts are Important

Reasons a clear knowledge of historical facts are important in any context:

- To preserve historical truth, understand how and why something began, progressed and arrived where it is currently; to be aware of shared roots; to know the history of one's ancestry, tribe, race, nation, religion or culture can provide deep and meaningful insights into oneself.
- To avoid repetition of errors and reinventing the wheel; to build on the framework of past knowledge and apply lessons learned for an improved future.
- To gain invaluable insight through hindsight; to fill in gaps, reasons and understanding; to provide clarity and sense.
- To more fully appreciate and value the individuals who lived in the past, e.g. their contributions, victories, achievements, challenges, setbacks, hardships. To be aware of the past fosters empathy, compassion, inspiration, gratefulness, praise and joy.
- To understand the true causes, contributing factors and consequences of the history and development of one's spiritual beliefs and methods; to provide a sense of spiritual

stability and to contribute to believers becoming more "rooted and grounded" in their faith (Eph. 3:17).

Value of Skepticism

Prove all things; hold fast that which is good (1 Thess. 5:21).

Skepticism is suspended judgment, an attitude of doubt. It is an approach that subjects all knowledge claims to scrutiny with the goal of sorting out true from false claims. A skeptic ponders. Truth is a skeptic's foundation for belief.

Learning about shocking news or painful disappointments that challenge or contradict current beliefs can create cognitive dissonance (when a person's beliefs do not align with facts). Skepticism is the natural, rational result that leads to questioning, searching for facts and reconciling beliefs so they conform with truth. (*See* Cognitive Dissonance below.)

A skeptic does not spontaneously trust, does not believe an authority without proof, does not accept anecdotal stories or personal experiences as reliable indicators of truth. In two words, the skeptic's position is: "Prove it." Without indubitable proof, claims are merely unfounded beliefs, opinions or preferences. A skeptic wonders, "why, who says, how do you know, what does that mean, where is it written, when was it said?" and more (Five Ws and 1 H).

Skepticism is healthy and wise. Great teachers promote skepticism. The Bible encourages it, "Prove all things; hold fast that which is good" (1 Thess. 5:21). Suspending judgment while investigating facts can prevent harm, e.g. jumping to unwarranted conclusions, unnecessary hurt, misplaced anger, needless heartache, missteps, errors or misunderstandings, to name a few.

Those who possess the facts and know the truth should welcome the skeptic and be more than willing to provide it. Such sharing can be meaningful, valuable and rewarding. The truth has nothing to hide.

A universally acknowledged truth is that all things on Earth have a beginning, and the 2x2 Sect is no exception. It is natural for humanity to question where something or someone came from; to want to establish reference points of cause, source and origin.

The preceding chapters show that:
- There were no Workers in any countries prior to 1897.
- There were no Fellowship Meetings or baptisms prior to 1902.

- There were no hymns written by Workers or Friends prior to 1897.
- The 2x2 Sect published no hymnal prior to the *Go-Preacher Hymn Book*, circa 1906.

Skeptical readers who remain doubtful that the 2x2 Church and Ministry did not exist prior to the twentieth century are encouraged to independently locate the following items **predating 1897:**

- A hymn written by a Friend or Worker
- A 2x2 hymnbook
- A photograph or name of a Worker or Friend
- A letter written by a Friend or Worker
- A 2x2 Convention announcement or speakers list
- A 2x2 Workers List
- Any notes from any 2x2 gathering/assembly
- A group that met in homes with pairs of itinerant ministers

As information, the printing press was invented in 1450; the first typewriter was invented in 1868; photography was invented in 1839; and the Kodak camera came on the market in 1888. All these reproduction options were available before 1897 and could have provided some of the above.

The complete absence of *any* earlier evidence of the above items is very telling. From a historiographic perspective, their absence is a "smoking gun." This is one of those times when absences speak louder than words. The inescapable past is part of the present—when it speaks and when it is silent.

At this late date there are no living primary witnesses with empirical knowledge of the 2x2 Sect's early days. However, many members left behind recorded eyewitness accounts and correspondence, e.g. William Irvine, John Long, Alfred Magowan, Joe Kerr, Ed. Cooney, Goodhand Pattison. There were also numerous secular eyewitnesses, e.g. reporters, journalists and legal court documents.

The history presented in this book is supported by extensive and diverse contemporary accounts, recollections, letters, notes, essays, photographs, public records, newspaper articles, books, ship passenger lists, census and genealogical records, etc., all dated *after* 1897. Most of these documents are easily accessed on the associated website *TellingTheTruth.info*.

❧❧❧

50

Why Truth Is Important

A good understanding is the surest way to avoid a misunderstanding.

Importance of Truth. Clarification is the best defense for avoiding the hazards of ambiguity. True communication is only possible when parties attach the same meaning to terms, i.e. are on the "same page." The idiom "comparing apples to oranges" is sometimes applied when two individuals understand something in totally different ways. Therefore, to minimize or eliminate equivocation, the following terms, as used in this book, are defined below.

Truth: That which is true; a statement that accords with fact or reality; an established, proven or verified fact.

Fact: An irrefutable, verifiable piece of information; something known to be true, proven correct—unlike a belief, which is a thought we have decided is true, but may or may not be true.

Belief: To accept (with or without proof) that something is true; to trust, have faith or confidence in someone or something; to credit with veracity. A set of beliefs is *a belief system*.

Rational and *Irrational*: Rational thought is based on facts, logic and reason (not feelings). Irrational thought is emotionally based and lacks facts, logic and reason.

Values: What one believes to be important, ranked by worth, desirability and goodness; beliefs that guide or motivate attitudes and/or actions. A set of values is a *value system*.

Logic: The study of the methods by which a conclusion is proven beyond all doubt. Given the truth of the premises, the conclusion must be true.

The truth does not mind being questioned.
A lie does not like being challenged.

**Truth is of *primary* importance to a rational person—more important than retaining one's current belief. In rational thought, truth is the foundation for belief. When their beliefs are proven to be incorrect or unfounded, the rational person changes and realigns them to reflect what is true. The rational person chooses to believe what actually occurred, based on evidence they have carefully examined, tested, weighed and evaluated. They are willing to risk safety for truth. Is the evidence true? Is it sufficient? Does the conclusion logically follow the facts?

Truth is *secondary* to an irrational person. Truth is not the foundation for their beliefs. They choose their beliefs without requiring proof. Often, they give primary importance to holding fast to their current beliefs or the status quo. Rejecting what they do not want to know in favor of what they prefer to believe, the irrational person is more concerned with securing an arrangement of *facts* that coincides with their current accustomed beliefs than in finding truth. They prefer safety over risking.

Unwilling to examine contrary evidence, the irrational person may make decisions and form beliefs from emotions (anger, fear, hope, love, etc.), vested interests, authority figures, traditions, suggestions, habits, repetition, familiarity, prejudice, propaganda, intimidation, whims, arbitrariness, gut feeling, apathy, submissiveness, etc. It is not uncommon for them to expend much effort to justify a challenged belief and to preserve fiction, fraud, fables, myths and errors rather than admit to or accept the truth. Their beliefs are not based on adequate evidence and sound logic, but rather on their desire to believe.

Beliefs and Values

Simply stated, a belief is something one considers to be true, whereas a value is something one considers to be important. *All i*ndividuals hold a personal belief system and a value system.

Children usually adopt the personal and spiritual beliefs and values of those in authority over them (parents, ministers, teachers, etc.) and regard them as their own, even though they may not have consciously chosen them. When children arrive at the age of accountability, they normally begin to question and challenge their instilled beliefs and values.

Through testing, proving and re-evaluating their personal and spiritual beliefs and values, an individual decides whether to accept, reject or wisely suspend belief, pending more information before they make a decision. From their examination, they formulate and internalize the ones they are firmly convinced are true or important— they take ownership of them. With the arrival of additional or corrected information, this re-evaluation decision-making process reoccurs.

> *A truth that is merely acquired from others only clings to us as a limb*
> *added to the body, or as a false tooth, or a wax nose.*
> *A truth we have acquired by our own mental exertion*
> *is like our natural limbs, which really belong to us.*
> *This is exactly the difference between an original thinker*
> *and the mere learned man.* **(Arthur Schopenhauer 1788–1860)**

Challenging events and tragic circumstances create questions that can cause one to re-examine their spiritual beliefs and values, such as discovering the 2x2 history and founder. Seeking for wisdom and understanding, some strive to "prove all things" (1 Thess. 5:21); and to "be fully persuaded in his own mind" (Rom. 14:5). This process often serves to deepen one's faith and often leads to a closer relationship with God.

Spiritual gravity may be obtained during the process of making certain one's faith is built on a solid foundation of truth. Individual Bible study and knowledge can lead to peace and a firmer commitment as truth seekers endeavor to avoid the error of "not knowing the scriptures nor the power of God" (Matt. 22:29).

Many people experience a deep innate need to get back to their roots, to know their past. Spiritual stability can result from knowledge of history regarding how, when, where and upon what principles one's church was founded. Historical insight into one's spiritual roots may enable one to become well-grounded and more firmly rooted in their spiritual life.

Reconciling History

Cognitive Dissonance is a theory in social psychology referring to the mental conflict that occurs when a person's beliefs do not align with facts. It happens when a person is confronted with additional or corrected information that contradicts their beliefs.

Cognitive dissonance often causes mental distress. Feelings of unease and tension arise. People attempt to relieve their discomfort in various ways. Some utterly reject the new information without investigation. Others may reconcile the inconsistencies by altering one belief so that it conforms with the other.

Many joined and remained in the 2x2 Church chiefly because they were told and believed its historical lineage traced back to the apostles and the **original** New Testament church. Therefore, it is not surprising that they felt spiritually defrauded, deceived and betrayed upon discovering at this late date that the true 2x2 Church history was withheld from them and their ancestors. Trust was broken. For some, the resulting spiritual agony triggered acute grief, distress, justifiable anger, panic attacks, depression and even PTSD. *See Reflections* and *Reflected Truth* in Appendix M.

For some, the historical knowledge was the catalyst that motivated them to verify the evidence. No longer complacent, some become determined to discover the truth, regardless of the consequences or cost. It takes courage to be willing to question, research and reassess information contrary to what one was taught and believed. The rational thought process of reconciling and integrating history into one's current beliefs and values facilitates spiritual growth and a deeper relationship with God.

Even so, many prefer to continue believing explanations that contradict verifiable historical records. Some Workers have misleadingly claimed the 2x2 Sect's direct lineage on Earth is impenetrable or unknowable, and that God ordained it to be that way. For example, US Worker Willie Pollock declared, "We can't explain it. By faith, we accept it. If we need too much explanation, we don't have faith." Pollock's reply employs willful ignorance and deception with an ad hominem attack on skeptics.

The *willfully ignorant* are those who lack information or facts because they have refused to acknowledge them (whereas the *uninformed* are those who have little to no knowledge about something). Leaders of the 2x2 Sect who remain uninformed and/or willfully ignorant about their church history are inexcusable. Facts do not cease to exist because they are ignored. Facts dismantle excuses.

God recorded in Scripture His universal plan to save mankind through faith and belief in Jesus Christ alone. Jesus stated, "I am the way, the truth, and the life: no man cometh unto the Father, but by me" (John 14:6). The Scripture pertaining to God's plan of salvation (Jesus Christ) has been misapplied by some Workers to the beginning and ministry of the 2x2 Church belief system.

When it can be shown that a similar belief system, way or method was started by two different sources (God and Irvine) at two vastly different times in history, with no traceable linkage to each other, it is not possible for them to be the *same* identical entity. One is God's plan of salvation, and the other is a man's restoration movement.

As recently as 2019, Brother Worker Donald Campbell misrepresented the origin of the 2x2 Sect at the Winchester No. 1 New Zealand Convention: "These things were decided and settled in Heaven long before this world was ... and it is not given to man just to know how it was ... we don't look to any man or woman and say, 'This person began this thing' ... There were a group of them in Ireland ... it didn't begin there. It was already begun in Heaven; all that did happen was that it was uncovered. Made known again."

The 2x2 origins are no longer vague or obscure. Far from being impenetrable, the 2x2 Church can be easily traced back as far as the turn of the twentieth century, when Irvine started what he called his "Great Experiment." On the other hand, God's way of salvation in and through Jesus Christ can be traced back to God Himself through recorded history, the Bible, which opens with the words *In the beginning*.

Just as one cannot legitimately plagiarize the work of another and pass it off as their own, neither can one *legitimately* take Scripture referring to a heavenly, spiritual beginning and pass it off as referring to the 2x2 Sect's beginning in Ireland. Doing so commits the fallacy of equivocation and falls short of "rightly dividing the word of truth" (2 Tim. 2:15). Equivocation is the use of a key word or phrase in more than one sense in the course of a statement.

At the Convention at Glen Valley, BC, Canada on Aug. 4, 1988, Don Wolfenden (from Pakistan) equivocated using this claim, "When did this start? Some said 100 or 200 years ago. But this was in the heart of God from the beginning. God's Way is in the Bible. Jesus the same, yesterday, today and forever. This is God's Way and we are in it."

With the sheer magnitude of broadly consistent, reliable data from the sect's early days, drawn from a variety of public and private sources, there is now a transparent, comprehensive picture of the birth of this movement.

This begs the question: Why have the 2x2 Sect leaders not recorded a true and accurate account of their history? It has been over 100 years since they expelled their founder, William Irvine, who initiated the ruling that there was to be no printed literature. Why continue to follow his manmade rules that are contrary in principle to recording history, when the Bible itself is a history book? When history is meant to be one of our greatest teachers, why not be willing to record it for posterity?

Followers have the right and responsibility to question and know the beliefs, practices and history of their faith, especially when "everyone of us shall give account of himself to God" (Romans 14:12).

The following letter addressed a Worker's diversionary reply cautioning the questioning writer not to be taken up with genealogies. The Worker is the highly esteemed US Overseer of Oregon, Howard Mooney (circa 1988). *Read more* correspondence by this writer on website *Expressions by Ex-2x2s (Ex2x2.info)*

Dear Howard,

I couldn't agree more wholeheartedly with your position towards natural genealogies and other endeavors mentioned in 1st Timothy which are counterproductive and wasteful to the preservation and growth of our fellowship and love for Truth.

However, when we preach that our lineage harkens from the beginning and has been shaped by the sure and sovereign will of God; and when we preach that out of humanity in general, God has been sifting and molding a particular and peculiar people who would embody and embrace His plan with whom he would give His special revelation and dispensation, then our genealogy must be set forth with meticulous detail and accuracy, as has been done by not only the Old Testament authors, but also Matthew and Luke.

Apparently, God felt the lineage of Christ was important enough to document it in exactitude and occupy the first 17 verses of Matthew in which the Jewish descent to Abraham was traced. Luke was divinely inspired to trace the genealogy of Jesus to Adam which represents a direct connection with not only the Jews, but all mankind. I believe, therefore, that it is incumbent upon us if we are preaching the sectarian doctrine of apostolic succession, either explicitly or implicitly, we must substantiate this factually as God moved Matthew and Luke to do. If indeed, we can't prove beyond all doubt that we have an unbroken connection with first century Christianity, then obviously, it should not be preached as an indisputable fact.

Conversely, if we lay no claim to unbroken succession, then we are in effect admitting to an earthly organizer, a person who in our particular instance began this movement and resurrected what he felt to be primitive Christianity through emphasis upon select and specific scriptural reference for this purpose.

If this is so, let us honestly admit to it and remove the questions and cloak of secrecy which have intentionally or unintentionally shrouded the origins of this way. If the early foundation of our fellowship be based upon anything less than a full disclosure of the pure and honest truth, then the entire structure, no matter how closely it may be aligned with specific scriptures, is in error and in grave jeopardy as an instrument through which God would desire to work.

Your Brother in Christ,

Jim Vail

The Law of Cause and Effect and the Law of Compensation.

The past is our history, the present seeds our tomorrows. Hindsight is a wonderful opportunity to obtain clarity, perspective and understanding. Those who fail to read, know and learn from past history may end up repeating its mistakes.

Lessons learned are past experiences that are considered in future decisions, actions and behaviors. The basic purpose of reviewing lessons learned is to promote the reoccurrence of desired outcomes and to prevent the reoccurrence of undesirable outcomes. Two principles that influence the future are the *Law of Cause and Effect* and the *Law of Compensation*.

Law of Cause and Effect. The world operates under this Law, i.e. for every cause, there is an effect or consequence, good or bad. All actions have a reaction. Future consequences are shaped by present actions. Every life choice has some kind of consequence to some degree.

Law of Compensation. A life principle and observation in the Bible is "A man reaps what he sows" (Galatians 6:7); also called the *principle of sowing and reaping*. Life is full of consequences from actions, both good and bad.

The unleashed consequences of 2x2 leaders' earlier actions continue to surface and plague Workers. The diminishing membership is not fulfilling biblical prophecies about the "falling away," and "love waxing cold." Rather, it is the result of the Workers reaping what they sowed and experiencing the boomerang effect.

Over time, the Workers have caused or seeded several major exoduses of 2x2 Sect members by (1) dealing dishonestly and consciously hiding and/or denying the sect's true history and founder; (2) non-uniform procedures applied to divorcees who remarry (*See* Chapter 29), (3) their method of dealing with 2x2 perpetrators of child sexual abuse (*See* Chapter 41), and (4) worldwide inconsistencies in policies, e.g. celebration of Christmas and weddings, consumption of alcohol, dress codes, hair, etc. (*See* Chapters 34–35).

Why Are 2x2s Leaving? Numerous in-depth accounts providing reasons for members' departures are posted on the website *Expressions by Ex-2x2s (Ex2x2.info)*. Besides the above-mentioned causes, some other problematic issues Ex-2x2 dissidents have cited that contributed to their exits (in no particular order) are:

Workers claiming that the 2x2 Sect is God's only/right way (Living Witness Doctrine, exclusivity); denying that the Holy Spirit is working in other Christians/believers; usurping the Holy Spirit's role as the believer's personal guide (John 16:13); teaching the traditions of men (Workers) as commandments of God (Matt. 15:3–9, Mark 7:6–13); lack of scriptural basis for many legalistic rules; withholding baptism and communion; immorality in the ministry; failure/refusal to answer sincere questions; unscriptural doctrine and doctrinal ambiguity (grace, works, trinity, sin, repentance, eschatology, etc.); inappropriate gospel sermons at funerals; taking official sect names while claiming to have none; incorporating in some countries (Alberta, etc.); idolization of Workers; judgment without mercy; no recourse for Workers' decisions (no appeal process), unconditional submission required, etc.

Long touted as "the perfect way," the numerous flaws and inconsistencies in a church claimed to be "the same all over the world" has many members experiencing cognitive dissonance and disillusionment. Therefore, a growing number of members have lost confidence in the 2x2 belief system and its leaders, and many have chosen to disengage from it.

Under the leaders' current ***modus operandi***, it appears the 2x2 Sect is not sustainable. So far, there have been at least five major 2x2 Exoduses. *See* First Exodus, Chapter 24, 1914; Second Exodus, Chapter 28, 1928; Third Exodus, Chapter 32, 1950s; Fourth Exodus, Chapter 33, 1982; and Fifth Exodus, Chapter 35, that began in the 1990s and is currently ongoing. These exoduses have been caused by 2x2 leadership reaping what they sowed.

Generally, the 2x2 Church leaders (with some exceptions) have underestimated the power of history and truth and have neglected their importance. By ignoring their past and making the same mistakes over and over, they have shown themselves to be slow learners and repeat offenders.

> ***Those who fail to learn from history are condemned to repeat it.***
> **(Winston Churchill)**

In Closing. This book is the most detailed historical account ever published about William Irvine and the Two by Two Church he founded. If the history had not been covered up, omitted and denied; and if false, erroneous information had not been substituted in its place; and if attempts to rewrite its history had not been circulated, there would have been no need for this book to be written.

In sharp contrast to the oft repeated mantra that the 2x2 Church is *the same the world over*, it is extraordinary that the answers to questions regarding its origins are so varied, contradictory and even obfuscatory. The labyrinth of replies varies considerably from Worker to Worker, member to member, place to place and time to time. Failure to provide a true, consistent and comprehensive narrative of 2x2 history is not honest and lacks integrity and credibility. Many questioners find this disappointing, disturbing, disheartening, even shameful and insulting.

What Will the Future Hold?

The previous chapters show some of the areas where the 2x2 Sect has transitioned and developed, and that process will continue. Just as in the past, there have been disputes and differences, and changes in doctrine and practices, so will there be more to come.

Currently, new issues are facing the church that are being processed consistent with the leadership's historic attitude toward disputes and differences (typically by Regional Overseers agreeing on internal policies that are then applied locally or worldwide). Many of these issues are also faced by other churches, such as addressing domestic violence, child sexual abuse, remarriage after divorce, systemic corruption and abuse of power. In some locations, Workers have recently been willing to take lessons from other churches and adopt or adapt minimal policies to address such issues.

As well, there are regional differences in many matters, such as divorce and remarriage, consumption of alcohol, communion wine, attendance at sports or entertainment venues, attitudes toward technology use, politics, health controversies, etc. Frequent international travel highlights these differences and may foster harmonization or heighten discontent.

Internal rules, such as the focus on women's attire, cosmetics and hair are being modified in some parts of the world, possibly as an attempt to retain members who might otherwise leave. Other current issues in wider society, such as gender and treatment of minorities may become more topical.

Current and future members will now be able to review and comprehend the evolution of the 2x2 Church Fellowship over time. In the future as new situations arise, perhaps beliefs and practices will be addressed, and changes made in a timelier manner.

Learning lessons from the past leads to forming wiser choices in the present and paves the way to an improved future. Workers and members alike now have the opportunity, perhaps as never before, to contribute to the positive future evolution of their Fellowship, while honoring and accepting the past. Acknowledging the past provides good reasons to act or not act and make timely changes and adjustments, individually and collectively.

Some changes that might lead to a restoration and resurgence of the movement are: an acceptance and admission that the history has been mishandled and misrepresented; a willingness to reassess and turn to the core doctrines of the Christian faith; members being allowed to be individually guided by the Holy Spirit; acceptance of believers outside the 2x2 Sect as fellow-Christians, as was the belief when the sect began. "Other sheep I have which are not of this fold" (John 10:16).

As the title, *Preserving the Truth,* indicates, the purpose of this book is to present, safeguard and preserve and make easily accessible the early historical details of the 2x2 Sect, and to cause William Irvine's name and role to become common knowledge among 2x2 members, former members and others. May this book help the reader to develop a deeper appreciation for history and lead them to a closer walk with God.

THE END.

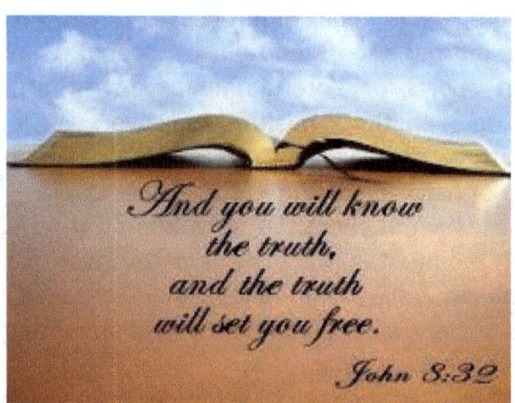

And you will know the truth, and the truth will set you free.

John 8:32

Appendix A   1905 Workers List and Married Workers

NAMES of WORKERS at JULY 1905.

Wm. Irvine	D. McLachlin 1904	M. McDougal 1902
John Kelly	Wilson Reid 1904	M. Knox 1902
John Long 1899	Alex. Walker 1904	Annie Smith 1903
Geo. Walker 1899	Tom Noble 1904	May Carroll 1903
T.M. Tunner 1899	Sam Aitchison 1904	T. Moore 1903
Alex. Givan 1899	Alex. Paterson 1904	M. Skerritt 1903
Albert Quinn 1900	Herbert Reid 1904	P. Hodgins 1903
Mat. Wilson 1900	Rob. Bash-ford 1904	J. Chapman 1903
W. Gill 1900	J. Smith 1904	Lily Coles 1903
John Sullivan 1900	J. Fawcett 1904	Alice Pipe 1903
Ben Boles 1900	Dave Christie 1904	Lizzie Sergent 1903
John Hardy 1900	Dick Watchorn 1904	Mrs. Carroll 1903
A. Alexander 1900	Jas. Martin 1904	M. Patton 1903
Irvine Weir 1900	J. Wrightman 1905	M. Gownes 1903
W. Clelland 1900	H. Gillespie 1905	A. Stanley 1903
Ed. Cooney 1901	John Grace 1905	A. McClung 1903
Noble Stinson 1901	Percy Abbot 1905	F.C. Carroll 1904
W. Abercrombie 1901	John Stone 1905	B. Baxter 1904
Jack Little 1901	W.G. Armstrong 1905	Mina Reid 1904
Andrew Robb 1901	Tom Betty 1905	Jean Allan 1904
J. Cavanagh 1901	W. Jones 1905	Cha. Ryan 1904
Ed. Rooney 1901	J. Williamson 1905	Bella Cooke 1904
D. McKay 1901	A. Armstrong 1905	Liz. Manning 1904
J. Jackson 1901	W. Jackson 1905	Lily Reid 1904
Joe Kerr 1902	Rob. Johnston 1905	Lottie Reid 1904
Chas. Glenn 1902	Frank Downie 1905	Aggie Hughes 1904
A. Hutchison 1902	John Andrews 1905	Tillie Moor 1904
John Breen 1902	Wm. Sneddin 1905	Annie Skerritt 1904
R. Moikle 1902	John McNeil 1905	Rob. Dane 1904
T. Elliott 1902	Bill Williams 1905	Bessie Rooney 1904
E.D. Armstrong 1902	Tom Paterson 1905	Annie McNaughton ... 1904
Geo. Beattie 1902	Jos. Boyd 1905	Annie McBride 1904
Chas. Guy 1902	C. Matthews 1905	Annie Irvin 1904
R. McClure 1902	Joe Burns 1905	Lillie Wood 1905
R. Skerritt 1902	Tom Purves 1905	F. Hodgins 1905
J. Hume 1902	Joe Foster 1905	Tilly Colhoun 1905
Sam Jones 1902	W. McIlrath 1905	H. Harrison 1905
Willie Weir 1903	Art. Greaves 1905	Lizzie McGregor 1905
J. Corcoran 1903	Crawford Crook...... 1905	J. Campbell 1905
T. Craig 1903	Geo. Manning 1905	H. Alexander 1905
D. Cameron 1903	Walter Smith 1905	A. Hutchison 1905
H. McNeary 1903	C. Somerville 1905	S. Skerritt 1905
C. Buttimor 1903	Thos. George 1905	S. Corcoran 1905
T. Haggart 1903	Abe. Myros 1905	Annie Davies 1905
Jn. Doak 1903	Thos. Hughes 1905	Edie Easy 1905
H. Olliver 1903	Robert Darling 1905	V. Jamieson 1905
Alf. Reading 1903	Geo. Samuel 1905	Bella Somers 1905
J Patrick 1903	John Byers 1905	Minnie McGurk 1905
W Carroll. 1903	Bo . Humphries 1905	Min. Pearson 1905
J. Fraser 1903	James Gordon 1905	Flor. Loftus 1905
Wilson McClung 1903	Alex. Gibson 1905	Beattie Holmes 1905
D. Doherty 1903	Chas. Ross 1905	Bella Reid 1905
J. Patterson 1903	W. Garvan 1905	Maggie Stewart 1905
Frank Scott 1903	H. Dennison 1905	Annie Taylor 1905
R. Bulleck 1903	H. McKay 1905	Edie Weir 1905
Tom Lynass 1903		Bella Kerr 1905
Tom Clarke 1903	**SISTERS.**	Mary Cook 1905
Alex. Pearce 1904	Sara Rodgers 1900	Ella McDougal 1905
Dave. Lyness 1904	Emma Gill 1900	M. Watson 1905
J. Jardine 1904	Jennie Gill 1900	Miriam Buttimor 1905
Hugh Doak 1904	M. McGivern 1901	Lily Wellwood 1905
Jim Hodgins 1904	M. McCauley 1902	Cha. Cavanagh 1905
H. Matthews 1904	L. Boyd 1902	F. Young 1905
Joe Gaskon 1904	L. Falkiner 1902	Edie Willis 1905
Jack Carroll 1904	Dot. Holland 1902	
Campbell Arrell 1904	Mary Spence 1902	
Jn. Elliott 1904	M. Moody 1902	
James McCreight 1904	Mrs. Elliot 1902	
Archie Russel 1904	M. Cooper 1902	

Many copies of the 1905 Workers List have been found with various formats and titles, including: *Names of Workers at July 1905, Names of English and Irish Workers up to 1905, British Isles Workers List, July 1905,* etc.

Regarding the date William Irvine and John Kelly entered the Work, one list shows 1897; another shows 1899 and nine lists leave the date blank. One list omits the names of Irvine and Edward Cooney. *See* detailed comparison of all 1905 Workers Lists on 2x2 History website. www.2x2church.info/early-workers

Eight Workers Lists contain a total of 201 Workers; one shows 194, one shows 199 and one shows 200. Of the 201 Workers, there were 76 Sister and 125 Brother Workers or 62% Brother and 38% Sister Workers. It is remarkable that all the Workers' surnames appear to be British; there is a noticeable lack of Swiss, German, French, Italian, etc. names.

A close analysis shows there are small differences, but the lists substantively agree. It is not known if any of these lists were created around 1905 or if they were recreated later. Summary numbers are:

	Year Entered Work									
	1897	1898	1899	1900	1901	1902	1903	1904	1905	Total
Male	2		4	9	9	13	20	25	43	125
Female				3	1	10	14	17	31	76
Total	2	0	4	12	10	23	34	42	74	201
Cumulative	2	2	6	18	28	51	85	127	201	

NOTE: The 1905 Workers List only includes Workers in/from the British Isles who were in the Work in July 1905. Workers who dropped out or died before 1905 are not listed. Workers who entered the Work after July 1905 are not shown.

Some who were or may have been Workers by the end of 1905 are Sam Boyd 1900; Elisabeth Jamieson 1905, Bob and Elizabeth Guy 1902; Abigail Armstrong 1905; Celia Conboy 1905; Mary Cook 1905; Maud Davis 1905; Anna Dodds 1905; Craig Fullerton 1905; Norman McBride 1905; George Thomas 1905. Frank Downie was married to Elsie (Ingram) who is not listed. Tom Betty was married to Elizabeth (Pendreigh) who is not listed.

List of All Known Married Worker Pairs

Last Name	First Names	Maiden Name	Children
Batstone	Verdun and Anna	Bryant	
Beattie	Ralph and Amy Constance Irene "Rene"	Lester	Four children
Betty	Tom and Elizabeth "Lily"	Pendreigh	Three sons
Brown	Joe and Grace	Prideaux	
Butler	Arthur and Emma		
Bye	Lars and Olga	Wold	
Carelse	Andrew and Ann		
Carroll	William "Bill" and Margaret "Maggie"	Hastings	Daughter May
Christie	David "Dave" and Emily	Wilson	Son and daughter
Cunningham	Bob and Isabella "Bella"	Fleming	Daughter Lucille
Dalrymple	Robert and Ruth	Brost	
deGroot	Albert J. and Emma M.	Besk	
Dennison	Tom and Shirley	Jesiek	
Dickson	Nathaneal "Nat" and Annie	Metcalf	One son
Doak	Hugh and Dessie	Dick	
Downie	Frank and Elsie	Ingram	Daughter Renee
Dunshee	Willard Amos and Ethel E.	McVicker	
Elliott **First married couple to enter the Work (1902)**	Tom and Ellen	Stinson	
Gard	Edward "Ed" and Caroline "Carrie"	Palmer	One son
Graham	Robert and Maude	Pryor	Five children
Guy	Bob and Elizabeth	Jones, Sam Jones' sister	
Harris	Vernandez and Edith		
Hartmann	Otto and Manny	Schneider	
Heselwood	Arther/Arthur and Elizabeth "Lily/Lizzie"	Ripley	Four children
Johnson	George and Ella	Powers	
Kilpatrick	Tom and Martha		
Kleven	Joseph "Joe" and Minnie	Propp	
MacLeod	Murdo and Dollie	MacLean	Son George
Magowan	Alfred and Sarah	Dawson	

Last Name	First Names	Maiden Name	Children
McClung	Walter and Christina "Chrissie"	McLennan	
McClung Entered the Work in 1903	Wilson and Anne "Annie"	Kerr	
McIlwrath	William "Willie" and Mildred "Millie" Olive	Spillett	Son Jimmie
Medica *Last married couple to enter the Work (1962) and last to die.*	Martin and Catherine Elizabeth "Betty"		
Micheletos	John and Anna "Annie"	McBride	
Peterson	Gus and ?		
Pitts	Jim and Mary		
Plaatjies	James and Gertrude "Gertie"		
Punke	Ernst and Finny		
Quick	Frank and Hilda	Vogt	
Richter	Charles "Charlie" and Belle	Weydt	
Robinson	Les and Evelyn		
Scott	Alexander "Sandy" and Eva	Idso	
Scott	Joseph "Joe" and Mary Ann "Millie"		
Smith	John Robert "Bob" or "João" and Martha	Hogg	
Steward	Andy and ?		
Thompson	Thomas and Annie	Swift	
Walker	George and Margaret "Maggie"	Dane	
Wilson	Matthew "Matt" and Leticia	Armstrong	
Winegard	Ellsworth and Caroline	Bedette	

Appendix B   William Irvine

Irvine Family Tree

Child No.	Birthdate	Death Date	Death Age	Name	Spouse	Marriage	Children
	07/08/1833	08/12/1913	80	John, Father	Elizabeth Grassam	12/09/1858	11
	11/10/1833	11/25/1897	64	Elizabeth, Mother	John Irvine	12/09/1859	11
1	03/14/1859	05/06/1918	59	John	Mary B. Stewart	11/14/1879	7
2	02/24/1861	07/18/1886	25	Margaret	unmarried		0
3	**01/07/1863**	**03/9/1947**	**84**	**William**	**unmarried**		**1**
4	10/05/1864	03/11/1928	63	James	Catherine Halkett	09/21/1888	0
5	06/23/1866	12/07/1938	72	Agnes	John Freebairn	11/16/1888	12
6	03/15/1868	06/23/1868	15 mo.	Henry #1	unmarried		0
7	01/26/1870	09/20/1872	2	Henry #2	unmarried		0
8	12/12/1871	06/15/1887	15	Elizabeth	unmarried		0
9	02/01/1874	04/28/1937	63	Jane "Jeanie"	Peter Comrie	04/28/1893	7
10	01/25/1876	11/23/1952	76	Helen "Nellie"	David Clelland	08/07/1896	7
11	02/09/1879	06/1963	83	Janet "Jennie"	Peter Clelland	10/27/1899	6

Statement of William Irvine
For the Trial of *Burfitt V. Hayward*, July 1913

Was born in Kilsyth, 1863, brought up Presberterian [sic], converted through Presberterian [sic] preacher in 1893. Instructed in the way of serving the Lord by the late John Colville, M.P. of Motherwell, N.B.

Studied in the Bible Training Institute, Glasgow for two years.

Preached for five years in the Faith Mission, (Scotland) and have just gone on preaching and practicing what I was taught, and what is generally called "Evangelical Christianity."

We seek to follow the pattern given by Jesus and the apostles and keep close to the practices of the early church, as there are so many different interpretations.

The Bible teaches, we preach and practice—that no drunkard shall inherit the Kingdom of God, or unclean or fornicator, or adulterer. Chastity, Charity, Righteousness and Integrity are the basis for all true Christian life and character, as well as service to God and man.

We emphasise the need for living Christ before our fellow men as well as preaching Him as Saviour. The Blood of Jesus Christ is our only plea for the forgiveness of sin for all men.

We encourage preachers to go and preach the Gospel freely to all men, two by two. Two women or two men or a married couple may go together. But never otherwise, or in violation of the laws of chastity as taught by both God and man.

We encourage people who want to live for God and worship and serve Him in spirit and in truth, to use their homes as the place of worship.

To show Christian hospitality.

To maintain good works before their fellows.

We hold yearly Conventions lasting from one or two weeks at convenient places, where preachers and saints, or Christians who live Christ at home, come and get help and encouragement to be true, chaste and useful to God in their daily life.

The Convention at Brewham 1912 lasted from June 14 to 24. About 200 people attended the meetings.

I was shown a leaflet on the 21st by Howard Burfitt, such as was said to be posted in Bruton outside the barber's shop occupied by Mr. Maidstone. This caused me to understand some of the language I had overheard from some of those who came to look on, rather than hear what was said in meetings.

I heard two women say, "Old Burfittt ought to be burned," and other remarks that made me wonder at their hostility as we are not accustomed to those things in other places.

Conventions are held at some worthy respected Christian home where accommodation is made for all who come, having due regard to Christian, Human, Moral and Spiritual; as well as health and sanitary considerations.

Women and men observe strict separateness in meetings, at meals and quarters for sleeping; and any violation of these conditions would at once be disciplined by asking them to go home. Half of the attendants at meetings are married people who have their families with them.

Out preaching there are many married people also. There are two, three, four, and five out of one family preaching, in many cases, brothers and sisters.

Our meetings and lives and preaching is always open to the public and we do nothing that any person who wants to see may not come and examine.

Our endeavour is to honour God, follow Jesus and obey the Scriptures as taught in the free churches of Great Britain today.

The charges Wilson has made are absolutely unfounded, both in the teaching and practice of those he seeks to libel with a view to hindering our work.

Yours very truly
William Irvine

~~~~~

The Palestine Post
March 10, 1947
Obituary of Mr. William Irvine

A well-known figure in Jerusalem passed away with the death yesterday, after a long illness, of Mr. William Irvine of Kilsyth, Scotland. Mr. Irvine died in his 84th year after having resided in Palestine since 1919, where he came in pursuit of his beliefs. He will be remembered by many who knew him as the kindly old white-haired gentleman seen on his daily walk between the Post Office and the Old City walls. He died with the full faith of better things to come. The interment will take place at the Zion Cemetery at 2:30 p.m. today.

~~~~~

Impartial Reporter, Enniskillen, N. Ireland
WILIAM IRVINE DEAD
March 16, 1947
THE APOSTLE OF THE 'PILGRIMS'

WILLIAM IRVINE is dead. His name means nothing to the younger generation, but those who can recall the great 'Pilgrims' or 'Dipper' Conventions in Co. Fermanagh of about 30 years ago, will recall the tall, hatless figure of William Irvine, who was at that time the 'teacher' and leader of the 'Pilgrims.' His rugged face, his dynamic personality, his strong and impressive address, swayed the thousands who gathered from all parts to hear him. The women folk adored him as a saint and listened to him with rapt attention as if they were hypnotised. He was a lovable man and a real Christian.

A recent issue of the *Sunday Post* [now the *Jerusalem Post*] contained an appreciation of William Irvine which will be read with interest by those who remember him. It was as follows:

"I was a soldier in Jerusalem. Maybe that makes you think of armed combats, of Arabs and Jews and strange scenes and customs. But my most vivid memory is of a tall Scotsman with a great head of white hair. Every morning I saw him striding out of the Holy City towards the Garden of Gethsemane. He wore a deerstalker's cap, heavy jacket, shorts and suede sandals. He greeted nearly everyone he met with a smile and a word of encouragement. And they felt the better for meeting him. You knew at once there was something remarkable about the man.

"He was William Irvine. Sixty years ago, at thirty-five years of age, he was general manager of William Baird and Company's Boswell Collieries in Lanarkshire. He was only in his twenties then and on the way to the top of his profession—a directorship. But he felt a higher call. He gave up his job. He founded in his native Kilsyth a movement which is still active. He did not believe in churches of stone. A tent or the open-air was all he wanted. He told his message with simple earnestness. Having founded his church in his native village, he felt he had to go with his message to foreign lands. He set out as a free-lance missionary. He went to Ireland, United States, Canada, South Africa, Australia, New Zealand, the Colonies. He became known all over the world as 'The Man with the Mission.'

"He lived frugally. His needs were slight. Money had no value for him. 'I have nothing,' he said. 'Yet—I lack nothing.' He quoted from Luke, 'Go your way. Behold, I send you forth, as lambs among wolves. Carry neither purse nor scrip nor shoes and salute no man by the way.' Between the two great wars he settled in Palestine. He received letters from all corners of the Earth where his message was still remembered. During the Second World War, he became a favourite of the British troops. They called him 'Jock.'

"Then last Sunday I learned that in Jerusalem, William Irvine had come to the end of his pilgrimage. He died, a single man, aged 84."

NOTE: Reportedly, the above article was written by Irvine Noble, a young English soldier. Very likely the last of his loyal followers to personally visit him, Irvine expressed, "I had Irvine Noble for half a day with a companion and enjoyed them" (to Everitts, Jan. 6, 1946, *TTT*).

Chronological Account of Irvine's Life
Excerpt from William Irvine's Letter to Dunbars
October 13, 1920

On November 1st [1893], I said, "Goodbye"—sold all I have and stepped out on the waters to walk by faith on a very troubled sea, and me a greenhorn like grass.

1893, on January 1st, I thought on finishing my course, so much disgusted was I with what the world looked upon as a successful life. It seemed so hollow and disappointing, both in pleasure, place and power.

1893, on January 8, I decided for the Lord and the battle began. Five days after, I gave public testimony to the men over whom I was taskmaster. I was 30 years of age on 7th of January, so that I began my 31st year by deciding whom I would serve and whom I would not. I very soon found out that neither church nor world fitted the New Testament service of the master I had chosen. All the holy hypocrites around came to me to be friends and work for me. I soon found out it was for profit every time and only to make more difficult what was already.

I was not satisfied with my knowledge of the Book [Bible] and wanted to get rid of much of my old infidelity and other things which I had learned. I had been in the yoke since I was eight years of age and could afford to take a little look around; and in spite of all my friends and enemies, I did what the Lord was prompting me to do. Thus acting, I was up against all sort of people who either held on to their good position, or were seeking a job in the religious world, or drawing a salary and shinning up the slimy path to glory amongst men. I had opportunities for joining something if I was willing to shut my eyes and mouth and take the price in mammon of unrighteousness.

As I opened my mouth the Lord filled it, but with what most people did not like. I benefited in the Bible Institute by getting to know the Book according to the teachings of the best and most holy and evangelical missionary people in the world. But these things only showed me that I would have to sell myself to someone of them if I wanted place. I had known too much of place, power and men to be hoodwinked or blindfolded—and finally chose to join the Faith Mission, which showed the most spiritual and fire, and so after two years, I started preaching with them in July 1895—and it was good, for here I found out a little more of myself and a little of the iniquity and bondage of being associated with a holy set of hypocrites who had more devil in them than where I had been, who would make any man a sinner for a word or a trifle—though I did not see it was devilry then.

In November 1896, I was sent to the West of Ireland to the hottest Roman Catholic spot in the world, and where this Irish trouble began at the beginning of this year. After 6 or 7 months there, I got to where the Carrolls were in Nenagh; and there BEGAN THE WORK that has spread so far.

In October 1896, I was working a mission quite near where the Sinn Féins are now getting more than they bargained for, in the burning of their town on October 3, 1920. I had been wondering when we would hear of it, but I did not know it would be on the day I STARTED the mission there that stirred the whole of that country for years to come, as I did in Southwest Ireland and finally all over Ireland.

In September 1893, I sent in my resignation for the Colliery and got free 1st of November. In September they refused to receive me as a student in the Bible Training Institute, Glasgow, though I attended the classes from outside.

In September 1898, I was put out of the Faith Mission for not being willing to conform to all their piccadilly discipline, etc.

In September 1903, I was put out of the church I had formed in my native town [Kilsyth] because I would not make it the head of the work I was doing.

On September 1903, I sailed for USA with George Walker and Irvine Weir, who quarrelled the first night they went out without me, which was the second day there. Then began pioneering and setting George and other to work, and I returned on September 5, 1904, next year to a day. Spent a year at home.

In September 1905, I sailed for South Africa with 17 Brothers and Sisters, half for Australia and New Zealand; landing in Frisco [San Francisco, California] on April 4, 1906, in time for the Frisco Earthquake. Then took my way to Paso Robles, and then to Los Angeles, where I had two weeks meetings in a tent where they were strong on all the healing and Pentecostal holiness of that time, out of which the Pentecostal movement began just as I left.

1907, I got back home in August after having Meetings in Canada in two places. Came back to the States that year and had Conventions and went back to Ireland for July again, by New Zealand, Australia and South Africa.

1908—Then back to States (and so for every year 'til 1913) on September, 11 years.

In 1914, I was rejected by The Testimony and crossed to USA on September 5th, the same day and from the same port I had left in 1903 on September 5th, 11 years ...

Calling in 1893 on January 8.

Left business 1893 on November 1.

Started preaching and got the Seal of God in September 1895 in Nenagh.

Was put out of Faith Mission and had first Convention in Ireland 1899.

Put out of Kilsyth Church and started for USA in 1903.

Had my first trip down California coast after the earthquake, April 1906.

Was rejected by Testimony in September 1914.

My last trip up coast in April 1919.

Left Los Angeles on June 4 or so, 1919.

Excerpt from William Irvine's Letter to Fay Sheeley
"I am also a Freemason"
January 30, 1929

You may tell your brother that I also am a Free and accepted Master Mason. My Mother Lodge being 547 – Stewart Scotch for past 45 years. So, I know all that it means. But if I were the Grand Master or the President of USA it could not avail me anything when wrath is being poured out on all that is prewar.

Obituary of Rev. Archibald Grassam Irvine
The Press (Christchurch, New Zealand)
June 16, 1952

The death occurred in Christchurch, on Saturday morning [June 14, 1952], of the Rev. A. G. Irvine, for nine years a Presbyterian minister at Ashburton. He was aged 66. Mr. Irvine came to New Zealand from Glasgow in 1900, when he was aged 14, and received a business training with the Union Steam Ship Company. He was at this period keenly interested in the work of the YMCA and the Sailor's Rest. He later studied at the University of Otago where he took the degree of Master of Arts and began his training for the Presbyterian ministry. In the First World War he served with the New Zealand Army as a chaplain. After the War he was a minister in North Otago for eight years, in Ashburton for nine years, and in Hawera for 18 years. Two years ago he retired to Christchurch, where he maintained his interest in church affairs, assisting at St. Stephen's Church at Bryndwr. Mr. Irvine was very popular with young people and specialised in Bible class work. He is survived by his wife.

The History of the Presbyterian Church of New Zealand provides the following details about Archibald Irvine:

- Master of Arts (M. A.) degree, University of Otago;
- Knox Theological Hall, Dunedin, NZ 1914–16;
- Ordained Waiareka (*sic*), 1916;
- Chaplain, WWI NZ Expeditionary Force in UK and France;
- Minister of Codford, NZ, 1919;
- Minister of Ashburton, NZ 1924;
- Minister of Hawera, NZ, 1933 (Elder 1940, 435).

References:
Register of New Zealand Presbyterian Church Ministers, Deaconesses & Missionaries from 1840, 171.
www.archives.presbyterian.org.nz/Page171.htm

~~~~~

Obituary of Irvine, Mary Jamieson Irvine
The Press, (Christchurch, New Zealand)
December 20, 1981

Irvine, Mary Jamieson (nee Murray). On December 19, 1982, at Windermere Hospital, loved wife of the late Rev. Archibald Irvine, loved sister of the late Donald, Murdoch, John, Catherine and Minnie, and loved aunt of her nieces and nephews; in her 94th year.

~~~~~

Note: Both Archibald and Mary Irvine were buried in Bromley Cemetery, Keighleys Road, Christchurch, New Zealand in Block 12, Plot 133. The funeral director for both burials, J. Lamb, Trotter & Son of Christchurch, New Zealand, stated in a letter dated February 21, 1996, that their records indicated Mary was born in Milton, New Zealand. Her father, Murdoch Murray was a farmer. Her mother was Margaret (Fletcher) Murray. Born April 25, 1889, Mary Jamieson Murray, age 26, married Archibald G. Irvine in 1916 in Milton, New Zealand. A niece from Christchurch was given as next of kin.

Appendix C   William Irvine's Omega Message

Information relative to William Irvine's Omega Message has been compiled from discussions with current and former followers; from over 1,000 letters he wrote to his followers; as well as letters written by Omega Message People to each other. No complete written statement of beliefs has surfaced to date. An example of a letter in his handwriting follows below.

Terminology. In his letters, Irvine usually referred to the Two by Two Sect as *The Testimony,* abbreviated as *The Testy.* He coined the terms *Alpha Gospel,* to apply to the sect from its inception to August 4, 1914, and *Omega Message, The Message,* or the *New Thing* for his latter teachings. He divided his teachings broadly into two time periods— before and after WWI. The Alpha Gospel was pre-WWI, and the Omega Message was post-WWI. Those who accepted and followed his Omega Message, he called *Little Ones* or t*hose who have ears to hear.* Current followers take no official name and are referred to as the *Irvinites, Message People* and *The Witnesses.*

Irvine's Comments about Himself

Through his letters, Irvine provides glimpses into his feelings about the role he sincerely believed he was divinely appointed to fill:

"If they would not hear me because of my leastness, they would not have heard Him [Jesus] ... For I am to Jesus, what Jesus was to His Father" (to Morgans, Dec. 18, 1931, *TTT*).

"You can see how much alone I have been in the conflict and how it has all centered around me and my Message. And I'm glad that these things were not made clear to me earlier, for there would have been more temptation to getting puffed up over them ... You may almost think me presumptuous in these readings, but I'm sure, else I would not give them to you" (to Skerritts, July 13, 1924, *TTT*).

"And to think that all that has happened is centered in me, rather than all the great men in worlds' eyes. People may think it vanity and pride of heart that would make me say these things, but it's the plain reading of the Book, and the key to unlocking all the mysteries of past and present things" (to Nobles, Nov. 17, 1927, *TTT*).

"Now I can see Jesus had it all planned and prophesied of, though I was all along quite ignorant and innocent ... and when the end of the Alpha Gospel came in 1914 and Judgment began, He broke up the House and cut asunder all who did not know or believe I was chosen to read Revelation and give 'meat in due season' to those who had ears to hear by my Alpha witness; in the world ripe for Judgment in 1914" (to Loitz, Jan. 14, 1946, *TTT*).

Irvine's Summary of His Omega Message

The following paragraph is an informative brief summary of Irvine's Omega Message in his own words:

> You ask how I can learn the things that should be taught at this time. Read Rev. 1:1–3 and you will find a perfect answer. Revelations which God gave to Jesus, and He to John by His Angel, that John should write them. "Blessed is he that readeth (meaning the Prophet) "and they that hear and keep the words, for the time is at hand." There was no Reader till the time was at hand.

> When the time of Tribulation comes, then John the Writer, and the Reader become the Two Witnesses. Rev. 10:11 and in quite a number of other places, Jesus speaks of John coming back and not suffering martyrdom till he is killed as in Rev. 11. John was the First Apostle of Jesus, and I am to be the Last, as there will be no need for such when Jesus comes with the meek to reign for 1,000 years as King of Kings and Lord of Lords ...

> Jesus told the Pharisees they searched the Scriptures, for in them they thought they had Eternal Life, while the Book teaches us the need of a Man sent of God, through whom He will speak words of Eternal Life. The Scripture is of no private interpretation, meaning we can only understand the words of inspired sent men, by the same Spirit; and men can pretend anything they want, and use the Scriptures any way they choose, they can never take the Spirit which God always can and will give only to the Man who is willing to fulfil the conditions revealed in all whom He ever sent.

> If you have ear to hear my Reading, you will soon find that you will have ears to hear what the Spirit saith for these days. Matthew 18 deals with The Man who is to be the Greatest in the Kingdom of Heaven and is The Test for all who know Jesus and will become the Little Ones." (to Law, Dec. 21, 1927, *TTT*)

Irvine's Explanation of the Need for a Prophet
October 11, 1930
PO Box 696
Jerusalem, Palestine

My Dear Friends;

Thanks for yours. The world is full of false prophets and prophecy, and every man seems to walk in his own thoughts and ways, iniquity and hypocrisy, so why not the need for a true Prophet? And don't think God will ask any man in the matter.

The Book is full of proofs that such a man is to be Prophet or mouthpiece of God for these days; if people can't see, then it is proof that they have no light, or worse, the light of them is darkness.

We have had 17 years of the Beginning of Sorrows according to what Jesus said in Matthew 24, etc., in diverse places, and **now we are to have worldwide war, famine, pestilence and plagues for seven years to end the whole fabric of religion, racialism and the language babble on the Earth**. What began at Babel is to end in the destruction of Babylon as you can see from Rev. 17 and 18. The Reader of Revelation and those who hear his reading are the new seed for the Kingdom of God being set up on the Earth.

You can see in Rev. 22 what it will mean for all who either add to or take from the words of this prophecy, by the reading of the Book by the Man. A Prophet is a man on the Earth for whom the Spirit of God is to see, hear and witness. People always loved the dead Prophets, but either did not feel the need of, or give ear to a living Prophet.

Jesus is on the Throne in Heaven, and most every form of righteousness on the Earth is carried on in His name and backed by His written record; SO WHY NOT A PROPHET?

Isaiah 55 is a record of this servant, whom Jesus makes Witness, Leader and Commander, for all who will hear Him. People's attitude toward God, Jesus and the Spirit is known by their attitude to the Servant. All who will hear my reading of Revelation, which is the program of Judgment of all man from 1914 to the end, will find a place of shelter, provision and comfort. All others will perish from the Earth. This is the reading of the whole Book, as it was in Noah's time to now.

My best wishes for you. Hear and your soul shall live, refuse and perish.

William Irvine

Irvine's Explanation of the Book of Revelation
William Irvine's Letter to Blackburns
September 14, 1936

My dear Blackburns:

Thanks for yours. I expect, by the time this reaches you, the World War will be on and John will not tarry much longer. Then you will see the drought and plagues following, according to Revelation 9:12, and the whole of what I have been showing His servants who were willing to hear and obey will shortly be done. Blessed are they who keep the sayings of the prophesy (sic) of this book, Revelation.

Revelation 22 is an outline of all that comes from the Throne. The River of Life flowing and the tree growing, its leaves for the healing of the smitten nations, while men fearing and war nearing, and our greater opportunity for witnessing and seeing the reward for those who hear and obey; and they who oppose and despise, wrath and more wrath to end all their silly cackle and lip service worship, so-called.

Revelation 22:6 shows you Him sending me, His Prophet-Angel.

Revelation 22:7 shows who are Blessed.

Revelation 22:8–9 the meeting of the TWO WITNESSES.

Revelation 22:10 Seal not the sayings of THIS BOOK, for they are NOW.

Revelation 22:11 The time at hand for men, unjust, filthy and righteous and holy are all in the same place and plane and will be rewarded according to the use they have made of the Witness. Revelation 22:12 as his work shall be.

Revelation 22:13 Jesus as Alpha, with the keys of Kingdom and Omega keys of Hell and Death. Revelation 22:14 shows who are Blessed and his commandments are not hard to keep which comes from the Throne, not Moses and Jesus, as in low (sic), or Alpha Days, but the Living God and Jesus as He gives us His Servant or Sent One.

Revelation 22:15 shows where the whole religious world now is and what their spiritual marks are. They can never have any part in the Tree of Life or entrance to the City by the Gates. The false preachers cannot climb up some other way this time.

Revelation 22:16 shows Jesus sending me to testify these things. Not in Babylon, but to those whom I got to know in pre-War days, called the seven churches.

Revelation 22:17 shows the Man to be the Angel.

Revelation 22:17 My message was to gather the Woman-Bride, who is to be the channel of the Spirit's Message, or Witness and all who hear my message will also say come; for my message is to whosoever will, as the Old Gospel was in pre-War days.

Revelation 22:18 shows how foolish any man is who tries to take from or add to the message and my reading of Revelation.

Revelation 22:19 they shall be as sure of death and Hell, as we who hear can be of LIFE, if we OBEY and so let the Spirit work in us and by us to all. He is preparing through trouble and suffering in the clouds now let loose on Earth, which will show who and what is what.

My love and best wishes in Him,

William Irvine

Irvine's Failed Prophecies

1923: "The 11th hour of the 11th day of the 11th month is Armistice Day. The year is probably from the year that Abram got the promise of the Land. If you look [it] up you will find it about 1923 BC as we see **1923 the probable year in which it will be fulfilled**" (to Skerritts, Dec. 1, 1922, *TTT*).

1932: "The Rapture comes at the end of the 1,000 years, and so shall we be with the Lord, not on the Earth, which will be finished so far as His purpose is concerned and burnt up ... There can be no Rapture of the church, for there is no church since 1914, and only such as have ears to hear and obey the Reader of Revelation or the Witness, Leader and Commander He has given to people, can have any hope ... **We are six months into Tribulation and no Rapture**" (to Chapmans, Feb. 12, 1932, *TTT*; Irvine believed in a seven-year Tribulation).

1934: "So Rev. IX is easier to read now than ever. 11.11.11 Jewish time was the hour, day, month of 1914 War. August 1st Jewish time it began and finished. 11.11.11 Christian time and the coming war hour, day, month and year may be **1st August 1934.** And John's coming at same time, for the World War, famine, pest and plagues I expect will begin together. **So our long expectations may now be in sight—20 years to a day from 1914 War**" (to Fountains, June 22, 1934, *TTT*).

1938: "We are now entering the 17th hour of His sufferings; and so the 18th year of Judgment; and now the 1st year of Tribulation, **which is the last 7 years** ... for this time **next year, when John will have come,** and the Woman be invited to come to Palestine" (to Fountains, Aug. 2, 1930, *TTT*).

1938: "So here I am awaiting my reward, with all the other 2,000 million on the Earth to be signed and sealed by John from Heaven— **probably at the end of the 24 years from 1914** ... Jesus' sufferings in the 24 hours ending in the tomb helps us to see the preparation in these 24 years ending in the tomb for the unregenerate world. The day, hour, month and year: 1914 + 24 = **1938** (to Edwards, Jan. 7, 1938, *TTT*).

1938: "This is my spiritual birthday and I expect we will be having a happy New Year and a real Xmas in John's coming at the end of 24 years from 1914 War, coming on when the 7 seals had been opened in Heaven. The 24 hours of Jesus' sorrow, death and burial have been well carried through since 1914, and now **six months ahead the end will come**" (to Skerritts, Jan. 6, 1938, *TTT*).

1938: "The Wall Street joke of raising a five million dollar fund to offer Roosevelt if he retires in five months—all these fives seem to draw our attention to our being in the last five months of the 24 years of Beginning of Sorrows and helps **to place the hour, day, month and year for Tribulation about 6th August**" [1938] (to Edwards, March 11, 1938, *TTT*).

1952: "So the great quake comes at the end, **about seven years from now**" (to Sutter & Pincetl, Nov. 18, 1945, *TTT*).

NOTE: A large collection of William Irvine's Letters are posted on the website *TellingTheTruth.info* in Founder, Irvine's Letter Collection. *See also* Chapter 25.

Telng. Addr : ALMASIE   Telephone 752

SUISSE PENSION
ALMASIE

JERUSALEM 25/4/36
P. O. Box 696

[Handwritten letter, largely illegible]

My Dear Walter + Annie

Thank for yrs. I expect you have been seeing in papers about what happened in Jaffa on 19/20 April 36 the Kings message days ago to the world came on 20th april the day the ark rested this is also the day Italy celebrates the founding of the Roman Empire over 2500 yrs ago which Italy had hoped to celebrate in addis abbaba but failed. The King took sick on 20th ...

Handwritten Letter by Wm Irvine to Walter, Neomi [Noble] & Co. from Jerusalem (April 25, 1936)

Appendix D   Edward Cooney

Books about Edward Cooney and His Followers.

The author of the only biography ever written about Edward Cooney, Dr. Patricia Thelda Roberts, born December 11, 1919, was one of eight children born to William Hamilton (1867–1943) and Emily (West) Roberts (1876–1952). Emily was the sister of John and William West, hosts of the Crocknacrieve and Mullaghmeen Convention grounds in Ballinamallard, Co. Fermanagh, Ireland.

Dr. Roberts attended the Enniskillen Model School and Enniskillen Collegiate. She obtained her B.A. at the University of California, Berkeley, and received her second degree from Sorbonne University in Paris. She received her M.A. from Columbia University, New York, and her Ph.D. from New York University. In 1984, she retired to her home village of Ballinamallard, Co. Fermanagh, Ireland, and passed away September 29, 2014.

Dr. Roberts' family became followers of Cooney around the turn of the twentieth century. In 1943, Edward Cooney officiated at her father's funeral. In 1950, she personally met Cooney in London, became one of his followers and was baptized by him in 1953. Fellow worshippers met in her home in Ballinamallard as long as she was able.

When my husband and I were visiting Enniskillen in 2004, Dr. Roberts invited us to have tea in her home. Also present were Fred Wood's daughter, Elizabeth McCord and Myrtle Doherty, also Cooneyites; Doherty is mentioned in the acknowledgments of all Dr. Roberts' books

Well placed to write a definitive account, Dr. Roberts compiled four books about Edward Cooney, all published by William Trimble Ltd., Enniskillen, N. Ireland; all are out of print. The titles are:

1. *The Life and Ministry of Edward Cooney, 1867–1960,* 1990 (ISBN 0 9510109 4 8). *Read* on website *TellingTheTruth.info* in Publications.
2. *Selected Letters, Hymns and Poems of Edward Cooney, 1867–1960,* 1991 (no ISBN)
3. *Selected Letters of Fred Wood 1890–1986,* 1997 (no ISBN)
4. *The Go-Preacher Movement: An Anthology,* 2000 (no ISBN)

Cooney Family Tree
Information provided by
Helena Halpin, Great Granddaughter of Mary Elizabeth Cooney and Russell C. Cooney, Grandson of Frederick George Cooney

(Verified with Ancestry.com)

Child No.	Birthdate	Death Date	Death Age	Name	Spouse	Marriage	Children
	01/1838	09/12/1924	88	William Rutherford	Emily Maria Carson	08/31/1863	8
	1842	12/16/1917	78	Emily Maria Carson	William Rutherford	08/31/1863	8
1	12/13/1864	05/28/1887	22	William McEffer	unmarried	n/a	0
2	02/16/1866	03/22/1953	87	Mary Elizabeth	Sydney Boyton Smith	09/9/1896	4
3	**02/11/1867**	**06/20/1960**	**93**	**Edward**	**unmarried**	**n/a**	**0**
4	04/18/1868	05/31/1945	77	Henry "Harry"	Ada Beatrice Gardiner	08/3/1895	3
5	09/03/1869	04/12/1940	70	Frederick George	Mildred Tatlow	08/28/1908	4
6	05/10/1871	08/29/1909	38	Alfred Carson	unmarried	n/a	0
7	04/23/1873	06/11/1898	24	James Ernest	unmarried	n/a	0
8	08/21/1875	08/03/1929	46	Edith Emily	James McConnell	07/1905	2

Rossorry Parish Church Cemetery. Several Cooney family graves are located in this church built in the 1840s, located on the outskirts of Enniskillen. Heading west out of Enniskillen, turn left onto Rossorry Church Road before Portora Royal School. The road twists and turns for about a mile into the countryside and the Rossory Church is on a hill on the left.

Tombstone Inscription:

COONEY

In affectionate remembrance of
William McEffer Cooney died 29th May 1887 aged 22 years.
James Ernest Cooney died 11th June 1898 aged 24 years.
Alfred Carson Cooney died 29th August 1909 aged 38 years.
Emily Maria Cooney died 16th December 1917 aged 78 years.
William Rutherford Cooney died 12th September 1924 aged 88 years.

Edward Cooney's Testimony, 1947

(Written soon after William Irvine's Death)

"Forasmuch as many took in hand to draw up a narration concerning the matters which have been fully believed among us as they delivered them to us they having been eye witnesses and attendants of the word, it seemed good also to me having been acquainted from the first with all things, accurately with method to write to thee, most excellent Theophilus, that thou mightest know the certainty of the things concerning which thou was instructed" (Luke 1:1–4).

There was in the days gone by, a certain man called **William Irvine**, upon whose heart God's spirit worked to raise him up like the judges of old, to lead back those in Christendom to the truth as it is in Jesus. In fact, he bore some resemblance to Samson. He was a strong man and warred with Spiritual Philistines effactually until Delilah so influenced him that he put her before God. **He has died recently in Jerusalem**. Let us hope that in his declining days, like Solomon, he discovered that to fear God and keep his commandments is the whole duty of man.

Some years ago, he wrote the writer to come and work with him in Jerusalem. The reply the writer gave was that when his hair grew again, as it was when first he met him, he would be glad to work with him, but not until then. The long hair of Samson seems to speak of revelation from God direct; not clipped, to suit his flesh, or the flesh of others. When Delilah clipped his hair to suit her flesh and the flesh of the Philistines who feared Samson, knowing that God was with him, Samson, although he shook himself not knowing that God had left him, found that Jehovah had departed from him, and that he was weak like any other man. 'Tis so with all God's Servants who depart from revelation from God direct and confer with flesh and blood.

In the year 1914 when we became aware of William's defeat, the writer was moved to go to see him personally and try and help him who had been such a help to him and others, and now needed help himself.

This desire he had was discouraged by his fellow Workers, but as he got to see he should obey God and not man, he went to Scotland to see the man of God who had lost the power he once had. The writer is glad ever since that he did this and believes he was of some help to his erring Brother.

At this time, the writer got to see that he should return to God as Jeremiah was exhorted by God to return to him; see Jer. 15:19, so that he might again stand before God, and in the light of his countenance separate between the precious and the vile; from what he had learned through William, from God, and what he had accepted from him which was not from God.

Jeremiah seems to have been influenced by flesh and blood revelation and mixing it with God's revelation to him direct, found his pain perpetual and his wound incurable, refusing to be healed. In this condition, he said to God, "Wilt thou indeed be unto me as a deceitful brook, as waters that fail?" [Jer. 15:18 KJV] The only remedy was to return to God and cease mixing God's revelation with that which proceeded from flesh and blood. This, the writer has sought to do with profit. William had been partially persuaded by Joe Kerr to accept the heresy that no one could be born again without meeting a living witness. Others held that that witness must be a sent preacher who had heard William or some other preacher who had heard him.

The writer got to see this flesh and blood revelation to be vile and gave it up in 1914, returning to the true Gospel preached by himself and William for four years after they met, which recognized John 20:30 to be true, and Paul's dialogue in Romans 10:14–18 answered by Psalm 19, where it shows God speaking through nature as he did to the magi through the law (which is perfect converting the soul), and finally through the preacher, the words of whose mouth and meditation of whose heart is acceptable in God's sight. The Lord knoweth them that are his and the writer's business is to depart from iniquity himself and exhort all who profess to be his to do so likewise; Iniquity meaning all that is not like Jesus who is equity.

Peter at the day of Pentecost thought that unless a man was circumcised by a living witness and kept the law, he could not be saved; but God showed him, as he showed me, this was not so, and God used him more after he got clear on this point—see Acts 10 and 11, also Gal. 2:11–21. Paul was a great help to Peter in this respect and has also been a great help to the writer.

An attempt has been made to give an account of God's dealings with us ignoring William Irvine. This is not honest. William Irvine was born again when a Presbyterian, through hearing John McNeill preach the

Gospel in Motherwell Town Hall, and I have in my possession a letter from him to me, claiming this to be so, written from Jerusalem before he died. He afterwards joined the Faith Mission denomination and was Pilgrim Irvine when I first met him in Borrisokane, Co. Tipperary, Eire.

In 1914, when all men of military age were required to register, Andy Robb registered himself as Independent Faith Mission. I registered myself as Christian and advised Willie Gill to council all to do likewise, but he said, "Let us take the name we call ourselves by *The Testimony of Jesus*." At that time, I am sorry to say I used to go contrary to my conscience, to avoid differing from my fellow Workers. I gave in to Willie in this respect and so erred, but have confessed my sin to God, and God has forgiven me. We have committed the same sin in the USA in calling ourselves *Christian Conventions*. We should repent and take the consequences.

Twenty years ago the writer declared to George Walker in Samuel Charlton's presence in Edgar Hawkins' home that it was his purpose to cut out of his life all that contradicted the Scriptures. George refused and excluded him from the fellowship of his brothers and sisters in the territory over which he claimed oversight. John Carroll had previously excluded him in his territory. James Jardine acquiesced in his territory and the exclusion has spread to British Isles.

He still goes on conscious that he has not been excluded by the One who prunes the vine. So the writer, after the way they call heresy, so worships the God of his fathers, believing all things written in the law and the prophets and signs himself Edward, which is the English for witness. His course is nearly run, but he hopes and purposes to go on.

By Edward Cooney, 1947

(Parker 1982, 115–17) *See also* Roberts 1991, 43–45, *TTT;* includes insignificant variations.

Statement by Edward Cooney for Court Case

July 1st, 1913

I, Edward Cooney, was born in Enniskillen, Ireland, and brought up in the Church of Ireland. Through the preaching of William Irvine, who was at the time an Evangelist in connection with a well-known mission called the "Faith Mission," I decided to become a disciple of Christ when about 32 years of age. Shortly afterwards, I decided to go forth and preach in fellowship with the said William Irvine and others in fellowship with him. Since then I have been preaching in England, Ireland, Scotland,

USA—Canada. During the last 12 months [I] have been preaching in Fermanagh, Ireland, my native county.

With regard to marriage, I hold [the] same views as taught by the Evangelical churches regarding it being honourable and that a man should have only one wife and a wife only one husband. I also hold in common with them that fornication is a grave sin and teach accordingly.

In common with the Evangelistic churches, I hold that Jesus Christ is our example and that His teaching and that of His apostles is to be received and practiced; that all that is contrary to their teaching and practice is wrong. Because Peter and Paul exhorted those who professed to be disciples of Christ not to adorn themselves with gold, pearls, or costly apparel, I teach likewise.

Mr. Wilson's statements that I and my fellow preachers encourage, or practice immoral conduct is absolutely without the slightest shadow of foundation. My brother-in-law, Sidney Boyton Smith M.A., Vicar of St. Clements, Bristol, can give evidence as to my personal character and as to my being incapable of teaching or practicing what is laid to the charge of my fellow preachers and myself in the leaflet published by Mr. Wilson, Cretingham, Framlingham, posted outside [the] barbers shop, Bruton, by the Vicar of Bruton.

Signed: E. Cooney

~~~~~

1928 Historic Meeting and Apostolic Council
Held in Andrew Knox's home in
Clankilvoragh, Lurgan, Co. Armagh, N. Ireland
By Edward Cooney

To God's children at present divided by the sleight of men and cunning craftiness whereby they lie in wait to deceive.

In Ephesians 4:14 Paul writes: "That no longer we may be infants tossed and carried about by every wind of the teaching in the sleight of men in craftiness with a view to the systematizing of error" (quoted from Greek text. Quotations in this letter from same).

God's revelation is Jesus the Christ, the Son of the Living God, progressively given to the heart of God's child from his father who is in the Heavens, Matthew 16:16–17. This revelation being progressive cannot be systemized; for we know in part, and in part we prophesy; any attempt to organize this revelation so that it becomes final produces stagnation—"for the path of the just is as the dawn that shineth more and more unto the perfect day." If the physical light was organized at the dawn stage, what a catastrophe it would be for the children of men. So, any attempt to systematize or organize the progressive revelation of the Christ, the Son of the Living God gradually given to God's children individually, with a view to its being received collectively, is equally a catastrophe with more fearful consequences, because the issues are eternal.

It seems to be unknown by many of God's children and unrealized by most that on October 12th, 1928, at Clankilvoragh, Lurgan, Ireland, at a meeting of those who might be called the apostles amongst the people of God—indeed there happened to be 12 present—a verbal agreement was submitted by the summer-up, James Jardine, expressed by John Carroll, called by the latter [at] different times a *Solemn Agreement* binding all the Workers not to express individual revelation even though true *IF* the Worker in whose field they were had not yet seen it. This verbal agreement was as declared at that historic meeting and apostolic council a **Basis of Fellowship for All Workers.**

When Edward Cooney refused to bind himself by it and declared he would retain the liberty God gave him when he started forth to preach, John Carroll, who seemed to be foremost apostle in the introduction of this agreement, rose up and left the room, declaring he would have no more fellowship with Edward Cooney; the other eleven apostles remained; but with the exception of the said Edward Cooney and one of his fellow apostles, Thomas Elliott, they all subsequently acquiesced in the graphic demonstration by which his fellow apostle, John Carroll, had excommunicated Edward Cooney from his fellowship.

This is a true description of what took place on that memorable occasion; and as the untruth has been spread that I went out of fellowship from my brethren and thereby caused a division, I write to let you know that I earnestly desired, and still earnestly desire, to remain in the fellowship of my brethren on the same condition as we had from the beginning, viz., that *the truth as it is in Jesus* be the only test by which His disciples are to be disciplined, and that the Scriptures are to be [the] only written revelation accepted as declaring the truth. One of the apostles has since said that it was not excommunication but withdrawal from a Brother walking disorderly and referred me to II Thes. 3:6–12. I appeal to my brothers and sisters in Christ to read the passage and see if it can with fairness be applied to me under the circumstances of which I have given an account.

Believe me still to be Christ's bondsman and yours for His sake.

Edward Cooney

P.S. I have written this letter in the first part impersonally, and in the latter part personally, purposely. [E. C.] (Roberts 1991, 5–6, *TTT*)

Letter by Edward Cooney to My dear Sister

1 Kingscourt Street
Belfast
May 1930
My dear Sister,

... I see now more clearly what was taking place, so seek ... to let you know some of the developments of the work of God and the adversary amongst us as God's people.

Undoubtedly God called us and separated us to be his people in the beginning; and most prominent and most used in this calling out a people for God's name was William Irvine who, at the time of his being sent forth to be a prophet, saw more clearly than any of us that the revelation of the Father to each individual child of His is the Rock alone on which Jesus Christ would build his church, and that the gates of Hades should not prevail against it ...

The kingdom about which Jesus spoke for the space of 40 days to his sent ones began when the Holy Spirit, the Paraclete, took control of the church, and like a rushing mighty wind impelled it into the good fight of faith. Barrenness and dearth are always the result of organization caused by flesh and blood revelation. We are slowly but surely drifting into this condition and prophecy has almost ceased amongst us. Our only hope is to get back to the simplicity and childlikeness of the beginning, especially those of us who have the oversight.

When I returned from abroad, the year before last, I had a long talk with Willie Gill about the situation. I told him that we who claim to have the apostolic oversight needed to be converted and become like little children so as to enter the kingdom, Matthew 18:3. He agreed with me regarding the necessity, that we, like the twelve whom Jesus desired should tend his lambs, feed and shepherd his sheep, needed conversion from the who-is-greatest-in-the-kingdom-of-Heaven spirit so as to become like little children as they did on the day of Pentecost, when they entered into the kingdom of which the Holy Spirit became the controller, as the executive of the Father and the Son.

From [when] Jesus spoke those words till Pentecost, the twelve were being converted and at that time with the 108 saints in fellowship with them became converted. The sent ones of Jesus got to the place where they were willing to do the will of God as recorded in Mark 3 and were brother and sister and mother to him. But they got away from that childlike trustfulness and so have we. A few of us see our need of turning again to this childlikeness that we had in the beginning; and I believe we are being converted toward it. But our brethren, who as yet fail to see their need of this, have put us out, even as the patriarchs put Joseph out. Hope we may so prove God to be with us even as Joseph did, that our fellow patriarchs may see their mistake and become again our brothers as in the case of Joseph and his brethren.

In the beginning, we were all free to express the revelation God made clear in our hearts. The proof that it was God's revelation being that it was according to the Scriptures and in agreement with Him who was the Word made flesh. Now a verbal agreement has been framed by apostolic Overseers. William Irvine, John Hardy [Hardie] and some others at the beginning believed they were born again in Babylon, but I am sorry to say that I accepted the flesh and blood revelation through Joe Kerr backed by William Irvine, that previous to meeting him we were unregenerate.

John Hardy [Hardie] for many years refused to accept this, then I took up the same position as John. In 1914, God showed me the pre-eminence William got through this error, leading together with other things to his ceasing to be the humble Brother amongst brethren he was at the beginning. I am sorry to say that John Hardy [Hardie] has embraced the error he stood out against for so long. Wilson McClung declared that this, which he calls *Babylonish testimony*, is my chief offence. But I am happy to be back at the place we occupied for four years after God called William Irvine and others of us to rebuild Jerusalem. I have been excommunicated by my fellow Workers and hundreds of Saints and eight Workers have been put outside the camp with me.

It would grieve me to think of, and grieve me more to write of, the appalling change in God's Servants and Saints who have actively promoted this ungodly course of action. So I ask you to forgive me for not giving you details which my love of those with whom I used to take sweet counsel and together walked in company to the house of God caused me to refrain from declaring what I hope they may yet turn from.

Believe me still to be Christ's bondsman and yours for his sake. I can humbly say more so than when we first met in Newcastle.
Edward Cooney
(Roberts 1991, 21–23, *TTT*)

~~~~~

Extracts of Letters from and to Alice Flett (circa 1930)
New Westminster, B.C. Canada

To Edward Cooney: We did not meet you when you were here but hearing of you and having had the privilege of reading some of your recent letters, I feel you love all the brethren even as many do, and as Joseph did, but like him, you have been kept in separation because of measures taken against you by them. I understand you could not agree in all things with them. You felt some of their works were not scriptural. My one reason for writing you is, I would love to hear from you of the first years and first experiences in this Testimony. I always thought, at least I hoped and always told strangers, since first realizing I had found the truth as it is in Jesus, that *The Testimony* had always been; had never ceased since it was given to the world by Jesus Himself. I would like to know from you about your first steps into the Truth, first years in fellowship and your separation. Signed: Alice Flett

~~~~~

Edward Cooney's Answer to Alice Flett, circa 1930

My dear Sister, [Alice Flett]

Your letter has just come, and I am inclined to reply without delay in the hope my answer may help others in similar circumstances. I am glad you gather from my letters I love all the brethren, even as Joseph did. I am far behind Joseph in the volume of my love, but I would like to increase more and more. The breadth of which takes in the whole world; the length of which is expressed by Paul in Ephesians 5:1 "Be ye therefore imitators of God as children beloved and walk in love even as also Christ loved and gave up himself for us, an offering and a sacrifice to God for an odour of a sweet smell." This love is beyond all natural love and needs to be poured into our hearts by the Holy Spirit which was given to us. Then we will be willing to die for sinners inside God's family and outside. See Romans 5:5–8.

You mention, "My one real reason for writing is to hear from you of the first years and first experiences in this Testimony." You write that since you believe the truth as it is in Jesus that *The Testimony* "had always been." You are right. Abel, the second son of Adam, was the first preacher to give the testimony of Jesus, and through ranks of messengers, this testimony has been passed on to this day. The church, so-called, has failed to give the testimony of Jesus. Hence Jesus has sent prophets, wise men and scribes—in the Old Testament, from Abel to Zacharias (whom those who sat in Moses' seat slew between the temple and the altar because he told them the truth: "Ye have forsaken the Lord, and the Lord has forsaken you" and in the New Testament times from the testimony given by Jesus at Pentecost till the present time.

I was born anew in the city of Armagh, Ireland, sometime during 1884. After that, a number of us who had been through the same experience, met in a room from time to time, to encourage one another to follow Jesus, still attending the same denominations we belonged to. After a few years, I got to see I should be a continuing disciple of Jesus.

I ceased to belong to any denomination, and with progressive light pressed on in the path of discipleship, preached in the open-air and in the synagogues when permitted. Some got won to Christ during this my ministry. In Enniskillen, my native town, we met in a Presbyterian man's home Sunday afternoons, and preached in the slums in a schoolhouse granted the use of by the Methodists.

I travelled for my father's business and preached inside and outside, as occasion offered, with some persecution, and whilst doing so, met William Irvine, through whom George Walker, Jack Carroll, William Carroll, Willie Gill and a number of the present leaders professed, including James Jardine. He and I were drawn together as brothers in Christ, each of us claiming liberty to follow Him as we received progressive light from God by the Spirit. He was at that time Pilgrim Irvine, a preacher in a denomination called the Faith Mission, into which May Carroll entered, and in which she preached for some time after being won to Christ by William Irvine.

At this time, we believed that all who were born anew including ourselves, in the denominations, were children of God, needing to become continuing disciples. Two heresies arose amongst us at this time, started largely by Joseph Kerr, who said no one could be saved who had not met William Irvine, or some of those in fellowship with him. Others held that only through Sister or Brother Workers could any be saved, and that these Workers must be William Irvine's associates. In 1914, I declared that I returned to the Gospel William Irvine and I, with others, preached for some years before these heresies were introduced.

Plans were made secretly to get me excluded, and in 1928, at Clankiborough, Lurgan, ten Workers put Thomas Elliott, since deceased, and me out, excluding us from fellowship, because we would not agree to two decrees which were additions to the Scriptures.

Now my dear sister, I could write much more, but if you get in touch with Andy Boyd, 10187 103rd Street, Room 8, Edmonton, Alberta, Canada, he was one of those who met with me in Enniskillen, and he may be able to answer some of your further questions. Am sure Sam Boyd has given you some light on our spiritual experience before we met William Irvine. Ask any further questions you wish when you reply.

Yours lovingly in Christ,

Edward [Cooney]

(Roberts 1991, 15–17, *TTT*)

Appendix E   The Keswick Convention

Keswick Convention Headquarters
Keswick Convention Centre, Keswick, Cumbria, England
Keswick Ministries, Rawnsley Centre, Keswick, CA12 5NP
E-mail: info@keswickministries.org
Website: www.keswickministries.org/

Convention Motto: *All One in Christ Jesus*.
Convention History: *See* keswickministries.org/history/
Convention Purpose: To promote Bible teaching with the aim of encouraging holy and biblical lifestyles.

Convention Description. "The Keswick Convention is a unique Christian event. It is free and everyone is welcome. The main event is held in a marquee, where we hold the morning Bible Readings from Monday to Friday and evening celebrations every day. We host interesting and inspiring seminars, the Keswick Lecture, Keswick Unconventional, and we run dedicated programmes for children, youth and young adults. We use different venues including local churches for these various seminars and programmes. Experience the sense of unity across generations and denominations as people gather to hear from God's Word. Join us at the Convention this summer and go home refreshed, equipped and inspired, to serve God and become more like His Son. All you need to do is book your accommodation and join us!" (Keswick Website)

The Keswick, England Convention is held annually for three solid weeks in the summer. The dates for 2019 were July 13–August 2. The Conventions are not only located in the town of Keswick. There are many annual meetings, some very large, that either use the Keswick label or owe their existence to the Keswick Convention, held in the UK and also around the world, including Japan, Jamaica, North America, India, parts of Africa and New Zealand. In Australia, the Belgrave Heights Convention is held about 45 km east of Melbourne, Victoria. Some of the Friends and Ex-2x2s attend this annual Convention.

The Keswick Convention is conducted by Keswick Ministries, the operational name for the Keswick Convention Trust. Trustees are drawn from a number of Christian organizations and denominations. The Trust employs a full-time operations manager and a small number of permanent staff, based at the Convention center. Many volunteers assist during the annual Convention event.

Additional Sources

The Keswick Convention: Its Message, Its Method and its Men
        by Charles F. Harford. London. 1907.
        (Harford, a son of the Keswick founder, edited this book;
        now available through *Forgotten Books*, 2012;
        www.forgottenbooks.org)

Transforming Keswick: The Keswick Convention, Past, Present &
        Future, by Charles Price and Ian Randall. OM Publishing, 2000.

The Keswick Story: The Authorized History of the Keswick Convention
        by J. C. [John] Pollock. Great Britain: Hodder and Stoughton,
        1964

Keswick Hymn-Book, compiled by Trustees of the Keswick Convention.
        London, England: Marshall, Morgan & Scott Ltd., Circa 1940.

Appendix F   *Presbyterian Evangelist John McNeill*

Background: On January 8, 1893, William Irvine professed through Presbyterian Rev. John McNeill in the Motherwell Town Hall, Scotland. At that time, Rev. McNeill was affiliated with Dwight L. Moody's evangelistic campaign; he was never a Worker in the Two by Two Sect.

Note: Brother Worker, John McNeill, shown on the 1905 Workers List is *not* the same person as the Rev. McNeill through whom Irvine converted.

~~~~~

At the request of John McNeill's widow, Alexander Gammie compiled the official biography of Rev. McNeill, titled *Rev. John McNeill: His Life and Work,* first published in 1933. This book is the primary source of the following summary of his life's work.

John McNeill was born on July 7, 1854, in Houston, Renfrewshire, Scotland, to John and Catherine "Katie" (McTaggart) McNeill. The eldest son, he was second in a family of seven children. When he was 12, the family moved to Inverkip where he went to work in a quarry. Beginning at age 15 (from 1869 to 1877), he worked for the railway, starting as a gateboy. He was described as "the burly youth with the frank, open countenance and the strong, cheery voice."

Brought up in a deeply spiritual home with family worship on Sunday mornings and evenings, he attended the Inverkip Presbyterian Free Church. In spiritual matters, he claimed he owed more to his parents than anyone else. "Our religion," he would say, "was dyed in the wool." In a letter to his minister, he declared his choice to become a Christian when he was about 19 years old. He lived a clean life, never smoked and was a teetotaler.

McNeill rose rapidly to the position of railway clerk after transferring to Edinburgh. After joining St. Bernard's Free Church, he became a Sunday school teacher and was ordained as a deacon. He became an active member of the Young Men's Christian Association (YMCA), a society made up of members of all churches founded in 1844. Had he not been connected with the YMCA, he declared, "Then, humanly speaking, I might never have been a minister."

So convinced was the YMCA vice-president that McNeill should be in the ministry that he helped finance McNeill's education. For three years, beginning in 1877, McNeill studied at Edinburgh University in Scotland and supported himself by performing missionary work for St. Bernard's

Free Church. He developed a fondness for open-air preaching and of mission work in general, which ultimately became the passion of his life.

While studying at Edinburgh University, he married Susan Spiers Scott on October 24, 1879; he was 25, and she was 28. Nine months later, their son, John Alexander, was born. But for Susan, it is said, he might not have persevered to the end of his studies. Soon after their marriage, Susan developed an illness from which she never fully recovered. After five years at Glasgow University, in 1886, he completed his Divinity Course at what is now known as the Church of Scotland's Trinity College.

At age 32, in July 1886, McNeill became the pastor of the McCrie-Roxburgh Free Church in Edinburgh, Scotland. There he suddenly burst into fame. Crowds flocked to hear him—both rich and poor, educated and illiterate. Before long, it was necessary to use a circus tent to accommodate the 3,000 plus attendees; some called it the "Circus Church." In a meeting at the huge Waverly Market, the low estimate was 12,000–14,000 attendees. He had come to Edinburgh, poor and unknown; he left as one of the most popular ministers and one of the best known public figures in the city.

Three and one-half years later, the McNeills moved to London where he became pastor of the Regent Square Presbyterian Church on February 28, 1889. Throngs of people followed him from the very beginning of his ministry. He and Charles Spurgeon (20 years his senior), pastor of the Metropolitan Tabernacle, became good friends. Charles Spurgeon (1834–1892) was an English Baptist Preacher, nicknamed *Prince of Preachers*. Rev. McNeill was nicknamed the *Scotch Spurgeon*, which name was used as the subtitle for the 1895 book, *Rev. John McNeill's (the Scotch Spurgeon) Popular Sermons.*

After 12 years of marriage and four children in ten years, his wife, Susan, died on July 7, 1891, aged 40, of pneumonia, just three weeks after giving birth to their fourth child.

About the same time, John Campbell White (soon to become Lord Overtoun) approached McNeill with the following offer: "Here we are, two Christian men deeply interested and engaged in Gospel work. Our Master has given me money, and He has given you preaching, and yours is the greater gift. Why should not we go into partnership? I will undertake to relieve you of worldly cares, and you will go wherever you will, preaching the Gospel."

McNeill accepted Lord Overtoun's offer and resigned from Regent Square Church in December 1891. Before long, McNeill was world famous, speaking in Toronto, New York, Chicago and other places. In October 1891, after hearing McNeill preach for a week in Chicago,

Dwight L. Moody invited him to join Moody's evangelistic campaign. Until this time, McNeill had no natural desire to be an evangelist. He claimed, "The Lord thrust me out" into evangelism to preach the Gospel.

His evangelistic work with Moody and Sankey commenced in January 1892 with a highly successful mission in Aberdeen, Scotland. He traveled far and wide in Scotland, England and Ireland, preaching in large cities, small villages and country districts. Crowds flocked to hear the popular traveling evangelist. At brief intervals, he returned home to be with his four motherless children.

During this period, in January 1893, Rev. John McNeill had a mission in Motherwell Town Hall, during which William Irvine converted. At that time, McNeill was affiliated with Dwight L. Moody's evangelistic campaign.

In 1893, at Moody's request, McNeill traveled to a special campaign connected to the World's Fair in Chicago, where he preached to huge crowds for five months and made a profound impression. Subsequently in 1894 and 1895, he went on world tours to South Africa, Australia, India, etc. In Melbourne, Australia, he regularly addressed 5,000 people on weekdays and 10,000 on Sundays.

His greatest campaign was held in London, from January to June 1898, concluding with 12 days in the Royal Albert Hall. "Over 10,000 attended his Sunday evening services; the aggregate for the whole campaign at the lowest estimate, was half million." While in London, after seven years of being a widower, he met his future wife, Margaret Lee Millar (1867–1960). They were married on July 14, 1898, and produced six children. Altogether, McNeill was father to ten children.

McNeill continued his evangelistic missions and tours for 16 more years, from 1891 to 1907, under the sponsorship of Lord Overtoun, although there had been no formal written agreement. On February 15, 1908, Lord Overtoun died, aged 69, without leaving any legal provision for the arrangement to continue. After 17 years, John McNeill, age 53, was suddenly left without any means to support his evangelistic tours and large family. Once again, he became a pastor. From 1908 to 1916, he pastored the following churches:

- Christ Church Westminster Bridge Road in London, England, September 1908, for one year.
- St. George's Presbyterian Church in Liverpool, England, April 3, 1910–Nov. 24, 1912.
- Cooke's Church in Toronto, Canada, on January 2, 1913, for about two years.

- Central Presbyterian Church, Denver, Colorado, US, 1915–1916, for nine months, 3,200 members.

After WWI broke out, at the request of the YMCA, McNeill returned to Scotland in September 1916, to work among the soldiers. He was sent to France, Egypt and Malta. After the War, in early 1919, he returned to America for a three-month evangelistic mission. After that, from 1919 to 1928, he was a pastor at the following churches:

- South Highlands Presbyterian Church in Birmingham, Alabama, US, June 4, 1919–July 1920.
- Fort Washington Presbyterian Church in New York, New York, US, on October 12, 1920–December 21, 1924.
- Tenth Presbyterian Church of Philadelphia, Pennsylvania, US, December 21, 1924, for two years. Church of the Open Door, Los Angeles, California, US, December 22, 1926–October 7, 1928.

~~~~~

"Though a loyal Presbyterian, it was evident that John McNeill was bound by no denominational fetters. If he heard that a number of Christian churches were uniting for a service, he rejoiced and was glad to do all he could to help." When asked why he was sometimes called *Dr. McNeill*, he replied, "I am not a D.D., [Doctor of Divinity]; I was offered the honor once by a college, but I declined it. It is not for me" (*New York Times* May 9, 1897).

"On October 20, 1928, the McNeills said a final farewell to America and returned to London due to Mrs. McNeil's health, where he resumed his role as a minister of the Presbyterian Church of England. His favorite recreations were swimming, golfing and riding horses. He learned to ride after he was 40 and claimed he had ridden over 600 horses" (*New York Herald Tribune*, May 5, 1933, p. 5).

Rev. McNeill was preacher, pastor and evangelist for the rest of his life. Whether he was pastoring a church or engaged in a special campaign, he was always an evangelist at heart. He was "not comfortable in keeping a full church full."

He experienced both roles of ministry—that of being a settled pastor and of being a traveling evangelist. A pastorate required preparing fresh discourses every week for the same people, feeding the flock. The work of an evangelist was mainly holding missions, preaching the Gospel, being always on the go, six days a week, often for weeks and even months on end. He gave new sermons and had another hundred prepared evangelistic sermons in his repertoire. He was famous throughout the world. One year he preached 330 times. He claimed there was as much hard work in one ministry role as the other.

Diagnosed with a heart attack in January 1933, he retired and died in his sleep on April 19, 1933, aged 79. Funeral services were held simultaneously in three Scotland locations, at Regent Square Church in London; George's Parish Church in Glasgow; and Charlotte Chapel in Edinburgh. He was buried in the old churchyard at Inverkip, Renfrewshire, Scotland, beside his parents. His widow died September 18, 1967, aged 93. Newspapers across the world carried his obituary and articles lauding his work.

John McNeill's son and wife, Archibald "Archie" and Evangeline (Duff) McNeill, developed the Cannon Beach Christian Conference Center in Oregon in 1945. After their passing, their oldest daughter, Heather (McNeill) Goodenough, took the helm as Executive Director. *See* website cbcc.net. *See also* website *TellingTheTruth.info* in History Articles, Walter Duff.

Note. As can be seen from the activities above, Rev. John McNeill was never affiliated with a group, sect or movement similar to the Two by Two Sect.

References:
Rev. John McNeill: His Life and Work by Alexander Gammie, 1933.
        Great Britain: Pickering & Inglis.
Evangeline – A Story of Faith by Bette Nordberg, 1996. Biography of
        Evangeline (Duff) McNeill and the development of the Canon
        Beach Conference Center in Oregon, US.
Rev. John McNeill's (The Scotch Spurgeon) Popular Sermons. 1896.
        Edited by J. B. McClure. Rhodes & McClure.

~~~~~~

Motherwell Times, Motherwell, Scotland:
*1893 Jan. 07. Announcement of Rev. John McNeill services to be held at
        Motherwell Town Hall*
1893 Jan. 14. Report of Rev. John McNeill week's mission in Motherwell

New York Times:
1897 May 01 p. 13. Dr. McNeill - "the Scottish Spurgeon" – "A Shaggy
        Master of Pathos"
1897 May 09 p. 12. Travels of Evangelist Rev. John McNeill – Preached
        all over the habitable globe - Even to Zulus

Death Notices:

1933 May 05 p. 5 *New York Herald Tribune*. Rev. John McNeill Was
    World Famous as an Evangelist

1933 April 29 p. 6 *Vancouver Sun*, Vancouver, BC, Canada. Service for
    Preacher

1933 April 20 p. 2 *The Gazette*, Montreal, QC, Canada. Rev. John
    McNeill dies in London

1933 April 22 p. 5 *The Province,* Vancouver, BC, Canada. Rev. John
    McNeill-Evangelist

Appendix G   Faith Mission

Faith Mission Headquarters
548 Gilmerton Road, Gilmerton, Edinburgh, Scotland EH17 7JD
Faith Mission Bookshop
5-7 Queen Street, Belfast, N. Ireland, UK BT1 6EA
Website: faithmission.org

~~~~~

The following letter by Rev. Colin N. Peckham, Principal of Faith Mission, is regarding William Irvine's time spent in the service of Faith Mission. *See* original letter on website *TellingTheTruth.info* in Photo Gallery, Workers, British Isles, Scotland, Faith Mission.

THE FAITH MISSION BIBLE COLLEGE
2 Drum Street Gilmerton,
Edinburgh, Scotland
Principal: Rev. C. N. Peckham, B.A., M.Th

29th. May, 1991.

Re: William Irvine.

Dear Mrs. Kropp,
    In reply to your request for information concerning William Irvine's connection with the Faith Mission, **William Irvine** joined the Faith Mission in 1895, and after working in Scotland, came across to Ireland probably around May of 1896. The Faith Mission was founded by J. G. Govan in 1886, as an evangelistic agency for the villages of Scotland, and the Work was extended to Ireland in 1892. At some time in 1897, Mr. Irvine went to work in the south of Ireland, where he is referred to in our magazine *Bright Words* as superintending the work there from 1898 to 1900. The last reference to him as such, is the issue of Nov./Dec. 1900.
    There is reference in what we call *Location of Pilgrims* to a mission in Rathmolyon beginning Oct. 10, 1897, by William Irvine, after which he went to Co. Tipperary.
    In the magazine issue for June/July 1898, the report of the work by Mrs. Pendreigh appeared as follows:
    "Since coming across to ... the south of Ireland, we have thoroughly enjoyed the work ... In some places the opposition was great, but by prayer and patient endurance battles were fought and won ... During

some missions several (Roman Catholics) were brought in, and I believe savingly converted ... most of the work has been in and around Co. Tipperary, and one or two fully successful missions in Kings and Queen's Counties ... I don't think any of us could go away with a grudge in our hearts ... as our **D. P. [District Pilgrim]** has the happy plan of making us cross hands ... and sing some chorus as a pledge of being true to God and to one another."

The D.P. referred to was, of course, **William Irvine**, and Mrs. Pendreigh later became one of his most devoted followers and remained so all her life.

In the August 1898 issue of our magazine, William Irvine's name appears for the first time as superintending the work in the South.

"A brief visit to Co. Tipperary occupied the remainder of my stay across the channel ... with Pilgrims Pendreigh and McLean, I attended five meetings at Nenagh ... it was a joy to meet so many bright and sympathetic children of God in that part of the country, and to see so much satisfactory fruit remaining from the missions held by **Pilgrim Irvine** and the sisters during the past 12 months."

In 1898, on the List of Workers in Govan's report of the work, Mr. Irvine's name appeared as superintending the work in the South of Ireland.

In 1899, Govan wrote, "As far as the South of Ireland is concerned, there has not been much work."

In the March 1990, [should be 1900] issue of *Bright Words*, Govan wrote "Pilgrim Irvine is in the south of Ireland. We have not had regular reports from him lately."

The last time William Irvine's name is given as superintending the work in the South is in the annual report for 1900, where Govan wrote as follows:

"The work in the south of Ireland has not been reported ... much of the time of the Pilgrim in charge having been taken up with the building of movable wooden halls, nearly all of which are worked on independent lines and workers unconnected with and not under the direction of the Faith Mission."

In the August 1901 issue, Govan writes: "When in Ireland, I came into close contact with a movement that has been going on for a year or two. A number of young people are going out on quite independent lines ... while there may be much that is good in the devotion and earnestness of those who thus leave all ... a number of the features of this movement do not commend themselves to us ... some have mistaken them for pilgrims, so we find it necessary to say that the Faith Mission is not responsible for this movement."

In the issue for September 1901, he wrote, "During the year several have dropped out of our list of workers. **Pilgrim Irvine** has been working on independent lines, chiefly in Ireland. Then quite recently **Pilgrim Kelly** has resigned and also aligned himself with these independent workers."

Around the end of 1901, a small leaflet was issued titled 'To Correct Misunderstandings.' A portion of it reads as follows: "As we continue to receive word that certain itinerant workers (associated with **Mr. Irvine and Mr. Cooney**) frequently pass under the title of "Pilgrims" or "Faith Workers," we wish it to be observed that the name "Pilgrim" was adopted for our evangelists from the formation of the Faith Mission in 1886, and that the workers of this new association differ very widely ... in aims, principles and methods from those of our Mission."

There is no reference to William Irvine in the volume of 1902, but in the magazine issue for May 1903, the following statement appears: "We regret that it seems needful, owing to the confusing statements that have been made, to state plainly that we have no responsibility for the work carried on in Ireland, and elsewhere by Mr. Irvine and his fellow workers. Having little organization or arrangements whereby to distinguish them, the agents of this anonymous work have been mistaken for our Faith Mission Pilgrims, and misleading references have appeared in the public press."

From these references, you can see that William Irvine definitely did not leave the Faith Mission to take over or become a part of an existing ministry. There certainly was no movement of that kind existing over here before Irvine's breakaway movement. As William Irvine spent some time in the Faith Mission before leaving it, there is no possibility that he founded the Cooneyite Sect before 1886, as it was in October 1886, that John George Govan began the Faith Mission.

Irvine went to the south of Ireland in 1897, and his superintendency must be understood in the light of the conditions there then. His work, and that of the few workers in that area, was merely that of holding pioneer missions. He was not a *superintendent* in the sense that we know that term to mean today. In fact, he was only in the Faith Mission for about three years before leaving to work on independent lines. He was separated from the main flow of Christian work in the North, and from the burgeoning Faith Mission work in Scotland. Because he worked in such isolation in an extremely Roman Catholic county not enjoying fellowship in any great measure with other members of the Faith Mission, he was able to deviate from the normal practice, methods and teachings of the Faith Mission.

I certify the above information is true and correct to the best of my knowledge and ability, so far as the records of Faith Mission are concerned. I hope this information will be helpful to you, and if I can be of any further assistance, please feel free to write again.

Sincerely yours,
Rev. C. N. Peckham.

~~~~~

In a personal visit to Faith Mission headquarters in 2004, Keith H. Percival, then the General Director, provided a copy of the Faith Mission "Official List of Workers" for the years 1895–1902. He gave permission to use the list with the following disclaimer: "This list was compiled by Mr. John Eberstein, former President of Faith Mission, who through research has produced a list of the early Pilgrim workers in the Faith Mission; giving details of when they joined the Mission, the date they left and giving notes as to what happened to them after that" (Eberstein, Official List, in author's possession). This list shows William Irvine left Faith Mission in January 1901, with the notation: "founded Cooneyites in S. Ireland," and shows John Kelly left in September 1901 with the notation: "joined Cooneyites."

Publications by or about the Faith Mission

The following books may be obtained through the Faith Mission headquarters or their bookshops.

Spirit of Revival by I. R. Govan

Publisher: Stanley L. Hunt Ltd., Rusheden, Northhamptonshire, GB UK, 1978
John G. Govan's daughter, Isabella Rosie Govan Stewart, wrote this biography of her father and the story of the early years of the Faith Mission.

Heritage of Revival – a Century of Rural Evangelism by Rev. Colin N. Peckham

Faith Mission Publishing, 1986, Edinburgh, Scotland UK
ISBN: 0–9508058–1–5
The early history and activities of the Faith Mission.
(Reprinted on *TTT*)

Faith Triumphant – A Review of the Work of The Faith Mission 1886–1936
  By J. B. McLean, and others (no publishing date)
Songs of Victory compiled by Andrew W. Bell, published by *Life Indeed*, third edition 1952; fourth edition, 1998
  (Hymnbook used by Faith Mission)

Bright Words, **Monthly Magazine of Faith Mission.** Since 1889, the Faith Mission has published a monthly magazine initially entitled *Bright Words,* then *Life Indeed* before being renamed First! Their monthly publication provides news and reports concerning their Pilgrim workers, their current locations, converts, missions, testimonies, as well as spiritual articles. **William Irvine is mentioned many times in the early issues of Bright Words.**

Appendix H   Three Groups Founded by William Irvine

What They Believe
GROUP NAMES and COMMON MONIKERS

(1) The Two by Two Sect (aka 2x2s, *The Truth, The Fold, The Way, The Testimony*)
(2) The William Irvine followers (aka *Irvinites*)
(3) The Edward Cooney followers (aka *Cooneyites*)

NOTE. While none of the three groups has an official name recognized by their members, outsiders and among themselves, they are known informally by many monikers. Sometimes, to satisfy government requirements, the 2x2 Sect has registered under various names. The monikers *2x2s, Irvinites* and *Cooneyites* are used respectfully for identification purposes in this book.

1. STARTING POINT.

2x2s: In 1897, the 2x2 Sect was started in Ireland by William Irvine. Contend they have no headquarters, are not an organization or denomination and are not incorporated or tax-exempt.

Irvinites: Beginning in 1918, Irvine began claiming he received a new revelation. His Senior Workers refused to accept and go along with it, resulting in a split. Irvine and some of his loyalists formed a loose-knit group following Irvine's Omega Message. They had no headquarters and were not affiliated with any group, church or organized religion and were against all organized religion. Contact with other followers was through letters and visits.

Cooneyites: In 1928, Edward Cooney was excommunicated. Many loyal members detached themselves from the 2x2 Sect or were disfellowshipped and formed a group. They were not an organized religious body.

2. INFORMAL NAMES MEMBERS USE AMONG THEMSELVES.

Two by Twos (2x2s) refer to their group as *the Friends and Workers, Saints, Children of God, Kingdom of God, Family of God,* etc.

Irvinites refer to their group as *Message People, Little Ones and Witnesses.* Informally, they refer to their beliefs as the *Omega Message.*

Cooneyites refer to themselves as Brothers and Sisters.

3. CLERGY, MINISTERS and SUPPORT.

2x2s: Ministers have no formal religious training, education and no knowledge of original Bible languages. They believe Jesus intended all preachers for all time (universally) to follow His instructions to His disciples in Matthew 10:5–14, Mark 6:7–11 and Luke 9:1–5. Workers are to be celibate, have no settled homes, travel in same-sex pairs (two by two), hold Gospel Missions and oversee the flock. They usually live as houseguests of members willing to host them; or if no homes are available, they rent temporary accommodations called a *bach,* especially in foreign fields. No public collections are taken; they do not accept a salary, taking literally Jesus' command: "freely you have received, freely give" (Matt. 10:8 *NKJV*). No accounting is made regarding donations to the ministry. Some members leave legacies; others make freewill contributions to various Workers and Overseers. Generally, they do not accept donations from non-members. The sect is established in the majority of countries worldwide. Most recruiting is by Workers holding a series of Gospel Missions.

Irvinites: The role of a preacher ceased in 1914; subsequently there were no leaders, preachers, Workers, or member hierarchy other than their self-proclaimed prophet, Irvine. His followers individually witnessed Irvine's Omega Message to outsiders as opportunities arose and "brought along" interested parties. Irvine encouraged one-on-one recruiting. While he lived, Irvine's followers mailed him money and gifts; he lived frugally and never needed to be employed.

Cooneyites: Following the deaths of Cooney and Fred Wood, they have sanctioned no missionaries, Workers, or Gospel Meetings. Individuals witness to others as opportunity arises.

4. SIN.

2x2s: Sin is possible after the age of accountability, usually around age 12–13. Transgression is a sin of presumption, or deliberately, knowingly sinning. Non-compliance to the Workers' dictates or interpretations of Scripture is considered sin. Sinners are (1) all those not walking in the 2x2 Sect; and (2) those in the 2x2 Sect who are being disobedient. There is a dispute in the sect as to whether remarriage after divorce is an unforgivable sin. *See* Chapter 29.

Irvinites: The unforgivable sin is not accepting William Irvine as God's prophet. Sin is human nature, including all thoughts and feelings. If a person "has an honest heart" (believes in William Irvine), God will forgive most things, including murder; the exception being wickedness; e.g. gossip, judging, despising or accusing others of sin, participation in church activities or religious rituals.

Cooneyites: Sin is disobedience to the Holy Spirit, who convicts believers of sin.

5. CHURCHES, ASSEMBLY SITES and WORSHIP SERVICES.

2x2s: Two types of services. (1) Their Sunday Fellowship Meetings have participatory worship by members with communion—a day of rest when most cease working. They also gather for a midweek Bible Study Meeting and in some areas, a Sunday Evening Meeting. (2) A series of Gospel Meetings (a mission) conducted by their evangelists for recruiting. No restrictions for sites used for Gospel or Special Meeting services. Most believe members of all other churches, sects, denominations and religions have been deceived; consequently, all their adherents will go to Hell.

Regional Conventions are held annually in most countries for four days, three meetings per day. Size in the US ranges from approximately 300 to 1,200 attendees. Members are strongly urged to attend one complete Convention per year. Convention property is usually owned by a member. Buildings constructed for the Convention are paid by funds controlled by the Overseer and/or donated by members. All-day Special Meetings are held semi-annually in most areas.

Irvinites: Contend God is not found in church buildings, nor in those who go to buildings to worship, their priests, ministers, etc. They do not assemble for regular meetings and infrequently socialize with each other in small groups; Irvine discouraged "bunching up." View everyone outside their group as deceived.

Cooneyites: Meet only in fellow-worshipper's homes on Sunday (with communion) and midweek meetings. All may participate (outside visitors included); there is freedom to use any Bible translation.

6. PRINTED LITERATURE and HYMNAL.

2x2: Use King James Bible primarily and their own hymnal compilation: *Hymns Old and New,* 1987 edition, published by R. L. Allan & Son, England. Publish no literature for public consumption.

Irvinites: Irvine recommended using the King James Version. No published hymnal or belief statement. Religious hymns are considered wicked trappings of corrupt churches. Irvine's letters about his Omega Message have been copied and handed down through the years but are not published. There is no central bank of letters, and no follower has all his letters; everyone has their own collection and rereads them.

Cooneyites: Use *Hymns Old and New,* 1951 edition.

7. ORDINANCES and PRAYER.

2x2s: Observe ordinances of communion weekly in Sunday Fellowship Meetings. Baptism is by complete immersion; oppose infant baptism and sprinkling. No foot washing. Address their prayers to the Father, in Jesus' Name, asking for His spiritual aid and forgiveness; rarely ask for material, natural items. Recommend private prayer at least twice daily, with audible prayer in Meetings and before meals.

Irvinites: Baptism, communion, funerals are not practiced. Do not pray. They talk to God about anything and anyone.

Cooneyites: Same as 2x2s. Private prayer is more important and should be as often as need is felt.

8. PROFESSIONS OR CONVERSION.

2x2s: Public profession in a Gospel Meeting is generally required to become a member. Previous baptisms are not recognized, and a convert must be baptized or rebaptized into the 2x2 Sect.

Irvinites: Converted when a person believes in their heart that Irvine is the prophet of God for the latter days. No other acknowledgment is required.

Cooneyites: Each person's journey is individual. Baptism is a symbol of dying to the past life and being raised to a new life in Christ—not into a sect.

9. AFTERLIFE – HEAVEN AND HELL.

2x2s: Believe all people receive either eternal life in Heaven or eternal punishment in Hell, depending upon their beliefs and lifestyle while on Earth.

Irvinites: Since 1914, believe everyone either receives eternal life in Heaven or eternal punishment in Hell, depending upon whether they believe and submit to Irvine's teachings.

Cooneyites: Accepting progressive revelation, many have come to see that Hell is the second death and is *aionion* and remedial, rather than eternal and pointless. Christ will reign on Earth during the Millennium and until then there will be neither resurrection nor judgment.

10. TABOOS.

2x2s: Some rules, taboos or expectations vary according to locality. The following unwritten taboos are generally recognized across the entire sect as being unacceptable: televisions, movies, stereos, smoking, drinking, illegal drug use, swearing, gambling, dancing, reading Christian books/literature, current fads and fashions and long hair for men. For women, no short hair, makeup, slacks, shorts, or jewelry (except for wedding rings, brooches and watches). Facial hair and long hair on men became unacceptable sometime after their early days— this is changing. Drinking alcoholic beverages was a taboo from their start, the exception being European Workers and Friends in some countries.

Irvinites: None. Dress and behavior are of no consequence to God. They use the rule of moderation—nothing excessive. No rules regarding smoking, alcoholic beverages, dancing, movies, TV. No outward appearance customs for women. William Irvine smoked a pipe.

Cooneyites: All should be in the world but not of the world. Follow the rules of moderation, modesty and morality. The Holy Spirit gradually reveals taboos to each individual.

11. HOLIDAY CELEBRATIONS.

2x2s: Customs vary. Observe the usual national and secular holidays, including Halloween and Thanksgiving. Easter and Christmas are not celebrated religiously.

Irvinites: Usual holidays observed except for Easter and Christmas.

Cooneyites: Christmas and Easter are heathen festivals and not celebrated religiously

12. EDUCATION.

2x2s: In general, they do not now discourage higher education, but did so in the past. Any profession that restricts the ability to rest on Sundays or regularly attend Meetings is considered less than ideal, except for farming.

Irvinites: Higher education is not encouraged, as "the more people are educated and exalted, the further from the possibility of hearing the voice of the Lord God by the Man [Irvine] whom He sends" (Irvine to Hooes, Nov. 24, 1927, *TTT*).

Cooneyites: Freedom for parent to decide.

13. MILITARY SERVICE.

2x2s: Pacifists. Approved method of serving in the armed services is as a Conscientious Objector non-combatant, refusing to bear arms, taking literally the commandment "Thou shalt not kill."

Irvinites: Serving in the military to defend your country when necessary is the duty of a citizen.

Cooneyites: Same as 2x2s.

14. MARRIAGE, DIVORCE and REMARRIAGE.

2x2s: Marriage is the second-best choice in life; the best choice is to be a Worker. Members are expected to intermarry in a civil ceremony. Workers do not perform marriages. Divorce is undesirable but accepted as sometimes necessary. After a spouse dies, remarriage to a fellow member is acceptable. In some areas, remarriage after divorce is considered an unforgivable sin, and depending on the Overseer in charge, privileges permitted to those divorced and remarried vary. Workers are not in agreement on this subject worldwide, nor in North America. *See* Chapter 29.

Irvinites: Families, eating, drinking, marrying and giving in marriage is all vanity and dust. Marriage is of no consequence to God; it is a civil contract, a human issue. Parties have free choice but should only intermarry with another Irvinite. Divorce and remarriage are considered to be "of the flesh" and of no consequence to God.

Cooneyites: Marriage is a civil ceremony performed by a registrar. They should not remarry while ex-spouse is alive; divorced individuals are not barred from fellowship.

15. WOMEN and CHILDREN.

2x2s: Women have an equal part in worship services. Wives are to be submissive to their husbands. It is preferred that wives stay at home and be full-time homemakers. Female Workers are subordinate to the male Workers. God does not hold children accountable for their actions until they reach the age of accountability, usually around 12–13 years of age.

Irvinites: Irvine took a dim view of women preachers or leaders. "No woman can be an apostle in going forth as He sent His chosen disciples to be, then, now and forever" (Irvine to Edwards, May 18, 1944, *TTT*). Children are in the covenant of either blessing or cursing with their parents until they become of age to choose for or against. Irvine strongly warned against having children, due to "woe to those who give suck in the last days."

Cooneyites: Women have freedom to pray or prophesy in Meetings. Wives should defer to their husbands. Bring up a child in the way he should go. At the age of majority, he is responsible for his actions.

16. DEATH – BURIAL.

2x2s: Funeral services officiated by male Workers; female Workers may have a part. They are usually held in funeral homes with interment. Attendance by members residing in the area is somewhat expected, even though the member may not be acquainted with the deceased.

Irvinites: Casket lowered into the ground without ceremony or preachers. Cremation and burial are acceptable.

Cooneyites: Officiated by brothers. Held in homes or funeral parlors. Mostly interment.

17. NUMBER OF FOLLOWERS.

2x2s: The 2x2 Sect does not provide membership statistics. In 2022, worldwide membership is roughly estimated to be 75,000.

Irvinites: No member list. Followers are scattered across the world, with most located in US West Coast area. Estimate for the year 2021 is less than 100 worldwide.

Cooneyites: Not followers of Edward Cooney, but of Jesus Christ. No record. Estimate less than 100.

18. HIERARCHY, AUTHORITY and DISCIPLINE.

2x2s: States, provinces or regions are controlled by a male head Worker (Overseer) who assigns fields to Workers under his authority. Each field contains a number of home churches, where up to around 30 meet with a presiding Elder. Overseers and head Workers are males.

Workers have absolute authority in all matters; members have no representation and no means of recourse. Unquestioning loyalty is expected. Discipline is implemented with talks, threats, shaming and shunning. Not unusual for communion, baptism or the offender's part in prayer and testimony to be withheld. Meeting may be removed from an offender's home. Infrequently, excommunications may occur when an Overseer sees no likelihood of submission from the offending member.

Irvinites: After Irvine died, no one took his mantle. There was no head or leader. (He was not supposed to die). Attempts to become a leader are considered wicked. Followers do what their conscience dictates. No formal process for discipline, as there is no ruling authority. Those who leave are often shunned by remaining members and family.

Cooneyites: Christ and the Holy Spirit should be in control. Discipline is by their heavenly Father by conscience and trials. Jesus said if your brother sins against you, go and show him his fault. An Elder presides over each home Meeting.

WHAT THEY BELIEVE

19. DOCTRINE.

2x2s: No doctrinal statement published; state the Bible is their doctrine. Accept both Old and New Testaments as the inspired Word of God.

Irvinites: Their doctrine is the Bible, as interpreted by William Irvine in his letters.

Cooneyites: Same as 2x2s.

20. AUTHORITY.

2x2s: Claim they believe and follow only the teachings of the New Testament. The Workers hold the final authority to interpret the Scripture and make decisions. Senior Workers have equal or more authority than younger Workers, with the Regional Overseer exercising the final decisions. Some Senior Overseers have influence across regional boundaries.

Irvinites: State they follow the teachings of God's prophet, Irvine, whose word supersedes the Bible.

Cooneyites: Christ is the head.

21. GOD.

2x2s: Believe in only one God, who is the heavenly Father, the Creator.

Irvinites: One God, God the Father, the Creator. The trinity is the three sides of God's personality.

Cooneyites: Same as 2x2s.

22. JESUS.

2x2s: Most view Jesus as God's only son, who is under the authority and position of His Father who alone is God. Jesus is not considered God the Son or regarded as God. Jesus was the promised Messiah, conceived by the Holy Spirit, born of the virgin Mary; lived a perfect life; came to Earth in a man's body to establish a ministry pattern (Matthew 10) to be followed universally for all time. He was crucified, died and rose again bodily, before ascending to Heaven. They look forward to Jesus' second coming.

Irvinites: Jesus is Lord of Hosts; Jehovah in the Old Testament; the God-child. Jesus came as Alpha to finish the Old Testament work, and to offer himself as the supreme sacrifice for sin. Since August 5, 1914, when Jesus "took the throne," salvation is only obtained through the Jesus of Revelation 1, via Irvine's teachings. Irvine is the gate to salvation.

Cooneyites: Same as 2x2s.

23. HOLY SPIRIT.

2x2s: God's Spirit. A force or power emanating from God or from Jesus to a child of God. It is often perceived as an emotional feeling or attitude. The Spirit comes and goes. Not considered a part of the trinity.

Irvinites: Believe the Holy Spirit is the mother side of the trinity; the one that leads, guides, teaches, nurtures and protects.

Cooneyites: He is the Spirit of Truth sent by Jesus to teach and guide his followers and to give them His power.

24. SALVATION and REWARDS.

2x2s: Salvation can only be obtained by hearing the Workers preach the Gospel, accepting Jesus (professing) through one of their Workers, following their particular belief system that meets in homes and continuing faithfully therein until death. They will only know after death if they are saved. Salvation is earned by good works. Faith is proved by one's adherence to the Workers' interpretation of the Bible and their traditions.

Irvinites: No one is saved now, not even William Irvine or the apostles. Only the people who accept and follow Irvine's Omega Message are God's people. Irvine's litmus test for salvation: "And men, good, bad or indifferent or perfect are to be Judged by their attitude to my reading of Revelation" (Irvine to Baessler, April 18, 1928, *TTT*). According to Irvine, "It don't matter whether people are unjust, filthy, righteous, or holy. Their reward depends on their attitude to His man [Irvine] and message of Revelation. They will either be for or against him and their reward according to" (to Hooes, Sept. 27, 1935, *TTT*).

Cooneyites: God's salvation is the Christ within, giving daily victory over sin. Good works are acts of obedience to the Holy Spirit. They follow salvation. Rewards are at the resurrection for being good and faithful servants of the Master.

25. GRACE.

2x2s: (1) Grace is a thankful prayer before meals. (2) Grace is God's graciousness, compassion and merciful empowerment that enables them to live right, to do His will to the end of their life, thus earning salvation through their good works. By contrast, biblical Christianity upholds that grace is what we receive that we do not deserve, merit or earn, alongside the definition of God's mercy, which is Him not giving us what we do deserve. The relationship of grace to salvation is not emphasized in the manner of evangelical Christian churches, who view grace as God's Riches At Christ's Expense, the unmerited favor of God, as God doing what we cannot do for ourselves, which justifies us.

Irvinites: God's favor. The grace and mercy God shows us should be seen, heard and felt by all we come in contact with—one cannot have the grace of God without showing grace to others.

Cooneyites: Grace is God's unmerited favor. It cannot be earned. It is His sovereign choice, given in Jesus Christ. By grace we are given the faith that enables us to believe in Jesus.

26. HEALING, MIRACLES, SPEAKING IN TONGUES, CASTING OUT DEMONS, SATAN.

2x2s: Viewed as divine signs occurring only in the first century to confirm and convince. They believe the term *speaking in tongues* means speaking in foreign languages. Satan is a fallen angel engaged in an age-long struggle to seduce men to follow him rather than obey God. He is evil, a deceiver, a murderer, a liar. They fear his power to deceive.

Irvinites: Satan is a fallen angel engaged in an age-long struggle to lure men to follow him rather than obey God. He will play a big part in the last days. Healing, tongues and deliverance ministries are viewed as works of Satan to deceive and lead people astray from God.

Cooneyites: Same as 2x2s. Satan is a deceiver, murderer and liar from the beginning and is the Prince of this world.

NOTE. Entries for Cooneyites provided by Mary (Wood) Rogers, from Northern Ireland, daughter of Fred and Sadie Wood (Fred was Edward Cooney's right-hand man.)

Appendix I   Black Stocking Correspondence

Excerpt of Jack Carroll's Sermon regarding Black Stockings, no date:

We gave you four words last year to guide you in connection with your purchases during the year—economy, simplicity, modesty and neatness. What the Scripture teaches about the dress question is covered by these four words, and we will have no complaint if the Daughters of Zion give evidence that in all their purchases during the year, they do it as unto the Lord, remembering that if they are to have a testimony of value, it will be well for them to be guided by these four words.

We don't want to make rules or laws for God's children that would bring them into unnecessary bondage. We believe we can safely trust our Sisters in Christ in this matter, which is such a serious matter, as far as they are concerned, if they will be guided by these four words. If they do this, it will result in their having a testimony for God that will be of value.

We would like our sisters here to look upon the Sister Workers as a safe guide in this matter. There is no need for an absolute uniformity. We know this is a very serious question, and we believe that in some cases at least, there could be a little improvement in this matter. **We don't like to see any wearing stockings so closely like having no stockings on at all**, and we feel perfectly sure that when you buy your next pair, if you remember these four words, especially the word modesty, you will be more careful not only with regard to material but also with regard to color.

~~~~~

Letter by George Walker, Philadelphia, Pennsylvania, no date.

Dear Friends,

A letter, containing a misleading statement concerning what I said in a Workers' Meeting regarding Black Stockings, having been circulated amongst my Friends, I feel I should write the following:

Over 17 years ago, a man who did not profess and with whom I was not acquainted came to me at a Special Meeting and complained that his wife, who had recently professed, was wearing Black Stockings at the advice of the Sister Worker she had professed through. Previous to this, I had given little thought to the color of hosiery worn by our Sisters. I knew when long dresses were worn it was considered all right to wear different colors.

I talked with some of the older Sister Workers that I had cause to have a great deal of confidence in. They believe it would be better for all to wear black. At Conventions that year, I asked this question: "IF all sisters were satisfied in there [sic] minds that their wearing black was pleasing to the Lord, would their doing so hurt the Lord's work?" I expressed my opinion that it would not.

I favored black because it was furthermost from the flesh color that many of us believed was unbecoming to 'women professing godliness.' At no time did I say black was the only modest color. I spoke against the wearing of it being a Condition of Fellowship. I did not, and I do not believe using pressure on people to make them go beyond what is in their heart, or to do what they are not convinced in their minds they should do, is profitable to them or to the Lord's work.

I am personally acquainted with a number of Sister's [sic] Workers and Saints who believe it is pleasing to the Lord for them to continue wearing the black they have always worn. I appreciate their willingness to bear reproach for being true to their convictions. I have seen other qualities in them that causes me to 'esteem them highly.' I am acquainted with other Sisters who believe their wearing other modest colors is pleasing to the Lord. I have no reason to doubt their tureens [sic] and sincerity. I have seen in them manifestation of the Spirit of Christ that causes me to 'esteem them highly.'

There are other parts of a woman's attire that it may be needful to mention. Is the wearing of a dress that does not come to a reasonable length below the knees when she is seated becoming to a 'woman professing godliness'? The Scriptures speak expressly about outward adorning, wearing of gold, plaiting of hair. We are sometime grieved to see some of our Sisters wearing large showy brooches, and we fear the wristwatch, when worn as an adornment especially a gold one, with gold band, is not in keeping with the instructions given in Peter's Epistle. We fear the tendency some of our sisters have to follow the latest fads in arranging their hair does not add weight to their testimony.

During the past few years, we have not said much in Conventions or other Meetings about outward appearance. We have had a strong desire to so speak and act that love would be increased amongst us. If we have in our hearts unfeigned love for the Lord, we will so love His work and people that we will be very careful not to hurt His work or cause the weakest amongst His people to stumble by what we wear or do or say.

We will be anxious to excel in graces and virtues that are mentioned so many times in both Old and New Testament, the forgiving spirit that enables us to forgive from the heart everyone who has wronged us or in any way hurt our feelings. The compassion, the sympathy, the brotherly love, that enables us to forbear and be patient with all and that causes our Fellowship to be profitable and pleasant. If we lack these things, we cannot 'adorn the doctrine,' though our outward appearance is correct according to the Scriptures. Seeing that the Holy Spirit inspired Paul and Peter to mention these things, we should not consider the outward unimportant. Our unwillingness to obey in this may indicate a rebellious spirit that prevents the Lord working in us, and us having the condition of heart and spirit that in the 'sight of God' is of great price.

Recently I have been impressed with the word *servant* as used by Paul. In RV Version it is translated *slave.* We know a slave has little to say regarding what he will do or say or how he will act towards others. I would like in the future to be more like a faithful slave.

With love and good wishes to all who Love His Name and Way,

Your servant for Christ's sake.
George Walker

See also Chapter 36, Black Stocking Church.

Appendix J   Australian Conflicts

1954 Record of Events Regarding the Guildford Report

As reports have gone forth regarding recent happenings in Victoria, we feel that it is necessary to put on record events which have led up to the present and so clarify the situation.

After the late leader of Victoria, W. C. Carroll, passed away and was buried, Tom Turner returned via Sydney to Queensland. While in Sydney, he had a talk with John Hardie, and they thought a meeting with the Elder* Workers was due to consider matters of general concern to the Work in Australia, including the matter of the oversight of the Work in Victoria. An Elder's Meeting of this sort had often been wished for and suggested in past years, but William Carroll was not in agreement, not considering it necessary, stating that Conventions were sufficient.

As John Hardie was not well, he asked Tom Turner to convene the Meetings.

All States and New Zealand were asked to send a representative and each leader, including Chris Williams (appointed leader of Victoria by William Carroll), accepted the invitation, but the other Workers in Victoria wrote back to Tom Turner, in a letter signed by all the Workers except Chris Williams, that they did not see the need for a Workers' Meeting. This was done while Chris wrote from Tasmania accepting the invitation.

The meetings at Guildford were to be held from February 20th and notice to that effect was sent out. Others invited to the meetings were Walter Pickering, Alex Mitchell, Les Hawse and Harry Morgan. Although Chris had earlier accepted the invitation, at a later stage he began to object to coming, and it was only by telephoning him at the last moment that his confirmation as leader in Victoria was sure, that he and Walter Pickering agreed to come.

In all, eleven attended the meetings which began with prayer and were conducted in a godly manner. Each day for four days, the same procedure was followed, and many items were brought forward. Tom Turner was asked to lead the meetings. It was recognized that the three youngest members at the meetings were not representing any State in Australia and their voting in the meetings did not influence the affirmation or negation of the matters in discussion. Alex Mitchell asked if it would be in order for them to vote and the Chairman said, "Why not?" If each State in Australia and New Zealand had one representative, giving each one a vote, then the findings at Guildford would remain the same. Without the extras, W. Pickering, J. Williamson,

A. Mitchell, L. Hawse and H. Morgan, there would have been no alteration to the decisions made. This should be borne in mind, as some objections have been made regarding the constitution of the meetings.

Meetings Held in Guildford NSW February 20–24, 1954

Present: John Hardie, T. M. Turner, J. Williamson, C. Williams, W. Pickering, W. F. Hughes, J. C. Baartz, L. Hawse, W. Schloss, A. Mitchell and H. Morgan. In Chair: T. M. Turner.

First Meeting:

1. Confirmation of Chris Williams as Worker in charge of Victoria.

2. Exchange of Workers between States as a good thing to encourage.

3. The 'border' question. Reference to perplexities—that they would be done away with as much as possible and all concerned seek to foster a spirit of love and give and take.

4. Agreed that Victorian Workers cooperate with other States and consider the opinion of others.

Second Meeting:

5. The question of Saints being put out of fellowship in Victoria without a hearing. Some cases dealt with. (Deferred until next day).

Third Meeting:

6. That all are agreed that we, as servants of God, should be on the same lines as at the beginning. (unanimous)

7. We are agreed that anything which would cause contention should be avoided. It would have been more expedient if objections to the permanent residence at "Rosebud," Victoria, had been considered. The "Rosebud" dwelling had been a cause of contention in other countries, as well as in Australia, and it should have been done away with to save trouble and brethren from stumbling. Paul said, "Wherefore, if meat make my brother to offend, I will eat no flesh while the world standeth." It is agreed that anything similar should not occur again. (eight for, three against)

8, 9, 10 omitted.

Fourth Meeting:

11. Proposed that for unity between countries on this side of the world, each country: India, Ceylon, Malaya, Indonesia, each State of the Commonwealth and New Zealand, at any future meeting of the Elder Workers be represented. (A Senior Worker should be appointed to oversight.) Eleven Workers (aka Elders) in all and one with the power to convene meetings to decide matters when called upon by Elders of any State or country. Something without a leader tends to lack of unity. The Elder appointed would also give the advice necessary.

Regarding Workers Being Sent to the East: It was proposed that John Hardie be appointed to this place. (Carried unanimously)

12. Will we all give an assurance that, as much as is in our power, we will go back to our States to show to our fellow laborers that we are all united and that we will foster this spirit of cooperation in this work of God? (Assurance given unanimously)

13. It is with great reluctance that we Brothers should have to register our disapproval of certain things that happened in connection with our departed Brother's life. Two Sister Workers and a Brother stayed with him at "Rosebud" to look after him, when there were open homes who would gladly receive him and cater for his needs and do the superintending of his meals necessitated by the fact that he was a diabetic. This went on for ten years. These Workers had no Gospel Meetings while at "Rosebud"—this, we greatly regret. We feel that what happened has been a digression from the way in which the Work began—both in our day and Jesus' day. We trust there will never be a repetition of these happenings. We feel the responsible Workers should have been consulted with regard to getting their approval of who should succeed our departed Brother in the oversight in Victoria.

This last paragraph was unanimously voted to be included in the Report. Each of the Workers present was given a copy and others were sent to responsible Workers throughout the world.

We separated at Guildford with high hopes that unity and harmony would prevail, and all would be well. Harry Morgan, Les Hawse and Alex Mitchell parted on friendly terms from Chris Williams and had his approval re-visiting in Victoria.

Within a few days of the return to Victoria of Chris Williams and Walter Pickering, a meeting of the Victorian Workers was held at Dandenong to discuss the Guildford Report. Those Workers drew up a circular which was signed by Chris Williams and delivered by hand to the Melbourne churches and sent by post to the churches throughout the State.

After making a solemn promise before God to cooperate with all States and work for peace and harmony, Chris and Walter sent this circular which showed that there was no desire whatever to cooperate. Men who were at Guildford were branded as traitors. It was stated that a personal attack had been made on the life and testimony of the late William Carroll, and that the meetings were held for that purpose. Others at the Guildford meetings can state that there was no such purpose and no attack was made on William Carroll's life and testimony. It was all through a matter of principles, not personalities. Many matters were brought up and dealt with concerning all States, New Zealand and overseas.

Then the Victorian Workers convened a meeting at the Dandenong Town Hall of all in and around Melbourne where the full report of the Workers Meeting held the previous week was read. This report was later read at various centres throughout the State. The following are extracts from this report.

"For these days are very evil and we are not fighting against flesh and blood, but against principalities, princes (those who have great dominion) and principalities and powers and spiritual wickedness in high places. Very subtle enemies and very powerful—"

"They explained about the Victorians not being willing to cooperate with other States. Well, I don't think there was any Brother more willing to cooperate with other States than our Elder Brother, but we know that the others would not cooperate unless they could dictate or interfere with Victoria, so therefore, they really would not cooperate with us unless they had that privilege, as it were. We know it is not the right thing for any man or Elder to interfere with another State. We know that the reason for this thing happening is because there is such lust for power and place.

"It is really only ungodly men that could speak against the work of God in Victoria, and all their meeting was really against Victoria, and they got all their evidence from ungodly men who had departed from the faith—"

~~~~~

Following a reading of this report in Geelong by John Hardie and helpers, at which Chris Williams and several Workers and Elders from Melbourne were present, Chris stated that he meant to stand behind the testimony of William Carroll, and John replied that he means to stand by the testimony of Jesus Christ.

——/3/1954, the day on which the meeting was held in Dandenong Town Hall, Chris wrote to John Hardie as follows:

My dear John:

We have plunged into a sea of sorrow since we came back from the meetings at Guildford. All the Victorian Workers and some of the Elders and Saints have felt it very much that the "Rosebud" question was brought up, involving our Brother who was so much loved and respected for the Christ he loved and preached.

We have told all the people around Melbourne that we did not stand for it ever being discussed and testimonies have been given by the Workers that lived with William Carroll, and we cannot deny that they received 'treat' benefits that helped in the Gospel. It has raised such a feeling that a breach even greater, seems imminent. Could it not all be withdrawn? If you would receive it, a copy of all that was said at the meeting would be sent to you. Only desiring that Christ shall be upheld in us and for His sake,

Yours by mercy,

Chris Williams

~~~~~

To this, John replied on March 16, 1954: that he expected, if his health permitted, to be in Albury in the near future and invited Chris to meet him there and talk the matter over, which would be far better than writing. Chris did not answer this letter, and although he was in Wodonga, just across the river, the weekend John came to Albury, he made no attempt to meet him, or even speak to him on the telephone.

Instead of taking the matter to the responsible Workers who were at Guildford, Chris Williams vented his feelings and the whole matter amongst the people of God. The circular was sent out to the churches, and this followed by the Dandenong report, caused great shock and suffering and confusion and even separating of the people.

As a result of this, many wrote to John from Victoria appealing for help, saying they could not associate themselves with the stand the Victorian Workers had taken. These appeals for help came not from those who were out of fellowship, but from those who were still in fellowship. Many had declared their determination to stand by the older Workers before any attempt was made to acquaint them of the true facts.

It was felt that these appeals could not be ignored, especially as Chris took no notice of John's offer to talk things over with him, and accordingly, early in April, John came into Victoria to help those who cried for help—those such as had been told by Workers that if they were not satisfied, the door was open. Alex and Harry Morgan also came with John, followed later by Tom Turner and Willie Hughes.

True fellowship for many had almost ceased since Workers and Saints in many churches were constant in their "preaching against" those in their midst who they felt were questioning the stand taken by the Victorian Workers. As a result of this end, the true facts being made known, a great many expressed their desire and determination to stand behind the Elder Workers in fellowship with the other States and countries against which the Victorian Workers have stood out.

Beside the attempt at conciliation made by John Hardie before the trouble was ventilated by the Victorian Workers, a further attempt was made by Tom Turner and Alex Mitchell with Chris Williams and Walter Pickering, but the latter two refused to discuss the matter.

Signed by:

John Hardie, T. M. Turner, W. J. Hughes, J. C. Baartz, W. Schloss, A. R. Mitchell, R. L. Hawse and H. Morgan

The Guildford Report Withdrawal
Dandenong, Victoria
April 20th, 1955

The Overseers of Australia and those from overseas being met together to consider the difficulties that exist concerning the Work in Victoria, are agreed that the statement contained in the Guildford Report reflecting on the life and ministry of our late Brother (W. C. Carroll) is now unconditionally withdrawn.

The Victorian Workers and Saints who met at Dandenong also wish to express their regret for the statements made reflecting on the Elders and Workers from other countries and these are unconditionally withdrawn, also the letter sent out from Dandenong to the several churches in Victoria.

Regarding the residence at Rosebud, we feel it is our duty to state that we cannot accept such an arrangement as a precedent that could be repeated.

We would add that, in our opinion, when an Overseer in any state or country, through infirmities or other circumstances, is unable to personally carry out his responsibilities, he should call to his aid a Brother who has the approval and confidence of his brethren and who can eventually assume the oversight.

In order to give assurance to all concerned that every effort will be made to restore confidence and promote unity and true fellowship amongst Workers and in the several churches in Victoria, we will endeavour to find an impartial Brother from overseas who will supervise and co-operate in the oversight of the Work for such time as may be considered necessary.

Dandenong, Victoria
April 20th, 1955

[Signed:] George Walker, J. Forbes, J. T. Carroll, W. J. Hughes, J. Hardie, T. Turner, J. Baartz, J. Williamson, C. Williams

*In Australia at this time, the term *Elder* was used for both the Senior Head Worker and Overseer of a state.

Appendix K   Military Miscellaneous

Sources:

Conscience in America: A Documentary History of Conscientious Objection in America 1757–1967; edited by Lillian Schlissel. E. P. Dutton, Pub., NY, 1968

Conscription of Conscience: The American State and the Conscientious Objector 1940–1947; by Mulford Q. Sibley and Philip E. Jacob, Cornell University Press, Ithaca, NY, 1952

War, Conscience and Dissent by Gordon C. Zahn, Hawthorn Books, NY, 1967

The CPS Story: An Illustrated History of Civilian Public Service by Albert N. Keim, Good Books, NY, 1969

Conscientious Objectors and the Second World War: Moral and Religious Arguments in Support of Pacifism by Cynthia Eller, Praeger Publishers, Santa Barbara, CA, 1991

Pacifism and Conscientious Objection by G. C. Field, Cambridge University Press, Cambridge, England, UK, 1945

Courage of Cowards: The Untold Stories of First World War Conscientious Objectors by Karyn Burnham, Pen and Sword Books Ltd, South Yorkshire, England, UK, 2014

Conscientious Objectors of the Second World War: Refusing to Fight by Ann Kramer, Pen and Sword Books Ltd, South Yorkshire, England, UK, 2013

We Will Not Go to War: Conscientious Objection during the World Wars by Felicity Goodall, History Press, Cheltenham, England, UK, 1997

Two by Two Veteran's Reunions

1989 Camp Barkley Servicemen Reunion, Sioux Falls, South Dakota
1989 World War II Reunion, Camp Barkeley, Texas
1992 World War II Reunion, Sioux Falls, South Dakota
1995 World War II Reunion, Charleston, South Carolina
1999 World War II Reunion, Sparks, Nevada
1992 Ft. Sam Houston 1965–1972 Army Reunion, San Antonio, Texas
2001 Ft. Sam Houston 1965–1972 Army Reunion, San Antonio, Texas
1996 Korean War Veterans Reunion, location unknown
2006 Korean War Veterans Reunion, Mesquite, Nevada

Difficulties Encountered in Obtaining C.O. Classifications in WWII

Carl D. Smith from Laredo, Texas: "Had a rough time with the C.O. classification, and spent many hours being grilled and questioned about it, but was finally cleared" (1995 Reunion Booklet, 2).

Carroll W. Leen from Auburn, California: "Had trouble getting my C.O. so Jack Carroll made a special plea to the Draft Board for me" (1995 Reunion Booklet, 4, 47).

Irwin Wahlin from Afton, Minnesota: "They ignored my C.O. papers, and I was put in the Infantry. I trained with men until the rifles were issued. Then I was sent to Ft. Lewis, Virginia, and instead of the Medics, they put me in the Engineers. It was there I carried a crowbar for a couple of weeks while marching. After that, I carried the flag!" (1999 Reunion Booklet, 88).

C. Burmeister from Walsh, Illinois: "In 1941, I was inducted into the US Army at Des Moines, Iowa. Tom Patterson, my father in the Gospel, helped me with my papers requesting non-combatant service. In spite of that, I was assigned to Anti-tank Co. 1st Infantry 6th Armored Div. and sent to Ft. Leonard Wood, Missouri ... they had no field medics at that date ... the regular Army hadn't heard of such. So, I verbally asked for it. The 1st Sgt sent me to the Company Commander, and he ended up calling the Post Commander ... He spoke with authority, 'Yes the Constitution provides for this status!' He instructed them to transfer me to the medics or to the Station Hospital. I served in the Station Hospital Dental Clinic until the spring of 1942" (1999 Reunion Booklet, 31).

Aubrey Oldham from Albuquerque, New Mexico: "When guns were issued, I was issued a scrub brush and ordered to scrub the garbage can, while the other soldiers were on the drill field. The temperature was ten above zero and I was in light fatigues. Every swipe left a sheet of ice on the can. Also had to clean guns, rake the yard and unload trash. I was eventually allowed to become Night Fireman where I kept the fire going through the bitter cold nights ... in Ft. Warren, Wyoming" (1999 Reunion Booklet, 66).

Ken Paginton from England: "Then War broke out, and I did four and one-half years non-combatant service in the Army ... Among regular soldiers, swearing and using God's name in vain is commonplace. I remember when it came to bedtime the first night, I stood for a long time getting courage to kneel by my bed and pray, but I'm glad to say I got the victory. They soon respected me and would keep quiet while I prayed. Then at mealtime, when I bowed my head to give thanks, they would tap me on the shoulder and say, 'Aren't you well?' When I told them I was giving thanks for my food, they exclaimed, 'What, giving thanks for an Army meal?!' Then they would snatch away my plate, and I had to hold on to it when bowing my head. It was a matter of 'watching and praying.' But after a while, they gave me every respect" (Paginton, 1992, TTT).

WWII Foreign Internees

South Africa. Four Dutch South African Workers who had been preaching in Bandenoeng (West Java), Indonesia, were interned in Indonesia during WWII when the Japanese landed there on March 1, 1942. For three and a half years, while Bernard Frommolt and Willem Boshoff were internees, they held Gospel Meetings and several professed. The Sister Workers, Gertie Maree and Esther Loots, were allowed to go free until 1942, when they also went to prison camp. All survived.

Norway. Edith Hanson and Alma Lee were arrested on October 14, 1942, as foreign nationals when the Germans invaded Norway during WWII. They were held in captivity in Germany and released in 1945. Matilda Smeenk and some other Workers in the Netherlands were interned by Germans.

Around 1942, Jack Carroll reported at a California Convention:

> Two Brothers and two Sisters were captured when the Island of **Java** fell. Two Brothers taken prisoners in **Singapore.** Several Workers in **Burma** able to get away from Gangoon and are now safe and at work in India. Through the British Red Cross, touch has been established with the Workers in **Greece**. All are safe. One lone Sister Worker is holding the fort in unoccupied **France**, doing what she can to strengthen the Lord's little flock there. Also, one Sister in **Belgium**. The fourteen Workers now in **Holland** able to carry on much as usual. There are four in **Denmark**, but their movements are somewhat restricted.
>
> In **Norway and Sweden**, they were able to have their Conventions much as usual. One Brother in **Czechoslovakia**, who was interned for a while. Two Brothers are interned in **Germany**. Another one was under sentence of death for several months, then suddenly given his freedom with no explanation. Fourteen Workers at present in **Germany**— somewhat hindered but may have Meetings in homes. One Brother Worker in Warsaw, **Poland**. He was captured twice, first by one side, then by the other. Now he is free. There are two Workers in **Egypt** and two in **Syria**.

Any other 2x2s imprisoned in wars are unknown to me and were not intentionally omitted.

See also Chapter 38, Military Service and Section C, International Development.

Appendix L   *Pioneers of Various Countries*

This list has been compiled with diligent research from verbal and written reports but there may be unintentional errors or omissions. Details are unknown for several countries.

Country / State	Year	Pioneer and Early Workers	Country / State	Year	Pioneer and Early Workers
Africa			Tanzania	1935	Arthur Robert, Jack Greene
Algeria	Early 1950s	Robert Sterling, Jim Ratcliffe		1961	Florence Hayes, Daphne Pratt
	Following year	Verna Munro, Glenna Mae Terry	Zimbabwe	1922	Willie Clark, Tom Bovine, Wilson Reid
Egypt	1931	Willie Brown, Wilson Reid	**Asia, Far and Middle East**		
	?	Amalia Bouzakis	Bangladesh	1990 2000	David Rundle, John Watt Adele Jeske, Fiona Muirhead
Kenya	1927	Willie Clark, Steve Penniall	Burma (Myanmar)	1924	Adam Hutchison, Alex Leadbetter
	?	Bernice Jelliman, Martha Roy		1927-28	Cora Bailey, Doreen Blair
Ethiopia	Aft 2008	Andy Robijn	Cambodia	Bef. 2002	Lloyd Morgan?
Madagascar	1964	Ken Paginton	China, Peoples Republic	1926	Willie Jamieson, Max Bumpus
Morocco	1947	Ray Bonds, Donald Karnes	East Timor	2006	Trevor Loechel, Daniel Bell
	?	Anna Neuhaus, Glenna Mae Terry	Hong Kong	1937	Charles Preston, Tom Fowler
Sierra Leone	1931	Unknown	India	1921-22	Adam Hutchison, Colin Watt, Ben Buys
South Africa	1905	Wilson Reid, Alex Pearce, Joe Kerr, John Cavanagh, Mary Moodie, Barbara Baxter, Lilly Reid, Martha Skerritt			

Country / State	Year	Pioneer and Early Workers
	1925	Syd Maynard, Gertie Barendilla, Doreen McKenzie, Teenie Walker
Indonesia	1929	George Absalom, James Bird
Japan	1926	Bert Middleton, Ernest Davis
	1947	Sam Lang, Cecil Barrett
Kazakhstan	1990	Dale Benjamin, Pahk Chansun
Korea	1920s	Willie Jamieson
	1949 & 1955	Sproulie Denio, Don Garland
Korea, South	1957	Gordon Winkler, Merlin Howlett, Jeanette Munn, Alice Ramsden
Lebanon	1939	Willie Brown, Eddie Lowe
Papua New Guinea	1954	Edwin Allen
Malaysia	1932	Lindsay Stratford, Bert Cameron
Nepal	1990	David Rundle
Pakistan	1989	David Rundle
Philippines	1936	Hubert Sylvester, Howard Ioerger
	1946	May Sylvester, Bernice Beaber
Siberia	Aft. 1962	Ruta Sprogis

Country / State	Year	Pioneer and Early Workers
Singapore	1932	Lindsay Stratford, Bert Cameron
Sri Lanka (Ceylon)	1927	Alex Mitchell, Jack Trigg
	1928	Alice Morris
Syria	1942	Charlie Addington
Taiwan	1956	Dellas Linaman, Chas. Preston, Wolfgang Klussmann
Thailand	1954-56	Ray Jamieson, Ralph Joll, Edgar Bell
Vietnam, South	1956-57	Fred Allen, Maurice Archer
	1960	Bonnie Dahlin, Phyllis Munn
Australia, New Zealand		
Northern Territory	?	Unknown
New South Wales	1907	John Hardie, Richard (Dick) McClure
Queensland	1906	John Sullivan, Jack Little, Polly Hodgins, Lizzie Sargent
South Australia	1908	Adam Hutchison, Jim McCreight
Tasmania	1908-10	Annie Smith, Fannie Carroll
Victoria	1904	John Hardie, Sandy Alexander
Western Australia	1905	Tom Turner, Jim McCreight, Laura Falkiner, Aggie Hughes

Country / State	Year	Pioneer and Early Workers
New Zealand	1904	John Hardie, Sandy Alexander
	1905	Adam Hutchison, Joe Williamson, Maggie McDougal, Frances Hodgins, Annie Smith, Fannie Carroll
The Caribbean / West Indies		
Jamaica was the first Caribbean country to be pioneered.		
Antigua & Barbuda	1932	Sam McNab
Aruba	1953	Minnie Collen, Nelie Blokker
Bahamas	1931	Frank Stephens, Archie Currie
Barbados	1928	Willie Donaldson, David McMechan
	1930	Florrie Elliott, Lily Miller
Bermuda	1986	Willie Thomas, Norman Nash
Cayman Islands	1928	Florrie Mahood, Florrie Elliott
Cuba	1952	Roy Lacy, Tom Law, Clarence Anderson
Dom. Rep	1971	Harold Eames, Howard Frederick
	1973	Lucy Rogers, Edna Hollister
Guyana	1937	Ernest Smith, Tom Law
Haiti	1971	Orin Taylor, Charles Lauchner

Country / State	Year	Pioneer and Early Workers
Jamaica	1922	Willie Snedden, Frank Stephens
	1925	Florrie Elliott, Lena Brindle
Puerto Rico	1950	Harold Eames, Clarence Anderson
St Kitts and Nevis	?	Ernest Smith, Sam Driver
St Vincent and The Grenadines	1932	Albert Joyce, Ernest Smith
Suriname	1948	Unknown
Trinidad & Tobago	1933	Willie Donaldson, John McDiarmid
Europe		
Europe	1926	Jack Craig & Jack Annand pioneered several East European countries
Albania	Mid-1990s	Doug Crompton, Frank Renteria
Armenia	1994-95	Eric Culbert alone, then Teo Bocancea
Austria	1931	Arnold Scharmen, Gustav Ege
	1935 & 1949	Bertha Schmidt, Irene Zahorkla
Belgium	1928	Joe Hogan, Jim Chapman
Bulgaria	1986-87	Richard Davis, Jeff Evans
Cyprus	1950	Fred Quick
Czechoslovakia (Now Czech Republic and Slovakia)	1926	Jack Annand, Tom Alexson

Country / State	Year	Pioneer and Early Workers
Denmark	1920	Peter Svinth
England	1900	John Long
Estonia (attached to work in Finland)	2005	Larry Stephens
Faroe Islands (attached to work in Denmark)	1925	Peter Svinth, Kristoffer Kristensen
Finland	1920	Adolph Pearson
France	1908	John Baillie, Harry Dennison
France	Aft. WWI	John Baillie, Ray Bonds, Kitty Westerby, Dorothy Brown
Germany	1913	Otto Schmidt, James Jardine
Germany	1920	Otto Schmidt, Heinrich Grefe
Greece	1920	John & Annie Micheletos
Greenland	WWII	Rasmus Prip
Hungary	1930	James Jardine, Alex Secker, Lena Secker
Iceland	Dur. WWII	Rasmus Prip maybe (from Denmark)
Ireland	1897	William Irvine
Italy	1910-13	Penny Barton, (Maggie Johnson?)
Italy	Aft. WWI	Alexander Scott, Robert Marshall
Italy	Aft. WWII	Edna Powell, Va. Micheletti
Latvia	Bef. WWI	Jack Craig, Carl Leonhardt
Latvia	1921	Wilson Reid

Country / State	Year	Pioneer and Early Workers
Netherlands / Holland	1923	Frank van de Merwe, Willie Smeenk
Norway	1913	Edgar Carlson, August Gustafson
Norway	1919	Otto Schmidt, Edith Hanson
Poland	1926	Jack Annand, Tom Alexson
Portugal	---	Combined with Spain
Romania & Moldova	1964	Richard Davis
Romania & Moldova	1965	Maria Hartig, Ruth Christian
Romania & Moldova	1968	Jim Wood
Scotland	1899	Wm. Irvine & Bicycle Tour
Slovakia	1990s	Richard Davis, Jurjen Pettinga
Spain	1933	Sandy Scott, Otto Kemich
Spain	1951	Basilio Alvarez
Sweden	1910	Edith Eklund, Edith Hanson
Sweden	1910-11	August Gustafson, Bob Skerritt,
Sweden	Aft. WWI	T. Larson, R. Carlson
Switzerland	1913	Penny Barton, Maggie Johnston, Otto Schmidt, James Jardine
Switzerland	1925-26	Eddie Schaer, George Wix, Lottie Wix, Katie Hay
Turkey	1964-66	Roy Price
Ukraine	1925	Tom Alexson, Jack Annand
USSR/Russia	Abt 1926	Jack Craig, Carl Leonhardt
USSR/Russia	Mid-1920s	Konstantin Petrochuk

Country / State	Year	Pioneer and Early Workers	Country / State	Year	Pioneer and Early Workers
Yugoslavia	Aft. WWII	Alec Secker	Nicaragua	1990	Carolyn Forsland, Lesvia Dominguiez
Latin America					
The Work in South America began in Buenos Aires, Argentina.	1919		Panama	1969	Willie Pollock, Jack Campbell
Argentina	1919	Jack Jackson, Herbert Vitzhum, Glenn Smith, Maurice Hawkins	Paraguay	1962	Jorge Webster, Steven Stivers
	1922	Ruby Pellett, Leah Hawkins		1968	Morelia Zapata, Margery Harrison
Belize	1985	Jack Campbell, Holmer Bolinger, Willie Pollock	Peru	1969	Willie Boles, Norman Campbell
Bolivia	1957	John Pattison, Fred Hogan	Uruguay	1920	Robustiano Ferreira
Brazil	1923	Jack Jackson, Robert "Bob" Smith	Venezuela	1980	Ted Rozema, Lynn Walker
Chile	1921	Jack Jackson, Maurice Hawkins	**North America - Canada**		
Colombia	1985	Munro MacAngus, Wm. Rosal, David Lockhart	Canada	1904	Harry Oliver, Tom Craig, John Doak, Geo. Buttimer
Costa Rica	1970	Lynn Walker, Jack Campbell	Alberta	1907	Noble Stinson, Robert Darling, Maggie Row, Grace Douglas
Ecuador	1974	Willie Boles, Norman Nash	British Columbia	1907	Jack Carroll, Kate Rankin, Jean Houston, May Carroll, Florence May
El Salvador	1973	Pat Daniels, Lilian Bateman	Manitoba - Ontario	1904-05	Harry Oliver, Tom Craig, John Doak, Geo. Buttimer, Dora Holland
Falkland Islands	1954	Jim Boles, Lawrence Blizard	New Brunswick	?	Galen Harrison
Guatemala	1962	Wilbur Walker, Lynn Walker	Newfoundland	1908	George Johnson, Tom McGivern, Blanche Chappell, Rosetta Miller
Mexico	1933	Lewis Murray, Daniel Leighty			

Country / State	Year	Pioneer and Early Workers
Nova Scotia	1908	Unknown
NW Territory	?	Unknown
Prince Edward Island	1907	Willie Snedden, Willie McAllister
Quebec	1908	First French-speaking: Harry Dennison, John Baillie
Saskatchewan	?	Unknown
Yukon Territory	?	Unknown
North America – USA		
USA	1903	William Irvine, Irvine Weir, Geo. Walker
	1904	Emma Gill, Maggie Rowe
Alabama	Between 1923-27	George Beatty, Tom Grooms
Alaska	1910	Bill & Sara Corcoran (siblings)
	1933	Jack Carroll, Harold Gibson
Arizona	1925	Frank Dennison, Willie Semple, Mae Dennison
Arkansas	1913	Sam Buchanan
California	1904-05	Irvine Weir, Walter Slater, Willie Jamieson
Colorado	By 1912	Geo. Walker, Ernest Gordon
Connecticut	Bef. 1922	
Delaware	Aft. 1927	
Florida	1915-16	Willie Snedden, Ross Huffman (possibly)

Country / State	Year	Pioneer and Early Workers
Georgia	1912	Ida Hawkins, Annie McLaughlin
Hawaii	1923	Dave & Emily Christie
Idaho	1913	Tom Lyness, Donald Davidson
Illinois	By 1912	
Indiana	1906	Geo. Walker, Herbert Reid
Iowa	1907	Maggie Stewart, Mamie Womer
Kansas	By 1912	
Kentucky	1907	Alfred Magowan, John Burns
Louisiana	1922	Arthur Benton, Ira Hamilton
Maine	Bef. 1922	
Maryland	Bef. 1922	
Massachusetts	Bef. 1922	
Michigan	1906	May Carroll, Annie Edwards
Minnesota	By 1912	
Mississippi	1925-26	Alphie Jewell, Max Bumpus
Missouri	1907	Hugh Matthews, Farring Hawkins, Jean Weir, Leroy Shaw (female!)
Montana	By 1912	
Nebraska	1906	Jean Craig, Violet Jamieson
Nebraska	1907	Tom Craig, Hugh Doak
Nevada	Aft. 1927	
New Hampshire	Aft. 1927	
New Jersey	Aft. 1927	

Country / State	Year	Pioneer and Early Workers	Country / State	Year	Pioneer and Early Workers
New Mexico	Bef. 1922		Pacific Islands		
New York	Bef. 1922		American Samoa	1972	Mary Hasper, Claire Brownlee
North Carolina	1924?	Robert Smith, Eddie Beacom			
North Dakota	1903-04	Emma Gill, Wm. Irvine	Federated States of Micronesia	1970s	Leo Stancliff
	1905	Tom Craig, Robert Bullock	Fiji	1922	Robert Blair, Robert Stockdill
Ohio	Bef. 1908				
Oklahoma	By 1912		Guam	1966	Leo Stancliff, Harry Henninger
Oregon	1907	Willie Jamieson, Jas. Martin, Elisabeth Jamieson, Esther Hanson	Marshall Islands	1985	Harry Henninger, Alan Vandermyden
Pennsylvania	Bef. 1922				
Rhode Island	Aft. 1927				
South Carolina	Between 1923-27				
South Dakota	By 1912				
Tennessee	1907	William Cleland, Tom Clarke			
Texas	By 1912				
Utah	Bef. 1922				
Vermont	Aft. 1927				
Virginia	Bef. 1922				
Washington	1907	Jack Carroll			
	1909	Esther Hanson, Maggie Marshall			
West Virginia	Bef. 1922				
Wisconsin	Bef. 1922				
Wyoming	By 1912				

Appendix M   Resources for Two by Two Material

1983. Booksellers USA, Richland, WA, distributors of *The Secret Sect.*
Not currently active

1989. Threshing Floor Ministries, Spokane, WA (TFM)

1992. *Research and Information Services Inc.*, Oregon (*RIS*)
(Workersect.org/index.html)

1996. The original *Veterans of Truth*, Canada, (*VOT*) reproduced on
The Lying Truth website

1997. *Telling The Truth*, Oklahoma/Texas (*TTT*) (*TellingTheTruth.info*)

2000. *The Lying Truth* website (*TLT*) (www.thelyingtruth.info**)**

2005–2014. The original website *Veterans of Truth—Past and Present*
(*VOT*); name changed to *VOT is Alive* (VIA). Not currently active.

2008. *WINGS for Truth* website (stands for: Working to INform, Guide
and Support Those Who Have Been Sexually Abused Within the
Fellowship of Friends and Workers (wingsfortruth.info/)

2008. Truth Archive (thetrutharchive.blogspot.com)

2012. *The Liberty Connection* website (TLC-WEB), rebranded in 2022 as
Expressions by Ex-2x2s (*EXP*) (Ex2x2.info)

2013. *2x2 History* (www.2x2church.info/)

2013. *Hymns Old and New–An Unofficial Compendium*
(www.hymnsoldandnew.info/)

2013. Timeline of key events in the early development of the sect:
(www.tiki-toki.com/timeline/entry/124167/History-of-the-
Friends-and-Workers-Fellowship)

2022. *CherieKroppEhrig.com*, author's website for *Preserving the Truth*

Timeline for Books Published about the 2x2 Sect.

1982. *The Secret Sect* by Doug and Helen Parker

1990 and 2004. *The Church without a Name* by Kathleen Lewis, 1st and
2nd editions (Lewis 1990, *EXP*)

1991 and 2012. *Has the Truth Set you Free?* by Gene and Grace Luxon,
1st and 2nd editions

1993. *Reinventing the Truth* by Kevin N. Daniel

1993 and 2019. *Reflections*, compiled by Daurelle Chapman, 1st and 2nd
editions.

1996. *A Search for 'the Truth'* by Lloyd Fortt

1996. *Reflected Truth* compiled by Joan F. Daniel

1996. *The Church with No Name* by Lynn Cooper (Cooper 1996, *EXP*)

2000. *In Vain They Do Worship* by Willis G. D. Young, a Canadian Ex-worker (Young 2000, *TTT*)

2003. *The Apostles' Doctrine and Fellowship: A documentary history of the early church and restorationist movements* by Dr. Cornelius Jaenen, a 2x2 Canadian man

2015. *From Cult to Christ: The Church With no Name and the Legacy of the Living Witness Doctrine* by Elizabeth Joy Coleman

2018. *I Will Disentangle Myself .... and Leave* by Bob Williston

2022. *Preserving the Truth: The Church without a Name and Its Founder, William Irvine* by Cherie Kropp-Ehrig

Forums created and used by 2x2s and/or Ex-2x2s.

1996. *2x2–Church List Serve,* first group e-mail network. No longer active

2001. The *Professing Message Board* (*PMB*), first Internet discussion forum. Renamed *Common Ground,* it is no longer active, but remains online with thousands of posts

2003. *Truth Message Board* (*TMB*) forum

2009. The *Liberty Connection* (*TLC*) forum for Ex-2x2s only

2016. *Truth Old & New-Christian Group* (Facebook)

2022. Ex 2x2 Support Group (Facebook)

Additional Resources

Chapman, Daurelle, Compiler. Reflections: The Workers, the Gospel and the Nameless House Sect. 1993; 2nd Ed. 2019. Bend, Oregon: Research & Information Services.

Coalter, George J. 1890. "Fermanagh's Sects." In *Memoirs or Selections from the Diary of Geo. J. Coalter.* Enniskillen, N. Ireland: William Trimble. 16, 54–56.

Coleman, Elizabeth Joy. 2015. *From Cult to Christ: The Church With No Name and the Legacy of the Living Witness Doctrine.* Australia: Adeline Press.

Cooper, Lynn. 1996. *The Church With No Name: Known as the Cooneyites, Two by Twos.* Self-published. *Expressions by Ex-2x2s.* Ex2x2.info

Daniel, Joan F. Compiler. 1996. *Reflected Truth: Former Workers and Followers Unmask Life in a Large, Little-known Sect.* Sisters, Oregon: Research & Information Services.

Daniel, Kevin. 1993. *Reinventing the Truth.* Bend, Oregon: Research & Information Services.

Lewis, Kathleen. 1990. *Church without a Name. Expressions by Ex-2x2s.* Ex2x2.info

Luxon, Gene and Grace. 2012. *Has the Truth Set You Free?* Self-published: CreateSpace.

Paul, William E. 1977. *They Go About Two by Two: The History and Doctrine of a Little Known Cult. Telling The Truth.*

Piepkorn, Arthur Carl. 1979. "Christian Fellowship (People on The Way, Disciples of Jesus, Friends, Two-By-Twos). In *Profiles in Belief: The Religious Bodies of the United States and Canada, Vol. IV.* San Francisco, CA: Harper & Row, Publishers. 58–62.

Veterans of Truth: Original VOT website. 1996. *See The Lying Truth website.* www.thelyingtruth.info/vot/home_splash.php

Wikipedia: Two by Twos. wikipedia.org/wiki/TwobyTwos

WINGS Website. wingsfortruth.info/

Appendix N   Marriage, Divorce and Remarriage

Letter regarding Marriage, Divorce and Remarriage by William P. Lewis, Eastern US Overseer (undated)

INTRODUCTION: It has come into my heart to write some of the facts of my experience and some of the personal visits and conversations I have had with various of my brethren and companions over the years concerning the matter of Marriage, Divorce and Remarriage in the light of the best understanding of the Scriptures, both Old and New Testaments, that we arrived at prayerfully and out of great concern for ourselves and for those we were responsible to guide and counsel in the fear of the Lord.

I have not held on to any interpretation that a good many of my closest brethren and companions did not agree with; just as all doctrine of the Lord is understood, so this was "precept upon precept, line upon line, here a little, there a little," Is. 28:10. Concern in these matters for me goes back to my earliest years in the work of the Gospel and the beginning of my studies of the Bible with my companion; a concern that has intensified as my responsibilities to enter into judgments affecting the souls of others has increased.

Let me say that I sought the counsel and aid of older brothers in deciding some cases that were in my field of responsibility, from the time I became responsible, nearly 30 years ago; and what some may look upon as being a change cannot appear so to me, due to that fact. Even then, we were considering cases, as we are now, and looking back have not been disappointed in the outcome of any of them, as there has been good evidence of the Lord's pleasure in them.

There was a general feeling and desire among us that discussed this, that there would be someday a meeting of our elders to settle this question definitely and for all, and in the area of my responsibilities it has been. There never was, in my mind, nor even voiced by those with whom I discussed it, any criticism of those who went before us, for we did then as now ... "weigh as one who dreads dissent and fears a doubt as wrong" to quote Whittier. It was just that we felt in our own souls that we were lacking. The decision (Par. 3) was that every case be examined and decided upon its own merits and the circumstances peculiar to it.

1. Matt. 5:32, 19:9, Ps. 56:5–6. Remarriage–exceptive clause of fornication. Attention is especially drawn to the exception Jesus made where fornication was concerned. It seems evident that remarriage was in question; if there had been no "marrying of another" involved, Jesus would have made no such exception, since no question of possible sin could arise if a union had been dissolved by death; but this was a case of putting away, questioning its legality.

2. Remarriage of the innocent party. (Ps. 55:11–15) Jesus included the exceptive clause to make it clear that the remarriage of the innocent party was not a sinful action where fornication was involved. I Cor. 7:27–28. This is confirmed by Paul. A difference is made here between those who were "bound to" or "loosed from" a wife, and one who had never been married, virgins. In both cases marrying was not a sin, which could not have been referred to if the "loosing from" had been by death. Again no questions in that case. **The questioning arose in my heart in view of the fact that we were treating all cases of abandonment and divorce of spouses amongst us, more or less, the same.**

3. Job 31:9–12. Remarriage only where fornication has taken place. In a meeting of our elders it was decided that only cases where fornication was involved would the question of remarriage be included. It was also agreed that 3 Overseers would consider and render judgment; not 1 or 2. This is very much in line with what Job said about it in his day before the law and in all probability before there was any written guidance. It was a matter for the Judges to decide; note the plural.

4. Meaning of fornication. As to the meaning of fornication, it has seemed to me that Jesus deliberately chose the word in order to cover all sexually related vice, forseeing our time and the perversion that would overspread the race. If He had said "except it be for adultery," He would have confined it to that particular form of fornication; fornication being a general term that did cover all as stated before. The man in I Cor. 5:1 was guilty of fornication because of an adulterous relationship with his father's wife and in both Old and New Testament, the word is used to describe the sins of married women.

5. Ezekiel 16:32–38, Jer. 3:1. Fornication dissolves the marriage bond, possibility of reconciliation. In one chapter in Ezekiel, ch. 16, the term harlotry, whoredom and adultery are referred to as being a multiplication of Israel's fornications, and she is called "a wife that committeth adultery" to be judged as women that break wedlock, from which we may rightly conclude that fornication dissolves the marriage bond. Not that it cannot be repaired, indeed that was the Lord's offer to Israel, contingent upon their repentance and return to Him. In Jer. He saw that is something the Law did not require a man to do, and it would be an act of great compassion and forgiveness for him to do it, an evidence of godliness in the man and testimony to a justice that only God could impart to him. The first attempt should be to effect such a reconciliation not where there is adamant pursuit of fornication and willful departure from one's faithful mate, that same justice demands that the guilty bear punishment and not the innocent.

6. II Kings 9:22, Hosea 2:2, Amos 7:7, I Cor. 5:1, Rev. 2:20–21. Fornication and adultery synonymous. It has been interesting to learn that the Greek word used in the Gospel for fornication is *porn*, which is employed in the Septuagint speaking of women (married) in the following cases, among others, (1st 3 above ... the last 2 using the word to fornicate.) The same Greek word issued in I Cor. 5 and Rev. 2, in one verse to commit fornication and in the other to commit adultery. Happily a knowledge of Greek is not necessary to understand the Scriptures, but it's reassuring when the Greek and Hebrew texts confirm what the Holy Ghost has given to us from what is available in our own language.

7. Lev. 20:10, Gen. 20:3, John 8. Death the penalty for adultery in the law. There are commandments in the law concerning these matters, one given by God carried the death penalty for both parties proven guilty of a willful act of adultery, and such punishment must have preceded the law. It seems to me that the only time Jesus dealt with this was in John 8, and He did not impose the death penalty that the Scribes and Pharisees were urging by the law, because He had come to abolish the death penalty of the law and bring life and immortality to light through the Gospel, to forgive repentant sins, except one, which we are certain was not fornication.

8. Deut. 24:1–4. Moses' commandment of divorce for restraint. The other commandment was written by Moses for hard hearted men, not to encourage or sanction divorce "for every cause," but to restrain and guide as much as possible a practice that was never pleasing or acceptable to God. Jesus confirmed this by His own words to those who questioned Him about it. If we are to understand His teaching on the subject, we must take this into account, for in all other places than John 8, He was dealing with Moses' commandment, explaining why He would say, "but I say unto you, that whosoever shall put away his wife, saving for the cause of fornication, causeth her to commit adultery." Matt. 5:32, 19:9, Mark 10:12 and "I say unto you, whosoever shall put away his wife, except it be for fornication and shall marry another, committeth adultery and whosoever marrieth her which is put away doth commit adultery." All the participants in this arrangement were held responsible, being the instigator. Is. 54:4–6. In those days it was not possible for a woman to readily support herself and her recourse was to find another man who would marry her. In Isaiah the Lord reveals His heart feelings for a woman so treated, according her the dignity and consolation of widowhood, when in reality she was a forsaken woman in youth. He was willing to take such to be His wife, to remove her shame and reproach, pleading with Israel in this vein.

9. I Cor. 7:25, 40. The innocent party divorcing. If a man or woman be put away for fornication, then they who put her away would not be the author of adultery in remarriage, since it was for that cause that he or she was put away. Doubtless the free and conscienceless use of Moses' precept; and the Pharisees instance that Jesus declare His interpretation of it was the reason for the Lord's words on the subject. He did not cover all the ground on it and the related circumstances that would arise. Thus Paul saying to the Corinthians, "I have no commandment of the Lord (concerning virgins), yet I give my judgment as one that hath obtained mercy of the Lord to be faithful," and "after my judgment, I think also that I have the Spirit of the Lord."

10. John 14:26, 16:13, Matt. 18:18–20. The guidance of the Holy Ghost. Jesus made it very clear that the Holy Ghost would come and teach them all things and bring to remembrance "all things that I have said unto you" and "He will guide you into all truth." We cannot escape the responsibility that was laid on the early Apostles in this regard if we are to be true to our profession to be followers of them. It is most awesome being charged to obtain the guidance of the Holy Ghost, so that judgment we give would be equitable and merciful, acceptable to and binding in Heaven, following this with the answer to Peter's question about forgiveness, emphasizing compassion and reminding us all of our utter dependence on the merciful and forgiving God, so that we would not deny to another what we must have ourselves.

11. Old Testament parallel teaching. Ps. 94:20–21. Again we have 2–3 involved in settling whatever controversy had arisen. A parallel teaching may be found in the O.T. showing that all matters were not covered by the law and had to be taken to Judges in that event. To attempt to settle questions that arise in our day by law would bring up the question that is asked in Ps. 94 and result in the answer in the following verse, I greatly fear.

12. I Cor. 7:8–11. Distinction between Classes. There are a number of classes, different classes, husbands and wives, married people, divorced people and widows. In two verses making a distinction between them, putting the woman who departed from her husband (not an adulterous mate) in the unmarried state and not responsible to remain so or to be reconciled to her husband.

13. I Cor. 7. Unbelieving partners. Paul also had advice for unbelieving mates, making it clear that their unbelief was not grounds for putting them away, if they were pleased to dwell with them, to do so would again, exercising Moses' precept, "for every cause." On the other hand if unbelieving depart, let him depart, a brother, a sister is not under bondage in such.

14. I Cor. 7:39. Wife bound by the law. The word bondage used here carries the same meaning as "bound by." The wife is bound by the law as long as her husband liveth. (Husband not an adulterous, departed mate.) It is significant that Paul uses the word bondage 6 times in the Galatian epistle in reference to the law and its bondage. Again I understand that the Greek words for "leave" and "put away" and "depart" are all correctly* translated to mean separation by divorce, permissible for the Christian for only one cause, fornication. (Gal. 2:4, 4:3, 9, 24, 25; 5:1)

*AUTHOR'S NOTE: This is an incorrect translation. *Put away* **does not** mean *divorce*. *See* Chapter 29 for correct definition of *put away*.

15. Hosea 2:2. Innocent party free to marry. The clear intent of the teaching every place is that the innocent victim of divorce for that cause is free from the law of husband and wife because an adulterous mate is no longer husband or wife. It was never possible for me to accept that the law offered a more equitable solution to the problem than our Lord, in that the penalty for the guilty under the law was death; harsh, but just; leaving the innocent free and not in an untenable position through a compelling human desire and God–given inclination to seek the love and compassion of a true mate.

16. The celibate life is of free will. Matt. 19:11–12, 1 Cor. 7:9, 37. Our Creator saw it was not good for a man to be alone, and Jesus confessed that every man could not live a celibate life in connection with His teaching concerning divorce. One might inject the question of the power and grace of God to enable a man or woman to remain unmarried in such circumstances, and far be it from me to minimize that possibility, but Jesus put it upon the individual's own ability to do so and so did Paul, "but if they cannot contain, let them marry," and "nevertheless he that standeth steadfast in his heart, having no necessity, but having power over his own will, and hath so decreed in his own heart that he will keep his virgin, doeth well."

17. I Cor. 7:37. Marriage is ordained of God and typifies Christ and the Church. This verse in I Cor., of course, was directed to ones who had never been married and by all understanding would find it easier to maintain a celibate life than those who had experienced the married state. It seems very clear that in all the Bible, God expected most men and women to seek a mate and enjoy the love and companionship that its union affords, the closest human tie as the most sacred. It is, in its purity, representing the relationship intended between Christ and His church. There is nothing in the Scripture to lead us to believe that any man or woman was expected to go through life alone, except by choice, and that, primarily, for the King of Heaven's sake. We have that example in Paul, Jesus and others, but not to the exclusivity of those who were married.

18. Adultery, an heinous crime. Job 31:11, Prov. 6:32–35. In conclusion, adultery is not unforgivable, but it is still what Job said it to be, an heinous crime, certain of punishment most damaging and dishonouring personally and with the longest lasting consequences for all those concerned. An offence that may not be purged by rewards and gifts, and we who have been called to try to mitigate these consequences know what a wounding it is, and we sadly conclude with Solomon, "but whoso committeth adultery with a woman lacketh understanding" [Prov. 6:32].

I have not written this to rebut arguments to the contrary, not even to try to convince skeptics, but that my friends might know my firm convictions and from whence they came.

William Lewis (1918-2000)
An Eastern US Overseer

Glossary

Frequently used definitions, explanations and terminology.

Alpha Gospel: Irvine's term for the original message of the 2x2 Workers, including the 2x2 ministry and church in the home founded by William Irvine in Ireland at the turn of the twentieth century.

Annual Meetings: *See* Convention.

Baptism: Only by immersion, often after a period of proving one is fully committed.

Bach: When unable to stay in homes of a member as a house guest, Workers rent temporary accommodations called a *bach*. This is very common in foreign fields.

Church in the Home: Sunday and midweek Fellowship Meetings are held only in a member's home.

Clergy, Clergyman: non-2x2 preachers, ministers.

Companion, Co-worker, Fellow-Laborer, Fellow-Servant, Associate: The other person in a pair of 2x2 Workers.

Convention, Annual: Also called Annual Meetings. Yearly regional assemblies of Friends and Workers; all are expected to attend. Typically lasting two–five days, including three daily meals. Three meetings per day, each with singing, preaching, prayer, and testimony and sermons by Workers and Friends. Usually some out-of-the-area visiting Workers are present. Attendance varies by location, from a few dozen to several hundred to over a thousand. Usually held at farms owned by Friends, with special purpose buildings, but sometimes in tents or a hired facility.

Cooneyites: In the sect's early days, the public and media commonly referred to the 2x2 preachers and members as *Cooneyites*, after Edward Cooney, one of their most prominent preachers. After Cooney was excommunicated in 1928, the splinter group of his loyal followers were also referred to as *Cooneyites,* while the Cooneyite moniker continued to be used for the 2x2 Sect also. Many published articles refer to the 2x2 group as *Cooneyites,* but the 2x2 Sect members have never referred to themselves by this name, and they usually deny any connection to it.

Elder, Bishop: A male 2x2 member who presides over a home church Meeting that is often, but not always, held in his home. In some countries the Overseers are called *Elders*.

Emblems, Breaking Bread (aka Communion, Eucharist, Lord's Supper): Ceremony in Sunday Fellowship Meeting in which thankfulness is expressed in prayer before consuming bread and fruit of the vine (wine or grape juice, depending on the location). From: "This do in remembrance of me" (Luke 22:19 *KJV*).

Evangelist: *See* Worker.

Ex-2x2s: Former members disassociated from 2x2ism; considered apostates, backsliders, dissenters, rebellious, unwilling.

False Church: Any church, sect, religion or movement and its members (other than the 2x2 Sect members) are viewed as sincerely wrong, misguided, deceived and will be going to Hell.

False Preachers: All other Christian ministers are considered false preachers or deceivers according to the Workers' teachings.

Fellowship: Refers to the church gatherings; weekly Fellowship Meetings are held on Sundays and sometimes midweek.

Field: The defined geographical area assigned to a pair of Workers to work/labor, usually for a 12 month period (apart from time away for Conventions and Special Meetings).

Friend, Saint: Refers to professing committed believers (lay persons) within the 2x2 Sect.

Gospel, the: According to the Workers, Jesus came to the Earth to establish a Two by Two ministry, to be a pattern and example of how believers should live; he died to pay for the sins of mankind. His blood only covers members of the Two by Two Sect. One must hear and accept the 2x2 Gospel through a Worker in order to be saved.

Handmaiden: *See* Worker, Sister.

Harvest Field: Refers to the whole world of the unsaved, spiritually lost individuals, who are not yet members of their church.

Home, Divided: A home where one member in a marriage is a 2x2 and the other is not.

Home, Open: A home known for hospitality among the members, especially one that accommodates Workers on a frequent basis and/or is available for Fellowship Meetings.

Labor: Workers are said to *labor* in various fields. Same as work and preach.

Living Witness Doctrine: The belief that "life begets life." As natural life comes from natural life, so also spiritual life is passed on from person-to-person. For someone to be saved, they must hear the Gospel in person from a "Living Witness"; that is, from a 2x2 Worker.

Meeting, Fellowship: Weekly member worship on Sunday. Typical Meeting protocol order: one to two hymns, members' audible prayer, hymn, members' testimonies (sharing from the Scripture), hymn, emblems (communion) with prayer before each, closing hymn. An Elder/Bishop presides, unless a Worker is present, and then the Worker does.

Meeting, Gospel: Public meeting conducted by a pair of Workers for the purpose of winning new converts and encouraging existing members. Consists of singing, praying and preaching. Usually held in public venues (e.g. schools, rented halls) and sometimes in members' homes. Outsiders are invited and welcome. No open collections are taken, although members may give privately.

Meeting, Midweek Bible Study: Usually a midweek and/or Sunday night Bible study on a given topic, theme or Bible passage is held. Same protocol as Fellowship Meeting without emblems. Typically, a Bible study subject list or series of chapters is supplied by Senior Workers for a given year. Not all areas have Sunday evening Meetings.

Meeting, Special: Held once a year for a geographical region where members of several individual Fellowship Meetings come together with a number of Workers. Usually consists of two meetings in a single day with singing, prayer, testimonies by Friends and sermons by Workers.

Meeting, Union: Two or more Sunday Fellowship Meetings may combine once a month in some areas.

Message People: Followers of William Irvine after he was dismissed in 1914, who accepted his Omega Message. Some were followers from the Alpha Gospel days, while others were new converts.

Ministers: *See* Workers.

Mission: A series of consecutive Gospel Meetings for the purpose of recruiting new converts.

Names for the 2x2 Church: The Church without a Name has many monikers. Some names insiders use to refer to their church have included *the Truth, the Way, the Fellowship, the Fold, the Kingdom, God's Way, God's People, Children/Family of God, The Testimony, the Meetings, the Jesus Way, the Friends and Workers Fellowship, Christian Church in England* and more.

Some of the nicknames outsiders have applied include *Two by Twos (2x2s), Cooneyites, Tramp Preachers, Dippers, Black Stockings, Irvinites, Reidites, Carrollites, No-Name Church, No-Secters,* etc. This book most frequently refers to this movement as the Two by Two Sect (2x2 Sect), the 2x2 Church, and 2x2 Fellowship.

Omega Message: After William Irvine was rejected as leader of the 2x2 Sect he founded, he began teaching an entirely different message he dubbed his *Omega Message.* It superseded his original Alpha Gospel that he claimed was finished in 1914. *See* Chapter 25 and Appendix C.

Outsider: Non-2x2. Any person who is not a follower of the 2x2 Sect.

Overseer: A supervisor over other Workers who oversees a large geographical region, such as a country, province, state or part of a state. They are said to have the "responsibility," "oversight" or "Eldership" of a region.

Pioneers: First Workers to go preach to a foreign country. Also used as a verb, e.g. "He pioneered Vietnam."

Preacher: Same as Worker; a minister. There are no lay preachers.

Preparations: Commonly called *preps*. A time when Workers and volunteers prepare the Convention facilities for an upcoming annual Convention, often taking four–six weeks for larger Conventions.

Profess, Make One's Choice, or to Decide: The public act of indicating in a Convention or Gospel Meeting that the person desires to commit to follow the beliefs and practices of the 2x2 Church. It may be framed as, "if you wish to follow Jesus in this Way, raise your hand (or stand to your feet)," or in some cases by talking to the Worker afterwards. The Worker's invitation is called *testing the Meeting*.

Professing: A status of a believer resulting from an individual publicly professing (converting) to the 2x2 Sect through a Worker, usually in a Gospel Meeting.

Servant: Same as Worker.

Standing Down, Stood Down: Not allowed to participate in Fellowship Meetings; different from being "put out" of the Sect or the Work (commonly used term used in Australia and New Zealand).

Taking part: Participating in prayer, testimony and communion in Meetings or Conventions. One's *part* (right to participate) may be taken away as a disciplinary measure for wayward Friends, which may include not taking communion.

Testimony: To give one's testimony in a Meeting or Convention context is to share one's thoughts and feelings on Bible passages or spiritual matters.

The Testimony, The Testy: The 2x2 Sect registered the name *The Testimony of Jesus* in the UK during WWI. William Irvine's preferred term used in his letters for the 2x2 Sect after he was expelled.

The Truth: The most common term English-speaking 2x2 members use among themselves to refer to their church. Same as "The Way," "The Fellowship," and "The Fold."

The Way: One of the terms commonly used by English-speaking 2x2 members among themselves to refer to their church. Same as "The Truth," "The Fellowship," "The Fold," etc.

Two by Two, 2x2 Sect: Most commonly used nickname by outsiders and the media for the church, including *Wikipedia*. Based on their practice of Workers preaching in pairs, or two by two.

Work, the: The individuals who volunteer to become 2x2 ministers and are accepted are said to have *entered the Work*, to be *in the Work*, and are called Workers, *servants, and handmaidens*.

Worker, Servant, Preacher, Minister, Evangelist, Laborer: A currently active and accepted member (man or woman) of the 2x2 ministry who has given up secular work and devoted their profession to that of proclaiming and teaching the Gospel. Entering the Work is a lifetime commitment: "No man, having put his hand to the plough, and looking back, is fit for the Kingdom of God" (Luke 9:62). Ideally, they were expected to "die in the harness"; however, many do leave due to poor health and other reasons. They officiate at funerals and when present, preside at Sunday, Midweek, Gospel and Convention Meetings. They are universally unmarried, homeless, roving evangelists and missionaries traveling from place to place (within their assigned fields), in same-sex pairs. Usually, they are welcome houseguests of followers or reside in temporary accommodations (baches) if no homes are available. Former Workers are referred to as *Ex-workers.* In earlier years there were married Worker pairs.

Worker, Head: Sometimes synonymous with term *Overseer.* Usually, the most Senior Worker in a geographical region. For example, the head Worker of Alberta, California, Victoria, New Zealand, Ireland, etc. Also called *the Elder* in some countries.

Worker, Senior: Usually the more experienced or older of a pair of Workers. Sometimes, loosely applied to a state head Worker.

Worker, Brother: A male Worker, aka servant, preacher, minister, evangelist.

Worker, Sister: A female Worker, aka handmaiden, servant, preacher lady, minister, evangelist.

World, the: Refers to the entire world system outside of the 2x2 Sect. All other churches, religions, secular philosophies, preachers, Christian believers, the material world and all socio-political movements.

References

The content of most references is reprinted on *TellingTheTruth.info* website. Newspaper articles are not included below and may be viewed on the website *TellingTheTruth.info* in History, Newspaper Articles-Old.

Note: n.d. indicates no date, undated; n.p. indicates not published.

Alberta Excommunication Tapes. 1999. *TellingTheTruth.info*, History, Divisions, Alberta.

Alberta Report. 1997. Edmonton, Alberta, Canada. Sept. 15.

Anderson, Kathie. 1983. "Church without a Name meets again amid Controversy." *Bellingham Herald*, Washington, US. Aug. 20. 4A.

Anton, Peter. 1893. *Kilsyth: A Parish History*. Glasgow, Scotland: John Smith & Son. www.electricscotland.com/history/kilsyth

Armstrong, Canon S. C. 1910. *Cooneyites or Dippers.* Dublin: Church of Ireland Printing & Publishing. *Telling The Truth.*

Ashby, Leonard 1939. *A Different Gospel: An examination of the teaching of the Cooneyites.* London, UK: Pickering & Inglis.

Atmore, Amelia A. 1927. *Secret Mormonism and Christian Science.* G. F. Vallance Publisher, Barkingside, Essex, Great Britain. *Telling The Truth.*

Baker, Paul. 1988. *King and Country Call – New Zealanders, Conscription and the Great War.* Auckland, NZ: Auckland Univ. Press. 173.

Ballinamallard Historical Society. 2004. *Ballinamallard, a Place of Importance.* n.p. 37, 50–51, 60, 64–72, 158–161.

Ballinamallard Methodist Church. 1903. Quarterly Meeting Minutes. *Telling The Truth.* Dec 14.

Baugh, Helen (Duff). 1984. *The Story Goes On.* Kansas City, Missouri, US: Stonecroft Inc.

Beaber, John S. *Deliverance—It Has Come!* ithascome.bravehost.com

Beattie, Joseph and Esther (Beattie) Gibson. 2001. *Ralph and Rene Beattie. Telling The Truth.*

Bence-Jones, Mark. 1978. *Burke's Guide to Country Houses, Ireland,* Vol. 1. Oxford, England: Burke's Peerage. Pergamon Press.

Berger, William. Account of William Berger. n.d. *Telling The Truth*

Berry, Dorothy "Dot":

———. 2008. "Black Stockings." *Expressions by Ex-2x2s* (*Ex2x2.info*).

———. 2009. "On Holy Ground." *Expressions by Ex-2x2s* (*Ex2x2.info*).

"Bethel Mission in South Australia." 1910. *Telling The Truth.*

Bone, James. 1975. "Account of the Spread of the Gospel in the Early Days in California"; owner of Gilroy, California, US Convention grounds. *Telling The Truth.*

Bright Words. 1895–1904. Edinburgh, Scotland: McFarlane & Erskine. *Telling The Truth.*

Burgess, Ethel (Anderson). 1915. "Account of Gospel Coming to West Point," Newfoundland, Canada. *Telling The Truth.*

Buck, Ann. 1984. *Victorian Costume and Costume Accessories,* 2nd rev. ed. Carlton, England: Ruth Bean Publishers. 142.

Carroll, Frances "Fannie." 1964. Sermon at Santee, California US Convention. *Telling The Truth.* October.

Carroll, John "Jack" Thomas (JTC):

———. 1923. Christie Marriage Announcement. *Telling The Truth.* Dec 1.

———. 1934. "The New Testament Church," Bakersfield, California US Convention. *Telling The Truth.*

———. 1940. Statement at Theodore, Saskatchewan, Canada. *Telling The Truth.* July 14.

———. 1942. Statement at Olympia, Washington, US. *Telling The Truth.* Sept. 4–7.

———. 1951. Statement at Arizona US Convention. Oct. 25–28.

———. n.d., n.p. "Matthew 13 Sermon." *Telling The Truth.*

———. n.d., n.p. Minister Statement; unsigned, probably by Jack Carroll. *Telling The Truth Photo Gallery.*

Carroll, William "Bill" Charles (WCC):

———. 1950. Sermon. *Telling The Truth.* Dec. 16.

Chandler, Russell. 1983. "Obscure, Silent Nameless Sect Travels 'Secret' Path." *Los Angeles Times.* Sept. 13. 3.

Christian History Magazine, Hudson Taylor & Missions to China. 1996. Carol Stream, Illinois: Christianity Today Int. Issue 52. *ChristianityToday.com/history/issues/issue-52*

Christian Workers Magazine. 1920. Mount Morris, Illinois: Moody Bible Institute. February. 454.

Cooney, Edward:

———. 1928. Explanation of 1928 Meeting. Appendix D.

———. 1947. Testimony of Edward Cooney. Appendix D.

"Corcoran Family Story of Faith." n.d. *Telling The Truth.* n.p

Cunnington, Willett, C. and Phillis. 1970. *Handbook of English Costume in the Nineteenth Century.* Boston, Massachusetts, US. Plays Inc. 567.

Dair Rioga Local History Group. 2005. *All in Good Faith*. Naas, Co. Kildare, Ireland: Leinster Leader. 322–336.

Daniel, Joan. *Reflected Truth: Former Workers and Followers Unmask Life in a Large, Little-known Sect*. Sisters, Oregon, US: Research & Information Services. 264

Doak, John. 1945. Sermon at Portage la Prairie, Manitoba, Canada Convention.

Dorey, Duncan P. and Margaret J. Dorey v. Janice L. Steingard, Case No. 9703–16174. 1999. Excerpt of Trial Transcript. Edmonton, Alberta, Canada. Feb. 8.

Drummond, Henry. 1884. *Natural Law in the Spiritual World*. London, England: Hodder and Stoughton. 59–94. *Telling The Truth*.

Eberstein, John G.:

———. 1964. "Who Are the Cooneyites?" *Life of Faith*. *Telling The Truth*. April 23.

———. 1895–1902. "Official List of Workers (in author's possession).

Elder, J. R. 1940. *History of the Presbyterian Church of New Zealand*. Christchurch: Presbyterian Bookroom. 435.

Ellis Island. *See* libertyellisfoundation.org/

Expressions by Ex-2x2s (EXP). 2012. Ex2x2.info

Faith Mission Aims and Principles. n.d. n.p.

Faith Mission Staff of Workers Lists. See *Bright Words*.

Federal Bureau of Investigation. 1943. Report of Kansas City Division File No. 100–6698. April 23.

First! Sept-Oct, 2011. Faith Mission Publication. 8. faithmission.org/first_magazine

"First Missions in New Zealand." n.d. *Telling The Truth*.

"First Two Workers to go to Australia and New Zealand." n.d. *Telling The Truth*.

"Friends Who Lived in the Hutt Valley 1901–2006." n.d. *Telling the Truth*.

Fruchtenbaum, Dr. Arnold G. 2020. *Footsteps of the Messiah*. San Antonio, Texas: Ariel Ministries. 91, 106, 126-140.

Gaebelein, Arno. C. 1923–1924. *Our Hope* Vol. 30. New York. January.

Galloway, Don. 1999. "Alberta Excommunication Events." *Telling The Truth*.

Gammie, Alexander. 1933. *John McNeill: His Life and Work*. Great Britain: Pickering & Inglis.

Gill, William. 1951. William Gill's Funeral. *Telling The Truth*. June 5.

Go-Preacher's Hymn Book. 1909. n.p. *Telling The Truth*.

Govan, I. R. [Isobel Rosie Stewart]. 1978. *Spirit of Revival*. Rusheden, Northhamptonshire, England: Stanley L. Hunt.

Govan, John George – See *Bright Words*.

Grant, David. 1986. *Out in the Cold, Pacifists & Conscientious Objectors in New Zealand during World War II*. Auckland, New Zealand: Reed Methuen Publishers. 157, 165–66.

Grass, Milton N. 1955. *History of Hosiery*. New York: Fairchild Publications. 251.

Haley, J. Evetts. 1983. *Charles Goodnight: Cowman and Plainsman*. University of Oklahoma Press. 462.

Hanowell, Manford. 2006. "Account of Fred Hanowell." *Telling The Truth*. Sept. 15.

Hardie, John. 1982."John Hardie – Concerning his Arrival in Australia and New Zealand." *Telling The Truth*. Feb. 20.

Heaney, Mavis. 2004. *To God be the Glory: The Personal Memoirs of Rev. William P. Nicholson*. Belfast, N. Ireland: Ambassador Publications; Greenville, South Carolina, US: Emerald House. 110.

Hanson, Richard. Ed. 1987–88. *James & Ina Hill Clan*. Portland, Oregon, US: Hanson Book Company. 9.

Hawkins, Maurice. Account of Maurice Hawkins. n.d. *Telling The Truth*.

Holland, Dora. 1913. Letter to Dear Brother. Aug. 11. *Telling The Truth*.

Hosfeld, Kathleen. *Skagit Valley Herald,* Mt. Vernon, Washington, US.

———. 1983a. "Criticism Clouds Church's Gathering." Aug. 17.

———. 1983b. "Former Members of No-Name Church Continue Quiet Protest." Aug. 18.

Hughes, Garrett. 1987. Funeral Notes for Erling Omdal, Eagle Bend, Minnesota, US. Oct. 6.

Hughes, Hazel. 1971. Transcript of Hazel Hughes talk. *Telling The Truth*.

Hughes, Willie:

———. 1928. Letterhead "The United Christian Conventions of Australasia and New Zealand." *Telling The Truth Photo Gallery*.

———. 1946. Statement at Te Ore Ore, Masterton, New Zealand. *Telling The Truth*. Jan. 6.

Humphries, R. A. and R. S. Ward. 1995. *Religious Bodies in Australia,* 3rd ed. Wantirna, Victoria, Australia: New Melbourne Press. 218–219.

Hutchison, James:

———. 1986. *Weaver, Miners and the Open Book: A History of Kilsyth*. Self-published, Scotland. 124–28.

———.2018. *Canal Boats & Miners Rows: Kilsyth 1750–1970*. Self-published, Scotland. 79.

Hymns Old and New. Ed. 1987. Basingstoke, Hants, England: R. L. Allan & Son.

———. www.bibles-direct.com

———. *Hymns Old & New: An Unofficial Compendium* website. www.hymnsoldandnew.info/

Irvine, W. C. Compiler. 1929, 1935. *Heresies Exposed,* 37th ed. Neptune, New Jersey, US: Loizeaux Brothers. 73–78; W. C. Irvine was no relation to William Irvine.

Irvine, William:

———. 1911–47. Collection of Letters by William Irvine. *Telling The Truth.*

———. 1913. Statement. *Telling The Truth.* July.

———. 1910–17. Sermons. *Telling The Truth.*

Jaenen, Cornelius. 2003. "Nameless spiritual fellowship." *Apostles' Doctrine and Fellowship.* Ottawa, Canada: Legas Publishing. 518–542.

Jackson, Jack. 1960. Sermon at Freedom, New York Convention. Nov. or Aug. 14, 1960.

Jamieson, Elisabeth. 1969. "Auntie Elisabeth's Reminiscences." Hayward, California, US. *Telling The Truth.*

Knight, Marti. 2000. "Black Stocking Memories." *Expressions by Ex-2x2s (Ex2x2.info).*

Laderer, Luise and Sofie. n.d. "Account of Luise and Sofie Laderer's Prison Experiences in WWII." *Telling The Truth.*

Latimer, William Thomas. 1902. *History of the Irish Presbyterians,* 2nd ed. Belfast, Ireland: William Mullan & Son. 496 (Google Books online).

Lying Truth, The website (TLT). 2000. www.thelyingtruth.info/

Long, John. *Journal of John Long, 1872–1927. Telling The Truth.*

———. n.d. "Why I am an Unsectarian Evangelist." In "Treatises and Writings." *Telling The Truth.*

Mac Annaidh, Seamas, ed. 2008. "Cooney's Family Background." In *Fermanagh Miscellany 2.* Enniskillen, N. Ireland: Fermanagh Authors Assoc. 45–49.

Magowan, Alfred:

———. 1931. *Outline of the History of a Peculiar People from 1900–1931.* Sydney, Australia: G.S. Publishers. *Telling The Truth.*

———. 1948. *Ideas and Beliefs of the Victorians.* 4–5.

———. 1956. *Testimony of a Witness for the Defence.* January 13. *Telling The Truth.*

———. c 1958. *Cross-Examination of a Witness and Address to the Jury. Telling The Truth.*

Martin, Sheila (De Jager). 1998. Personal communication with Author; Martin was a 2x2 from Cape Town, South Africa, who immigrated to Ontario, Canada, in 1971.

Massey, Edgar. 1992. "Constitution of Kristna i Sverige" (Christians in Sweden). In *Another Step: Our Story.* www.anotherstep.net

McDonald, John. n.d. *Go-Preachers or Cooneyites.* Sydney, Australia: Christian Workers' Depot. *Telling The Truth.*

McLean, J. B. n.d. *Faith Triumphant – A Review of the Work of the Faith Mission 1886–1936.* Edinburgh, Scotland: Faith Mission Book Rooms. 27.

McPhail, Mrs. Alex (Verna). n.d. "Early Days in California 1904–1910." *Telling The Truth.*

Meetings of Senior Workers:

———. 1928. Senior Workers Meeting at Lurgan, Ireland. Appendix D. October 12.

———. 1930. Senior Workers Meeting at West Hanney, England. *Telling The Truth.* July 19–21.

———. 1938a. Senior Workers Meeting at West Hanney, England. *Telling The Truth.* July.

———. 1938b. Senior Workers Meeting in Colorado, US *Telling The Truth.* Dec. 1.

———. 1954. Senior Workers Meeting at Guildford, NSW, Aust. Guildford Report and Withdrawal. Appendix J. Feb. 20–24.

———. 1955. Senior Workers Meeting at Dandenong, VIC, Australia. April 20. Appendix J.

———. 1975. Senior Workers Meeting in Minneapolis, Minnesota, US; Report by Tharold Sylvester. Jan. 24, 1987. *Telling The Truth.*

Milton, Elma (Wiebe), n.d. "When the Gospel Came to the Weibe Family." *Telling The Truth.*

Mooney, Howard. n.d. "The Origin of Christmas." *Truth Archive website.* thetrutharchive.blogspot.com.

National Archives of Ireland Census. 1891, 1901, 1910, 1911.

National Records of Scotland Census. 1881, 1891, 1901.

Nguyễn Huu Bau, Nguyễn Thị Minh Thanh and Nguyễn Xuân Hoàn. 2014. Account of the Vietnam Division. *Telling The Truth.*

Noble, James L. Grand, Secretary of the Grand Lodge of Ancient Free and Accepted Masons of Scotland of Edinburgh. 2010. *Telling The Truth Photo Gallery.* Nov. 19.

Nordberg, Bette. 1996. *Evangeline: A Story of Faith.* Canon Beach, OR: Canon Beach Conference Center; Seaside, Oregon: Frontier Publishing. 25, 65, 71.

Oman, Everett C. 1992. *Bigots of Boscobel.* Anacortes, Washington: Pandoran Publishing. 59.

Palmer, Phoebe. 1859. *The Promise of the Father,* 1981 Ed. Salem, Ohio: Schmul Publishers.

Park, Ada. 1985. "When the Gospel came to Oregon in December 1907." *Telling The Truth.*

Parker, Doug and Helen Parker. 1982. *The Secret Sect.* Sydney, Australia: MacArthur Press.

———. 1954. *A Spiritual Fraud Exposed.* Padstow, NSW, Australia: Utility Press. *Telling The Truth.*

———. 1995. Transcript of Testimony of Doug Parker. Bellview, Washington. *Expressions by Ex-2x2s (Ex2x2.info)* June 9.

Pattison, Bert. 1951. "A Review of Hymns Old and New." *Telling The Truth.*

Pattison, Goodhand. 1935. "Account of the Early Days. " Cloughjordan, Ireland. *Telling The Truth.*

Pattison, John, compiler. n.d. "Princess Victoria's Contact with the Workers 1917–1920." *Telling The Truth.*

Preecs, Bart. 1983. "Two by Twos: Victims of Anonymous Cult?" In *Spokesman-Review* [Spokane, Washington]. June 5. 1.

Price, Charles and Ian Randall. 2000. *Transforming Keswick.* Berkshire, Great Britain: Cox and Wyman. 54.

Register of New Zealand Presbyterian Church Ministers, Deaconesses & Missionaries, 1840. 171.
www.archives.presbyterian.org.nz/Page171.htm

Research and Information Services (RIS). 1993. Sisters, Oregon, US. workersect.org

Richardson, Alan. 2020. Statement regarding Coronavirus (Covid-19). March 14. *Telling The Truth.*

Roberts, Dr. Patricia:

———. 1990. *The Life and Ministry of Edward Cooney, 1867–1960.* Enniskillen, N. Ireland: Wm. Trimble.

———. 1991. *Selected Letters, Hymns and Poems of Edward Cooney, 1867–1960.* Enniskillen, N. Ireland: Wm. Trimble.

———. 1997. *Selected Letters of Fred Wood 1890–1986.* Enniskillen, N. Ireland: Print Factory.

———. 2000. *The Go-Preacher Movement-An Anthology.* Enniskillen, N. Ireland: Print Factory.

Roddie, Robin P. 2013. *Bulletin of the Methodist Historical Society of Ireland.* 150.

Rule, William Murray (W.M.). 1929. *Cooneyites or Go-Preachers and Their Doctrine.* London, England and Sydney, Australia: Central Bible Truth Depot. *Telling The Truth.*

Sanderson, Neville. 2001. "100 Years in a Professing Family." *Expressions by Ex-2x2s (Ex2x2.info).*

Schmidt, Mervyn. n.d. Why We Left. *Expressions by Ex-2x2s (Ex2x2.info).*

Schnitzer, Pauline. n.d. "A Little of my Experiences at Stuttgart." *Telling The Truth.*

Schroeder, Thomas V. "Tom":

———. 2018. Black Stockings. *Expressions by Ex-2x2s.* Last rev. May 16.

———. 2016. Tom's Story. Why We Left. *Expressions by Ex-2x2s.* Last rev. July 10.

Scrutator. 1905. "A New Sect." *Irish Presbyterian.* March. 38.

Sibley, Mulford Q. and Philip E. Jacob. 1952. *Conscription of Conscience: The American State and the Conscientious Objector 1940–1947.* Ithaca, NY: Cornell Univ. Press. 7–9, 16.

Silvernail, Harold. 1984. "Milltown, Washington Convention Story." *Telling The Truth.*

Smith, Sid. n.d. "The History of Hosiery" (President of The Hosiery Association. E-mail to Cherie Kropp-Ehrig, 2000). n.p.

Stancliff, Jack. 2009, Version 7.3. "Early History of the Gospel in Bakersfield, California, US." *Telling The Truth.*

Stanley, Alan. 2005. *I met Murder on the Way–The Story of the Pearsons of Coolacrease.* Naas, Co. Kildare, Ireland: Leinster Leader. 13.

Strong, James. 1990. *New Strong's Exhaustive Concordance of the Bible.* Nashville, Tennessee, US: Thomas Nelson Publishers.

TA. See *Truth Archive*

Telling The Truth (TTT). 1995. *TellingTheTruth.info*

Telling The Truth Photo Gallery. TellingTheTruth.info/photogallery/

Tenniswood, Eldon:

———. 1977. "Family Counseling Meeting." Santee, California, US. *Telling The Truth.*

———. 1981. "Early Days in Michigan." *Telling The Truth.* October.

Thornblad, Debra. 1992. "Multitude of the faithful flocks to Milford every year." In *Milford (NH) Cabinet and Wilton Journal.* Aug. 5.

Toft, Susan. 1984. "Church with No Name Packs in Crowds." In Coeur d'Alene Press [Idaho, US] June 8.

Trimble, William C. 1910. *The Tramp or Go-Preachers (Sometimes called Pilgrims)*. Enniskillen, Northern Ireland: Impartial Reporter Printing Works. *Telling The Truth*.

TTT. See Telling The Truth website. *TellingTheTruth.info*

Truth Archive (TA). thetrutharchive.blogspot.com. Collection of documents produced by and circulated among members of the 2x2 Sect.

Two by Two History (2x2 History Website):

———. Australian History. www.2x2church.info/australian-history

———. New Zealand History. www.2x2church.info/nz-history

———. UK History. www.2x2church.info/uk-history

US Military Reunion Booklets: See Appendix K.

Vine, W. E. 1985. *Vine's Expository Dictionary of Biblical Words*. Nashville, Tennessee, US: Thomas Nelson Publishers. 465, 477.

Vogt, Margaret. 2008. "Memories of Margaret Vogt." *Telling The Truth*.

Waddingham, Mary Elizabeth "Lizzie" (Coles). n.d. "Mary Elizabeth Waddingham Testimony." n.p. *Telling The Truth*.

Walker, George:

———. 1942. Statement to US Selective Service. *Telling The Truth*. March 24.

———. 1970. Hector, MN Convention. *Telling The Truth*. Oct. 3.

———. 1972. Charles A. Hughes' Funeral. *Telling The Truth*. Aug. 19.

———. 1979. "Notes on George Walker's Early Days in America" *Telling The Truth. Oct. 29.*

———. 1981. Account of Last Days, Death and Funeral. *Telling The Truth*. n.d.

———. 1988. Account of George Walker's Early Days. *Telling The Truth*. Feb. 16.

West, Ida. 1954. Statement. *Telling The Truth*. Aug.

West, Sara. 1954. Statement. *Telling The Truth*. Aug. 31.

West, William. 1929. Statement. *Telling The Truth*. Oct.

Williams, Roche. 1999. *In and Out of School: In the Home of the MacDonaghs*. 202 (citing *Nenagh News and Tipperary Vindicator*, April 29, 1911).

Wood, Fred. 1985. "Early Memories." n.p. *Telling The Truth*.

Wood, Iona (Hill). 1977. "Early Memories of Iona R. (Hill) Wood. California, US." *Telling The Truth*. May 18.

Young, Willis G. D. 2000. *In Vain Do They Worship. Telling The Truth*.

Index